Social Change

John Eric Nordskog

PROFESSOR OF SOCIOLOGY
UNIVERSITY OF SOUTHERN CALIFORNIA

McGRAW-HILL BOOK COMPANY, INC.

New York   Toronto   London

1960

SOCIAL CHANGE

III

47172

HM
101
N.5

Preface

Every element in man's culture is subject to change, but a textbook on social change must be limited in its scope and in the nature of its emphasis. Former works have differed in these respects, and there is no fixed pattern for the study of social change. Nevertheless, certain theoretical, descriptive, and evaluative aspects of courses in social change have become traditional. Such material has been accounted for in so far as it provides perspective and insight, and it has influenced the selection of readings which are a feature of this book.

The purpose of the text is not only to present in general basic sociological principles of social change, but to examine several specific areas of change involving fundamental social institutions. Throughout the book, textual development and readings have been integrated to maintain structural unity.

The study begins with a survey of concepts, theories, and social processes especially significant in social change. Attention is also given to the implications of societal self-direction and to the interrelatedness of personality, culture, and society as aspects of social change.

The effects of growth in population over the world have so many ramifications in social and cultural change that an understanding of population as a process is important enough to merit the consideration given it here.

All forms of social change come within the province of culture, and a statement of the nature of culture, its structural features, and how culture changes, is generally regarded as essential. The concept of progress, emphasized in several previous texts, is explained here as a subjective evaluative aspect of social change. Ideas and ideologies need to be understood as powerful agents in social change, and concrete examples are given of contemporary ideologies and their influence in social reform movements. Thus a general foundation is laid for the consideration of change in several institutionalized areas of human behavior—the economic, political, religious, and legal.

Everyone is affected by changes in attitudes and policies regarding war and by the constant jeopardy of militarism to our social institutions. On the other hand, any hopeful trends toward peaceful world organization should be credited as factors in social change.

In the present survey civilizations are shown not only to be changing, but to be constantly on trial; no doubt existing civilizations will, in time, be superseded by others. The perspective of change may be relatively narrow if confined to contemporary events; or it may be more broadly historical in terms of civilizations changing throughout the centuries.

This study of social change is meant to be objective, realistic, and practical; it is meant also to be both positive and constructive. Some readings have been drawn from classics which have meaning for present-day trends and events. Most readings, however, are from recent publications. With few exceptions the readings, whether from books or journals, have been reprinted as completely as space permits. The social elements in change have been stressed in preference to the material elements in culture, though the latter receive their due share of attention.

Acknowledgment is given to the authors and publishers as each selection appears, and for their splendid cooperation the present author is indeed grateful. Appreciation is also due the staff of the Doheny Memorial Library, the Library of International Relations, and Mudd Memorial Library, all at the University of Southern California, for their generous assistance in facilitating research.

John Eric Nordskog

Contents

I

Introduction to
Social Change

Everything in man's culture is subject to change, a process which may be referred to as social change or cultural change, or as a combination of social and cultural change. The process may be slow or fast, evolutionary or revolutionary. The term "social change" is relatively simple, although as a sociological concept it is especially comprehensive.

Social change means simply the process of becoming different in any sense. When changes grow in a connected order out of earlier phases of change, the process is called evolution. In evolution, the latter changes *are* by virtue of the fact that the former *were*. The evolutionary changes appear in a connected sequence because of certain potentialities which were present in some sense at the beginning and continue to unfold within the series of changes. The term "development," which involves change in the sense of unfolding gradually or evolving the possibilities of something gradually, is also frequently applied to social phenomena.

Change and evolution are not evaluative concepts, for they denote merely the process of becoming different. Both terms are, however, significant in defining "progress," the implication being that what emerges through change or evolution is for the better. Progress exists only as an evaluative and subjective concept, and its nature as a value judgment depends upon the perspective of the observer. Evolution may in some instances appear to be progressive, in others regressive.

Social and cultural aspects of change are in some respects distinguishable, though they are at the same time related to each other. The difference lies in the fact that "social" refers to "society," which is not synonymous with "culture." Culture includes both material and nonmaterial elements, all of which are products of human society. But society is usually described in psychological terms not applicable to material things, e.g., sociability, gregariousness, association, the capacity to respond to social stimuli, the ability to communicate socially, etc. If the adjective "social" be restricted to these characteristics of society, it follows that social change refers to changes in mechanisms of human association.[1] The more precisely *social* elements of culture are thus apparent in aspects of social organization and in social behavior as exemplified in customs, mores, institutions, laws, language, ideologies, and all other societal aspects of culture.

All data considered in this study of social change, whether they pertain to material things or the techniques of making them, or to patterns of social interaction and organization, are to be thought of as cultural.

Change and evolution are generalized concepts whose concrete meanings depend upon the categories or events to which they are applied. The changes are very different when speaking of, say, organic evolution, individual development, human history, cosmic genesis, and chemical transformation. When considering change with reference to living things, it is significant that their experience counts in the process and enables them to gather up the effects of their own past and carry them forward, cumulatively, into their future. This conception reaches its highest significance for human beings because, not only have they experienced evolution physically and mentally to reach the plane of Homo sapiens, but their experience in human association has enabled them to create culture and transmit it socially from generation to generation.

Whether or not man has potentialities for further evolution lies in the realm of speculation. It is certain, however, that for thousands of years man has depended on his rational faculties for adaptation to his natural and social environment. The record of this adaptation, which has culminated in the social and cultural heritage, makes it possible to trace the evolution of man's culture, beginning with the earliest known artifacts made by the precursors of Homo sapiens. The anthropological story of mankind reveals a vast process of social change and evolution which can be analyzed in terms of culture traits, complexes, and patterns.

PREHISTORIC CULTURAL DEVELOPMENT

The older the prehistoric culture, the fewer artifacts have been found to represent its phases. Artifacts, sometimes called "fossils of the mind," have at times been found buried with fossils of the individuals who made or used them. Though the record is a meager one, enough is available to enlighten us concerning the evolution of man and his culture in prehistoric times.

The earliest known elements in man's cultural heritage are generally conceded to be the so-called "eoliths" or "dawn stones." These objects were flint fragments bearing curious chippings which, it is thought, were caused by man's grasping them by the hands and using them for the cruder motions of striking, prying, or cutting. Bones also have been found with unusual scratches upon them which point to a similar conclusion. Eoliths have been attributed to upper Pliocene time by some archeologists, though others hesitate to place eoliths earlier than Pleistocene time.

[1] *Cf.* William Fielding Ogburn, *Social Change with Respect to Culture and Original Nature*, B. W. Huebsch, Inc., New York, 1922, p. 59; new edition, The Viking Press, New York, 1950, p. 59. For discussion of social evolution, see pp. 56-61 in either edition.

The Pleistocene phase in geological chronology has been familiarly called the Glacial or Great Ice Age, marked by four major glacial periods—the Günz, Mindel, Riss, and Wurm glacial periods. Of special significance, however, are the three major interglacial periods, known respectively as the Günz-Mindel, the Mindel-Riss, and the Riss-Wurm interglacial periods. During these periods there was a retreat of the ice. The earlier periods were of longer duration, the length of time for each period growing gradually shorter. The present may be another interglacial period, the fourth in a major sequence, to be followed by another advance of the cold. Only a few degrees of difference in annual temperature might cause these major oscillations of ice ages over thousands of years. During the postglacial period there have been several lesser ice intervals, known as the Bühl, the Gschnitz, and the Daun ice periods. Between each of these came warmer interglacial intervals. The present-day Alpine glaciers are remnants of the last, or Daun, glaciation. The range of glaciation was not limited to the area which now constitutes Europe but has been particularly significant for its influence on prehistoric cultural development in the European area. Glacial periods in other regions of the world have had comparable advances and recessions, and doubtless have affected man's habitation and culture building. Geologists and archeologists differ greatly in the time periods allotted to Pleistocene chronology of man's evolution and cultural innovations. They differ in their dating of fossils of the precursors of man and the appearance of artifacts representing cultural stages comprising the Paleolithic (Old Stone) Age, which fell within Pleistocene and post-Pleistocene time. There is no real consensus in dating the finds of the Neolithic (New Stone) Age or of the Copper, Bronze, and Iron Ages, though deviations in the latter instances are more nominal. In any case, it is likely that man the culture-builder has experienced all phases of the Great Ice Age and his record of achievement must have been affected by it. For countless ages, the evolution of man and the evolution or development of his culture moved very slowly indeed.

During the first or Günz-Mindel interglacial period, approximately 500,000 B.C., Heidelberg man was extant, and lower Paleolithic culture was represented by such artifacts as the *coup de poing*, or fist ax, and by flint scrapers, perforators, knives, and flake tools. During the second or Mindel-Riss interglacial period, about 300,000 B.C., Swanscombe man represents the hominid type extant, and the lower Paleolithic culture of that phase included improved hand axes and flake implements. During the third or Riss-Wurm interglacial period, which began about 120,000 B.C., Neanderthal man had arrived on the scene, and lower Paleolithic culture was marked by hearths and burials, flint quarrying, and the making of side scrapers, points of various kinds, and cleavers.

The ice of the fourth or Wurm glacial period retreated enough between 40,000 B.C. and 30,000 B.C. to make the greater part of Europe ice-free; and then Cro-Magnon, the immediate precursor of modern man, appeared on the scene. The culture then developed was different enough to merit distinction as upper Paleolithic. Among its characteristic artifacts were beautifully worked laurel-leaf points, lance points of bone and horn, backed blades, awls, chisels, and there was some sculpture and engraving on bone and ivory. Later in this period appeared harpoons, and polychrome frescoes on cave walls. Thus the Paleolithic or Old Stone Age culture can be divided into lower and upper, to indicate the evolution of artifacts and techniques which were in some respects distinctive.

The cultural contributions of Cro-Magnon and modern man make for a more continuous record during the Holocene or postglacial period. Modern man may be placed at approximately 10,000 B.C., and associated with him was a transitional Mesolithic culture, indicated by crude geometric art, painted pebbles, and microliths. By 5000 B.C. modern man was well along in the Neolithic culture period, with its pottery, the dog, the hewn ax, the bow and arrow. Neolithic (New Stone Age) culture was distinctive for the grinding and polishing of stone implements and the use of celts; for its elementary agriculture which produced barley, millet, peas, and flax; also for the domestication of cattle, swine, sheep, and goats. Other notable features were the wheeled carts, loom weaving, megaliths, and dolmens. By 1900 B.C., modern European race types were introducing the Bronze Age, marked by the casting and alloying of metals, the making of swords, shields, and helmets of bronze; another trait of importance was the domestication of the horse. About 1000 B.C. or 900 B.C. modern European race types introduced the Iron Age, distinguished by cast- and wrought-iron weapons and tools, and by the invention and use of metallic money, glass, and the spoked wheel.

This brief outline of prehistoric cultural development shows how slowly man's discovery and invention added to his culture through many thousands of years. Paleolithic man, who occupied the earth for all but the last 1 or 2 per cent of human time, nevertheless built up a cultural heritage which became the basis for more rapid cultural achievement during historic times. Our knowledge about prehistoric man and culture provides a perspective for appreciating the terrific acceleration in cultural growth within historic times, and the achievements since the beginning of the Industrial Revolution appear all the more remarkable when one looks backward to man the food gatherer and man the fire maker.

Different aspects of man at the cultural threshold could be emphasized, following the prehistoric perspective given above, but only two have been selected owing to limitations of space. In the first of these selections Felix M. Keesing gives his answer to the question, What is known of the origin and early development of culture?

The actual "origins" of particular cultural elements, such as marriage, religion, or art, are not known, and establishing a base line for the origin of culture is in itself a difficult matter. However, beginning with the Eolithic or prepaleolithic period, archeologists have made it possible to reconstruct in broad terms man's artifacts and the core or flake industries which produced them. Findings such as these have also been credited, in so far as possible, to the fossil remains of ancestral Homo types culminating in Homo sapiens, particularly when the artifacts and fossils have been found in close association or in similar geological strata. Such a reconstruction has been made by Professor Keesing, built around his conception of man as a food gatherer.

1

MAN AS FOOD GATHERER*
Felix M. Keesing

What is known of the origin and early development of culture?

Discussions of particular cultural elements, such as marriage, religion, or art, often present quite glib accounts of their origin, as though it were possible to reconstruct with scientific precision what the ways of life of early man were like. Anthropologists regard these theories with the utmost skepticism, to say the least. In actual fact, as represented by the archaeological record, there is only the most fragmentary knowledge even of material objects. The number of specialists capable of analyzing this evidence scientifically is very small indeed.

Establishing a base line for "the origin of culture" is in itself a difficult matter. What was called earlier "protoculture" appears to have been characteristic in some degree of prehuman animals, especially the generalized anthropoids in the zone immediately behind man. The early hominids or "manlike" anthropoids, in adapting to bipedal locomotion and an upright position, freed their forelimbs for other uses. It is a fair hypothesis that they would have used sticks, stones, and other extensions of the hands as tools long before they developed habits of shaping them artificially for greater efficiency—hence enabling those capable of being preserved to be recognizable by the archaeologist. Again, the refinement of symbolic communication was undoubtedly a very slow and selective process, and in spite of various theories relating to the origin of language it is pure guesswork to say what patterns of learned symbolic behavior came first. Even such an amusing remark as the physical anthropologist Hooton's statement that "man must have descended from a particularly babbling kind of ape" has no necessary validity. Our picture remains necessarily one of inference and of great generality: that at the time for which archaeologically recognizable elements have become available, their users were living in tiny groups as mobile food gatherers (judged from caves and other living sites, and from animal bones, shells, and other food remains); that a group typically consisted of a few related and congenial "families" (but of their family organization we know nothing); that one or more groups occupied a territory, using and guarding its resources; that strong individuals emerged as leaders; and that members of the group had a sense of identity and submitted for the most part to habits of "social order" as modern men do.

Now come the "eoliths" into the picture, sometimes, as at Red Crag in southern England, found together in large numbers at what appears to be a "workshop" and showing some crude regularities of form. Together with "paleoliths" from early time zones of the Paleolithic, they sort out into basic tool types. One is the *hammer*, in this case a usually rather rounded hammerstone showing marks of percussion. The hammered stone materials fall mechanically into two types:

* From Felix M. Keesing, *Cultural Anthropology: The Science of Custom*, Rinehart & Company, Inc., New York, 1958, pp. 87–94. Reprinted by permission of the publishers.

the *core* or nucleus from which pieces are struck, and the *flake* or piece struck off. An *anvil* in the form of another stone may also be used. Cores and flakes, after the primary fracture, may be *retouched* by secondary working to produce one face or edge (unifacial, or a "uniface") or to produce two faces or edges (bifacial, or a "biface"). Archaeologists infer from shape and sometimes from use marks that, besides the hammer and the anvil, even very early tools fall into some familiar types: the ax or chopper, the knife, the scraper, the borer, the chisel, and (probably coming later) the point, most familiar in projectile tools and weapons.

The most efficient of stone materials is *flint,* which is hard, yet tends to fracture in a controllable way. It has been aptly said that wherever deposits of flint were located, early man thrived. Another material with these qualities is the black volcanic "glass," obsidian. But many other hard types of stone were flaked by early man. One chopper type, known as the "pebble ax" or "pebble tool," has as its basis a more or less rounded pebble such as could be picked up along a shore or river bed. Judging by the distances that flint and other desirable stone materials were carried in some localities, an early type of "trading" among groups is suggested.

Fire might also be listed in the "tools" of early man. Apart from an unproved hypothesis that some of the fossil anthropoid and "apeman" types of Africa used fire, the earliest evidence is from the cave living-site of "Peking Man" at Choukoutien, near Peking, China. Here not only remains of early fires and charred bones have come to light, dating from perhaps 350,000 years ago, but also dried-up berries which were part of the diet of this early *Homo* type.

Given certain technological alternatives, even in these beginning tool types, cultural variation appears to have begun almost immediately. In western Europe, Africa, southwest Asia, and south India, both cores and flakes were used as tools. But in some sites the so-called "hand ax" or "fist ax" (a core biface held in the hand) predominates, while

in others most or even all of the tools were based on the flake. In eastern Europe and Asia north of the Himalayas to east Asia flake industries predominate. In north and east India and southeast Asia, and on to the caves of Peking Man, a uniface "pebble tool" or chopper is characteristic. Choppers also have a very early distribution in east Africa. The implication is that, as with genetic heritages discussed earlier, isolation in small scattered populations favored a selection among alternatives in behavior—a process which was to become vastly magnified as cultural innovations became cumulative.

Lower Paleolithic finds have by now been located widely over the warmer zones of the Old World, and have been equated with a considerable number of "type site" names. In Europe an older development sequence into "Pre-Chellean," "Chellean," and "Acheulian" has been undergoing revision, particularly in terms of the core-flake distinction. Of somewhat varying new classifications, perhaps this should now go into the opening section of standard texts on "Western Civilization":

Period	Core Industries	Flake Industries
Lower Paleolithic	Acheulian (various periods)	Levalloisian
	Abbevillian (formerly Chellean, Pre-Chellean)	Clactonian
Eolithic, or Pre-Paleolithic	Ipswichian, etc.	

Unless one were specializing in archaeological study it would be cumbersome to learn a number of special type-site names for collateral traditions of various regions in Africa. For Asia, some important traditions are the

Soanian (from the Soan River terraces of northeast India), the Anyathian (from Anyathia in Upper Burma), the Patjitanian (from Patjitan in Java, and probably associated with the so-called "Java Man," *Pithecanthropus*), and the Choukoutienian (from the Choukoutien caves near Peking). The last-named type site is of very great importance as it is the only place where such tools have been found to date directly associated with a fossil form of early man; they have come to light in large numbers and their manufacturing processes are well understood.

Hundreds of generations were to pass without much perceptible shift in the tool kit and presumably only minor changes in the way of life generally. Control of stone flaking improved in some zones, particularly the working of flint. An artistic modern eye might also infer that, over and above pure utility, some objects began to show an appreciation of symmetry and other aesthetic qualities. Then, by perhaps 60,000 to 40,000 years ago some new elements come into the archaeological picture.

The time is around the Third Interglacial, and the cold of the Fourth Glacial is gathering in Europe and in the more northerly zones of Asia. *Homo* types called "Neanderthal" are the actors, and they are moving into rock shelters and caves for at least the winters. There, fire is put to use for light, employing simple lamps; bones of animals are worked into tools; burials are placed in holes discernibly cut into the floors; the large hand ax becomes small, and emphasis is placed upon flake tools including scrapers, which suggest the use of body coverings: "Micoquian" cores, and flake tools of "Tayacian" and especially "Mousterian" types. This is the Middle Paleolithic or "Mousterian" period—the latter name from a type site in the cave of Le Moustier in France. Its characteristic features have come to light, sometimes associated directly with fossil skeletal remains of Neanderthal Man, at points through Europe and as far east as Uzbekistan in middle Asia. Earlier it was spoken of above as a regional, not a universal, horizon of culture.

Some archaeologists have suggested that, in colder zones, Neanderthal groups may have been "refrigerated," because evidence of their occupation of caves ceases toward the height of the Fourth Glacial. In Palestine and Iraq, however, skeletal remains of "Mount Carmel Man" and "Shanidar Man" suggest a hybridizing process between Neanderthalers and early types of modern man, *Homo sapiens*. Some fossil finds, moreover, suggest that early *Homo sapiens* groups were living in parts of Europe at least by the Third Interglacial, that is, over the same time period as the Neanderthalers, e.g., "Fontechavade Man" of France, "Swanscombe Man" of England. There are possibilities that, besides some intermarriage, these larger-brained peoples may have contributed to the demise of Neanderthaloid ("Neanderthallike") groups not only here but also in Africa (e.g., "Rhodesia Man") and southeast Asia ("Solo" or "Ngandong" Man, of whom eleven skulls have come to light in that ocean-bound migration pocket, Java).

The zone of final evolution toward *Homo sapiens* from earlier, more generalized, *Homo* forms is not yet known. Howells (1942) and perhaps most other specialists consider it to be that vital crossroads region in human history, the Iran-Iraq plateau south of the Caspian, now so dried up. Some believe it to be in Africa, from which, in such a warm period as an Interglacial, migrating groups moved into Europe. What is clear, however, is that the modes of living of some at least of these "early moderns" show marked advances in technology, in art and religion, and presumably in other types of cultural growth. The "Cro-Magnon" men, best known from extensive archaeological remains in Europe associated with the later phases of the Fourth Glacial, evidently brought with them a complex of cultural traditions which had already been basically worked out in whatever were their zones of former occupation.

This is the Upper Paleolithic, dating in Europe from perhaps 35,000 to 12,000 years ago. Immediately striking are new techniques of working stone. Instead of knocking off flakes by percussion, a much more controlled method is developed for removing chips, even down to tiny size: *pressure flaking*. A bone or hardwood tool, pressed with skill against the stone matrix, will flake out even delicate and intricately shaped artifacts, as with arrowheads or Solutrean leaf points. Again, the skilled craftsman could strike off—not always with success, of course—long flat pieces called *blades*. Near the end of this period a *pecking and grinding* technique was developed by which stone which does not fracture well could be shaped out, even if the surface was left more or less roughly pitted. The tool kit often became greatly elaborated, and has called for a quite technical vocabulary in archaeological classification: keeled scrapers, busked gravers, battered-back blades, and so on.

The Upper Paleolithic is also marked by great elaboration of bonework. In its final stages in Europe, the extensive use of bone, horn, and tusk materials caused some scholars to call this particular subtype (the Magdalenian) the *Bone Age*. Among bone artifacts were borers and projectile points, including an important new invention, the harpoon, with a detachable head, often barbed; spear throwers to add force to projectiles; needles and toggles (for buttoning) indicative of clothing; carved figurines; necklaces and other bodily ornaments; and a perforated "baton" of unknown use. Many ethnologists hypothesize that these bone industries of Glacial man in Europe have their modern continuity in the circumpolar traditions of bonework still so important to groups scattered along northernmost Asia, and on into the Eskimo zones of North America.

Animal remains in their refuse dumps indicate the great reliance of these people for food upon larger cold-weather mammals: among them the reindeer, the woolly mammoth, the European bison, the wild horse. Fishing was also a source of food. The food quest is also the main theme of the well-known "cave art" traditions so much publicized since the first "galleries" came to light in southern France and northern Spain in the 1860's. From early and mostly crude gravings in outline on objects and on cave walls, these visual representations became elaborated in the later Upper Paleolithic into often realistic sculptures and cave paintings. Judged by our art standards (we know nothing except by inference of the standards of these early peoples), these traditions represent a first great efflorescence of aesthetic creativity. As indicated earlier, representations of animals, and the much less frequent and cruder representations of men, are judged to have meanings connected with religious belief, especially hunting and fertility magic. African Bushmen, Australian Aborigines, and certain other hunting peoples of modern times have cave art traditions broadly involving such meanings. Not least interesting are numerous minor markings, among them tectiform (tentlike) drawings which suggest summer outdoor dwellings; hand outlines, sometimes with missing fingers; circles, chevrons, and other geometric forms, including some which might be forerunners of writing. It must be noted that such art has limited regional distribution. It occurs selectively in parts of Europe and in some forms (e.g., bone carving) through north Asia. The great number of Upper Paleolithic traditions, found widely over the world, show little tendency to artistic elaboration.

In the older archaeology, the Upper Paleolithic subdivided into a threefold sequence of "Aurignacian," "Solutrean," and "Magdalenian." Later classifiers have been trying out new type schemes, even for Europe, to bring out regional traditions. Two new names have been more recently emphasized for this period in Europe: "Chatelperronian," so named for a small type of stone "point" located initially in the type site of Chatelperron, and "Gravettian," so named after a characteristic type of long slender stone gravette or graver tool which was used notably in ornamentation. In turn, these are sometimes called Lower and Upper "Périgordian." A diagram for the Upper Paleolithic is therefore likely to show a sequence or regional emphasis somewhat as follows: Périgordian (Chatelperronian, followed by Gravettian), Aurignacian, Solutrean, Magdalenian. As with the Lower Paleolithic, there is also an ever-increasing elaboration of type names for traditions outside Europe: in Africa, Asia, and (more tentatively) America.

The question of classifying the earliest American traditions as paleolithic deserves more space than can be given here. Many archaeologists specializing in American studies have held that even the oldest types of materials were of mesolithic or early neolithic derivation, i.e., offshoots of less elaborated forms of these traditions which had reached northeast Asia. A post-Glacial crossing of the Bering Strait could then be visualized as very recent in archaeological time: perhaps 12,000 to 8,000 years ago.

Evidence has been accumulating, however, suggestive of an earlier timetable, at least for the initial Indian migrations. Bird (1946) found in caves near the tip of South America materials closely like those of circumpolar cultures such as the Eskimo. De Terra (1949) located paleolith-like tools on old beaches in the Valley of Mexico. Former lake areas in the Colorado and Mohave deserts, as well as in shore areas in southern California, have yielded some typologically old tool industries, "stone circles," refuse middens, and other elements which may approximate to the earliest levels of occupation. Possibilities of Bering Strait crossings during Fourth Glacial times, via pockets free of ice, or even along the edge of the ice with sea mammals as the main basis of subsistence, are currently being taken into account. This view could push datings back to anywhere between 30,000 and 15,000 years ago.

An amazingly wide range of cultural types is found among the surviving food-gathering groups still existing in more isolated parts of the world. They have adapted to different habitats, with quite different resources—far-ranging animals like the reindeer or caribou, seasonal ones like the salmon, nonmoving ones such as shellfish; scattered root and fruit plants, seasonal seeds and nuts, a bulky resource in the case of the sago palm. Some groups with stationary resources, or with seasonal staples which they can store in quantity, have even been able to develop larger and more sedentary types of community of village size in place of their earlier tiny roving bands. Many of these adjustments must have been initiated by the time of which we are speaking. In some of them the dynamic was evidently lodged which led to the food-producing, or neolithic, revolution.

Every human population, at all times, has needed to organize its life about its natural environment in terms of the skills available to it and the values which it accepted. And every population has, from the beginning, changed the face of the earth in some degree. This was true of Paleolithic man and man the food gatherer, as well as of his more cultured successors. And fire may be considered the first great force employed by man to change and exploit his habitat. Far back in the dim past ancient man abandoned his campfires and allowed them to ignite vegetation; and it is likely that then, as in later cases, he deliberately started conflagrations which swept over the country. In ancient as in recent times, thick forests and dense jungles of brush offered little use to the hunter or collector. Narrow trails through tangled and heavy growth were dangerous because of the concealment provided to human, as well as animal, enemies. It is a known fact that aborigines have, whenever possible, set fire to jungles and thick woods in order to "open them up." Widely spaced trees and clear meadows and plains offer better and safer hunting. Man has resorted to broadcast burning, not only to reduce the danger from enemies, but also to rouse or drive game during hunting, to improve pasture for game, to procure and maintain the yield of certain wild plants, to improve the berry harvest, and under certain conditions as an act of war. Whatever the most ancient reasons for burning have been, they persist and are joined to the motives of the planter and herder.[2]

Loren C. Eiseley deals with "man the fire maker" from another angle. His position is that man's unique evolution is largely due to his ability to turn heat to his own ends. Man did not invent fire; he discovered it and made it one of the giant powers on the earth. It is true that man the fire maker, in cooking, extending grasslands, baking pottery, and making tools, found in fire a means to change and control his environment. But that is a far cry from man's present-day scientific uses of fire, and its potentialities seem to be limitless. Thus primitive man as fire maker contributed the initial discovery of fire which has had a great variety of functions throughout the ages and which continues to have untold potentialities in the atomic age.

2

MAN THE FIRE-MAKER[*]
Loren C. Eiseley

Man, it is well to remember, is the discoverer but not the inventor of fire. Long before this meddling little Prometheus took to experimenting with flints, then matches and finally (we hope not too finally) hydrogen bombs, fires had burned on this planet. Volcanoes had belched molten lava, lightning had struck in dry grass, winds had rubbed dead branches against each other until they burst into flame. There are evidences of fire in ancient fossil beds that lie deep below the time of man.

Man did not invent fire but he did make it one of the giant powers on the earth. He began this experiment long ago in the red morning of the human mind. Today he continues it in the midst of coruscating heat that is capable of rending the very fabric of his universe. Man's long adventure with knowledge has, to a very marked degree, been a climb up the heat ladder, for heat alone enables man to mold metals and glassware, to create his great chemical industries, to drive his swift machines. It is our intention in this article to trace man's manipulation of this force far back into its ice-age beginnings and to observe the part that fire has played in the human journey across the planet. The torch has been carried smoking through the ages of glacial advance. As we follow man on this journey, we shall learn another aspect of his nature: that he is himself a consuming fire.

At just what level in his intellectual development man mastered the art of making fire is still unknown. Neanderthal man of 50,000 years ago certainly knew the art. Traces of the

[*] Reprinted by permission of the author and *Scientific American,* vol. 191, no. 3, pp. 52–57, September, 1954.
[2] See Omer C. Stewart, "Fire as the First Great Force Employed by Man," in *Man's Role in Changing the Face of the Earth,* William L. Thomas, Jr., et al. (ed.), University of Chicago Press, Chicago, 1956, pp. 115–133.

use of fire have turned up in a cave of Peking man, the primitive human being of at least 250,000 years ago who had a brain only about two thirds the size of modern man's. And seven years ago Raymond Dart of Witwatersrand University announced the discovery in South Africa of *Australopithecus prometheus,* a man-ape cranium recovered from deposits which he believed showed traces of burned bone.

This startling announcement of the possible use of fire by a subhuman creature raised a considerable storm in anthropological circles. The chemical identifications purporting to indicate evidence of fire are now considered highly questionable. It has also been intimated that the evidence may represent only traces of a natural brush fire. Certainly, so long as the South African man-apes have not been clearly shown to be tool users, wide doubts about their use of fire will remain. There are later sites of tool-using human beings which do not show traces of fire.

Until there is proof to the contrary, it would seem wise to date the earliest use of fire to Peking man—*Sinanthropus.* Other human sites of the same antiquity have not yielded evidence of ash, but this is not surprising, for as a new discovery the use of fire would have taken time to diffuse from one group to another. Whether it was discovered once or several times we have no way of knowing. The fact that fire was in world-wide use at the beginning of man's civilized history enables us to infer that it is an old human culture trait—doubtless one of the earliest. Furthermore, it is likely that man used fire long before he became sophisticated enough to produce it himself.

In 1865 Sir John Lubbock, a British banker who made a hobby of popular writing on science, observed: "There can be no doubt that man originally crept over the earth's surface, little by little, year by year, just, for instance, as the weeds of Europe are now gradually but surely creeping over the surface of Australia." This remark was, in its time, a very shrewd and sensible observation. We know today, however, that there have been times when man suddenly made great strides across the face of the earth. I want to review here one of those startling expansions—a lost episode in which fire played a tremendous part. To make its outlines clear we shall have to review the human drama in three acts.

The earliest human-like animals we can discern are the man-apes of South Africa. Perhaps walking upright on two feet, this creature seems to have been roaming the East African grasslands about one million years ago. Our ancestor, "proto-man," probably emerged from the tropics and diffused over the region of warm climate in Eurasia and North Africa. He must have been dependent upon small game, insects, wild seeds and fruits. His life was hard, his search for food incessant, his numbers were small.

The second stage in human history is represented by the first true men. Paleoanthropic man is clearly a tool user, a worker in stone and bone, but there is still something of the isolated tinkerer and fumbler about him. His numbers are still sparse, judging from the paucity of skeletal remains. Short, stocky and powerful, he spread over the most temperate portions of the Afro-Eurasiatic land mass but never attempted the passage through the high Arctic to America. Through scores of millennia he drifted with the seasons, seemingly content with his troglodyte existence, making little serious change in his array of flint tools. It is quite clear that some of these men knew the use of fire, but many may not have.

The third act begins some 15,000 or 20,000 years ago. The last great ice sheet still lies across northern Europe and North America. Roving on the open tundra and grasslands below those ice sheets is the best-fed and most varied assemblage of grass-eating animals the world has ever seen. Giant long-horned bison, the huge wild cattle of the Pleistocene, graze on both continents. Mammoth and mastodon wander about in such numbers that their bones are later to astonish the first American colonists. Suddenly, into this late paradise of game, there erupts our own species of man—*Homo sapiens.* Just where he came from we do not know. Tall, lithe, long-limbed, he is destined to overrun the continents in the blink of a geological eye. He has an excellent projectile weapon in the shape of the spear thrower. His flint work is meticulous and sharp. And the most aggressive carnivore the world has ever seen comes at a time made for his success: the grasslands are alive with seemingly inexhaustible herds of game.

Yet fire as much as flesh was the magic that opened the way for the supremacy of *Homo sapiens.* We know that he was already the master of fire, for the track of it runs from camp to buried camp: the blackened bones of the animals he killed, mute testimony to the relentless step of man across the continents, lie in hundreds of sites in the Old and the New Worlds. Meat, more precious than the gold for which men later struggled, supplied the energy that carried man across the world. Had it not been for fire, however, all that enormous source of life would have been denied to him: he would have gone on drinking the blood from small kills, chewing wearily at uncooked bone ends or masticating the crackling bodies of grasshoppers.

Fire shortens the digestive process. It breaks down tough masses of flesh into food that the human stomach can easily assimilate. Fire made the difference that enabled man to expand his numbers rapidly and to press on from hunting to more advanced cultures. Yet we take fire so much for granted that this first great upswing in human numbers, this first real gain in the seizure of vast quantities of free energy, has to a remarkable degree eluded our attention.

With fire primitive man did more than cook his meat. He extended the pasture for grazing herds. A considerable school of thought, represented by such men as the geographer Carl Sauer and the anthropologist Omer Stewart, believes that the early use of fire by the aborigines of the New World greatly expanded the grassland areas. Stewart says: "The number of tribes reported using fire leads one to the conclusion that burning of vegetation was a universal culture pattern among the Indians of the U. S. Furthermore,

the amount of burning leads to the deduction that nearly all vegetation in America at the time of discovery and exploration was what ecologists would call fire vegetation. That is to say, fire was a major factor, along with soil, moisture, temperature, wind, animals, etc., in determining the types of plants occurring in any region. It follows then, that the vegetation of the Great Plains was a fire vegetation." In short, the so-called primeval wilderness which awed our forefathers had already felt the fire of the Indian hunter. Here, as in many other regions, man's fire altered the ecology of the earth.

It had its effect not only on the flora but also on the fauna. Of the great herds of grazing animals that flourished in America in the last Ice Age, not a single trace remains—the American elephants, camels, long-horned bison are all gone. Not all of them were struck down by the hunters' weapons. Sauer argues that a major explanation of the extinction of the great American mammals may be fire. He says that the aborigines used fire drives to stampede game, and he contends that this weapon would have worked with peculiar effectiveness to exterminate such lumbering creatures as the mammoth. I have stood in a gully in western Kansas and seen outlined in the earth the fragmented black bones of scores of bison who had perished in what was probably a man-made conflagration. If, at the end of Pleistocene times, vast ecological changes occurred, if climates shifted, if lakes dried and in other places forests sprang up, and if, in this uncertain and unsteady time, man came with flint and fire upon the animal world about him, he may well have triggered a catastrophic decline and extinction. Five thousand years of man and his smoking weapon rolling down the wind may have finished the story for many a slow-witted animal species. In the great scale of geological time this act of destruction amounts to but one brief hunt.

Man, as I have said, is himself a flame. He has burned through the animal world and appropriated its vast stores of protein for his own. When the great herds failed over many areas, he had to devise new ways to feed his increase or drop back himself into a precarious balance with nature. Here and there on the world's margins there have survived into modern times men who were forced into just such local adjustments. Simple hunters and collectors of small game in impoverished areas, they maintain themselves with difficulty. Their numbers remain the same through generations. Their economy permits no bursts of energy beyond what is necessary for the simple age-old struggle with nature. Perhaps, as we view the looming shadow of atomic disaster, this way of life takes on a certain dignity today.

Nevertheless there is no road back; the primitive way is no longer our way. We are the inheritors of an aggressive culture which, when the great herds disappeared, turned to agriculture. Here again the magic of fire fed the great human wave and built up man's numbers and civilization.

Man's first chemical experiment involving the use of heat was to make foods digestible. He had cooked his meat; now he used fire to crack his grain. In the process of adopting the agricultural way of life he made his second chemical experiment with heat: baking pottery. Ceramics may have sprung in part from the need for storage vessels to protect harvested grain from the incursions of rats and mice and moisture. At any rate the potter's art spread with the revolutionary shift in food production in early Neolithic times.

People who have only played with mud pies or made little sun-dried vessels of clay are apt to think of ceramics as a simple art. Actually it is not. The sun-dried vessels of our childhood experiments would melt in the first rain that struck them. To produce true pottery one must destroy the elasticity of clay through a chemical process which can only be induced by subjecting the clay to an intense baking at a temperature of at least 400 or 500 degrees centigrade. The baking drives out the so-called water of constitution from the aluminum silicate in the clay. Thereafter the clay will no longer dissolve in water; a truly fired vessel will survive in the ground

for centuries. This is why pottery is so important to the archaeologist. It is impervious to the decay that overtakes many other substances, and, since it was manufactured in quantity, it may tell tales of the past when other clues fail us.

Pottery can be hardened in an open campfire, but the results can never be so excellent as in a kiln. At some point the early potter must have learned that he could concentrate and conserve heat by covering his fire—perhaps making it in a hole or trench. From this it was a step to the true closed kiln, in which there was a lower chamber for the fire and an upper one for the pottery. Most of the earthenware of simple cultures was fired at temperatures around 500 degrees centigrade, but really thorough firing demands temperatures in the neighborhood of 900 degrees.

After man had learned to change the chemical nature of clay, he began to use fire to transform other raw materials—ores into metals, for instance. One measure of civilization is the number of materials manipulated. The savage contents himself with a few raw materials which can be shaped without the application of high temperatures. Civilized man uses fire to extract, alter or synthesize a multitude of substances.

By the time metals came into extended use, the precious flame no longer burned in the open campfire, radiating its heat away into the dark or flickering on the bronzed faces of the hunters. Instead it roared in confined furnaces and was fed oxygen through crude bellows. One of the by-products of more intensified experiments with heat was glass—the strange, impassive substance which, in the form of the chemist's flask, the astronomer's telescope, the biologist's microscope and the mirror, has contributed so vastly to our knowledge of ourselves and the universe.

We hear a good deal about the "Iron Age," or age of metals, as a great jump forward in man's history; actually the metals themselves played a comparatively small part in the rise of the first great civilizations. While men learned to use bronze, which demands little more heat than is necessary to produce good ceramics, and later iron for tools and ornaments, the use of metal did not make a really massive change in civilization for well over 1,500 years. It was what Leslie White of the University of Michigan calls the "Fuel Revolution" that brought the metals into their own. Coal, oil and gas, new sources of energy, combined with the invention of the steam and combustion engines, ushered in the new age. It was not metals as tools, but metals combined with heat in new furnaces and power machinery that took human society off its thousand-year plateau and made possible another enormous upswing in human numbers, with all the social repercussions.

Today the flames grow hotter in the furnaces. Man has come far up the heat ladder. The creature that crept furred through the glitter of blue glacial nights lives surrounded by the hiss of steam, the roar of engines and the bubbling of vats. Like a long-armed crab, he manipulates the tongs in dangerous atomic furnaces. In asbestos suits he plunges into the flaming debris of hideous accidents. With intricate heat-measuring instruments he investigates the secrets of the stars, and he is already searching for heat-resistant alloys that will enable him to hurl himself into space.

How far will he go? Three hundred years of the scientific method have built the great sky-touching buildings and nourished the incalculable fertility of the human species. But man is also *Homo duplex*, as they knew in the darker ages. He partakes of evil and of good, of God and of man. Both struggle in him perpetually. And he is himself a flame— a great, roaring, wasteful furnace devouring irreplaceable substances of the earth. Before this century is out either *Homo duplex* will have learned that knowledge without greatness of spirit is not enough for man, or there will remain only his calcined cities and the little charcoal of his bones.

Small groups of men who live in the Stone Age may still be studied in remote corners of the world. However, as they are fast dying out, they present anthropologists with an emergency. The Tasmanians, who lived by hunting and food gathering, and whose artifacts were of Old Stone Age quality, were hunted like wild animals by the white settlers who followed the explorers to the South Pacific island. By 1830 no more than 200 of the thousands of natives who had inhabited the island were left, and the last Tasmanian died in 1876. Easter Island has been regarded as a lost opportunity, but Thor Heyerdahl, in his book *Aku-Aku*, has revealed important areas of research still available.[3]

Still extant hunting and food-gathering tribes have been investigated among the Eskimos, the Australian aborigines, the Pygmies of central Africa, and the Negritos of the Malay Peninsula. Many others have been completely neglected, and disease and changed conditions of life are destroying them, or at least their cultures, with appalling rapidity. While opportunity remains, social scientists should acquire as much information as possible about such peoples as the following: the primitive Indian tribe known as the Yamana on the island of Tierra del Fuego off the tip of South America; the natives on the small island of Engano, southwest of Sumatra; the Kubus who rove the jungles of southern Sumatra, reported to be the most primitive tribe still left on earth; some of the natives of the Great Andaman Islands of the Bay of Bengal. A complete list of obscure tribes of our world would be a very long one. Large areas of India, Burma, and Indochina, some islands of Indonesia, parts of Africa, great tracts in South America—these and other places remain prac-

[3] Thor Heyerdahl, *Aku-Aku*, Rand McNally & Company, Chicago, 1958.

tically unexplored from the anthropological point of view. Studies of such peoples would fill important gaps in the structure of the human heritage.[4]

The nineteenth-century idea that cultures evolve in the same way as plants and animals was abandoned when anthropologists found that it did not jibe with their observations. Now the evolutionary approach is being revived, with this difference: The facts, instead of limiting the approach to linear evolution, suggest multilinear cultural evolution. On this new basis evolutionists today are seeking to build an understanding of the development of human cultures. It is an ecological approach. The purpose is to learn how the factors in each given type of situation shaped the development of a particular type of society. Multilinear evolution is not merely a way of explaining the past; it is applicable to changes occurring today.[5]

NATURAL FACTORS IN SOCIAL CHANGE

Natural factors in social change are usually discussed in terms of three kinds of determinism—biologic, racial, and geographic. These will be discussed before dealing with technological and cultural factors.

Biologic Determinism. The law of evolution, formulated with reference to biology, soon appealed to philosophers as the key to group development and transformation, and all social change was traced to biological conditions and changes. One aspect of the theory was Social Darwinism, which stressed intergroup struggle as the means of selection. Among the Social Darwinists, who became known as the "conflict school" of sociologists, were the following men: Walter Bagehot (1826–1877), Ludwig Gumplowicz (1838–1909), Benjamin Kidd (1858–1916), Jacques Novicow (1849–1912), G. Vacher de Lapouge (1854–1936), Otto Ammon (1842–1916), and Gustav Ratzenhofer (1842–1904). The members of this school interpreted social evolution merely as a phase of biological evolution.

After about a generation of Social Darwinism, interest shifted to the so-called science of eugenics, which assumed that human evolution could be socially directed. The eugenists believe in natural selection, though they claim that in human society it works badly most of the time; hence the need for social direction of the process. The father of eugenics as a cult was Sir Francis Galton (1822–1911); among others in Europe who contributed to the movement were Karl Pearson, Otto Ammon, Wilhelm Schallmayer, and G. Vacher de Lapouge. In the United States, H. F. Osborn, C. B. Davenport, and others have helped popularize ideas of this cult. Of its postulates, we are primarily concerned with the one that social change comes through selection of the hereditary qualities of the population. Some eugenists believe that civilized society has greatly spurred the selective process, though it has at the same time thwarted its beneficent effects, causing it to favor the less capable instead of the most competent stock. As civilization has advanced, man's inherent fitness has declined. Modern society is undermining its genetic constitution by

[4] *Cf.* Robert Heine-Geldern, "Vanishing Cultures," *Scientific American,* vol. 196, no. 5, pp. 39–45, May, 1957.
[5] *Cf.* Julian H. Steward, "Cultural Evolution," *Scientific American,* vol. 194, no. 5, pp. 69–80, May, 1956.

abrogating the law of the survival of the fittest. The main difficulty is in reproductive selection, which eugenists assume is the chief factor which brings about social change and determines the direction of evolution.

To arrest the genetic trend, the eugenists' program involves the consideration of three types of environmental influence on the population, namely, therapeutic agencies, methods of altering the germ plasm, and selective measures. To criticize these propositions briefly: the therapeutic agencies have only temporary results and are of no value for race improvement; although changing the germ plasm might still be considered a possibility, it has not as yet been done; family eugenics offers nothing of lasting value in the direction of race improvement; racial eugenics, which proposes to purge the population of all poor genes by preventing reproduction among the bearers of such genes, has too many imponderables to deal with and has not been successful. And, finally, the major hypothesis of the eugenics movement, that society is undergoing change by means of biological selection, is without foundation in fact. Society has undergone great change, but its civilization has evolved without either the need or intimation of measurable alteration in its biological constitution.[6]

Racial Determinism. Racialism is a method of accounting for social evolution, not simply by hereditary selection, but by the presence or absence of a particular ethnic element in the population. The theory assumes that the so-called "Aryan" or "Nordic" race has been superior to all others and that it alone has been the creator and sustainer of civilization. The doctrine has been sponsored under such names as Aryanism, Teutonism, Celtism, Anglo-Saxonism, and Nordicism.

The cornerstone of the racialist doctrine was laid long ago by the historian Tacitus in his *Germania* (A.D. 98), in which he described the barbarians about whom he wrote as virtuous, individualistic, adventurous, sensitive to racial purity, and liberty-loving. The term "Aryan" was apparently introduced into European usage and associated with the Germanic stock by a German philologist, Max Müller, in 1853. He applied the term to a group of languages which he called Aryan, and assumed that there also was an Aryan race, which, of course, was a fallacy. The real founder of racialism was the French writer and diplomat, Joseph de Gobineau (1816–1882), who elaborated his theory in a work entitled *Essai sur l'inégalité des races humaines* ("Essay on the Inequality of Races"). His explanation of history's rise and fall of civilizations in terms of race is fallacious. His assumption that the white races are intellectually superior to the colored, and that the Aryans (whom he identified with the Aryas of India, the Iranians, the Hellenes, and the Sarmates or ancestral Germans) are leaders and world rulers by nature has been thoroughly discredited.

Houston Stewart Chamberlain, Oswald Spengler, Madison Grant, T. Lothrop Stoddard, and others have also been identified with fallacious racial doctrines. The Nazis made racialism one of their cardinal principles, motivated by extreme fanaticism. Perhaps the most disgraceful aspect of Nazism was its persecution and extermination of members of minority groups, which was rationalized on "racial" grounds.

[6] For additional details, see Newell LeRoy Sims, *The Problem of Social Change,* Thomas Y. Crowell Company, New York, 1939, pp. 91–122, which includes a useful bibliography. Also see Clarence Marsh Case, *Social Process and Human Progress,* Harcourt, Brace and Company, Inc., New York, 1931, pp. 103–128; eugenics is discussed here with reference to its possibilities in societal self-direction, and its fallacies are clearly exposed.

Since there has been no measurable change in the biological heritage of society within historic times, it is reasonable to conclude that race per se is not directly a factor in social change. The consensus of scientists is that there is no valid ground for assuming that any one race is of a higher order or better endowed by nature than another. Theories of difference in degree of mental endowment among races and populations and of inborn racial "psyches" have not been sustained. Racial prejudices, however, are apt to have some effect on social change, but such prejudices are founded largely on culture rather than on biological factors.

Geographic Determinism. The influence of the geographic environment was recognized in the writings of antiquity. Greek and Roman philosophers, and several during the Middle Ages, were intrigued by the ideas of environmentalism. Hippocrates, Plato, Aristotle, and Ibn Khaldun represent these early contributors to the theory. Jean Bodin (1530–1596), a Renaissance scholar, is given even more credit for establishing the doctrine in social theory. But beyond all these, Montesquieu (1689–1755) emphasized environmentalism in his work *The Spirit of Laws,* in which he described numerous ways in which the environment affected man and social institutions. A century later, full-fledged geographic determinism was enunciated in England by H. T. Buckle (1821–1862) and in Germany by Karl Ritter (1779–1859). These two writers were the principal sources for the present-day schools of human geography. Friedrich Ratzel (1844–1904), building directly on the works of Ritter, formulated the modern concept of human geography, which was introduced into America by Ellen Semple and Ellsworth Huntington. Topography, natural resources, and climate are the principal geographic influences claimed by this school to be determiners of social life.

Throughout this long development of environmentalist theory, fact and fancy have been confused, and certain impressions have been exaggerated. Our primary concern, however, is with *environmental limitations.* The material culture of an area reflects the "permissive" character of the environment. Certain values may be absent in an environment and consequently certain activities may be excluded. As W. I. Thomas illustrates this principle, "The Eskimo will not be able to cultivate corn or build houses and boats of wood, and the tropical African will not wear furs, build houses of snow, or construct blubber lamps." [7] Populations are generally dependent upon the fertility of the soil, the nature of their agriculture, the domestication of animals, the utilization of mineral resources, and the influences of their political history. Thus cultural change occurs subject to the opportunities and limitations of the environment. However, if the situation permits, populations find ways to circumvent unfavorable conditions; on the other hand, they may fail to utilize what is favorable.

The principle that different types of culture may emerge successively in an identical environment has been demonstrated repeatedly in the development of communities and nations. In modern times, the industrialization of European nations, of progressive nations in the American hemisphere, or of Japan and Russia, illustrates the emergence of scientific and technological culture in several different environments. There are national variations in this emergence, though cultural succession is evident. British

[7] W. I. Thomas, *Primitive Behavior,* McGraw-Hill Book Company, Inc., New York, 1937, pp. 6–7.

influence has been paramount in Australia, New Zealand, Canada, South Africa, and elsewhere; yet the Dominions are not copies of Great Britain. Two groups living side by side in the same general environment may be very different in some of their behavior and culture patterns. This is evident in American sectionalism, in the contrasts between life in Mexico and that in neighboring American states, and in the uniqueness of French Canada as compared with the rest of the Dominion and the neighboring New England states. The culture area rather than the natural environment should be emphasized in studies of social change, though environmental limitations should always be considered in cultural development.

In the following selection by W. D. Wallis it is shown that the dependence of civilization upon geographic environment must be accepted. But, however favorable the surroundings, the culture must have attained a certain advance, or it has taken no advantage of environment. Nature may give the blessing, but it is not really a blessing until man accepts it and learns to utilize it. Since the term "geographic environment" has been defined in different ways, Wallis makes it a point to dispose of the confusion that has arisen. As civilization advances, man seeks more and more to escape the exactions of the environment, to impose his will more masterfully upon nature, to conquer his conqueror. Adaptation to physical environment depends upon the will, the training, and the social inheritance of those who inhabit a given locality. With this orientation, Wallis presents a practical interpretation of the relations between physical environment and social development. The conclusion reached with reference to geographic environment and culture is, "The importance of physical environment to social evolution is in direct proportion to the advance of the culture. It is the lever as well as the fulcrum, but its leverage is determined by the civilization."

3

GEOGRAPHICAL ENVIRONMENT AND CULTURE*

Wilson D. Wallis

The view that nature has made or has unmade man is suggested by man's dependence upon nature. He is a creature of the earth's surface. Only by keeping touch with her can he maintain life. Out of her womb is he born, from her he receives nourishment, to her embrace he ultimately returns. Yet her children have not received impartial treatment. Some have nestled in favored spots where bounteous nature fills all needs; others have been put

* Reprinted by permission of *Social Forces,* vol. 4, no. 4, pp. 702–708, June, 1926.

down in hard places where life is a constant struggle with environment, a niggardly provider from whom blessings are wrung with sweat of brow and horny hands, or sought under dangerous and precarious conditions.

Herodotus remarked that Egypt is the gift of the Nile. Though he meant geographical Egypt cultural Egypt was almost coterminous with it and the one could scarcely be separated even in thought from the other. Egyptian civilization depended upon the fertility of the land, a fertility attributable to inundations providing a constantly renewed alluvium, and to a warm and abundant sunlight. Wheat is native to the Mediterranean area. It is plausible that nature herself provided the wild seed, covered it with a rich soil, watered it, and by the warmth of a southern sun nurtured it into a grain whose rare virtues were manifest. Thus were offered to the natives who dwelt along the turgid Nile advantages not vouchsafed those inhabiting colder and less happy regions beyond the Mediterranean. Nature had been kinder to those who dwelt along the river bank than to those whose abode was in desert or on bleak mountain height. Bodin stressed the fact that civilization is limited by degrees of latitude and of longitude, and also by altitude, noting the superiority of plains and river valleys as seats of civilization. Inspired by Bodin, Montesquieu pointed to climatic zones as delimitations of culture. The natives in the tropics did not advance beyond savagery because heat was enervating and because every need was supplied by nature. Those living in frigid zones were equally unfortunate, nature in that region being as niggardly as in the tropics she was beneficent, the polar inhabitants being forced by the inclemency of the region to spend most of their time and energy in securing food and clothing. The temperate zones furnish the happy mean; here man's needs are not fully supplied by nature; he must exert himself in order to satisfy them; the requisite labor stimulates without exhausting his efforts and capacities. For proof of his assertion Montesquieu pointed to the geographical distribution of civilization. The centers of civilization lie within the temperate zone and diminish in quality as we proceed toward the tropics or toward the polar regions. In the present century the views of Bodin and of Montesquieu have been championed by Miss Semple and by Ellsworth Huntington, who describe the extent to which not only effort and ability but civilization as well are matters of climate.

The dependence of civilization upon geographical environment must be accepted. But these writers leave out of the reckoning factors which are an intimate part of the situation. However favorable the surroundings, the culture must have attained a certain advance or no advantage is taken of environment. The Nile doubtless had long been irrigating and enriching the soil of Egypt, scattering the land with wild grains out of which man was destined to make cultivated cereals.

Nature may give the blessing but it is not really a blessing until man accepts it and learns to utilize it. Whether he does one or both depends upon himself as well as upon nature. Lucky accidents are not lessons to those not already alert. While the effects of climatic conditions upon mentality and upon physical stamina are not to be underrated, the fact remains that climatic conditions act differently upon different individuals as well as upon different civilizations. The balmy climate of Southern California has acted in one way upon the early Mexican-Spanish population, in another way upon the later European-American. Within certain bounds, heat does not kill intellectual or physical effort but merely handicaps it.

Again, by the theory of Montesquieu and of Huntington it is difficult to explain the shiftings in the centers of civilization from millennium to millennium, or even from century to century. Races which in the last thousand years have achieved greatness in art, literature, and science, lie within the cooler temperate zones. But what shall we say of the preceding thousands of years?

Moreover, the shiftings of civilization within a given geographical area make it difficult to accept the hypothesis that the environment accounts for the civilization, since the same conditions yield widely different products. If the Nile made ancient Egyptian civilization, must we not say that it made the civilization of medieval times, and that of modern times? Yet these products are of the most varied character.

In explaining everything the environment explains nothing. We know that in some parts of the world the climate has remained constant throughout thousands of years, whereas the civilization in that area has undergone manifold change. Whether we speak of the valleys of the Nile, the Euphrates and Tigris, the Rhine, or the Po, contrasts in successive civilizations stand out against a background of a same geographical environment maintaining itself through kaleidoscopic changes in social life, religion, art, and science.

Huntington does not save the day by pointing to a change in climatic conditions in Palestine and Italy, changes which he assumes account for the shiftings of civilization in those areas. The climatic changes have been trivial compared with the momentous changes in civilization which those lands have witnessed in the past three thousand years. The attempts to show the direct effects of environment upon national character must be rated equally unsuccessful. Gomperz fails to convince us that the intellect of Greece was the outcome of a rugged interior and an indented coastline. His theory will not account for the fact that Greek civilization developed in the sixth and fifth centuries B.C., arts, sciences, and philosophies which culminated in a period of brilliancy never achieved previously nor subsequently. Geographical conditions in Greece have not changed in any noteworthy respect, if they have changed at all; meanwhile, in this land of brilliant sunshine, civilization has waxed and waned, has died and found new birth.

Nor can we accept Taine's view that the spirit of English literature has been dictated by the environment. If the fogs and bogs of the North made morose and phlegmatic Saxons and Danes, how could they make light-hearted and vivacious Celts? When Sir William Ramsay assures us that the rugged mountains of Anatolia could not fail to arouse the religious sense, and Draper and Miss Semple declare that the monotony of the desert inspires belief in monotheism, we can only conclude that they have not read the evidence aright, because they have not read all of it. Must they not first explain why Mohammed arose when he did, and why the same desert region produced monotheism in one century and polytheism in another? Must they not also demand that the deserts of China, of Australia, and of North and South America deliver up their secrets of a monotheistic faith? In a word, those who support the thesis that the geographical environment is responsible for culture show nothing more than that culture must subsist in an environment, and that, given the culture and the environment, a correlation between the two can be made.

The defenders of the view that geographical environment constitutes the determinants of culture have been loth to define the meaning which they attach to "geographical environment." Their use of the term shows that they employ it now in the sense of what exists for the culture in question, now in the sense of what exists for the civilized man but does not exist for the culture in question. The two meanings are not synonymous. Shall we say that the Alleghany Indian of two centuries ago lived in an environment of coal, or that he lived in an environment of a useless black substance which we call coal and which we recognize, but he did not, as a substance capable of giving light, heat, and power? Was aluminum a part of our environment fifty years ago? There seems but one answer: Coal, a substance capable of giving light, heat, and power, was no part of the environment of the Alleghany Indian, though, as we now know, it was all about him; aluminum, a useful metal, was no part of our environment fifty years ago, though the substance, unknown, was about us on every side awaiting discovery and utilization.

Civilization has created these portions of the environment.

By environment we mean those things and influences with which we come into contact directly or indirectly. Though Captain Kidd's treasure lies buried at my doorstep, so long as I am uninfluenced by its presence it can not be said to constitute a part of my environment. At some future date knowledge may make it such.

Some years ago, accompanied by a friend, I boarded a train at Bischofsheim, in southern Germany. We rode through a beautiful country romantic with historic associations. Our enjoyment of these was now and then interrupted by the conversation of two ladies from Iowa, mother and daughter. The burden of their talk was: What should they do with the chicken-house and the back porch when they returned to their Iowa home? They had no eye for scenery nor for historical associations. Our physical bodies passed through the same physical surroundings, but our environments were as far apart as mediaeval Germany and the henroost in Iowa.

America was no part of the environment of the ancient Roman nor of the mediaeval Londoner, but today America is part of the environment of the inhabitants of these cities. Civilization created this change in environment. The new environment of America gave us a new civilization, but the old civilization of Europe gave us the new environment, the Americas. The nature of the actual environment of a people can not be settled by the cartographer. How can he describe the environment of the New Yorker? The environment of some New Yorkers is the region of Long Island Sound and Hudson River. But many a New Yorker lives in an environment as large, almost, as the national boundaries. Not only do his wanderings make this actual: he may travel as far in a museum or with a book as others with an unlimited ticket. Nor do we forget the subtlety and indirectness of the geographical influences. These so-called influences, however, are merely the medium in which human forces and motives find resisting fulcrum.

By adapting itself to environmental influences human life shows its reasonableness, its balance, its ingenuity, its freedom. It makes the most of them in order that it may rise above their compulsions. Without geographical environment civilization is as impossible as war without gravitation, but environment does not explain nor cause civilization more than gravitation causes or explains war. The shiftings in the center of civilization from one region to another, and the various changes in civilization which a given geographical area witnesses can be explained only by reference to the human life there resident. This human life possesses cultural traits received from another geographical horizon which it will transmit to some further region. The environment which accounts for these shiftings is a culture environment overleaping geographical barriers or even annihilating them and setting up new ones.

At one time to some peoples rivers are a means of separation; at other times and to other peoples they are a means of communication. What the geographical environment signifies, which is almost equivalent to saying what the geographical environment is, depends upon the peoples concerned. They create it to a much larger extent than it creates them. Countries once the white man's grave have been made habitable. Mortality decreases as man remakes the environment. In regions where formerly environment had complete mastery of man he has subjected it to his will and now is its master. As Buffon expressed it: "The more, therefore, he observes and cultivates nature the more means he will find of making her subservient to him and of drawing new riches from her bosom without diminishing the treasures of her inexhaustible fecundity." To attribute social advance to geographical environment is to place ourselves by the side of the old lady who marvelled at the providential way in which big rivers were made to run past big towns. The teleology is inverted.

Man is not an automaton, but a creature with a will. As Kirchhoff says:

The suggestions thrown out by the nature of his birthplace sometimes find him a docile, sometimes an indifferent pupil. What is now the world-harbor of New York once served the Indians as nothing but a hunting place for edible mollusks. On the same rock-bound coast that educated the Norwegians into intrepid sailors, the Lapps are at present eking out a paltry existence as fishermen. . . . If, however, man ventures to pit his strength against the elemental power of the sea; if he goes further and elects as his vocation the sailor's struggle with storm and seething breaker, then the poet's word in its full significance may be applied to him: "Man's stature grows with every higher aim." The mariner's trade steels muscle and nerve, it sharpens the senses, it cultivates presence of mind. With each triumph of human cleverness over the rude forces of nature it heightens the courageousness of well-considered, fearless action.

Geographical environment is the cradle in which man's genius awaits the promptings of motives which give him mastery over his fate.

In many ways he is and always has been dependent upon the geographical environment; he can no more escape it than he can dodge the forces of gravitation; the one as surely as the other fashions him and accounts for some of his characteristics. It may be that our arboreal ancestors—if they were arboreal! —climbed down from the trees because the trees were degenerating in that area, forced to earth while our unfortunate, because too fortunate, simian cousins remained within their leafy bowers.

Man, possibly, is an example of the fact that unfavorable environment in the end may prove to be a favorable one, eliciting potencies which else lie dormant or atrophy in disuse. Conformity to environment can not guarantee survival, much less can it ensure progress. When one speaks in terms of conformity to environment one thinks of mollusks and the smaller parasites, admirably adapted to the environment. The failure or refusal of higher forms to conform closely with environment is a distinguishing trait. Or shall we say they conform to different environments, though these environments lie within the same latitudes and longitudes, as drawn by the cartographer? The oyster and man live in much the same environment if only they knew it, but knowing it or not knowing it is the element which makes the environment what it is. The dyne of selection is as important as the array of things upon which selection operates.

Rational selection of environment is taken for granted when it is alleged that environment is a determining factor in economic, social, or political life, that it makes or unmakes a people, determining whether a given tribe or nation is to rise to prominence in world affairs or is to sink into inoffensive and powerless rivalry for a place in the sun.

Undoubtedly certain environments are favorable and other environments are unfavorable; yet, the advantages they offer are conditional upon the response of the culture. Man can do well where conditions are unfavorable; he can do poorly where conditions are favorable. He is more than a creature of the environment, or he is no human being. The story of his conquest of nature and of his utilization of her forces is evidence that he is a creator as well as a creature of environment. What he has become is to be explained in part by nature, but much more by nurture; it is more a matter of race than one of place.

The murders committed by Labrador Eskimo have an environmental background, for they are committed at the time of the year when the seasons most dispose to outrage.

In the dark days of midwinter, when polar winds blow and the men can not go out to hunt, they sit inside the huts, gorge with meat, and take little exercise. A congested body harbors an irritable nervous system, the amiable, good-natured Eskimo becomes sullen and moody. Mental depression reflects his gloomy surroundings. Old slights and grudges which he recalls in this abnormal condition assume exaggerated proportions. Under such conditions most of the murders occur. We see no objection to considering this a case of the influence of geographical environment. But it must be recalled that not all Eskimo subjected to these conditions commit murders, and that all peoples subjected to these conditions do not react to them as do the Eskimo.

With advance in civilization man is able more and more to escape the exactions of the environment, to impose his will more masterfully upon nature, to conquer his conqueror. The correlation between man's economic life and his geographical environment is not evidence of the influence of physical environment. The correlation shows the extent to which man has adapted himself to the environment, the extent to which he has compelled it to minister to his needs, to serve his purposes, to respond to his will. We do not find canoes in the Sahara Desert. If the converse of the picture is that the environment does not drive man to build canoes, the obverse is that enterprises other than canoe-building ensure salvation.

Moreover, where geographical conditions are the same or similar we do not find a same and often not a similar reaction.

The reaction to the geographical environment depends not so much upon the nature of the environment as upon the nature of the culture transplanted to the environment.

Adaptation to physical environment depends upon the will, the training, the social inheritance of those who inhabit a given locality. If we wish to predict what a people will do when they move into a new environment, it is more important to know the people than to know the place—or better, one must know both.

Nietzsche leaves out of the reckoning an important factor when he declares: "If thou knewest a people's need, its land, its sky, and its neighbor, then wouldst thou divine the law of its surmountings, and why it climbeth up that ladder to its hopes." The people themselves are one of the factors in their progress, and usually the most important of the factors. As Horace says, "They change their sky, not their spirit, those who travel across the seas."

Within limitations which shift with the civilization, almost any kind of culture can flourish in almost any kind of physical environment. But culture can not flourish independently of surrounding cultures. Savagery can not persist indefinitely when its neighbors are civilized peoples. Civilization can not maintain itself in a sea of savagery, but ultimately will give way to savagery or bring savagery into line with civilization.

An analysis of the geographical environment does not afford as valuable insight into the culture of a people as does a knowledge of the culture of its neighbors. The distribution of cultures confirms this induction. There is a geography of culture as clearly marked, as distinct in demarcating outlines, as different in content, as is the physical geography.

The lines which mark out culture areas are not coterminous with those which delimit river, valley, mountain systems, plateaus, plains. Culture boundaries in some cases to an extent respect geographical lines, as, for example, in aboriginal North America; yet in the main, culture lines cross and interpenetrate geographical boundaries as though the latter did not exist. Where geographical features impose limitations the limitations are respected; but not until we know the culture do we know the limitations. Geographical features do not break up civilized America as they do, or did, aboriginal America.

To a forest-dwelling people the region of wood imposes limiting conditions upon the construction of houses; yet the Eskimo disregard such limiting conditions, finding at hand other materials out of which to make habitations.

Were the Eskimo isolated groups, not intermingling and not exchanging articles in trade, their isolation would be pointed to as imposed by environment. But they rise above these specious limitations and do trade, travel, visit, and intermingle. Were art wholly absent from their culture the lack of suitable materials for the operation of the artistic impulse would be pointed to as responsible for the absence of art. Here again they rise above our expectations, refuse to acknowledge obviously limiting conditions, are artists. The limiting conditions can not be inferred apart from the culture which inhabits a given environment. To this extent the poet is right: "In thine own breast stands the star of thy fate."

Physical environment is not a matter apart from social development, nor one to which the culture can be indifferent. The culture shows its wisdom by acquaintance with environment and by making the most of it. If 'being influenced' by the environment means making the most of it, then it is the part of wisdom to be influenced. Adaptation to environment illustrates the freedom and rationality of the group. With advance in civilization man attains relative freedom from environment. He may acquire freedom by changing place of abode, escaping to regions where the preferred environment is to be found, though this at best usually is a matter of individual rather than one of group choice; or he may protect himself through his own devices from the inclemency and extremes of the environment.

Man learns to make nature do his bidding. Where there is dearth of rainfall he supplies rivers of irrigating canals. The water which will not come from the heavens shall be induced to come up through the earth. The wilderness and the desert are made to blossom like the rose; in the dreariest wastes man induces nature to be prodigal of her blessings. As man develops power, as his devices become more ingenious, environment is reinterpreted and remade.

In early stages of social development nature may determine man's activities; later he gives the emphasis to the environment. He no longer trembles at nature's threat for he can throttle the threat in its utterance. Sun, wind, and wave are made to generate power which man uses to his enhancement. As a factor in progress physical environment is important in the case of two peoples of the same level of culture, possessing the same handicrafts, the same mechanical ability. As between widely diverse cultures differences in environment do not much matter. The superior advantages of the physical environment of North America mean much to the culture of Canadians and to the peoples of the States; they mean much less to the Spanish in Mexico; they mean still less to unenlightened Indian tribes. The environment of Australia is a factor in the social evolution of Europeans who now govern that continent; it is a much weaker factor in the life of the aborigines. In one case the culture is able to utilize the environment, in the other it is not. The importance of physical environment to social evolution is in direct proportion to the advance of the culture. It is the lever as well as the fulcrum, but its leverage is determined by the civilization. As Voltaire says, though climate has influence, government has a hundred times more, and religion in conjunction with government has still more.

Technological Factors of Social Change. Technological factors include not only changing techniques in production and distribution, but various ideologies which have emphasized economic determinism of social change. Karl Marx, for example, offered a materialistic conception of historical change. He believed that the stage of technological development determines the mode of production and the relationships and institutions that constitute the economic system. This set of relationships is claimed to be the chief determinant of the whole social order. The cultural life of man, his intellectual, aesthetic, and spiritual life, his creeds and his philosophies, and the social forms which are their vehicles are said to be the reflection of the economic order. Thorstein Veblen also believed that the difference in environment explains the difference in the social structure and, therefore, man's habits of thought and action.[8]

[8] Thorstein Veblen, *Theory of the Leisure Class,* The Viking Press, New York, 1922, pp. 192–193. Chapter VIII as a whole is recommended on the subject.

The following selection from an analysis of society by R. M. MacIver and Charles H. Page sketches realistic relationships between changing techniques and changing society. The effects of the machine age on modern society are broad and fundamental. Mechanization has brought changes in attitudes, beliefs, traditions, and many social values; it has greatly affected social structure and function. Examples of how technological advance initiates social change have been given with reference to agricultural techniques, advances in communication, and the control of atomic energy. Advancing technology tends consistently to promote specialization.

4

CHANGING TECHNIQUES AND CHANGING SOCIETY*

R. M. MacIver and Charles H. Page

MODERN SOCIETY AND THE MACHINE AGE

The approach through technology has on other grounds a particular appeal and significance for our own age. The rapid changes of our society are obviously related to and somehow dependent upon the development of new techniques, new inventions, new modes of production, new standards of living. We live more and more in cities, and "in the city—and particularly in great cities—the external conditions of life are so evidently contrived to meet man's clearly organized needs that the least intellectual . . . are led to think in deterministic and mechanistic terms." † *The most novel and pervasive phenomenon of our age is not capitalism but mechanization,* of which modern capitalism may be merely a by-product. We realize now that this mechanization has profoundly altered our modes of life and also of thought.

(1) *Mechanization and Social Changes.* Attitudes, beliefs, traditions, which once were thought to be the very expression of essential human nature, have crumbled before its advance. Monarchy, the divine ordering of social classes, the prestige of birth, the spirit of craftsmanship, the insulation of the neighborhood, traditions regarding the spheres of the sexes, regarding religion, regarding politics and war, have felt the shock. The process, beginning with the external change and ending with the social response, is easy to follow and to understand. Take, for example, the profound changes which have occurred in the social life and status of women in the industrial age. Industrialism destroyed the domestic system of production, brought women from the home to the factory and the office, differentiated their tasks and distinguished their earnings. Here is the new environment, and the new social life of women

* From *Society: An Introductory Analysis,* Rinehart and Company, Inc., New York, 1949, pp. 553–557. Reprinted by permission of the publishers.

† R. E. Park, chapter on "Magic, Mentality, and City Life," in Park and E. W. Burgess, *The City,* Chicago, 1925.

is the response. The rapid transitions of modern civilization offer a myriad of other illustrations.

The swift transitions of our industrial mechanized civilization have not only been followed by far-reaching social changes, but very many of these changes are such as appear either necessary accommodations or congenial responses to the world of the machine. In the former category come the higher specialization of all tasks, the exact time-prescribed routine of work, the acceleration of the general tempo of living, the intensification of competition, the obsolescence of the older craftsmanship, the development, on the one hand, of the technician and, on the other, of the machine operative, the expansion of economic frontiers, and the complicated, extending network of political controls. In the latter may be included the various accompaniments of a higher standard of living, the transformation of class structures and of class standards, the undermining of local folkways and the disintegration of the neighborhood, the breaking up of the old family system, the building of vast changeful associations in the pursuit of new wealth or power, the increasing dominance of urban ways over those of the country, the spread of fashion, the growth of democracy and of plutocracy, the challenge of industrial organized groups, particularly the organizations of labor, to the older forms of authority.

(2) *Mechanization and Changes in Values.* With these conditions are bred corresponding attitudes, beliefs, philosophies. A great mass of contemporary social criticism seeks to depict and often to arraign the cultural concomitants of the machine age. Its tenor is generally as follows: Different qualities are now esteemed because the qualities which make for success, for wealth, and for power are different. Success is measured more in pecuniary terms, as possession is more detachable from social and cultural status. A form of democratization has developed which measures everything by units or by quantities and admits no differences in personal values save as they are attached to external goods or are the means of their acquisition. Men grow more devoted to quan-

tity than to quality, to measurement than to appreciation. The desire for speed dominates, for immediate results, for quick speculative advantages, for superficial excitations. The life of reflection, the slow ripening of qualitative judgments, is at a discount. Hence novelty is sought everywhere, and transient interests give a corresponding character to social relationships. The changing interests of civilization absorb men to the relative exclusion of the more permanent interests of culture. Men grow pragmatic in their philosophies. "Things are in the saddle and ride mankind." The mechanistic outlook explains life itself in behavioristic terms, as a series of predetermined responses to successive stimuli. The unity of life is dissipated, since from the mechanistic point of view all things are means to means and to no final ends, functions of functions and of no values beyond.

(3) *Direct and Indirect Effects of Technological Change.* That the tendencies thus described are at least accentuated by the mechanization both of work and of the means and conditions of recreation is clearly established by a great mass of evidence. It can scarcely be a mere coincidence that in the periods and in the countries of rapid technological advance there should have developed corresponding or congenial ways of thinking and of living. Nevertheless we should be wary of concluding too hastily that social relations are in all important respects predominantly determined by technological changes. This conclusion would hold only if culture also, the values men set before them as ends for which to live, were essentially the product of technology. But culture in turn seeks to direct technology to its own ends. Man may be the master as well as the slave of the machine. He has already rejected many of the conditions that accompanied and seemed to be imposed by the earlier technology of the industrial revolution. He has taken some steps in all civilized countries to place a variety of controls on factory toil, on the squalor of factory towns, on the shoddiness and ugliness of many factory-made goods, on the risks and fatigues of many factory operations. Man is a

critic as well as a creature of circumstance.

Therefore we should distinguish between the more direct and less direct social consequences of mechanization or other technological process. Certain social consequences are the inevitable results of technological change, such as a new organization of labor, the expansion of the range of social contacts, the specialization of function, and the encroachment of urban influences on rural life. Other concomitants, not being inevitable conditions of the operation of the new techniques, are more provisional or more precarious, such as the increase of unemployment, the intensified distinction between an employing and a wage-earning class, the heightening of competition, and the prevalence of mechanistic creeds. In the remaining sections of this chapter we shall endeavor to show that the deterministic theories which make technological change the dominant or overruling cause of social change are one-sided or misleading. But first it is well to insist on the positive aspect, and show by citing some recent developments how real and how important an agency of social change is the quest of modern man to discover and to utilize new techniques, new and more efficient methods of accomplishing his ends.

HOW TECHNOLOGICAL ADVANCE INITIATES SOCIAL CHANGE

Every technological advance, by making it possible for men to achieve certain results with less effort or at less cost, at the same time provides new opportunities and establishes new conditions of life. The opportunities, or some of them, are frequently anticipated in the development or exploitation of the new devices; the new conditions of life are in large measure the necessary and unanticipated adjustments to the new opportunities. A few illustrations will bring out the distinction.

(1) *New Agricultural Techniques and Social Change*. Take, for example, the advance of agricultural technology. The improvements in the breeds of cattle, in the use of fertilizers, in the varieties of seed, in mechanical laborsaving devices, and so forth, have

had as their direct objective the increase in the quantity and quality of agricultural production. But as concomitants of the attainment of this objective there have gone changes in farm economy and in the manner of life of the farming household. And beyond these again there have gone changes in the relation of agriculture to industry, migrations from the farm to the city because of the lessened numbers required to supply the agricultural needs of the whole community, the decay or abandonment of marginal farm lands, tendencies to agricultural depression, new struggles for foreign markets and new tariff barriers. And these changes in turn have stimulated new and difficult economic problems. Thus the achievement of the immediate objective of agricultural technology has led by an inevitable nexus to changes of an entirely different order.

(2) *Advances in Communication and Social Change*. Even more far reaching and complex are the social changes that spring from the development of the techniques of communication. For communication is at once a primary condition of social relations and a basis of nearly all other forms of technological advance. The course of civilization has been marked by a constant development of the means of communication, but never so rapidly as in our own days, when electricity is not only being adopted as motive power in place of steam, not only is a factor in the improvement of automobile and airplane, not only makes the motion picture a vast commercial enterprise and television a promising adventure, but also, resuming its distance-annihilating range, becomes in the radio a voice that is heard simultaneously by millions over the face of the earth. The impact of these changes on society is too enormous and too multifarious to be dealt with here except by way of incidental illustration. Every step of technological advance inaugurates a series of changes that interact with others emanating from the whole technological system. The radio, for example, affects a family situation already greatly influenced by modern technology, so that its impetus toward the restora-

tion of leisure enjoyment within the home is in part counteracted or limited by opposing tendencies. Again, the radio combines with other technological changes to reduce the cultural differentiation of social classes and of urban and rural communities. On the other hand, by enabling an individual speaker to address great multitudes, it makes possible the rapid rise of new parties or social movements, provided the broadcasting system is not itself politically controlled. In the latter event it tends to produce the opposite result, becoming a most powerful agency of propaganda monopolized by the ruling power. This last illustration should serve to show that what we call the "effects" of invention are in large measure dependent variables of the social situation into which they are introduced.

(3) *The Control of Atomic Energy and Social Change.* The most spectacular illustration, however, is that afforded by the epoch-making discovery of a way to make atomic energy serviceable to human objectives. Like so many other discoveries of modern science, this new agency is available equally for destructive or for constructive purposes. As an agent of war it forebodes the most appalling annihilation of all the works of man. As an agent of peace it may ultimately bring an unprecedented era of plenty.

THE GENERAL DIRECTION OF SOCIAL CHANGE WITH ADVANCING TECHNOLOGY

Bearing in mind the caution contained in the last paragraphs we may still ask whether there is any major direction in which society moves under the continual impact of technological change.

(1) *Specialization.* We have seen that technology itself tends always in the same direction, attaining ever greater efficiency in the performance of *each* of the various functions to which its devices are applied. In doing so it specializes functions more and more, and thus tends to create an ever-increasing division of labor, with whatever social consequences depend thereon. The social significance of this growing division of labor has been given

classic treatment by Durkheim, though some of his conclusions, such as that greater liberty and a diminution of class differences are concomitants of specialization, are stated in too sweeping and universal a form. More certain is the correlation between technological advance and a more elaborate social organization with higher interdependence between its parts, greater mobility of the members with respect to location and to occupation, more elaborate systems of laws and of governmental controls, new concentrations both of economic and of political power, greater instability of the institutional order, greater leisure and generally higher standards of living for large numbers. These conditions seem to be directly bound up with growing technological efficiency, and they in turn have further repercussions on every aspect of social life. They also create some extremely important social problems, one being the unbalance of the economic system that accompanies the accelerated processes of technological change. But within our limits we can do no more than suggest some of the immediate social concomitants of technological advance.

(2) *The Modern Significance of the Technological Factor.* It is scarcely too much to say that every major problem of modern society is either initiated by or at least strongly affected by technological change. Conflicts between states, as they strive for dominance, for security, or for prosperity, are in no small measure concerned with competing ambitions to secure or control areas rich in oil, coal, or other resources of crucial importance to modern industry. Again, the specialization of functions in a modern economy gives rise to a multitude of organized groups, each of which seeks its own economic advantage and each of which has the power of withholding a service that modern interdependence renders indispensable. On the other hand, these groups are affiliated with or incorporated into massive federations or combinations. These in turn exercise a correspondingly greater power, so that the disputes arising out of their clashing interests sometimes threaten to disrupt the whole social order. . . .

Cultural Factors of Social Change. W. F. Ogburn has formulated a hypothesis of *cultural lag* as a factor in social change. The thesis of cultural lag is that the various parts of culture do not change at the same rate, some of the parts changing more rapidly than others. Within a culture there is a correlation and interdependence of parts, so that a rapid change in one part of culture may require readjustments through other changes in the various correlated parts of culture.[9]

To explain what is meant by the correlation and interdependence of parts of culture, let it be assumed that two cultural variables are related, one being an independent variable and the other dependent on the first. As changes occur in the independent variable, adjustments will be called for in the dependent or adaptive variable; but since changes in the dependent variable occur later than those in the other which disrupted the equilibrium, the result is "cultural lag." Ogburn takes industrial change to represent an independent variable, and education, a dependent variable; then, if industrial change occurs more rapidly than that required in education, the result will be a lag in education as the adaptive variable.

This hypothesis has been criticized on various counts, but it continues to be a favorite one with sociologists.[10] Whether or not one reduces it to statistical measurement, its philosophical implications are important. MacIver and Page suggest the need for a more refined analysis of cultural lag because of the complexity of modern social organization. There are so many ways in which parts of culture are interdependent. Cultural lag has been referred to by various writers in terms of technological lag, also as technological restraint. Restraint may be determined by bureaucratic interest, by economic interest, or by cultural interest. The new technology may be introduced from without into a community or country where culture is wedded to a quite different system, which acts as a restraint; cultural unity and harmony is disrupted if an alien culture is forced upon the society. This is evident in the impact of Western culture in Oriental and Asiatic regions. Another factor is culture clash; this occurs wherever two ways of life or modes of thought within the same community are so opposed that they cannot live side by side, and the very presence of the one implies the suppression of the other. On the other hand, there is such a thing as cultural ambivalence, meaning a simultaneous attraction toward and a repulsion from certain aspects of culture.[11]

Culture as Determinant of Social Change. Culture does not *cause* cultural growth or change, though culture is a dynamic of social change. There is an intimate connection between our beliefs and our institutions, our valuations and our social rela-

[9] William F. Ogburn, *Social Change with Respect to Culture and Original Nature,* B. W. Huebsch, New York, 1922; new edition, The Viking Press, Inc., New York, 1950. See pp. 200–207 and 210–213 for statement and development of the hypothesis of cultural lag. *Cf.* Ogburn's article, "Cultural Lag as Theory," in *Sociology and Social Research,* vol. 41, no. 3, pp. 167–174, 1957.

[10] See, for example, James W. Woodward, "A New Classification of Culture and a Restatement of the Cultural Lag Theory," *American Sociological Review,* vol. I, pp. 89–104, 1936. Hornell Hart has a chapter, "The Hypothesis of Cultural Lag: A Present-day View," in *Technology and Social Change,* by Francis R. Allen et al., Appleton-Century-Crofts, Inc., New York, 1957, pp. 417–434.

[11] For more extended development of these points of analysis, see MacIver and Page, *op. cit.,* pp. 575–580.

tionships. And it may be reiterated that all cultural change involves social change, for the social and the cultural are closely interwoven. The cultural factor not only is responsive to technological change but also acts back on it so as to influence its direction and its character. That cultural elements have a directional role is indicated by the influences of historic religions and ideologies. Max Weber, for example, developed a theory that the ethics of Calvinism were not only in conformity with, but an important preparation for the growth of capitalism.[12] Since the "Protestant ethic" traditionally has emphasized those virtues of thrift, discipline, personal responsibility, self-help, and unremitting toil which were congenial to the capitalist spirit, this determinist theory had some plausibility.

It should be noted, however, that social institutions are reciprocally interrelated and their influences are not apt to be limited to one direction; also their influences may be multiple and subject to dispersion in various aspects of the culture. The effects of the airplane, for example, are dispersed in many directions, as is evident in war, transportation, government, commerce, agriculture, and other relationships. Similarly the social institutions influence one another according to the dynamics of the situation, and caution must be observed in weighing the importance of any one factor in directing social change. The directional role of Protestantism, in so far as it has been judged favorable toward capitalism, was necessarily qualified by other economic, political, and social reforms in process at the time. The religious code would reflect adjustments to the changing moral code.

Other Cultural Determinants. Societies may be thrown violently into a dynamic condition because of their reactions to catastrophes such as floods, drought, earthquakes, or storms. They may become dynamic because of population factors, the sudden increase or decrease in numbers, the effects of destructive epidemics or plagues. Societies may become dynamic because of social determinants such as invasion, conquest, or the migrations of peoples. These factors may involve racial and cultural conflict and are likely to hasten the cross-fertilization of cultures.

Victory in warfare has historically been a major factor in the ascendancy of nations and empires, and, conversely, defeat in war has meant the subordination of the victims. Usually the culture of the stronger nation will prevail over that of the weaker nation, though in the process of cross-fertilization the conquered people may have more to offer for cultural advancement than the more militant conqueror.

Immigration is another agency for change; through peaceable penetration, the newcomers may introduce traits from a different culture area. The culture of the United States is an outstanding example of the results of this process. However, even in prehistoric times migrations were leaving their traces in the amalgamation of racial stocks and the blending of cultures. Racial and class conflicts may result from invasion, conquest, or the migratory movements of peoples who differ in race, culture, and history.

[12] Max Weber, *The Protestant Ethic and the Spirit of Capitalism,* trans. by Talcott Parsons, George Allen & Unwin, Ltd., London, 1930. For criticism of Weber's theory, see R. H. Tawney, *Religion and the Rise of Capitalism,* Harcourt, Brace and Company, Inc., New York, 1926, and J. Milton Yinger, *Religion in the Struggle for Power,* Duke University Press, Durham, N. C., 1946, pp. 85–118.

Discovery, invention, diffusion, and other social processes are sometimes referred to as culture determinants. They will be discussed along with other processes that produce social and cultural change.

SOCIAL PROCESSES INVOLVED IN SOCIAL CHANGE

Social change itself is a process, but in its fulfillment one or more of several social processes may be in action. The processes defined below are fundamental but are not to be thought of as exclusive of others. Ordinarily, several processes are functioning at the same time in the same culture area.

Acclimatization. The process by which an organism becomes adapted to a new climate is called acclimatization. The term may be applied to plants, animals, and human beings. The test of acclimatization is not the survival of the individual, but of the species or variety. Two fundamental principles are significant in acclimatization. First, every species is subject to climatic limits imposed by temperature, humidity, sunshine, wind, and other factors. The individual can survive within certain climatic limits; within more restricted limits the individual can permanently reproduce its kind. The second principle is that every species thrives best under definite conditions of climate, but the optimum for the individual and for conditions of reproduction may differ widely. Moreover, the optimum and the limits vary appreciably from one individual to another. The main problem of acclimatization centers around the white man who moves to the moister parts of the tropics. However, increased exploration and development of the polar regions may arouse special interest in problems of acclimatization in those sectors of the earth.

Accommodation. This social process is to be differentiated from adaptation, although both are forms of adjustment. Whereas adaptation may be defined as structural change in the organism which takes place through biological variation and selection, the term "accommodation" is reserved for functional changes in the habits and customs of persons and groups—changes which are transmitted socially rather than biologically. Through accommodation, old habits are broken up and new coordinations are made. Social organization is the product of accommodations to past and present situations. Social heritages, traditions, sentiments, culture, and technique are accommodations; they are acquired adjustments which may be transmitted only socially. Accommodation to conflict situations may take the form of domination, toleration, compromise, conciliation, and conversion. Thus accommodation may function in interpersonal relations, in labor-management adjustments, in international conflict, and in countless other social situations requiring adjustments.

Adaptation. This term denotes a process of organization, i.e., the gradual development of an integrated scheme of structures and functions suited to a rather definite mode of life under specific conditions. The different races of men have obviously undergone more or less environmental selection, notably in adaptation to temperature, moisture, sunlight, and altitude. The Caucasian, Mongoloid, and Negro stocks have different climatic optima and different ranges of climatic toleration. Such physical adaptations are necessarily more general than specific, and achieved only over long periods of time. However, man adapts himself to his habitat not so much by mutational differences as by cultural achievements; this fact largely accounts for differences in the cultures of peoples living in such widely different habitats as arctic and desert, or wet and torrid. It should be remembered, however, that migration, trade, travel, and war diffuse culture traits across considerable distances; moreover, man may to some degree adapt the environment to his own purposes. In their physical sense, adaptation and acclimatization over periods of time would have something in common. Various animals undergo such adjustments seasonally, while man depends upon and adjusts his culture to ensure his survival in a given habitat.

Social Assimilation. As popularly used, assimilation is a political rather than a cultural concept. It ordinarily denotes the process or processes by which peoples of diverse racial origins and different cultural heritages, occupying a common territory, achieve a cultural solidarity sufficient at least to sustain a national existence. Its root meaning is "to make similar or alike." Assimilation may take place so gradually that its phases are scarcely observable. As immigrants acquire the language of their adopted country and gradually become able to participate economically and politically in the common life of the people, without encountering prejudice, they are being assimilated. They are becoming culturally similar to their neighbors and associates, a part of a cultural solidarity. Some foreigners and minority groups are so markedly different in race and culture that it is exceptionally difficult for them to become assimilated.

Competition. Competition implies a struggle or contest between two or more persons for the same object. The genus of competition is rivalry, which is universal in life and in society. Whether competition refers to rivalry for prestige and income or for power and wealth, its sociological function is to promote organization. It is by competition—whether of persons, firms, industries, nations, races, beliefs, habits, or cultures—that the fittest survive. Through competition, individuals and institutions of different capacities are given places in a going society; and competition is a basic factor in the adaptation of an industrial system to new conditions. Thus competition functions as a process of selection, as an economic organization, and as an agency of social development.

Competition determines the distribution of population territorially and vocationally. The division of labor and the organized interdependence of individuals and groups are products of competition. Workers compete impersonally in the ranks of labor; there is competition at the level of management; and competition is more or less constant between management and labor. The factors in production—land, labor, capital, and the entrepreneur—theoretically and actually operate in competition with one another; and now governmental interference has become another factor in competition. Nations engage in economic struggles which affect specific industries and national economies as a whole. The current agitation about automation is a phase of the competition between labor and management in industry. In periods of crisis, competition may be converted into conflict. This may happen when labor organizations resort to strikes or other coercive methods of a more personal and intermittent nature. When competition becomes so critical that social welfare is jeopardized, the society will very likely turn to some political process for remedial action.

Conflict. As sociological concepts, competition and conflict are closely related but distinguishable forms of interaction. Whereas competition is regarded as continuous and impersonal, conflict is intermittent and personal. In conflict, an indispensable condition is the contact of those engaged in the struggle; the struggle is conscious and evokes emotions, passions, and drives beyond those usually associated with competition. Competition is concerned with location, position, and ecological interdependence and determines the position of the individual in the *community*. Conflict, on the other hand, is concerned with status, subordination and superordination, and control, and fixes the individual's place in *society*. Both terms can be applied to groups and nations, as well as to struggle between individuals.

There are many types of situations in which tensions are built up to the stage of overt conflict; among the more common examples are war, feud and faction, litigation, and the conflict of impersonal ideals or ideologies. Conflict itself is the resolution of the tension between the contraries.

The rivalry of social groups may be friendly and competitive; at times, however, rivalry develops into conflict. This is not infrequently the case among gangs and political organizations. Culture conflicts may arise among religious sects and denominations, especially with reference to sects that are struggling for recognition. Conflict situations that arise among racial and caste groups are likely to be charged with emotionally motivated cultural prejudices.

Invention and Discovery. New culture traits come into existence through invention, which frequently is associated with discovery. Invention is defined as an active combination of social elements into a new form, and discovery is a more passive perception of existing relations of such elements. The two processes are, however, closely interrelated. Discovery of new facts or principles in physical or mental nature presupposes the invention of new methods of acting or thinking; on the other hand, invention of new influences and reactions, whether in nature or in society, is rarely devoid of newly discovered facts as assisting, inspiring, or even originating its conditions.

That which one "discovers" existed before, but had remained unknown. Discovery may be essentially accidental, as when gold was discovered in California or the diamond found in South Africa. Many formulas or processes have been discovered accidentally while conducting experimental research in physics, chemistry, astronomy, and other sciences, including the social sciences. Two factors usually are necessary for discovery to be made: first, opportunity for the phenomenon to manifest itself; and second, intelligent observation of the manifested phenomenon. These factors may operate in response to one's curiosity, or the drive of necessity, or that intangible quality called genius. These factors suggest the role of the inventor.

An invention is, in simple terms, a device, contrivance, or the like, originated after study or experiment. Invention and discovery are so closely coupled that it may be said they go hand in hand, each contributing to the usefulness of the other. The inventor begins with the knowledge he has acquired from the cultural heritage or base and tries new combinations of facts or ideas or principles, hopeful that he may be able to solve some specific problem. Thus mentally equipped, the inventor tends to be alerted toward discovery; and invention and discovery continue to complement each other while experiments are conducted.

The teamwork of invention and discovery is evident in instances such as these: when Archimedes of Syracuse (287?–212 B.C.) discovered specific gravity by noticing the displacement of water while taking a bath; when Aristotle (384–322 B.C.), curious concerning the development of the chick in the egg, began to experiment and thus initiated the science of embryology; as when Benjamin Franklin (1706–1790) proved the identity of lightning and electricity; when Lee De Forest (1873–   ) developed his audion tube (1921) which made practicable transcontinental telephony, both wire and wireless; when Albert Einstein (1879–1955) developed his theory of relativity and discovered new factors in the research on the atom.

If man had depended only on discovery, the cultural heritage would no doubt be rather negligible. Inventors do not wait; they search, as did Louis Pasteur (1822–1895), August Weismann (1834–1914), Charles R. Darwin (1809–1882), Gregor Johann Mendel (1822–1884), and many other scientists and inventors whose names have become household words. An excellent illustration of man's inventive sensitivity is shown in the manner of discovering Pluto, the ninth major planet, which revolves around the sun about once every 248 years. This planet was discovered in 1930 by Clyde W. Tombaugh, while working on reckonings which had been made in 1914 by Percival Lowell from perturbations in the orbits of Neptune and Uranus. Pluto's orbit is outside that of Neptune, at a mean distance of 3 billion 670 million miles from the sun. Thus knowledge already in existence was used to discover a fact which hitherto had been unknown.

Beyond all doubt, the best example of what one man can achieve in his own lifetime through a combination of invention and discovery is provided by Leonardo da Vinci (1452–1519), the most versatile man in history. This Italian was justly famous as painter, sculptor, architect, musician, engineer, and scientist. Not only was he one of the greatest masters of the arts, but he was intensely interested in investigations of problems in geology, botany, hydraulics, and mechanics. He was even interested in ballistics and the principles of flying. This man was the supreme example of Renaissance genius.

The Borrowing of Culture Elements. Culture may be added to by borrowing from some other contemporary culture. This method may be associated with *adoption,* which means the act of taking and applying something or putting into practice as one's own a trait or complex which was not so originally. Another related concept is *imitation,* which means to copy some object or idea or to follow it as a pattern, model, or example. The process whereby a trait spreads from one culture to a place of acceptance in another is called *diffusion.* Some culture traits may experience *modification* and adaptation as they are diffused from one culture area to another.

Diffusion. Simply defined, diffusion is the process, usually but not necessarily gradual, by which elements or systems of culture are spread; it is the process by which an invention or a new institution adopted in one place is adopted in neighboring areas and in some cases continues to be adopted in adjacent ones until it may spread over the whole earth. Economic, political, and religious institutions have traveled far and wide through the process of diffusion, as is also true of conflicting ideologies such as democracy, socialism, and communism. More concretely, the products of discovery and invention in the physical sciences have traveled quickly from continent to continent in modern times, and the influences of the Industrial Revolution are becoming increasingly evident over the whole world.

Diffusion is allied to tradition in that both pass culture material from one group to another. However, tradition usually refers to the transmission of cultural content from one generation to another of the same population, while diffusion transmits from one population to another. Tradition and diffusion are conservative factors in culture history, as contrasted with the creative one of invention. Among the mechanisms of diffusion are migration and colonization, conquest, missionization, commerce, revolution, and gradual infiltration, which may be conscious or unconscious.

Sometimes it is difficult to determine whether a custom has come into practice through diffusion or has had an independent origin in more than one culture. In cases where traits or customs have come into practice independently, they are examples of what we call *parallelism*. It is also possible for certain cultures that are markedly different in some of their characteristics to evolve independently toward similarity in those characteristics—a process known as *convergence*. For example, A. L. Kroeber reports that the English language ". . . has gone approximately nine-tenths of the way towards attaining a grammar of the Chinese type." [13] He mentions a third language of independent origin, that of the Polynesians, which has traveled about the same distance in the same direction. Thus three languages—Chinese, English, and Polynesian—have been converging toward a similar type of grammar. As another example of parallelism, consider the quaint practice called the "couvade." Now there may be elements of diffusion of this custom in certain regions, but the fact that the custom existed independently among the Basques of France and the Indians of Brazil suggests independent evolution of the custom. At the same time, proverbs are found in the cultures of Europeans, Africans, Asiatics, and Oceanians, but they were not present in the cultures of native American Indians; it is therefore probable that the custom was borrowed from a common source in the four eastern continents.

The zodiac, with its specific arrangement of twelve constellations, seems to have originated among the Chaldean Babylonians about a thousand years before Christ; from this source, the pattern traveled to the Persians, the Greeks, the Roman Empire, and thence to the whole of Western civilization. Diffusion coupled with adaptation of traits is illustrated by the names given the days of the week in different cultures. Babylonian, Greek, Egyptian, and Syrian influences on naming the days of the week have spread in all directions. The alphabet is another clear case of borrowing and adaptation in culture. It is believed that the idea of the alphabet originated among the Phoenicians; from them it spread to the Greeks, who adapted it to the sounds of their language, and symbols for the vowels were added. All subsequent European alphabets are modifications of the Greek alphabet. All the alphabetic systems now in use—Roman, Greek, Hebrew, Arabic, Indian, as well as other systems that have become extinct, can be traced to a single source. Our zero, along with the other

[13] See A. L. Kroeber, *Anthropology,* 1st ed., Harcourt, Brace and Company, Inc., New York, 1923, pp. 124–125. Cf. with his section on convergent languages in the 1948 edition, pp. 242–244.

nine digits, is attributed to Hindu invention approximately twelve to fifteen hundred years ago. The tobacco complex and the horse complex are outstanding examples of how culture diffusion has encircled the world.

Acculturation. Acculturation is the subjective phase of culture formation. This term covers all the various ways in which individuals or groups take on new culture traits. Education is the chief method of acculturation. Informal conditioning in social relationships also works to that end. Cultural assimilation on the part of immigrants is an example of acculturation.

Of all these social processes which have been defined and illustrated, invention and diffusion are no doubt the most important. However, social processes, like other factors in cultural development and change, do not function singly, but in multiple relationships. Social processes do not operate by and of themselves; they depend upon what human beings do, wittingly or unwittingly, in response to social stimuli and in efforts to solve their problems. The ways in which human beings utilize social processes will eventually mold their culture. The question remains, then, Can societies direct cultural and social change to desired ends?

SOCIETAL SELF-DIRECTION

Has sufficient knowledge about the social and cultural heritage been accumulated, and human ability developed, so that society may purposefully direct its own course of social change? Can society decide what is best for itself and plan accordingly? Lester F. Ward believed in social planning, and he coined the term "social telesis" to express his conception of it. Clarence M. Case was hopeful, yet realistic, about the planning of social change, and converted Ward's phrase to "societal self-direction."

The Utopian Approach to Planning. Historically, the idea of social planning, or even of a planned society, is ancient. Lycurgus and Plato were advocates of social planning in their day, and Plato's *Republic* is commonly regarded as the first great utopia of literary record. Sir Thomas More (1478–1535), an English philosopher and statesman, wrote an idealized conception of society under the title *Utopia,* which later became the name for this genre of literature. More's *Utopia* (1516) is a classical description of an ideal state to be contrasted with the undesirable social and political institutions of his day. Back in the fifth century, St. Augustine's *City of God* had outstanding influence on social thought; it enunciated the theocratic ideal which was to dominate visionary thinking throughout the Middle Ages. Among the famous utopias written after More's venture, the following rate well in popularity: Campanella's *The City of the Sun* (1623); Francis Bacon's *The New Atlantis* (1627); Harrington's *Oceana* (1656); Samuel Butler's *Erewhon* (1872); Edward Bellamy's *Looking Backward* (1888); William Morris's *News from Nowhere* (1891); H. G. Wells's *A Modern Utopia* (1905) and *Men Like Gods* (1923); and Aldous Huxley's *Brave New World* (1932). Most utopias have suggested ideals for the amelioration of the principal social problems observed in the social environments of their respective authors.

None of the utopias could offer an actual blueprint for realizing the society described as ideal. Since society is always changing more or less, and sometimes in unexpected ways, no plan or schedule of action could have been projected with reasonable accuracy. The utopian writer could only criticize or satirize existing conditions and state his conception, or dream, of an ideal state or society. It is significant that Karl Marx's exposition of socialism—or "communism," as Marx and Engels preferred to call it in their *Communist Manifesto*—never was anything more than a dialectical generalization and, because of its fallacious premises and assumptions and predictions, largely utopian. National socialistic planning based on Marxian premises also has proved to be utopian. Various experiments in communal cooperative organization, influenced by the doctrines of Saint-Simon, Fourier, Cabet, and Robert Owen, failed because they were founded on unrealistic propositions. These experiments should not be confused with the consumers' and producers' cooperatives which have been successful in many countries and which, in fact, are opposed to socialism. The ideas and "potentialities" of social planning have long been attractive to social scientists and philosophers. Ideologies have their positive side in their emphasis on amelioration, but ideals are abstractions, while the problems are realities.

Social Maturation—a Prerequisite for Planning. Societies have to grow and mature, just as individuals do. Individuals go through life more or less bound by the social norms and expectations of the community, and it is exceptional for them to venture to become self-directing in their behavior. Their personality patterns are for the most part molded according to the structure of the society. Societies, like their individual members, live largely in their mores and institutions and seldom possess the ideals or the energy needed to strive for independent action. Nevertheless, before there can be societal self-direction, there must be a deliberate and purposeful self-realization, a societal growing up.

Some phases of societal growth are stored and transmitted in the social heritage, so that it is possible for the society concerned to know what it has been in the past and how it came to be what it was and is, as a basis for planning toward what it would like to be. This factor is in a sense "social memory," to borrow Giddings's phrase. Along with this factor must go a developed social self-consciousness which Case understood to consist of "simultaneous thinking along similar lines by many different persons who are mutually aware of this concerted thinking." [14] This, in turn, means intercommunication, discussion, and the development of a true public opinion. Finally, societal self-direction requires a process of collective evaluation, resulting in the feeling that certain things are worth striving for.

Since societies live largely in their mores and institutions, societal self-direction could not depend directly on modifying the mores, which characteristically are conservative. If the conception of social change or progress were introduced as an element in the mores, some planned changes in mores would no doubt be forthcoming. Societal self-direction, if dependent on planning the mores, would progress too slowly. More speedy by far is change through legislation, though the laws must be in harmony with the mores and public opinion if they are to be enforceable and practicable.

[14] Clarence M. Case, *Social Process and Human Progress*, Harcourt, Brace and Company, Inc., New York, 1939, p. 86.

Rationality as a Factor in Change. The "growing up" of both individuals and societies involves a maturation of intellectual qualities. Ward and Comte, who had great faith in human ability to assume responsibility for progressive welfare planning, placed too much emphasis on intellectualism, or the rationality of mankind. They ascribed unwarranted power to education, and held an excessively idealized conception of social guidance through the imparting of knowledge to the masses. Their assumption was that certain classes were privileged because of their superior knowledge, while other classes were underprivileged and exploited because of disparity in their education. They believed that, by imparting knowledge more equitably among all social classes, the masses would become more dynamic in improving their mode of life. Perhaps "the revolt of the masses," as conceived by the philosopher José Ortega y Gasset (1883–1955) and contemporary trends toward a laboristic economy in the United States and elsewhere imply some effects of education among the masses. However, ideals like those of Ward and Comte are not necessarily realistic. Societies are apt to be governed less by reasoning than by tradition and custom; that is, societies are more likely to be influenced by emotional than by intellectual leadership. Nevertheless, societal self-direction requires rational planning and the application of social engineering.

National Planning. Experimentation in social planning on a national scale has become general among nations since about 1913 or 1914. National controls over production and distribution were applied in some areas of social life during World War I, as temporary expedients. Sovietized Russia, after the Bolshevik Revolution of 1917, resorted to national planning on a grand scale, with five-year programs carefully detailed to govern production and distribution in industry and agriculture, as well as education and other areas of life. The ultimate objective was not only a state-planned economy, but a state-planned society. Soviet planning was watched with intense interest, and some aspects of its governmentalism became too strongly tempting to be resisted. The circumstances of the world-wide depression, which was an economic consequence of World War I, caused many nations to increase the sphere of governmental control and to resort to national planning to meet the emergency. It was thought that economic maladjustments could be solved by political action; economic problems were exploited as political issues. But it should not be overlooked that in Soviet Russia and other communist-motivated states national planning is equivalent to a planned nation, whereas in democratic states the ultimate problem is to use national planning wisely in essential areas of life without permitting the government to become arbitrary or autocratic.

Societal self-direction on a national scale (or for lesser self-governing political divisions) therefore involves alternative choices: democratic freedoms, liberty, and individualism, or the opposite values—identified with arbitrary regimentation characteristic of collectivist systems—socialism, communism, and fascism. These two sets of values are obviously incompatible. Arbitrary collectivist planning is determined by a ruling elite, and scarcely qualifies as "societal self-direction," while democratic methods of planning, within the Western conception of "democratic," exemplify more directly and completely the meanings of societal self-direction. However, enhancing the power of the government for planning or for other functions may cost the people some of their democratic privileges or rights.

National planning as a form of societal self-direction would, presumably, utilize every possible branch of knowledge for the guidance of specialized planning. The emphasis should be rational rather than unduly emotional, though the planners and even the populace influenced by their propaganda may be motivated by ideologies that tend to be mythical, unrealistic, and highly emotional. Moreover, planning begets more planning, and societies need to be constantly alert to the possible abuses of planning. The problem of society then is to *direct* social change in its behalf without becoming the victim of the process. No other elements in societal self-direction are as important as the human beings whose way of life will be affected by the plans to be enforced.

Desirable aspects of societal self-direction are applicable to national, state, or local planning. National issues may appear more distant and abstract and of less immediate concern to the individual. Citizens may depend upon legislators and administrators to the point of becoming apathetic. However, societal self-direction and individual indifference or apathy are incompatible, whether the issues are national, state, or local. In countries where local self-government is minimal or nonexistent, governmental dominance tends to be conservative about its own continuance; governing becomes a vested interest.

Evolutionary Versus Revolutionary Change. Social change may be achieved by evolutionary or revolutionary methods, and either of these may yield to the other as social situations or movements run their course. When the process of change is voluntary and peaceful, and does not particularly disrupt the mode of life of a society, it is termed "evolutionary." When changes are effected suddenly with the use of force, and involve a violent seizure of power and possibly a change in the location of sovereignty, the process is said to be "revolutionary." Revolutions do not and can never change everything in a society's culture, but they may destroy or alter components of culture so drastically as to cause extreme social suffering. Revolutionary methods of change have ordinarily been pertinent to local and national regions. However, revolutionary movements have now taken on international aspects, as manifested in the Communist Revolution which aims at the conquest of the free world.[15]

THE INTERRELATEDNESS OF CULTURE, PERSONALITY, AND SOCIETY

Culture, personality, and society are interrelated and function reciprocally in the process of social change. Many definitions of culture state that it is always acquired by human individuals as a social product, or that culture is our social heritage passed on from generation to generation by a process of learning or conditioning; but such definitions have not explained *how* culture is acquired or *how* the social heritage is

[15] For a discussion of socialism, communism, and the Soviet-planned Communist Revolution, see John Eric Nordskog, *Contemporary Social Reform Movements,* Charles Scribner's Sons, New York, 1954. Other chapters deal with the meanings of liberalism and democracy.

passed on. From the standpoint of the dynamics of human adjustment, the explanation seems to lie in the fact that there can be no natural cleavage in the psychological organization of the individual, culture, and society.[16]

Culture does not cause culture, nor is it able to transmit itself from person to person or from one generation to the next as a cultural heritage. Culture is not only the product of, but is transmitted through, human interaction and communication, which are psychological phenomena. Society and culture are organized and structured psychologically. Social structure refers to the characteristic uniformities and regularities in social life in accordance with which the members are expected to pattern their behavior.

Each child is born potentially equipped to understand and acquire a patterned integration of culture which becomes a part of himself. The process whereby individuals are conditioned and adjusted to live harmoniously with others in the same society is called "socialization"—a process without which there would be no culture, no personality structure, and no social structure. The process of acculturation is a subjective phase of culture formation and covers the ways in which individuals or groups take on new culture traits.

Both socialization and acculturation, as processes, work through education and the informal conditioning which occurs in social relationships; as a result the individual becomes aware of other individuals and the social norms and expectations —i.e., the social structure—of the society in which he lives. Socialization depends for its effectiveness on the human being's capacity to develop self-awareness, which in turn comes only through an awareness of others. This "self and other" awareness enables human beings to communicate intelligently and thus to transmit the meanings of cultural objects from oneself to another.[17] Socialization directs this intercommunication so that human beings become psychologically structured to live according to the social structure of the community. Through socialization, then, the individual acquires a personality structure which reflects the social character of the society.

Mead says, in unmistakable terms, that the self, as that which can be an object to itself (self-awareness), is essentially a social structure, and it arises in social experience.[18] The unity and structure of the complete self is a reflection of the unity and structure of the social process as a whole. Or, viewing the matter from the standpoint of the group or society instead of the individual, Mead believes that "the organization and unification of a social group is identical with the organization

---

[16] See Abram Kardiner, "The Concept of Basic Personality Structure as an Operational Tool in the Social Sciences," Ralph Linton (ed.), *The Science of Man in the World Crisis*, Columbia University Press, New York, 1945, pp. 107–122. Also the interpretation by A. Irving Hallowell, "Culture, Personality, and Society," A. L. Kroeber (ed.), *Anthropology Today*, The University of Chicago Press, Chicago, 1953, pp. 597–620; an imposing bibliography is included.

[17] See George H. Mead, *Mind, Self and Society*, The University of Chicago Press, Chicago, 1934, part III for his discussion of "The Self," and part IV for his treatment of "Society."

[18] *Ibid.*, p. 140. Mead's views may be compared with those of Charles H. Cooley, *Social Process*, Charles Scribner's Sons, New York, 1918, pp. 249 ff. Also compare these two with Arthur James Todd, *Theories of Social Progress*, The Macmillan Company, New York, 1918, who devotes several chapters to the primitive notions of the self, the psychological analysis of the self, and self as a social product.

and unification of any one of the selves arising within the social process in which that group is engaged, or which it is carrying on." [19]

The conception that self-awareness grows out of the awareness of others is clearly supported by Mead; he refers to the organized community or social group which gives to the individual his unity of self as "the generalized other." [20] Finally, the reciprocal relationship of self-awareness and other-awareness may be explained in terms of control; that is, it is in the form of the generalized "other" that the social process influences the behavior of the individuals involved in it and carrying it on; thus the community exercises control over the conduct of its individual members.[21]

All this process of developing self-awareness and other-awareness, which is an aspect of the socialization process, is psychological and is integrated with culture, which must also be regarded as psychological if there is to be any cultural communication. Culture, which is a social product, provides the bridge between self-awareness and other-awareness. Culture provides the medium for both societal structure and personality structure. And cultural change—or social change (either term will do)—will necessarily reflect its reciprocal relationships with personality and society. Thus culture, personality, and society reflect social change which originates in their functional interrelatedness and which can be transmitted from generation to generation because of their continued interrelatedness.

The continuity of society is provided for as new members are born into the group; each new member acquires, through the processes of socialization and maturation, a patterned integration of culture determined largely by the social character of the group. The new members thus socialized and culturally integrated make the process of transmitting culture—i.e., a gradually changing culture—a continuous operation.

[19] *Ibid.,* p. 144.
[20] *Ibid.,* p. 155.
[21] *Ibid.*

II

The Challenge of Population Growth

Every species has a birth rate which, unhindered, would swamp the earth. The characteristic result, however, because of the utter ruthlessness of natural selection and the struggle for existence to which all species are subject, is the maintenance of a balance among the species as related to the life-sustaining properties of their habitat. In this struggle thousands of species have become extinct, among them some of the precursors of man.

Man's fecundity (natural ability to produce offspring) was once a survival guarantee, but now, in terms of fertility (the actual number of children born), it has become the root of a most pressing social problem. As a self-domesticated being, man has become an end in and of himself. Man alone among the animals has, because of his cultural heritage and inventiveness, freed himself to some extent from factors in natural selection and the struggle for existence which limited his numbers more effectively in former times than they have in recent centuries.

Human life, like that of all species, depends upon the supplies of the bases of life, for which the demand is insatiable. An increase in supply, by encouraging the birth rate, may be accompanied by an increase in the number of consumers; or, as another possibility, the standard of living may be raised. Man's insatiable demand for consumption goods is complicated by his fecundity and the tendency for populations to increase in number rather than to remain stationary. The problem, basically, is to strike a balance between two variables—a changing supply of consumption goods and a usually increasing number of consumers. Hundreds of millions of people on the earth at the present time are in relative or actual want, suffering from starvation diets lacking in calories and essentials for health, and yet the increase in world population has become so phenomenal as to be called explosive. Current estimates are that the world population will be nearly doubled within about five decades. Demographers realize that all forms of human grouping will be greatly affected by overwhelming forces working within population as a social process.

43

Population Theories and Social Change. Only a few selected theories will be referred to here. Foremost among them is Thomas Robert Malthus's belief that the power of population to reproduce is indefinitely greater than the earth's power to produce subsistence for man. Population, when unchecked, increases in a geometrical ratio, and subsistence increases only in an arithmetical ratio. Disregarding, however, these mathematical comparisons, Malthus's references to two classes of checks which operate to keep down man's numbers do have implications for social change: hunger and disease were held to be the chief *positive* checks, that is, the principal factors keeping the death rate high; but there also are *preventive* checks through which the birth rate may be reduced, and in this connection Malthus thought primarily of late marriage and abstinence within marriage. Populations in different parts of the world are becoming increasingly conscious of the importance of preventive checks. Methods of contraception are being encouraged in various countries—as in Puerto Rico, Ceylon, and Japan—and abortion and sterilization have been legalized under stipulated conditions.

Herbert Spencer's theory of the antagonism between individuation and genesis is also of interest for social change. He held that, as complexity of life increases, a reduction in fecundity takes place. The more strenuous the adjustments the individual must make to ensure his own existence and success, the weaker are his efforts toward reproduction. Somewhat similar was Arsène Dumont's emphasis on social capillarity as a limiting factor in population growth. According to his theory, as man strives to mount to higher levels in his social environment he becomes less and less likely to reproduce himself.

Carr-Saunders has been a leading exponent of the theory of the optimum number —that man's growth in numbers is determined by his notions of the economically desirable numbers under his conditions of life. The assumption is that increase or decrease in the population, once the hypothetical optimum point has been reached, would tend to reduce productivity per capita. Economic changes would, of course, be accompanied by other social effects. Improvement in economic methods of production and distribution would have some proportional effect on the optimum number, and negative trends in the economy would affect the optimum adversely.

Population Policies. Population policies include forms of control over numbers, resources, economic arts, consumption, and other factors influencing population changes. Population policies aim to promote the general welfare; so they would not be those of families or nominal groups, but of the society as a whole. Patterns of reproduction have generally been established to serve one of four ends:

1. To slow up or prevent an increase in numbers
2. To encourage an increase in the group size or to maintain it at about the same size
3. To improve the quality of the population
4. To distribute the population better in relation to resources available for their support

Policies or practices to control population have traditionally been restrictive, expansive, eugenic, or distributive. The restrictive policies include infanticide, abortion, sexual taboos, killing or abandoning the aged or sick, acceptance of disaster (pestilence, plague, famine), war, marriage restrictions, migration, and contraception. Expansive policies may be devised to increase resources, to meet needs for defense, to promote dynastic and national interests, or because of religious and other cultural influences. Proposed eugenic policies would, it was believed, improve the quality of population. Distributive policies have involved immigration, urbanization, and other forms of mobility.

Factors in Population Growth. The supply of land and the effectiveness of its utilization would be of primary importance. More land area is available, but it is said to be, for the most part, inferior and at or near the point of marginal utility. About 93 per cent of the world's land surface lacks one or more of the factors necessary for satisfactory food production. Not many decades will pass before the world's population will be doubled if its present rate of increase is maintained, whereas the agricultural food-bearing area may possibly be increased by about 32 per cent. Improvements in agricultural methods, soil chemistry, and soil conservation will no doubt increase the means of subsistence, though not indefinitely, and such means are subject to "diminishing returns."

Sociopsychological factors are important in population growth. Man's rational qualities, and the internal and spiritual aspects of his life, influence human population. Only man can think in terms of optimum numbers for the best man-to-land ratio and plan accordingly. Societies are influenced by styles in the size of families—large, medium, or small—for different classes, or for urban and rural families. Public opinion has changed with reference to some factors involved in securing a mate and establishing a family, freedom before and after marriage, woman's sphere in contemporary society, and the social values associated with home and family life. Legal and religious sanctions affect the use of contraceptives, abortions, prostitution, illegitimacy, sterilization, and various aspects of marriage and family relations; however, some changes are occurring in these particulars. Personal values, the individual's manner of life and standard of living, poverty, economic success or failure—all may affect the birth rate and population growth.

The quality of a population or of the individuals composing it depends partly on heredity, but also on nurture and the influences of social and cultural environment. Heredity determines the inherent capacity of all individuals, but inherited potentialities may be limited or developed according to environmental conditions. Good heredity provides a favorable bond between successive generations, and good environment provides favorable opportunity for each generation to develop. Euthenic programs may be designed to improve the social and environmental conditions of life. Eugenic programs, on the other hand, are concerned with the breeding out of unfit individuals carrying some hereditary taint, such as feeble-mindedness, epilepsy, or physical deformity; but much scientific investigation remains necessary to determine the boundaries and relationships of heredity and eugenics. Regulations concerning the health of persons planning marriage are, of course, generally approved. Among more arbitrary selective measures, the institutionalization of mental defectives is the one which has been most frequently used or advocated. Sterilization of the unfit is no doubt the most drastic eugenic policy; but, although twenty-nine states have such laws, the practice remains subject to question in the United States. In present-day Japan, legal attitudes toward abortion and sterilization have become more favorable. However, cause and effect have been confused in some eugenic assumptions, and eugenic legislation has not been enforced consistently.

Population movements may greatly affect the numbers occupying a given land area, and may be considered spatially (as regards movement from one locality to another) and numerically (as populations are increased or decreased by migration). Such movements are bound to involve cultural readjustments. Population movements affect the composition of population in terms of age, sex ratio, ethnic qualities, and the religious, educational, political, economic, and other social criteria used in analyzing population grouping. Immigration problems are complementary to those incident to emigration. Though both movements are taking place simultaneously in most countries, one or the other of the movements tends to predominate and is more likely to force social adjustments. Immigration laws may work for selective immigration, as has been characteristic within the United States for some decades.

Famine, disease, pestilence, plague, and war are at times major influences on population growth or decline; these factors of course work for decline in population. Throughout history, famines in European countries, Asia and the Orient have acted as positive checks against population growth. In some areas famines have been accepted as incidental phases, though millions of persons were victims in famines recorded for various countries. In other areas which are more culturally advanced, ways have been devised for alleviating the ravages of famine. The same is true with reference to disease, pestilence, and plague. War appears to be more beyond control than these other evils. War has become far more destructive, and more costly in terms of property and lives, as well as fantastically expensive to maintain.

DEMOGRAPHIC CHANGES

Within the century from 1850 to 1950 the population of the United States increased from 23.2 million to 150.7 million. Within the same period the relative influence of immigration changed greatly: the 1850 census reported a total immigration of 1.7 million during the previous decade, and these immigrants constituted 27.9 per cent of the population increase during that decade; during each of the next three decades, between 2 and 3 million immigrants arrived, yet their relative percentage of the population increase remained approximately the same. Far more startling were the census reports in 1890 and 1910. The 1890 census reported 5.2 million immigrants for the previous decade, which accounted for 40.6 per cent of the population increase during that decade; and the 1910 census reported a total immigration of 8.8 million during the previous decade, which accounted for 55.0 per cent of the population increase for the period. Since that time the number of immigrants has of course dwindled considerably because of restrictive legislation. The 1950 census reported that the total immigration for the decade was 0.9 million, which accounted for 4.7 per cent of the population increase during the ten-year period. Not only has the total foreign-born white population varied considerably during the century; the Negro population has increased from 3.6 million in 1850 to 15.0 million in 1950. These population changes have certainly had great influence on the economic, political, and social development of the United States. All these millions of people, whites, Negroes, and immigrants, affected the development of American culture in their roles as producers and consumers.

Demographers differ in their predictions of population growth in the United States, though all of them now promise tremendous changes. One such report estimates an increase of United States population from 167 million on July 1, 1956, to 227 million on July 1, 1975. The same source estimates that within the eighteen-year period the East will add 13 million people, the South 15 million, the Midwest 14 million, and the West 18 million.[1]

The individual states will differ considerably in their percentages of population increase. In the Midwest, the more rural and agricultural the states are, the more nominal will be their percentage of increase. Percentage gains among the Eastern states will be stronger than those of the midwestern agricultural states. Gains among the Southern states will range from nominal in Arkansas and Mississippi to stronger among the rest, with Texas and Florida exceeding the others. The greatest increases are predicted for the Western states, with California leading the nation in this respect.

The distribution of population will reflect the influences of the flight from the farms, the development of "strip" cities extending for miles along the main highways of the nation, the fact that "farm states" are becoming relatively fewer, the boom in the development of the desert states, industrial trends, and other factors.

It is estimated that the number of people living on farms will drop from 22.2 million to 15.3 million by 1975; that the number residing in towns of less than 2,500 will increase from 37.9 million to 46.9 million; the number residing in central cities of metropolitan areas will increase from 53.3 million to 61.1 million; and the number of people residing in suburbs of metropolitan areas will increase from 46.9 million to 85.2 million, which is by far the greatest area of change predicted.[2]

Owing to the influences of science, medicine, and Western technology, death rates have declined sharply in many countries, and have tended downward over the world in general. Death rates for 1950, selected from the United Nations *Demographic Yearbook* of 1955, are listed in Table 2-1. Death rates specific for age and sex vary considerably for different nations, not only for the populations as a whole, but for males as compared with females and for age groups from infancy to old age.

In many countries of the world where the modes of life have been modernized there has been a change in life expectancy. The proportions of children that survive the first year of life and the relative numbers who live to maturity and old age continue to increase. In the United States, the expectation of life at birth reported for 1952 was 68.6 years for the total population. In general, the expectation of life at birth and for each successive year is more favorable for the white than for the non-

---

[1] Data used by permission, from a copyrighted article, "Where Will U.S. Put 60 Million More People?" *U. S. News & World Report,* vol. 43, pp. 46–54, August 9, 1957.
[2] *Ibid.,* pp. 46–54.

TABLE 2-1. DEATH RATES FOR 1950

Country	Deaths per 1000 of population
Egypt	19.1
Mexico	16.2
United States	9.6
Chile	15.0
Argentina	9.0
Peru (including Indian jungle inhabitants)	12.6
Japan	10.9
Finland	10.1
France	12.7
Iceland	7.9
Italy	9.8
Netherlands	7.5
Norway	9.1
Portugal	12.2
Spain	10.9
Sweden	10.0
Switzerland	10.1
United Kingdom	11.7
Yugoslavia	13.0

white population and more favorable for the females than for the males in both white and nonwhite groups.

Marital status within the American population has changed considerably from 1890 to 1950, as reported for single, married, widowed, and divorced groups for both whites and nonwhites.[3] The percentage of males remaining single decreased from 43.6 per cent in 1890 to 26.4 per cent in 1950; comparable figures for females were 34.1 per cent and 20.0 per cent. Conversely, the percentage of the married population increased from 1890 to 1950; whereas 52.1 per cent of the males were married in 1890, 67.5 per cent of the males were married in 1950; of the females, 54.8 per cent were married in 1890, and 65.8 per cent were reported as married in 1950.

The percentages of widowed males changed little from 1890 to 1950, but the percentage of widowed females tended to increase. The percentage of divorced males in 1950 was ten times as large as that reported for 1890, and the percentage of divorced females was six times as large as reported for 1890.

From 1890 to 1950 the median age at first marriage in the United States has consistently been lowered for both males and females. The median for males was 26.1 years of age in 1890, and 22.7 years in 1950; the median age for females dropped from 22.0 years in 1890 to 20.3 years in 1950.[4] Clearly, then, the marital situation of the United States population has changed along with social attitudes and economic conditions.

[3] Source of marital status statistics, U.S. Bureau of Census, Census of Population: 1950, Detailed Characteristics, Bulletin P-Ci, adapted from Table 102, pp. 179–180.
[4] Source: J. Frederick Dewhurst and Associates, America's Needs and Resources, The Twentieth Century Fund, Inc., New York, 1955, Table 18, p. 57.

WORLD POPULATION TRENDS

The challenge of population growth is felt very unevenly in different parts of the world, but becomes more meaningful when considered from the standpoint of world population as a whole. Most observers agree concerning the gravity of the population trend, though they may vary somewhat as to details, as is seen in the following selections: "World Population" by Julian Huxley, "World Population Trends" by Philip M. Hauser, "A Generation of Demographic Change" by Pascal K. Whelpton, and "Recent Population Trends in the New World: An Over-all View" by Kingsley Davis.

Huxley reveals the present status of the race between the increase in the number of people and the rise of their food production. People living in regions of the world which are not crowded and still have room to spare are not likely to be conscious of the oncoming dangers from an explosive world population. But the traveler is almost certain to be impressed by the sheer numbers of people in China, Java, Japan, and India; he may be shocked into realizing that the increase of human numbers has initiated a new and critical phase in the history of our species. Huxley indicates in graphic terms how fantastic the rate of population growth actually is; he considers changes in birth rates and death rates as factors and gives some attention to possible population policy as a remedy. This selection deals with the general world situation only, though the article may be consulted further for data concerning Japan, India, Indonesia, Thailand, Fiji, and Australia.

5

WORLD POPULATION*

Julian Huxley

The problem of population is the problem of our age. In the middle of the 20th century anyone who travels around the world, as I have recently done, cannot fail to be struck by the signs of growing pressure of population upon the resources of our planet. The traveler is impressed by the sheer numbers of people, as in China; by the crowding of the land, as in Java; by the desperate attempts to control population increase, as in Japan and India; and at the same time by the erosion, deforestation and destruction of wildlife almost everywhere. The experiences of travel merely highlight and illustrate a fact which for some time has been obtruding itself on the world's consciousness: that the increase of human

* From article, "World Population," in *Scientific American*, vol. 194, no. 3, pp. 64–67, March, 1956. Reprinted by permission of author and journal.

numbers has initiated a new and critical phase in the history of our species.

This crisis was recognized by the holding of a Conference on World Population in Rome in 1954. Held under the aegis of the United Nations, the Conference was a milestone in history, for it was the first official international survey of the subject of human population as a whole. In 1949 the UN had convened a scientific conference on world resources at Lake Success. As Director General of UNESCO, invited to collaborate in this project, I had suggested that a survey of resources should be accompanied by a similar survey of the population which consumed the resources. I was told that there were technical, political and religious difficulties. Eventually these difficulties were smoothed over; censuses were taken; and a conference on popualtion was duly held in 1954. During the five years it took to arrange for a look at the problem the world population had increased by more than 130 million.

Let me begin by setting forth some of the facts—often surprising and sometimes alarming—which justify our calling the present a new and decisive phase in the history of mankind. The first fact is that the total world population has been increasing relentlessly, with only occasional minor setbacks, since before the dawn of history. The second fact is the enormous present size of the population—more than 2.5 billion. The third is the great annual increase: some 34 million people per year, nearly 4,000 per hour, more than one every second. The human race is adding to its numbers the equivalent of a good-sized town, more than 90,000 people, every day of the year. The fourth and most formidable fact is that the rate of increase itself is increasing. Population, as Thomas Malthus pointed out in 1798, tends to grow not arithmetically but geometrically—it increases by compound interest. Until well into the present century the compound rate of increase remained below 1 per cent per annum, but it has now reached 1⅓ per cent per annum. What is more, this acceleration of increase shows no sign of slowing up, and it is safe to prophesy

that it will continue to go up for at least several decades.

In short, the growth of human population on our planet has accelerated from a very slow beginning until it has now become an explosive process. Before the discovery of agriculture, about 6,000 B.C., the total world population was probably less than 20 million. It did not pass the 100 million mark until after the time of the Old Kingdom of Egypt, and did not reach 500 million until the latter part of the 17th century. By the mid-18th century it passed the billion mark, and in the 1920s it rose above two billion. That is to say, it doubled itself twice over in the period between 1650 and 1920. The first doubling took nearly two centuries, the second considerably less than one century. Now, at the present rate of acceleration, the population will have doubled itself again (from the 1920 figure) by the early 1980s—i.e., in the amazingly short space of 60 years.

Each major upward step in numbers followed some major discovery or invention—agriculture, the initiation of urban life and trade, the harnessing of non-human power, the technological revolution. During the present century the most decisive factor in increasing population has been of a different sort—the application of scientific medicine, or what we may call death control. In advanced countries death rates have been reduced from the traditional 35 or 40 per thousand to less than 10 per thousand. The average life span (life expectancy at birth) has been more than doubled in the Western world since the mid-19th century. It now stands at about 70 years in Europe and North America, and the process of lengthening life has begun to get under way in Asian countries: in India, for example, the life expectancy at birth has risen within three decades from 20 to 32 years.

BIRTH RATES V. DEATH RATES

Population growth appears to pass through a series of stages. In the first stage both the birth rate and the death rate are high, and the population increases only slowly. In the second stage the death rate falls sharply but the birth rate stays high; the population therefore expands more or less explosively. In the third, the birth rate also falls sharply, so that the increase of population is slowed. Finally both the birth and the death rates stabilize at a low figure; thereafter the population will grow only slowly unless it is spurred by some new development, such as access to new food sources or a change in ideas and values.

In the Western world the reduction of the death rate came gradually, and its effect on population growth was buffered by factors which tended at the same time to reduce the birth rate—namely, a rising standard of living and industrialization, which made children no longer an economic asset.

Matters have been very different in the still underdeveloped countries of Asia. There death control has been introduced with startling speed. Ancient diseases have been brought under control or totally abolished in the space of a few decades or even a few years. Let me give one example. In England malaria took three centuries to disappear; in Ceylon it was virtually wiped out in less than half a decade, thanks to DDT and a well-organized campaign. As a result of this and other health measures, the death rate in Ceylon was reduced from 22 to 12 per thousand in seven years—a fall which took exactly 10 times as long in England. But the Ceylon birth rate has not even begun to drop, and so the population is growing at the rate of 2.7 per cent per annum—about twice the highest rate ever experienced in Britain. If this rate of growth continues, the population of Ceylon will be doubled in 30 years.

Almost all the underdeveloped countries are now in this stage of explosive expansion. When we recall that rates of expansion of this order (2 to 3 per cent) are at work among more than half of the world's 2.5 billion inhabitants, we cannot but feel alarmed. If nothing is done to control this increase, mankind will drown in its own flood, or, if you prefer a different metaphor, man will turn into the cancer of the planet.

Malthus, a century and a half ago, alarmed the world by pointing out that population

increase was pressing more and more insistently on food supply, and if unchecked would result in widespread misery and even starvation. In recent times, even as late as the 1930s, it had become customary to pooh-pooh Malthusian fears. The opening up of new land, coupled with the introduction of better agricultural methods, had allowed food production to keep up with population increase and in some areas even to outdistance it. During the 19th century and the early part of the 20th food production increased in more than arithmetical progression, contrary to the Malthusian formula. We now realize, however, that this spurt in food production cannot be expected to continue indefinitely: there 's an inevitable limit to the rate at which it can be increased. Although Malthus' particular formulation was incorrect, it remains true that there is a fundamental difference between the increase of population, which is based on a geometrical or compound-interest growth mechanism, and the increase of food production, which is not.

There are still some optimists who proclaim that the situation will take care of itself, through industrialization and through the opening of new lands to cultivation, or that science will find a way out by improving food-production techniques, tapping the food resources of the oceans, and so on. These arguments seem plausible until we begin to look at matters quantitatively. To accelerate food production so that it can keep pace with human reproduction will take skill, great amounts of capital and, above all, time—time to clear tropical forests, construct huge dams and irrigation projects, drain swamps, start large-scale industrialization, give training in scientific methods, modernize systems of land tenure and, most difficult of all, change traditional habits and attitudes among the bulk of the people. And quite simply there is not enough skill or capital or time available. Population is always catching up with and outstripping increases in production. The fact is that an annual increase of 34 million mouths to be fed needs more food than can possibly go on being added to production year after year. The growth of population has reached such dimensions and speed that it cannot help winning in a straight race against production. The position is made worse by the fact that the race isn't a straight one. Production starts far behind scratch: according to the latest estimates of the World Health Organization, at least two thirds of the world's people are undernourished. Production has to make good this huge deficiency as well as overtake the increase in human numbers.

A POPULATION POLICY

Is there then no remedy? Of course there is. The remedy is to stop thinking in terms of a race between population and food production and to begin thinking in terms of a balance. We need a population policy.

The most dangerous period lies in the next 30 or 40 years. If nothing is done to bring down the rate of human increase during that time, mankind will find itself living in a world exposed to disastrous miseries and charged with frustrations more explosive than any we can now envision.

Even primitive societies practice some form of population control—by infanticide or abortion or sexual abstinence or crude contraceptives. Since the invention of effective birth control methods in the 19th century, they have been very generally practiced in all Western countries. Their spread to other cultures has been retarded by various inhibitions —religious, ideological, economic, political. It is worth noting that one retarding factor in the past has been the reluctance of colonial powers to encourage birth control in their colonies, often out of fear that they might be considered to be seeking to use population control as a weapon against an "inferior" race.

Today the underdeveloped countries are making their own decisions; what is needed is a new and more rational view of the population problem everywhere. We must give up the false belief that mere increase in the number of human beings is necessarily desirable, and the despairing conclusion that rapid increase and its evils are inevitable. We must reject the idea that the quantity of human beings is of value apart from the quality of their lives.

Overpopulation—or, if you prefer, high population density—affects a great many other needs of mankind besides bread. Beyond his material requirements, man needs space and beauty, recreation and enjoyment. Excessive population can erode all these things. The rapid population increase has already created cities so big that they are beginning to defeat their own ends, producing discomfort and nervous strain and cutting off millions of people from any real contact or sense of unity with nature. Even in the less densely inhabited regions of the world open spaces are shrinking and the despoiling of nature is going on at an appalling rate. Wildlife is being exterminated; forests are being cut down, mountains gashed by hydroelectric projects, wildernesses plastered with mine shafts and tourist camps, fields and meadows stripped away for roads and aerodromes. The pressure of population is also being translated into a flood of mass-produced goods which is washing over every corner of the globe, sapping native cultures and destroying traditional art and craftsmanship.

The space and the resources of our planet are limited. We must set aside some for our material needs and some for more ultimate satisfactions—the enjoyment of unspoiled nature and fine scenery, satisfying recreation, travel and the preservation of varieties of human culture and of monuments of past achievement and ancient grandeur. And in order to arrive at a wise and purposeful allocation of our living space we must have a population policy which will permit the greatest human fulfillment.

If science can be applied to increase the rate of food production and to satisfy our other needs, it can and should also be applied to reduce the rate of people production. And for that, as for all scientific advance, we need both basic research and practical application. Basic research is needed not only on methods of birth control but also on attitudes toward family limitation and on population trends in different sections of the world. Once we have agreed on the need for a scientific population policy, the necessary studies and measures to be applied will surely follow. This does not mean that we should envisage a definite optimum population size for a given country or for the world as a whole. Indeed, to fix such a figure is probably impossible, and to use it as a definite target is certainly impracticable. For the time being our aim should be confined to reducing the over-rapid population growth which threatens to outstrip food supply. If we can do this, our descendants will be able to begin thinking of establishing a more or less stable level of population.

Philip M. Hauser uses the word "explosive" to describe the population growth of the world during the past 300 years, but it has become exceptionally explosive within the last few decades. More than 2.7 billion people on the earth today are forced to subsist upon the products of 3 billion acres of cultivated land and 6 billion acres of pasturage. Even if all productive land were cultivated, there would be only 2 acres available for each person now alive. If the present rate of increase is maintained, the population will be doubled in seventy years, and some estimates predict the doubling will come sooner than that. In any case, the rate of increase is such that it cannot continue long without catastrophic consequences, and the need for some forms of population control is immediately apparent.

6

WORLD POPULATION TRENDS*
Philip M. Hauser

About 2½ billion human beings today inhabit the globe. More than half of them are in Asia, about one fourth are in Europe, and the remaining fourth are distributed approximately equally among North America, South America, and Africa. About two thirds of the earth's peoples live in four regions containing only one tenth of the land surface of the globe, namely, in the densely settled portions of southeastern Asia, in South Asia, in Europe, and in northeastern United States. The distribution and trend of the world's population are to be understood in terms of two major factors: (1) the relatively small portion of the surface of the globe which provides human sustenance, and (2) the history of population growth, which is an important and inseparable aspect of culture history.

With respect to the first of these factors it should be observed, in the interest of gaining a quick perspective, that of the earth's total surface of about 197 million square miles about three fourths is water and only one fourth is land. Of the land surface about one half is either too cold or too dry to be cultivated. Almost an additional fourth of the

* Reprinted by permission of *Sociology and Social Research*, vol. 39, no. 2, pp. 73–80, November-December, 1954.

world's land surface is similarly not available for cultivation by reason of infertile soil, mountainous or rocky terrain, excessive rainfall, or the works of man, such as cities, industrial establishments, roads, etc. Slightly more than a fourth of the world's land surface (about 27 per cent), including pasture, produces food and fibers for human consumption. These approximately 3 billion acres of cultivated land and 6 billion acres of pasture provide an average of only about 2 acres of cultivated land for each person now alive. Most of the world's population is concentrated in or near the relatively small portion of the earth's surface which produces the world's major food supply, rice in Southeast Asia and India, and wheat in Europe and on the North American plains.

The history of the world's population growth cannot be fully reconstructed. For the greater part of man's presence on the earth there are no records of the size and composition of populations. Even today, the exact number of people in the world is unknown; for there has never been a complete population census for most of Asia, including China, for most of Africa, or for parts of Latin America. Reasonably adequate data, however, are available for many parts of the globe and estimates of varying reliability for the remainder on both a historical and a contemporary basis. From the available data it is possible to reconstruct in broad strokes the growth of world population and differential growth in major parts of the globe for the past 3 centuries.

Historical Growth. In 1650, it has been estimated, there were approximately ½ billion people in the world. Thus, in the 3 centuries which have elapsed since that date the population of the world has increased about 5-fold. It more than doubled in the 2 centuries between 1650 and 1850 and more than doubled again in the past century. Over the entire 300-year span, the world's population increased at an average annual rate of about 5.6 per 1,000. The average annual rate of growth increased during this period, however, having been about 4 per 1,000 in the first of these centuries (1650 to 1750), 5 per 1,000 in the second century (1750 to 1850), and 8 per 1,000 in the last century (1850 to 1950). From 1920 to 1950, despite the war, the population of the world has grown at a rate of 9 per 1,000 or almost 1 per cent per year.

In the anthropologist's perspective of the history of man, the increase in the population during the last 300 years must be regarded not only as unprecedented but as explosive in character. This statement may be documented by a simple calculation. An increase of 1 per cent per year, while it may seem low as a rate of return on investment, is in reality a fantastically high rate of increase for a population over any prolonged period of time. It means a doubling of the population in about every 70 years. For example, 100 persons reproducing at this rate for only 5,000 years would produce a population of 3,981,000,000 times 10 raised to the 15th power—a population which would result in a density of 2,746,000,000 persons per square foot of land surface on the globe. Looking to the future, a 1 per cent average annual increase of the present world's population would produce a population of about 4 billion by the year 2000, over 500 billion by the year 2500, and even more astronomical figures if projected further.

It would seem reasonably safe to conclude that throughout most of man's residence on the globe, population grew very slowly indeed and at only fractions of the rates of increase observed during the modern era. Furthermore, it would also seem reasonably safe to conclude that contemporary rates of world population increase cannot possibly continue for a prolonged period of time. In this connection, it is perhaps worth noting the futile discussions, on the whole, of the population-carrying capacity of the earth. Baker, Thompson, and Salter, taking into account foreseeable increases in agricultural productivity, estimate a maximum potential world population of about 5 billion persons. Hollstein, among those with relatively high estimates, calculates a maximum possible population of over 13 billion. Pearson and Harper, at the lowest extreme, conclude that 2.8 billion persons is the maximum that the world can support even at an Asiatic standard of living, and that a population of only 900 million can be supported by the earth at the North American standard of living.

Judged by any calculations, it is clear that the world has experienced an unprecedented demographic revolution in the modern era—one which is still in process and one which cannot possibly continue for long. Let us consider the factors underlying this demographic revolution, its differential impact on the various regions of the world, and some of its attendant problems and implications.

Regional Differences. The rate of population growth during these 3 centuries has varied greatly for the different continents. The 5-fold increase of world population represents an averaging of a 166-fold increase in North America, a 23-fold increase in Latin America, a 6½-fold increase in Oceania, a 6-fold increase in Europe (including the USSR), a 5-fold increase in Asia, and only a doubling in Africa. The special place of Europe and areas of European settlement in the demographic revolution is noteworthy. The population of areas of European settlement increased 8- to 9-fold from 1650 to 1950 and of Europe plus the area of European settlement about 7 times.

The differential rates of population increase in the various portions of the globe are interrelated with general historical and cultural changes in these areas. Fertility, mortality, and migration are to a considerable extent functions of culture, and the basic changes in fertility and mortality schedules and in human migration which account for world and regional population growth are products of basic cultural changes.

Patterns of Population Dynamics. Patterns of population dynamics, that is, patterns of birth and death rates, disregarding migration which does not affect the world total, can in terms of historical population growth be classified into three convenient, ideal-type categories: preindustrial, transitional industrial, and industrial. It is in an understanding of these patterns of population dynamics that the demographic revolution and differential rates of population growth throughout the world can be understood, and that the projection of the world's population can be made meaningful and its implications grasped.

Preindustrial Population Dynamics. The preindustrial pattern of population dynamics is essentially a pattern of high fertility and high mortality. Typically, the relation of the death rate to the birth rate is such as to produce a relatively low rate of natural increase and, in effect, to maintain a population equilibrium through an extremely wasteful process of large numbers of deaths offsetting large numbers of births. The high birth rate and the high death rate are functions of preindustrial societies. Although elaborate explanations or rationalizations are frequently assayed in explanation of high fertility, there is probably adequate explanation to be found in Malthus's observation that the "sex urge is persistent and permanent." The high mortality of preindustrial cultures is to be understood in terms of low productivity, famine, chronic malnutrition, debilitating disease, and often political disorder with attendant internecine warfare. This pattern of population dynamics undoubtedly characterized population growth during most of man's presence on earth. It is exemplified by such evidence as is available for Japan during the Tokugawa period or for India between 1872 and 1921.

Transitional Population Dynamics. The transitional pattern of population dynamics is characterized by a relatively rapid and great decline in mortality with a lag in the decline of fertility. In consequence, the gap between fertility and mortality—natural increase—is greatly increased. Under the initial impact of increased productivity in agriculture, the development of commerce, and the emergence of industry, relatively rapid strides are made in the reduction of the death rate. This reduction in mortality is associated with changing culture in the early stages of the "industrial revolution," including, particularly, improved means of transportation and communication, increased productivity, the introduction of at least elementary sanitation and public health methods, and the achievement of relative political order and peace.

In contrast to the relatively quick drop in mortality, the birth rate of the preindustrial order tends to remain high during the initial stages of industrialization. The lag in the decline in fertility is attributable to the fact that there are more institutional, cultural, and personal factors operating to resist the control of fertility than operate to resist the control of mortality. In general, it may be pointed out that there tend to be relatively few religious, moral, political, or cultural barriers to reducing mortality and that the programs which involve the reduction of mortality require governmental action, collective and impersonal, rather than individual and personal action. The control of fertility tends more to involve individual motivation and behavior and is usually beset with varying forms of religious, moral, political, and cultural barriers.

Populations in the industrial-transitional stage of population growth increase rapidly, and, in fact, it is this type of growth that accounts for the relatively rapid increase of the populations of Europe and the Americas during the past 3 centuries. This type of increase is well illustrated by the experience of the British Isles, the United States, Japan, and the Union of Soviet Socialist Republics, among others.

Industrial Population Dynamics. The pattern of industrial population dynamics is characterized by both low mortality and low fertility. In the later stages of industrialization, as a result of basic institutional changes and changes in personal values and human motivation which are not yet fully understood, control is exerted not only over mortality but also over fertility. In cultures in the later stages of industrialization greatly decreased birth rates reflect voluntary parenthood, achieved largely through various methods of birth control. The Western countries are, on the whole, in this stage of population growth.

It is possible to document the great declines in fertility in the more advanced industrial nations, and through the utilization of demographic-analytical techniques to demonstrate that Western countries have reached a stage in the balance of fertility and mortality in which, once their age and sex structure reflect contemporary birth and death rates, they will no longer be reproducing themselves. That is, even though most Western countries still have an appreciable natural increase, this increase is attributable to the present favorable age structures of their populations which reflect the relatively high fertility of preceding generations. It is necessary at this point to take note of the remarkable upswing of marriage and birth rates in Western countries, including the United States, in the postwar period. Some have heralded this upswing as an indication of a reversal of the downward secular trend in fertility. It is clear that the great increase in marriages and births is of a magnitude to require many short-run adjustments to a substantially increased total and youthful population. It is not so clear, however, as yet, that the secular trend has been significantly reversed.

Population Projections. In the present state of knowledge it is not possible to predict the future population of the world or of its component areas. An ability to predict future population would imply an ability to predict the future course of technological advance, the impact of induced economic programs, of business cycles, of human motivation, of government policies, and of war, among other things. It is possible, however, to construct population projections for the world and its constituent parts based on previous trends and explicitly stated assumptions. Although it is almost certain that the assumptions made as bases for such projections will not hold, projections nevertheless have utility for analytical and planning purposes.

A number of projections of world population in various areas of the world have been made both prior to and since the war. Let us examine the most recent ones for the world and its broad regions—those prepared by the staff of the United Nations.*

The projections of the United Nations consist of the calculations of a "hypothetical 1980 population" for the world, the continents, and regions based on the assumption of birth and death rates continuing at observed 1946-48 levels; and a "hypothetical 1980 population" for the world and three groups of regions according to explicitly stated "high," "medium," and "low" assumptions. The former simply projects population growth on the basis of the relatively high postwar rate of natural increase without regard to variations in trends in the various regions of the world or the stage they have reached in their population growth pattern. The latter projections are based on three sets of assumptions—high, low, and medium—taking into account differential trends and the stage of each region in the demographic revolution. These projections are made for only three groups of regions which correspond roughly in their vital rates to the patterns described above.

The hypothetical 1980 population of the world, based on the assumption that birth and death rates would continue at 1946-48 levels, may be estimated as 3,523 million. This would represent an increase for the 30-year period of over 1,100 million persons, or 46 per cent. It would represent an average annual rate of growth of about 1.3 per cent.

The hypothetical populations of the world in 1980, resulting from the "high," "medium," and "low" assumptions, are as follows: "high," 3,636 million; "medium," 3,277 million; "low," 2,976 million.

The high projection results in an increase of over 1,200 million persons, or about 50 per cent, representing an average annual rate of growth of 1.4 per cent. The medium assumption results in an increase of about 800 million persons, or 35 per cent, with an average annual rate of growth of about 1 per cent. The low assumption results in an increase of less than 600 million persons, or 23 per cent for the period, representing an average annual rate of growth of .7 per cent.

As is indicated by the United Nations in its analysis of its projections, "one may conclude that the population of the world is likely to increase during the next 30 years by at least 500 million, barring major wars or other unforeseen calamities. If conditions are favorable, the increase may be by as much as 1,200 million." The smaller of these increases would mean an increase in 30 years approximately equal to the total 1950 population of Europe and the Soviet Union. The larger of these increases represents a population equal to that of all of Asia in 1950. As is pointed out in the United Nations report, "it would mean a larger growth in 30 years than occurred in the thousands of years from the first appearance of *homo sapiens* to as recently as 1850."

Some Implications. The world, as a whole, will increasingly be faced with the problem of controlling its numbers. This is a relatively new problem in human experience. It arises from cultural changes which have destroyed the prehistoric and historic patterns of population equilibrium. It is a problem, more specifically, which arises from human interventionism in the control of mortality without sufficient interventionism, as yet, in the control of fertility to re-establish an equilibrium. We live on a finite globe. We have experienced during the last 3 centuries an unprecedented demographic revolution. The world is now increasing at an average annual rate of growth of about 1 per cent per year. This is a fantastic rate of growth which, as we have seen, cannot possibly be sustained. It inevitably follows that if we continue to control mortality even at present levels, let alone at the reduced levels which are in prospect, we must also control fertility.

The projections of world population document these assertions in a somber way. They indicate the necessity for great increase in the world's productivity even if present levels of living, as they now exist in the various regions of the world, are to be maintained; and for a prodigious increase in productivity if the levels of living of the various peoples

* *Population Bulletin,* No. 1, United Nations, New York, December, 1951.

on the earth are to be raised. The 64-dollar population question may be stated as follows: Is it possible for the less-developed areas of the world, which already contain more than half of the earth's population, to experience what we loosely call the "industrial revolution," without a repetition of the demographic revolution experienced by the Western world? More specifically, is it possible for the less-developed areas to reap the benefits of the potentially great declines in mortality without a more rapid decline in fertility than that experienced by the Western world?

Attempts to raise levels of living through programs of economic development cannot ignore the mortality-fertility balance. The initial impact of such efforts is to produce great declines in mortality. To raise the levels of living of the peoples in these areas will therefore require a more rapid increase in productivity than in population. Obviously, an increase in the level of living could be more easily effected if decreases in mortality were accompanied by decreases in fertility. The twentieth century does not afford the same setting for a demographic revolution in the less-developed areas that the seventeenth century provided for Western nations. Moreover, the contemporary world possesses techniques for reducing mortality at much faster rates than that ever achieved by the West. It has available not only means of reducing famine, achieving potable water and food, and practicing public sanitation but also a relatively advanced medical art which includes the antibiotics. But it as yet offers no new means of, or even tangible prospects for, rapidly modifying value systems and human motivation to reduce fertility or miraculous ways of producing incentive in mass populations to increase productivity.

The maintenance of world peace and order, it is increasingly recognized, will in large measure depend on the reduction of the great differences in the levels of living of the "haves" and "have-nots" of the world. Differences of 10 to 1 in per capita income, and in infant mortality, reflecting the differences in levels of living, underlie the international tensions and hostilities of our day. Economic development programs represent perhaps the most powerful weapon we have yet devised to promote peace and to prevent war. Economic development programs, however, are ensnarled in the Gordian knot of "the population problem." It is a problem precipitated by long-time cultural changes. It is a problem that will ever press more urgently to the end that a more equitable balance is achieved between the distribution of the world's peoples and the world's resources and that an equilibrium is attained between human mortality and human fertility.

As a unit for analysis, Pascal K. Whelpton uses the growth of world population during the last generation—approximately the last thirty years—though contemporary trends are seen in a perspective going back to the time of Christ's birth. This selection refers briefly to the population trends in several countries where population policies have been initiated experimentally to retard population growth. The basic question has become one of reducing fertility rather than reducing mortality.

7

A GENERATION OF DEMOGRAPHIC CHANGE*

Pascal K. Whelpton

It is desirable to consider first the growth of the total population of the world during the last generation, or roughly the last thirty years, and to compare it with that of the preceding generation. During the last thirty years, the world population has been growing by about 27 million per year. During the preceding thirty years it was growing by about half as large an amount—14 million per year. The rate of increase has not risen so rapidly, however. During the last thirty years it has been about 12 per thousand per year, compared with about 8 per thousand during the preceding thirty years. In other words there has been roughly a 50 per cent increase in the rate of increase from one generation to the next.

One term we frequently hear used in connection with the world's population growth is "explosion." Is this an appropriate term, or is it an unjustified scare word? During the last generation, as I have said, the number of people has been rising annually about 12 per thousand—or about 1.2 per cent. When businessmen borrow money at an interest rate of 1.2 per cent, they think they are getting it cheaply. And when people who are dependent on investments receive a return of 1.2 per cent per year they feel that it scarcely paid them to save. In the short run the world's recent rate of growth seems rather small.

But when one realizes what such a rate can amount to if it continues over a long time, one's attitude changes radically. When Christ was born the world's inhabitants numbered about 350 million. If that population had grown from 1 A.D. to 1957 at the rate of growth of 1900–1930—8 per thousand per year which seems quite small on an annual basis—there would at present be in this world nearly 8 million people for every one person who is now here. If the rate of growth of the last thirty years—about 1.2 per cent which also seems small—had started at the beginning of the Christian Era, we would now have more than 3,000 people per square foot of the world's land area. And if the rate of growth of the last five years—which is only about 1.5 per cent per year—had been in effect we would now have more than one million people per square foot of land. So from the long-time point of view, it seems very appropriate to say that the world is having a population explosion.

Let us look at a crude diagram of the growth of the human species. We are told that mankind first appeared on the earth's surface between five hundred thousand and a million years ago. Let us be conservative, assume that it was five hundred thousand rather than a million years ago, and begin with two people. (Some begin with one person but I prefer starting with one of each

* From Roy G. Francis (ed.), *The Population Ahead,* University of Minnesota Press, Minneapolis, copyright 1958.

sex.) We know very little about man's numbers during most of the five hundred thousand years, merely that from a modern viewpoint the globe had comparatively few inhabitants five thousand years or more before the birth of Christ. At that time, as I have said, the world's population was approximately 350 million. In other words, during nearly all the first 498,000 of the 500,000 years that we are assuming to have passed since the origin of man, the species was increasing at an average rate of about 4 per hundred thousand. Nowadays a city or nation with such a rate would be sure it was standing still rather than growing. And well it might, for if we represent this rate of growth graphically (see Figure 1) the population line for these 498,000 years appears to be practically horizontal. In great contrast is the skyrocketing of people from 350 million to 2,700 million in the last 2,000 years. This appears as an almost vertical line on our diagram, so that the whole picture resembles a right angle.

Before discussing developments in various countries during recent years it may help to reconsider what is referred to as the demographic revolution. In nearly all parts of the world a century or two ago—and in important parts of it today—birth and death rates were at a relatively high level and of approximately the same magnitude; hence little, if any, population increase occurred. Then in some parts the death rate began to go down, fell rapidly for a few decades, and finally began to level off. In a few countries of Europe the birth rates have now also fallen until they approach the death rates on this low level, and again there is very little population growth. But the death rate has been the first to fall, only later followed by a decline in the birth rate, and this is what has brought rapid population increase. A model of these changes is shown in Figure 2.

Now in general, the countries of the world have been moving along the path of the demographic revolution during the last generation, and even during the eight years since the previous symposium on population was held. This may be seen by comparing birth and death rates for 1955 or 1956 with rates for thirty years earlier. In the United States, the crude death rate (the number of deaths per thousand population) has declined from 12 to 9. The crude birth rate (about which I'll say more later) is 25 per thousand —the same now as it was a generation ago. (A major decrease in the 1930s was balanced by an increase in the 1940s.) The United States is not behaving quite properly in terms of our schematic diagram, for the rate of natural increase is now about 16 per thousand compared with about 13 a generation earlier. Nevertheless, our country undoubtedly is in the latter part of the demographic revolution, and the changes of the last thirty

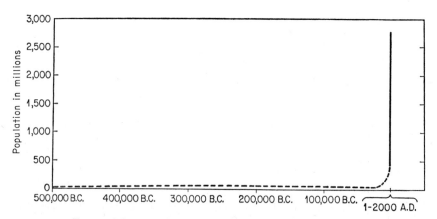

FIG. 1. Schematic diagram of the world's population growth.

years probably should be regarded as short-time fluctuations rather than as long-time secular trends.

If we consider the countries to the south of us in Middle and South America, we find a quite different type of change. Thirty years ago, the crude death rate of most of those countries was between 20 and 30 per thousand and falling. We know less about the birth rate because fewer of these countries had fairly complete birth registration, but the indications are that it was high—40 to 45 per thousand—and close to what is usually thought of as the upper level. The rate of increase for this large region as a whole was in the neighborhood of 15 per thousand. In other words, most of these countries were in an early phase of the demographic revolution.

In the last thirty years there has been a substantial drop in the crude death rate in Middle and South America. In some countries the rate has almost been cut in half and is now down to 10 per thousand. In contrast, the crude birth rate has remained fairly high as a rule—still between 40 and 45 per thousand—although small declines have occurred in some countries, and Chile and Argentina now report rates of 34 and 24, respectively. The larger drop in mortality than in fertility has raised the annual rate of natural increase (population growth) of the region from about 15 per thousand to about 25 per thousand. In other words, most of the American countries to the south of us have been moving toward the middle of the demographic revolu-

tion. This region now has a more rapid rate of population growth than any other large area in the world.

Next, let us consider the other extreme —the European countries (excluding the U.S.S.R.) for which we have good information. In this part of the world the crude death rate thirty years ago usually was between 12 and 20—along the latter part of the death rate line in Figure 2. Since then, it has declined to between 9 and 12 per thousand—nearly as low as it can go. In the same period of time the birth rate has declined from 20-30 per thousand to between 15 and 25 per thousand in most cases. The net result is a small decrease in the rate of population growth, from about 9 to 7 per thousand. Europe is in the second half of the demographic revolution, with some countries much farther along than others.

The situation of Canada, Australia, and New Zealand has been quite like ours, so I won't say anything about them.

We know much less about what has happened in the Asian countries than we do about what has happened in Europe or the Americas. Even now we don't have good vital statistics for a majority of the population of Asia. The best estimates—those of the United Nations—indicate that thirty years ago the crude death rate in most Asian countries was between 30 and 40 per thousand, and that it has declined by now to between 20 and 35. The birth-rate situation resembles that of Middle and South America—the crude rate

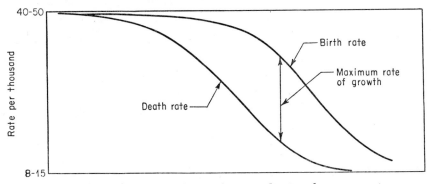

Fig. 2. Model of the demographic revolution, indicating changes over time.

of most countries being estimated at between 40 and 45 per thousand thirty years ago, and in the neighborhood of 40 per thousand at the present time. In consequence, the rate of natural increase in the Asian region has risen from roughly 10 per thousand to 15 per thousand. Nearly all these countries are in the first part of the demographic revolution.

Japan is an outstanding exception to the general Asian picture. In the last eight years the birth rate has been lowered drastically—from 33 to 19 per thousand. This probably is the most abrupt peacetime drop that has ever occurred in any country during the world's history. Compared with thirty years ago, however, the death rate has gone down nearly as much as the birth rate, and the rate of population growth has only declined from 13 to 11 per thousand. Recently, however, Japan has moved rapidly along the later stages of the demographic revolution.

One of the outstanding cases of rapid population increase is Singapore—another Asian area with very good statistics available. In that city the death rate has been brought down to about 9 per thousand, and the birth rate has remained high (in 1956 it was 48 per thousand), so the rate of natural increase is now 39 per thousand, or 3.9 per cent per year!

It would be interesting to consider some other unusual situations, but instead let me summarize. Broadly speaking, we find that the world's population is now increasing at about 1.5 per cent per year, that the United States, Canada, Australia, New Zealand, the U.S.S.R., Asia, and Africa are close to the world average, that the rate of 2.5 per cent for Middle and South America is well above the world average, and that Europe's rate of 0.7 per cent is not quite half as large as the world average.

Next, it may be desirable to think about the outlook for future population growth in various areas. Let us begin with the countries in which the demographic revolution has gone furthest, and which have annual growth rates of less than 1 per cent. Nearly all these countries are in Europe. In most of them the crude death rate is about as low as it can go. In fact, in some cases this rate is likely to rise as the proportion of middle-aged and older people in the population increases. Birth rates also are relatively low, in most cases because a large majority of married couples wish to have small families and are successful in their efforts to prevent unwanted pregnancies. In these countries the rate of growth during coming years will depend chiefly on the average number of children that married couples want to have. This number may go up in some countries if economic conditions improve, if programs to favor larger families are adopted, or if changes in value systems place more emphasis on children as compared with economic goods. On the other hand, changes in the opposite direction may occur, and tend to reduce the average number of children wanted. Predicting the future trends of such conditions is highly speculative. Moreover, little is known about the relative importance of the numerous factors influencing the decisions of couples on having another child; hence we lack an adequate basis for evaluating the extent to which a known change in a given factor—for example, in economic conditions—would raise or lower the number of children wanted. We can be fairly sure, however, that actual family size will move closer to desired family size as married couples become better informed about contraceptive methods, and as more effective and acceptable methods are developed. On the whole, therefore, I expect these countries will continue to move along the path of the demographic revolution, and to have slowly decreasing rates of growth. In the short run, if important fluctuations in economic conditions occur, there undoubtedly will be important short-run changes in fertility and population increase.

Among the countries with medium growth rates—that is, between 1 and 2 per cent per year—we find such a wide variation in conditions that generalization is impossible. I mentioned Africa as growing on the whole at about the world rate of 1.5 per cent per year. In some parts of Africa it is practically certain that death rates will be lowered and that the number of people will rise more rapidly. If out of each thousand babies that are born in a year, four hundred die before their first birthday, as has been the case in some Egyptian villages in recent years, there is plenty of opportunity for reducing death rates substantially! In contrast, other countries or groups of people—for example, the French in North Africa and the white population of the Union of South Africa—are in the latter part of the demographic revolution, and their rate of growth is more likely to taper off than to go up.

There are others who can speak better than I about what is likely to happen in the U.S.S.R., another country with a medium rate of growth. I expect some reduction to occur, for I think that more and more of the Russian people will come to realize that having too many children tends to depress the level of living of a family.

Eastern Asia as a whole has a rate of growth only slightly above the world average. In China I think the likelihood is that population growth will become somewhat more rapid as death rates are reduced through public health measures. Recently, however, some of the Communist leaders have been pointing out the need for family limitation so that the lower death rates which are desired (and anticipated) will not mean large additions to the 600,000,000 people now present whose living levels are to be raised. It is possible that these discussions will lead to a program enforced with the power that a Communist regime can use, which will lower birth rates more quickly than death rates and slow down population growth rather than speed it up. If this happens, China will go through the demographic revolution much more rapidly than the United States and the countries of northwestern Europe.

Southeastern Asia has a rate of growth of about 1.8 per cent per year according to the United Nations' estimates. It is likely to go even higher for a time, for the reasons first mentioned in discussing China.

South central Asia, of which India has a major part of the population, is now thought to be growing at about 1.2 per cent per year. There too, I think some increase in the rate of growth is to be expected, for public health programs and other changes are likely to reduce death rates. But here again a major uncertainty is what will happen to the birth rate. Will the government of India be successful with the program it is planning to spread information about a relatively simple and fairly effective method of contraception among married couples throughout rural India? Ten million rupees is budgeted for that project over a five-year period as a part of the second five-year plan. That is only a little more than 2 million dollars, which to us is not a large amount, and which certainly doesn't seem large on a per capita basis for India. But one must remember that in terms of human time a rupee will buy as much in India as a dollar here, so from the standpoint of purchasing power 10 million rupees is not too far from 10 million dollars.

So far as I know India is the first country to make a large-scale attempt to reduce birth rates by spreading information about contraception. In this respect it is a great pioneer for the heavily populated and underdeveloped countries. Many people are quite pessimistic about what can be done, while others are moderately optimistic. It is possible that the program will have little impact, but it is also possible that it will be surprisingly effective and that a substantial beginning will be made in the next five years in lowering the birth rate in India and speeding it toward the end of the demographic revolution. The results will be awaited with great interest.

Reserving for the end of my paper a more detailed discussion of the United States, which is also among the countries with a medium rate of growth, I would like now to pass on to the last of the three groups I mentioned.

The rapidly growing areas, with a rate of more than 2 per cent per year, consist mainly of Middle and South America, the Philippines, and parts of Oceania. For Middle and

South America the outlook for the next few years probably is for little reduction in the rate of growth. While fertility probably will decline, there is a good chance that this change will be balanced by a further decline in mortality. In other words, this region as a whole probably has not reached the midpoint of the demographic revolution. Argentina is an important exception. Its rate of natural increase already has been lowered to 16 per thousand, and the downward trend is likely to continue.

I have been talking so far about birth rates, death rates, and rates of natural increase, and have not said anything about international migration because during most of the world's history it has had only a very slight effect on the rate of growth of the total population. In theory, international migration should take people from areas where there is over-crowding to areas with greater economic opportunity, which should speed up the world's growth. In practice, large-scale movements concentrated in a few decades have occurred only intermittently. European migration to the Americas was one of the major movements, but even here the crucial factor was not the number of people who crossed the ocean. Vastly more important was the fact that the comparatively few who came brought a different civilization which replaced the indigenous hunting and fishing economy and enabled a given amount of land to support far more people than it had supported previously.

Within the last generation, one of the largest movements of people across national boundaries has been the migration of Moslems from India to Pakistan and of Hindus from Pakistan into India. It is estimated that about 10 million Hindus went to India, and a substantially smaller number of Moslems went to Pakistan. But even this huge interchange has had relatively little effect on the total number of people in each country, and no measurable effect on the growth rate of the world. If we define international migration more strictly, and rule out movements like the foregoing on the ground that they reflect

changes in national boundaries following a war or other unusual event, we find that during the last thirty years the United States has received more immigrants than any other country. But the net inward movement has amounted to only about 3 million people, or an average of about one hundred thousand a year, which is of minor importance compared with our rate of natural increase from the excess of births over deaths.

Because we are Americans we are especially interested in what has been happening to population growth in the United States and what is likely to happen in the future. Our population on January 1, 1957, was very close to 170 million. For the last ten years we have been growing by about 2.7 million per year. During the last thirty years, and the preceding thirty years as well, the increase was close to 50 million people, or 1.7 million per year. Many persons have read so much about the postwar jump in the birth rate and know of so many families in which young married couples are having more children than their parents that they think the United States has been growing recently at a record-breaking rate as well as by record-breaking numbers. This is incorrect. In the last ten years our annual rate of growth has averaged about 1.5 per cent. Although this is well above the rate of about 1.2 per cent for the last thirty years as a while, it is well below the rate of 1.7 per cent for the preceding thirty years and barely half the rate which prevailed most of the time from 1700 to 1860.

It is interesting to consider different portions of the last thirty years, because of the great contrasts that are found—for example, the depression decade of the 1930s and the decade of prosperity since World War II. If we compare these two periods we find for one thing that there were about 22 million births in the former and about 38 million in the latter. This is a jump of more than 70 per cent, which is most unusual. People are right in speaking of the great upsurge in numbers of births and in the birth rate since the war—the baby boom, as it is sometimes called. But are they right in saying (as so many do) that the chief cause is larger families? Let us see, for that will help us to understand what is likely to happen in the next decade or two.

First, however, let us rule out about 25 per cent of the increase in the number of births, because it merely reflects the fact that the population was larger in the last ten years than it was during the 1930s. We can do this by considering the crude birth rate instead of the number of births. The crude birth rate averaged 17.3 per thousand during the 1930s and 24.6 per thousand during 1947 to 1956. This rise of 42 per cent is much smaller than that of 70 per cent for the number of births; nevertheless, it too is unusual in world history.

When I ask people what they think has been the most important factor in raising our birth rate so greatly, the answer almost always is "Families are getting larger." There has been a change in that direction, but if we measure family size on the basis of the average number of births per couple with children, we find that the increase in this number has contributed only about one-sixth of the birth-rate rise we are discussing.

Other explanations are that more women are marrying, and that those who do so are marrying younger. The former is not important, because for many decades about 90 per cent of American women married before reaching the end of the childbearing period, and the rise so far has not reached 94 per cent. Even if it were to continue to 100 per cent (which is most unlikely) the relative change would not be large. Much more important as a cause of the postwar baby boom is the younger marriage of more women. For example, at the end of the 1930s approximately 53 per cent of the women aged 20–24 (and born in 1916–20) had already married, but in 1955 the proportion married by ages 20–24 had risen to 71 per cent for women born in 1931–35. This is a large increase. Together with the small decrease in the number of old maids it has contributed about 40 per cent of the rise in

the crude birth rate from the 1930s to 1947–56.

The third (and last) change I shall mention is the tendency for more married women to have at least one child and to start childbearing sooner after marriage. In 1940 approximately 33 per cent of the women aged 20–24 who had married had not yet borne a child. By 1955 the corresponding proportion had fallen to 25 per cent. Similarly, among women aged 25–29 who had ever been married those without children decreased from 26 per cent of the total in 1940 to 13 per cent in 1955. Such changes have contributed more than 40 per cent of the rise in the crude birth rate from the 1930s to the postwar decade.

You may say that if fewer wives are childless and more have one child, this helps just as much to increase average family size as having three children instead of two. This is correct. I have mentioned the two types of change separately in order to emphasize the fact that the increase in family size that is under way results chiefly from some couples having one or two children instead of none, some having two or three instead of one, and some having three or four instead of two. This is far from a return to the large-family pattern of a century ago.

If we put all types of increase together we still find that less than half of the rise in annual fertility from the depression low to the postwar high is attributable to more children per married couple, and more than half to the fact that women are marrying younger and having their first child at a younger age. The latter circumstance has moved to the past ten years some millions of births that would have occurred during the next ten years if the former pattern of age at marriage and the first confinement had continued.

Most of us who are concerned with population problems professionally tend to overestimate the increase in size of family that has been going on, because it has been larger on the whole in the upper educational and income groups—the groups that we are likely to know about firsthand—than in the rest of the population. We tend to judge the situation as a whole by what happens to the people we know about. We have fewer friends in the lower educational and income classes where average size of family has still been going down.

What is the outlook for the future? Will the high annual birth rate of recent years be maintained? The tendency for women to marry and start childbearing younger is a temporary factor. As long as the age at marriage is dropping, the birth rate will be supported at a relatively high level by that influence. But once the age at marriage stops going down, the birth rate does not remain on that plateau but declines to a lower level. A big question, then, is how much longer will the age of women flocking to the altar and to the maternity ward a year or two later decline? I think age of marriage may continue to decline, but there certainly is a limit below which it is not likely to go. It is one thing for the median age—the age by which half the women who will marry have done so—to decrease from between 21 and 22 among the women born during 1916–20 to less than 20 among those born during 1926–30. But it will be another thing if the decline continues to 18 or younger. Similarly, the shortening of the average interval between marriage and the first baby is a temporary factor, which raises the annual birth rate while it is going on, but lets it fall once the new shorter interval is established. Here again it is one thing for the average length of the first interval to decline from about 34 months for women born during 1916–20 to 24 months for those born during 1926–30, and another thing for it to decline to 14 months. There is no chance of its going as low as nine months in our population!

It is evident from what I have said that only a substantial increase in the average number of children per family can keep our birth rate from declining. Such an increase would not be temporary in its influence (as is the case with younger marriage and earlier childbearing) but would help to maintain a higher birth rate even though family size should become stable at a level only somewhat above that of the recent past. But what is likely to happen to family size in coming years? The best information now available comes from a study of a representative sample —what the statistician calls a "probability sample"—of the white married couples in the United States with the wife between the ages of 18 and 39. This information was collected about two years ago and is now in the process of being analyzed. It shows that some increase in the size of completed families is almost certain to occur, but not as large an increase as is commonly thought. For example, among the women who were at the end of the childbearing period at the beginning of 1955 (i.e., who were then 45–49 years old) there had been an average of about 2.40 births per woman who had married. This lifetime birth rate is certain to go higher in coming years, for in 1955 among the women aged 35–39 who had ever been married there had already been about 2.50 births per woman and another .15 to .45 were expected. Among still younger women—aged 25–29— the rate by 1955 had been lower, but these women confidently expected to have at least 2.7 births each and possibly as many as 3.3, and gave 3.0 as a most probable figure. An increase from 2.4 to 3.0 children per ever-married woman would represent a substantial reversal of the long-time downward trend of family size in the United States. It would regain only a fraction of the past decrease, however, for the average married woman aged 45 in 1910 had borne 4.3 children, and half a century earlier the average probably was about 6.0. In consequence, I think it is quite likely that the crude birth rate and the rate of population growth will start down within five or ten years, and certainly will do so within fifteen years.

The speed and size of the decline will depend in part on economic conditions, but the desires of our millions of married couples will play a more important role. The birth rate in the United States, as in several other countries, is largely under voluntary control.

Among the white married couples with the wife between the ages of 18 and 39 in the study to which I referred earlier, about 70 per cent had tried to space their children or to limit their number. Another 9 per cent, mostly young married couples, had not done so as yet, but expected to do so in the future. So 79 per cent can be called family planners, at least in intent. The remaining 21 per cent include 5 per cent that were definitely sterile and not interested in contraception. Another 9 per cent were probably sterile or had had so much difficulty in conceiving that they felt little need for control measures. This leaves only about 6 per cent that conceived easily and did not expect to use some method of birth control to space children or limit their number. If we consider only the fecund couples—those that conceived easily—we find that about 83 per cent had already used contraception, another 7 per cent expected to do so, and only about 10 per cent said they would not try any type of family planning. The latter group contains a substantial number of younger couples who have not been married long, some of whom are likely to change their minds after they have three, four, or five children. The experience of the older couples shows numerous additions to the ranks of the family planners after the birth of an additional baby. In fact, having an additional child seems to be a strong incentive to the practice of contraception.

If we look at the relation between the family size desired by the fecund couples and the actual number of their children, we find that only about 14 per cent said they had more children than they wanted, and that in most cases the excess was only one. As would be expected, few of the younger couples had more than they wanted, though some of them no doubt will as time passes. But even among the fecund couples with the wife aged 35–39, only 22 per cent are in the excess fertility group. (Among those who had not tried control measures the percentage is 40.) It seems fair to say that a rather high degree of success in controlling fertility has been achieved.

It is clear that population growth in the United States during the next few decades will depend primarily on marriage patterns and on the attitudes of married couples regarding family size. These can change quite rapidly, as we have seen by comparing the last ten years with the 1930s. The United States has been unusually prosperous since World War II. If prosperity is maintained we probably shall have for a time a continued trend toward somewhat larger families, but shall soon see the stabilization of marriage and the first confinement at ages only a little below those now customary. The result will be a decrease in the birth rate and the rate of population growth to somewhat lower levels. If there is a recession we undoubtedly shall see sharper decreases in both these rates. And if we have a major depression like the 1930s—which does not seem likely but might possibly happen—the birth rate probably will go down with startling rapidity, because the tendencies to marry younger, to have the first child come sooner, and to want larger families will all be reversed. This is an extreme that we should not overlook entirely even though it now appears quite improbable.

In contrast to the outlook for some slowing down of population growth in the United States, the global outlook is for more rapid growth. The underdeveloped countries with a large proportion of the world's population can reduce death rates rapidly by developing good public health programs, and speed up population growth accordingly. The crucial question is what will happen to their birth rates. Will countries like India and China be as successful in reducing fertility as in reducing mortality? If so, their demographic revolution will be over in much less time than in most of the developed countries, and the explosive growth of the world's population shown in Figure 1 will be brought under control, perhaps within a century. If not, man's ingenuity faces the staggering task of providing for his rapidly growing numbers, and doing so not as in the past but on the rising level of living that is so widely wanted.

In the following selection Kingsley Davis gives an over-all view of recent population trends in the New World. The abstract accompanying the article provides sufficient introduction.

8

RECENT POPULATION TRENDS IN THE NEW WORLD: AN OVER-ALL VIEW*

By Kingsley Davis

Abstract: The Western Hemisphere has been leading the world in population growth. Although the United States-Canadian rate of increase is high in comparison to most other industrial nations, it is the Latin American countries that are contributing most to the over-all increase. These countries as a whole exceed the growth rate in any other major area of the world. Whereas industrial northern America has experienced a postwar upsurge in population due to increased fertility, the tremendous gains in Latin America have been made because of sharply declining mortality. The consequences of the amazing rate of population growth depend in part upon whether economic development itself or external factors have brought down the death rate.

The Western Hemisphere, perhaps because of its extreme contrasts, has seldom been treated demographically as a single region. Yet without wasting words to define a mythical "true region," we can say that the Americas have more in common than is ordinarily stated and that their differences are in many ways complementary and interdependent. Each American nation is nearer to several other American countries than to any non-American country, and each has peculiarities that give it specialization within the diversified economy of the entire hemisphere. The foreign trade of these countries is predominantly within the region. Recently, for example, 55 per cent of the exports of twelve Latin American states went to, and 62 per cent of the imports came from, other American countries; in 1956 the United States exports going to the rest of the Americas represented 41.5 per cent of the total value, and the imports coming from the Americas represented 54.3 per cent of the total. Foreign travel is also heavily within the hemisphere, as is foreign investment. In 1955 the value of United States direct investment in Canada and the Latin American republics (excluding dependencies) was estimated to be 68 per cent of all of this country's foreign direct investment. In general, barriers are lower for intra-American commerce and for intra-American migration than for external movements of goods and people.

This interdependence would be less if it were not for at least two broad bases of similarity which, in addition to geographical

* Reprinted by permission of *The Annals of the American Academy of Political and Social Science*, vol. 256, pp. 1–10, March, 1948.

contiguity, the Americas possess in common: first, the dominant institutional structure and intellectual outlook derive from Europe; second, these elements have everywhere been modified by New World conditions. Sharp cultural differences exist—some growing out of the divergent regions of Europe itself and some out of the persistence of indigenous cultures or the stage of economic development —but the common European background and common transplantation into a new region have given the peoples of this part of the world a broadly similar outlook. They share a sense of being part of a new and expanding region with enormous potentialities. They share a sense of freedom from some of the constrictions and historical antagonisms of Europe. They are less divided by linguistic diversity than any major region of the world.

The Western Hemisphere is by no means self-contained, and its unity rests as much upon profound but complementary differences as it does upon similarities. It may not therefore be a "region" by some definitions, but precisely because its demographic characteristics bear a systematic relation to both its diversities and its resemblances, it is a fruitful area for the study and interpretation of population trends. The present volume of THE ANNALS attempts to utilize the natural laboratory that the hemisphere thus provides. The several authors give not only the salient demographic facts, but also their views as to how these facts bear upon or derive from the economic and sociological evolution of the Americas. The purpose of this first essay is to provide an over-all view as an introduction to the more specialized contributions that follow.

THE WORLD'S FASTEST GROWING POPULATIONS

Demographically speaking, the outstanding fact concerning the Western Hemisphere in recent decades can be briefly stated. During a period when the earth's population has been increasing faster than it ever did before, our half of the world has exceeded the world rate. Furthermore, that part of the hemisphere

which lies south of the United States—that is, the Caribbean islands, Middle America, and South America—has exhibited the most rapid human increase of any major region of the world. This all-time record in sheer multiplication deserves close attention.

As for the entire hemisphere, in 1940 it contained approximately 277 million people; in 1955, about 366 million—an increase of something like 89 million (or 32 per cent) in fifteen years. The average increase per decade since 1920 has been 17.5 per cent or half again as fast as the average shown by the rest of the world taken as a whole. Like the rest of the world, however, the rate of growth in our hemisphere has tended to accelerate, as the following figures show:

Percentage increase per decade *

Location	1920– 30	1930– 40	1940– 50	1950– 60
Western Hemisphere	17.3	11.4	19.5	21.7
Rest of World.	10.4	11.3	8.9	17.3

* Calculated from populations given in the United Nations *Demographic Yearbook* 1956, p. 151, and 1960 projections on medium assumptions given in forthcoming United Nations publication, "Population Estimates for World Regions, 1955–1975 and 1975–2000."

The first step in understanding the rate of increase in the whole hemisphere is to recall that the various subregions do not contribute equally to it. The biggest dividing line is that between the highly industrial part comprising Canada and the United States and the less industrial part to the south. If for the sake of convenience rather than strict accuracy we designate all of the area south of the United States as "Latin America," we find that this section expanded its population from 90 million in 1920 to 183 million in 1955—an increase of 100 per cent in 35 years. Northern America—Canada, United States, Alaska, Greenland, Bermuda, St. Pierre, and Miquelon—also reached 183 million in 1955; since, however, it had started with 117 rather than 90 million in 1920, its increase over the entire period was only 56 per cent or a little more than half the rate of increase for "Latin America."

The fact that the United States and Canada have been lagging behind the other American countries does not mean that, by ordinary standards, their populations are growing slowly. Their performance must be judged in comparison to other industrial countries. Taking the industrial countries of the world as a whole, we find that since about the time of World War I, in contrast to earlier periods, they have been exhibiting a slower rate of population growth than the underdeveloped countries as a whole. But among the industrial countries, Canada and the United States have rates of increase that are among the highest. Since 1920, in fact, their average growth rate is about three times that of the industrial countries of northwest and central Europe.

Rates of Increase. Among the less developed nations of the world where population increase has generally reached unprecedented proportions, the countries and territories of Latin America are far and away in the lead. The high rate of population growth in the entire hemisphere is thus a function of both the fast rate of increase in Canada and the United States compared to other industrial nations and the extraordinarily fast rate in Latin America compared to other underindustrialized areas. This can be seen by classifying the world's regions and computing their rates of increase.

Regions	Percentage gain 1920–1960
Underdeveloped regions	70.5
Latin America	126.3
Asia (excluding Japan)	68.4
Africa	67.6
Pacific Islands	63.6
Southern Europe	42.6
Developed regions	41.1
Australia–New Zealand	92.4
Japan	71.7
Northern America	68.4
U.S.S.R.	36.1
Northwest and Central Europe	23.3

Source: *Demographic Yearbook 1956*, United Nations, p. 151. Also 1960 projections on medium assumptions given in forthcoming United Nations publication, "Population Estimates for World Regions, 1955–1975 and 1975–2000."

TABLE 1. MEDIUM ESTIMATES OF FUTURE POPULATIONS IN MAJOR REGIONS

Country	Population (in millions)			Percentage gain
	1960	1975	2000	1960–2000
Northern America	197	240	312	58.4
Latin America	205.8	304.1	592.8	188.0
Central America	46.3	72.3	150	224.0
Caribbean	19.6	27.1	48	144.9
Tropical South America	107	163	339	216.8
Temperate South America	32.9	41.7	55.8	69.6
Africa	235	303	517	120.0
Asia	1,620	2,210	3,870	138.9
Europe	424	476	568	34.0
Oceania	16.3	21.0	29.3	79.8
U.S.S.R.	215	275	379	76.3
World	2,910	3,830	6,270	115.5

Source: From Population Branch, United Nations, "Population Estimates for World Regions, 1955–1975 and 1975–2000." These are estimates based on medium assumptions. Since at the moment of writing they have not been published, they are of course subject to revision. Columns do not add to world total because of rounding.

One should note that Northern America does not show the fastest growth among the industrial areas; since, however, most of the world's industrial population is still found in Europe, the United States and Canada are above average for this type of region.

As for the future, there is scant reason to expect that rapid population growth in the Americas will soon cease. Recent projections by the Population Branch of the United Nations show, on the basis of medium and rather conservative assumptions, what may be reasonably expected. According to these figures, contained in Table 1, the entire hemisphere will grow from 403 million in 1960 to 905 million in 2000 representing a gain of 125 per cent in 40 years, second only to Asia in rate of increase. Latin America, however, will gain faster than any other major region, primarily because of the extraordinary multiplication in those parts lying in the tropical latitudes.

Necessarily, no responsible demographer pretends to "predict" future populations, and the Population Branch of the United Nations certainly does not do so. The population of the American hemisphere in the year 2000 may actually turn out to be only a few million, or more than a billion, depending on what happens between now and then. The projections given here are simply estimates made systematically on the basis of recent population dynamics. They are reasonable deductions as to the future implications of recent developments. On the whole, the Population Branch considers its projections for 1975 more likely to prove true than those for 2000, and it believes that its "medium" estimates are conservative. The "high" estimate for the Western Hemisphere in 2000 runs to 976 million, the "low" estimate to 719 million. The general assumption in all of the projections is that there will be an orderly pattern of population change, that no unprecedented world calamity or completely new development will intervene to destroy the pattern. One should regard the projections, therefore, as simply rough indications of the order of magnitude implicit in

present dynamics if they continue their general evolutionary pattern.

Demographically speaking, the main reason for the hemisphere's fast population growth is the widening spread between birth and death rates. This widening breach is recently common to the entire region, but its magnitude has been greater in Latin America; also, the direction and relative influence of the two variables—fertility and mortality—have been different in Northern and Latin America.

The secondary reason for the population growth is continued immigration. This factor has had greatest influence in Canada, less in the United States, and still less in much of Latin America; but it should not be ignored.

DEMOGRAPHIC CAUSES IN CANADA AND THE UNITED STATES

Let us look more closely at the differences between Northern and Latin America in the way fertility and mortality have behaved. As is well known, Canada and the United States underwent a long decline in birth rates beginning far back in the nineteenth century and extending to the 1930's. After 1940, however, they sustained a marked *rise* in births. The United States crude birth rate, for example, in 1951–1956 reached the level it had shown in 1925 (though never equalling any year prior to 1925). Average rates by five-year periods were as follows:

ANNUAL BIRTHS PER 1,000 POPULATION

Year	United States	Canada
1920–24	26.8	27.4
1925–29	23.2	24.1
1930–34	19.7	22.2
1935–39	18.8	20.3
1940–44	21.2	23.0
1945–49	24.1	26.9
1950–56	24.9	27.9

Although crude rates, because they are influenced by the age structure, are defective indices of fertility, the figures nevertheless indicate a substantial reproductive recovery in both countries.

If, now, we look at the United States-Canadian death rates, we find that they apparently declined during the entire time from at least the middle of the nineteenth century onward. In the United States the drop in the death rate was on the whole slower than the drop in the birth rate up until the late 1930's, and for this reason, despite very substantial immigration, the rate of population growth declined steadily. In Canada the picture is not so clear, but it appears that the drop in the death rate was at least no faster than the decline in fertility, for there was no upward trend in population growth even with immigration. Table 2 shows that the rate of increase in the United States population fell regularly from 1860 to 1940, while the rate in the Canadian population fell regularly from 1910 to 1940.

When the birth rate rose in these two countries after 1940, thus reversing the long downward trend, the death rate continued its steady decline. As a result, the spread between the two rates widened markedly and, as Table 2 makes clear, the rate of population growth rose sharply. The change in the birth rate, upward this time, was however again much faster than the change in the death rate, which continued downward. It can be calculated that in the United States the rise in the birth rate since 1940 has been more than four times as important in producing the increased population growth as was the decline of the death rate; and in Canada it has been more than five times as important.

Postwar immigration into both Canada and the United States, as Helen Eckerson shows in the present volume, has been substantial. The United States, still the world's greatest immigrant-receiving country, has accepted a larger number than Canada, but not in relation to population. Immigration has consequently made a bigger contribution to Canada's postwar upsurge in population than it has to the United States rise.

In sum, it is the changes in fertility that provide the main explanation of rising or falling rates of population growth in industrial Northern America. The unpredicted population growth since the war has been due

TABLE 2. GROWTH RATE OF UNITED STATES AND CANADIAN POPULATIONS

Year	Per cent increase per decade	
	United States	Canada *
1850–60	35.6	32.6
1860–70	26.6	14.2
1870–80	26.0	17.2
1880–90	25.5	11.8
1890–1900	20.7	11.1
1900–10	21.0	34.2
1910–20	14.9	21.9
1920–30	16.1	18.1
1930–40	7.2	10.9
1940–50	14.5	18.6
1950–60	18.4 †	28.4 †

* In the case of Canada the census is taken one year after the turn of the decade. The last figure, however, is based on the 1950 population.

† Estimates from United Nations, Population Branch, "Future Population Estimates for World Regions," forthcoming publication.

principally to an increased birth rate and only secondarily to lower mortality and enhanced immigration. A rough assessment of the relative contribution of each demographic variable to the postwar spurt in growth yields the following:

Country	Rise in birth rate	Fall in death rate	Increased immigration
United States	74%	18%	8%
Canada	58%	12%	30%

THE PATTERN OF DEMOGRAPHIC CHANGE IN LATIN AMERICA

In most of the countries to the South, the pattern of change is different from that just described for Canada and the United States. With respect to fertility, for example, there has been no long decline in the birth rate except in Argentina and perhaps in Uruguay. Instead the birth rate has tended to persist at a high level, usually between 40 and 50 per thousand when registration is reasonably accurate. Thus no low point was reached in births during the depression, nor has there been much of a rise since then. The acceleration of population growth in Latin America is clearly not due to a rise in fertility.

Nor is the acceleration due particularly to increased immigration. The majority of immigrants to the New World have been going, as in the past, to Northern America; and in Latin America itself, as Richard Robbins points out, only three countries have received a substantial influx since the war.

We are left, then, with a decline in mortality as the predominant demographic factor causing the rise in the growth rate of Latin American populations. Whereas the Canadian-United States death rates showed a continued but gradual drop from what was in 1920 already a low level, the rates in most of the other American countries have fallen precipitously from very high levels, the rate of decline tending to increase. Unfortunately, the data on mortality in Latin America are generally poor; but I have taken eleven countries which have the better death registration systems and have computed the average percentage decline in the crude death rate by five-year intervals with the following results:

Years	Average percentage decline in annual death rate
From 1920–24 to 1925–29	6.0
From 1925–29 to 1930–34	7.7
From 1930–34 to 1935–39	8.1
From 1935–39 to 1940–44	7.8
From 1940–44 to 1945–49	16.2
From 1945–49 to 1950–54	17.1

Since crude death rates reflect changes in the age structure and in the accuracy of registration, the declines noted here may either overstate or understate the actual trend; but there can be no doubt about the unprecedented speed and recent acceleration of the fall in the death rate. A similar precipitous decline has been occurring in most of the other less-industrial parts of the world.

In Latin America, therefore, it is the tumbling of the death rate, rather than a rise of fertility as in Canada and the United States, that explains the phenomenal increase in population growth since 1940. At the present time the human tide in Latin America appears to be ascending about 36 per cent faster than in Northern America. Mexico, for example, has more than doubled its population since 1925, reaching 30½ million by 1956. The Mexican birth rate for 1955 is recorded as 46, nearly twice that of the United States, and the death rate as only 13, having dropped 43 per cent since 1940. It looks as though Mexico's population (already augmented by about a million each year) will soon be growing at a rate of 3½ per cent per year. At this rate it will double every twenty years and increase tenfold in 67 years. Other countries in the area are also approaching this situation, including El Salvador, Venezuela, Guatemala, Honduras, Panama, and the Dominican Republic.

During the next two or three decades the growth-rate difference between Northern America and most of the other countries is likely to expand. The main factor supporting higher growth rates in Canada and the United States—the postwar rise in fertility —is apparently leveling off, while the main factor in Latin America—mortality decline— is continuing. Birth rates in Latin America show little sign of receding from their customarily high level, although Argentina's— and probably Uruguay's—rate has behaved more like that of the United States than like that of Mexico; and Puerto Rico's rate has declined since 1947. It seems likely that the first broad area of Latin America to achieve a modern birth level will be the temperate and more industrial southern part of South America, and this is the reason the United Nations estimates a lower future population growth for that region.

BEHIND THE DEMOGRAPHIC PATTERN

If we ask why, among the world's underdeveloped areas, Latin America leads in population growth, and why the United States and Canada are close to the lead among the industrial nations, a full answer is too complex to be given here. However, it is helpful to recall two features of the Western Hemisphere already mentioned—first, that it is still a "new" region of the world, and, second, that it is a region in which European culture is everywhere dominant.

Significantly, Latin America is the only major part of the world which is peopled by colonizing Europeans and yet is preponderantly agrarian and non-industrial. All other underdeveloped areas, aside from parts of Europe itself, are non-European in race and culture. Among the less industrial regions of the earth, therefore, the Latin Americans have the advantage of both a European background and a new and relatively empty territory. This fact helps to explain why it has been easier to transmit to them the modern techniques of death control than it has been in most other underdeveloped areas. It also helps to explain the expansionist attitude. Although parts of the Caribbean and Central America are crowded, the region as a whole has a comparatively low population density in relation to resources. South America, in fact, is still an empty shell, fully peopled near the coasts but almost empty in the interior. With 16 per cent of the world's inhabitable land area and, as of 1955, only 6.8 per cent of the world's people, Latin America as a whole still feels that its opportunities are abundant. This translates itself into the belief that an increased population is a good thing, that high birth rates and brisk immigration should be favored.

In Northern America the social order brought by the colonists was not the more feudal and stratified type found in southern Europe, but the more competitive and industrialized type found in northwest Europe. This order thrived in the New World, with the result that, until about 1920, its population grew faster than that of Latin America. However, the demographic effects of mature industrialism kept slowing the rate of increase by depressing fertility. When a rebound came in the 1940's and 1950's, it was destined to be greater and to last longer than the similar rebound in industrial Europe because the United States and Canada are still new countries in which the restraints on fertility do not derive mainly from lack of economic opportunities.

It will be noticed from figures given earlier that the only industrial countries exceeding Northern America in rate of population growth between 1920 and 1960 are Australia and New Zealand. (Japan, which was slightly ahead, is a special case of late industrialization, too far afield to treat here.) The reason is that both Australia and New Zealand are "newer." Their period of fast numerical increase therefore came later than that of Canada and the United States, and their rebound after the depression was at least equal if not greater.

Australia, New Zealand, Canada, and the United States are not likely to repeat the very rapid human increase they exhibited earlier. Remarkable as their postwar upsurge has been, it has not enabled them to match the underdeveloped areas, especially Latin America, because their rise in births has not equaled the latter's fall in deaths.

TABLE 3. RELATIVE SIZE OF UNITED STATES POPULATION

Countries	Ratios: U. S. ÷ other unit			
	1920	1960	1975	2000
United States ÷ second country (Brazil)	3.9	2.7	2.1	1.3
United States ÷ next five countries	1.6	1.2	1.0	0.6
United States ÷ rest of hemisphere	1.1	0.8	0.7	0.5

SOME FUTURE IMPLICATIONS

One likely consequence of the trends so far described is a radical shift in the numerical balance within the hemisphere. Whereas in 1920 the ratio of the United States-Canadian population to that in the rest of the hemisphere was 1.3 to 1, it will probably be reduced to 0.8 to 1 by 1975, and to 0.5 to 1 by the end of the century. Heretofore, the United States has been the demographic giant of the region. In 1920 it had more people than the rest of the two continents combined; at present its ratio is down to 0.8 to 1. It will probably retain its position as the largest nation up to at least the end of the century, but its ratio to the second and third will decline (see Table 3). The first six nations seem destined to retain their 1920 ranks, though not their relative ratios, through 1975; but if the United Nations projections hold true beyond that date, Peru and Colombia will both eclipse Canada, and Colombia will eclipse Argentina.

One should not assume that political positions will shift correspondingly. National strength does not rest solely on population size, particularly as science and economic efficiency take precedence over sheer manpower. However, when other things are roughly equal, sheer numbers count heavily. If Canada and the United States are to keep their positions of leadership, they will have to rely increasingly upon human capacities rather than upon human numbers.

If rapid population growth intensifies economic problems, it may weaken rather than strengthen a nation. Such a prospect, if found anywhere in our hemisphere, is to be found in Latin America where the population growth is greater and the economies weaker. The question of whether population expansion in this region is impeding the rate of economic gain really turns on the extent to which the swift drop in mortality is due to economic advance itself or to external factors. If it is mainly due to the former, there is no necessary economic disadvantage (whatever other disadvantages there may be) in population growth. If, on the other hand, the drop in deaths is chiefly the result of other factors, the chances are that it is reducing *per capita* income below what it would otherwise be. George Stolnitz presents reasons for crediting much of the mortality reduction in Latin America to extraeconomic factors. These reasons seem convincing to me, especially since there are signs of population pressure in many of the Latin American economies.

Any adverse economic effects, however, are hard to see because they are partially masked by the wave of postwar prosperity characterizing this region. Should this wave continue until the economies are transformed into modern industrial systems, the birth rate would ultimately turn downward and the rate of population increase would drop. There is no guarantee, however, that the rise in national incomes will continue uninterruptedly. To the extent that mortality control is coming from external sources—foreign science, personnel, and funds—a halt in economic growth would not stop it. Instead, the death rate would continue downward, the birth rate would probably remain high, and the population expansion would continue until the unfavorable effects of poverty on mortality more than matched the favorable effects of outside influence.

Characteristics of Latin American Economy. Some of the danger signals in the present Latin American economic situation are these: * (1) Although the rise in *per capita* gross product was rapid during 1945-1955, averaging 2.3 per cent per annum, the increase was greater in the first half than in the latter half of the period. (2) Per capita agricultural production for export fell in 1956 to the lowest level in 15 years, due partly to increased domestic needs as well as to bad weather and bad markets. (3) Despite the rapid urbanization and heavy rural-urban migration which Mr. Browning describes in

* These points are summarized from the excellent survey in the United Nations *Economic Bulletin for Latin America,* vol. 2, February, 1957.

the present volume, the increase of the rural population has not diminished during 1925 to 1955. Thus the tendency of the agricultural population to cease to grow, so characteristic of advancing economies, is not occurring except in a few countries such as Chile, Cuba, Uruguay, Venezuela, and, over a long period, Argentina. (4) Partly because of the shortage of land in some countries and lack of opportunity in others, there is widespread underemployment of males in the agricultural sector. (5) Although industrial output has risen, the proportion of the labor force employed in manufacturing has tended to remain stationary. At the same time the proportion employed in services has increased rapidly; in 1950 it embraced 25.3 per cent of the labor force as compared to 18.1 per cent in industry (only half of which was in manufacturing proper as opposed to handicraft). The ratio of services to industry, which normally moves downward instead of upward in the middle stages of industrial development, is so high as to appear excessive. (6) Within the manufacturing sector the production of capital goods and of intermediate products is not commensurate with the emphasis on final consumer goods.

These characteristics of the Latin American economy point to serious imbalances that must be overcome if the current boom is to continue uninterruptedly. Some of them suggest that excessive population growth may be a factor. Whether it is or not at the present time, the current human increase seems to be too fast to be sustained over the long pull. Either the economy will eventually fail to move ahead, in which case the death rate will ultimately be pushed up; or the economy will continue to gain, in which case fertility will eventually be depressed. We know that at the present time the number of living children in each family is greater than it ever was before, with greater strain on the resources of parents. We know too that the movement of millions of people to the towns and cities increases the costs and inconvenience of children. The effect of present trends is therefore such as to cause those trends eventually to subside. Accordingly, the important question is not whether the amazing population growth of today can be sustained indefinitely, but when it is likely to cease. We can agree with Harrison Brown that a billion people in the hemisphere can be supported fairly well (and agree with him also that the prospect of that many is unpleasant), but maintain at the same time that half a billion could be supported just as well or perhaps far better.

III

How Culture Changes

The character of social life in every community is determined largely by the culture of which it is a part. The cultural heritage or base of a community is distinguishable from that of other communities in so far as contact between them has been limited. The culture base provides the opportunities and sets the limitations for social and cultural change within all communities, and to the extent their culture bases are unlike, the potentialities for change would be different. What, then, is this phenomenon called culture, and how does it change?

The Nature of Culture. Culture includes everything that man has done to raise himself above his natural limitations. Culture is the sum-total of human achievement possessed by the group; or, more broadly, it is the sum-total of human achievement in the possession of mankind. The most frequently quoted definition of culture is the one offered by Edward B. Tylor in 1871: "Culture or civilization, taken in its wide ethnographic sense, is that complex whole which includes knowledge, belief, art, morals, law, custom, and any other capabilities and habits acquired by man as a member of society." [1] This definition stood virtually alone for about thirty-two years (1871–1903), but by 1950 the number of definitions had increased to 164.[2] Descriptive definitions that contain enumerations of culture traits tend to be criticized on different counts. Tylor's statement, for instance, is said to be incomplete, or too intellectualistic, or it implies too great a stability of culture and too passive a role on the part of man.

Since there is such an abundance of other definitions, at least two others merit consideration because of their implications for social and cultural change. Clarence Marsh Case introduced new terminology which is significant: "Culture consists essentially in the external storage, interchange, and transmission of an accumulating fund of personal and social experience by means of tools and symbols. . . . Culture is the unique, distinctive, and exclusive possession of man, explainable thus far only in terms of itself." [3] This conception of culture is more dynamic, and indicates the

[1] Edward B. Tylor, *Primitive Culture,* John Murray, London, 1871, vol. I, p. 1.

[2] A. L. Kroeber and Clyde Kluckhohn, *Culture: A Critical Review of Concepts and Definitions,* Peabody Museum of American Archaeology and Ethnology, Harvard University Press, Cambridge, Mass., 1952.

[3] Clarence M. Case, "Culture as a Distinctive Human Trait," *The American Journal of Sociology,* vol. 32, p. 920, May, 1927.

processual nature of culture—storage, interchange, transmission, and accumulation—all this by means of tools and symbols which man alone knows how to use. The fact that culture is explainable thus far only in terms of itself shows that it is an abstraction for which no integrative theory has yet been found.

Ellsworth Faris, in his treatise on human nature, held that culture and personality are correlative terms—twinborn products of human life. He thought of culture as the collective side of personality, and personality as the subjective aspect of culture. His assumption that ". . . society with its usages and personalities with their variations are but two ways of looking at human life" suggests that a common denominator for society and personality is found in culture.[4]

More definitions would bear analysis, but they would be found complementary to one another. Those quoted above denote what culture is as a generalization and suggest areas within which social and cultural change takes place. Yet the term "culture" must have not only general but specific meanings. As a generalization, culture is a structure which embraces all cultures no matter how different they are or how greatly separated in time or place. In this sense, culture includes man-made environments as diverse as those of the Eskimos in the Arctic region, the head-hunting Jivaros of South America, the aborigines of Australia, the Pygmies and Bantus of Africa, and, at the other extreme, the most advanced peoples of Europe, the Americas, and the Orient.

The term "culture" may be used to represent the totality of man's achievements from the earliest-known artifact of the Old Stone Age to the most recent invention which has been accepted as socially useful. On the other hand, the culture concept may be limited to a particular people or area. There are distinctive qualities or elements in German culture, French culture, English culture, Brazilian culture, and so on; and Western culture is in many respects different from Asiatic and Oriental cultures.

Organizational Concepts for Cultural Analysis. The details and complexities of relationships within a culture can be classified and ordered under the following concepts: (1) the culture *trait,* (2) the culture *complex,* (3) the culture *pattern,* and (4) the culture *base.* The culture base is a functional reference to the culture *heritage,* considered more concretely as the cultural environment operative at a certain time and place.

Units in culture, whether material or nonmaterial, from which all larger blocks of culture are compounded, are called *culture traits.* The culture of any people would in a sense be the sum total of its traits, but the significance of any culture or of its parts could not be determined merely by listing traits. The recognition and enumeration of traits is the initial step in an analysis of culture; it becomes evident at once, however, that the meaning of every trait depends upon its function within a specific social and cultural context.

Artifacts—physical objects made by man—are culture traits. The *coup de poing* (the flint pick or fist hatchet identified with Chellean culture) was a true artifact, about as early an example as is known. The modern steel hatchet and all other tools,

[4] Ellsworth Faris, *The Nature of Human Nature,* McGraw-Hill Book Company, Inc., New York, 1937, p. 278.

utensils, and weapons made by man are artifacts. A canoe or a ship, thought of as a culture unit, is an artifact; a wigwam or a house would qualify equally as a man-made artifact, and so would a cart or an automobile. Thus it appears that an artifact may be one simple object, or it may be something which is made up of many parts which have been assembled and fitted together to form a cultural unit. The actual meaning of the man-made objects mentioned depends upon the socially recognized functions in particular contexts. The fact that any one of the objects mentioned is made up of a multiplicity of parts does not make it any the less an artifact, nor does it convert it into a culture complex.

Besides artifacts, culture includes many nonmaterial elements which have been differentiated by Earle Edward Eubank as "mentifacts." [5] Mentifacts are not merely forms of overt behavior but are things having externality. Language, a body of mental concepts apart from the written or printed page, constitutes a mentifact. Since language is the *sine qua non* of culture—without it there could be no rational communication—the vital nature of other kinds of mentifacts is also suggested. Accordingly, under the head of mentifacts comes the great body of knowledge which has accumulated throughout the centuries, i.e., various systems of thought, codes of morals, the great mythologies and philosophies of the world. Mentifacts, then, are creations that exist in nonmaterial form quite independent of any mechanical device which embodies them. Both artifacts and mentifacts are purely impersonal creations, and entities in themselves. The meanings of mentifacts, as of artifacts, depend upon the social conception of their functions in the culture of which they are elements. And mentifacts, like other cultural elements, are subject to social change.

Group feelings and beliefs, folkways, and mores also are group creations; they exist subjectively as forms of behavior and feeling which are inseparable from the person holding them. In that respect these categories differ from mentifacts, which are not merely forms of overt behavior but things having externality. These "subjective" aspects of culture are also significant factors in social change.

Evidently it is not characteristic of traits to appear and function singly. They are commonly associated with other traits and are organized with reference to some common center. Major interests or activities in the mode of life of any body of people become focal points about which cultural features develop and arrange themselves into distinguishable combinations known as "trait complexes." In American Pueblo Indian life the maize complex is the nucleus about which much of the culture is integrated. Among the Bedouin tribes the camel concept ramifies a culture complex extensive enough to involve six thousand terms for "camel" qualified by its contexts. The automobile, a cultural trait in American life, is the focal point about which a vast automobile complex derives, including factories, highways, gas stations, garages, motels, and many other things which did not exist before the automobile was invented. Similarly there is the airplane complex, the railroad complex, the trucking complex. In the sports world, there is the baseball complex, the football complex, the tennis complex, and many others.

A trait and a trait-complex having been defined, what is meant by a *culture pat-*

[5] Earle Edward Eubank, *The Concepts of Sociology*, D.C. Heath and Company, Boston, 1932, p. 357.

tern? A social norm as a mode of behavior may be referred to as a pattern. A configuration of culture traits may be said to form a pattern or to have a pattern. Trait-complexes grouped into a larger organization of distinctive features which characterize a culture may be called "patterns." In this sense, the patterns of Eskimo culture comprise their whole series of adjustments to the arctic way of life. The patterns of American culture include the use of machines, rapid communication, purposive education through schools, etc. Languages differ in their grammar and in their general patterning; they differ in content according to whether the mode of life of the people is pastoral, agricultural, industrial and commercial, or some combination of the arts of life.

This survey of the nature of culture and the means available for analyzing and comparing the elements of any culture (no matter how primitive or advanced) and for noting characteristic trends in cultural changes has been arranged to provide a perspective not only for the several readings which follow immediately but also as a general foundation for this text as a whole.

The readings have been selected to develop and apply basic culture concepts in harmony with contemporary theory and practice. Their titles comprise ample indication of their content: "The Nature of Culture" by Wilson D. Wallis, "How Diffusion Enriches Individual Cultures" by Ralph Linton, "How Culture Changes" by George Peter Murdock, "Does Human Nature Change?" by John Dewey, "The Effects of Technology on Man" by Leslie Paul, "The Changes of Half a Century" by George J. S. King, and "A Century of Engineering Progress: 1852–1952" by James Kip Finch.

Wallis's definitions of culture will prove to be familiar, at least in part; but of special significance will be his seven generalizations about aboriginal cultures. These generalizations point out the essential uniqueness and unity of cultures of specific peoples, the importance of the culture trait in the diffusion of culture, and the relative effects of innovations in culture. Instead of thinking of culture in the abstract, it is important to comprehend actual cultures as unique phenomena, and to realize that culture is changing continually, however slowly or rapidly, as influenced by the circumstances that prevail. Wallis assures us that the problems of social reconstruction are largely problems of culture, and that they can be dealt with intelligently only by taking account of culture traits.

9

THE NATURE OF CULTURE[*]
Wilson D. Wallis

It has been said,

A nation's culture includes the points of view every one has about individual conduct and social relations; his attitude toward government and toward other peoples; his habit of mind about the family, the duty of parents to children and children to parents; his standards of taste and of morals, his store of accepted wisdom which he expresses in proverbs and aphorisms; his venerations and loyalties, his prejudices and biases, his canons of conventionality; the whole group of ideas held in common by most of the people. This body of culture comes to every individual mainly through well-recognized channels, through parents and elders who hand it down by oral tradition, through religion, through schools, and through reading, both of books and of newspapers and periodicals.[†]

This description refers to non-material culture; culture, however, includes material as well as non-material things, and may be defined as the artificial objects, institutions, and modes of life or of thought which are not peculiarly individual but which characterize a group; it is "that complex whole which includes knowledge, belief, art, morals, law, custom, and any other capabilities and habits acquired by man as a member of society." [‡] Culture, therefore, is supra-individual. The individual is a carrier and transmitter of it and may modify it, but no individual creates a major portion of the culture in which he participates. A tribe, usually the smallest unit investigated by the ethnographer, is a culture unit, but it has not created all of its culture. Its traits resemble those of neighbors, or of some neighbors, in so many respects that the resemblances cannot be attributed to independent origins, but imply a common source. A culture area, therefore, may include several tribes. Thus the culture traits of the Plains Indians have such marked similarities that the tribes collectively constitute a culture area. The culture of the Eskimo extends over a long narrow strip of the arctic New World and a small portion of the Old World, including many localities which have no direct contacts with one another. Indeed, practically the whole of the known aboriginal New World can be divided into culture areas. An attempt has been made to describe the culture areas of Negro Africa, though not with the same success as in the case of North America, owing, partly perhaps, to the more rapid diffusion of culture traits through much of the African continent, and partly to the nature of the ethnographical data, which are not as adequate for Africa as for North America. There are distinct culture areas in

[*] Reprinted by permission from Wilson D. Wallis, *Culture and Progress*, McGraw-Hill Book Company, Inc., New York, copyright 1930, pp. 9–12.

[†] Mark Sullivan, *Our Times. The United States 1900–1925*, vol. II, "America Finding Herself," New York, 1927, p. 1.

[‡] Edward B. Tylor, *Primitive Culture*, vol. I, p. 1.

Oceania, notably Polynesia, Melanesia, and Micronesia, and certain culture areas in the Philippines have been identified. Although much of the aboriginal world can be divided into culture areas, there is little information with regard to some large ethnographical areas. Enough is known about aboriginal cultures, however, to justify the following conclusions:

1. A culture is unique. This is true not merely of the larger culture area which includes tribes, but also of each component tribal culture. The culture of the Plains area, for example, is nowhere duplicated. Moreover, no two tribes within the Plains area have identical cultures. Many culture traits of the Omaha are shared by neighbors, but there is no exact counterpart to Omaha culture. The Osage resemble the Ponca and the Kansa in many traits, but each tribal culture has individuality and uniqueness. Throughout the known ethnographical world the respective cultures are unique.

2. A culture does not travel *in toto* into other culture areas, though the peoples who carry it may extend their territory and so enlarge the geographical boundaries of their culture. Moreover, when people travel to new territory, usually their culture is modified; it does not remain identical with its old self, though of course it may preserve many old traits. Thus the culture of the Old World was not transplanted entire to the New; but only certain traits crossed the Atlantic. No culture area of the New World, therefore, is an exact duplicate of one in the Old World.

3. Despite the uniqueness of tribal culture, no tribe is culturally a self-complete unit. Each is a borrower from others, *i.e.*, the culture is affected by adjacent cultures. The Dakota, for example, were influenced by the art, mythology, and ceremonial organizations of neighbors, and by the latter's use of the horse. Invariably a culture is influenced by the cultures with which it comes into contact. So considerable is this influence that from a knowledge of contiguous cultures one can usually, but not always, correctly predict the general characteristics of a given culture.

4. Though a culture does not travel as a unit, *i.e.*, intact, many culture traits travel. So strong is the tendency for a culture trait to travel beyond the boundaries of the group in which it originated that it is difficult to find examples of culture traits which do not show this disposition. Thus ceramics, art designs, ceremonial organizations, methods of disposing of the dead, birth-rites, naming-customs, styles of dress and of personal adornment, initiation ceremonies, stories and plots, proverbs, omens, portents, animistic interpretations, and a thousand other traits spread from tribe to tribe, and sometimes permeate large culture areas. As a rule, therefore, a culture does not supplant another, but various traits seep into neighboring soil where they take root and sometimes flourish more luxuriantly than in the place of origin—as happened when the messianic religion was introduced from the Paiute into the Plains area, when Christianity was introduced from the Near East into Western Europe, and when maize was introduced into the Plains area by the whites.

5. A culture is a functioning dynamic unit and the various traits which compose it are interdependent. A culture trait does not function in isolation nor independently of other traits of the culture, but each is influenced by a change in any phase of the culture. Thus the Manitoba Dakota recount the order in which the animals and the "elements"—soil, stone, water—were created and this order reflects the hierarchy of the supernatural power of these animals and substances. The folklore and mythology fit into this framework of cosmogony and theology. Fighting, hunting, magic, religion, and ceremonialism are interrelated activities which interdigitate with the Dakota theory of evolution and the philosophy of *wakan*.* A similar statement holds for every culture. When, for example, Margaret Mead studied Samoan

* See, for example, W. D. Wallis, "Beliefs and Tales of the Canadian Dakota," *J. Amer. Folk-Lore*, vol. 36, pp. 36–101, 1923.

individuals she found that "a knowledge of the entire culture was essential for the accurate evaluation of any particular individual's behavior." * Similarly, Malinowski says of the matrilineal system among the Trobriand Islanders: "the whole system is based on mythology, on the native theory of procreation, on certain of their magico-religious beliefs and it pervades all the institutions and customs of the tribe." † There are conflicts and maladjustments, but even these imply interdependences and at least a partial unification of tribal life. "A native tribe bound by a code of disconnected inorganic customs would fall to pieces under our very eyes," ‡ as would any culture group.

6. Since the traits which comprise a culture are interrelated, an innovation affects the entire culture. The ethnologist is familiar with many instances in which this has been disastrous. The introduction of the horse doubtless modified many phases of Plains area culture. Later the extinction of the buffalo and the confinement of the Indians to reservations destroyed tribal morale and shattered the culture. When the white man's stove became a part of the culture equipment of the Chilkat of Alaska, the voices of ancestors who had spoken through the crackling of the wood in the open fire no longer came to cheer or to warn descendants, and an important influence in the morale of the tribe disappeared. Degeneration in ethical standards followed and the culture deteriorated. Normally, however, when culture changes are gradual rather than abrupt, there is continuous accommodation to the new trait.

7. Individuals do not participate in the culture to the same degree or in the same way. One individual may be more efficient in art, another in industrial technique, another may be more deeply steeped in tribal lore. Perhaps, "savages are more like one another than are civilized men," § for, as compared with civilized men, the individuals in a primitive group conform more closely to a pattern. If, however, allowance is made for the more limited range of tribal culture, the individualities of men in primitive life are perhaps as marked as those of civilized men.

Wallis explains that Western civilization is both a culture and a composite of cultures, blending Germanic, Graeco-Roman, and other cultural influences. Many traits of our Western culture have been borrowed from Babylonia, Egypt, Greece, Rome, Palestine, Persia, China, Japan, the American Indians, and others. Nevertheless, Western civilization should be viewed as *a* culture in which an essential unity or equilibrium is as characteristic as that in the simpler societies and their cultures. In spite of the diversity in culture, there is unity; few things in themselves have much cultural significance; and what the cultural traits contribute depends upon how they are utilized and also upon how much they utilize.[6]

Ralph Linton has shown, in a discussion of diffusion, how even a small segment of an American's daily life is a composite of cultures. The title of the following excerpt has been adapted for our purpose.

* Margaret Mead, *Coming of Age in Samoa*, New York, 1928.
† Bronislaw Malinowski, *Crime and Custom in Savage Society*, New York, 1926, p. 75.
‡ *Ibid.*, pp. 125–126.
§ C. Delisle Burns, *Political Ideas, Their Nature and Development*, Oxford, 1915, p. 181.
[6] W. D. Wallis, *Culture and Progress*, McGraw-Hill Book Company, Inc., New York, 1930, pp. 12–34.

10

HOW DIFFUSION ENRICHES INDIVIDUAL CULTURES*

Ralph Linton

The service of diffusion in enriching the content of individual cultures has been of the utmost importance. There is probably no culture extant today which owes more than 10 per cent of its total elements to inventions made by members of its own society. Because we live in a period of rapid invention we are apt to think of our own culture as largely self-created, but the role which diffusion has played in its growth may be brought home to us if we consider the beginning of the average man's day. The locations listed in the following paragraphs refer only to the origin points of various culture elements, not to regions from which we now obtain materials or objects through trade.

Our solid American citizen awakens in a bed built on a pattern which originated in the Near East but which was modified in Northern Europe before it was transmitted to America. He throws back covers made from cotton, domesticated in India, or linen, domesticated in the Near East, or wool from sheep, also domesticated in the Near East, or silk, the use of which was discovered in China. All of these materials have been spun and woven by processes invented in the Near East. He slips into his moccasins, invented by the Indians of the Eastern woodlands, and goes to the bathroom, whose fixtures are a mixture of European and American inventions, both of recent date. He takes off his pajamas, a garment invented in India, and washes with soap invented by the ancient Gauls. He then shaves, a masochistic rite which seems to have been derived from either Sumer or ancient Egypt.

Returning to the bedroom, he removes his clothes from a chair of southern European type and proceeds to dress. He puts on garments whose form originally derived from the skin clothing of the nomads of the Asiatic steppes, puts on shoes made from skins tanned by a process invented in ancient Egypt and cut to a pattern derived from the classical civilizations of the Mediterranean, and ties around his neck a strip of bright-colored cloth which is a vestigial survival of the shoulder shawls worn by the seventeenth-century Croatians. Before going out for breakfast he glances through the window, made of glass invented in Egypt, and if it is raining puts on overshoes made of rubber discovered by the Central American Indians and takes an umbrella, invented in Southeastern Asia. Upon his head he puts a hat made of felt, a material invented in the Asiatic steppes.

On his way to breakfast he stops to buy a paper, paying for it with coins, an ancient Lydian invention. At the restaurant a whole new series of borrowed elements confronts him. His plate is made of a form of pottery invented in China. His knife is of steel, an alloy first made in southern India, his fork a

* From *The Study of Man*, Appleton-Century-Crofts, Inc., New York, 1936, pp. 325–327. Reprinted by permission.

medieval Italian invention, and his spoon a derivative of a Roman original. He begins breakfast with an orange, from the eastern Mediterranean, a canteloupe from Persia, or perhaps a piece of African watermelon. With this he has coffee, an Abyssinian plant, with cream and sugar. Both the domestication of cows and the idea of milking them originated in the Near East, while sugar was first made in India. After his fruit and first coffee he goes on to waffles, cakes made by a Scandinavian technique from wheat domesticated in Asia Minor. Over these he pours maple syrup, invented by the Indians of the Eastern woodlands. As a side dish he may have the egg of a species of bird domesticated in Indo-China, or thin strips of the flesh of an animal domesticated in Eastern Asia which have been salted and smoked by a process developed in northern Europe.

When our friend has finished eating he settles back to smoke, an American Indian habit, consuming a plant domesticated in Brazil in either a pipe, derived from the Indians of Virginia, or a cigarette, derived

from Mexico. If he is hardy enough he may even attempt a cigar, transmitted to us from the Antilles by way of Spain. While smoking he reads the news of the day, imprinted in characters invented by the ancient Semites upon a material invented in China by a process invented in Germany. As he absorbs the accounts of foreign troubles he will, if he is a good conservative citizen, thank a Hebrew deity in an Indo-European language that he is 100 per cent American.

The foregoing is merely a bit of antiquarian virtuosity made possible by the existence of unusually complete historic records for the Eurasiatic area. There are many other regions for which no such records exist, yet the cultures in these areas bear similar witness to the importance of diffusion in establishing their content. Fairly adequate techniques have been developed for tracing the spread of individual traits and even for establishing their origin points, and there can be no doubt that diffusion has occurred wherever two societies and cultures have been brought into contact.

George Peter Murdock, in the following selection, addresses himself to the problem of describing *how* culture changes. The processes he discusses are grouped under the terms "innovation," "social acceptance," "selective elimination," and "integration." In the development of the subject, however, he gives attention to the processes of innovation, variation, invention, tentation, cultural borrowing, and of course diffusion. These processes are so defined and illustrated as to indicate their fundamental interrelationships in cultural change. All these processes apply whether the aspects of culture concerned are material or nonmaterial in nature.

11

HOW CULTURE CHANGES*
George Peter Murdock

It is a fundamental characteristic of culture that, despite its essentially conservative nature, it does change over time and from place to place. Herein it differs strikingly from the social behavior of animals other than man. Among ants, for example, colonies of the same species differ little in behavior from one another and even, so far as we can judge from specimens embedded in amber, from their ancestors of fifty million years ago. In less than one million years man, by contrast, has advanced from the rawest savagery to civilization and has proliferated at least three thousand distinctive cultures.

The processes by which culture changes are by now reasonably well known to science. They cannot be understood, however, without a clear comprehension of the nature of culture, and this must be summarized here. . . .

Culture is the product of learning, rather than of heredity. The cultures of the world are systems of collective habits. The differences observable among them are the cumulative product of mass learning under diverse geographic and social conditions. Race and other biological factors influence culture only in so far as they affect the conditions under which learning occurs, as when the presence of people of markedly different physique operates as a factor in the development of race prejudice.

Culture is learned through precisely the same mechanism as that involved in all habit formation. Hunger, sex, fear, and other basic drives, as well as acquired motivations, impel human beings to act. Actions encounter either success or failure. With failure, especially when accompanied by pain or punishment, an action tends to be replaced by other behavior, and its probability of recurring under similar conditions is diminished. Success, on the other hand, increases the tendency of responses to occur when the same drive is again aroused in a like situation. With repeated success, responses are established as habits, and are progressively adapted to the situations in which they are appropriate.

A culture consists of habits that are shared by members of a society, whether this be a primitive tribe or a civilized nation. The sharing may be general throughout the society, as is normally the case with language habits. Often, however, it is limited to particular categories of people within the society. Thus persons of the same sex or age group, members of the same social class, association, or occupational group, and persons interacting with others in similar relationships commonly resemble one another in their social habits, though diverging behaviorally from persons in other categories.

The social sharing of habits has several causes. The fact that the situations under which behavior is acquired are similar for many individuals conduces in itself to parallel learning. Even more important is the fact that each generation inculcates on the next,

* From Harry L. Shapiro (ed.), *Man, Culture, and Society*, Oxford University Press, New York, 1956, pp. 247–260. Reprinted by permission of Oxford University Press.

through education, the cultural habits which it has found satisfying and adaptive. Finally, the members of any society exercise pressure upon one another, through formal and informal means of social control, to conform to standards of behavior which are considered right and appropriate. This is particularly true of behavior in interpersonal relationships, where the success or failure of an action depends upon the reaction of another person to it, rather than, for example, upon its adaptiveness to the innate qualities of natural objects. Once one has acquired a limited number of stereotyped patterns of social behavior one is equipped to cope successfully with widely diversified social situations, and one is also provided with a body of reliable expectations regarding the probable responses of others to one's own behavior. This gives confidence and spares the individual an immense amount of individualized learning, which is ever a painful process. It is with good reason, therefore, that every society lays great stress on social conformity.

The habits that are variously shared within a society, and which constitute its culture, fall into two major classes, namely, habits of action and habits of thought. These may be termed, respectively, 'customs' and 'collective ideas.' Customs include such readily observable modes of behavior as etiquette, ceremonial, and the techniques of manipulating material objects. Collective ideas are not directly observable but must be inferred from their expression in language and other overt behavior. They include such things as practical knowledge, religious beliefs, and social values. Moreover, they embrace a mass of rules or definitions, which specify for each custom the persons who may and may not observe it, the circumstances in which it is and is not appropriate, and the limits and permissible variations of the behavior itself. Collective ideas also include a body of social expectations—anticipations of how others will respond to one's own behavior, especially of the sanctions, i.e. social rewards and punishments that can be expected from conformity and deviation. With every custom and with

every organized cluster of customs, such as a 'culture complex' or 'institution,' there is ordinarily associated a mass of collective ideas.

Actual social behavior, as it is observed in real life, must be carefully distinguished from culture, which consists of habits or tendencies to act and not of actions themselves. Though largely determined by habits, actual behavior is also affected by the physiological and emotional state of the individual, the intensity of his drives, and the particular external circumstances. Since no two situations are ever exactly alike, actual behavior fluctuates considerably, even when springing from the same habit. A description of a culture is consequently never an account of actual social behavior but is rather a reconstruction of the collective habits which underlie it.

From the point of view of cultural change, however, actual or observable behavior is of primary importance. Whenever social behavior persistently deviates from established cultural habits in any direction, it results in modifications first in social expectations, and then in customs, beliefs, and rules. Gradually, in this way, collective habits are altered and the culture comes to accord better with the new norms of actual behavior.

Changes in social behavior, and hence in culture, normally have their origin in some significant alteration in the life conditions of a society. Any event which changes the situations under which collective behavior occurs, so that habitual actions are discouraged and new responses are favored, may lead to cultural innovations. Among the classes of events that are known to be especially influential in producing cultural change are increases or decreases in population, changes in the geographical environment, migrations into new environments, contacts with peoples of differing culture, natural and social catastrophes such as floods, crop failures, epidemics, wars, and economic depressions, accidental discoveries, and even such biographical events as the death or rise to power of a strong political leader.

The events which produce cultural change by altering the conditions under which social behavior proves adaptive, i.e. is or is not rewarded, are invariably historical, i.e. specific with respect to time and place. Events occurring at different places and times may resemble one another, however, and exert parallel influences upon different cultures. It is thus possible to view changes in culture either in relation to their spatial and temporal setting or in relation to comparable events wherever and whenever they have occurred. The former or 'historical' approach answers such questions as what? when? and where? The latter or 'scientific' approach, by illuminating the processes by which change occurs, answers the question how? Both approaches are valid and completely complementary.

Historical anthropologists commonly discuss particular traits of culture, such as the use of tobacco, the wheel, the domesticated horse, the alphabet, or money, treating of their 'invention' at specific times and places and of their 'diffusion' from the points of origin to other parts of the world. Since our problem is to describe *how* culture changes, we must abandon the bird's-eye view of the historian and examine the processes within societies by which all changes, and not merely particular ones, take place. These processes may be conveniently grouped under the terms 'innovation,' 'social acceptance,' 'selective elimination,' and 'integration.'

Cultural change begins with the process of *innovation*, the formation of a new habit by a single individual which is subsequently accepted or learned by other members of his society. An innovation originates through the ordinary psychological mechanism of learning, and differs from purely individual habits only in the fact that it comes to be socially shared. It is nevertheless useful to distinguish several important variants of the process.

An innovation may be called a *variation* when it represents a slight modification of pre-existing habitual behavior under the pressure of gradually changing circumstances. The slow evolution in the forms of manufactured objects over time usually represents an accumulation of variations. In the same manner, tattooing can be extended over a wider area of the body, additional barbs may be added to a harpoon, skirts may be lengthened or shortened, folk tales may grow by accretion, or ceremonial may become increasingly elaborate and formalized. Variation occurs in all cultures at all times. The individual increments of change are often so slight as to be almost imperceptible, but their cumulative effect over long periods may be immense.

When innovation involves the transfer of elements of habitual behavior from one situational context to another, or their combination into new syntheses, it is called *invention*. At least some degree of creativeness is always present. Most of the important technological innovations are of this type. Thus the invention of the airplane involved the synthesis of such elements as the wings of a glider, an internal-combustion engine from an automobile, and an adaptation of a ship's propeller. Though less well known, inventions are equally common in the non-material aspects of culture. The city-manager plan, for example, represents an obvious transfer of techniques of business management to the sphere of local government, and most forms of religious worship are modeled on behavior toward persons of high social status, e.g. sacrifice upon bribery, prayer upon petitions, laudation upon flattery, ritual upon etiquette.

Since invention always involves a new synthesis of old habits, it is dependent upon the existing content of the culture. A synthesis cannot occur if the elements which it combines are not present in the culture. It is for this reason that parallel inventions so rarely occur among unconnected peoples of differing culture. With the exception of such simple and obvious combinations as the hafting of tools, anthropologists know of only a handful of genuine inventions that have been arrived at independently by historically unrelated peoples. Among them perhaps the most famous are the fire piston, invented by the Malays and a French physicist, and the dome, developed by the ancient Romans from the arch and independently invented by the Eskimos for their snow igloos.

Among peoples of the same or related cultures, on the other hand, parallel inventions are extraordinarily common. The culture provides the same constituent elements to many people, and if one person does not achieve the synthesis others are likely to do so. The Patent Office furnishes thousands of examples. In one famous instance, the telephone, applications for a patent were received on the same day from two independent inventors, Bell and Gray. Another noted case is the independent formulation of the theory of natural selection by Darwin and Wallace. So common is this phenomenon that scientists often live in dread of the anticipation of their discoveries by rivals. Parallel invention thus appears to be frequent and almost inevitable among peoples of similar culture, though so rare as to be almost non-existent among peoples of different culture.

A third type of innovation may be called *tentation*. Unlike the previous types, which merely modify or recombine elements of habit already in existence, tentation may give rise to elements that show little or no continuity with the past. The mechanism by which these are acquired is that which psychologists call 'trial-and-error learning.' Tentation may occur in any situation in which established habits prove ineffective and individuals are so strongly motivated that they try out other modes of behavior in a search for an adequate solution to their problems. They will ordinarily try out first a number of variations and recombinations of existing habitual responses, but if all of these fail they will resort to 'random behavior,' in the course of which they may accidentally hit upon some novel response which solves the problem and thereby becomes established as a new cultural element.

Crises are particularly conducive to tentation. In a famine, for instance, people try out all sorts of things that they have never eaten before, and if some of them prove nutritious and tasty they may be added to the normal diet. An epidemic similarly leads to a search for new medicines, and both primitive and civilized peoples have discovered useful remedies in this way. War also leads to improvisation, as do economic crises. The New Deal in the recent history of the United States, for example, reveals numerous instances of tentation. Scientific experimentation, it should be pointed out, is often a form of controlled tentation, as when a new series of chemical compounds are systematically put to test. The saying that 'necessity is the mother of invention' applies more forcefully to tentation than to invention proper.

When accidental discoveries lead to cultural innovations, the process is commonly that of tentation. The origin of the boomerang in aboriginal Australia will serve as an example. Over much of that continent the natives used curved throwing sticks to kill or stun small animals, and in a limited part of the area the true boomerang was used for this purpose. Almost certainly the first boomerang was produced by sheer accident in the attempt to fashion an ordinary throwing stick. Observing the unique behavior of the particular stick in flight, the maker and his fellows doubtless attempted to duplicate it. They must have resorted to tentation, or trial-and-error behavior, until they eventually succeeded, and thereby established boomerang manufacture as a habit. The history of modern 'inventions' is full of such instances, the discovery of the photographic plate by Daguerre being one of the most familiar examples.

Tentation also accounts for a type of cultural parallel which is distinct from genuine independent invention. There are certain universal problems which every people must solve and for which there are a limited number of easy and obvious solutions, so that peoples in different parts of the world have often hit upon the same solution quite independently. Rules of descent provide a good illustration. In all societies, each individual must be affiliated with a group of relatives to whom he regards himself as most closely akin and to whom he can turn for aid in time of need. There are only three possibilities: patrilineal descent, which relates an individual to kinsmen in the male line; matrilineal descent, which affiliates him with relatives through females; and bilateral descent, which associates him with a group of his closest relatives irrespective of their line of descent. Every society must choose one of these alternatives or some combination thereof, and, since the possibilities are limited to three, many peoples have, of necessity, arrived independently at the same cultural solution. Funeral customs present another example, since there are only a limited number of feasible ways of disposing of a dead body. In all such instances, if a society is compelled for any reason to abandon its previous custom it will inevitably, through tentation, arrive at an alternative solution which other peoples have independently adopted.

The fourth and last type of innovation is *cultural borrowing*, which is what the historical anthropologist, with his bird's-eye view, calls 'diffusion.' In this case the innovator is not the originator of a new habit, but its introducer. The habit has previously been part of the culture of another society; the innovator is merely the first member of his social group to adopt it. From the point of view of psychology, cultural borrowing is merely a special case of the learning process known as 'imitation.' The innovator, faced with a situation in which the shared habits of his own society are not fully satisfactory, copies behavior which he has observed in members of another society, instead of resorting to variation, invention, or tentation to solve his problem.

Of all forms of innovation, cultural borrowing is by far the most common and important. The overwhelming majority of the elements in any culture are the result of borrowing. Modern American culture provides a good illustration, as can be shown by a few random examples. Our language comes from England, our alphabet from the Phoenicians, our numerical system from India, and paper and printing from China. Our family organization and system of real property derive from medieval Europe. Our religion is a composite of elements largely assembled from the ancient Hebrews, Egyptians, Babylonians, and Persians. Metal coinage comes from Lydia, paper money from China, checks from Persia. Our system of banking, credit, loans, discounts, mortgages, et cetera, is derived in its essentials from ancient Babylonia, with modern elaborations from Italy and England. Our architecture is still largely Greek, Gothic, Georgian, et cetera. Our favorite flavors in ice creams, vanilla and chocolate, are both borrowed from the Aztecs of Mexico and were unknown to Europeans before the conquest by Cortez. Tea comes from China, coffee from Ethiopia, tobacco from the American Indians. Our domesticated animals and plants, virtually without exception, are borrowed. If the reader were to make a list of absolutely everything he eats during the next week, analysis would probably show that one third are products that were already cultivated in Neolithic times and that at least two thirds were being raised at the time of Christ, and it would be surprising if the list contained any item that was not cultivated for food somewhere in the world when Columbus sailed for America.

Our own culture is not unique in this respect, for it is doubtful whether there is a single culture known to history or anthropology that has not owed at least ninety per cent of its constituent elements to cultural borrowing. The reason is not far to seek. Any habit that has become established in a culture has been tried out by many people and found satisfactory. When a society finds itself in a dilemma, therefore, the chances that an element already present in the culture of another people will turn out to be an adequate solution to its own problem are vastly greater than those of any random and untested innovation of another type. Cultural borrowing is thus highly economical, and most peoples tend to ransack the cultural resources of their neighbors for adaptive practices before they resort to invention or tentation.

Cultural borrowing depends upon contact. Obviously the opportunity for borrowing is lacking in the case of a completely isolated society. Other factors being equal, the extent to which one culture will borrow from another is proportionate to the intensity and duration of the social intercourse between their bearers. Contact need not always be face-to-face, however, for there are numerous instances of cultural borrowing at a distance through the medium of written language or through copying of articles received by trade. By and large, however, societies borrow mainly from their immediate neighbors, with the result that the products of diffusion are ordinarily clustered in geographically contiguous areas.

Trade, missionary enterprise, and political conquest create conditions conducive to cultural borrowing. Peculiarly important, however, is intermarriage, for this brings individuals of differing culture together within the family, where children can learn from both parents. Diffusion then proceeds through the socialization process, which produces far more perfect copying than does cultural borrowing on the adult level. The American 'melting pot' operates largely through this mechanism. Primitive peoples practicing local exogamy, i.e. requiring individuals to obtain spouses from another village or band, commonly reveal considerable cultural uniformity over wide areas, as in aboriginal Australia and among the Indians of the Northwest Coast. By contrast, in areas like Melanesia and Central California where marriage normally takes place within the community, even villages a few miles apart may differ strikingly in dialect and customs. In the one case culture is diffused through the same process by which it is transmitted; in the other, even adult contacts tend to be restricted to a minimum.

Incentive—a need or drive—is as essential in cultural borrowing as in other types of innovation. A people rarely borrows an alien cultural element when they already possess a trait which satisfactorily fills the same need. Thus the blubber lamp of the Eskimos was not borrowed by the Indians to the south, who had plenty of wood for fires to heat and light

their dwellings. On the other hand, the extraordinarily rapid diffusion of tobacco over the earth after the discovery of America reflected the general absence of competing traits. It has been observed that the first individuals in a society to borrow alien customs are likely to be the discontented, underprivileged, and maladjusted. Thus in India Christian missionaries have made many more converts among the 'untouchables' than in the higher strata of society, and in our own country fascism and communism attract an unduly high proportion of unsuccessful and neurotic people.

The presence in a receiving society of some of the habit elements involved in a new trait greatly facilitates borrowing. It is for this reason that diffusion occurs most readily among peoples of similar culture, who already share many elements of habit. Thus Englishmen and Americans borrow more frequently and easily from each other than from Russians, Chinese, or Hottentots. Conversely, aboriginal peoples are greatly handicapped in taking over the complex technology of modern civilization. They cannot, for example, begin to manufacture the steel products which they want without also taking over such things as blast furnaces and rolling mills.

Cultural borrowing will occur only if the new habit is demonstrably rewarding. The native quickly adopts steel knives and axes from the white man because their superiority to his former stone implements becomes immediately apparent. On the other hand, Europeans were slow to borrow paper manufacture from the Chinese because the advantages of paper over parchment appeared very slight at first. The Chinese and Japanese have not yet adopted the alphabet from western civilization because, however great its ultimate advantages, it would impose heavy burdens and discomforts upon all literate persons during the necessary period of readjustment. Geographic and climatic factors may prevent diffusion by withholding or reducing the possibilities of reward, and social prejudices such as ingrained conservatism may counterbalance potential advantages by inflicting disapprobation upon innovators.

Borrowing need not be exact. Oftentimes, indeed, all that is borrowed is the external 'form' of a custom and not its 'meaning,' i.e. the collective ideas associated with it. The familiar caricature of the cannibal chief wearing a silk hat provides a good illustration. Frequently an imperfect copy is quite adequate. Thus when the Plains Indians took over horses and riding equipment from the Spaniards they omitted the horseshoe, which was quite unnecessary on the prairie. Sometimes changes are imposed by the conditions of the geographical environment. When the Iroquois Indians adopted the birchbark canoe from their Algonkian neighbors, for example, they altered the material to elm bark because of the scarcity of birch trees in their habitat. Frequently cultural factors favor a modification. The original Phoenician alphabet lacked characters for vowels, the nature of their language being such that consonant signs sufficed for the identification of words. Since this was not true of the Greek language, when the Greeks borrowed the Phoenician alphabet they converted characters for which they had no need into symbols for vowels.

Modifications are so common in cultural borrowing that authorities like Malinowski have regarded the process as scarcely less creative than other forms of innovation. Often, indeed, it is inextricably blended with invention or tentation. This is well illustrated in instances of 'stimulus diffusion,' in which only the general idea of an alien cultural trait is borrowed, the specific form being supplied by improvisation. Thus a famous Cherokee chief named Sequoyah, though an illiterate man, had noticed that white men could somehow understand messages from pieces of paper on which peculiar marks were inscribed, and he came to the conclusion that this would be a useful skill for his own people to acquire. He therefore set himself the task of devising a system of marks by which the Cherokee language could be written. Inventing some signs of his own and copying some from

pieces of printed matter—numbers and punctuation marks as well as letters, upside down or on their sides as often as upright—he produced a novel form of writing, a syllabary rather than an alphabet, which his tribesmen learned and still use to this day.

The second major process in cultural change is *social acceptance*. So long as an innovation, whether original or borrowed, is practiced by the innovator alone in his society, it is an individual habit and not an element of culture. To become the latter it must be accepted by others; it must be socially shared. Social acceptance begins with the adoption of a new habit by a small number of individuals. From this point it may spread until it becomes part of the sub-culture of a family, clan, local community, or other sub-group, or until it becomes a 'specialty' characteristic of persons belonging to a particular occupational, kinship, age-graded, or other status category, or until it becomes an 'alternative' widely but optionally practiced. Eventually it may even become a 'universal,' shared by all members of the society. The term 'degrees of cultural saturation' has been proposed for the various steps in social acceptance.

The learning mechanism involved in social acceptance is imitation, as in the case of cultural borrowing, but the model whose behavior is copied is a member of one's own rather than another society. So similar are the two processes that the term 'diffusion' is often applied to both; social acceptance is called 'internal' or 'vertical' diffusion to differentiate it from cultural borrowing, which is termed 'external' or 'horizontal' diffusion. With minor exceptions, most of what has previously been stated about the latter process applies equally to the former. Since close contact and similarity of culture can be taken for granted, however, copying is usually far more exact, and this is accentuated by social control.

A factor of considerable importance in social acceptance is the prestige of the innovator and of the group who are first to imitate him. Changes advocated by an admired political or religious leader are readily adopted, whereas few will follow an unpopular or despised innovator. Clothing styles accepted by 'the four hundred' quickly diffuse throughout the masses, but the 'zoot suit' does not spread from the taxi dance hall to the ballroom. Women imitate men more readily than *vice versa*. In our own society, for example, many women have adopted masculine garments, smoking and drinking habits, and occupations, but there appears to be no concerted movement among men to wear skirts, use cosmetics, or apply for positions as nurses, governesses, or baby-sitters.

Selective elimination constitutes a third major process of cultural change. Every innovation that has been socially accepted enters, as it were, into a competition for survival. So long as it proves more rewarding than its alternatives a cultural habit will endure, but when it ceases to bring comparable satisfactions it dwindles and eventually disappears. The process superficially resembles that of natural selection in organic evolution. It should be noted, however, that cultural traits do not compete directly with one another but are competitively tested in the experience of those who practice them. Oftentimes the competition is carried on between organized groups of people with contrasting customs and beliefs, as between nations, political parties, religious sects, or social and economic classes, and the issue is decided indirectly by the victory of one group over the other. By and large, the cultural elements that are eliminated through trial and error or social competition are the less adaptive ones, so that the process is as definitely one of the survival of the fittest as is that of natural selection.

Few of the genuine gains of culture history —the achievements of technology, of science, of man's control over nature—have ever been lost. The so-called 'lost arts of antiquity' are largely mythical. To be sure, particular peoples have declined in civilization, but not until they have passed on their contributions to others. What man has lost, in the main, is a mass of maladaptive and barbarous practices, inefficient techniques, and outworn superstitions. New errors arise, of course, in each generation, but it is comforting to realize that the mortality of error is vastly greater than that of truth.

It is the genuine achievements of man that anthropologists have in mind when they say that culture is cumulative, comparing culture history to the growth of a snowball as it is rolled down a hill. Even achievements that are superseded rarely disappear. Today the electric light has proved superior to earlier methods of lighting, but the gas mantle, the kerosene lamp, and the tallow candle still survive in out-of-the-way places or under special conditions. Survival is often assured through a change in function. The use of outmoded weapons has been preserved, for example, in athletic sports like fencing and archery and in boyhood toys such as the sling and the peashooter. Other ancient usages survive in legal, religious, and academic ceremonial. Written records, of course, preserve much of the culture of the past from oblivion. Our libraries bulge with the puerilities as well as the achievements of history.

The fourth and last important process of cultural change is that of *integration*. The shared habits that constitute a culture not only fluctuate in their degree of social acceptance, and compete for survival, but they also become progressively adapted to one another so that they tend to form an integrated whole. They exhibit what Sumner has called 'a strain toward consistency.' Every innovation alters in some respect the situations under which certain other forms of habitual behavior occur, and leads to adaptive changes in the latter. Similarly it must, in its turn, be adjusted to modifications elsewhere in the culture. While each such change is in itself, of course, an innovation, their reciprocal interaction and cumulative effect deserve special recognition as an integrative process. . . .

Certain anthropologists have erroneously assumed that the elements of any culture are in a state of nearly perfect integration, or equilibrium, at all times. Actually, however, perfect equilibrium is never achieved or even approached. The adjustment of other elements of culture to an innovation, and of it to them, requires time—often years or even generations. In the meantime other innovations have appeared and set in motion new processes of integration. At any given time, therefore, a culture exhibits numerous instances of uncompleted integrative processes as well as examples of others which have been carried through to relatively satisfactory completion. What we always encounter is a strain toward internal adaptation, never its full realization.

The period of time which must elapse between the acceptance of an innovation and the completion of the integrative readjustments which follow in its train Ogburn has aptly called 'cultural lag.' During such a period of lag people attempt, through variation, invention, tentation, and cultural borrowing, to modify old customs and ideas to

accord with the new, and to adjust the new to the old, so as to eliminate inconsistencies and sources of friction and irritation. In a modern democratic society, politics is a major scene of such efforts.

The net effect of the various processes of cultural change is to adapt the collective habits of human societies progressively over time to the changing conditions of existence. Change is always uncomfortable and often painful, and people frequently become discouraged with its slowness or even despair of achieving any genuine improvement. Neither history nor anthropology, however, gives grounds for pessimism. However halting or harsh it may appear to participants, cultural change is always adaptive and usually progressive. It is also inevitable, and will endure as long as the earth can support human life. Nothing—not even an atomic war—can destroy civilization.

John Dewey is concerned with the question of whether important, almost fundamental, changes in the ways of human belief and action have actually taken place and still are capable of taking place; or, he asks, have people just imagined that certain changes have occurred in social values? To any individuals who contend that certain changes would be contrary to human nature, Dewey asserts that there are few social changes which could be opposed on the ground that they are contrary to human nature itself. In support of his viewpoint, he considers war as an institution and its relation to such psychological factors as combativeness, pugnacity, and fear, which are commonly regarded as native elements of human nature.

For additional evidence that human nature changes, economic institutions and relationships are cited as an area most susceptible to change. Changes in law are changes in human nature; law is one of the most conservative of human institutions, yet it changes, sometimes slowly, sometimes rapidly. Education is, of course, a primary agent for social change, and, therefore, for change in human nature. The history of social institutions everywhere is evidence of the plasticity of human nature.

12

DOES HUMAN NATURE CHANGE?*
John Dewey

I have come to the conclusion that those who give different answers to the question I have asked in the title of this article are talking about different things. This statement in itself, however, is too easy a way out of the problem to be satisfactory. For there is a real problem, and so far as the question is a practical one instead of an academic one, I think the proper answer is that human nature *does* change.

By the practical side of the question, I mean the question whether or not important, almost fundamental, changes in the ways of human belief and action have taken place and are capable of still taking place. But to put this question in its proper perspective, we have first to recognize the sense in which human nature does not change. I do not think it can be shown that the innate needs of men have changed since man became man or that there is any evidence that they will change as long as man is on the earth.

By "needs" I mean the inherent demands that men make because of their constitution. Needs for food and drink and for moving about, for example, are so much a part of our being that we cannot imagine any condition under which they would cease to be. There are other things not so directly physical that seem to me equally engrained in human nature. I would mention as examples the need for some kind of companionship; the need for exhibiting energy, for bringing one's powers to bear upon surrounding conditions;

the need for both coöperation with an emulation of one's fellows for mutual aid and combat alike; the need for some sort of aesthetic expression and satisfaction; the need to lead and to follow, etc.

Whether my particular examples are well chosen or not does not matter so much as does recognition of the fact that there are some tendencies so integral a part of human nature that the latter would not be human nature if they changed. These tendencies used to be called instincts. Psychologists are now more chary of using that word than they used to be. But the word by which the tendencies are called does not matter much in comparison to the fact that human nature has its own constitution.

Where we are likely to go wrong, after the fact is recognized that there is something unchangeable in the structure of human nature, is the inference we draw from it. We suppose that the manifestation of these needs is also unalterable. We suppose that the manifestations we have got used to are as natural and as unalterable as are the needs from which they spring.

The need for food is so imperative that we call the persons insane who persistently refuse to take nourishment. But what kinds of food are wanted and used are a matter of acquired habit influenced by both physical environment and social custom. To civilized people today, eating human flesh is an entirely unnatural thing. Yet there have been

---

* From *The Rotarian Magazine*, vol. 52, no. 2, pp. 8 ff, February, 1946. By permission of the publisher.

peoples to whom it seemed natural because it was socially authorized and even highly esteemed. There are well-accredited stories of persons needing support from others who have refused palatable and nourishing foods because they were not accustomed to them; the alien foods were so "unnatural" they preferred to starve rather than eat them.

Aristotle spoke for an entire social order as well as for himself when he said that slavery existed by nature. He would have regarded efforts to abolish slavery from society as an idle and utopian effort to change human nature where it was unchangeable. For according to him it was not simply the desire to be a master that was engrained in human nature. There were persons who were born with such an inherently slavish nature that it did violence to human nature to set them free.

The assertion that human nature cannot be changed is heard when social changes are urged as reforms and improvements of existing conditions. It is always heard when the proposed changes in institutions or conditions stand in sharp opposition to what exists. If the conservative were wiser, he would rest his objections in most cases, not upon the unchangeability of human nature, but upon the inertia of custom; upon the resistance that acquired habits offer to change after they are once acquired. It is hard to teach an old dog new tricks and it is harder yet to teach society to adopt customs which are contrary to those which have long prevailed. Conservatism of this type would be intelligent, and it would compel those wanting change not only to moderate their pace, but also to ask how the changes they desire could be introduced with a minimum of shock and dislocation.

Nevertheless, there are few social changes that can be opposed on the ground that they are contrary to human nature itself. A proposal to have a society get along without food and drink is one of the few that are of this kind. Proposals to form communities in which there is no cohabitation have been made and and the communities have endured for a time. But they are so nearly contrary to human nature that they have not endured long. These cases are almost the only ones in which social change can be opposed simply on the ground that human nature cannot be changed.

Take the institution of war, one of the oldest, most socially reputable of all human institutions. Efforts for stable peace are often opposed on the ground that man is by nature a fighting animal and that this phase of his nature is unalterable. The failure of peace movements in the past can be cited in support of this view. In fact, however, war is as much a social pattern as is the domestic slavery which the ancients thought to be an immutable fact.

I have already said that, in my opinion, combativeness is a constituent part of human nature. But I have also said that the manifestations of these native elements are subject to change because they are affected by custom and tradition. War does not exist because man has combative instincts, but because social conditions and forces have led, almost forced, these "instincts" into this channel.

There are a large number of other channels in which the need for combat has been satisfied, and there are other channels not yet discovered or explored into which it could be led with equal satisfaction. There is war against disease, against poverty, against insecurity, against injustice, in which multitudes of persons have found full opportunity for the exercise of their combative tendencies.

The time may be far off when men will cease to fulfill their need for combat by destroying each other and when they will manifest it in common and combined efforts against the forces that are enemies of all men equally. But the difficulties in the way are found in the persistence of certain acquired social customs and not in the unchangeability of the demand for combat.

Pugnacity and fear are native elements of human nature. But so are pity and sympathy. We send nurses and physicians to the battlefield and provide hospital facilities as "naturally" as we change bayonets and discharge machine guns. In early times there was a close connection between pugnacity and fighting, for the latter was done largely with the fists. Pugnacity plays a small part in generating wars today. Citizens of one country do not hate those of another nation by instinct. When they attack or are attacked, they do not use their fists in close combat, but throw shells from a great distance at persons whom they have never seen. In modern wars, anger and hatred come after the war has started; they are effects of war, not the cause of it.

It is a tough job sustaining a modern war; all the emotional reactions have to be excited. Propaganda and atrocity stories are enlisted. Aside from such extreme measures there has to be definite organization, as we saw in the two World Wars, to keep up the morale of even non-combatants. And morale is largely a matter of keeping emotions at a certain pitch; and unfortunately fear, hatred, suspicion, are among the emotions most easily aroused.

I shall not attempt to dogmatize about the causes of modern wars. But I do not think that anyone will deny that they are social rather than psychological, though psychological appeal is highly important in working up a people to the point where they want to fight and in keeping them at it. I do not think, moreover, that anyone will deny that economic conditions are powerful among the social causes of war. The main point, however, is that whatever the sociological causes, they are affairs of tradition, custom, and institutional organization, and these factors belong among the changeable manifestations of human nature, not among the unchangeable elements.

I have used the case of war as a typical instance of what is changeable and what is unchangeable in human nature, in their relation to schemes of social change. I have selected the case because it is an extremely difficult one in which to effect durable changes, not because it is an easy one. The point is that the obstacles in the way are put there by social forces which do change

from time to time, not by fixed elements of human nature. This fact is also illustrated in the failures of pacifists to achieve their ends by appeal simply to sympathy and pity. For while, as I have said, the kindly emotions are also a fixed constituent of human nature, the channel they take is dependent upon social conditions.

There is always a great outburst of these kindly emotions in time of war. Fellow feeling and the desire to help those in need are intense during war, as they are at every period of great disaster that comes home to observation or imagination. But they are canalized in their expression; they are confined to those upon our side. They occur simultaneously with manifestation of rage and fear against the other side, if not always in the same person, at least in the community generally. Hence the ultimate failure of pacifist appeals to the kindly elements of native human nature when they are separated from intelligent consideration of the social and economic forces at work.

William James made a great contribution in the title of one of his essays, *The Moral Equivalents of War*. The very title conveys the point I am making. Certain basic needs and emotions are permanent. But they are capable of finding expression in ways that are radically different from the ways in which they now currently operate.

An even more burning issue emerges when any fundamental change in economic institutions and relations is proposed. Proposals for such sweeping change are among the commonplaces of our time. On the other hand, the proposals are met by the statement that the changes are impossible because they involve an impossible change in human nature. To this statement, advocates of the desired changes are only too likely to reply that the present system or some phase of it is contrary to human nature. The argument *pro* and *con* then gets put on the wrong ground.

As a matter of fact, economic institutions and relations are among the manifestations of human nature that are most susceptible of change. History is living evidence of the scope of these changes. Aristotle, for example, held that paying interest is unnatural, and the Middle Ages reëchoed the doctrine. All interest was usury, and it was only after economic conditions had so changed that payment of interest was a customary and in that sense a "natural" thing, that usury got its present meaning.

There have been times and places in which land was held in common and in which private ownership of land would have been regarded as the most monstrous of unnatural things. There have been other times and places when all wealth was possessed by an overlord and his subjects held wealth, if any, subject to his pleasure. The entire system of credit so fundamental in contemporary financial and industrial life is a modern invention. The invention of the joint stock company with limited liability of individuals has brought about a great change from earlier facts and conceptions of property. I think the need of owning something is one of the native elements of human nature. But it takes either ignorance or a very lively fancy to suppose that the system of ownership that exists in the United States in 1946, with all its complex relations and its interweaving with legal and political supports, is a necessary and unchangeable product of an inherent tendency to appropriate and possess.

Law is one of the most conservative of human institutions; yet through the cumulative effect of legislation and judicial decisions it changes, sometimes at a slow rate, sometimes rapidly. The changes in human relations that are brought about by changes in industrial and legal institutions then react to modify the ways in which human nature manifests itself, and this brings about still further changes in institutions, and so on indefinitely.

It is for these reasons that I say that those who hold that proposals for social change, even of rather a profound character, are impossible and utopian because of the fixity of human nature, confuse the resistance to change that comes from acquired habits with that which comes from original human na-

ture. The savage, living in a primitive society, comes nearer to being a purely "natural" human being than does civilized man. Civilization itself is the product of altered human nature. But even the savage is bound by a mass of tribal customs and transmitted beliefs that modify his original nature, and it is these acquired habits that make it so difficult to transform him into a civilized human being.

The revolutionary radical, on the other hand, overlooks the force of engrained habits. He is right, in my opinion, about the indefinite plasticity of human nature. But he is wrong in thinking that patterns of desire, belief, and purpose do not have a force comparable to the momentum of physical objects once they are set in motion, and comparable to the inertia, the resistance to movement, possessed by these same objects when they are at rest. Habit, not original human nature, keeps things moving most of the time, about as they have moved in the past.

If human nature is unchangeable, then there is no such thing as education and all our efforts to educate are doomed to failure. For the very meaning of education is modification of native human nature in formation of those new ways of thinking, of feeling, of desiring, and of believing that are foreign to raw human nature. If the latter were unalterable, we might have training but not education. For training, as distinct from education, means simply the acquisition of certain skills. Native gifts can be trained to a point of higher efficiency without that development of new attitudes and dispositions which is the goal of education. But the result is mechanical. It is like supposing that while a musician may acquire by practice greater technical ability, he cannot rise from one plane of musical appreciation and creation to another.

The theory that human nature is unchangeable is thus the most depressing and pessimistic of all possible doctrines. If it were carried out logically, it would mean a doctrine of predestination from birth that would outdo the most rigid of theological doctrines. For according to it, persons are what they are at birth and nothing can be done about it, beyond the kind of training that an acrobat might give to the muscular system with which he is originally endowed. If a person is born with criminal tendencies, a criminal he will become and remain. If a person is born with an excessive amount of greed, he will become a person living by predatory activities at the expense of others; and so on. I do not doubt at all the existence of differences in natural endowment. But what I am questioning is the notion that they doom individuals to a fixed channel of expression. It is difficult indeed to make a silk purse out of a sow's ear. But the particular form which, say, a natural musical endowment will take depends upon the social influences to which it is subjected. Beethoven in a savage tribe would doubtless have been outstanding as a musician, but he would not have been the Beethoven who composed symphonies.

The existence of almost every conceivable kind of social institution at some time and place in the history of the world is evidence of the plasticity of human nature. This fact does not prove that all these different social systems are of equal value, materially, morally, and culturally. The slightest observation shows that such is not the case. But the fact in proving the changeability of human nature indicates the attitude that should be taken toward proposals for social changes. The question is primarily whether they, in special cases, are desirable or not. And the way to answer that question is to try to discover what their consequences would be if they were adopted. Then if the conclusion is that they are desirable, the further question is how

they can be accomplished with a minimum of waste, destruction, and needless dislocation.

In finding the answer to this question, we have to take into account the force of existing traditions and customs; of the patterns of action and belief that already exist. We have to find out what forces already at work can be reinforced so that they move toward the desired change and how the conditions that oppose change can be gradually weakened. Such questions as these can be considered on the basis of fact and reason.

The assertion that a proposed change is impossible because of the fixed constitution of human nature diverts attention from the question of whether or not a change is desirable and from the other question of how it shall be brought about. It throws the question into the arena of blind emotion and brute force. In the end, it encourages those who think that great changes can be produced offhand and by the use of sheer violence.

When our sciences of human nature and human relations are anything like as developed as are our sciences of physical nature, their chief concern will be with the problem of how human nature is most effectively modified. The question will not be whether it is capable of change, but of how it is to be changed under given conditions. This problem is ultimately that of education in its widest sense. Consequently, whatever represses and distorts the processes of education that might bring about a change in human dispositions with the minimum of waste puts a premium upon the forces that bring society to a state of deadlock, and thereby encourages the use of violence as a means of social change.

What do we mean by the "technical age" if it is to be distinguished from what we used to call the machine age, or the industrial age, or the electrical age? Leslie Paul's answer emphasizes the growth and perfection of certain *methods* of dealing with problems, in which the key concept is "streamlining." Technical foresight is a factor, and is a function of research to solve problems and prevent mishaps in industry. Technics, then, is not only machine, but method, tempo, research, and organization. The modern machine, modern bio-technics, and technics in terms of tools or instruments which extend human powers, all have their roots in the far distant past.

Thus far the technical aspects of change appear to be of a positive nature. But Paul's article carries a note of warning, for he mentions aspects of the machine age and technical age which ought to give us great concern. These aspects are three: first, that mechanics and technics have become a source of idolatry; second, that they are a source of slavery; and third, that they are a means whereby man is dehumanized. The author's explanations of these criticisms show that social and cultural change needs to be considered pro and con, because material gains may be offset by human costs.

13

THE EFFECT OF
TECHNOLOGY ON MAN*
Leslie Paul

What does the ordinary man mean by technics? I am sure, to begin with, that he does not mean what we mean, and that he is not afflicted by our fears, which would strike him as odd or affected. And a title like "The Effect of Technology on Man" would still, even if he understood it, be meaningless to him. For the ordinary man, "technics," if he uses the term at all, would mean some ingenious new machine like radar, or a decoding machine, or an electronic brain; or else some new and clever process for streamlining the production of some commodity, or the substitution of a new substance like a plastic for an old and expensive metal. In any case, the ordinary man is prone to admire rather than fear these developments, and the epithet "technical" applied to our age would have the effect of praise to him. There would not be very much point to him in making a "fuss" about technics, for civilization would

appear to him to be all of one piece and the technical would to him be difficult to distinguish from the non-technical. I think we ought to be aware that to the common man many attacks on technics must appear high and rarefied, the unintelligible resentment of the highbrow at the things from which he (the highbrow) benefits too. Perhaps, therefore, we have to state very clearly what we mean by technology, or the technical age. What *do* we mean by the technical age as against, for instance, what we used to call the machine age, or the industrial age, or electrical age? We do not only mean the spread of machinery over the face of the globe, or its greater perfection, for these things have been going on a long time. We do not only mean the invasion, as with the calculating machine or the electronic brain, of realms once believed to be the prerogative of the reasoning mind. Or if we mean these

* From the *Hibbert Journal*, vol. 55, pp. 20–29, October, 1956. Reprinted by permission of the author, the *Hibbert Journal*, and George Allen & Unwin, Ltd., London, publishers.

things, we mean a greater process which encompasses them too—we mean the growth and perfection of certain *methods* of dealing with problems—all that which is understood in industrial circles by the term *streamlining*.

Let me give examples of what I mean. The machine is most efficient when it has to deal with uniform units, and is not faced with exceptions. If there are enough exceptions, then one may be forced to invent new machines to handle the exceptions, and there is an obvious economic limit to this process. Therefore it is important to begin with units of uniform size, shape and weight in industry, or to create them if they do not exist. Before the Second World War, for instance, someone invented a rice machine. The average housewife likes her rice pure white, and shies away from the darker sort, and this machine was created to separate the white from the darker grains. Grains of all shades were fed into a chute which handled them in such fashion that it got them all moving tail to head like sausages from a machine, and then it shot the stream of grains in a straight line over a photo-electric cell which reacted to the darker grains and released a jet of compressed air of razor-blade width, and fractional duration, which expelled the discoloured grain from the stream. This machine had only to deal with variations in colour. But had the offending grains been of twice the size of the white ones, or curled like bananas, then the process of sorting might have been insuperable. The importance of uniform units is demonstrated by Robert Jungk in his book *Tomorrow is Already Here,* which deals with the technological age which has descended on the United States. One story he tells is of the effect of technology on the tomato crop of California. As every gardener knows, tomatoes ripen irregularly. The home gardener must look round his shrubs periodically and hunt for the ripe ones. This goes on quite a long time—there is a lengthy harvest, with irregular output of fruit of irregular shape. In terms of industry that means high labour costs, high marketing costs, and the irregular flow of products on to the

market. But presently some ingenious engineer came along to the Californian fruit grower with a mechanical tomato-picker which could run down the rows of plants, gently shaking each in turn to dislodge the ripe fruit. But it was of little use, just because of the harvesting irregularities I have described. And so the botanist was called in to invent a plant in which all the fruit would ripen together and be of uniform size, but in which the stalk was weak, so that the gentle shaking would dislodge the fruit without breaking the bush, but in which the skin of the tomato was strong and elastic to prevent bruising when the fruit fell into the net held out, by the machine, to catch it. And presently, the right kind of tomato plant *was* bred—a plant, you see, which fitted the machine. Then with regularity in output, and with fruit of uniform size and dependable ripeness, other processes—the packing or canning, the dispatch or marketing—were quickly mechanized. And these two stories illustrate for us that the age of technics is more than the age of machines, it is *the age of the organization of the materials*—all the materials which contribute to the success of an industry—the raw materials, the factory materials, the labour material, the consumers.

For once the flow is organized, the worst catastrophe occurs if it dries up, or a block ensues. And what could cause such a thing as a block or a failure? Disease in the fruit, failure in the supply of boxes or wrapping paper, a strike of packers or carmen, or a sudden preference on the part of the consumer for paprika. Of course when an industry is small it has to take a chance about these things. But the larger it grows and the more capital it eats up, the less inclined it is to take chances. And it exerts all its power to streamline all its material on to a conveyor belt system. By psychological pressures, economic incentives, and loyalty incentives to keep labour sweet and to even out its output, it tries to avoid stoppages and it tries to overcome consumer resistance in advance by advertising. For the public, too, must be induced to keep up, or step up, its consumption of tomatoes to a uniform pace, or to a uniform acceleration. The most difficult thing is to slow the whole process down. It is often easier to stop it altogether. And this co-ordination, this conveyor belt leading from plant to stomach, is technics too. Technics therefore is as much a method as a matter of machines, but it is a method deriving from the machine, the pace of which has to be dictated by the optimum pace of the machine, and that again is organized upon the basis of an economic optimum.

Then there is a further problem—that of technical foresight. The investment in the industry must be protected. In the tomato industry the whole thing could be ruined by a plant disease: therefore constant research is necessary into the incidence and conquest of tomato plant diseases. In other problems involving technical foresight, the tomato industry may be a bad example, I'm not sure. But we might make it a better one. Supposing for example (which I think is not true in California) that the tomato ripened only once a year. The tomato-less months would yield scarcity prices, and so then botanical research would be directed to the discovery of a fruit with a shorter ripening time; or improvements in refrigerating technics would be asked for; anything to level out the flow to the market. Or the organization would look for a popular fruit to ripen in the months in which the tomato did not, or even if necessary try to invent one, in order that organization could be maintained at one hundred per cent. A great part of the technical problem is the research problem—so that industry can plan not for this year or the next, but for ten years ahead, and against the ruin which would otherwise come upon an expensive plant if a new substance or new method caught the old one unprepared. One thousand million pounds per annum are spent on industrial research in the United States: and needless to say that research, too, is technically organized. Such research may be directed to fascinating ends like electronic brains, but equally to such humdrum domestic problems as the invention of a melon which fits the

standard refrigerator, or the discovery of a doughnut which tastes better after dunking in coffee than before.

Technics, then, is not only machine, but method, tempo, research, organization, no matter of what kind. It is even, where labour and the consumer are concerned, an imperialism of persuasion, for certainly no consumer industry carries on without investigation of psychological techniques. But never forget that it is also, where the housewife is concerned, the sorcerer.

Now all this has very grave consequences for man, and we will look at them presently. But first let me say that I see this as the fruit of a long process of human effort, not as something which has been suddenly and horribly sprung upon us. Man is a technical being: he has been described as a toolmaking animal: the birth of modern technics is to be discovered in the human efforts of the very earliest man. I am inclined to think that the first conveyor belt was the woodpile. It was obviously useless to go to all the labour of lighting a fire with a rubbing stick or flint and tinder unless you could ensure a proper flow of fuel to keep it alight. So that the discovery of fire first posed for man the problem of the organization of the raw material. And in the first fire-minder we have, perhaps, the embryo of the first machine-minder!

One of the great human glories has been man's slow conquest of his natural environment. We rightly regard the work of man in history as being in some sense the expression of the Holy Spirit. When man acquired speech and other forms of expression and communication—dancing, or architecture, or dress, or flags, or so forth—are we not right to see in this a deepening of human solidarity, a maturing of human consciousness, a means whereby men learnt to speak not only to each other, but to God? Let us recognise also that toolmaking, and primitive technics in general, are all part of this process of the civilization of man. The knife, the saw, the hammer, the nail, the plough, the harrow, the wheel, the sail, the boat, the oar—all these formed part of the process by which man saw himself as separate from nature. He saw himself not as a part of nature, bound by his own nature to his bare physical gifts, but as one who by his God-given powers, those powers spoken of in Genesis, looks at the nature from which he is separate and sees it not only as it is but as it might be after his intervention. Man's intervention in natural processes did not begin with the ingenuity of the Californian botanist in producing a standard tomato, but long ago in the discovery of wheat, in the breeding of horses and domestic cattle, in the taming of the dog and the enslavement of the hen. Did not all these events, in their time, revolutionize society in some degree? They must have done, but we recognize them, not as disasters, but as steps in the civilization of men.

The modern machine, and modern biotechnics, have their roots in the far distant human past. So too have technics in their application to human beings, such as tools or instruments which extend human powers, like the scholar's spectacles, or the compass, telescope, microscope, chronometer and the hundreds of variations on the instruments which increase man's power of touch, or sight, or awareness of time. Medicine too, one of the oldest of the human arts, has always concerned itself with just that interference with the body, or that invasion of the personality, which would enable a disease to be cured. And how can one regard all these advances through the ages except as the triumph of human ingenuity over the countless inert or hostile forces which stood in the way of man's will to civilize himself, to lift himself out of the animal into the truly human, and to look from the human to God?

All this, it seems, makes nonsense of Ruskin or William Morris, or Georges Bernanos, or the other opponents of the machine. On the whole they hate the machine *qua* machine, believing it to be the real source of the corruption and decivilization of modern man. They are the modern Rousseauists, and they believe that the machine is the villain where Rousseau thought that civilization was

the villain. But if you put the machine process of our contemporary civilization into reverse and, like one of Professor Toynbee's archaists, move back in time, where do you land? Not certainly into a pure, natural society of uncorrupted men, but quite probably into something like 18th-century France before the revolution, into an artificial, elaborate, cold society every bit as much of an artifact as a machine, and standing implacably (as Rousseau discovered) between man and nature. And a society by no means technically ill-equipped! No, to get to anything modern man would consider to be a natural society, you would have to travel back to a primitive tribal society: but even the most primitive society has its rituals, its tabus, its totemistic marriage regulations, its mythical history, its sophisticated sex-relationships, and it is as remote from "natural" man as perhaps modern man is. And even such a society would possess weapons, fishing tools, stores, nets, pots, houses—in fact, for all its apparent simplicity, a complicated technical background. Indeed where *is* this "natural man" unspoilt by machine or civilization, or anything else? He does not exist except as a convenient excuse for the social contract theory, and the best that one can say of him is that if he ever did exist his life must have been, as Hobbes saw, "solitary, poor, nasty, brutish, and short."

No, we have no right to condemn either machines or the technical age. We have even a right to rejoice in it, as far as it is a means of lifting up humanity. We have to accept it as a challenge of the Holy Ghost, and to recognize that the whole of human history witnesses to a "stretching" of man. Throughout history man is being continually remade, or lifted out of his old self. He is not allowed to rest. And nothing is so ridiculous as to pick and choose in the technical age, as if the technical age were only just that part of it one personally disliked. Nothing is so absurd as the man who comes to Oxford by train or car to denounce machinery, and who complains if the hot-water system in his hotel does not work, if the radio is out of order, or if he cannot get hold of a telephone in a hurry, and maybe returns to London at the end of the week to denounce the age of technics over the radio. We could quite easily make ourselves ridiculous out of a kind of pedantic fear or scholarly distrust of the machine which no worker surely has.

But there are at least three aspects of the machine age and technical age which ought to give us grave concern. They are, first, that mechanics and technics have become a source of idolatry; secondly, that they are a source of slavery; thirdly, that they are a means whereby man is "dehumanized." In all conscience, these are serious enough charges. Let us look at them.

Idolatry. Science to-day is not quite as sure of itself as once it was. This is certainly true of pure science, of physics, mathematics, geometry, astronomy and so forth. A. N. Whitehead has spoken of that unparalleled revolution in knowledge which has gone on in the last seventy or so years and has knocked the bottom out of the tidy Newtonian universe. The present knowledge of the atom, the extraordinary qualities which Einstein and Minkowski have discovered in the space-time universe, the quantum theory of Max Planck and the uncertainty principle of Heisenberg —all these revelations of this century demonstrate the wobbliness of much scientific knowledge, and they have produced a new humility in scientists, especially in those who are prepared to look at the findings of physics from a metaphysical point of view. In this connection the researches and findings of Jeans, Eddington, Whitehead, Einstein, Coulson and many others must be familiar to most of us. But with applied science there is no such humility, and just no inclination at all to look at its own activities and findings from any transcendent plane. And applied science is, in this context, technics. In technics we find only the greatest arrogance. A repair workshop in the field at the Normandy beachhead put out the notice (or so I'm told): "We achieve the impossible immediately: the miraculous takes a little longer." One recognizes the fun in that; it is part of the high

spirits which win wars; but it might serve also as a motto for modern technics.

Is there a problem which technics cannot solve? No technician really believes that. The world is a plastic one for him. Granted sufficient force, it can be moulded in any direction one chooses. "The miraculous takes a little longer than the impossible." No matter what problems of soil, of growth, of breeding, of mechanical handling, of split-second timing, of consumer unreliability, or workshop absenteeism—all can be graphed, broken down into unitary problems, reshuffled, organized into a foolproof system. Almost any technician would say that, granted there is no financial ceiling or deadline, any problem requiring the technician can be solved—possibly even church attendance. I can think of no greater proof of the idolatry of technics than the present craze for space-travel. Reaching the moon, or Mars, or maybe any part of space is just another technical problem to be solved along with others. Indeed, the rockets of the Nevada desert are already probing into the airless space above the earth. Technics does not ask whether this is humanly worth while: it has its own answer, that any problem which defies present technical knowledge is technically worth solving. Technics therefore develops its own imperialism—it is its own justification and its own reward.

The recent conference on Gerontology suggests that old age is a "problem" which will be solved, and death too. One will, in the gerontological view I suppose, live as long as one likes, and then decide to die, even to the day, and die with the convenience of turning off a tap. Of course this is worship: it is worship of scientific power. But this scientific power does not exist in a vacuum: it is not something which streams into our atmosphere unasked, like rays from outer space. Science is the accomplishment of man, and worship of science is worship of man. It is self-worship: it is the view that nothing is impossible to man. Which is as much as to say that man is god. Of course such incredible arrogance, such *hubris,* calls down its nemesis. In the hydrogen bomb man has a power vast enough to wipe out the human race, and he cannot control it, and he is understandably frightened. But it would be a rash man who would argue that this has shaken the confidence of the world in man's own technical ingenuity to bring about the redemption of man.

Slavery. Some men are now travelling regularly at supersonic speeds. Rocket trips for humans are going to test out the capacities of the human organism to an extraordinary degree. What is the limit of the human body under such stresses? There is a base in the United States which Robert Jungk wrote about in *Tomorrow is Already Here,* where pilots and navigators are tested to discover what they can endure. I have absolutely nothing against that. These men are volunteers. But the driving theme of the research station is that unfortunately "man is a faulty construction," and somehow, by a combination of mathematics and medicine and psychology, one has got to get over his annoying deficiencies, whether by plating him like an insect, or by increasing his internal resistance, or by organizing his mental equilibrium, so that he may be as reliable as the machines he has to control. Certainly psychology is used to quieten his anxieties. At this station they are trying to produce a man who is physically and psychologically foolproof (and maybe drunkproof too) and who can therefore marry himself to the dangerous and expensive machines he has to navigate. Let us be quite clear what this implies—it is the relationship I first exposed when I spoke of the tomato industry in California. The machine demanded a certain kind of fruit. In this case the machine demands a certain kind of technician. And technics are being used to breed or organize a uniform kind of technician. And certainly this pressure to adapt man to his machine environment is going on everywhere. In Russia, the technics of Pavlov's conditioning are used to produce the docile tools that Russian industry requires.

But conditioning goes on in many places where volunteers are not concerned. There are great commercial halls in America where

girls sit before typewriters under the view of a supervisor on an elevated platform. Letters are piped to the typists through strip-recording devices: the girls receive them through earphones and play them straight on to the typewriters before them. The only human contact they have is the voice at the end of a piece of dictation with its calculated "Thank you, miss." There are many such places: and when recently I talked with some students from the Butler University about this method, one of them said, with a gasp, "You find this system not only in the commercial houses, but in at least one great religious organization."

The human relationship which once existed between typist and employer is gone; the typist is merely an unfortunately indispensable part of a mechanism. Now this might not be too bad, but in order to compensate for the lost human relationships many enterprises seek to build up a spurious loyalty to the firm: the leader or owner is built up by propaganda into a benevolent Caesar. His photo is everywhere, and loyalty badges and slush magazines are all part of the psychological gush intended to keep the typist—or whatever other worker may be concerned—from becoming neurotic and hostile. Here again the worker is being regarded as so much material to be streamlined for the sake of the general output, and to be prepared or adapted psychologically for the demands of the machine. It is just another example of the conveyor-belt technique.

Now this process has not gone very far, I think. We must not over-rate it. But it has gone far enough for us to see what dangers it entails, and to recognise that certain psychological and spiritual pressures, when applied to loyalties that run deeper than loyalties to a firm, can be enslaving. Hitler and Stalin have shown us the consequences of the application of these techniques of mass indoctrination when applied to our inflammable loyalties to nation, race and class. And when they lead to an effort to achieve psychological control of a whole nation then we peep already into the Big Brother horror of Orwell's

1984. The totalitarian state is the streamlined state in which government by technics has replaced government by consultation or consent.

Dehumanization. Slavery dehumanizes of course, but I have been thinking of the dehumanization which comes from within, and I mean especially that withering up of certain springs of life which is really the source of complaint of Morris, Ruskin, Bernanos and others. One feels that in a machine world, in which problems are solved by technics or else not regarded as problems at all, there is a loss of the meditative, the creative, the spiritual enrichments which early periods of human history certainly enjoyed. The poor man ploughing in silence the lonely hill could commune with God and nature. It is a little difficult to think of the atomic worker communing with anything except the geiger counter, or for that matter believing in anything but that. The *Manchester Guardian* recently had an article about the decay of the Lake District as a recreational centre. Of course it asked, Why? One tentative conclusion was that there had been a change in holiday habits; crowds flocked to crowds; they sought the mass amusements; the mechanical amusements, the cinema, the radio, the television, the funfair, the Battersea Pleasure Gardens were their quite unconscious standard. They looked for the amusement on tap which involved no effort; they had the feeling that only that which technics provided was really worth having.

In this sense the technical age brings a great malaise, which no one has yet discovered how to define or how to cure, but which may not be unrelated to the waves of racial violence, persecution, terror and war which have afflicted the world in this century—as though man is taking out of his fellows what he should take out of the machine. Men become frustrated without the opportunity to work creatively and aggressively. Things to-day are solved too easily for the common man by technics; even his job becomes less exacting. Then too man is protected by a social cocoon which takes over from him, problems of sickness, death, disaster and unemployment. Good perhaps, but it narrows the area in which a man may move on his own. The stark realities of the universe are lost, except in war. And so man is in retreat from his own powers. They atrophy: he not only accepts the slavery of the technical age, but is indignant when it is not laid on! The technical age obscures birth, death, God, love. It takes responsibility from the man in the street, but it lays too much on others, on the man in the lab, or the cabinet room, or the bomber control tower.

This is a terrific problem, especially when we recollect that the call from God to man to be human is the call to risk and adventure, the call to move into the unknown, and that fewer and fewer are free to exercise that call to-day.

That which is a source of idolatry, even for the slaves it enslaves, is a source of idolatry because it produces results. It is in the sphere of the practical that man has done so marvellously well. But it is the temptation of all temptations to-day because it promises the Mescalin paradise—all the kingdoms of the world, life without death, body without ill-health, sex without remorse or risk; it promises to man even the omnipotence and omniscience of God. But it is an idol with feet of clay. It does not produce a streamlined morality to go along with the streamlined power: on the contrary the power seems to make the morality unnecessary, even a hindrance to its complete exploitation. Men still are greedy, and lust for power: the prize is big, the weapons grow bigger, the risks will always be taken in the end. The greatest of all successes to-day for technics is in military weapons; military power to-day exceeds industrial power by a very wide margin. And what in the end the technical race seems to lead to is power over men without end. The sorcerer's apprentice, who started an energy working which he had not the right spell to stop, was lucky, for there was, after all, the sorcerer who knew the answers and called the whole thing off. We are in the position of the sorcerer's apprentice whose spell has murdered the sorcerer and left him without means to end the dance. Who can take off our spell to-day, except God? But there can be no *human* effort to end it unless we first know where we are going and what we expect of man and society. But do we want to end it, and on what terms? Unless we first ask what we are prepared to re-nounce, then all attacks upon the menace of technology are likely to prove short-lived.

The first half of the twentieth century has an unparalleled record of human achievement, as denoted by the ways in which the period has been described—the age of speed, the age of science, the electrical age, the atomic age, and from the standpoint of more strictly human values the age of woman and the century of the common man. Even more objectively, however, Geo. J. S. King surveys representa-tive changes which have taken place in the populations of leading nations—ideologi-cal changes, political succession—and reminds us of the many inventions which have so greatly altered modern living.

Fully as remarkable, however, are the social and political changes evident in fiscal reform, trade unionism, pensions, self-government, and the distribution of wealth through the "welfare state." Changes have occurred in the arts, in music, in the theatre, and in the cinema. New religious cults have arisen, new philosophical ideas have developed, psychiatry has won recognition. And, not least, the East and West await "the outcome of a cleavage which is in part a battle of creeds, as well as of policies." There is scarcely an area of culture in which important changes have not taken place during this half century, and the stream of change flows on.

14

THE CHANGES OF HALF A CENTURY*

Geo. J. S. King

Problems, both national and international, mount so rapidly, and the sum of human achievement accumulates so impressively, that each succeeding half-century seems more mo-mentous than any that has gone before; and it is certain that none has been so memorable as the first half of the twentieth century. In science, in education, in ideological evolution, in physical development, in the mastery of the elements, in man's relation to man, and in every department of human effort—except, perhaps, the fine arts—the fifty years that

* From the *Hibbert Journal*, vol. 49, no. 3, pp. 277–283, 1951. Reprinted by permission of the author, the *Hibbert Journal*, and George Allen & Unwin, Ltd., London, publishers.

ended on December 31, 1950, have accomplished more, whether for good or evil, than any similar period in history. It might even be claimed, perhaps, that the changes and achievements of the half century have exceeded those of all previous centuries combined.

This half-completed century has been variously described as the Age of Speed, the Age of Science, the Electrical Age, the Atomic Age, the Age of Machinery, the Age of Woman, and the Century of the Common Man. It might also be described as the age of the test tube and the laboratory—the age in which the experimenter and the scientist displaced the soldier, the politician, and the pamphleteer as the men with the greatest influence over their fellows.

When the century began Britain was an undisputed first among the nations. But that same geographical accident that had been in part the secret of her strength ensured that her hegemony must cease when nations unfettered and unrestricted by nature fitted themselves to challenge her. Her territorial limitations had given her security for centuries, but they had prevented expansion, enforced insularity, and had made emigration essential, since she could not support an indefinitely increasing population. Inevitably she looked to the Empire for the development she could no longer continue, and whereas between 1901 and 1950 her population increased only by some eleven millions, that of the United States practically doubled in the same period—an increase of more than seventy millions; and whereas a decrease of several millions is expected in the population of Britain by 1965, it is anticipated that the U.S.S.R. will increase by nearly fifty millions in the same period. The "teeming millions" of Asia have multiplied, moreover, until the "yellow peril" that was merely a product of the new journalism in the early years of the century becomes, with the impetus of an ideological incentive, a potential threat to world peace.

These ideological changes that have transformed Asiatic or near-Asiatic decayed empires into powerful nations are, perhaps, the greatest of the problems bequeathed by the first half of the century to the second, and they have demolished, incidentally, the theory that empires never "come back." It is now obvious that fallen powers can rise again if invigorated by economic changes. The German Empire, dead in 1919, made a recovery under the impetus of Nazi rule which, although temporary, was none the less effective enough to cause a universal upheaval by plunging the world into the cataclysm of the Second World War. Russia, humbled in 1905, and prostrate in 1919, shed her effete imperialism to become, under Communism, more menacing a power than she was in the Czarist years, before Port Arthur, Mukden, and Tannenberg had shattered the legend of the "steam-roller"; and it is her relentless resurgence that confronts the world as the new half-century dawns, and prevents the economic recovery of the rest of Europe by forcing its nations to devote their industry and manpower to defensive armament. And finally China, which, like Russia and Germany, was an Empire in 1901, is in 1950 a strong and united totalitarian state, whose mounting strength and uncertain intentions repeat in the Far East the problems that Russia presents in Europe.

Only in the West is there an accession of strength without a change in the way of life, and the United States, aided by her geographical situation, her far-flung frontiers, the accumulation within her own borders of practically everything needed to sustain a great nation, and her comparative immunity while Europe twice bled in war, faces the new order in the East across a Europe that is uneasily aware of its precarious situation as a buffer between the two great powers of the world, and its destiny as the potential cockpit of a third world war.

The advance of America was, in fact, almost inevitable, whereas the advance of Russia is a miracle. Here is no case of profiting by evasion of war, for Russia has been grievously stricken by both world wars of the century. The first left her shattered, with her frontiers rolled back, and with her resources so sapped that she seemed to be at the mercy of any determined enemy. In those days anti-Communistic propaganda need employ only the weapon of ridicule. Russia's weakness was surely a proof that Communism wrecked and dispirited a country to such an extent that she could not compete with the smallest state that was unhampered by amateur doctrinaires! That was thirty years ago; but to-day Russia, although she has endured another war that has devastated a great part of her terrain, inspires no longer derision but fear. It is not now the ineptitude but the ruthless efficiency of Communism that impresses the democracies of the West.

The disappearance of the great autocracies that were empires when the century began reminds us of the paradox that—apart from backward states in Africa and Asia—it is mainly in the democracies of Europe that monarchy has survived and, to make the paradox more striking, it is often in Socialist or near-Socialist countries. In Britain, in Scandinavia, in the Low Countries (and in Greece alone among the Balkan nations) kingdoms survive, but there is not a single monarchy in the New World, and in the Old World republics have superseded kingdoms even in nations that are politically to the Right.

In 1901, on the other hand, France and Switzerland were the only republics in Europe. Russia, Austria-Hungary and Turkey were empires, and the other states (including those in the Balkans and the Iberian peninsula) were kingdoms. When the year began Victoria was still on the throne of Britain, although only a few weeks were to pass before her death ended an epoch. The Boer War was then a serious distraction, despite which fact income tax was only 1s. 2d. in the pound. There were still horse trams and horse buses. Man had never flown in a heavier-than-air machine; he had not been on the roof of his own world (he has still not done so); neither had he seen the poles of his globe. Britain had not yet enfranchised her women, and she had not given her people

old age pensions, benefit during sickness, provision for unemployment, adequate workmen's compensation, nor a compulsory half-day's holiday a week. She had not yet paid her Members of Parliament, and her Second Chamber was as powerful as in the days of George III. As late as 1903 Sir Henry Campbell-Bannerman could say without fear of contradiction that one-third of her people were on the verge of starvation in a world of plenty.

Swiftly, as the early years of the new century passed, man consolidated his conquest of Nature, and she yielded to his dominion amenities that were soon regarded as necessities. In that new year of the century the first wireless messages flashed across the Atlantic, the first Zeppelin airship took the air, and the submarine became a definite naval force. Another early arrival was the electric tram. The birth of the internal combustion engine and the pneumatic tyre belonged to the closing years of the old century, and soon, as their use developed, there came the first of the motor omnibuses which were to supersede the electric tram in the streets. The horseless carriage, primitive though it was, was one of the most popular of free spectacles in the early 1900's, and while the century was still young the carriage was displaced by the automobile, the hansom-cab by the taxi, and the horse-drawn brake by the char-à-banc.

Already the dirigible airship was banishing the balloon from the lordship of the sky; and in 1903 history was made in North Carolina by the first lifting from the ground of a machine that was heavier than air. Thenceforth the successive stages of man's mastery of flight followed rapidly. By 1914 the aeroplane was an important factor in war, and by 1939 it was decisive. And so to the monster air-liner, the distance-bomber, and the supersonic speed of jet-propulsion.

The complement to the physical mastery of the air was its intellectual conquest, which had begun before Marconi flashed his famous message across the Atlantic in 1901, and reached its consummation in the dual miracle of radio and television. The adaptation of electricity to rail transport began in the early years of the century in the London area, although it was only slowly that electrification was extended to main line railways in Britain.

Before the century began Pierre and Marie Curie gave radium to the world. Rœntgen had discovered X-rays in the 'nineties, almost simultaneously with Ronald Ross's discovery of the malarial parasite; but the numerous by-products of the X-ray belong to the twentieth century, which has been enriched also by the many legacies of Lister and Pasteur, and has seen such tremendous achievements as Einstein's theory of relativity, the foundation of chemotherapy, the alliance of medicine and chemistry, and the discovery of insulin, penicillin, streptomycin, and the iron lung; also the application of mechanism to agriculture, and even the fearful prospect of celestial adventures inspired by visions of inter-planetary communication. Above all it has witnessed that crowning achievement of science, with which the name of Rutherford is so honourably associated—the conquest of the atom, with its potentialities alike of good and evil for the future of mankind.

With the perfecting of the internal combustion engine—extended in its turn to war by the armoured car and the invention of the "tank"—and the development of the aeroplane, came the realisation that this is the century of speed. Only steam had previously enabled man to travel faster than in the days of Cæsar or Charlemagne. But with new acceleration on the road and in the air his rate of propulsion increased so rapidly that by the end of the half century he could travel (though not on ground) faster than sound. Inevitably the tempo of life had to quicken to keep pace with faster travel. Gone was the leisurely tranquillity of Dickensian or Gladstonian days. There was the paradox, moreover, that every device planned to make life easier made it more intense. How leisurely and peaceful was the life in a Dickens office, before the telephone and the typewriter arrived to destroy both its privacy and its repose!

The Dickensian-Gladstonian man of business emerged, top-hatted and frock-coated, from a house devoid of central heating and electric labour-saving devices (and which had probably not even a bath or indoor sanitation). It was a quiet house, because there was no wireless or gramophone, and he stepped from it into a silent street, with no roar of motor-traffic, and with no buzz of aircraft overhead, to enter his noiseless office. Even his pleasures he took quietly, and although there were theatres and concerts there was no cinema to lure him from his fireside, and no speedway, ice-hockey or greyhound-racing. He was more likely to remain at home, reading while his wife sewed. If he danced it would be the sedate and genteel Victorian jog-trot, instead of frenzied leaping to the accompaniment of syncopated music.

Even the tremendous advances in science and industry of the twentieth century are not more remarkable than social or political changes. In Britain the new century began with the Conservative administration under Lord Salisbury confirmed in office as a result of the "Khaki Election" of the previous year. Among its new parliamentary recruits was the twenty-six-years-old son of that stormy petrel of Victorian politics, Lord Randolph Churchill; and on the other side of the House was a fiery young Welsh attorney who, in that same year, narrowly escaped man-handling at Birmingham on the charge of being "pro-Boer." The one, of course, was Winston Spencer Churchill, and the other David Lloyd George. Before long they were to sit side by side on the Treasury bench as leaders of that brilliant Liberal administration which began the modern programme of social reform—and each in turn was to lead the nation in the two great wars that were to follow.

The first outstanding political episode of the century was the declaration of Joseph Chamberlain that the moment was ripe for fiscal reform. His Protectionist proposals of 1903 at first disrupted the Unionist ranks, but were eventually accepted with varying degrees of enthusiasm. But the result was overwhelming defeat at the polls in 1906, and the beginning of that Campbell-Bannerman-Asquith era which gave trade unionism its charter, conferred pensions on the aged, sponsored Lloyd George's revolutionary Budget of 1909 (an Insurance Act of 1911), curtailed the powers of the House of Lords by the Parliament Act, and made a determined attempt to solve the Irish problem. The strength of Liberalism was so great in those days as to suggest that the Party was almost impregnable, but the swift changes of war ordained that Liberalism as a potential government, though not as a political faith, was to disappear, apparently for ever.

Another—and perhaps a greater—political achievement of that régime was to grant self-government to South Africa. Before the century began the accepted policy in foreign affairs was the "splendid isolationism" associated with the name of Lord Salisbury, reinforced by the spectacular Imperialism typified in various phases by such men as Joseph Chamberlain, Rudyard Kipling, Alfred Milner, and, above all, by Cecil Rhodes, whose dream of an all-British Cape to Cairo route was almost the last great vision of Empire expansion. In contrast with such narrow imperialism the decision to grant South Africa autonomy at a time when the Boer War was still a vivid memory was an act of courage and statesmanship that was an outstanding landmark in British history. Almost simultaneously New Zealand became a Dominion, following Australia, which had achieved nationhood in the first year of the century. By such successive stages the Empire was being transformed into a Commonwealth of Nations. It was the practical re-birth of the British Empire, and an appropriate commemoration was the institution of Empire Day in 1904. Following the First World War Ireland also acquired freedom—but it took a second war to establish India as a dual nation, and to give independence to Egypt and Burma. Thus ancient animosities and rankling prejudices were softened, if not completely assuaged, by new conceptions of statesmanship.

While Britain was consolidating her Empire on a new basis the world was attempting —at first timorously, but later more wholeheartedly—to free itself for ever from the threat of war. The Hague Conferences of 1899 and 1907 were a prelude to the League of Nations which, though subsequent events discounted its value, was the most valuable legacy any war had ever bequeathed, and was an heroic attempt by such idealists as Woodrow Wilson to pacify the human race. But the world had to endure the horrors of another war before a second American President replaced Wilson's fourteen points with the "four freedoms," and, more fortunate than his predecessor, carried the American nation with him. And so to UNO which, veto-distracted though it was, was the greatest effort yet made to preserve the peace of the world. The old alliances, such as the *Entente Cordiale,* had gone for ever; and in their place, within the framework of the United Nations, came such conventions as the Atlantic Pact, Western Union, and the Council of Europe. The nations were progressing, though slowly and with many stumbles, and harassed with many threats, towards a new federation of man which concerned itself not only with the preservation of peace, but with those many unostentatious offshoots of UNO which are concerned with food, health, cultural, labour and other interests common to men of every race and every nation.

The problems of one generation are the historical curiosities of another, and some of the controversies that aroused angry passions earlier in the century will seem strangely unreal to a present generation. The Chinese Labour question in South Africa, the Taff Vale judgment that transformed Labour into a parliamentary party, the "Little Englander" movement (countered by the "We want eight and we won't wait" slogan), the reawakening of the "Nonconformist conscience" by the Education Act of 1902, the "Limehousing" campaign of "L.G." in 1909, the "Marconi Scandals," the "Agadir Incident," the Sidney Street episode, the "Home Rule means Rome Rule" campaign, the "Votes for Women" years, the "Campbell Case," the General

Strike, the trial of the British engineers in Russia—these are some of the many problems that distracted the British people on various occasions during the past fifty years.

And steadily, through it all, the nation's social structure was undergoing a change that was in effect a revolution accomplished by easy stages, with an ever-quickening move to a more equitable distribution of wealth, until, with the closing years of the half century, the "Welfare State" ended the insecurity that had always hitherto been the lot of the artisan and the labourer—although those whose watchwords were initiative, enterprise, and independence, did not welcome the new order with genuine enthusiasm.

With improved social and hygienic conditions came an increase in the expectation of life, and a notable advance in the physical and medical standards of the nation, accompanied by a world-wide improvement in the measure of athletic achievement, to confound the pessimists who extolled every century but their own.

In the arts—whether in literature, painting, sculpture, or music—the theme of the century has been the exploitation of new forms of expression rather than a continuance of the tradition of the classics. Some of the outstanding writers of the period—even Bernard Shaw, who so narrowly failed to survive the year 1950—overlapped from the previous century. In 1901 Samuel Butler, Bret Harte, Herbert Spencer, Ibsen, Lecky, George Meredith, Swinburne, Mark Twain, Zola, Tolstoi, Strindberg, Rostand, Alfred Austin, Anatole France, Conrad, Kipling, Henry James, Thomas Hardy and Robert Bridges were still alive; and among the newer generation were H. G. Wells, Arnold Bennett, D. H. Lawrence, Rupert Brooke, John Masefield, Barrie, Chesterton, Galsworthy, Maeterlinck, Maxim Gorki, Yeats, Sean O'Casey, James Joyce, and T. S. Eliot. A rugged realism in sculpture was represented by such men as Rodin and Epstein; and in art the Impressionism of the previous century was followed by Cubism and Futurism.

In music again the conviction that classicism had reached its zenith with Brahms inspired new experiments that seemed so often to the uninitiated merely a series of dissonances. Verdi, Grieg, Debussy, Leoncavallo, Rimsky-Korsakov, and Puccini were survivors from the old century, but the composer of the twentieth century is surely Sibelius. In Britain Elgar overshadowed all others in the early nineteen-hundreds, and other famous names are those of Delius, Bax, Vaughan Williams, Benjamin Britten, Rutland Boughton, William Walton, and Gustav Holst; and on the Continent Richard Strauss, Mussorgsky, Prokofiev, and Scriabin. But although the "Proms" were a new educational force in British music, and although the National Brass Band Festival was a feature of the new century, "Jazz," which was of American origin, swept across oceans and frontiers, to convert millions of people from music to rhythm.

In the early years of the century musical comedy enthralled Edwardian England, and the bygone greatness of the stage was still represented by such as Irving, Beerbohm Tree, Forbes-Robertson, J. L. Toole, Ellen Terry, Eleonora Duse, and Sarah Bernhardt; and the variety stage by such as Dan Leno and Marie Lloyd. Some of the finest plays of Shaw belonged to the new century; and a feature of the age was the advance of Ballet, with Anna Pavlova as its most notable exponent. And there was, of course, the Cinema, developing from its immature crudities at the beginning of the century to an expression of the genius of Charles Chaplin and Walt Disney.

The twentieth century has seen the growth of such new cults as Christian Science and Spiritualism, the development of new philosophical ideas, and the recognition of psychiatry. There have been such colourful episodes as the pageantry of three Coronations, the Silver Jubilee of 1935, the Delhi Durbar, the Wembley Exhibition, and the London Olympiads of 1908 and 1948. Other memorable events of the century, whether in Britain or outside it, will be recalled by brief phases—the *Entente Cordiale,* the Russo-

Japanese War, the discovery of the North and South Poles, the Balkan Wars, the sinking of the *Titanic,* improved general and technical education, the first garden cities, the evolution of the "new journalism," the commercialisation of sport, the Caillaux-Calmette tragedy, rapid and bewildering changes in French politics, "Daylight Saving," the rise and fall of Fascism, and the emancipation of women (culminating in the appearance of the first woman M.P., and the first woman Cabinet Minister). There were the Irish Rebellion, the Russian Revolution, the Spanish Civil War, the Declaration of Human Rights, Labour's coming to power in Britain (from the "One-Man Party" comprising Keir Hardie when the century began to nearly 400 seats in 1945), the nationalisation of coal, transport, electricity, and steel, the rationalisation of dress (both male and female), racial intolerance in South Africa, the inauguration and jettisoning of America's "New Deal," and the repression of political freedom in liberty-loving America. And the close of the period left Britain uncertain over the vexed question of deciding where the line should be drawn between the freedom of the individual and the welfare of the community.

Inevitably the scientific genius that has bestowed so many benefits on the human race in the last fifty years has been diverted to destruction, and has intensified the horrors of war. Atomic energy, which has such a golden promise for the future, also releases new forces of frightfulness, and makes mass slaughter possible on a scale no mediæval barbarian could have contemplated. Yet neither threats nor their fulfilment retard the increase in the population of the world, which has proceeded at such a pace that there is danger, for the first time since man's discovery of agriculture, that there will not be sufficient food on the globe to feed him.

And so, in 1951, East and West, divided ideologically as well as racially, now face each other in potential hostility, with the invisible iron curtain of the "Stalin Line" between them—an uneasy world awaiting the outcome of a cleavage which is in part a battle of creeds, as well as of policies.

The changes in culture during the first half of the twentieth century are indeed remarkable, but an examination of a century of engineering progress (1852–1952) reveals something else of importance concerning the relations between engineering and science. Engineering and science are factors intimately interwoven in modern culture, first in the sense that they created this new culture, and secondly from the social standpoint because the ever-changing economic and social demands of the day are primary incentives to continued and more rapid engineering and scientific development. Engineering as a potent instrumentality in the rise of Western civilization has a history of at least fifty centuries. What developments, then, in the scope and character of modern engineering account for the remarkable changes of the past century? James Kip Finch recounts the outstanding achievements of the Industrial Revolution in answer to this question, noting material and organizational features. Fundamental distinctions between science and engineering are pointed out. Finch believes that new and revolutionary inventions have played a far less important role in creating the age in which we live than is generally assumed. He finds more intriguing the role which science has played in increasing the scope and power of engineering in the past hundred years, and finds the answer in the improved technique which science has helped to develop within the engineering field itself. The final resultant is a more fully rationalized, scientific, quantitative technique of design.

15

A CENTURY OF ENGINEERING PROGRESS: 1852-1952*
James Kip Finch

Any attempt to summarize the advances that have taken place in engineering during the past hundred years leads inevitably to generalizations that demand qualification—to statements that immediately raise, in the mind of the reader, a host of reactions that begin, "Yes, but. . . ." Clearly, we are dealing with a century of ever-increasing complication and complexity. The older, largely independent, isolated, and self-sufficient rural life, which most of our people led a hundred years ago, has been in the process of replacement by nothing less than a completely new culture. No longer are we a nation of small, self-sustaining units. A family economy has been replaced by a highly interdependent national—in some respects international—exchange of goods, the majority of which were formerly produced at home. Man—or even the family—can no longer stand alone. We are dependent upon others for the bare necessities of life, not to mention new services we now regard as essential. The economy under which we live is no longer under individual control and one in which we may, with relative ease, visualize our needs and wants and adjust our resources to meet them. It is, in fact, so involved that even the economic doctors, although aware of many symptoms, dispute causes and differ widely as to cures.

Engineering and science are intimately interwoven in the complicated fabric of modern life, for they have, on the one hand, created this new culture and, on the other, the ever-changing economic and social demands of the day are primary incentives to continued and more rapid engineering and scientific development. One naturally expects, therefore, to encounter cross-currents and conflicting influences in a field that has played a dominating part in creating a new and complex way of life.

Engineering is no newcomer in the life of man. For fifty centuries, at least, engineering has been a potent instrumentality in the rise of Western civilization. What developments, then, in the scope and character of modern engineering account for the remarkable changes of the past century, in bringing about which engineering has been the prime force? Certainly one of these has been the part played by the engineer in the Industrial Revolution, for we are still struggling with economic, social, and political problems that arise from the mechanization of industry, and what a famous president of the American Society of Civil Engineers, George S. Morison, once called "the manufacture of power."

The main stream of engineering history may by followed back to at least 3000 B.C., in the fertile valleys of the Nile in Egypt and the Tigris-Euphrates in Mesopotamia. The accomplishments and experiences of those earlier days were brought together in ancient Greece and enriched with improved

* Reprinted by permission of *Scientific Monthly*, vol. 75, no. 2, pp. 99–108, August, 1952.

technical understanding and practices. Building on this foundation Rome, in her turn, spread all over the ancient world standards of urban life that were not to be equaled for a thousand years. The Middle Ages intervened, ages when man went to school to learn to be civilized again. After the brief fruition of this schooling in the Italian Renaissance, France took over the leadership of the Western world and held it almost up to the time of the French Revolution.

The rise of engineering and Western civilization had thus been concurrent, but the engineering of the great period of French leadership was still unchanged, was still, in essence, ancient engineering. It was still public-works engineering—roads and bridges, canals, harbors, and water supplies. The vast domain of industry and manufacturing remained almost untouched. French industries were mainly rural, with those in the few urban centers dominated by the guilds, unprogressive and unchanging. Construction materials remained the timber, stone, and brick of ancient times—metals were too costly to use except for weapons, tools, and fastenings—and power was limited to the physical exertions of men and animals, plus the uncertain contributions of wind and water. But during the eighteenth century, the last great century of French leadership, the changes that were to form the basis for Britain's outstanding world position in the Victorian era, as well as for our life today, were in the making across the Channel.

Based on the development of the coal (i.e., coke) process in lieu of the charcoal which had almost denuded Britain of her forests, the British iron trade was revived by the Darbys. Wilkinson added to the cast-iron era which followed, and, by the close of the century, Cordt had developed his puddling process and rolls for wrought iron. A real Age of Metal was inaugurated. The first iron bridge in the world was built at Coalbrookdale in 1779. Kay, with his fly-shuttle of 1732, began the mechanization of the textile industry, which, carried forward by Cartwright, Arkwright, and others, has, until the past thirty years or so, been the dominating industry of industrialized nations. Then, about the time of our own American Revolution, Watt, first making economically practicable Newcomen's mine pump—in response to the growing demand for coal—went on to develop the rotative engine and, thereby, to start a new era. The development of industrial tools and machinery had been going on for centuries and was certain to continue. It was the advent of steam power to turn the wheels of industry that made it possible to replace hands by machines. The steamboat and the steam railroad followed in the early nineteenth century, providing another essential—adequate transportation for the exchange of goods.

When the American Society of Civil Engineers was founded in 1852, therefore, it was at a time when the United States was in the process of adopting and adapting these fruits of Britain's newly evolving way of life to our own needs and problems. Transportation facilities were the major requirement. Here each state of the Union sought, not primarily to strengthen union by intercommunication, but to secure the advantages of trade with the West. The Erie Canal of 1817–25 gave New York an outstanding advantage, but the Baltimore and Ohio railroad and the Pennsylvania canals and railroad also reached the Ohio. The westward movement was not to stop until the American people had spread across a continent, and the Pacific Coast had been linked by rail with the East. The Union and Central Pacific railroads met in 1869, but our greatest decade of railroad building—over 70,000 miles of track—came in 1880–90.

In other words, the nineteenth century in the United States was almost completely dominated by the transportation problem, and, after the early canal era and the Cumberland road venture of the federal government, it was the railroads that took the center of the stage. This is not to say that there were no other engineering or industrial developments. Our major cities—first Philadelphia, then New York, and then Boston—had their water supply problems. There was also some vitally important industrial pioneering. But in view of what was to take place after 1900—in the second half of these hundred years under review—America's industrial growth of the nineteenth century seems puny indeed—merely a making ready of the way.

The Philadelphia Centennial of 1876 forms a convenient reference date. The power needs of this exhibition were met by the giant engine designed by Corlis—a 1400-horsepower, low-speed, low-pressure, reciprocating engine far more perfect mechanically, of course, but differing in no basic way from the Watt engine of a century earlier.

This was clearly a showpiece, which did not reflect American power needs. American manufacturing was still localized in the New England states and around New York City and Philadelphia. The numerous smaller industries of the East still relied on the small water powers around which New England towns and villages had grown. Lowell on the Merrimac and then Holyoke on the Connecticut offered larger water-power sites. The industries of the coastal cities required steam power, but the demand was for relatively small units, say, 25 horsepower or less—usually small, noncondensing, inefficient reciprocating engines. As a matter of fact, if one seeks for the best in steam power in the nineteenth century, he must turn to steamships. The largest stationary reciprocating engines ever built (7500 horsepower) went into the powerhouses for electrification of the Elevated Railroad and the first New York subway in 1902–04, whereas two engines each twice this size on a single shaft had driven the screws of the *Campania* and the *Oceanic* in 1893 and 1899.

It was not until the eighties that the Indians were finally subdued and we realized that our geographic frontiers had been reached and we could turn around and take stock of our winnings. It is true that Eli Whitney, of cotton gin fame, had adopted interchangeable manufacture in the making of muskets in 1792, that we had stolen textile machines from Britain in spite of her best efforts to prevent their export, and that, by the time of her great London exhibition of 1851, "the American system" of manufacture had created a great stir abroad. But the real American Industrial Revolution was yet to come. Our earlier advances had been primarily those of territorial conquest. Those of the twentieth century were to be based on the technological and industrial exploitation of our resources.

There is hardly a single curve of engineering or industrial growth which does not turn sharply upward after 1900. Possible exceptions are railroad building (we reached our maximum railroad mileage—253,000 miles, enough to encircle the world ten times—in 1920) and coal mining which, after a World War I peak, declined with the advent of by-product coke ovens and oil competition. Our first billion-dollar corporation, U. S. Steel, came in 1901. The American Portland cement industry was born at the beginning of the century. Brick and stone gave way to mass-produced concrete. The development of the automobile not only created a major industry but ushered in the Highway Era, with demands for highways and superhighways we have yet fully to meet, and, happily for the bridge engineer whose railroad employment had run out, a period of great bridges that surpass in span anything the world has ever known. Steel began to replace wrought iron immediately after the Philadelphia Centennial, and by 1950 we were turning out over 1000 pounds for every man, woman, and child in the country as compared with possibly 15 to 20 pounds of iron a century ago. Copper also was on the way up, but by 1946 aluminum had become less costly per pound than the red metal.

World War I marked in many respects a climactic date in American engineering, as we shall note. It also marked the rise—or at least a remarkable expansion—in the American chemical industry. Discovering that we had been dependent upon Germany for many of our chemical needs, older companies, such as Du Pont, began to broaden their fields of interest, and new industries were built on the German patents confiscated during the war years. The astounding growth of the American chemical industry followed.

But in no field of human endeavor has the American Industrial Revolution been more marked than in that of the generation and utilization of power. It has been reliably estimated that in 1900 there was available in the United States power equipment totaling about 25 million horsepower, or about two man power per capita. In other words, earlier centuries had produced two silent slaves to relieve man of physical toil. The past fifty years have seen more than a fifty-fold per capita increase.

The power manufactured by, and purchased for, industry in 1900 was about two horsepower per industrial worker. It is now in the neighborhood of ten horsepower. Recalling that it takes from six to ten men to equal a horsepower, this means that the physical power of our modern industrial worker has in the past century been multiplied a hundred-fold. Every man, woman, and child in the world could not provide the power to turn the wheels of American industry alone.

It should be noted also that a large part of modern power equipment is in portable gas engine form. The number of motor vehicles in the United States today is some 50 million, or the equivalent of one for every three inhabitants, and there are in addition the millions of gasoline- or oil-powered farm, construction, and other machines.

Back of this tremendous expansion, there have of course been many stimulating forces: a widespread demand sustained by a widespread purchasing power; the remarkable increases in the wages of labor since 1900, which have forced the substitution of machines and power for men; and, certainly a basic influence, the development of electrical means of transmitting and utilizing power. Electric lighting may claim perhaps 10 or 15 per cent of power service but, whereas only 4 per cent of our tools and machines were electrically operated in 1900, over 75 per cent were so individually driven in 1927, and one seldom sees another type of machine today.

And what has this all meant to the American people? On the material side, American production has been increased five- to sixfold in the last half-century. In these same years our population has about doubled, so that this means that each of us has today two and one-half to three times the goods and services that were available fifty years ago. But this is not all. Mass production demands mass consumption. We have had to find, and still have to find, useful, productive employment for some 600,000 new workers every year in order that they may have the purchasing power to enjoy this increased production. We hear much of the monotony of modern industrial life, of the loss of the pride and incentive, the creative satisfactions, of our earlier craftsmanship era. The answer is, of course, that a craftsmanship era could not maintain our standards of living of the present day. And how many of us have any gifts of craftsmanship? We forget also that in earlier days "man's work was from sun to sun and woman's work was never done." Those were the days when the majority of men were "brothers to the ox." Since the turn of the century American technology and industry have created useful, productive employment for millions who possess no unusual gifts yet who can, thanks to modern machines and power, and in a forty-hour week, afford standards of living never before paralleled in human history.

Engineering has been, indeed, the great leveling force in the history of man. It has done much to compensate for the differences of night and day, of heat and cold. Through transportation and power it has made possible the equalization of differences of location. The farmer, as well as the city dweller, can enjoy the comforts and conveniences of the Power Age. Industry, with its higher standards of living, has spread from New England over all the states, until today there is not a state in the Union that produces less than $25,000,000 annually of manufactured products and only four that produce less than $100,000,000. And the end is not yet. We are apt to forget that this modern age has also done much to man's productive abilities. Millions who operate machines do not possess the natural gifts essential to manual production. Indeed, the great danger of this era of equal opportunity which modern technology has brought about is that, in our search for equality, we may easily fall into the error of failing to recognize the importance of quality —of the special gifts from which these advances spring.

Yes, it is a complex and complicated life we lead and it has raised many new economic, social, and political problems. At times it seems that man has, in this past century, come in the grip of a new evolutionary force —a dominating power which urges him ever onward to new developments, new problems, and new adjustments, but one from which he cannot sever his connection and from the continued and ever-more rapid evolution of which he cannot restrain his efforts.

Certainly one of the most important factors in increasing the scope and tempo of this movement over the past century has been the liaison between the natural sciences and engineering. Although the general pattern of modern engineering development was well established in 1852, the past hundred years have witnessed a long-delayed *rapprochement* between the two activities. As A. North Whitehead has remarked, it was just about a century ago that a developed science wedded itself to a developed technology and a new era in the life of man began. This story fits perfectly into the brackets of time we have been reviewing. Has this wedding, then, been the determining factor in creating the new epoch? What part has science played in modern engineering progress? What is the relationship of science to engineering?

Today's engineering is, of course, but the modern version of several ancient practical arts: the art of construction, the mechanical and chemical arts, and the arts of mining and metallurgy. One is immediately impressed with the fact that the majority of the areas of engineering interest and the methods or means used in engineering practice are thus of very early origin. Engineers built roads

and bridges, harbors, aqueducts, and water supplies, developed steam power, the steam boat and railroad, extended the scope of engineering activities into our industrial life, all before, and sometimes centuries before, there was any relationship between natural science and engineering. Why, then, should there be any liaison between these two interests now?

There is, of course, a fundamental difference of purpose between natural science and engineering. Science seeks to explain, to explore causes, and to increase our understanding of nature. Engineering is, on the other hand, creative, seeking to satisfy man's material needs and wants within the economic framework of the times. Their common interest derives from the fact that the engineer, in shaping our environment and exploiting our resources for the better use and convenience of man, is inevitably working with or against natural forces or making use of nature's gifts. What we may not always remember, however, is that this dual interest in a common area is not the full story. It has been said that the pure science of today becomes the applied science of tomorrow. There may possibly be some exceptions, and it is undoubtedly true that, through modern organized developmental research, we are shortening the gap between scientific discovery and its application and use in engineering and industry; but if history teaches us anything it is that the quick transformation of discovery to use is simply a bit of wishful thinking.

There is a clearly defined sequence of events between scientific discovery, on the one hand, and its practical, creative use, on the other. Several factors are involved in the process. In the first place, the engineer has never been able to wait until he had all pertinent information before attempting to meet the material needs and wants of his day. The doctor does not refuse to treat a patient because he does not fully understand the disease from which the afflicted one suffers. Engineers built stone arch bridges for at least two thousand years before they had more than a shrewd idea of what made them stand up. Even today, although an empirical, rule-of-thumb design based on these centuries of experience is quite simple and easy, a rigid, scientific, quantitative analysis of the stresses in this ancient structural form is almost impossible.

The steam engine, the steamboat, the railroad, as well as the truss bridge, the suspension, and the arch, were all well developed before the science behind them was known in more than the purely intuitive, empirical, qualitative manner which resulted from years of training, observation, and practice. In short, we had bridges before we had even an approximate bridge theory, steam engines before the modern theory of heat, and, in our own day, the science of aerodynamics has followed the invention of the Wright brothers.

The first step in the birth of a new engineering product is invention—the marriage of an idea with the means of its realization. And, contrary to popular belief, the role of science in this process has usually been secondary. Natural science is, after all, a quite modern growth. For centuries, as a result of the narrowness of Greek thought and, later, the dominance of the church, the growth of science was impossible. It was not until the sixteenth century that science was made free, and not until well into the nineteenth that the term "natural philosophy" passed out of use. The eighteenth century marked a notable advance, but in the earlier ages such science as existed offered little or nothing to the engineer. Watt made it clear that he owed nothing in his steam engine invention to his friend Dr. Black's discoveries—nothing to more than a quite obvious common sense, experience, and observation. Bell's invention of the telephone was, of course, made possible by the use of the electromagnet, but the idea of transmission of speech was pure Bell —it did not originate with the magnet. The Wrights learned to fly through actual trial and error rather than as the result of any scientific discovery. It has been argued that Faraday was the real inventor of the dynamo. He unquestionably discovered magnetic induction, but it took at least fifty men fifty years to produce a practical, useful dynamo. It is undoubtedly true that within the past century scientific knowledge has made it increasingly possible to realize inventive ideas. It is also true that within the past fifty years or less we have passed into another phase in invention in which, occasionally, the process is reversed; that is, we seek an inventive idea that will make use of a scientific discovery. But to assume that any scientific discovery will, as the public has been led to believe, find practical use and application tomorrow is sheer nonsense. Actually, new and revolutionary inventions have played a far less important role in creating the age in which we live than is generally assumed. We must look elsewhere for the major and vitally important role which science has played in increasing the scope and power of engineering in the past hundred years of their married life. The answer is to be found in the improved technique which science has aided in developing within the engineering field itself.

Before the middle of the last century the technique of engineering design was based almost entirely on an intuitive sense or feeling for design, ripened and developed by experience. It was empirical design, largely rule of thumb, purely qualitative, and dependent on rather rare, natural gifts. Beginning in France in the late eighteenth century, and greatly strengthened and extended by British workers in the first half of the nineteenth century, more rigid, more fully rationalized scientific, quantitative techniques of design were slowly developed. The history of a single structural element, the simple beam, illustrates the difficulties involved. Until about 1830–40, the size of a beam to carry a load over a span was a matter of judgment and experience. We did not have what is known today as the common theory of flexure by means of which, knowing the load and the span and having tested the material to be used, we may compute the size of a beam needed to meet these conditions. Galileo had worked with the problem in the sixteenth century, but on erroneous assumptions. Euler and Bernoulli had been interested in the mathematics of the elastic curve of a beam. About 1820 Navier, a professor in the Ecole des Ponts et Chaussées, developed the basic theory in practically the form in which we have it today. But it took such practical workers as the British engineers Tredgold and Barlow to test beams, discard the unnecessary mathematical complications of the earlier "elasticians," and produce a workable technique of design. That is, progress in engineering science, although based on the understandings of natural science, is developed and made useful and applicable not by scientists but by engineers.

This search for more fully rationalized, more accurate, quantitative techniques of design to replace the older empirical, qualitative, and thus uncertain judgment techniques of the past still goes forward today of course —at an ever-increasing tempo. World War I may be said, however, to have marked a turning point in the general character of this search. The nineteenth century was marked by what may be called the "coefficient method of attack." Engineering science was a curious combination of a few basic scientific formulas modified by experimentally determined coefficients which allowed for the many, still unknown factors that were always encountered in practice. A notable example was hydraulics, in which the flow through an orifice, to take a simple case, was based on the Torricelli theorem: $q = av = a\sqrt{2gh}$; but a coefficient, varying with the shape and size of an opening and determined by experiment, was introduced to reconcile theory with practice. Large-scale experimentation was the order of the day. With the turn of the century we began to analyze the behavior of the coefficients, what had been called the factors of ignorance. Viscosity, inertia, basic parameters such as the Reynold's number, not only led to new understanding, but to the ideas of dimensional and dynamic similarity that made it possible to relate model tests to prototypes. Fluid dynamics was born. Large-scale experimentation was, in many cases, no longer necessary.

There is probably nothing so exasperating

to the natural scientist as the time-lag between theory and practice. He is apt to regard the engineer as a slowpoke if not actually an incompetent. There are two obvious answers to this criticism. In the first place, the scientist naturally has his own interests, and they are seldom those that furnish direct grist for the engineer's mill. As in the case of the medical profession, the engineer has had to dig out the great bulk of his practical science himself. Of the group of subjects which have long been known as engineering science, this has been true especially of thermodynamics, hydrodynamics, and the mechanics of materials and structures. Furthermore, the problems involved in such digging are often complicated. Take, for example, one of the most recent areas of engineering interest to succumb, at least in part, to rational, scientific analysis, namely, soil mechanics. There are at least a dozen complex, interrelated variables involved in the physical behavior of any one soil. In addition, there are few conditions in nature where any such thing as uniform soil conditions occur. Physics, of course, aids us in explaining such basic phenomena as cohesion, capillarity, grain shape and size, but these are only elements in a complex problem; and the engineer wants more than explanations, he wants to know in advance how much a bridge pier will settle, or what is the stable slope for an earth embankment. These are clearly not problems in which the scientist would be interested.

There is also another fundamental fact that is too often ignored. The main service of natural science to engineering has been in the development of a more fully rationalized, scientific, quantitative technique of design, but design is not an end in itself; it is merely a means to more effective and efficient production or construction. The most highly scientific and accurately designed device or product man can conceive has no merit unless it offers better service at less cost than some existing device or product. It is because more scientific design offers possibilities of such economy that the search for further rationalization of engineering design never ends. It would be almost impossible to mention a single engineering device, product, or method which has not been improved through specialized scientific study and analysis. But there are external factors that strongly influence this trend and that demand attention. They can best be exemplified by the rather wide differences between American and European engineering development.

In the first place, one of the major advantages of scientific design is that it results in a saving of materials. Overdesign is avoided, and parts of a structure or machine are made no larger than is necessary to meet the loads coming upon them. Similarly, the scientifically designed steam engine uses less coal, the improved electric light fewer watts per lumen. But, in many cases, such exact and materially economical design involves more labor, and more highly skilled labor, to produce.

As early as 1838 a British engineer visiting the United States remarked that American design differed from European practice primarily because, although we had an abundance of materials, skilled labor was scarce and costly. Throughout the nineteenth century the basic desiderata in engineering design were ease and speed of production. We did not hesitate to use a few more pounds of steel or a yard or two of concrete if this would result in a saving of labor or reduce the period during which capital would be idle and unproductive. These ideas have influenced all our engineering activities, from the development of labor-saving machinery to the design of bridges that could be largely shop-made and in which field operations were reduced to a minimum. We have been the greatest labor savers and producers the world has ever known, but until recent years, we have paid little attention to "unnecessary refinements" in design.

In Europe, on the other hand, skilled labor has been relatively plentiful and materials relatively costly. As a result, European engineers have sought the utmost in the refinement of design. In 1851 an American, Squire

Whipple, published the first text dealing with the analysis of truss bridges, but with few exceptions we have contributed little to the development of engineering science since. We have left this to European workers and not infrequently have regarded them as "mathematical geniuses without a practical hair on their heads."

This situation began to change about the time of World War I. To what extent it was influenced by a change in the relative cost of materials and labor and the increasing cost of supplies is problematical. In the structural field the demand for larger structures, in which economy demanded more exact analysis, and secondary stresses could no longer be ignored or provided for by generous overdesign, played a part. The development of the airplane, a flying structure of intricate design, was another factor. The replacement of direct current by a far more complex alternating service posed new problems. The coming of the steam turbine, and the growth of demand to the point where Corlis' giant steam engine of 1876 of 1400 horsepower became a joke as compared with modern turboelectric units of 280,000 horsepower, stimulated a far more exact study of thermodynamic and similar problems. Edison's famous Pearl Street Station in New York of 1882 probably used 30 or 40 pounds of coal per kilowatt hour produced. By 1900 this had been reduced to 7 in the better plants and today it is 1 or less—an over-all heat efficiency of about 30 per cent. And there is still room for improvement.

Where have we secured the basic theory and understanding by which these more recent advances have been made possible? There are, of course, exceptions, but in general we have imported them, ready-made, from Europe, mainly from Germany. It seems safe to say that American engineering has gained far more in power and refinement of techniques from such importations than it has from any American advances in natural science. We have been backward in the development of engineering science in this country, and our contributions in some fields of natural science have correspondingly not been outstanding.

It is of course true that scientific knowledge has generally been made quickly and readily available to the entire world and it is, thus, as Ewart Smith has observed, on the technical and industrial use of knowledge, on industrial practice and know-how, on the state of engineering science, that the industrial and economic position of a nation depends. It has been frequently noted that World War II made it impossible for us to rely any longer on European sources for either the research that leads to scientific discoveries or the basic studies that result in improved engineering science and practice. Furthermore, Russia has "imported" extremely able German talent and is not revealing the results of their labors to the world. The fate of the world rests today, as never before, on scientific and technological leadership. And this, in turn, is primarily a problem of our understanding the relationships of science and engineering. We have a tremendous backlog of scientific knowledge on which to draw for improved engineering practice, but we must be the

first to discover new scientific knowledge. We must also be the first to learn how to use and apply such knowledge in improving and advancing our engineering and industrial knowledge. One activity that grew and developed greatly during the depression years and that has been further stimulated by World War II is research. We must see that in this development we do not overemphasize either research in natural science at the expense of research in engineering science or vice versa.

Unlike Russia, we are aiding the backward nations of the world financially and with technical advice and direction in attaining the same standards of life that the American Industrial Revolution has brought to us. But we would be blind indeed if we failed to realize that not only the dislocations of World War II but also this widespread gift of technological and industrial know-how pose a challenge to American science and engineering that must be met in the years that are to come. The challenge of the past Century of Progress in Engineering, great as it has been, is completely overshadowed by the challenge we face today.

IV

Conceptions of
Social Progress

The root meaning of progress is "to go forward," but when considered as a quality of social change or evolution progress can hardly be "defined." At best, progress can only be described or characterized; but description is not definition. Is anyone perfectly sure *where* and *when* and *how* progress on the whole has taken place, or *if* it has actually occurred? Nevertheless, progress is an important evaluative concept which denotes change for the better, whether the cultural elements considered are material or nonmaterial. In any case, progress is purely subjective and exists only in the mind of the observer.

Criteria of Progress. L. T. Hobhouse describes progress as the "social growth of social life in respect to those qualities in which human beings attach or can rationally attach value." [1] N. I. Karayev says, "Progress . . . is the gradual elevation of the standard of human development, accompanied by conditions which make it possible for a larger and larger number to attain this standard." [2] Statements like these make it clear that societal progress is a movement toward some general and greater human good. The emphasis is upon a societal or *general* human good. How are we to know what constitutes such human good? Several tests of progress have meaning for different aspects of "progress."

Materialistic tests judge change in terms of the "biggest," the "greatest," or "newest" and "most modern," thus emphasizing size or quantity or recency. Excellence is confused with magnitude of results.

Statistical tests may be applicable to the increase of the total population of a country, as if greater numbers mean national progress; or to an increase in expectancy of life; or to the degree there is racial, linguistic, educational, religious, or other forms of uniformity and homogeneity among a people; or to an increase of literacy; or to

[1] L. T. Hobhouse, *Social Evolution and Political Theory*, Columbia University Press, New York, 1911, p. 87.
[2] Quoted from Karayev's *Principal Queries of the Philosophy of History*, vol. III, p. 214, by J. Hecker, *Russian Sociology*, John Wiley & Sons, Inc., New York, 1934, p. 167.

the divorce rate as a criterion of the status of the family life and the domestic virtues in a society. These tests measure mere quantitative change and are not decisive with reference to questions of general welfare.

Ideological tests, whether in terms of religions, or of economic and political ideologies and the social movements motivated by them, have little practical value. Ideological criteria tend toward the abstract and metaphysical, the unrealistic and mythical.

Order and harmony have been suggested as the great good by the Russian philosopher Peter Lavrov (1823–1900), as well as by Auguste Comte, Leonard T. Hobhouse, Charles A. Ellwood, and A. J. Todd. Lavrov looked upon progress as "a harmonizing and synthesizing of the social forces of solidarity and individuality." [3] Throughout his writings Hobhouse frequently refers to the growth of harmony as the social good. Ellwood prescribes harmony through adaptation as one of the chief ends of progress, and Todd suggests that harmony is the standard for measuring progress. Todd expresses his conception thus: "Social progress involves the harmonious development of every constituent member and group in society, this harmony to be determined by the fitness of the society to meet the exigencies of nature and self-conscious life, to grapple with its problems of today, and to provide for going on tomorrow." [4]

Happiness has been held to be the criterion and goal of progress. As an ardent champion of this criterion, Ward defined human progress as that which secures the increase of human happiness. All happiness, as interpreted by Ward, consists in the gratification of desire. J. K. Folsom held that progress is change for the better, this "betterness" to be measurable in terms of human happiness, the latter meaning a minimum of suffering and a maximum of enjoyment. Hertzler, however, maintains that happiness is not the goal of progress, and he says that biology, psychology, and sociology have not been able to establish a sound foundation for the hedonistic philosophy that pleasure is the sole or chief good in life, that moral duty is fulfilled in the gratification of pleasure-seeking instinct and dispositions, or, more briefly, that "the greatest happiness for the greatest number" is the chief good in life. There are higher and truer values than the maximization of pleasure and the minimization of pain. [5]

The development of individuality is another criterion of progress. For the Russian Kareyev, the emancipation of the individual is thought to be the great good. It involves the self-liberation of the personality through the recasting of cultural ideas and social forms of institutions. Man's freedom is derived through social organization involving reciprocally related institutions—moral, social, political, economic, and religious.

The adaptation test is another to consider. Ellwood thought of progress as adaptation or adjustment which results from the increasing control over life and its condi-

---

[3] See Newell LeRoy Sims, *The Problem of Social Change*, Thomas Y. Crowell Company, New York, 1939, p. 346.
[4] See A. J. Todd, *Theories of Social Progress*, The Macmillan Company, New York, 1918, p. 124.
[5] J. O. Hertzler, *Social Progress*, Appleton-Century-Crofts, Inc., New York, 1928, p. 86.

tions.[6] Progress thus means a better adaptation of social groups to the requirements of their existence, and adjustments to a wider, more universal environment. Hobhouse regarded social progress as the growth in the harmonious adjustment of man to society, of the different types of social organization to each other, and of society as a whole to its environment. Thomas Nixon Carver was also interested in adaptation, but distinguished between passive adaptation—i.e., the modification of the species to suit the conditions of the environment—and active adaptation—i.e., the modification of conditions to suit the species.

The agents of progress should not be confused with the criteria of progress. Hertzler discusses the following agents: intellect and knowledge, science and invention, exceptional individuals, ideals and programs, public opinion, and education.[7]

Clearly it is difficult to reduce something which is as subjective as the concept of progress to genuinely objective reality. However, the several readings which follow will prove useful in connection with the present exposition of social change. The titles of the selections suggest the nature of their content: "The Idea of Progress" by John B. Bury, "Progress: A Western Notion" by Clarence M. Case, "Culture Development and Progress" by Wilson D. Wallis, "Is Progress a Delusion?" by Will Durant, "Progress" by John Dewey, and "Is History Predictable?" by Reinhold Niebuhr.

John B. Bury considers the validity of the idea of human progress. Among the criteria for judgment are these: that progress has an aim, that civilization has a destination, and that man's capacity to acquire knowledge of nature or of his environment may continue indefinitely. The idea of human progress resolves into a theory which involves a synthesis of the past and a prophecy of the future. Theoretically, man is assumed to be slowly advancing in a definite and desirable direction; there is also the inference that this progress will continue indefinitely. Such a theory of progress belongs to the same order of ideas as providence or personal immortality; that is, belief in progress is an act of faith.

---

[6] See Charles A. Ellwood, *Introduction to Social Psychology*, Appleton-Century-Crofts, Inc., New York, 1917, pp. 289–291, and same topic as developed later in his *Psychology of Human Society*, Appleton-Century-Crofts, Inc., New York, 1925, pp. 423–428.

[7] J. O. Hertzler, *op. cit.*, chaps. 9–14.

16

THE IDEA OF PROGRESS*
John Bagnell Bury

When we say that ideas rule the world, or exercise a decisive power in history, we are generally thinking of those ideas which express human aims and depend for their realisation on the human will, such as liberty, toleration, equality of opportunity, socialism. Some of these have been partly realised, and there is no reason why any of them should not be fully realised, in a society or in the world, if it were the united purpose of a society or of the world to realise it. They are approved or condemned because they are held to be good or bad, not because they are true or false. But there is another order of ideas that play a great part in determining and directing the course of man's conduct but do not depend on his will—ideas which bear upon the mystery of life, such as Fate, Providence, or personal immortality. Such ideas may operate in important ways on the forms of social action, but they involve a question of fact and they are accepted or rejected not because they are believed to be useful or injurious, but because they are believed to be true or false.

The idea of the progress of humanity is an idea of this kind, and it is important to be quite clear on the point. We now take it so much for granted, we are so conscious of constantly progressing in knowledge, arts, organising capacity, utilities of all sorts, that it is easy to look upon Progress as an aim, like liberty or a world-federation, which it only depends on our efforts and good-will to achieve. But though all increases of power

and knowledge depend on human effort, the idea of the Progress of humanity, from which all these particular progresses derive their value, raises a definite question of fact, which man's wishes or labours cannot affect any more than his wishes or labours can prolong life beyond the grave.

This idea means that civilisation has moved, is moving, and will move in a desirable direction. But in order to judge that we are moving in a desirable direction we should have to know precisely what the destination is. To the minds of most people the desirable outcome of human development would be a condition of society in which all the inhabitants of the planet would enjoy a perfectly happy existence. But it is impossible to be sure that civilisation is moving in the right direction to realise this aim. Certain features of our "progress" may be urged as presumptions in its favour, but there are always offsets, and it has always been easy to make out a case that, from the point of view of increasing happiness, the tendencies of our progressive civilisation are far from desirable. In short, it cannot be proved that the unknown destination towards which man is advancing is desirable. The movement may be Progress, or it may be in an undesirable direction and therefore not Progress. This is a question of fact, and one which is at present as insoluble as the question of personal immortality. It is a problem which bears on the mystery of life.

Moreover, even if it is admitted to be

* From John Bagnell Bury's *The Idea of Progress*, pp. 1–7. Reprinted through permission of Dover Publications, Inc., New York 10, New York.

probable that the course of civilisation has so far been in a desirable direction, and such as would lead to general felicity if the direction were followed far enough, it cannot be proved that ultimate attainment depends entirely on the human will. For the advance might at some point be arrested by an insuperable wall. Take the particular case of knowledge, as to which it is generally taken for granted that the continuity of progress in the future depends altogether on the continuity of human effort (assuming that human brains do not degenerate). This assumption is based on a strictly limited experience. Science has been advancing without interruption during the last three or four hundred years; every new discovery has led to new problems and new methods of solution, and opened up new fields for exploration. Hitherto men of science have not been compelled to halt, they have always found means to advance further. But what assurance have we that they will not one day come up against impassable barriers? The experience of four hundred years, in which the surface of nature has been successfully tapped, can hardly be said to warrant conclusions as to the prospect of operations extending over four hundred or four thousand centuries. Take biology or astronomy. How can we be sure that some day progress may not come to a dead pause, not because knowledge is exhausted, but because our resources for investigation are exhausted—because, for instance, scientific instruments have reached the limit of perfection beyond which it is demonstrably impossible to improve them, or because (in the case of astronomy) we come into the presence of forces of which, unlike gravitation, we have no terrestrial experience? It is an assumption, which cannot be verified, that we shall not soon reach a point in our knowledge of nature beyond which the human intellect is unqualified to pass.

But it is just this assumption which is the light and inspiration of man's scientific research. For if the assumption is not true, it means that he can never come within sight of the goal which is, in the case of physical science, if not a complete knowledge of the cosmos and the processes of nature, at least an immeasurably larger and deeper knowledge than we at present possess.

Thus continuous progress in man's knowledge of his environment, which is one of the chief conditions of general Progress, is a hypothesis which may or may not be true. And if it is true, there remains the further hypothesis of man's moral and social "perfectibility," which rests on much less impressive evidence. There is nothing to show that he may not reach, in his psychical and social development, a stage at which the conditions of his life will be still far from satisfactory, and beyond which he will find it impossible to progress. This is a question of fact which no willing on man's part can alter. It is a question bearing on the mystery of life.

Enough has been said to show that the Progress of humanity belongs to the same order of ideas as Providence or personal immortality. It is true or it is false, and like them it cannot be proved either true or false. Belief in it is an act of faith.

The idea of human Progress then is a theory which involves a synthesis of the past and a prophecy of the future. It is based on an interpretation of history which regards men as slowly advancing—*pedetemtim progredientes*—in a definite and desirable direction, and infers that this progress will continue indefinitely. And it implies that, as

The issue of the earth's great business,

a condition of general happiness will ultimately be enjoyed, which will justify the whole process of civilisation; for otherwise the direction would not be desirable. There is also a further implication. The process must be the necessary outcome of the psychical and social nature of man; it must not be at the mercy of any external will; otherwise there would be no guarantee of its continuance and its issue, and the idea of Progress would lapse into the idea of Providence.

As time is the very condition of the possibility of Progress, it is obvious that the idea would be valueless if there were any cogent reasons for supposing that the time at the disposal of humanity is likely to reach a limit in the near future. If there were good cause for believing that the earth would be uninhabitable in A.D. 2000 or 2100 the doctrine of Progress would lose its meaning and would automatically disappear. It would be a delicate question to decide what is the minimum period of time which must be assured to man for his future development, in order that Progress should possess value and appeal to the emotions. The recorded history of civilisation covers 6000 years or so, and if we take this as a measure of our conceptions of time-distances, we might assume that if we were sure of a period ten times as long ahead of us the idea of Progress would not lose its power of appeal. Sixty thousand years of *historical* time, when we survey the changes which have come to pass in six thousand, opens to the imagination a range vast enough to seem almost endless.

This psychological question, however, need not be decided. For science assures us that the stability of the present conditions of the solar system is certified for many myriads of years to come. Whatever gradual modifications of climate there may be, the planet will not cease to support life for a period which transcends and flouts all efforts of imagination. In short, the *possibility* of Progress is guaranteed by the high probability, based on astro-physical science, of an immense time to progress in.

It may surprise many to be told that the notion of Progress, which now seems so easy to apprehend, is of comparatively recent origin. It has indeed been claimed that various thinkers, both ancient (for instance, Seneca) and medieval (for instance, Friar Bacon), had long ago conceived it. But sporadic observations—such as man's gradual rise from primitive and savage conditions to a certain level of civilisation by a series of inventions, or the possibility of some future additions to his knowledge of nature—which were inevitable at a certain stage of human reflection, do not amount to an anticipation of the idea. The value of such observations was determined, and must be estimated, by the whole context of ideas in which they occurred. It is from its bearings on the future that Progress derives its value, its interest, and its power. You may conceive civilisation as having gradually advanced in the past, but you have not got the idea of Progress until you go on to conceive that it is destined to advance indefinitely in the future. . . .

Bury traces in broad terms the emergence of the idea of progress in the culture of Greece and Rome as well as of Europe during the Middle Ages and the Renaissance. During all these epochal cultural phases, the conditions were not favorable to the appearance of the idea of progress.

It was in the last stage of the Renaissance, which includes the first quarter of the seventeenth century, that soil was being prepared in which the idea of progress could germinate. The history of its origin definitely begins with interpretations of universal history written by Jean Bodin; some credit is also due the works of another Frenchman, the classical scholar Louis Le Roy. Especially significant in the origin of the concept of progress was Francis Bacon's conception of utility as the end of knowledge. Bury points out that the guiding star of Bacon's intellectual labor was the principle that knowledge's proper aim is to ameliorate human life, to increase men's happiness, and to mitigate their sufferings. Bacon also believed that the true object of the investigation of nature was to establish the reign of man over nature. Thus man arrives, after thousands of years of intellectual growth, at the threshold of the concept of progress.

Clarence Marsh Case, building on the perspective given by Bury, goes on to emphasize the degree to which progress is a Western notion. Further glimpses into the social mentality of the Greeks and Romans, and of some contemporary philosophers, support the view that the concept "progress" emerged as an element in modern culture.

17

PROGRESS: A WESTERN NOTION*
Clarence Marsh Case

The history of this modern and Western notion that the kind of change which we call "progress" is the normal course of human affairs, if not of the natural world and the entire universe, has been minutely traced by Professor J. B. Bury, in his scholarly work entitled *The Idea of Progress: An Inquiry into Its Origin and Growth,* published in 1920. A detailed report of the course of this remarkable idea would carry us beyond the scope of the present work, but taking note only of some of the most outstanding facts, it seems that the *Greeks* never attained the idea because they were dominated by certain conditions and viewpoints that rendered a clear notion of progress impossible. Being impressed with the notion of Fate, personified in the three portentous sisters who spun and severed the cords of every life, they could hardly picture that atmosphere of free human agency essential to the movement called social progress today. Moreover, the thinkers of that day conceived the history of the cosmos as a series of cycles, endlessly recurring, during each one of which the world ascended through thirty-six thousand years and then descended for an equal period. According to

the most rigid adherents of this theory every point in each cycle exactly duplicated the corresponding point on the cycles preceding and following it—the same people living, and doing precisely the same things. It is evident that there could be no conception of social progress in the light of such teaching. It was further rendered impossible by the fact that the Greeks possessed at that stage no history of their own past or that of any other people, and so could not look back over a long course of events through which they had ascended, or at least seemed to have ascended, as can modern nations rich in the records of their own past. Couple with this their further lack of any considerable body of applied science, by means of which man's power over environment can be asserted, and it does not appear strange that even this most advanced people of antiquity never formulated the concept of social progress. They looked backward upon better times, which were known as the Golden Age—a myth which still endures in many lands very far removed from Greece.

During the Middle Ages little advance toward the idea of progress was made. The idea of the Golden Age was still dominant, though

* From C. M. Case, *Social Process and Human Progress,* Harcourt, Brace and Company, Inc., New York, copyright 1931, pp. 10–23.

it took the form of a lost Eden. It is true that Christianity laid a basis for the idea of Progress in its teaching of redemption and its conception of a Divine plan or purpose which was destined to realize itself through the power of God, not largely in this world, to be sure, but none the less surely in the world to come. But along with this vision of an onward-moving progression of world events there stood out such ideas as that of the Fall of Man and of the total depravity of the human race, neither of which, as taught in the current theology, left room for any large notion of possible improvement for mankind on this planet.

The large place held, in those times, by otherworldliness and the doctrines of the end of the world and the Day of Judgment must be regarded as a powerful factor in producing the social pessimism that long prevailed.

With the opening of the Modern Age there arose a movement of thought which has radically transformed the ideas of the earlier periods. The Golden Age was now transferred to the future. Men no longer looked backward, but forward, to the best days of our race on this earth. The Greek notion of Fate, with its successor, the Medieval belief in an actively Intervening Providence, gave way, particularly among the disciples of Descartes, before the conception of a world governed by natural and invariable law. The gap left by earlier ignorance of history came to be filled by a vision of the history of civilization, later differentiating into scientific history proper with its several branches, archeology, anthropology, and ethnology, the last three vastly extending the range of man's vision into the past. Simultaneously a body of scientific knowledge began to form, at the same time that it came to be perceived, under the leadership of Sir Francis Bacon, that the legitimate object of knowledge is the utilitarian service of mankind.

The prestige of the Ancients, imposed by the Revival of Classical Learning, gradually gave way to a growing conviction that we moderns are just as capable as were the men of ancient Greece or Rome. At the same time

there slowly emerged, in place of the theological conception of a preconceived and predestined Divine plan of world history, the theory of an evolutionary scheme of gradual and fortuitous development. This, itself devoid of logical foundation, carried with it the three equally unwarranted corollaries of the indefinite ascent of man, the feasibility of perfecting human nature, and the optimistic belief in an indefinite future for the human race on this globe.

It should not be overlooked that we have sketched here in the briefest possible way a vast movement of thought, and especially a growth of sentiment, which required some centuries for its completion. Moreover, the different phases of it were discontinuous, irregular in rate of advance, and the whole thing a largely unconscious, groping process, finely illustrating that "tentative method of growth" which, as Professor Cooley has so clearly shown, is characteristic of all living things, whether organisms or organizations.

In the course of this process venerable misconceptions were discarded, while new and more valid conceptions came to be accepted. But along with these better and truer views there crept in also errors peculiar to these times. Chief among them is a very widespread tendency to confuse the two concepts, "progress" and "evolution." This loose way of thinking has already proceeded so far that it is in danger of penetrating the *folk-thought* of the Occident, despite the fact, as will be pointed out on other pages, that there is no logical justification for such a notion. In this respect the modern movement has made for confusion, rather than clarity, of thinking. Perhaps Herbert Spencer is chiefly responsible for this misinterpretation. His leadership along this line is probably the product of his intellectual enthusiasm for the idea of evolution, coupled with an emotional and sentimental approval of things as he found them in his mid-Victorian England. As Bury remarks, "the optimism of Spencer's view could not be surpassed. . . . Above all he is struck with the inherent sufficingness of things." Bury clearly perceives what Spencer and his school apparently fail to see, that evolutionism admits of either pessimism or optimism, but "in an age of prosperity and self-complacency the affirmative answer was readily received, and the term evolution attracted to itself in common speech the implications of value which belong to progress."

A second phase of the modern thought movement has witnessed an alternate expansion and contraction in the *scope* accorded to our notions of social progress. Following the Revival of Learning the incipient moderns first succeeded, after "a literary war a hundred years long," as Bury phrases it, in believing that their own artistic powers were equal to those of the ancient Greeks and Romans. This led to a conception of progress along *intellectual* lines exclusively. Gradually this expanded into a vision of *social* welfare in general. But even when thus enriched in content its extent was still narrow —wider, to be sure, than the Greek conception of the city-state, but for a long time limited to the world then enlightened by Roman civilization. Nevertheless such thinkers as Bodin, Fontenelle, Condorcet, and Kant caught glimpses of international and even world progress.

After the Fall of Rome the Empire shattered into feudalistic particularism and provincialism. Then after long centuries of social confusion the great national states—England first, then France, Germany, Italy and the rest in order,—arose, and the nationalistic provincialism of the present era was born. Group selfishness in this nationalistic form has become the real religion, vastly more binding than their professed Christian faith, of the vast majority among modern populations, and now, only after the catastrophe of 1914, the nations are groping to recover their recent and too quickly dimmed vision of a more inclusive ideal of human welfare and world progress, so ably championed by President Wilson.

A third current characteristic of modern thinking on social progress began in the Seventeenth Century with Le Roy, Malebranche and others, including the entire school of French Encyclopedists. Its teaching may be called the *optimism* of progress. It is essentially emotional and sentimental, and is based, not upon a cool induction from adequate and well-scrutinized facts or even a logically sound inference from accepted premises, but upon three square meals a day, along with the other assured securities, comforts, and luxuries of a social era based upon a "pleasure economy" rather than a "pain economy." It is essentially the rosy philosophy of a good digestion and of satisfaction with one's own achievements, or those of his group, bulking large in the more or less subconscious background. Perhaps Bury is right in thinking that this materialistic optimism of progress began with Prince Albert of England, who, in 1855, had the principal hand in staging the first International Exposition. There the various improvements of recent decades, particularly along scientific, artistic and mechanical lines, were most impressively displayed. The resulting ocular demonstration was taken at the time as the final overthrow of those thinkers who bewailed the waning powers of nature, the degeneration of mankind, and the alleged consequent stagnation of the world. At the same stroke there entered in the shallow modern notion that progress consists "in more things," a distinctly modern puerilism which has been so trenchantly ridiculed by Mrs. John Martin, in her brilliant book, *Is Mankind Advancing?*

On the other hand, among the better tendencies developed by the more modern philosophy of progress, should be mentioned one of the utmost significance for the clarification of this problem. That is the tendency to distinguish three distinct factors in social evolution, namely Physical Environment, Racial Factors, and Culture. Most thinkers, from Montesquieu and others even earlier, have, to be sure, distinguished environment from the human factor, but their analysis was incomplete and ineffective. This was due to their failure to subdivide the human factor into the biological or racial, on the one hand, and the truly social or cultural elements on the other. So recent is this potent distinction that not only the unschooled masses, but also most biologists and psychologists, many of them making considerable pretension to authority on social questions, have thus far failed to sense the real existence and profound significance of *culture,* or, if preferred, of the social heritage, as distinguished from organic heredity. For example, the essential fallacy of most "eugenicists," a fallacy now slowly becoming recognized, lies in the fact that they start out to talk about social problems and proceed to discourse about biological facts connected only remotely, if at all, with the subject in hand. Nowhere is this more true than in the consideration of social progress. The discovery, by contemporary ethnologists and sociologists, of the importance of folkways, *mores,* social attitudes, social values, and culture in general, is of the utmost significance for the solution of this mystery of human improvement. The bare assertion must suffice for the present, leaving its elaboration and application to succeeding chapters.

The explanation just given of the idea of Progress as a distinctive Western notion, stood thus apparently complete in historical terms, until Professor Oswald Spengler's analysis of Western culture appeared.* His masterly, but somewhat baffling, argument makes it appear at least plausible that this limitation of the idea of progress to the modern West is a consequence of a more basic factor than had been previously adduced. This is the apparent fact that the peoples (or as Spengler would say, the "cultures") of classic Greece, and of the Orient both then and now, *have not been able to conceive the notion of progress at all because they lack a comprehensive sense of time.* Spengler argues that it is only the Western mind that stresses history, change, and progress. The others live in an *eternal present,* with no feeling for duration, evolution, or *becoming* in any sense. The evidence adduced in support of this startling assertion is more or less familiar in detail, and its

combined weight strongly supports the conclusion that "we men of the Western culture are, with our historical sense, an exception and not a rule. World-history is our world picture and not all mankind's. Indian and Classical man formed no image of a world in progress, and perhaps when in due course the civilization of the West is extinguished, there will never again be a culture and a human type in which world-history is so potent a form of the waking consciousness." †

The evidence referred to, which we have not been accustomed to see set in all the significance of its togetherness, shows further that the classical mind was as unfamiliar with our notion of empty and limitless Space as it was with that of a constantly flowing and endless Time. As for the last named, the Greeks had no clocks or other mechanical devices designed to mark with monotonous rhythm the never-ceasing time-flow. In Germany about the century of the Crusades the chiming wheel-clock and tower-clocks made their first appearance. Again, classical music was devoid of counter-point, according to Spengler, and classical mathematics was purely static, being without the *time*-element whose introduction produced the Western mathematics of "fluxions," i.e. calculus, and of the fourth dimension. He might have added even more emphatically that the time factor seems to have been largely responsible for the very recent retreat of the old Euclidean geometry before the relativity mathematics of Einstein, although, to be sure, the time of mathematics and of natural science is not the real time of experience, but a *form of the space concept, pure science being both timeless and dateless.*

In practical affairs of State the same lack of a strong time-feeling limited both the works undertaken and the materials of their execution. Says Spengler: "In Classical cities nothing suggested duration, or old times or times to come—there was no pious preserva-

* Oswald Spengler, *The Decline of the West,* Alfred A. Knopf, New York, 1926, translated from the German by Charles Francis Atkinson.
† *Ibid.,* p. 15.

tion of ruins, no work conceived for the benefit of future generations; in them we do not find that durable material was deliberately chosen." * With the example of Mycenaean and Egyptian stonework before him, the Dorian Greek, we read, ignored that technique and built with wood or clay. So much for the fleeting materials; as for the undertakings themselves, "No (Greek) city ever made it its business to drain or to afforest a district, or to introduce advanced cultivation methods or new kinds of live stock or new plants . . . one let the future come, one did not attempt to work upon it." † In short, whether in literature, art, politics, or philosophy, *the Classical Greeks lived solely in the present*.

The Classical conception of *Space* is less directly, but nevertheless vitally, connected with the Greek inability to grasp the concept of progress, for, as already shown, the idea itself has expanded in its geographical scope as well as its content. Professor Spengler maintains that the notion of space, as we conceive it, was simply not known to the mathematics and physics of the classical world. Their language possessed no word to express it. That "eternal problem" of the nature of abstract space, which Kant tackled with such passionate interest "in the name of humanity," we suddenly find, says Spengler, "is a *purely Western* problem that simply does not arise in the intellects of other Cultures." ‡ The Greek's world was everywhere occupied, complete in outline, and he could not conceive of purely empty space as even theoretically existent.

It is a commonplace that the Greeks held the circle to be the most perfect figure, because it is perfectly symmetrical and fully enclosed. Smugly enclosed was their human world also, surrounded by the enclosing spheres of air and sky, and the fatherland itself, as Spengler puts it, was bounded by the encircling horizon visible from the citadel of one's native city. That definitely limited geographical area nevertheless gave plenty of room for the social idealism of those children of the pure present (an idealism perfectly embodied, according to Spengler, in the sensuous completeness of their statuary, architecture, and drama) who simply had no inkling of our Western vision of an ideal social order evolving through a far perspective in time, and expanding to embrace a vast concourse of peoples and nations in the wide worldspaces.

The same limitations mark the life of India. "The Indians have no sort of time-reckoning (the absence of it in their case expressing their Nirvana) and no clocks, and *therefore no history, no life memories, no care*. What the conspicuously historical West calls 'Indian history' achieved itself without the smallest consciousness of what it was doing." § While Indian philosophies and cults stress extraordinarily the idea of the "evolution" of the individual ego, it is always just that—purely individualistic, never social and organic. As the experience of the present writer itself testifies, the merest tyro in the study of Indian Brahmanic literature is quickly impressed with its essentially non-historical character, a deficiency, if such it may be called, supplied in part, but only in part, by Buddhism, as a later and more socially aggressive movement, and also one richer in historical personages and events.

Against these two great static Cultures that of the West, with its limitless Space, endlessly flowing Time, and forward-marching Progress, stands in profound and striking contrast. But along with us stand the Chinese, with their ancient traditional classics, their ancestor worship, showing their overweening sense of the Past, and the Egyptians with their intense feeling for the Future, expressing itself in their colossal, Time-resisting architecture and their pathetic mummification of the dead, which their concern for the

* *Ibid.*, p. 132.
† *Ibid.*, p. 138.
‡ *Ibid.*, p. 176.
§ *Ibid.*, p. 133.

Future drove them to develop upon such an astonishing scale.

When two out of four of the great civilizations of antiquity stand thus at the intellectual antipodes of our Progress-concept and its deepest logical implications, we need not marvel longer at the unprogressiveness of the so-called "savage." As Spengler puts it forcibly: "For primitive man the word 'time' can have no meaning. He simply lives, without any necessity of specifying an opposition to something else. He *has* time, but he knows nothing of it." * And if he can see no meaning in Time, he can probably find nothing significant in our Occidental notion of Progress, which is inextricably tied up with the Time process itself.

The word "process," on its part, raises a very difficult question concerning its meaning in sociology and in history, but that must be postponed to a later chapter. Just here one needs only to add that we do not assume that Spengler has given a perfectly exact picture of Greek Classical thought on these matters. His portrait is done in high colors, by way of contrasting the two periods, and doubtless suffers to some extent from overemphasis. Yet it carries conviction when one reads the evidence on his heavily weighted pages, despite the fact that another competent student of the subject has averred that these same Greeks developed a method of explaining natural phenomena that was essentially historical, namely the *genealogical*. Thus Professor Teggart says that when faced with any phenomenon, the early Greek Philosophers were accustomed to ask two questions: "Of what elements is it composed?" and "How did it originate?" † The latter involves history, and, obviously, an account of things in terms of Time. The *genealogy* involves the three elements of (1) a present person; (2) a series of ancestors; (3) a first source. This pattern the Greeks generalized into the "genealogical method," which "was cap-

able of wide extension, and could be applied to other than human or even animal relationships. Hesiod's Theogony is a genealogy of heaven and earth, and all that in them is. According to Aeschylus, gain is bred from gain, slaughter from slaughter, woe from woe. . . . The ascending lines of ancestry were followed up until they led to a common father of all; every series of outrages was traced through successive reprisals back to an initial crime; and more generally every event was affiliated to a preceding event, until the whole chain had been attached to an ultimate self-existing cause." ‡ Teggart goes on to say, "In the hands of the earlier Greeks, then, the genealogical method provided a form into which could be fitted an explanation either of a situation in the affairs of men or of a condition of things in the world of nature."

But in affirming its application to conditions in "the world of nature" he confirms the suspicion already arising as one reads, namely, that after all it is not really a historical method in the true sense of portraying unique irreversible events in the real Time (duration) of a living being or group of such beings, but simply an abstract logical chain of antecedents and consequences, aimed at a *causal* series in the world of nature, a series reversible in direction, and dealing in a statically mathematical way with "dead" things in space. The suspicion becomes conviction when Professor Teggart argues, on a later page, that "a theory of development appears, in Aristotle's writings, only in connection with his discussion of social organization, of science, and of art. Here, however, we find the recognition of an ascent from lower to higher forms, a progress gradually realized in the course of time." This to be sure seems the very concept that we have found lacking among the Greeks, but the next sentences, which he quotes from Gomperz's *Greek Thinkers*, spoil the whole thing: "This movement he [i.e. Aristotle] thought has already

---

* *Ibid.*, p. 122.

† *Cf.* Frederick J. Teggart, *Theory of History*, New Haven, 1925, chap. 8, "The Idea of Progress and the Foundations of the Comparative Method."

‡ *Ibid.*, quoting Benn.

reached its goal times without number, and has as often been compelled to ebb back to its starting-point. For secular catastrophes, repeated with immeasurable frequency, have laid the earth waste, destroyed the race of mankind down to a small remnant, and then allowed that race to rise anew and enter upon and retravel its ascending path of civilization again and again." "Clearly, then," concludes Teggart, "Aristotle held the view that human advancement goes through a determined, or natural, series of steps in successive 'cycles.' " * If so, Aristotle by the same token did *not* entertain the modern concept of Progress, which indicates an essentially historical, irreversible, unique process, which could never repeat itself—in a word what Spengler calls a Destiny. As an organic whole it probably includes minor processes of the repetitional type. . . .

Quite different from the approaches of Bury and Case is that taken by Wilson D. Wallis in his analysis of culture development and progress. Although he refers to theorists of historical importance, he is more interested in dealing with culture objectively and places emphasis on the following criteria: (1) culture development as increase in complexity, (2) culture development as increase in power, (3) the trend of culture development. He considers unconscious motivation which may promote culture development. Among the present-day effects of cultural development Wallis refers to specialization, friction, and integration, all of which have complex social implications.

18

CULTURE DEVELOPMENT AND PROGRESS†

Wilson D. Wallis

I. CULTURE DEVELOPMENT AS INCREASE IN COMPLEXITY

Thomas Aquinas interprets development as proceeding from simple to complex. He says,

It is the way of nature to proceed from the simple to the complex, for we find invariably in the workings of nature that the most complex is the perfection, completion, and end of the others, as is clear in every whole in respect to its parts. The mind of man, therefore, in its artistry must no less proceed from the simple to the complex as from the imperfect to the perfect.‡

Lamarck defines organic evolution as increase in complexity, and Herbert Spencer

---

* *Ibid.*, pp. 79–80.
† Reprinted by permission from W. D. Wallis, *Culture and Progress,* McGraw-Hill Book Company, Inc., New York, Copyright 1930, pp. 200–206.
‡ Thomas Aquinas, "Commentary on the Politics of Aristotle."

applies this principle to organic and social life. Its implications, however, have been grasped by many earlier writers. Compared with the Bronze and Iron ages, Hesiod's Gold and Silver ages are periods of simplicity and tranquility. Plato appeals to the principle of simplicity when he traces the origin of society to an economic stage in which each man was his own artisan for all the needs of life, before specialization led to trade, markets, and the internationalism evoked by increasing economic, social, and political complexity. Aristotle appeals to the principle of simple to complex when he interprets social evolution as development from the family to groups of families, and to village communities. The principle is accepted by Lucretius, who finds primitive social life devoid of the complexities which accompany civilization, and the concept is implicit in seventeenth and eighteenth-century philosophers who attribute the origin of society to contract. Archeology confirms the view that evolution proceeds from simple to complex. The social life of prehistoric man is not known but stone and metal implements reveal part of the story of his industrial development. The first of these stages, the eolithic, is characterized by simple forms of implements which scarcely vary in type except as accident would account for the variation. In the Early Paleolithic period the types are more numerous. During the passing of thousands of years the types of implements increase and the techniques improve. In the Late Paleolithic period the types are more clearly demarked and are more numerous. From Paleolithic through Neolithic, the Bronze age, the Iron age, to the latest phases of the present industrial age, there is increasing complexity. The unprecedented developments of the last century, the century of the engine and of electricity, have been accompanied by an increase in complexity, which is now so great that no one can master more than a small portion of the industrial field. "A wagon hath a hundred pieces (of wood)," says Hesiod,* with pride, of his agricultural

* Hesiod, "Works and Days," line 456.

Bronze-Iron age; he would have received with incredulity the information that a future civilization would make with ten thousand pieces, mainly of a harder metal than he knew, a self-propelling wagon which could outspeed and outdistance the swiftest birds.

Men make progress whether they will or not, says Spencer, for the cosmic process from undifferentiated homogeneity to differentiated heterogeneity goes on, and this is progress. Yet Spencer lived a simple life. He saw a complex world, but kept aloof from most of its entanglements. His statement of the principle is simple rather than complex, and it is not highly differentiated. With a simple pen he wrote his simple English, and he probably did not desire multiple differentiated hands, one for each letter of the alphabet. This biped of simple bilateral symmetry did not complain because his locomotion was much less differentiated than that of the crab or the lobster. He did not deplore the fact that man shows no tendency to develop into a centipede, a hydra, or a Janus, or to acquire as many stomachs as a camel.

As a matter of fact, development is not always from simple to complex. The devices of travel, for example, have become more complex, but traveling is simpler. The traveler takes more baggage than formerly, but conveying it is simpler than it used to be. If complexity has value it is because it simplifies the goals or the methods of reaching them, and facilitates the accomplishment of a purpose, or stimulates new purposes which afford more or deeper satisfactions. The superiority of the implements of the Upper Paleolithic over those of the Eolithic and the Lower Paleolithic lies in their greater efficiency. Bronze marks an advance over stone, iron over bronze, and steel over iron, because each new material is more efficient than the old. With these more efficient devices man attains power. Our industries are superior to those of fishers and hunters, pastoral peoples, and primitive agriculturists, because our devices are more efficient servants.

2. CULTURE DEVELOPMENT AS INCREASE IN POWER

Though development may bring greater complexity, the complexity is the form rather than the content, the body rather than the spirit of development. Development is the process by which latent powers reach fruition. To become an adult the child must develop from few and weak functions to many and vigorous ones. But the complexity of the adult organism does not constitute adulthood, it is merely accessory to it; and even though the organism becomes more complex, if latent powers do not function there is no progress. Complexity is a handicap if society flounders in the increasing number of phases in which it is involved or which it has evolved. No especial significance attaches to the fact that Paleolithic man evolves new types of implements. The significance lies in the fact that he makes types of implements better adapted to his purposes. Neolithic shows advance over Paleolithic man, not because the former has more implements and more activities, but because he acquires power. Ceramics, agriculture, and domestication, which come in the Neolithic period, are new sources of power. The value of complexity in culture must be judged by a like test. Civilization is not superior to primitive culture because it is more complex; its complexity is an attribute, not the essence of its superiority; it is superior in spite of its complexity. In early stages, when the economic order has not become specialized and the activities and interests of one are those of all, there is little complexity in the culture. But when specialization is under way there must be new adjustments if all demands are to be satisfied.

Increase in devices and growth in specialization enhance the power to attain objectives. To preserve these means of power new forms of social organization come into existence, and social life grows more complex. Each new trait increases the potential power of the culture. Social purposes can find more channels for expression, and new demands can be satisfied. Yet increasing complexity does not, in itself, constitute advance; it may be the outer garment of development, or the means to an end, but it is not the goal. Indeed, in many phases of social life development is from complex to simple, and to good purpose. Usually the marriage regulations in tribal culture are more complex than those in advanced civilizations, and frequently personal relationships are more involved—though this is not equivalent to more evolved. The elaborate ceremonialism of feudalism disappears when social life rests on other foundations and men have a different appreciation of position and personality. With intellectual development language grows simpler in form and in structure, for linguistic complexity is a handicap rather than an advantage. In actual vocabulary there is increase, because there is need for new words to denote new things, new relations, and new concepts. Improvement, however, does not lie in the greater complexity of language but in its more apt and effectual service. If culture develops greater complexity, this is not because men so desire, but because in their endeavor to realize their purposes they utilize many agencies. Though the phases of culture increase, we seek to simplify the culture and the scope and aim of life; our motto might be, "Seek simplicity and distrust it." Complexity is a mathematical concept and cannot measure values. Civilized man possesses power undreamed of by the savage. Life is power, civilization is socialized power, and the absence of power is death and decay. Progress, therefore, implies increase in power.

3. THE TREND OF CULTURE DEVELOPMENT

The evidence for the earliest stages of man's advance consists of those material objects which have resisted the disintegrations of time. The first implements are crude, for Eolithic man is little superior to the beasts save in the ability to select from nature the useful sticks and stones. Yet this selective ability makes him a tool-using animal, and the tool-using animal develops into a tool-making animal—*homo faber*. We know something of the development of tool making through many thousand years, far back into the Pleistocene era. Progress is slow but there is improvement in stone implements from the dawn of human history to the development of a metal civilization, when man learns to hammer copper, to mold bronze, to smelt iron and fashion out of it implements which enhance his power. Throughout these long periods of time he is continually specializing, in response to developing needs, providing himself with implements better adapted to his demands, though in turn increasing his wants. Development is conditioned by the culture already attained, and there is an intimate relation between the arts of one period and those of preceding and subsequent periods. Though there are stages of accelerated improvement, the rapidity of which is a measure of the growth in interdependence and specialization, there is no break in continuity. One stage of culture does not so much give place to a later one as develop into it, and much that was of value in the past is preserved in the ensuing stage. New stone implements supplement the old; bronze and iron supplement paleoliths and neoliths and only gradually and partially supplant them. Man grows stronger by augmenting his resources, carving out a new career by expanding the old one. There is continuity in development, for achievement is conditioned by previous accomplishments, and the past and the present contain the stimuli for the future. "Every fresh addition to knowledge opens out new vistas of previously unsuspected problems. We may be certain that when more is known of the Lower Paleolithic, its history will be found to be full of complexities of which we have as yet no conception." * This observation applies to every phase of culture. Certain stages of development must precede certain others. The wheel must come before the wheeled vehicle;

simpler types of watercraft must precede the sailboat; long voyages presuppose large vessels equipped with oars or with sails. Similarly,

> . . . a discovery in medicine is not only limited by the status of the knowledge in medicine, but it is dependent upon the existing knowledge in other fields . . . An analysis of any phase of medicine at any period of its history will reveal a . . . dependence upon, and limitation by, the existing knowledge in other fields.†

Man is not merely a conservative but a conserving animal as well, and seldom puts aside devices which have been tried and found useful. The civilization of which they are a part may be swept away and these things be lost to the world for all time or until they are rediscovered, but seldom have the useful arts, once adopted, been given up deliberately. A people who have developed metallurgy do not abandon it and revert to stone culture; a people who have evolved writing do not forget it. There are exceptions, but taking human history in its entirety, so far at least as mechanical devices are concerned, man not merely learns but remembers the lessons of useful experience. In the realm of social experience this, alas, is less often the case; social advantages, unlike material advantages, are not objectified, and seldom are they obvious to those who share them.

4. UNCONSCIOUS MOTIVES MAY PROMOTE CULTURE DEVELOPMENT

Usually the forces which stimulate culture development are not understood by those who respond to them. The motive of self-preservation may be exhibited by the group, whereas the individual who rises to the occasion may be ignorant of the more fundamental motives which prompt his response, for he is inclined to interpret the significance

* R. A. S. Macalister, *A Text-book of European Archæology*, Cambridge, 1921, p. 348.
† Bernhard J. Stern, *Social Factors in Medical Progress*, Columbia University Press, New York, 1927, pp. 106–107.

of events according as they serve or thwart his purposes. Hence he thinks that he freely fights for defense of country, rather than is subtly impelled by social influences. Influences external to the individual do not interest him until they are incorporated in his conscious motives. He then is interested in the fact that they are his motives; and their externality appears to him largely accidental. Culture development is largely a matter of knowing how rather than knowing about, and the group may act intelligently even when but vaguely aware of the circumstances which motivate it. It stumbles along its path, maintaining an acquired momentum, seeking points of least resistance, but guided by no charted course or compass. Although members of the group are only dimly conscious of their path and of their purpose, and culture development consists more in knowing how than in knowing about, the latter plays a larger part in human history when man understands himself both as individual and as a carrier of culture. For to know about is incipiently to know how; and such knowledge, if not the open door to progress, is at least the key which will unlock the door, the open sesame if there is one.

5. SPECIALIZATION, FRICTION, AND INTEGRATION

Many phases of civilization seem like,

A tale told by an idiot,
Full of sound and fury—signifying nothing.

The story of civilization leaves one guessing at the *motif* and wondering whether it embodies a rational plot. Scientific knowledge forges ahead but develops conditions, such as those exhibited in the industrial stage, which are worse than those of previous decades. Poison gas and high explosives give greater power for evil than had hitherto been achieved. Advance brings specialization, and specialization causes frictions which in turn necessitate a new integration of old forces. Then come further specialization, new fric-

tions, and a new integration to solve the new problems. It is a never-ending series of mistakes and corrections followed by further mistakes. Whether the spectacle arouses optimism or pessimism depends upon the part of the circle which arrests attention; but attention should not be limited to any one of these phases, for each one of them is consequent upon the others. Specialization develops new power and also new potential evil; the clash of powers leads to antagonisms, the friction which puts the brake on progress. Integration releases the brake by a redistribution of power, and a focusing upon new ends recognized as common. At this point man raises the question of the value of his culture and of the reality of progress. Social forces play a relatively independent part, though they may conflict with the economic régime at many points. With every thrust into new fields new conflicts arise, for a phase of culture developed to the full may impede the development of other phases unless there is deliberate and determined effort to prevent this result. Development of economic power, for example, may occasion conflicts with other phases of culture, and necessitate readjustments. The gregariousness which protects the individual when social development is feeble may later become a tyrant. There arise problems of adjustment of individual demand to social demand, and of class to class. Indeed, in civilization, the individual, once the center of his world, as man was once the center of the universe, now seems precariously on the periphery. Man controls nature but not human nature. Satisfaction of demands at one point leaves them unsatisfied at others, and while man makes gains along some lines he loses ground at others. To attain power he must attend to one thing at a time, but to retain power he must attend to all the means of salvation, for they are interdependent; and, apparently, he "cannot focus all good things at the same time." * A way out of this dilemma he has not found; and not until he finds it will development be equivalent to progress. As man attains a fuller

* Herbert G. Wells, *A Modern Utopia*, New York, pp. 233, 235.

knowledge of his world it becomes larger in meanings as well as in spatial dimension. Copernicus, Giordano Bruno, Galileo give him a new knowledge of the universe and of his position in it, as Darwin, Wallace, Huxley give him a new realization of his place in the animal kingdom. History, anthropology, prehistoric archeology pave the way to a new conception of the place of contemporary life in the larger scheme of human culture. Man can no longer be content to see the world in relation to himself, he must also see himself in relation to the world of which he is a part. Only through awareness of the forces with which he deals can he learn to command.

Without the truth there is no knowing,
Without the way there is no going.*

Only when man learns the course of culture development can he control it. He cannot wisely deflect a tendency until he wisely detects it.

The will to learn bringeth of learning
  growth;
Learning makes insight grow, and by insight
We know the Good; known Good brings
  bliss along.

In many respects man seems the victim rather than the hero of the drama of culture change. The progress of Western civilization has brought not only modern science and internationalism but also a World War. The Industrial Revolution brought comforts to many and misery to more. Man has acquired power, but meanwhile many lives and many goods have been snuffed out. New values have been gained, but old ones have been lost; and we are not yet able to assess the results.

Progress is a modern concept. We know that the Greeks and Romans characteristically were hostile or apathetic to the idea of progress; Durant, in his attempt to answer the question, Is Progress a Delusion? searches anew for explanations or causes of such attitudes. Durant states that the notion of progress found its first definite expression in the optimism of the eighteenth century, as revealed in the works of Turgot, Condorcet, Comte, and Buckle. But apparently there is a case against progress, as there are always inconsistencies and hindrances, and there are differences between physical and moral progress. This selection from Durant's voluminous writings is interesting from another standpoint, that of considering history's bold outlines of cultural development as a way of revealing the meaning of the concept progress. Man's achievements may thus be arranged in sequence as follows: speech, fire, conquest of the animals, agriculture, social organization, morality, tools, science, education, and writing and print. Would such a scheme of cultural development prove that progress is real?

* Thomas a Kempis, *Imitation of Christ.*

19

IS PROGRESS A DELUSION?*
Will Durant

I. THE YOUTH OF PROGRESS

The Greeks, who seem, in the enchantment of distance, to have progressed more rapidly than any other people in history, have left us hardly any discussion of progress in all their varied literature. There is a fine passage in Æschylus (*Prometheus,* 451–515), where Prometheus tells how his discovery of fire brought civilization to mankind, and gives in fifty lines such a summary of the stages in cultural development as would be considered immorally modern in certain American states. And there is a fleeting reference to progress in Euripides (*Supplices,* 201–18). But there is no mention of the idea in Xenophon's Socrates, nor in Plato; and Aristotle's cold conservatism puts the notion implicitly out of court. The Greeks conceived history, for the most part, as a vicious circle; and the conclusion of the Stagyrite, that all arts and sciences had been invented and lost "an infinite number of times," strikes the note of classical opinion on the subject from Thales to Marcus Aurelius. The Stoics counseled men to expect nothing of the future. Even the Epicureans took their pleasures sadly, and seem to have felt, like Mr. Bradley, that this is "the best of all possible worlds, and everything in it is a necessary evil." Hegesias the Cyrenaic pronounced life worthless, and advocated suicide; doubtless he lived as long as Schopenhauer.

Pessimism was to be expected in an Athens that had lost its freedom; but the same despair sounds in Latin letters at every stage of Roman history. Lucretius speaks of men *pedetentim progredientes*—progressing step by step; and yet he gives a brutally brief answer to the question of our chapter when he says, *Eadem omnia semper*—all things are always the same. Would the great poet and philosopher, if he could return to us, use the same word to describe our contemporary civilization? Surely he would be impressed by our immense multiplication of mechanisms and instrumentalities for the achievement of every desire; but probably he would ask, in his unhappy way, whether the men and women who use these magnificent machines are finer human beings, mentally, physically or morally, than those unfortunate ancestors who had to use their legs. He would be interested to know that a young wife had killed her husband with a sashweight, and he would be driven to concede that mankind had taken many centuries to discover the admirable utility of sashweights in this regard. Inevitably, however, he would suggest that this was a difference of means and not of ends—that the business of killing husbands was a very ancient industry. *Plus ça change, plus c'est la même chose.* What if all our progress is an improvement in methods, but not in purposes?

The other Romans are worse than Lucretius; they not only doubt the future, but they praise the past. Horace is a *laudator temporis acti;* Tacitus and Juvenal deplore the degeneracy of their age; and Virgil turns from pleasant fancies of a new Saturnian glory to phrase with his melodious felicity the gloomy vision of an Eternal Recurrence, a perpetual cycle and aimless repetition of identical events.

> *Alter erit tyum Tiphys, et altera quæ*
>   *vehat Argo*
> *Delectos heroas; erunt etiam altera bella,*
> *Atque iterum ad Trojam magnus mitte-*
>   *tur Achilles—*

"there will be another Tiphys" (an ancient prophet) "and another Argo to carry beloved heroes; there will be also other wars, and great Achilles will again be sent to Troy." * The hour-glass of æons will turn over and pour out the unaltered past into an empty and delusively novel present. There is nothing new under the sun; all is vanity and a chasing after the wind. And Marcus Aurelius, after achieving almost the highest form of human existence—the union of statesman and philosopher in one man, writes:

> The rational soul wanders around the whole world and through the encompassing void, and gazes into infinity, and considers the periodic destructions and rebirths of the universe, and reflects that our posterity will see nothing new, and that our ancestors saw nothing greater than we have seen. A man of forty years, possessing the most moderate intelligence, may be said to have seen all that is past and all that is to come; so uniform is the world.†

What were the causes of the hostility or apathy of the Greeks to the idea of progress? Was it due, as Professor Bury thinks, to the brevity of their historical experience, the very rapidity with which their civilization reached its apex and sank again? Or was it due to their comparative poverty in written records

of the past, and a consequent absence of the perspective that might have made them realize the measure of their own advance? They too had had a medieval era, and had climbed for a thousand years from barbarism to philosophy; but only towards the end of that ascent had writing graduated from bills of lading to the forms of literature. Parchment was too costly to be wasted on mere history. Or again, was this unconcern with progress due to the arrested development of Greek industry, the failure of the Greeks to move appreciably beyond the technology of Crete, or to produce in quantity those physical comforts that are at the basis of the modern belief in progress?

In the Middle Ages it was a like dearth of luxuries that kept the notion of progress in abeyance, while the hope of heaven became the center of existence. Belief in another world seems to vary directly with poverty in this one, often in the individual, always in the group. When wealth grows, heaven falls out of focus, and becomes thin and meaningless. But for a thousand years the thought of it dominated the minds of men.

Wealth came to Western Europe with the Renaissance and the Industrial Revolution; and as it multiplied, it displaced the hope of heaven with the lure of progress. That greatest single event in modern history—the Copernican revelation of the astronomic unimportance of the earth—made many tender souls unhappy; but its reduction of heaven to mere sky and space compelled the resilient spirit of man to form for itself a compensatory faith in an earthly paradise. Campanella, More and Bacon wrote Utopias, and announced the imminence of universal happiness. Europe, *nouveau riche,* imported luxuries, and exported ascetics and saints. Trade made cities, cities made universities, universities made science, science made industry, and industry made progress. Gargantua writes to Pantagruel: "All the world is full of

---

* Fourth Eclogue, quoted by J. B. Bury, *The Idea of Progress,* p. 12.
† Bury, *op. cit.,* p. 13.

savants, learned teachers, vast libraries." "In one century," says Pierre de la Ramée, meaning 1450–1550, "we have seen a greater progress in men and works of learning than our ancestors had seen in the whole course of the previous fourteen centuries." This has an ironically contemporary sound; what century has not crowned itself with some spacious estimate of this kind? But such self-confidence was the key-note of the Renaissance: we hear it as an organ-point in every line of Francis Bacon, striking the dominant chord of the European as against the Asiatic soul; obviously the conception of progress is for industrial and secular civilization what the hope of heaven was for medieval Christendom. The dearest dogmas of the modern mind, the *crura cerebri* of all our social philosophy, are the beliefs in progress and democracy. If both of these ideas must be abandoned we shall be left intellectually naked and ridiculous beyond any generation in history.

II. PROGRESS IN EXCELSIS

The notion of progress found its first definite expression in the exuberant optimism of the eighteenth century. Rousseau was out of key, and preferred American savages, whom he had not seen, to the cruel Parisians who had rasped his nerves; he thought thinking a form of degeneracy, and preached a Golden Age of the past that echoed the Garden of Eden and the Fall of Man. But when we come to the irrepressible and undiscourageable Voltaire we catch at first breath the exhilarating air of the Enlightenment. This *"Grand Seigneur* of the mind" had no delusions about Indians; he knew that man was better off under civilization than under savagery. He was grateful for the slow and imperfect taming of the human brute, and he preferred Paris to the Garden of Eden.

It was his disciple Turgot and Condorcet who made the idea of progress the moving spirit of modern times. In the year 1793 a French aristocrat by the name of Condorcet (or, to do him full justice, Marie Jean An-

toine Nicolas Caritat, Marquis de Condorcet) was hiding from the guillotine in a little *pension* on the outskirts of Paris. The incorruptible Robespierre, that consistently savage Rousseauian, had invited him to come and be abbreviated because, like Tom Paine, he had voted against the execution of the King. There in a lonely room, far from any friend, without a book to help him, and in a situation that might have warranted a pæan to pessimism and despair, Condorcet wrote the most optimistic book that has ever come from the hand of man, the great classic in the literature of progress—*Esquisse d'un tableau des progrès de l'esprit humain.* Having finished this magnanimous prophecy of the coming glory of mankind, Condorcet fled from Paris to a distant village inn; and there, thinking himself secure, he flung his tired body upon a bed, and fell asleep. When he awoke he was surrounded by *gendarmes,* who arrested him in the name of the Law. The next morning he was found dead on the floor of his cell in the village jail. He had always carried about with him a phial of poison to cheat the guillotine.

To read his book is to realize to what a bitterly disillusioned and sceptical generation we belong. Here was a man who had lost apparently everything, who had sacrificed privilege, position and wealth for the Revolution, who was now hunted to death by empowered barbarians, and who had to bear the culminating bitterness of seeing the Revolution, hope of the world, issue in chaos and terror; and yet his book represents the very zenith of man's hopefulness for man. Never before had men so believed in mankind—and perhaps never again since. What eloquence Condorcet pours forth, for example, on the subject of print! He is sure that it will redeem and liberate men; he has no premonition of the sensational press. "Nature," he writes, "has indissolubly united the advancement of knowledge with the progress of liberty, virtue, and respect for the natural rights of man." Prosperity will "dispose men to humanity, to benevolence, and to justice."

And then he formulates one of the most famous and characteristic doctrines of the Enlightenment: "No bounds have been fixed to the improvement of the human faculties; the perfectibility of man is absolutely indefinite; the progress of this perfection, henceforth above the control of every power that would impede it, has no other limit than the duration of the globe upon which nature has placed us."

And in conclusion he draws a tempting picture of the future—by which he means our time. As knowledge spreads, slavery will decrease, both among classes and among nations; "then will come the moment in which the sun will observe free nations only, acknowledging no other master than their reason; in which tyrants and slaves, priests and their stupid or hypocritical instruments, will no longer exist but in history and upon the stage." Science will double and treble the span of human life; woman will be emancipated from man, the worker from the employer, the subject from the king; perhaps, even, mankind will unlearn war. And he ends, passionately:

> How admirably calculated is this view of the human race to console the philosopher lamenting the errors, the flagrant acts of injustice, the crimes with which the earth is still polluted! It is the contemplation of this prospect that rewards him for all the efforts to assist the progress of reason and the establishment of liberty. He dares to regard these efforts as part of the eternal chain of the destiny of mankind; and in this persuasion he finds the true delight of virtue, the pleasure of having performed a durable service which no vicissitude will ever destroy. . . . This sentiment is the asylum into which he retires, and to which the memory of his persecutors cannot follow him; he unites himself in imagination with man restored to his rights, delivered from oppression, and proceeding with rapid strides in the path of happiness; he forgets his own misfortunes; . . . he lives no longer to adversity, calumny and malice, but becomes the associate of these wiser and more fortunate beings whose enviable condition he so earnestly contributed to produce.*

What generous optimism! What courageous idealism, and what passion for humanity! Shall we scorn more the naïve enthusiasm of Condorcet, or the intellectual cowardice of our time, which, having realized so many of his dreams, no longer dares to entertain the rest?

Behind this bright philosophy lay the Commercial and Industrial Revolutions. Here were marvels, called machines; they could produce the necessaries, and some of the luxuries, of life at unprecedented speed and in undreamed-of quantity; it was only a matter of time when all vital needs would be met, and poverty would disappear. Bentham and the elder Mill thought, about 1830, that England could now afford universal education for its people; and that with universal education all serious social problems would be solved by the end of the century. Comte saw all history as a progress in three stages, from theology through metaphysics to science. Buckle's *History of Civilization* (1857) stimulated the hope that the spread of knowledge would mitigate all human ills. Two years later Darwin spoke: the secularization of the modern mind was enormously advanced, and the idea of a coming Utopia replaced not merely Dante's filmy heaven but Rousseau's golden past. Spencer identified progress with evolution, and looked upon it as an inevitable thing. Meanwhile inventions poured from a thousand alert minds; riches visibly grew; nothing seemed hard or impossible to a science at last free from theological chains; the stars were weighed, and men accepted bravely the age-long challenge of the bird. What

* Jean-Jacques Rousseau, *A Sketch of the Progress of the Human Spirit,* English translation, p. 15.

could not man do? What could we not believe of him in those undoubting days before the War?

III. THE CASE AGAINST PROGRESS

Nevertheless, even in the midst of that mounting wealth and power, and that ever accelerated speed, which have characterized the civilization of the West, voices were raised to question the reality or the worth of progress. "At all times," said Machiavelli, at the height of the exuberant Renaissance, "the world of human beings has been the same, varying indeed from land to land, but always presenting the same aspect of some societies advancing towards prosperity, and others declining." * Fontenelle, in his *Dialogues of the Dead* (1683), pictured Socrates and Montaigne discussing the problem of progress, apparently in Hell, where all philosophers go. Socrates is anxious to hear of the advances that mankind has made since his fatal drinking bout; and he is chagrined to learn that men are still for the most part brutes. Montaigne assures him that the world has degenerated; there are no longer such powerful types as Pericles, Aristides, or Socrates himself. The old philosopher shrugs his shoulders. "In our days," he says, "we esteemed our ancestors more than they deserved; and now our posterity esteem us more than we deserve. There is really no difference between our ancestors, ourselves, and our posterity." And Fontenelle sums the matter up pithily: "The heart always the same, the intellect perfecting itself; passions, virtues, vices unaltered; knowledge increasing." †

"The development of humanity," said Eckermann, "seems to be a matter of thousands of years." "Who knows?" replied Goethe, "perhaps of millions. But let humanity last as long as it will, there will always be hindrances in its way, and all kinds of distress, to make it develop its powers. Men will become cleverer and more intelligent, but not better, nor happier, nor more effective in action, at least except for a limited

period. I see the time coming when God will take no pleasure in the race, and must again proceed to a rejuvenated creation." "The motto of history," said Schopenhauer, "should run, *Eadem, sed aliter*"—the same theme, with variations. Mankind does not progress, said Nietzsche, it does not even exist; or it is a vast physiological laboratory where a ruthless nature forever makes experiments; where some things in every age succeed, but most things fail. So concludes Romantic Germany.

Disraeli was one of the first to sense the difference between physical and moral progress, between increase in power and improvement in purposes. "The European talks of progress because by the aid of a few scientific discoveries he has established a society which has mistaken comfort for civilization." "Enlightened Europe is not happy. Its existence is a fever which it calls progress. Progress to what?" Ruskin, a rich man, questioned the identity of progress and wealth: were these wealthy shopkeepers and shippers better specimens of humanity than the Englishmen of Johnson's or Shakespeare's or Chaucer's days? Carlyle and Tolstoi acknowledged the enormous advance in man's means for achieving his ends; but of what use were these unprecedented powers if they had merely multiplied the ability of men to realize purposes as contradictory, as stupid, and as suicidal as ever before?

About 1890 Sir Arthur Balfour suggested, in his genial and devastating way, that human behavior and social organization are founded not on thought, which progresses, but on feeling and instinct, which hardly change from thousand years to thousand years; this, he believed, was the secret of our failure to transmute our growing knowledge into greater happiness or more lasting peace. Even the increase of knowledge may be part cause of the pessimism of our time. "He that increaseth knowledge increaseth sorrow," said Ecclesiastes. And his modern avatar confirms him: "In all the world," says Anatole France

---

* Bury, *op. cit.*, p. 31.
† Nordau, *Interpretation of History*, p. 286.

(if we may believe secretaries), "the unhappiest creature is man. It is said, 'Man is the lord of creation.' Man is the lord of suffering, my friend."

The socialist critique of modern industry did some damage to our faith in progress. The endeavor to make people vividly realize the injustices of the present took the form of idealizing the contentedness and tranquillity of the past. Ruskin, Carlyle, Morris and Kropotkin painted such pictures of the Middle Ages as made one long to be a serf bound to the soil and owing to some lord an aliquot portion of his produce and his wife. Meanwhile the liberal critique of modern politics, exposing corruption and incapacity in almost every office, made us doubt the divinity of democracy, which had been for a century our most sacred cow. The development of printing and the Hoe press resulted, apparently, in the debasement of the better minds rather than in the elevation of the worse; mediocrity triumphed in politics, in religion, in letters, even in science; Nordic anthropology and will-to-believe philosophy competed with barn-yard eugenics and Viennese psychology. Journalism took the place of literature; the "art" of the moving picture replaced the drama; photography drove painting from realism to cubism, futurism, *pointillisme* and other fatal convulsions; in Rodin sculpture ceased to carve, and began to paint; in the twentieth century music began to rival the delicacy of Chinese pots and pans.

It was the passing of art and the coming of war that shook the faith of our century in progress. The spread of industry and the decay of aristocracy coöperated in the deterioration of artistic form. When the artisan was superseded by the machine he took his skill with him; and when the machine, compelled to seek vast markets for its goods, adjusted its products to the needs and tastes of vast majorities, design and beauty gave place to standardization, quantity, and vulgarity. Had an aristocracy survived as a source of esthetic judgment trickling down among the people, it is conceivable that industry and art might have found some way

of living in peace. But democracy had to pay the price of popular sovereignty in art as well as in politics; the taste of innumerable average men became the guide of the manufacturer, the dramatist, the scenario-writer, the novelist, at last of the painter, the sculptor, and the architect: cost and size became the norm of value, and a bizarre novelty replaced beauty and workmanship as the goal of art. Artists, lacking the stimulation of an aristocratic taste formed through centuries of privileged culture, no longer sought perfection of conception and execution, but aimed at astonishing effects that might without doubt be called original. Painting became pathological, architecture halted its splendid development before the compulsion to build for a decade and not for centuries, music went down into the slums and the factories to find harmonies adapted to the nervous organization of elevated butchers and emancipated chambermaids. Sculpture decayed despite the growing unpopularity of clothing, and a million lessons in anatomy from every stage. But for automobiles and cosmetics, the twentieth century seemed to promise the total extinction of art.

Then the Great Madness came, and men discovered how precariously thin their coat of civilization was, how insecure their security, and how frail their freedom. War had decreased in frequency, and had increased in extent. Science, which was to be the midwife of progress, became the angel of death, killing with a precision and a rapidity that reduced the battles of the Middle Ages to the level of college athletics. Brave aviators dropped bombs upon women and children, and learned chemists explained the virtues of poison-gas. All the international amity built up by a century of translated literatures, co-operating scientists, commercial relationships, and financial interdependence, melted away, and Europe fell apart into a hundred hostile nationalities. When it was all over it appeared that the victors as well as the fallen had lost the things for which they had fought; that a greedy imperialism had merely passed from Potsdam to Paris; that violent dictatorships were replacing orderly and constitutional rule; that democracy was spreading and dead. Hope faded away; the generation that had lived through the War could no longer believe in anything; a wave of apathy and cynicism engulfed all but the least or the most experienced souls. The idea of progress seemed now to be one of the shallowest delusions that had ever mocked man's misery, or lifted him up to a vain idealism and a colossal futility.

IV. MINOR CONSIDERATIONS

"If you wish to converse with me," said Voltaire, "define your terms." What shall we mean by "progress"? Subjective definitions will not do; we must not conceive progress in terms of one nation, or one religion, or one code of morals; an increase of kindness, for example, would alarm our young Nietzscheans. Nor may we define progress in terms of happiness; for idiots are happier than geniuses, and those whom we most respect seek not happiness but greatness. Is it possible to find an objective definition for our term?—one that will hold for any individual, any group, even for any species? Let us provisionally define progress as increasing control of the environment by life; and let us mean by environment all the circumstances that condition the coördination and realization of desire. Progress is the domination of chaos by mind and purpose, of matter by form and will.

It need not be continuous in order to be real. There may be "plateaus" in it, Dark Ages and disheartening retrogressions; but if the last stage is the highest of all we shall say that man makes progress. And in assessing epochs and nations we must guard against loose thinking. We must not compare nations in their youth with nations in the mellowness of their cultural maturity; and we must not compare the worst or the best of one age with the selected best or worst of all the collected past. If we find that the type of genius prevalent in young countries like America and Australia tends to the executive, explorative, and scientific kind rather than to the painter of pictures or poems, the carver of statues or words, we shall understand that each age and place calls for and needs certain brands of genius rather than others, and that the cultural sort can only come when its practical predecessors have cleared the forest and prepared the way. If we find that civilizations come and go, and mortality is upon all the works of man, we shall confess the irrefutabilty of death, and be consoled if, during the day of our lives and our nations, we move slowly upward, and become a little better than we were. If we find that philosophers are of slighter stature now than in the days of broad-backed Plato and the substantial Socrates, that our sculptors are lesser men than Donatello or Angelo, our painters inferior to Velasquez, our poets and composers unnameable with Shelley and Bach, we shall not despair; these stars did not all shine on the same night. Our problem is whether the total and average level of human ability has increased, and stands at its peak today.

When we take a total view, and compare our modern existence, precarious and chaotic as it is, with the ignorance, superstition, brutality, cannibalism and diseases of primitive people, we are a little comforted: the lowest strata of our race may still differ only slightly from such men, but above those strata thousands and millions have reached to mental and moral heights inconceivable, presumably, to the early mind. Under the complex strain of city life we sometimes take imaginative refuge in the quiet simplicity of savage days; but in our less romantic moments we know that this is a flight-reaction from our actual tasks, that this idolatry of barbarism, like so many of our young opinions, is merely an impatient expression of adolescent maladaptation, part of the suffering involved in the contemporary retardation of individual maturity. A study of such savage tribes as survive shows their high rate of infantile mortality, their short tenure of life, their inferior speed, their inferior stamina, their inferior will, and their superior plagues. The friendly and flowing savage is like Nature—delightful but for the insects and the dirt.

The savage, however, might turn the argument around, and inquire how we enjoy our politics and our wars, and whether we think ourselves happier than the tribes whose weird names resound in the text-books of anthropology. The believer in progress will have to admit that we have made too many advances in the art of war, and that our politicians, with startling exceptions, would have adorned the Roman Forum in the days of Milo and Clodius,—though Mr. Coolidge was an appreciable improvement upon Nero. As to happiness, no man can say; it is an elusive angel, destroyed by detection and seldom amenable to measurement. Presumably it depends first upon health, secondly upon love, and thirdly upon wealth. As to wealth, we make such progress that it lies on the conscience of our intellectuals; as to love, we try to atone for our lack of depth by unprecedented inventiveness and variety. Our thousand fads of diet and drugs predispose us to the belief that we must be ridden with disease as compared with simpler men in simpler days; but this is a delusion. We think that where there are so many doctors there must be more sickness than before. But in truth we have not more ailments than in the past, but only more money; our wealth allows us to treat and cherish and master illnesses from which primitive men died without even knowing their Greek names.

There is one test of health—and therefore in part of happiness—which is objective and reliable: we find it in the mortality statistics of insurance companies, where inaccuracy is more expensive than in philosophy. In some cases these figures extend over three centuries. In Geneva, for example, they show an average length of life of twenty years in 1600, and of forty years in 1900. In the United States in 1920 the tenure of life of white people averaged fifty-three; and in 1926 it was fifty-six.* This is incredible if true. Nevertheless, similar reports come to us from Germany: the Federal Statistical Bureau of

Berlin tabulates the average length of life in Germany as twenty in 1520, thirty in 1750, forty in 1870, fifty in 1910, and sixty in 1920.† Taking the figures for granted, we may conclude, with the permission of the pessimist, that if life is a boon at all, we are making great strides in the quantity of it which we manage to maintain. Recently the morticians (*nés* undertakers) discussed in annual convention the dangers that threatened their profession from the increasing tardiness of men in keeping their appointments with death.‡ But if undertakers are miserable, progress is real.

V. THE OUTLINE OF HISTORY

Having made these admissions and modifications, let us try to see the problem of progress in a total view. It is unnecessary to refute the pessimist; it is only necessary to enclose his truth, if we can, in ours. When we look at history in the large we see it as a graph of rising and falling states—nations and cultures disappearing as on some gigantic film. But in that irregular movement of countries and that chaos of men, certain great moments stand out as the peaks and essence of human history, certain advances which, once made, were never lost. Step by step man has climbed from the savage to the scientist; and these are the stages of his growth.

First, Speech. Think of it not as a sudden achievement, nor as a gift from the gods, but as the slow development of articulate expression, through centuries of effort, from the mate-calls of animals to the lyric flights of poetry. Without words, or common nouns, that might give to particular images the ability to represent a class, generalization would have stopped in its beginnings, and reason would have stayed where we find it in the brute. Without words, philosophy and poetry, history and prose, would have been impossible, and thought could never have reached the subtlety of Einstein or Anatole

* I. Fisher, *National Vitality*, p. 624.
† New York *Times*, Sept. 7, 1928.
‡ Siegfried, *America Comes of Age*, p. 176.

France. Without words man could not have become man, nor woman woman.

Second, Fire. For fire made man independent of climate, gave him a greater compass on the earth, tempered his tools to hardness and durability, and offered him as food a thousand things inedible before. Not least of all it made him master of the night, and shed an animating brilliance over the hours of evening and dawn. Picture the dark before man conquered it; even now the terrors of that primitive abyss survive in our traditions and perhaps in our blood. Once every twilight was a tragedy, and man crept into his cave at sunset trembling with fear. Now we do not creep into our caves until sunrise; and though it is folly to miss the sun, how good it is to be liberated from our ancient fears! This overspreading of the night with a billion man-made stars has brightened the human spirit, and made for a vivacious jollity in modern life. We shall never be grateful enough for light.

Third, The Conquest of the Animals. Our memories are too forgetful, and our imagination too unimaginative, to let us realize the boon we have in our security from the larger and sub-human beasts of prey. Animals are now our playthings and our helpless food; but there was a time when man was hunted as well as hunter, when every step from cave or hut was an adventure, and the possession of the earth was still at stake. This war to make the planet human was surely the most vital in human history; by its side all other wars were but family quarrels, achieving nothing. That struggle between strength of body and power of mind was waged through long and unrecorded years; and when at last it was won, the fruit of man's triumph—his safety on the earth—was transmitted across a thousand generations, with a hundred other gifts from the past, to be part of our heritage at birth. What are all our temporary retrogressions against the background of such a conflict and such a victory?

Fourth, Agriculture. Civilization was impossible in the hunting stage; it called for a permanent habitat, a settled way of life. It came with the home and the school; and these could not be till the products of the field replaced the animals of the forest or the herd as the food of man. The hunter found his quarry with increasing difficulty, while the woman whom he left at home tended an ever more fruitful soil. This patient husbandry by the wife threatened to make her independent of the male; and for his own lordship's sake he forced himself at last to the prose of tillage. No doubt it took centuries to make this greatest of all transitions in human history; but when at last it was made, civilization began. Meredith said that woman will be the last creature to be civilized by man. He was as wrong as it is possible to be in the limits of one sentence. For civilization came through two things chiefly: the home, which developed those social dispositions that form the psychological cement of society; and agriculture, which took man from his wandering life as hunter, herder and killer, and settled him long enough in one place to let him build homes, schools, churches, colleges, universities, civilization. But it was woman who gave man agriculture and the home; she domesticated man as she domesticated the sheep and the pig. Man is woman's last domestic animal; and perhaps he is the last creature that will be civilized by woman. The task is just begun: one look at our menus reveals us as still in the hunting stage.

Fifth, Social Organization. Here are two men disputing: one knocks the other down, kills him, and then concludes that he who is alive must have been right, and that he who is dead must have been wrong—a mode of demonstration still accepted in international disputes. Here are two other men disputing: one says to the other, "Let us not fight—we may both be killed; let us take our difference to some elder of the tribe, and submit to his decision." It was a crucial moment in human history! For if the answer was No, barbarism continued; if it was Yes, civilization planted another root in the memory of man: the replacement of chaos with order, of brutality with judgment, of violence with law. Here, too, is a gift unfelt, because we are born within the charmed circle of its protection, and never know its value till we wander into the disordered or solitary regions of the earth. God knows that our congresses and our parliaments are dubious inventions, the distilled mediocrity of the land; but despite them we manage to enjoy a security of life and property which we shall appreciate more warmly when civil war or revolution reduces us to primitive conditions. Compare the safety of travel today with the robber-infested highways of medieval Europe. Never before in history was there such order and liberty as exist in England today,—and may some day exist in America, when a way is found of opening municipal office to capable and honorable men. However, we must not excite ourselves too much about political corruption or democratic mismanagement; politics is not life, but only a graft upon life; under its vulgar melodrama the traditional order of society quietly persists, in the family, in the school, in the thousand devious influences that change our native lawlessness into some measure of coöperation and goodwill. Without consciousness of it, we partake in a luxurious patrimony of social order built up for us by a hundred generations of trial and error, accumulated knowledge, and transmitted wealth.

Sixth, Morality. Here we touch the very heart of our problem—are men morally better than they were? So far as intelligence is an element in morals, we have improved: the average of intelligence is higher, and there has been a great increase in the number of what we may vaguely call developed minds. So far as character is concerned, we have probably retrogressed; subtlety of thought has grown at the expense of stability of soul; in the presence of our fathers we intellectuals feel uncomfortably that though we surpass them in the number of ideas that we have crowded into our heads, and though we have liberated ourselves from delightful superstitions which still bring them aid and comfort, we are inferior to them in uncomplaining

* J. B. S. Haldane, *Possible Worlds*, p. 302.

courage, fidelity to our tasks and purposes, and simple strength of personality.

But if morality implies the virtues exalted in the code of Christ, we have made some halting progress despite our mines and slums, our democratic corruption, and our urban addiction to lechery. We are a slightly gentler species than we were: capable of greater kindness, and of generosity even to alien or recently hostile peoples whom we have never seen. In one year (1928) the contributions of our country to private charity and philanthropy exceeded two billions of dollars—one half of all the money circulating in America. We still kill murderers if, as occasionally happens, we catch them and convict them; but we are a little uneasy about this ancient retributive justice of a life for a life, and the number of crimes for which we mete out the ultimate punishment has rapidly decreased. Two hundred years ago, in Merrie England, men might be hanged by law for stealing a shilling; and people are still severely punished if they do not steal a great deal. One hundred and forty years ago miners were hereditary serfs in Scotland, criminals were legally and publicly tortured to death in France, debtors were imprisoned for life in England, and respectable people raided the African coast for slaves.* Fifty years ago our jails were dens of filth and horror, colleges for the graduation of minor criminals into major criminals; now our prisons are vacation resorts for tired murderers. We still exploit the lower strata of our working classes, but we soothe our consciences with "welfare work." Eugenics struggles to balance with artificial selection the interference of human kindliness and benevolence with that merciless elimination of the weak and the infirm which was once the mainspring of natural selection.

We think there is more violence in the world than before, but in truth there are only more newspapers; vast and powerful organizations scour the planet for crimes and scandals that will console their readers for stenography and monogamy; and all the villainy and politics of five continents are gathered upon one page for the encouragement of our breakfasts. We conclude that half the world is killing the other half, and that a large proportion of the remainder are committing suicide. But in the streets, in our homes, in public assemblies, in a thousand vehicles of transportation, we are astonished to find no murderers and no suicides, but rather a blunt democratic courtesy, and an unpretentious chivalry a hundred times more real than when men mouthed chivalric phrases, enslaved their women, and ensured the fidelity of their wives with irons while they fought for Christ in the Holy Land.

Our prevailing mode of marriage, chaotic and deliquescent as it is, represents a pleasant refinement on marriage by capture or purchase, and *le droit de seigneur*. There is less brutality between men and women, between parents and children, between teachers and pupils, than in any recorded generation of the past. The emancipation of woman, and her ascendancy over man, indicate an unprecedented gentility in the once murderous male. Love, which was unknown to primitive men, or was only a hunger of the flesh, has flowered into a magnificent garden of song and sentiment, in which the passion of a man for a maid, though vigorously rooted in physical need, rises like incense into the realm of living poetry. And youth, whose sins so disturb its tired elders, atones for its little vices with such intellectual eagerness and moral courage as may be invaluable when education resolves at last to come out into the open and cleanse our public life.

Seventh, Tools. In the face of the romantics, the machine-wreckers of the intelligentsia, the pleaders for a return to the primitive (dirt, chores, snakes, cobwebs, bugs), we sing the song of the tools, the engines, the machines, that have enslaved and are liberating man. We need not be ashamed of our prosperity: it is good that comforts and opportunities once confined to barons and earls have been made by enterprise the prerogatives of all; it was necessary to spread leisure—even though at first misused—before a wide culture could come. These multiplying inventions are

the new organs with which we control our environment; we do not need to grow them on our bodies, as animals must; we make them and use them, and lay them aside till we need them again. We grow gigantic arms that build in a month the pyramids that once consumed a million men; we make for ourselves great eyes that search out the invisible stars of the sky, and little eyes that peer into the invisible cells of life; we speak, if we wish, with quiet voices that reach across continents and seas; we move over the land and the air with the freedom of timeless gods. Granted that mere speed is worthless: it is as a symbol of human courage and persistent will that the airplane has its highest meaning for us; long chained, like Prometheus, to the earth, we have freed ourselves at last, and now we may look the eagle in the face.

No, these tools will not conquer us. Our present defeat by the machinery around us is a transient thing, a halt in our visible progress to a slaveless world. The menial labor that degraded both master and man is lifted from human shoulders and harnessed to the tireless muscles of iron and steel; soon every waterfall and every wind will pour its beneficent energy into factories and homes, and man will be freed for the tasks of the mind. It is not revolution but invention that will liberate the slave.

Eighth, Science. In a large degree Buckle was right: we progress only in knowledge, and these other gifts are rooted in the slow enlightenment of the mind. Here in the untitled nobility of research, and the silent battles of the laboratory, is a story fit to balance the chicanery of politics and the futile barbarism of war. Here man is at his best, and through darkness and persecution mounts steadily towards the light. Behold him standing on a little planet, measuring, weighing, analyzing constellations that he cannot see; predicting the vicissitudes of earth and sun and moon; and witnessing the birth and death of worlds. Or here is a seemingly unpractical mathematician tracking new formulas through laborious labyrinths, clearing the way for an endless chain of inventions that will multiply the power of his race. Here is a bridge: a hundred thousand tons of iron suspended from four ropes of steel flung bravely from shore to shore, and bearing the passage of countless men; this is poetry as eloquent as Shakespeare ever wrote. Or consider this city-like building that mounts boldly into the sky, guarded against every strain by the courage of our calculations, and shining like diamond-studded granite in the night. Here in physics are new dimensions, new elements, new atoms, and new powers. Here in the rocks is the autobiography of life. Here in the laboratories biology prepares to transform the organic world as physics transformed matter. Everywhere you come upon them studying, these unpretentious, unrewarded men; you hardly understand where their devotion finds its source and nourishment; they will die before the trees they plant will bear fruit for mankind. But they go on.

Yes, it is true that this victory of man over matter has not yet been matched with any kindred victory of man over himself. The argument for progress falters here again. Psychology has hardly begun to comprehend, much less to control, human conduct and desire; it is mingled with mysticism and metaphysics, with psychoanalysis, behaviorism, glandular mythology, and other diseases of adolescence. Careful and modified statements are made only by psychologists of whom no one ever hears; in our country the democratic passion for extreme statements turns every science into a fad. But psychology will outlive these ills and storms; it will be matured, like older sciences, by the responsibilities which it undertakes. If another Bacon should come to map out its territory, clarify the proper methods and objectives of its attack, and point out the "fruits and powers" to be won,— which of us, knowing the surprises of history and the pertinacity of men, would dare set limits to the achievements that may come from our growing knowledge of the mind? Already in our day man is turning round from his remade environment, and beginning to remake himself.

Ninth, Education. More and more completely we pass on to the next generation the gathered experience of the past. It is almost a contemporary innovation, this tremendous expenditure of wealth and labor in the equipment of schools and the provision of instruction for all; perhaps it is the most significant feature of our time. Once colleges were luxuries, designed for the male half of the leisure class; today universities are so numerous that he who runs may become a Ph.D. We have not excelled the selected geniuses of antiquity, but we have raised the level and average of human knowledge far beyond any age in history. Think now not of Plato and Aristotle, but of the stupid, bigoted and brutal Athenian Assembly, of the unfranchised mob and its Orphic rites, of the secluded and enslaved women who could acquire education only by becoming courtesans.

None but a child would complain that the world has not yet been totally remade by these spreading schools, these teeming bisexual universities; in the perspective of history the great experiment of education is just begun. It has not had time to prove itself; it cannot in a generation undo the ignorance and superstition of ten thousand years; indeed, there is no telling but the high birth rate of ignorance, and the determination of dogma by plebiscite, may triumph over education in the end; this step in progress is not one of which we may yet say that it is a permanent achievement of mankind. But already beneficent results appear. Why is it that tolerance and freedom of the mind flourish more easily in the northern states than in the South, if not because the South has not yet won wealth enough to build sufficient schools? Who knows how much of our preference for mediocrity in office, and narrowness in leadership, is the result of a generation recruited from regions too oppressed with economic need and political exploitation to spare time for the ploughing and sowing of the mind? What will the full fruitage of education be when every one of us is schooled till twenty, and finds equal access to the intellectual treasures of the race? Consider again the instinct of parental love, the profound impulse of every normal parent to raise his children beyond himself: here is the biological leverage of human progress, a force more to be trusted than any legislation or any moral exhortation, because it is rooted in the very nature of man. Adolescence lengthens: we begin more helplessly, and we grow more completely towards that higher man who struggles to be born out of our darkened souls. We are the raw material of civilization.

We dislike education, because it was not presented to us in our youth for what it is. Consider it not as the painful accumulation of facts and dates, but as an ennobling intimacy with great men. Consider it not as the preparation of the individual to "make a living," but as the development of every potential capacity in him for the comprehension, control, and *appreciation* of his world. Above all, consider it, in its fullest definition, as the technique of transmitting as completely as possible, to as many as possible, that technological, intellectual, moral, and artistic heritage through which the race forms the growing individual and makes him human. Education is the reason why we behave like human beings. We are hardly born human; we are born ridiculous and malodorous animals; we *become* human, we have humanity thrust upon us through the hundred channels whereby the past pours down into the present that mental and cultural inheritance whose preservation, accumulation and transmission place mankind today, with all its defectives and illiterates, on a higher plane than any generation has ever reached before.

Tenth and Last, Writing and Print. Again our imagination is too weak-winged to lift us to a full perspective; we cannot vision or recall the long ages of ignorance, impotence and fear that preceded the coming of letters. Through those unrecorded centuries men could transmit their hard-won lore only by word of mouth from parent to child; if one generation forgot or misunderstood, the weary ladder of knowledge had to be climbed anew.

Writing gave a new permanence to the achievements of the mind; it preserved for thousands of years, and through a millennium of poverty and superstition, the wisdom found by philosophy and the beauty carved out in drama and poetry. It bound the generations together with a common heritage; it created that Country of the Mind in which, because of writing, genius need not die.

And now, as writing united the generations, print, despite the thousand prostitutions of it, can bind the civilizations. It is not necessary any more that civilization should disappear before our planet passes away. It will change its habitat; doubtless the land in every nation will refuse at last to yield its fruit to improvident tillage and careless tenancy; inevitably new regions will lure with virgin soil the lustier strains of every race. But a civilization is not a material thing, inseparably bound, like an ancient serf, to a given spot of the earth; it is an accumulation of technical knowledge and cultural creation; if these can be passed on to the new seat of economic power the civilization does not die, it merely makes for itself another home. Nothing but beauty and wisdom deserve immortality. To a philosopher it is not indispensable that his native city should endure forever; he will be content if its achievements are handed down, to form some part of the possessions of mankind.

We need not fret then, about the future. We are weary with too much war, and in our lassitude of mind we listen readily to a Spengler announcing the downfall of the Western world. But this learned arrangement of the birth and death of civilizations in even cycles is a trifle too precise; we may be sure that the future will play wild pranks with this mathematical despair. There have been wars before, and wars far worse than our "Great" one. Man and civilization survived them; within fifteen years after Waterloo, as we shall see, defeated France was producing so many geniuses that every attic in Paris was occupied. Never was our heritage of civilization and culture so secure, and never was it half so rich. We may do our little share to augment it and transmit it, confident that time will wear away chiefly the dross of it, and that what is finally fair and worthy in it will be preserved, to illuminate many generations.

Conditions in the world are so troublesome and uncertain that some persons probably see only irony in a discussion of progress at this time. The circumstances were very similar back in 1916 when John Dewey wrote the following selection, and what he said then is just as pertinent today. Grounds for optimism and pessimism exist for the present generation just as they did fifty years ago, and it is as necessary now, as then, to be wakened from illusions. For one thing, people continue to confuse rapidity of change with progress; yet fears of war and assurances against war on a vast scale continue to haunt mankind.

Dewey says progress depends, not on the existence of social change, but on the direction which human beings deliberately give that change. Secondly, the ease of social change is a condition of progress. On the other hand, while the modern man was deceived about the amount of progress he had made, and especially deceived about the automatic certainty of progress, he was right in thinking that for the first time in history mankind is in command of the possibility of progress. The future of progress depends upon man to say whether he wants it or not. Progress must be conceived as a responsibility, not as an endowment. But, if progress is to have its chance, certain conservative attitudes which propagate disbelief in the possibility of constructive social engineering will have to yield to or at least be tempered by progressive attitudes.

20

PROGRESS*
John Dewey

Some persons will see only irony in a discussion of progress at the present time. Never was pessimism easier. Others will recognize in it a fine exhibition of courage and faith, and find the manifestation heartening. There is indeed every cause for discouragement. But discouragement affords just the occasion for a more intelligent courage.

If our optimism was too complacent, it is because it was too thoughtless, too sentimental. Never was there a time when it was more necessary to search for the conditions upon which progress depends, until we can reaffirm our faith in its possibility upon grounds better than those upon which we have too blindly relied.

* From *International Journal of Ethics*, vol. 26, no. 3, pp. 311–322, April, 1916. Reprinted by permission of *Ethics* and the University of Chicago Press.

If we have been living in a fools' paradise, in a dream of automatic uninterrupted progress, it is well to be awakened. If we have been putting our trust in false gods, it is a good thing to have our confidence shaken, even rudely. We may be moved to find truer gods. If the reeds upon which we relied have broken, it is well for us to have discovered their frailty. If we have been looking in the wrong direction, we now have a sufficiently strong stimulus to direct our attention elsewhere. We can hardly welcome the war merely because it has made us think, and has made us realize how many of the things we called thoughts were asylums for laziness. But since the war has come, we may welcome whatever revelations of our stupidity and carelessness it brings with it; and set about the institution of a more manly and more responsible faith in progress than that in which we have indulged in the past.

For there can be no blinking the fact that much of that faith was childish and irresponsible. We confused rapidity of change with advance, and we took certain gains in our own comfort and ease as signs that cosmic forces were working inevitably to improve the whole state of human affairs. Having reaped where we had not sown, our undisciplined imaginations installed in the heart of history forces which were to carry on progress whether or no, and whose advantages we were progressively to enjoy. It is easy to understand why our minds were taken captive by the spectacle of change, and why we should have confused progress with change. It is not necessary to rehearse an account of the barriers which for thousands of years kept human society static. Nor is it necessary to do more than allude to the various inventions which by facilitating migration and travel, communication and circulation of ideas and reciprocal criticism, and the production and distribution of goods in a world-wide market, have broken down those barriers. The release of energies has gone on for a century and a half to a degree which we are still impotent to realize. Persons and things have been endlessly redistributed and mingled. The

fixed has given way to the mobile; the settled to the free. It was doubtless inevitable that, in its contrast with static conditions and ideals, this mobility and freedom should be taken for progress. Such it doubtless is in some respects. But the present crisis is in vain, so far as our intelligence is concerned, if it does not make us see that in the main this rapid change of conditions affords an *opportunity* for progress, but is not itself progress.

We have confused, I repeat, rapidity of change with progress. We have confused the breaking down of barriers by which advance is made possible with advance itself. Except with respect to the conservatives who have continuously bemoaned all change as destructive, these statements seem to me to sum up fairly well the intellectual history of the epoch that is closing. The economic situation, the problem of poverty by the side of great wealth, of ignorance and absence of a fair chance in life by the side of culture and unlimited opportunity, have, indeed, always served to remind us that after all we were dealing with an opportunity for progress rather than with an accomplished fact. It reminded us that the forces which were revolutionizing society might be turned in two ways: that they actually were employed for two diverse and opposed ends. But the display was not dramatic enough, not sensational enough, to force the lesson home. The war stages the lesson in a sufficiently striking way.

We had been told that the development of industry and commerce had brought about such an interdependence of peoples that war was henceforth out of the question—at least upon a vast scale. There are men now fighting who had written and lectured to that effect. But it is now clear that commerce also creates jealousies and rivalries and suspicions which are potent for war. We were told that nations could not long finance a war under modern conditions: economists had demonstrated that to the satisfaction of themselves and others. We see now that they had underrated both the production of wealth and the extent to which it could be mobilized for destructive purposes. We were told that the advance of science had made war practically impossible. We now know that science has not only rendered the enginery of war more deadly, but has also increased the powers of resistance and endurance when war comes. If all this does not demonstrate that the forces which have brought about complicated and extensive changes in the fabric of society do not of themselves generate progress I do not know what a demonstration would be. Has man subjugated physical nature only to release forces beyond his control?

Two things are apparent. First, progress depends not on the existence of social change but on the direction which human beings deliberately give that change. Secondly, ease of social change is a condition of progress. Side by side with the fact that the mere substitution of a dynamic or readily changing social structure for a static society does not accomplish progress, stands the fact that this substitution furnishes the opportunity for progress. We cannot too much insist upon the fact that until men got control of natural forces civilization was a local accident. It depended upon the ability of a small number of men to command, with assurance, the labor and services of other men. Any civilization based mainly upon ability to exploit the energies of men is precarious; it is at the mercy of internal revolt and external overflow. By exploring the heaps of rubbish scattered over the face of the earth, we are just beginning to learn how many civilizations have arisen in the past only to sink into rubbish heaps. The dominion of man over the labor of other men is a shaky basis for civilization. And civilization never attained stability upon such a basis. The scientific conquest of nature has at least given us another basis. We have now a sure method. Wholesale permanent decays of civilization are impossible. As long as there exists a group of men who understand the methods of physical science and are expert in their use, recovery, under the worst of circumstances, of the material basis of culture is sure and relatively speedy. While the modern man

was deceived about the amount of progress he had made, and especially deceived about the automatic certainty of progress, he was right in thinking that for the first time in history mankind is in command of the possibility of progress. The rest is for us to say.

I might almost as well stop here. For it seems to me that about all which I can say about the future of progress at the present time is that it depends upon man to say whether he wants it or not. If we want it, we can have it—if we are willing to pay the price in effort, especially in effort of intelligence. The conditions are at hand. We do not of course wholly control the energies of nature; we shall never wholly do so. But we are in possession of a method which enables us to forecast desirable physical changes and to set about securing them. So much is the secure result of the scientific revolution of the last three hundred years. We also know that it is not possible to bring about these physical changes without effecting at the same time vast social changes. The men who invented the stationary and locomotive steam engine, and the men who have since then harnessed both steam and electricity to all sorts of ends, have produced social changes by the side of which those produced by Alexander, Cæsar and Napoleon are insignificant. And the same process is going on as long as applied science goes on, whatever we may think about its worth. But, I repeat, while social change, thus brought about, represents an indispensable condition of progress, it does not present a guarantee for progress. The latter depends upon deliberate human foresight and socially constructive work. Hence we have first of all to change our attitude. Instead of congratulating ourselves upon its presence and certainty as a gift of the gods, as we have been wont to do, we have to recognize that it is a human and intentional product—as much so in principle as a telephone or irrigation or a self-binding reaper, and as much more so in fact as the factors upon which it depends are more complex and more elusive.

The doctrine of evolution has been popularly used to give a kind of cosmic sanction to the notion of an automatic and wholesale progress in human affairs. Our part, the human part, was simply to enjoy the usufruct. Evolution inherited all the goods of Divine Providence and had the advantage of being in fashion. Even a great and devastating war is not too great a price to pay for an awakening from such an infantile and selfish dream. Progress is not automatic; it depends upon human intent and aim and upon acceptance of responsibility for its production It is not a wholesale matter, but a retail job, to be contracted for and executed in sections. I doubt if the whole history of mankind shows any more vicious and demoralizing ethic than the recent widespread belief that each of us, as individuals and as classes, might safely and complacently devote ourselves to increasing our own possessions, material, intellectual, and artistic, because progress was inevitable anyhow.

In dwelling upon the need of conceiving progress as a responsibility and not as an endowment, I put primary emphasis upon responsibility for intelligence, for the power which foresees, plans and constructs in advance. We are so overweighted by nature with impulse, sentiment and emotion, that we are always tempted to rely unduly upon the efficacy of these things. Especially do we like to entrust our destiny to them when they go by eulogistic names—like altruism, kindliness, peaceful feelings. But spite of the dogma which measures progress by increase in these sentiments, there is no reason that I know of to suppose that the basic fund of these emotions has increased appreciably in thousands and thousands of years. Man is equipped with these feelings at birth as well as with emotions of fear, anger, emulation and resentment. What appears to be an increase in one set and a decrease in the other set is, in reality, a change in their social occasions and social channels. Civilized man has not a better endowment of ear and eye than savage man; but his social surroundings give him more important things to see and hear than the savage has, and he has the wit to devise instruments to reinforce his eye and ear—the telegraph and telephone, the microscope and telescope. But there is no reason for thinking that he has less natural aggressiveness or more natural altruism—or will ever have—than the barbarian. But he may live in social conditions that create a relatively greater demand for the display of kindliness and which turn his aggressive instincts into less destructive channels. There is at any time a sufficient amount of kindly impulses possessed by man to enable him to live in amicable peace with all his fellows; and there is at any time a sufficient equipment of bellicose impulses to keep him in trouble with his fellows. An intensification of the exhibition of one may accompany an intensification of the display of the other, the only difference being that social arrangements cause the kindly feelings to be displayed toward one set of fellows and the hostile impulses toward another set. Thus, as everybody knows, the hatred toward the foreigner characterizing peoples now at war is attended by an unusual manifestation of mutual affection and love within each warring group. So characteristic is this fact that that man was a good psychologist who said that he wished that this planet might get into war with another planet, as that was the only effective way he saw of developing a world-wide community of interest in this globe's population.

I am not saying this to intimate that all impulses are equally good or that no effective control of any of them is possible. My purpose is, in lesser part, to suggest the futility of trying to secure progress by immediate or direct appeal to even the best feelings in our makeup. In the main, there is an adequate fund of such feelings. What is lacking is adequate social stimulation for their exercise as compared with the social occasions which evoke less desirable emotions. In greater part, my purpose is to indicate that since the variable factor, the factor which may be altered indefinitely, is the social conditions which call out and direct the impulses and sentiments, the positive means of progress lie in the application of intelligence to the construction of proper social devices. Theoretically, it is possible to have social arrangements which will favor the friendly tendencies of human nature at the expense of the bellicose and predatory ones, and which will direct the latter into channels where they will do the least harm or even become means of good. Practically this is a matter of the persistent use of reflection in the study of social conditions and the devising of social contrivances.

I have already said that the indispensable preliminary condition of progress has been supplied by the conversion of scientific discoveries into inventions which turn physical energy, the energy of sun, coal and iron, to account. Neither the discoveries nor the inventions were the product of unconscious physical nature. They were the product of human devotion and application, of human desire, patience, ingenuity and mother wit. The problem which now confronts us, the problem of progress, is the same in kind, differing in subject-matter. It is a problem of discovering the needs and capacities of collective human nature as we find it aggregated in racial or national groups on the surface of the globe, and of inventing the social machinery which will set available powers operating for the satisfaction of those needs.

This is a large order. But it is not, with reasonable limits, one hopeless to undertake. It is much more within the bounds of legitimate imagination than would have been, five centuries ago, the subjugation of physical nature which has since been achieved. The chief difficulty lies in the primary step: it consists in getting a sufficiently large number of persons to believe in its desirability and practicability. In spite of its discipline by the achievements of physical science our imagination is cowardly and irresponsible. We do not believe that study, foresight and planning will do for the human relations of human beings what they have done for our relationship to physical nature.

We are living still under the dominion of a laissez-faire philosophy. I do *not* mean by this an individualistic as against a socialistic philosophy. I mean by it a philosophy which trusts the direction of human affairs to nature, or Providence, or evolution, or manifest destiny—that is to say, to accident—rather than to a contriving and constructive intelligence. To put our faith in the collective state instead of in individual activity is quite as laissez-faire a proceeding as to put it in the results of voluntary private enterprise. The only genuine opposite to a go-as-you-please let-alone philosophy is a philosophy which studies specific social needs and evils with a view to constructing the special social machinery for which they call.

So far I have avoided any contrast of the so-called progressive attitude with the so-called conservative attitude. I cannot maintain that reserve any longer. While in general, the opposite of the progressive attitude is not so much conservatism as it is disbelief in the possibility of constructive social engineering, the conservative mind is a large factor in propagating this disbelief. The hard and fast conservative is the man who cannot conceive that existing constitutions, institutions and social arrangements are mechanisms for achieving social results. To him, *they* are the results; they are final. If he could once cure himself of this illusion, he would be willing to admit that they grew up at haphazard and cross purposes, and mainly at periods quite unlike the present. Admitting this, he would be ready to conceive the possibility that they are as poor mechanisms for accomplishing needed social results as were the physical tools which preceded the mastery of nature by mind. He would then be free: Not freed just to get emotionally excited about something called progress in general, but to consider what improved social mechanisms or contrivances are demanded at the present day.

All this, you will say (and quite justly), is very general, very vague. Permit me, in concluding, to give a few illustrations suggested by the present international situation, which may make my conception a little less vague. A friend was in Japan at the time when the war broke out. He remarked to an acquaintance who happened to be the United States consul in the town where he was, that he supposed he would have no difficulty in getting an American draft cashed. His friend replied: On the contrary; he himself had had to spend almost two days in getting even a government draft cashed. My friend proceeded to generalize from this incident. He said in effect that in commerce we are proceeding upon an international basis; commerce depends upon a system of international credit. But politically we are doing business upon the basis of ideas that were formed before the rise of modern commerce—upon the basis of isolated national sovereignty. The deadlock due to this conflict could not continue, he surmised; either we must internationalize our antiquated political machinery or we must make our commercial ideas and practices conform to our political. Personally I agree with his account of the needed remedy; it makes little difference, however, for purposes of my illustration whether any one else agrees or not. The situation is one which is real; and it calls for some kind of constructive social planning. Our existing human intercourse requires some kind of a mechanism which it has not got. We may drift along till the evil gets intolerable, and then take some accidental way out, or we may plan in advance.

Another similar illustration is the condition in which neutral countries find themselves at the present time. They are in the position of the public when there is a strike on the part of street-railway employees. The corporation and the employees fight it out between themselves and the public suffers and has nothing to say. Now it ought to be clear that, as against contending nations, the nations not at war have the superior right in every case—not by any merit of theirs, usually only by accident. But nevertheless in the existing situation they are the representatives of the normal interests of mankind, and so are in the right against even the contending party that with respect to other contenders is most nearly in the right. But if the present situation makes anything clear, it is that there is almost a total lack of any machinery by which the factors which continue to represent civilization may make their claims effective. We are quite right in prizing such beggarly elements of international law as exist; but it is evidence of the conservative or laissez-faire mind that we cling so desperately to the established tradition and wait for new law to be struck out by the accident of clash and victory, instead of setting ourselves in deliberate consultation to institute the needed laws of the intercourse of nations.

The illustration may be made more specific. It was comparatively easy to unify the sentiment of the nation when previous international custom was violated by the sinking of the *Lusitania*. It would not be very difficult to inflame that sentiment, in the name of a combination of defence of national honor and defence of international custom, to the point of war. But it is always defence, mind you; every war is *ipso facto* defensive on the part of everybody nowadays. And defence is always retrospective and conservative, even when most offensive. A proposition to call for a conference of nations which would formulate what their rights are henceforth to be, whatever they may have been in the past, would be a constructive use of intelligence. But it would hardly call forth at present the enthusiastic acclaim of the populace and consequently makes no great appeal to the political authorities who are dependent upon the support of the populace.

One more illustration from the international situation. The relative failure of international socialism in the present crisis has been sufficiently noted, with grief by some, with ill-disguised glee by others. But the simple fact of the case is that at present workingmen have more to gain from their own national state in the way of legislative and administrative concessions than they have from some other state, or from any international organization. That they should make use of war to strengthen their claims for concessions from the only power which can make these concessions is but to be human. When the day dawns when the workingmen have more to gain in the way of justice from an international organization than from a purely national one, that day war will become an impossibility. But it is easier to try to do away with war by appeal to personal sentiment than it is to strive to institute even the first steps of any such organization—futile in comparison as the former method must prove.

I hope these remarks at least illustrate what is meant by the dependence of progress upon a foreseeing and contriving intelligence as well as what is meant by saying that it is a retail job. I can only point out the need, so far as they coincide in the further interests of peace with the interest of progress, of an international commerce commission; of an international tariff board; of an international board for colonies and one for the supervision of relations with those backward races which have not as yet been benevolently, or otherwise, assimilated by the economically advanced peoples. Such things are not counsels of perfection. They are practical possibilities as soon as it is genuinely recognized that the guarantee of progress lies in the perfecting of social mechanisms corresponding to specific needs.

Reinhold Niebuhr says our present total historical situation is a vivid reminder of the unpredictability of history. The miscalculations in regard to historical events in the immediate past are but instances of many miscalculations in recent history which prove the unpredictability of history. At best, we may speak of future events as being "probable," but not as "inevitable."

The falsity of some predictions is rooted in failure to discern all the factors and forces in the situation; some are due to an effort to fit history into some preconception; in other instances, dogmas underlying certain views have tended to produce miscalculations; in some instances, mistaken analogies are drawn. These and other factors are illustrated and interpreted by Niebuhr.

21

IS HISTORY PREDICTABLE?*
Reinhold Niebuhr

Everyone knows that history is drama; yet we persistently try to make it into something else. Drama, as art, must have at least two characteristics. The characters must act with a certain degree of consistency and not be arbitrarily manipulated to suit the necessities of a plot. But a drama must also present unpredictable events and reactions to situations. If actions were wholly predictable they would not impress the audience as "true"; for the audience knows instinctively that persons have a certain degree of freedom over

* Reprinted by permission of the author and *The Atlantic Monthly,* vol. 194, no. 1, pp. 69–72, July, 1954.

all the pressures of events and causal chains in which they are involved. The unpredictability of human actions makes the drama interesting, including the drama of history itself.

If this be true, every historian must be something of a dramatist as well as scientist. He must be a scientist in his search for the facts. But he must have artistic imagination to discern the dramatic pattern which is spelled out by the facts. If he imagines himself merely a scientist, he will suffer from the illusion that he could predict the future if he only knew all the facts. If he seeks to become a "philosopher of history," he will be under the illusion that he has discerned some permanent metaphysical pattern under the vast variety of historical events. That illusion will tempt him to even bolder and more hazardous predictions. For while there are undoubtedly historical patterns, every effort of philosophers to interpret events upon the basis of these alleged patterns has resulted in error and confusion.

Our present total historical situation is a vivid reminder of the unpredictability of history. We are involved in a cold war and an armaments race. Some wise men, relying upon historical analogy, tell us that a cold-war tension must inevitably make for a hot war. But when some of them insisted that the Korean war was the beginning of another world war, their predictions were refuted.

The miscalculations in regard to historical events in the immediate past are but instances of many miscalculations in recent history which prove the unpredictability of history. Since there are discernible patterns in history, we are right in speaking of "probable" events. But we can never speak of future events as "inevitable." If war should come, a thousand historians of subsequent ages would bend their energies to explaining just how it came about. And some would even prove that, given certain factors now known to us, the war was inevitable. That is wisdom after the fact. There is no way of turning it into wisdom before the fact. We have a right,

and even a duty, to distinguish between a highly probable eventuality and an inevitable one. In our situation a war is highly probable; but no amount of accurate analysis of the present factors and forces which a future historian might regard as the basis of its inevitability could justify a present historian in predicting its inevitability. The difference between prospect and retrospect is caused by the fact that the actors in the historical drama are partly determined by the pressures upon their decisions but they also remain free to make their choices. These choices can be fitted into a dramatic pattern after the event but not before.

Some of the false predictions of recent history are derived from failure to discern all the factors and forces in the situation, and some are caused by dogmatic efforts to press the drama of history into a false framework. Chamberlain predicted "peace in our time" because he failed to gauge the demonic force in Nazism correctly. He may have thus made the war he wanted to avoid more inevitable. But who will say that he may not also have made victory more possible in a war which his miscalculations made more inevitable? If we are to believe some very sober historians, the radar defenses and the airplanes which saved Britain in 1939 were not ready in 1938. Such a consideration incidentally makes Stanley Baldwin, rather than Chamberlain, the culprit of the piece. It also introduces the intriguing notion that a man stupid enough to trust the Nazis was required to buy the time necessary to ensure Britain's survival. Such factors add to the charm of history as a drama. Chamberlain's error reminds us that predictions of future events may be wrong not only because unpredictable factors enter into the web of history but because we may fail to estimate some constant factors correctly. In this case the underestimated constant was the consistent evil in Nazism.

Most frequently, faulty predictions are due not only to the effort to fit history into some preconception but to a fault in the preconception about the character of history itself. Thus Hegel anticipated the fulfillment of

Western culture in Prussia. The error may seem to have been caused by national arrogance, but it was prompted by a more basic fault in Hegel's dogma, which erroneously tried to fit historical events into a particular "dialectical" logic. Marx reconstituted the Hegelian conception of historical logic and saw the future in terms of even more serious miscalculations. His basic error was to regard a particular institution, that of property, as the root of all evil. This error prompted the erroneous prediction that civilizations which had eliminated property would be free of all egotism, individual and collective. Thus the corruption of the Marxist dream in Stalinist tyranny could not be foreseen even though it was an "inevitable" rather than a fortuitous corruption. Trotsky was so enamored of the Marxist dogma that he continued to predict that the Stalinist corruption would be eliminated, even while he suffered as a victim of it. He believed that the change in "property relations" would ultimately bring forth fruits of justice.

According to the Marxist dogma the "class struggle" would become more and more severe and would result in the increasing misery of the poor, until their resentments would set the world on fire with revolution. This prediction is in fact refuted by the increasing well-being of the working classes in advanced technical civilizations. This result is due to the creation of balances of power in technical societies which proved to be more, rather than less, flexible and adequate than those of agrarian societies. The complex class structure of modern technical societies is a complete refutation of the Marxist notion of a progressive simplification of the class structure, so that only owners and the dispossessed would remain at the historical climax. Significantly, the Marxist dogma can produce some very false predictions even when it is not held in its most rigorous form.

Many social scientists and economists confidently predicted a major depression in America after the war. The Swedish economist Gunnar Myrdal went so far as to suggest a hazardous trade agreement between Sweden and Russia as a "hedge" against the prophesied American depression. Many incalculable factors accounted for this miscalculation. The "cushions" against a depression built into our economy by ten years of legislation were not considered. But the error was probably due chiefly to a failure to note that the American businessman, despite his ideological inflexibility, possessed a practical flexibility which made him come to terms with historical contingencies in a way which was, for instance, beyond the wisdom of the French businessman.

One must incidentally attribute a great deal of the fury of the Communists to their frustration and bafflement when history does not follow the logic which they projected for it. Thus they have to lie ever more desperately to show that American workers are living in abject poverty. Had not their logic assigned such a fate for the workers?

The "dogma" which underlies the "liberal" world view is almost as productive of miscalculations as the Marxist dogma. The dogma assumes that historical development will inevitably solve the main problems of human existence, including the problems of the human community. Since the primary fruit of historical development is man's increasing freedom and power over nature, and since this power and this freedom create new problems in new dimensions for every former problem solved, the dogma naturally has resulted in many serious miscalculations, from the day that the aging French encyclopedists hailed Napoleon as the great servant of the "liberal" movement. They made the mistake of associating the misuse of power only with the traditional monarchic political forms, just as Marxism subsequently associated the misuse of power only with "bourgeois" forms. Wilson's hope that the First World War would make the world "safe for democracy" was part of this liberal dream of progress. Actually the war's aftermath resulted in new perils to democracy, and the rise of unanticipated tyrannies.

We have dwelt too long on the miscalculations which are due to dogmatic frames of meaning which contain some basic miscalculation of the human and historical situation. The fact is that, even upon the basis of the most flexible pattern of meaning for history, we still would make mistakes about the future. How could anyone have anticipated, for instance, that the "bourgeois" or capitalist movement would become merged with the aristocracy in Britain and borrow some virtues from the traditional society; that it would destroy the traditional society in France but take over some of its vices; and that in Germany the businessman would grow more efficient and powerful than in France while remaining politically incompetent and impotent? All these developments are not wholly incomprehensible in retrospect, but they are unpredictable in prospect.

Many of the historical miscalculations are due to mistaken analogies. History is fruitful of recurrences and therefore of analogies. If it were not so, no "lessons" could be learned from history. But since history also elaborates endless dramatic variations, none of the analogies are exact enough to become the basis for prediction. It is now fairly clear that both Roosevelt and Eisenhower looked hopefully to the future of Russian-American relations. Eisenhower told our Congress in 1945 that we understood each other because of our common "anti-imperialism." The barb at Britain was obvious. But the analogy could not comprehend the virtue of democracy at the heart of British "imperialism," nor the tyrannical corruption at the heart of the Communist "anti-imperialism."

Now, in the days of our disillusionment, another analogy is popular but equally dubious as a source of wisdom. Are not the Nazis and Communists very much alike? it is asked. Are not both equally tyrannical and cruel? Indeed they are very much alike; but not so much so that we ought to predict confidently that the Communists will inevitably go to war as the Nazis did. Communism is primarily a political conspiracy rather than a military movement. It relies on a dogma which promises its ultimate victory over us by a logic of history. Communists will there-

fore not have the same desperation as the Nazis had. Furthermore, Communism is a tyranny which rests upon utopian illusions rather than cynically nationalist aspirations, a difference which makes it more dangerous than the Nazis politically but not in a military sense. It is as "irrational" as Hitlerism, but its irrationality is of a different order. It relies, not upon mystic intuitions, but upon cool calculations rendered irrational by the restrictions upon the mind which its dogmas create. Finally, it has a wide expanse of territory, contrasted with the narrow geographic base of the Nazis. It is therefore not liable to be as desperate as Nazism.

These differences do not encourage complacency. The Communists remain dangerous foes who might become desperate and who might stumble into war in their dogmatic blindness. But the differences should refute the idea of an inevitable war and of the corollary idea: a "preventive" war. For all we know, there may be an analogy between Communism and Mohammedanism. It may, like Islam, persist as an historic force after it has lost its dynamic. But let us not press this or any analogy too far. For Islam did not subside as a dynamic force until it was defeated by European civilization in military conflict. We can learn from historical analogies, but we must not rely upon them too much, simply because when "history repeats itself" it never does so exactly. There is an endless emergence of novel factors in each situation which makes every analogy and comparison inexact.

Reliance upon historical analogy is frequently unreflective. When it is based upon an explicit philosophy of history the philosophy is rooted in a similar error, as that which underlies the idea of progress. Both equate historical drama too simply with the processes of nature. The one thinks that there is an essential similarity between natural and historical recurrences. The other rests its dogma on the similarity between natural and historical development. Both ideas are refuted by the radical nature of human freedom, which is able to elaborate endless dramatic variations upon the woof of recurrence and the warp of development furnished by nature.

Spengler and Toynbee have given us an interpretation of history based upon the classical idea that nature and history have similar cycles of recurrence, the only difference being that the cycles in which the rise and fall of historic cultures occur are larger than the cycles of birth, growth, decay, and death of natural organisms. Toynbee's recent effort to illumine our conflict with Communism in terms of an analogy between Eastern and Western Christendom leads to more confusion than illumination; for Communism is a novel factor for which there is no analogy in that ancient struggle, however intriguing may be the subordinate similarities which Toynbee finds in the attitudes of contemporary and medieval Russia. We are, after all, dealing with Russia now as the homeland of a world-wide secular and demonic religious movement. There is no analogy for this conflict in history.

Historians are notoriously hostile to, or critical of, the efforts of Toynbee and Spengler. Sometimes their hostility springs from their implicit acceptance of a more popular but equally implausible philosophy of history: the idea of progress. Sometimes their criticisms are prompted by their knowledge that these patterns of history falsify the historical details in some field in which the particular historian knows most. But partly the hostility springs from the dramatic instincts of a true historian. He senses that the drama of history is falsified and obscured by any "philosophy of history," for if it is a rigorous philosophy it claims to discover metaphysical channels for the stuff of history. That means that historical events are regarded as necessary actualizations of possibilities. The historian knows that what happens to persons and what happens in history are not necessary actualizations. History is an endlessly varied dramatic encounter between people and groups in which every event is so closely related to a previous event that the historian can give an account of the causal chain. But nothing happens with such a compulsion of natural or rational necessity that the future may be predicted upon the basis of past events. Some historians still believe that they might be able to predict the future if they only knew a little more. If they give themselves to this illusion they are not as wise as the most reflective statesmen, Churchill for instance. Such practical men have learned that the secret of wisdom is not to rely too much on any large patterns of history or upon any seeming exact analogies. They feel, even more than the historian, that the present occasion and responsibility are unique and cannot fit nicely into any pattern or yield their secret in terms of any analogy.

We mortals are so proud of our knowledge of the past that we are inclined to impatience and embarrassment because we know so little about the future. We try to overcome this embarrassment by all kinds of scientific and philosophical devices designed to penetrate the veil which hides the future. These devices, when not too ambitious, can be the servants of wisdom; for we are not creatures of the day and must prepare for the morrow. But too ambitious and pretentious anticipations of an essentially unpredictable future not only destroy the drama of history: they also increase its perils. We know how much havoc has been wrought by believers in an inevitable revolution. It would be tragic if we added to the havoc by believing in an inevitable war. Significantly, the worst damage is done when a bogus omnipotence seeks to come to the aid of a bogus omniscience.

V

Ideas and Ideologies

The power of ideas and ideologies in social change is evident in social movements, whether they be liberal, progressive, conservative, collectivist, evolutionary, or revolutionary. These terms indicate the association with characteristic attitudes in public opinion, usually called reactionary, conservative, progressive or liberal, or radical. The ideas or the tenets of ideologies will usually be accepted or rejected according to the attitudes which prevail in the society, somewhere within the range from radical to reactionary. Attitudes toward social values are, of course, changeable. Values or policies once regarded as radical may in time become acceptable to conservatives; things once objected to may later be defended as established social norms. Persons who have placed faith in the promises of socialism or communism may become disillusioned when its promises fail to materialize and turn toward some other cause.

Ideologies are freighted with words to conjure with, some of them essentially mythical in nature. American democracy has its inalienable rights, among which are life, liberty and the pursuit of happiness, government by consent of the governed, and other terms or phrases which have acquired mythical significance. Marxian socialism has its doctrine of class struggle, contests between exploiting and exploited classes, ruling and oppressed classes, its proletariat to be emancipated from the bourgeoisie, its doctrine of surplus value, and so on. All ideologies and religions have mythical terms or concepts of this kind; their effects as ideas are not necessarily bad, though they sometimes are exploited for ulterior purposes, and thus may be harmful in directing change. Several ideologies are so dynamic in world affairs today and so involved in major social conflicts that some consideration should be given to their nature.

It must be understood at the outset, however, that ideologies are tendencies, not revealed dogmas, and that they gradually change in content and meaning. Our conceptions of certain ideologies today are the product of changes in social context and in the interpretations of theories and programs concerned. Moreover, merely as an attitude, a conceptual term such as liberalism, democracy, or socialism is not necessarily related to any particular historical period or to any particular social groups. That is, terms which are significant in social movements may also become *abstractions* and thus more readily drift in meaning. Liberalism is such a term; democracy and capitalism likewise have drifted in meaning; *laissez faire,* liberty, freedom, individualism, free enterprise, and rugged individualism have been distorted as shibboleths; and, although the New Deal and Fair Deal have run their course within recent decades, their symbolism has been subject to political confusion.

Our primary interest in ideologies is with their significance in social movements now in process, and several of them have been selected for consideration: liberalism as opposed to collectivism; democracy; socialism and communism; capitalism; and nationalism.

Liberalism. As a social movement, liberalism may be concerned with the development of democratic political forms and institutions essential to political liberty; political liberty is not thought of as an end in itself, but as one of the prerequisites for the attainment of liberty in the broader sense. Liberalism is a deep-seated mental attitude whose primary postulate is the spiritual freedom of mankind. It rallies against unduly coercive interference in any sphere of life, and against unreasonable encroachment of government which jeopardizes or takes away man's liberties and freedoms. Liberalist movements have traditionally championed the cause of freedom, in contradistinction to certain collectivist movements which have tended to distort or destroy freedom. Such was the nature of liberalism as identified with social reform in Great Britain from about 1776 onward, and such has been its nature in the development of American economic, political, and other institutions.

Liberalism originated as a political philosophy devoted to the freedom of the individual, democratic institutions, and free enterprise. Politically, liberalism proclaimed the basic democratic liberties and demanded constitutional government based on popular representation, though the details vary in different countries. Economically, liberalism stood for free enterprise, private property, free trade at home and abroad. Liberalism became identified with progress. But liberalist movements run their course, as all movements do, and the issues involved in the struggle for freedom and liberty change; consequently the meaning of liberalism is subject to change with the passing of time. Liberalism in the United States, from the New Deal period onward has become identified with the enhancement of governmental power and administration and with more government planning and government spending, which is incompatible with the classical meaning of liberalism. But the United States is not alone in experiencing this "liberalist" trend; it has become characteristic in England and in some of its Dominions, in the Scandinavian countries, and elsewhere because of the influence of collectivism. Radical liberalism, which is "leftist" in its sympathies and programs of change, is virtually socialistic in its philosophy; conservative liberalism tends to oppose excessively radical change but is less negative toward governmental action than was characteristic of liberalism from about 1776 to 1871.

Collectivism. This is a generic term embracing several movements and systems aiming at the collective as opposed to the individual direction of the economy. Thus defined, collectivism includes socialism, communism, corporatism, fascism, and national socialism. From an entirely different standpoint, collectivism may represent voluntary social efforts in which individuals act in concert with others for their mutual welfare, independent of state action. But this latter meaning is not the one which concerns us at the moment. Collectivist movements are militant in method, purpose, and spirit. The ultimate purpose of collectivist movements is the directing of the entire society. Once the collectivist movement has gained sufficient momentum, it is difficult, almost impossible, to stop the drive toward autocracy. The marked trends toward centralization of government and the increase in state interference in national economy have been symptomatic of the collectivist drift in a number of Western countries, particularly Great Britain, the United States, and Scandinavia. The most developed example of collectivism at present of course is Soviet Russia with her satellites and her neighbor Communist China. Tito's Yugoslavia, with its national brand of communism, ought not to be overlooked. The basic choices between liberalist and collectivist ideals may be represented by such concepts as *laissez faire* versus state interference, self-reliance versus state paternalism, individual property and liberty versus state ownership and control.

Democracy. This word expresses a theory of society as well as a theory of government. As a political concept, it denotes a form of government in which the people rules itself, either directly or through representatives. Constitutional or limited monarchies may qualify as democracies, depending on the degree of popular participation in government. Democracy may be associated with federal forms of organization, as in the United States, or with unitary state organization, as in France. In either case, the nature and amount of the exercise of authority at national, state or provincial, and local levels are highly important. As a principle, democracy depends upon the exercise of self-government at all functional levels. These several areas of government should function cooperatively and harmoniously, without a race for power on the part of either. Contemporary examples of nationalization of industry and the socialization of economies have shown how democracy has been undermined and placed on the defensive. In democracy there is supposed to be a government of law instead of a government of men, but when vested interests in government arise, this principle may be disregarded. If democracies tend to become "welfare states" emphasizing paternalism and political pressure, the people become subject to an undemocratic form of despotism. The more subservient and dependent upon the government a people becomes, the less chance there is for a liberal, wise, and energetic government to spring from the exercise of popular suffrage.

Socialism. Since it takes various forms a comprehensive definition of socialism is not easy to formulate, but the following offered by G. D. H. Cole will serve for orientation purposes: "Socialism is essentially a doctrine and a movement aiming at the collective organization of the community in the interests of the mass of the people by means of the common ownership and collective control of the means of production and exchange." [1] Another working definition is that offered by Jesse W. Hughan: "Socialism is the political movement of the working class which aims to abolish exploitation by means of the collective ownership and democratic management of the basic instruments of production and distribution." [2] Thus generalized,

[1] From his article, "Socialism," *Encyclopaedia Britannica* (14th ed.), vol. 20, pp. 888–895.
[2] Cited from Jerome Davis, *Contemporary Social Movements,* Appleton-Century-Crofts, Inc., New York, 1930, p. 75.

the problem would remain of distinguishing between Marxian socialism, state socialism, guild socialism, syndicalism, Christian socialism, National Socialism, and any
other forms. Then, too, there are philosophical examples, as seen in Fabian socialism
in England. Socialism, as a generic term, includes communism, the former term
representing the initial phases of its development, and communism its ultimate
achievement.

Varieties of socialism differ in their ideals of justice, their motivation, their attitudes
toward the state, and their methods of attaining their ideals. State socialism, of
course, advocates state ownership and state control of production; anarchism, which
sometimes is included within the scope of socialism, would go as far as to destroy
the state. In general, the methods of socialism may be experimental, evolutionary, or
revolutionary. One way of distinguishing between socialism and communism is to
say that the former is evolutionary, the latter revolutionary; yet the terms are not
strictly limited either way. Communism, for example, may be revolutionary in certain
phases and evolutionary in others. The distinction between socialism and communism
is, however, more a matter of tactics and strategy than of objective. Soviet Russia,
which claims to be a socialist republic, has developed totalitarianism comparable to
that achieved through Italian Fascism and German National Socialism. Thus socialism, communism, and fascism provide the way to the same end result.

The term "communism" was originally used almost synonymously with "socialism,"
especially because Marx and Engels adopted the former word to make their brand
of socialism appear more scientific. But saying something is scientific doesn't necessarily make it so. Several features of communist theory and practice need to be
understood. Theoretically, the working classes are capable of seizing the power of
the state but not of maintaining it with success; consequently there must be a
"committee" to act for them—i.e., the Communist Party. To the Communist, the
organized state is the embodiment of force; the worker must gain control of and
use this form of force to achieve his final emancipation. The modern practice of
communism, especially the dictatorship of the proletariat and its maintenance by
terror, has its theoretical basis in the Marxian doctrine of the state. Both socialists
and Communists criticize free enterprise and agree in their desire for a society where
individual incomes derived from rent, interest, and profit will be eliminated. In lieu
of the profit motive in the capitalist system, the socialists and Communists advocate
conscious planning, the net result being a planned economy and eventually a planned
society.

It is significant that Lenin had to adapt Marxian doctrine to the circumstances
prevailing in Russia, and this phase of socialism (or communism) became known as
Leninism. Stalin in turn modified the doctrine still further, while claiming that
his program of development was founded on Marxism and Leninism.[3] Here we have
an example of how ideologies pass through phases of development both in theoretical
interpretation and in practice.

The Soviet Russian Constitution of 1936 contains a so-called "Bill of Rights"

[3] For a statement of Leninism, see John Eric Nordskog, *Contemporary Social Reform Movements*, Charles Scribner's Sons, New York, 1954, pp. 187–188; communism discussed as an
ideology, pp. 183–199; the Soviet Bill of Rights, pp. 229–230.

(Articles 118–133), which might just as well be said to define areas of regimentation. The values which Western Europeans or Americans associate with the phrase "civil liberties" are nonexistent in Soviet Russia and tend to disappear among the satellites. Yet the Russian Communists claim that their system provides more liberty than exists in other countries or under any other system. One of the principal objectives of Soviet Russia is a classless society, but actually the number of classes has been increased. Between 1936 and 1940, the number of social-class groups had increased to ten, according to a study by Alex Inkeles.[4] The former class structure has been replaced with one more suitable for a totalitarian hierarchy of power. With each phase of revolution, there have been new vested-interest groups with a political source of power to dominate the population. The present arrangement is not necessarily final. The transitions which have been made in Russia since the death of Stalin do not in any manner indicate the abandonment of the objectives of the Communist Revolution to rule the world.

Among the forms of arbitrary control in Soviet Russia, wages, hours, and working conditions in industry are regulated by collective agreements concluded between the factory administration and the industrial labor union. The conditions stipulated in the collective agreement are based on instructions from Moscow. The workers have no choice but to accept the collective agreement as presented. All agencies of control operating in the factory are integrated into a comprehensive system of control, requiring four distinct sets of agencies: government offices, the Communist Party, public organization, and voluntary groups. Broadly speaking, there is an over-all hierarchical system with the Communist Party in a position of supreme authority. Party control is directly effective within the factory organization. Elections in Russia are not free and democratic; voting is virtually a nominal procedure.

The systems of control reach down below the adult level. In the Young Communist League, boys and girls are deliberately and rigorously trained to become active builders of a Communist society. They are thoroughly drilled in the theories of communism, Marxism and Leninism being interpreted to suit the purposes of the dictator. Education in the Soviet Union is used to mold the mentality of its citizens from the cradle to the grave; nothing is left to chance. The distorted conception of liberty in Russia is exemplified in the attitude of the government toward religion. For example, Article 124 in the Constitution of 1936 provides: "In order to ensure to citizens freedom of conscience, the church in the U.S.S.R. is separated from the state, and the school from the church. Freedom of religious worship and freedom of antireligious propaganda is recognized for all citizens." For some time the Soviet government tried to eradicate religion in Russia, confiscated thousands of churches, and raised every possible obstacle to the continuation of the established religious institutions in Russia. The youth of the land have been indoctrinated with atheism. But faithful adherents kept the Greek Orthodox Church alive, and after World War II some policies against the church were relaxed to some extent. Nevertheless, "freedom of antireligious propaganda is recognized for all citizens."

Perhaps the blackest spot in the Soviet Russian system is that its forced labor

[4] Alex Inkeles, "Social Stratification and Mobility in the Soviet Union: 1940–1950," *American Sociological Review,* vol. 15, no. 4, pp. 465–479, August, 1950.

camps are an integral part of the economic system. These camps contain millions of workers who are nominally political prisoners, the victims of secret-police espionage. It is a system of slavery under the most abject conditions.

The sinister program of conquest engineered from the Kremlin in the name of a Communist Revolution points up the greatest threat of communism as an ideology. The techniques used are such that anyone can observe them day by day in countries the world over. The cold war may wax and wane, blow hot or cold, but for the peoples of the West it is necessary, at all costs, to guard their mistrust of Communist aggressiveness.

The social consequences of fascism and communism are in many respects similar. Sixteen points of similarity have been listed by Representative Fred E. Busbey of Illinois in the monograph *Fascism in Action,* as reproduced here: [5]

1. The wiping out of all independent trade-unionism with the result that those trade-unions which are permitted, exist only under the tolerance of the totalitarian state, to serve as its servile adjuncts.

2. The elimination of political parties except the ruling Nazi, Fascist, or Communist Party.

3. The subordination of all economic and social life to the strict control of the ruling, single-party bureaucracy.

4. The suppression of individual initiative, and the liquidation of the system of free enterprise, and a tendency toward government control of supercartels.

5. The abolition of the right to freedom of speech, press, assembly, and religious worship.

6. The reduction of wages and, in the case of communism, living standards.

7. The use of slave labor on a vast scale and the establishment of concentration camps.

8. The abolition of the right to trial by jury, habeas corpus, the right to independent defense counsel, and the innocence of the defendant until proven guilty.

9. The glorification of a single leader or Fuehrer or Duce, who is all-powerful and subject neither to criticism nor to removal through the ballot.

10. The utilization of a special form of social demagogy—for example, incitement of race against race and class against class—the elimination of all opposition, and the concentration of power into the hands of the ruling dictatorship.

11. The subordination of all economic and social life and the everyday needs of the population to the requirements of an expanding military machine seeking world conquest.

12. The establishment of a system of nation-wide espionage to which the entire population is subject.

13. The severance of social, cultural, and economic contact between the people of the totalitarian state and those of other countries, through a rigorous press and radio censorship, travel restrictions, etc.

[5] *Fascism in Action: A Documented Study and Analysis of Fascism in Europe,* House Document no. 401, 80th Cong., 1947.

14. The open disregard for the rights of other nations and the sanctity of treaties.

15. The maintenance and encouragement of fifth columns abroad.

16. The reduction of parliamentary bodies to a rubber-stamp status automatically approving all decisions of the one-party dictatorship and the omnipotent leader.[6]

Capitalism. This term denotes a way of life, an ideology, and a social movement. It does not mean merely the factory system, the machine, or the use of capital in any of its forms. Capitalism, as an economic system, acknowledges the rights of private property and leaves subject to free enterprise the whole machinery of production, from the acquisition of the raw material to the disposition of the final product.

Socialists criticize capitalism because they find fault with its system of production and distribution. They disparage both the existence of many "unearned" incomes and the great difference between the low incomes of the many and the high incomes of the few. (It is significant that in Soviet Russia, which is a "Socialist Republic," there is extreme disparity in the distribution of incomes.) Unearned incomes criticized by the socialists include those from land rent, interest and inherited funds, monopoly profits, and incomes based on the employment of the labor of others.

Capitalistic business is typically private, and the characteristic motivation is the quest for private gain. Capitalistic economy rests upon an exchange basis; capitalistic production is intended for the market and limited to the production of salable goods. One of the factors in production is labor, which is bought on the market. It is the labor service which is bought and paid for, not the worker himself as a commodity in commerce. Since the guiding principle of capitalism is gain, there is production from the capitalist viewpoint only if there is a profit. The distribution of the results of production is regulated through the mechanism of pricing.

Recurrent changes between prosperity and depression or employment and unemployment suggest that capitalism may undergo marked changes in form and function within short periods of time. As changes occur in the capitalist system, modifications are bound to take place in other social institutions, owing to the reciprocal relationships among them. The principles on which the capitalistic system rests—the right of private property, the right of free enterprise, and the liberty of contract—change gradually in response to the needs of a developing nation. The meaning of capitalism for the United States would not necessarily be applicable to other nations.

The capitalism of the machine age represents an adaption to new technological and social conditions. It has altered with the development of finance capitalism, and it will no doubt undergo further changes in response to automation and to, no less a factor, governmental interference in industry. Economic and political systems are always on trial, and this is certainly true of capitalism.

Capitalism has frequently been condemned because of abuses of power of control from the standpoint of ownership or management. It has been claimed that capitalism has failed because of excessive *laissez faire* in exploiting workers and the economy in general. Nevertheless, the concept of *laissez faire* is largely mythical, for controls

[6] Originally cited from *The Congressional Record*, vol. 93, no. 107, p. A2847, June 6, 1947.

over the way of life of immigrants to the United States began with the Mayflower Compact, and regulations ever since have varied from very strict to nominal in business relationships and even in the home. Controls over business and industrial enterprise developed according to the population's concern over resources and opportunities, but as long as natural resources and land seemed almost limitless, restrictions were comparatively nominal. That people eventually awakened to the need for conservation of natural resources became evident in the administration of Theodore Roosevelt, and regulations to that end began to come into effect. That Americans have not been indifferent to the ill effects of industrial and business trends in the United States has been manifested in dozens of acts of Congress from 1900 to the present, covering a great variety of problems—railroad rates, pipelines, pure food and drugs, telephone and telegraph, transportation of liquor, banking and investment, unreasonable restraint of trade, and so on.

Has capitalism broken down? Definitely not in production, for no other system can compare with it in productivity; but in the system of distribution there have been grave faults, and readjustments need to be worked out in that aspect of the system. To indicate change from the quantitative standpoint, the total labor force of the United States, consisting of persons 14 years of age and over and including the Armed Forces, was 64,599,000 in 1950 and increased to 70,387,000 in 1956. For the civilian labor force only, the total was 63,099,000 in 1950 and rose to 67,530,000 in 1956. The male civilian labor force was 44,442,000 in 1950 and 45,756,000 in 1956. The female civilian labor force was 18,657,000 in 1950 and 21,774,000 in 1956.[7]

The number of corporations in the United States has been irregular, the mortality among them indicating their lack of security and vulnerability in the business cycles, of which at least twenty-four have been noted between 1854 and the present. The success or failure of corporations would, of course, depend on a great number of factors. Of interest here is their relative number in successive years: in 1936 there were 478,857 active corporations and 51,922 reported as inactive; in 1944 the number was down to 412,467 active and 34,329 inactive; after that the trend was upwards, reaching a total of 623,570 active and 36,095 inactive corporations in 1950.

The total number of firms in operation in the United States on March 31, 1948, as reported by the U.S. Department of Commerce, was 3,966,800. The total number of operating businesses was reported as 3,965,000 in 1949, increasing to 3,980,000 in 1950, to 4,009,000 in 1951, and to 4,043,500 in 1952.

Conversely to the growth in number of business firms and corporations, the number of separate farms in the United States has been decreasing. In 1910, when the census of farm population was 32,077,000, there were 6,361,502 farms. In 1950, when the farm population was 24,335,000, the number of farms was 5,382,162.

Especially significant are the changes in the urban-rural distribution of population in the United States. In 1790, only 5.1 per cent of the population was urban, and 94.9 per cent rural; by 1950, 64 per cent of the population had become urban, and only 36 per cent remained rural in its way of life.

[7] U. S. Department of Commerce, *Annual Report on the Labor Force, 1956*, ser. P-50, no. 72, March, 1956.

Many people do not realize that oscillations of the business cycle are characteristic in the production and distribution of goods in a monetary system of exchange. These business cycles are usually taken in their stride as nominal trends upward or downward in business activity—they may be three or four years in duration or more—and only in the more extreme situations are they coupled with serious recessions or depressions.

Another aspect of capitalism which may be misinterpreted is the growth in size of corporations. Most corporations depend for their capital on the sale of stocks or bonds, some of the larger corporations having thousands of stockholders. Although the characteristic thing about democracy is its diffusion of power among the people, the people in America have been exceptionally tolerant of the trend toward concentration of economic power. Corporations and big business generally have forged ahead in acquiring more and more power with the intention of using it, so that in the end some business organizations have become as powerful as states. The question is whether democratic political power will absorb and use economic resources, bigness and all, to serve its ends, or will big economic power take over state power? The situation at present is that we have big business, big labor organization, and big government, and this three-way relationship constitutes the greatest challenge to the internal welfare of the nation.

Nationalism. This term also merits consideration as an ideology and as a social movement. The idea of nationality has been associated with ideals of political freedom in the sense that any given national group has the right to become or remain a separate state, independent of any other nation. But nationalism has greatly influenced the methods and objectives of reformist groups and revolutionaries. Fascism, for example, is essentially nationalistic, and nationalism has become so dynamic in Soviet Russia as to make other ideologies subordinate to it, as is evident in its intolerance of Titoism or other forms of national communism.

Fascist nationalism would be incompatible with that ordinarily associated with the democratic concept of the state or nation in which the individual is respected and has rights as a citizen. In modern times nationalism has characteristically been associated with imperialism and militarism, and perhaps this association is a reason why nationalism is more powerful as an ideology today than is commonly understood. Blended with statism in its fascist or totalitarian aspects, and thus resolved into "nation-statism," nationalization takes on almost frightening possibilities.

One of the factors that strengthened the dynamic influence of nationalism throughout the world was the phrase "self-determination," coined by Woodrow Wilson. This phrase pointed the way to the creation of group consciousness in Asia, China, India, and the Philippines; it led to the home-rule movements in the British Empire, in the empires of France and the Netherlands, and is presently dynamic in northern Africa and the Near East. Nationalism is a phase of maturation essential for membership in the United Nations. The development of national status is a phase in the trend toward world organization. Thus considered, the development of national unity should be a means, not an end in itself. Possibly the nation-state is more deep-rooted in the emotions of the masses than any previous form of political organization, yet it is likely that the present age of nationalism is a phase of national and international cultural growth and that it, like other phases, will be superseded by some greater form of social organization.

Although nationalism is a factor in the solidarity of the United Nations, it also happens to be a force for separation and division of interests. Psychologically it is one of the most emotionally charged causes of international conflict, even war. Excessive feelings of nationalism put states on much the same plane as primitive tribes who regarded all outsiders as enemies. A solution may be achieved through regional unions among nations in terms of their common interests, thus enlarging the "in-group" and economically or politically disposing of grounds for conflict. Nationalism might thus give way to regional federation, and federations of states now extant, notably the United States, show that this is possible.

With this survey of ideologies in mind, it will become evident why the ideas in the following selections have a bearing on social change. Moreover, they throw light on the following chapters. The readings, to be introduced in sequence, are: "The Age of Discussion" by Walter Bagehot, "Creeds and Ideologies" by Bertrand Russell, "The Decline of the Protestant Ethic" by William H. Whyte, Jr., "Democratic Apologetics" by T. V. Smith, "Of the Grounds and Limits of the Laisser-Faire or Non-interference Principle" by John Stuart Mill, and "Conservative Liberalism vs. Radical Liberalism" by David Lawrence.

Walter Bagehot (1826–1877), an English economist and journalist, observed that the peoples of the East were puzzled by the West's penchant for social change. In the East, people are more characteristically ruled by ancient custom, and they are skeptical of what Westerners may purport to do to "improve" their way of life. The feeling of the Hindus, for example, is typically an *old* feeling, and that of the West is a *modern* feeling. How may one account for the difference?

Bagehot attributes the difference to the growth of government by discussion in the West, particularly the discussion of subjects that concern matters of principle. He notes that discussion of this nature began in the small republics of Greece and Italy, where an increasing awareness of common actions and interests became the root of change and progress, though originality in life was then, for the most part, forbidden and repressed by fixed social norms. In the course of time, the development of "free thought," advance in science, and religious tolerance were factors favoring freedom of discussion. Discussion breaks down "the yoke of custom"—a famous Bagehot phrase; it provides incentives to progress, inasmuch as it places a premium on intelligence, teaches and requires tolerance, and is an instrument of social and cultural elevation.

22

THE AGE OF DISCUSSION*
Walter Bagehot

The greatest living contrast is between the old Eastern and customary civilizations and the new Western and changeable civilizations. A year or two ago an inquiry was made of our most intelligent officers in the East, not as to whether the English government were really doing good in the East, but as to whether the natives of India themselves thought we were doing good. In a majority of cases, the officers who were the best authority answered thus: "No doubt you are giving the Indians many great benefits: you give them continued peace, free trade, the right to live as they like, subject to the laws; in these points and others they are far better off than they ever were; but still they cannot make you out. What puzzles them is your constant disposition to change or, as you call it, improvement. Their own life in every detail being regulated by ancient usage, they cannot comprehend a policy which is always bringing something new; they do not a bit believe that the desire to make them comfortable and happy is the root of it; they believe, on the contrary, that you are aiming at something which they do not understand —that you mean to 'take away their religion'; in a word, that the end and object of all these continual changes is to make Indians not what they are and what they like to be, but something new and different from what they are, and what they would not like to be." In the East, in a word, we are attempting to put new wine into old bottles—to pour what

we can of a civilization whose spirit is progress into the form of a civilization whose spirit is fixity, and whether we shall succeed or not is perhaps the most interesting question in an age abounding almost beyond example in questions of political interest.

Historical inquiries show that the feeling of the Hindus is the old feeling, and that the feeling of the Englishman is a modern feeling. "Old law rests," as Sir Henry Maine puts it, "not on contract but on status." The life of ancient civilization, so far as legal records go, runs back to a time when every important particular of life was settled by a usage which was social, political, and religious, as we should now say, all in one—which those who obeyed it could not have been able to analyze, for those distinctions had no place in their mind and language, but which they felt to be a usage of imperishable import, and above all things to be kept unchanged. In former papers I have shown, or at least tried to show, why these customary civilizations were the only ones which suited an early society; why, so to say, they alone could have been first; in what manner they had in their very structure a decisive advantage over all competitors. But now comes the further question: If fixity is an invariable ingredient in early civilizations, how then did any civilization become unfixed? No doubt most civilizations stuck where they first were; no doubt we see now why stagnation is the rule of the world, and why progress is the

* From *Physics and Politics*, Beacon Press, Inc., Boston, 1956, pp. 114-121. (Originally published in 1873, by D. Appleton and Co., New York.)

very rare exception; but we do not learn what it is which has caused progress in these few cases, or the absence of what it is which has denied it in all others.

To this question history gives a very clear and very remarkable answer. It is that the change from the age of status to the age of choice was first made in states where the government was to a great and a growing extent a government by discussion, and where the subjects of that discussion were in some degree abstract or, as we should say, matters of principle. It was in the small republics of Greece and Italy that the chain of custom was first broken. "Liberty said, Let there be light, and, like a sunrise on the sea, Athens arose," says Shelley, and his historical philosophy is in this case far more correct than is usual with him. A free state—a state with liberty—means a state, call it republic or call it monarchy, in which the sovereign power is divided between many persons, and in which there is a discussion among those persons. Of these the Greek republics were the first in history, if not in time, and Athens was the greatest of those republics.

After the event it is easy to see why the teaching of history should be this and nothing else. It is easy to see why the common discussion of common actions or common interests should become the root of change and progress. In early society, originality in life was forbidden and repressed by the fixed rule of life. It may not have been quite so much so in ancient Greece as in some other parts of the world. But it was very much so even there. As a recent writer has well said, "Law then presented itself to men's minds as something venerable and unchangeable, as old as the city; it had been delivered by the founder himself, when he laid the walls of the city, and kindled its sacred fire." An ordinary man who wished to strike out a new path, to begin a new and important practice by himself, would have been peremptorily required to abandon his novelties on pain of death; he was deviating, he would be told, from the ordinances imposed by the gods on his nation, and he must not do so to please

himself. On the contrary, others were deeply interested in his actions. If he disobeyed, the gods might inflict grievous harm on all the people as well as himself. Each partner in the most ancient kind of partnerships was supposed to have the power of attracting the wrath of the divinities on the entire firm, upon the other partners quite as much as upon himself. The quaking bystanders in a superstitious age would soon have slain an isolated bold man in the beginning of his innovations. What Macaulay so relied on as the incessant source of progress—the desire of man to better his condition—was not then permitted to work; man was required to live as his ancestors had lived.

Still further away from those times were the "free thought" and the "advancing sciences" of which we now hear so much. The first and most natural subject upon which human thought concerns itself is religion; the first wish of the half-emancipated thinker is to use his reason on the great problems of human destiny—to find out whence he came and whither he goes, to form for himself the most reasonable idea of God which he can form. But, as Mr. Grote happily said, "This is usually what ancient times would not let a man do. His *gens* or his φρατρια required him to believe as they believed." Toleration is of all ideas the most modern, because the notion that the bad religion of A cannot impair, here or hereafter, the welfare of B is, strange to say, a modern idea. And the help of "science," at that stage of thought, is still more nugatory. Physical science, as we conceive it—that is, the systematic investigation of external nature in detail—did not then exist. A few isolated observations on surface things —a half-correct calendar, secrets mainly of priestly invention, and in priestly custody— were all that was then imagined; the idea of using a settled study of nature as a basis for the discovery of new instruments and new things, did not then exist. It is indeed a modern idea, and is peculiar to a few European countries even yet. In the most intellectual city of the ancient world, in its most intellectual age, Socrates, its most intellectual inhabitant, discouraged the study of physics because it engendered uncertainty and did not augment human happiness. The kind of knowledge which is most connected with human progress now was that least connected with it then.

But a government by discussion, if it can be borne, at once breaks down the yoke of fixed custom. The idea of the two is inconsistent. As far as it goes, the mere putting up of a subject to discussion, with the object of being guided by that discussion, is a clear admission that that subject is in no degree settled by established rule, and that men are free to choose in it. It is an admission too that there is no sacred authority—no one transcendent and divinely appointed man whom in that matter the community is bound to obey. And if a single subject or group of subjects be once admitted to discussion, ere long the habit of discussion comes to be established, the sacred charm of use and wont to be dissolved. "Democracy," it has been said in modern times, "is like the grave; it takes, but it does not give." The same is true of "discussion." Once effectually submit a subject to that ordeal, and you can never withdraw it again; you can never again clothe it with mystery, or fence it by consecration; it remains forever open to free choice and exposed to profane deliberation.

The only subjects which can be first submitted, or which till a very late age of civilization can be submitted, to discussion in the community are the questions involving the visible and pressing interests of the community; they are political questions of high and urgent import. If a nation has in any considerable degree gained the habit, and exhibited the capacity, to discuss these questions with freedom, and to decide them with discretion, to argue much on politics and not to argue ruinously, an enormous advance in other kinds of civilization may confidently be predicted for it. And the reason is a plain deduction from the principles which we have found to guide early civilization. The first pre-historic men were passionate savages, with the greatest difficulty coerced into order and

compressed into a state. For ages were spent in beginning that order and founding that state; the only sufficient and effectual agent in so doing was consecrated custom; but then that custom gathered over everything, arrested all onward progress, and stayed the originality of mankind. If, therefore, a nation is able to gain the benefit of custom without the evil —if after ages of waiting it can have order and choice together—at once the fatal clog is removed, and the ordinary springs of progress, as in a modern community we conceive them, begin their elastic action.

Discussion, too, has incentives to progress peculiar to itself. It gives a premium to intelligence. To set out the arguments required to determine political action with such force and effect that they really should determine it is a high and great exertion of intellect. Of course, all such arguments are produced under conditions; the argument abstractedly best is not necessarily the winning argument. Political discussion must move those who have to act; it must be framed in the ideas, and be consonant with the precedent, of its time, just as it must speak its language. But within these marked conditions good discussion is better than bad; no people can for a day bear a government of discussion which does not, within the boundaries of its prejudices and its ideas, prefer good reasoning to bad reasoning, sound argument to unsound. A prize for argumentative mind is given in free states, to which no other states have anything to compare.

Tolerance too is learned in discussion and, as history shows, is only so learned. In all customary societies bigotry is the ruling principle. In rude places to this day, anyone who says anything new is looked on with suspicion, and is persecuted by opinion if not injured by penalty. One of the greatest pains to human nature is the pain of a new idea. It is, as common people say, so "upsetting"; it makes you think that, after all, your favorite notions may be wrong, your firmest beliefs ill-founded; it is certain that till now there was no place allotted in your mind to the new and startling inhabitant, and now that it has conquered an entrance you do not at once see which of your old ideas it will or will not turn out, with which of them it can be reconciled, and with which it is at essential enmity. Naturally, therefore, common men hate a new idea, and are disposed more or less to ill-treat the original man who brings it. Even nations with long habits of discussion are intolerant enough. In England, where there is on the whole probably a freer discussion of a greater number of subjects than ever was before in the world, we know how much power bigotry retains. But discussion, to be successful, requires tolerance. It fails wherever, as in a French political assembly, any one who hears anything which he dislikes tries to howl it down. If we know that a nation is capable of enduring continuous discussion, we know that it is capable of practicing with equanimity continuous tolerance.

The power of a government by discussion as an instrument of elevation plainly depends —other things being equal—on the greatness or littleness of the things to be discussed. There are periods when great ideas are "in the air," and when, from some cause or other, even common persons seem to partake of an unusual elevation. The age of Elizabeth in England was conspicuously such a time. The new idea of the Reformation in religion, and the enlargement of the *moenia mundi* by the discovery of new and singular lands, taken together, gave an impulse to thought which few, if any, ages can equal. The discussion, though not wholly free, was yet far freer than in the average of ages and countries. Accordingly, every pursuit seemed to start forward. Poetry, science, and architecture, different as they are, and removed as they all are at first sight from such an influence as discussion, were suddenly started on-

ward. Macaulay would have said you might rightly read the power of discussion "in the poetry of Shakespeare, in the prose of Bacon, in the oriels of Longleat, and the stately pinnacles of Burleigh." This is, in truth, but another case of the principle of which I have had occasion to say so much as to the character of ages and countries. If any particular power is much prized in an age, those possessed of that power will be imitated; those deficient in that power will be despised. In consequence an unusual quantity of that power will be developed, and be conspicuous. Within certain limits vigorous and elevated thought was respected in Elizabeth's time, and, therefore, vigorous and elevated thinkers were many; and the effect went far beyond the cause. It penetrated into physical science, for which very few men cared; and it began a reform in philosophy to which almost all were then opposed. In a word, the temper of the age encouraged originality, and in consequence original men started into prominence, went hither and thither where they liked, arrived at goals which the age never expected, and so made it ever memorable.

In this manner all the great movements of thought in ancient and modern times have been nearly connected in time with government by discussion. Athens, Rome, the Italian republics of the Middle Ages, the communes and states-general of feudal Europe have all had a special and peculiar quickening influence, which they owed to their freedom, and which states without that freedom have never communicated. And it has been at the time of great epochs of thought—at the Peloponnesian War, at the fall of the Roman Republic, at the Reformation, at the French Revolution—that such liberty of speaking and thinking have produced their full effect.

Creeds and ideologies mean more when considered in the context of conflict issues with which they are identified. However, differences of creed are not necessarily a cause of strife; they only become so when they are combined with fanatical intolerance. Bertrand Russell says that, so far as ideologies are concerned, the troubles of our time show themselves in an increase of fanaticism.

The fanaticism which characterizes the Communist Party today arises from a combination of two forces: the doctrines of Marx and the traditions of Russia. When communism was introduced into Russia, it had to undergo a considerable transformation, which is explained by Russell. What emerged in Russia, however, was not what Marx had in mind. Marx's views were not based on the conditions of life in Russia; they were largely derived from a study of British factory workers in the early 1840s. The hatred then germinated by existing conditions was erected by Marx into a cosmic principle which, it was claimed, was the source of all progress.

Modern communism has been molded by two men, Lenin and Stalin, so it is a compound of Marxism, Leninism, and Stalinism, in which fanaticism has been a constant ingredient. Fascism and Nazism are also examples of strongly fanatical movements. All these movements were motivated by self-preservation and the lust for power. The cure for fanaticism of the kind evident in these ideologies rests on the assurance of security, prosperity, and a liberal education. Russell explains his conception of the functions of these factors as they concern the West and the Communist states.

23

CREEDS AND IDEOLOGIES*

Bertrand Russell

The most bitter struggles between different groups of mankind have been caused by one or more of three differences: of economic interest, of race, or of creed. In the First World War only economic interest was concerned; in the second, economic interest and creed. In the third, if it comes, economic interest, race and creed will all be involved. In this chapter I wish to consider fanatical differences of creed as a source of conflict, first historically and then in the present day.

The word "ideology," which is now common, means nearly the same thing as was formerly meant by "creed." An "ideology" may be defined as a system of beliefs leading to a line of conduct, both public and private, and supported, whenever it is politically important, by a priesthood or something analogous. The word was brought into general use by Napoleon, who objected to what he called *"idéologues"* because in his day they were mostly republican. I shall use the word "ideology" as practically synonymous with the word "creed," but with slightly less implication of dogmatic definiteness. One can speak of the "ideology" of American capitalism, but it would be stretching the use of words to call it a "creed."

Differences of creed are not necessarily a cause of strife; they only become so when they are combined with fanatical intolerance. Buddhism came to China and Japan peace-

* From *New Hopes for a Changing World*, pp. 111-125. Copyright 1951 by Bertrand Russell. Reprinted by permission of Simon and Schuster, Inc., New York, publishers.

ably, without disturbing the ancient religions of those countries. No one in either China or Japan thought that only one religion could be true. The Chinese came to believe in both Buddhism and Confucianism, the Japanese in both Buddhism and Shinto. In the Greco-Roman world similar views were generally held. The Romans identified their gods with those of Greece. Temples to Egyptian and Babylonian gods were built in Rome. The worship of Mithra was allowed to spread freely, and people who took to worshiping foreign gods did not on that account reject their native religions.

In the ancient world before the rise of Christianity there was only one exception: the Jews. The First Commandment says: "Thou shalt have no other gods before me." This was a new conception, inaugurated by the prophets. In their day it met with considerable opposition from the Jews, as may be seen in Jeremiah's complaints about the Jewish worship of Ashtaroth, but during the Captivity it won a complete victory. This intolerance (as it seemed to pagans) provoked hostility, and at various times the Jews suffered persecution, which never succeeded in changing their views.

Christianity inherited this theological exclusiveness from the Jews. Any concession to pagan worships was "idolatry," and was regarded as gravely sinful. The persecution of Christians by the Roman Government was caused by this exclusiveness, which was regarded as subversive, especially because it involved rejection of the divinity of the Emperor. When the Empire became Christian exclusiveness was carried much farther. It was not enough to be Christian: it was necessary to be orthodox, and to reject all the many subtle heresies that afflicted the Church in the fourth and fifth centuries.

Wars of religion begin with the rise of Mohammedanism. The Moslems, like the Christians and the Jews, held that there could be only one true Faith. They were less intolerant than the Christians, but sufficiently so to make any genuine peace between Christian and Moslem States impossible.

All through the Middle Ages war was used as an ideological weapon. Charlemagne converted the Saxons by massacring those who showed a reluctance to be baptized. The Templars and the Knights of St. John fought the Moslems. The third Crusade turned its arms against the Greek Orthodox Church. Simon de Montfort exterminated the Albigensian heretics. Henry V and the Council of Constance burnt the followers of Wycliffe. In Spain the Jews and Moors were first persecuted and then expelled. In the Balkans the Bogomil heresy was rooted out.

But all these wars and persecutions sank into insignificance by comparison with the wars of religion in the sixteenth and seventeenth centuries. Everywhere throughout what had been Catholic Europe the religion of the reigning sovereign, whichever it happened to be, was enforced with such severe penalties that the great majority acquiesced. Both sides held that it is right to assassinate a monarch of the opposite party; Guy Fawkes attempted it on behalf of the Catholics, and Ravaillac succeeded. Charles I's head was cut off, and Cromwell's body was hung in chains. The Thirty Years' War halved the population of Germany, but made almost no change in the balance of forces. At length, in view of the inconclusiveness of the struggle, a few enlightened nations, led by the Dutch, discovered that it was possible for Protestants and Catholics to live peaceably side by side. English fanatics had fled to America to escape persecution, and were able there to perpetuate the evil practices objection to which had caused them to leave England. But persecution in America ceased towards the end of the seventeenth century, except in the comparatively mild forms in which it still subsists. In Catholic countries religious persecution persisted until the French Revolution, after which political passions took its place.

Some opponents of Communism are attempting to produce an ideology for the Atlantic Powers, and for this purpose they have invented what they call "Western Values." These are supposed to consist of toleration, respect for individual liberty, and brotherly love. I am afraid this view is grossly unhistorical. If we compare Europe with other continents, it is marked out as the persecuting continent. Persecution only ceased after long and bitter experience of its futility; it continued as long as either Protestants or Catholics had any hope of exterminating the opposite party. The European record in this respect is far blacker than that of the Mohammedans, the Indians or the Chinese. No, if the West can claim superiority in anything, it is not in moral values but in science and scientific technique.

In the Book of Judges it says from time to time "And the land had rest forty years." The land of Europe had rest ninety-nine years, from 1815 to 1914. True, there were several Russo-Turkish wars, there was the Crimean War, there were Bismarck's three wars, there was the Boer War, and at the end of the period there was the Russo-Japanese War; but none of these produced at the time any profound upheaval, and none of them gave rise to a feeling of general insecurity such as now haunts us even in our dreams.

I was 42 when this era of tranquility ended. All of us who grew up at that time took for granted, almost without conscious thought, that the nineteenth century had set the pattern for the future. It had seen great changes, almost all beneficent; we expected more changes of the same sort. The practice of toleration, liberty and enlightenment had spread with astonishing rapidity. Nobody thought of the nineteenth century as a brief and exceptional interlude between two dark ages. Looking back, it is clear that we ought to have foreseen coming troubles: overpopulation, the end of great undeveloped food-producing areas, the bitter competition produced by the spread of industrialism in a number of countries all avid for power, the intoxication caused by Western ideas in intellectuals belonging to countries with other traditions and other circumstances. All this we ought to have foreseen, but we did not, and so when war came we found ourselves in a world for which we were intellectually and imaginatively unprepared. Our statesmen found old maxims inapplicable, but could not think of new ones. Blindly the nations blundered on from folly to folly. If we are to understand our own time, we must find the key to it, not in the eighteenth and nineteenth centuries, but in earlier, wilder and darker epochs.

So far as ideologies are concerned, the troubles of our time show themselves in an increase of fanaticism. There was, of course, some fanaticism in the period which now seems in retrospect to have been comparatively free from it. There was fanaticism in the French Revolution, but it was in control for only about two years. There was fanaticism in the German resistance to Napoleon, but it seemed to die down after 1815. There was fanaticism on both sides in the American Civil War and in the struggle between Russian revolutionaries and the Tsardom. But except in Russia the fanatics never seemed to gain control for any length of time.

Since 1914—largely, I think, as a result of sufferings caused by war—we have seen fanaticisms of various kinds controlling governments and making sensible statesmanship impossible. There was anti-German fanaticism in the years after the First World War; there was answering German fanaticism, leading to the victory of the Nazis. There was anti-Semitic fanaticism, with the inevitable response of Zionist fanaticism. Most important of all, there was, and is, Communist and anti-Communist fanaticism. While mankind remains in this temper, the sort of co-operation required for the inauguration of world Government is clearly out of the question.

The fanaticism which characterizes the Communist party at the present day arises from a combination of two forces: the doctrines of Marx, and the traditions of Russia. Something must be said about both. Before Marx, the leading Socialists—Owen, Saint-Simon and Fourier—were mild and philanthropic optimists, whose appeal was to reason and benevolence. Marx ridiculed these men as "Utopians." His own doctrine was fiercer and more dynamic. He did not expect or attempt to convert the propertied classes to his views. On the contrary, he held that, with negligible exceptions, men's political opinions express the economic interests of their class. Political divisions accordingly express the conflict between the interests of different classes. In the French Revolution the bourgeoisie had overthrown the feudal aristocracy; in the Communist revolution the proletariat would overthrow the bourgeoisie. The proletariat would be victorious because, by an inherent necessity, capitalism, as it developed, would diminish the number of the rich and increase the number of those who had "nothing to lose but their chains." The whole process, he held, was governed by a logical scheme standing above human volitions. If you were wise you would put yourself on the winning side, but it would win in any case.

The dynamic force of the doctrine, both in Marx and in his followers, was derived from hatred—illogically, since (in his view) the barbarities of the capitalists were fated, and were not due to their individual wickedness. His views were largely derived from a study of British factory workers in the early '40's—a horrible period, of child labor and famine artificially induced by the Corn Laws. Hatred was a natural reaction, but what Marx did was to erect hatred into a cosmic principle and the source of all progress. Naturally the propertied classes, wherever his creed spread, were terrified into violent reaction, and the vague good-natured liberalism of the middle nineteenth century gave way to a blacker and fiercer outlook.

There is in Marx a cold logic which is reminiscent of Calvin. Calvin held that certain people—chosen not for their virtues but arbitrarily—are predestined to go to heaven, and the rest are predestined to go to hell. No one has free will: if the elect behave well that is by God's grace, and if the reprobate behave badly, that again is because God has so willed it. So in Marx's system if you are born a proletarian you are fated to carry out the purposes of Dialectical Materialism (as the new God is called), while if you are born a bourgeois you are predestined to struggle

vainly against the light, and to be cast into outer darkness if you live until the coming Revolution.

The whole process of history proceeds according to a logical system, which Marx took over, with slight modifications, from Hegel. Human developments are as irresistible and as independent of human will as the movements of the heavenly bodies. The force that brings about change in social affairs is the conflict of classes. After the proletarian revolution there will be only one class, and therefore change will cease. For a time the dispossessed bourgeoisie will suffer, and the elect, like Tertullian, will diversify their bliss by the contemplation of the damned in concentration camps. But Marx, more merciful than Calvin, will allow their sufferings to end with death.

This curiously primitive myth appealed to the less fortunate sections of mankind much as Christianity had appealed to slaves in the Roman Empire. It brought the hope of a great reversal, in which the oppressed would come to enjoy happiness, power and—sweetest of all—revenge. It should, according to the word of the new gospel, have appealed first to industrial workers in the most advanced countries, namely Britain and America. But in America wage-earners were always prosperous (unless they were immigrants or colored people), and in Britain the prosperity of wage-earners increased very rapidly during the second half of the nineteenth century. In both these countries, therefore, Marx won few adherents. He won many in Germany, but there, too, increasing prosperity led to a softening of the orthodox doctrine. It was in Russia, the most backward and the least industrialized of the Great Powers, that Marx's adherents first achieved the conquest of the Government.

When Communism became Russian it underwent gradually a very considerable transformation. When I was a young man I knew Bebel and the elder Liebknecht, who were the leaders of the Marxist party in Germany. Both were kindly humanitarians, psychologically very similar to other Radicals of that time. They did not hate their political opponents; they would speak of the Kaiser with good-natured derision. They felt convinced that the future was with them, but so did all the other reformers—the vegetarians, the teetotalers, the pacifists, the Armenians, the Macedonian patriots, and all the rest. This belief, at that time, was part of nineteenth-century optimism, and had not the character of a desperate revenge phantasy. The German Marxists of that time, of whom I knew many, were for the most part likable as individuals; one did not sense in them the vein of cruelty which has since become characteristic of Communists.

Modern Communism has been molded by two men, Lenin and Stalin. Lenin had lived long years in the West, and so had most of his colleagues. He wanted not only to introduce Communism in Russia, but also to Westernize the country. In this respect he stood much nearer to Marx than Stalin does.

Lenin was undoubtedly one of the most remarkable men of our time. His intellect, it is true, was narrow and second-rate; he could not think outside the framework of Marxian orthodoxy, and would consider a contention proved if it could be shown to be in accordance with the scriptures of Marx and Engels. Where he was remarkable was in his inflexible faith and his indomitable will. Russia in 1917 was defeated and disorganized; the army had almost ceased to exist, the Germans held much of the country, and there were no forces capable of opposing their further advance; industry had collapsed, the peasants were in chaotic revolt, and various political parties were waging a bitter struggle with each other in spite of universal ruin. Lenin, immediately on his return from exile, marked out a narrow undeviating party line. First, with great difficulty, he persuaded the other leading Bolsheviks; then, by confidence and a show of inexorable logic, he converted the populace of Petrograd (as it then was). He won over the soldiers, who were returning from the front and refusing to go on fighting, by promising them peace and land. Within a few months he had made himself strong

enough to frighten Kerensky's Provisional Government into abdication and to proclaim the seizure of power by his own party.

This, however, was only a beginning. The Provisional Government had decreed the election of a Constituent Assembly, and the elections were completed shortly after the Bolshevik *coup d'état*. When it appeared that the majority in this democratically elected Assembly were opposed to the Bolsheviks it was dissolved; from that time to the present the Bolsheviks have had no title but naked force to the government of Russia. Lenin's next step was to induce his colleagues, with great difficulty, to accept a humiliating peace with Germany. No sooner was this concluded than a civil war broke out, in which defeat often seemed imminent. America, Britain, France and Japan, as soon as they had defeated the Germans, sent troops to help the opponents of the Bolsheviks in the civil war. Nevertheless the Bolsheviks won, and the world had to acquiesce while they consolidated their power. Throughout the first two years or more the Bolsheviks themselves expected defeat, and the rest of the world was confident that they would fall, but they survived, and set to work to organize Russia in accordance with Marxian theory.

Russia, however, was very different from Western countries, and what emerged was not quite what Marx had had in mind. Russia was largely illiterate; the immense majority of the population were peasants; the Tsarist autocracy had accustomed people to autocratic government; the Church was more subservient to the State than in Western countries; superstition was as widespread as it had been in Western Europe in the Middle Ages. These things facilitated what was called the dictatorship of the proletariat, which was in fact the dictatorship of the inner ring of the Communist party. Lenin had always been ruthless, and the experiences of the civil war did not make him less so. The dangers of the situation hastened the return to autocracy and the police State, to which the country had been accustomed before the Revolution.

Russia had always been prone to fanaticism. There were many heretical sects which heroically endured persecution. Ivan the Terrible and Peter the Great were fanatics. The anarchist leader Bakunin was much more fanatical than Marx. The reactionaries who supported the Tsarist Government paved the way to their own downfall by fanatical resistance to modern ideas; down to 1917 even the mildest liberalism led to Siberia. The atmosphere of fanaticism survived the Revolution, and was if anything intensified by precarious success.

With the coming of Stalin the Soviet regime entered upon a new phase. Lenin was a cosmopolitan, who had lived in Western countries and had no special feeling for Russia. Stalin knew only Russia, and had no respect for the West. He liquidated the old Bolsheviks, and invoked traditional Russian patriotism to help out the Communist ideology. Just as, in Elizabethan England, patriotism went hand in hand with Protestantism, so in Stalin's Russia patriotism goes hand in hand with Communism. Since most Russians are intensely patriotic, this gives great added strength to the regime. It must be acknowledged that Russia under Stalin has had amazing success. Communism is now in control in China, the Balkans, Poland and a large part of Germany, and there is every reason to expect further accessions of territory in Asia.

No success since the rise of Islam has been so rapid or so astonishing as the success of Communism. It is no wonder if the rest of the world is asking itself whether any limits short of the whole planet can be put to Soviet conquests.

Ten years ago another fanatical ideology, Fascism, seemed almost as threatening as Communism does now. Fascism has now gone underground, but perhaps only temporarily. At any rate the fanatical disposition which produced it is ready to be called out by the same kind of circumstances. The Nazis got their hold on Germany owing to the misery produced by the great depression, which, itself, was caused by the fanatical folly of American reactionaries. If America were again to pursue as mad an economic policy as that of the '20's, it is by no means impossible that correlative follies would again be generated in other countries.

Fanaticism in control of a Government is dangerous because it finds co-operation with others scarcely possible. Nazis and Communists alike have made treaties and agreements seem useless to the outside world, because their fanaticism makes them incapable of good faith. As things stand, a world Government is not possible unless Communism is overthrown or conquers the whole world. We must hope that its fanaticism will lessen, and that the hostile fanaticism of the United States will not meanwhile develop into an equal obstacle to co-operation.

Let us consider in a more general manner the nature of fanaticism, its causes, and the possible ways of diminishing it. The essence of fanaticism consists in regarding some one matter as so important as to outweigh everything else. The Byzantines, in the last days before the Turkish conquest, thought it more important to avoid unleavened bread in the communion service than to preserve Constantinople for Christendom. A large proportion of the inhabitants of the Indian peninsula are willing to bring their country to ruin on the question whether the eating of pork or the eating of beef is the more abhorrent sin. American reactionaries would rather lose the next war than employ in atomic research anyone whose second cousin once met a Communist at a party. During the First World War Scottish Sabbatarians, in spite of the food shortage caused by German submarines, protested against the planting of potatoes on Sundays, and maintained that Divine wrath at this sin explained our lack of military success. Those who have theological objections to birth control are willing that destitution, famine and war shall continue till the end of time because they cannot forget one misinterpreted text in Genesis. The ardent friends and the bitter enemies of Communism are alike willing to see the human race radioactively exterminated rather than compromise with the evil thing—capitalism or Communism as the case may be. All these are examples of fanaticism.

In every community there is a certain percentage of temperamental fanatics. Some fanaticisms are essentially harmless, and others do no harm so long as their adherents are few and not in power. The Amish in Pennsylvania hold that it is wicked to use buttons; this is completely harmless except in so far as it shows an irrational state of mind. Some extreme Protestants would like to revive the persecution of Catholics; these people are only harmless so long as they are very few. Fanaticism only becomes a serious menace when some fanatical creed is held by a sufficient number of people to endanger the peace, either internally by civil war or externally by a crusade, or when, without civil war, it establishes a Rule of the Saints involving persecution and mental stagnation. Of this last the greatest example in history is the rule of the Church from the fourth century to the sixteenth. The greatest example in our time is the rule of the Communist Church, as it may be called.

Historically, the main causes of fanaticism have been misfortune and poverty. Fanaticism among Jews became common during the Babylonian captivity; it was promoted by persecution in the time of Antiochus IV and the Maccabees, and again after the destruction of Jerusalem; in our time, the fanaticism of the Nazis has, as was inevitable, generated a counter-fanaticism among a certain number of Jews. In Mohammedan countries, where Jews were well treated, they were never fanatics.

The fanaticism of the Nazis only became tolerable to ordinary Germans as a result of the poverty and humiliation brought about by the Treaty of Versailles and the great depression.

The fanaticism of Russian revolutionaries was caused by Tsarist persecution; in particular, Lenin's fanaticism was first generated by his brother's execution. In 1917, defeat in war, chaos, and ruin produced in large sections of the Russian population a proneness to fanaticism and a readiness to follow any leader who knew his own mind and was genuinely convinced that he could lead the way to salvation. After the Bolsheviks had broken with democracy by dismissing the Constituent Assembly, self-preservation and lust for power were added to fanaticism. These motives, which exist also in rich imperialist nations, have a causation different from that of fanaticism. This makes a difficulty in dealing with Russia, where both kinds of motives co-exist.

To cure fanaticism, except as a rare aberration of eccentric individuals, three things are needed: security, prosperity and a liberal education.

Lack of security exists throughout the world at the present time. We have all been told horrors about hydrogen-bombs and bacteriological war; we all know that war may break out at any moment. The atmosphere of terror is driving men into superstition, and into forms of intolerance which intensify the danger instead of diminishing it. If fanaticism is to grow less, whether in Russia or elsewhere, the first step must be to find some way of diminishing insecurity. This is difficult in the present state of world politics, but it must be done if disaster is to be averted.

Prosperity is generally admitted in the West to be the best preventive of Communist fanaticism, but no one seems to draw the conclusion that it would be a good thing if Russia were prosperous. Trade across the Iron Curtain ought to be encouraged. Everything possible should be done to turn the attention of Russians to the internal development of their own country. I admit that the Russians make these things difficult, but it is bound to take time and patience to dispel their suspicions.

Liberal education is the most difficult to secure of our three requisites. Russians will have none of it; the United States has less of it year by year. Consider the case of Dr. Lattimore, who was accused of being a traitor for saying things about China which every well-informed person knew to be true, and which it was to America's interest to have known by those who make American policy. In this respect matters will not improve until there is more sense of security, at least for a few years ahead. To create such a sense, on both sides of the Iron Curtain, is the main duty of statesmen in our time.

But how is this to be done? There must be a change of emphasis: we must devote ourselves to showing, not how to secure victory for our side, nor how desirable our victory would be, but how disastrous to everybody on all sides a war must be. In the West, where free discussion is possible, important men, especially scientists, of all shades of political opinion, should meet together. It should be agreed that never, in their discussions, must anyone raise the question as to which system is best, the Russian or the American. What should be made clear is: first, that if there is a war, then even if one side is completely victorious (which is unlikely) the victors will still be worse off than if there had been no war; second, that there is no reason, except mutual suspicion, why the two kinds of regime should not exist peaceably side by side; third, that it is possible to divide the world into spheres, leaving each side free in its own sphere, but agreeing not to interfere in the other. If in the West men of sufficient importance and sufficient political diversity, including Communists, had

agreed on such a solution, it is not irrational to hope that Governments, on both sides of the Iron Curtain, would examine the proposals carefully, and would perhaps reach a basis of agreement. The alternative is disaster, not to this or that group, but to mankind.

If once the fear of imminent war were removed, I do not doubt that there would be a very rapid improvement. Russia would grow less illiberal, and the growth of intolerance in the United States would be checked.

World government, I repeat, must be our goal. I have dealt as candidly as I am able to do with the difficulties of population, of race, and of creed. I do not think these difficulties can be overcome in less than fifty years. Meanwhile the peace of the world must be preserved somehow by expedients and makeshifts and a general realization of what is at stake for mankind. The world has to learn economic common sense; different races have to treat each other as equals; and there must be tolerance as regards differences of creed. If there is no great war, natural tendencies will probably promote these things. And if, at last, it becomes possible to create a stable world government, mankind may enter upon a period of prosperity and wellbeing without parallel in the past history of our species.

The nature of the Protestant ethic which was in full flower in the United States at the turn of the century is revealed in a speech given to Yale University students in 1908. In the following article, this speech is cited in part and interpreted by William H. Whyte, Jr. The active words in the excerpt are "climb, force, compel, and control." According to Protestant rationalization at the time, one's success in the struggle against one's environment, which paid off in material rewards, was moral as well as practical; also it was spiritually justified. Moreover, if everyone could believe that seeking his self-interest automatically improves the lot of all, then the application of hard work should eventually produce a heaven on earth.

It may be thought that capitalism would have been impossible without this ethic. But the very Industrial Revolution which was partly brought about by the Protestant ethic, began, in time, to confound it. In retrospect, the turn of the century seems a golden age of individualism, yet by the 1880s the corporation had already shown the eventual bureaucratic direction it was going to take. Corporate organization became a standing taunt to this dream of individual success; and yet subservience to bureaucratic organization is found incompatible with the Protestant ethic. What, then, is the significance of thrift, hard work, and self-reliance for the present generation?

24

THE DECLINE OF THE PROTESTANT ETHIC*
William H. Whyte, Jr.

Let us go back a moment to the turn of the century. If we pick up the Protestant Ethic as it was then expressed we will find it apparently in full flower. We will also find, however, an ethic that already had been strained by reality. The country had changed. The ethic had not.

Here, in the words of banker Henry Clews as he gave some fatherly advice to Yale students in 1908, is the Protestant Ethic in purest form:

Survival of Fittest. You may start in business, or the professions, with your feet on the bottom rung of the ladder; it rests with you to acquire the strength to climb to the top. You can do so if you have the will and the force to back you. There is always plenty of room at the top. . . . Success comes to the man who tries to compel success to yield to him. Cassius spoke well to Brutus when he said, "The Fault is not in our stars, dear Brutus, that we are underlings, but in our natures."

Thrift. Form the habit as soon as you become a money-earner, or money-

maker, of saving a part of your salary, or profits. Put away one dollar out of every ten you earn. The time will come in your lives when, if you have a little money, you can control circumstances; otherwise circumstances will control you. . . .

Note the use of such active words as *climb, force, compel, control.* As stringently as ever before, the Protestant Ethic still counseled struggle against one's environment—the kind of practical, here and now struggle that paid off in material rewards. And spiritually too. The hard-boiled part of the Protestant Ethic was incomplete, of course, without the companion assurance that such success was moral as well as practical. To continue with Mr. Clews:

Under this free system of government, whereby individuals are free to get a living or to pursue wealth as each chooses, the usual result is competition. Obviously, then, competition really means industrial freedom. Thus, anyone may choose his own trade or profession, or, if he does not like it, he may change. He is free to work hard or not; he may make his own bargains and set his price upon his labor or his products. He is free to acquire property to any extent, or to part with it. By dint of greater effort or superior skill, or by intelligence, if he can make better wages, he is free to live better, just as his neighbor is free to follow his example and to learn to excel him in turn. If anyone has a genius for making and managing money, he is free to exercise his genius, just as another is free to handle his tools. . . . If an individual enjoys his money, gained by energy and successful effort, his neighbors are urged to work the harder, that they and their children may have the same enjoyment.

It was an exuberantly optimistic ethic. If everyone could believe that seeking his self-interest automatically improves the lot of all, then the application of hard work should eventually produce a heaven on earth. Some, like the garrulous Mr. Clews, felt it already had.

America is the true field for the human race. It is the hope and the asylum for the oppressed and downtrodden of every clime. It is the inspiring example of America—peerless among the nations of the earth, the brightest star in the political firmament—that is leavening the hard lump of aristocracy and promoting a democratic spirit throughout the world. It is indeed the gem of the ocean to which the world may well offer homage. Here merit is the sole test. Birth is nothing. The fittest survive. Merit is the supreme and only qualification essential to success. Intelligence rules worlds and systems of worlds. It is the dread monarch of illimitable space, and in human society, especially in America, it shines as a diadem on the foreheads of those who stand in the foremost ranks of human

enterprise. Here only a natural order of nobility is recognized, and its motto, without coat of arms or boast of heraldry, is "Intelligence and integrity." *

Without this ethic capitalism would have been impossible. Whether the Protestant Ethic preceded capitalism, as Max Weber argued, or whether it grew up as a consequence, in either event it provided a degree of unity between the way people wanted to behave and the way they thought they *ought* to behave, and without this ideology, society would have been hostile to the entrepreneur. Without the comfort of the Protestant Ethic, he couldn't have gotten away with his acquisitions—not merely because other people wouldn't have allowed him, but because his own conscience would not have. But now he was fortified by the assurance that he was pursuing his obligation to God, and before long, what for centuries had been looked on as the meanest greed, a rising middle class would interpret as the earthly manifestation of God's will.

But the very industrial revolution which this highly serviceable ethic begot in time began to confound it. The inconsistencies were a long while in making themselves apparent. The nineteenth-century inheritors of the ethic were creating an increasingly collective society but steadfastly they denied the implications of it. In current retrospect the turn of the century seems a golden age of individualism, yet by the 1880s the corporation had already shown the eventual bureaucratic direction it was going to take. As institutions grew in size and became more stratified, they made all too apparent inconsistencies which formerly could be ignored. One of the key assumptions of the Protestant Ethic had been that success was due neither to luck nor to the environment but only to one's natural qualities—if men grew rich it was because they deserved to. But the big organization became a standing taunt to this dream of individual success. Quite obviously to anyone who worked in a big organization,

* Henry Clews, *Fifty Years in Wall Street,* Irving Publishing Company, New York, 1908.

those who survived best were not necessarily the fittest but, in more cases than not, those who by birth and personal connections had the breaks.

As organizations continued to expand, the Protestant Ethic became more and more divergent from the reality The Organization was itself creating. The managers steadfastly denied the change, but they, as much as those they led, were affected by it. Today, some still deny the inconsistency or blame it on creeping socialism; for the younger generation of managers however, the inconsistencies have become importuning.

Thrift, for example. How can the organization man be thrifty? Other people are thrifty *for* him. He still buys most of his own life insurance, but for the bulk of his rainy-day saving, he gives his proxy to the financial and personnel departments of his organization. In his professional capacity also thrift is becoming a little un-American. The same man who will quote from Benjamin Franklin on thrift for the house organ would be horrified if consumers took these maxims to heart and started putting more money into savings and less into installment purchases. No longer can he afford the luxury of damning the profligacy of the public; not in public, at any rate. He not only has to persuade people to buy more but persuade them out of any guilt feelings they might have for following his advice. Few talents are more commercially sought today than the knack of describing departures from the Protestant Ethic as reaffirmations of it.

In an advertisement that should go down in social history, the J. Walter Thompson agency has hit the problem of absolution head-on. It quotes Benjamin Franklin on the benefits of spending. "Is not the hope of being one day able to purchase and enjoy luxuries a great spur to labor and industry? . . . May not luxury therefore produce more than it consumes, if, without such a spur, people would be, as they are naturally enough inclined to be, lazy and indolent?" This thought, the ad says, in a meaningful aside, "appears to be a mature afterthought, quali-fying his earlier and more familiar writings on the importance of thrift."

"Hard work?" What price capitalism, the question is now so frequently asked, unless we turn our productivity into more leisure, more of the good life? To the organization man this makes abundant sense, and he is as sensitive to the bogy of overwork and ulcers as his forebears were to the bogy of slothfulness. But he is split. He believes in leisure, but so does he believe in the Puritan insistence on hard, self-denying work—and there are, alas, only twenty-four hours a day. How, then, to be "broad gauge"? The "broad-gauge" model we hear so much about these days is the man who keeps his work separate from leisure and the rest of his life. Any organization man who managed to accomplish this feat wouldn't get very far. He still works hard, in short, but now he has to feel somewhat guilty about it.

Self-reliance? The corporation estates have been expanding so dynamically of late that until about now the management man could suppress the thought that he was a bureaucrat—bureaucrats, as every businessman knew, were those people down in Washington who preferred safety to adventure. Just when the recognition began to dawn, no one can say, but since the war the younger generation of management haven't been talking of self-reliance and adventure with quite the straight face of their elders.

That upward path toward the rainbow of achievement leads smack through the conference room. No matter what name the process is called—permissive management, multiple management, the art of administration— the committee way simply can't be equated with the "rugged" individualism that is supposed to be the business of business. Not for lack of ambition do the younger men dream so moderately; what they lack is the illusion that they will carry on in the great entrepreneurial spirit. Although they cannot bring themselves to use the word bureaucrat, the approved term—the "administrator"—is not signally different in its implications. The man of the future, as junior executives see him, is not the individualist but the man who works through others for others.

Let me pause for a moment to emphasize a necessary distinction. Within business there are still many who cling resolutely to the Protestant Ethic, and some with as much rapacity as drove any nineteenth-century buccaneer. But only rarely are they of The Organization. Save for a small, and spectacular, group of financial operators, most who adhere to the old creed are small businessmen, and to group them as part of the "business community," while convenient, implies a degree of ideological kinship with big business that does not exist.

Out of inertia, the small business is praised as the acorn from which a great oak may grow, the shadow of one man that may lengthen into a large enterprise. Examine businesses with fifty or less employees, however, and it becomes apparent the sentimentality obscures some profound differences. You will find some entrepreneurs in the classic sense—men who develop new products, new appetites, or new systems of distribution—and some of these enterprises may mature into self-perpetuating institutions. But very few.

The great majority of small business firms cannot be placed on any continuum with the corporation. For one thing, they are rarely engaged in primary industry; for the most part they are the laundries, the insurance agencies, the restaurants, the drugstores, the bottling plants, the lumber yards, the automobile dealers. They are vital, to be sure, but essentially they service an economy; they do not create new money within their area and they are dependent ultimately on the business and agriculture that does.

In this dependency they react more as antagonists than allies with the corporation. The corporation, it has become clear, is expansionist—a force for change that is forever a threat to the economics of the small businessman. By instinct he inclines to the monopolistic and the restrictive. When the druggists got the "Fair Trade" laws passed it was not only the manufacturers (and customers) they were rebelling against but the whole

mass economy movement of the twentieth century.

The tail wagged the dog in this case and it still often does. That it can, in the face of the growing power of the corporation, illustrates again the dominance mythology can have over reality. Economically, many a small businessman is a counterrevolutionist and the revolution he is fighting is that of the corporation as much as the New or Fair Deal. But the corporation man still clings to the idea that the two are firm allies, and on some particulars, such as fair trade, he often makes policy on this basis when in fact it is against the corporation's interests to do so.

But the revolution is not to be stopped by sentiment. Many anachronisms do remain; in personal income, for example, the corporation man who runs a branch plant on which a whole town depends is lucky to make half the income of the local car dealer or the man with the Coca-Cola franchise. The economy has a way of attending to these discrepancies, however, and the local businessman can smell the future as well as anyone else. The bland young man The Organization sent to town to manage the plant is almost damnably inoffensive; he didn't rent the old place on the hill but a smaller house, he drives an Olds instead of a Caddy, and when he comes to the Thursday luncheons he listens more than he talks. But he's the future just the same.

I have been talking of the impact of organization on the Protestant Ethic; just as important, however, was the intellectual assault. In the great revolt against traditionalism that began around the turn of the century, William James, John Dewey, Charles Beard, Thorstein Veblen, the muckrakers and a host of reformers brought the anachronisms of the Protestant Ethic under relentless fire, and in so doing helped lay the groundwork for the Social Ethic. It would be a long time before organization men would grasp the relevance of these new ideas, and to this day many of the most thorough-going pragmatists in business would recoil at being grouped with the intellectuals. (And vice versa.) But the two movements were intimately related. To what degree the intellectuals were a cause of change, or a manifestation, no one can say for certain, but more presciently than those in organization they grasped the antithesis between the old concept of the rational, unbeholden individual and the world one had to live in. They were not rebels against society; what they fought was the denial of society's power, and they provided an intellectual framework that would complement, rather than inhibit, the further growth of big organization.

It is not in the province of this book to go into a diagnosis of the ideas of Dewey and James and the other pragmatists. But there is one point of history I think very much needs making at this time. Many people still look on the decline of the Protestant Ethic as our fall from grace, a detour from Americanism for which we can blame pragmatism, ethical relativism, Freudianism and other such developments. These movements have contributed much to the Social Ethic, and many of their presuppositions are as shaky as those they replaced. To criticize them on this score is in order; to criticize them as having subverted the American temper, however, is highly misleading.

Critics of pragmatism, and followers too, should remember the context of the times in which the pragmatists made their case. The pragmatists' emphasis on social utility may be redundant for today's needs, but when they made their case it was not a time when psychology or adjustment or social living were popular topics but at a time when the weight of conservative opinion denied that there was anything much that needed adjusting. Quite clearly, revolt was in order. The growth of the organization society did demand a recognition that man was not entirely a product of his free will; the country did need an educational plant more responsive to the need of the people. It did need a new breeze, and if there had been no James or no Dewey, some form of pragmatism would probably have been invented anyway. Nonphilosophical Americans sensed that changes were in order

too; what the philosophers of pragmatism did was to give them guidance and tell them in intellectually responsible terms that they were right in feeling that way.

Pragmatism's emphasis on the social and the practical, furthermore, was thoroughly in the American tradition. From the beginning, Americans had always been impatient with doctrines and systems; like the Puritans, many came here because of a doctrine, but what they came to was a new environment that required some powerful adapting to, and whenever the doctrine got in the way of practicality, the doctrine lost out. Few people have had such a genius for bending ideals to the demands of the times, and the construction of fundamental theory, theological or scientific, has never excited Americans overmuch. Long before James, *Does it work?* was a respectable question to ask. If impatience at abstract thought was a defect, it was the defect of a virtue, and the virtue, call it what you will, has always been very close to pragmatism as Dewey and James defined it. By defining it they gave it coherence and power at a time when it needed assertion, but the inclination to the practical antedated the philosophy; it was not the product of it.

Reform was everywhere in the air. By the time of the First World War the Protestant Ethic had taken a shellacking from which it would not recover; rugged individualism and hard work had done wonders for the people to whom God in his infinite wisdom, as one put it, had given control of society. But it hadn't done so well for everyone else and now they, as well as the intellectuals, were all too aware of the fact.

The ground, in short, was ready, and though the conservative opinion that drew the fire of the rebels seemed entrenched, the basic temper of the country was so inclined in the other direction that emphasis on the social became the dominant current of U.S. thought. In a great outburst of curiosity, people became fascinated with the discovering of all the environmental pressures on the individual that previous philosophies had denied. As with Freud's discoveries, the findings of such inquiries were deeply disillusioning at first, but with characteristic exuberance Americans found a rainbow. Man might not be perfectible after all, but there was another dream and now at last it seemed practical: the perfectibility of *society*.

T. V. Smith begins his article in the following engaging manner: "It is rumored at home, and echoed abroad; or it is rumored abroad, and echoed at home, that our American democracy moves too slowly for survival in a rapid world; that we are economically too competitive when the aspirations of men are for comradeship and cooperative living; that we are too partisan in politics and too irresponsible in talk; and that we are too secular in our philosophy of life."

These charges and their implications are examined by Smith in the light of the American way of life. There are evidences of truth in the indictments, but it is important to realize that erroneous conclusions may be drawn from them.

25

DEMOCRATIC APOLOGETICS*
T. V. Smith

It is rumored at home, and echoed abroad; or it is rumored abroad, and echoed at home, that our American democracy moves too slowly for survival in a rapid world; that we are economically too competitive when the aspirations of men are for comradeship and co-operative living; that we are too partisan in politics and too irresponsible in talk; and that we are too secular in our philosophy of life. It is true that we sometimes move slowly, that our economy in general is competitive, that our politics is strident, and that our main bearings are secular. The degree to which each of these is true is a matter for investigation and definition. But neither the fact nor yet the degree of each is enough to condemn the democratic way of life that is practiced in America. Indeed, a defense of de-mocracy may be constructed upon the basis of general admission of the charges but of detailed demurrer to the conclusions drawn therefrom. Democratic apologetics may indeed rear a stately structure upon the very ruins of the prevailing indictment. It is that very task which we now undertake.

1. *It is rumored at home, and echoed abroad, that our democracy moves too slowly in a world now stuck in high gear.*—Majority decision does take time, though varying with exigencies. When arrived at, however, majority decision prevents backing and filling, or wholesale reaction full of waste, all of which are themselves time-consuming in countries totalitarian in their processes and revolutionary in their hopes. Majority support is a solid resource for the implementation of any policy.

* Reprinted from *Ethics*, vol. 63, no. 2, pp. 100–106, January, 1953. By permission of the author, the journal, and the University of Chicago Press, publishers.

It is arguable that democracy evens up to a fair comparison with other systems in the total time elapsed between conception and consummation of public policy.

Take crucial cases. Since war is usually thought of as crucial, take Pearl Harbor. It was only a matter of hours from Japanese action in this case to decisive American reaction. But, one answers, that was foregone. Well, then, some rapid decisions *are* foregone in a democracy, as indeed some slow decisions are commendable. The Civil War came slowly, maturing through half a century. Should the decision in that case have been made faster? Had it been made even more slowly, it perhaps need not have been made at all. Take a recent martial decision which was certainly not foregone: *Korea!*

It was far from certain that aggression in Korea must be met by the armed forces of our democracy, and more slowly by the armed forces of the free world through the cumbersome machinery of the United Nations. In Manchuria such aggression was not so met in the twenties. In Ethiopia it was not so met in the thirties. At Munich it was not so met. In Korea it *was* so met. Within something like one rotation of the earth on its axis we were at (limited) war in Korea, though with all but mythical forces. Democracy, that is to say, can act rapidly upon occasion. Whether it does or does not do so depends largely upon the necessity of the case and upon its desirability. It is no virtue to do rapidly what should not be done and only a qualified virtue to do rapidly what should be done more slowly. Decisiveness of action depends upon heavy concurrence in the desirability of collective action; and such time as is required therefore must be allowed. Haste no less than lethargy can make waste.

It is arguable that free peoples have learned the lesson that aggression unresisted is a sure way to jeopardize the peace: Manchuria, Ethiopia, Czechoslovakia. Three lessons in a generation appear to have proved something unambiguously. And when the proof of action is decisive, democracy can act quickly. When proof is lacking, quick action

is no test of wisdom and no standard, therefore, for condemning democracy.

> All experience hath shown that mankind is more disposed to suffer while evils are sufferable, than to right themselves by abolishing forms to which they are accustomed.

Thus Jefferson in explanation of slow action toward our then mother, England; but at the same time in defense of decisive action when the last hour of fruitful forbearance had struck. The same Jefferson later defended the snail pace of his own "domestic revolution" by cautioning an impatient constituent in these weighty words:

> I am sensible how far I . . . fall short of effecting all the reformation which reason would suggest, and experience approve, were I free to do whatever I thought best; but when we reflect how difficult it is to move or to inflect the great machine of society, how impossible to advance the notions of a whole people suddenly to ideal right, we see the wisdom of Solon's remark that no more good must be attempted than the nation will bear.

There is much to be said in favor of slowly matured action rather than mere quickness of response. So much, indeed, that the burden of proof is upon those who think that democracy errs as to the tempo of policy decisions. Meantime, Roosevelt's tempo in dealing with the depression, the quickness with which we have declared war upon unambiguous occasions, and in general the capacity of large populations to make up their mind about some things instantaneously— these all tend, while awaiting proof to the contrary, to balance the account and to bring the scales to rest in favor of our average rate of progression. Even atomic wars may yet be won by losing atomic battles. Confidence in the tempo of our decisions is inextricably involved with faith in our way of life. It is to be guessed that critics at home, as it is known that foes abroad, are enemies, not friends, of our way of life when they accept as proved our incapacity to meet fate at the crossroads, and to meet it masterfully. We may fool such critics again, as we have fooled them before, by being quick enough when decisiveness is called for and by being deliberate enough for victory when haste could only make for moral waste.

2. *It is charged abroad (hardly less from the Vatican than in the Kremlin), and echoed at home, that capitalistic economics is selfish, rapacious, and immorally competitive.*—General Eisenhower reports Marshal Zhukov unforgettably upon this matter. "He felt," says the General of the Marshal, "our system appealed to all that was selfish in people. He said that we induced a man to do things by telling him he might keep what he earned, might say what he pleased, and in every direction allowed him to be largely an undisciplined, unoriented entity within a great national complex."

"He asked me," our General continues of the Marshal, "to understand a system in which the attempt was made to substitute for such motivations the devotion of a man to the great national complex of which he formed a part." Eisenhower adds: "There was no doubt in my mind that Marshal Zhukov was sincere." Nor need there be any doubt in anybody's mind that critics of our capitalistic democracy at home, as well as its enemies abroad, are sincere. But that has literally nothing to do with *it,* though much to do with *them.* "Certitude," says Justice Holmes, "is never the test of certainty."

The question is of facts, not of fancies, however sincere the fancies be. *Is* there any better way of arranging the production of goods, of effecting their distribution, and of enjoying their consumption? Whoever disavows the economy that has grown up in the West, flowering in America, and which has proved itself compatible with personal liberty and with great political leeway, is either committing himself to the alternative system of communism, utterly incompatible with either personal liberty or political freedom, or is merrily tugging at the bootstraps of his own

theorizing. The choice today must be one or the other of these realities, as objects of loyalty. There is no ideal way of exploiting the earth and of supporting mankind upon it, now available as alternative to the hard choice between prevailing realities. But American capitalism constitutes meantime a most effective way of supporting with increasing standards of life a population redoubling itself each generation or so. One need hardly grieve for the luxury of pure ideality when the necessities of reality are made so tolerable.

The realities of capitalism raise the presumption that we have something differentially good in our economic system, whatever its enemies abroad or its critics at home may say. To set over against individualism and the resulting principle of competition as our main regulatory device some vague notion of co-operation is to understand neither men nor society. Men have always competed, and will always compete, no less in theories than in practices. It is a question, then, not of competition but as to what should be the prime object of competition. We make the object money, property, goods—things objective and capable of isolation and identification and control. The Russians make the object of competition deference, pride, power. Now the strange thing is that competition over the "spiritual" things, like theirs, is much more inhumane than is competition over material things, like ours. Private property gets no stronger commendation than the observation that men will not often kill each other over money. When, however, it is not money but "is the principle of the thing," then somebody must not infrequently get killed. Property would be justifiably kept private if there were no other reason for it than to provide men something relatively harmless to quarrel about. Those who quarrel about "truth," "the party line," "deviations"—they are the ones who actually perpetrate what is only charged in theory against capitalism: man's deepest inhumanity to man.

Co-operation covers a multitude of vices as well as certain virtues. Men do not have to kiss in order to co-operate; co-operation is compatible with a certain decent social distance. To make co-operation a sweety-sweety thing of brotherhood is to force men to find their bitters in places more stark than in capitalistic competition. Truth to tell, competition, as practiced in our capitalistic system, under certain rules of the game or at least with a certain feeling of *noblesse oblige,* is a *form* of co-operation. Indeed, competition is the best form of co-operation for daily living. It is the only form which has proved able to support itself without the recurrent necessity of liquidating erstwhile comrades in the high name of brotherly kindness. Romantic co-operation in the name of heaven seldom fails to make of earth a hell. An oriental philosopher could put this matter with more grace, however, as Hu Shih indeed has put it with more cogency, than can an occidental apologist for our own way of life.

The term "materialistic civilization," which has often been applied to stigmatize the modern civilization of the West, seems to me to be a more appropriate word for the . . . backward civilizations of the East. For to me that civilization is materialistic which is limited by matter and incapable of transcending it; which feels itself powerless against its material environment and fails to make the full use of human intelligence for the conquest of nature and for the improvement of the condition of man.

3. *It is rumored abroad, and echoed at home, that our politics is too partisan in nature and too strident in conduct.*—In a national campaign year one could not hear himself deny—even if he tried it!—that American politics is both strident and highly partisan. What are the options? We would not get rid of the stridency by suppressing the partisanship. Parties must bicker; for most of life lies beyond indisputable facts and so falls inside the permissible and inexorable zone of dispute. But must there *be* parties? Yes, there must be parties, on pain of something much worse than parties, namely, The Party!

What we now know to have happened behind the scenes in Mussolini's nonpartisan Italy and in Hitler's antipartisan Germany makes us guess that in Russia the presence of only one party does not spell the quiescence, as it attempts to delineate the doom, of dissent. There may be over a decade less noise from the retail output of a democratic country than there is in any totalitarian country with its stormy quiet, its revolutionary outburst, and the consequent slow and murmurous recovery from a thunder-and-lightning regime. The way it averages up is, again, what counts for humanity.

And the average, even admitting the general charge, is most likely in favor of democracy. At any rate partisanship is not to be dismissed by a wave of the wand. Though communism proposes as end the achievement of utter quiet, of pure comradeship, through the "withering away" of all partisan power, Russia approaches this idyllic end—if she does—by a succession of brutal means in which the state is more strident than any regime this capitalistic country has ever known. What they call "peace," even at home boils down to what is worse than our wars.

We think it, therefore, more fruitful to allow the partisan spirit to channel it and to exploit it than to command the sea of dynamic impulses to cease from surging. So, accepting party politics as inevitable, we are able to see in it much that is desirable. This acceptance of politics as normal and inevitable has characterized American democracy from the beginning. This is indeed the most fundamental difference between us and communism: we believe in politics; Communists do not. It was James Madison, "Father of the Constitution," who spoke at our national prime the words that still carry weight in our political maturity:

As long as the reason of man continues fallible, and he is at liberty to exercise it, different opinions will be formed. . . . The latent causes of faction are thus *sown in the nature* of man; and we see them everywhere brought into different degrees of activity, according to the different circumstances of civil society . . . *of speculation as of practice*. . . . So strong is this propensity of mankind to fall into mutual animosities, that *where no substantial occasion* presents itself, *the most frivolous and fanciful distinctions* have been sufficient to kindle their unfriendly passions and to excite their most violent conflict. [Italics mine.]

There it is, and stated like a true philosopher. Madison goes on to see and to say that property is the avenue through which much of the passion is drained off—and politics takes care of much of the rest.

Now it ill becomes those who sneer at the stridency of our partisanship to change "the party line" on one another without warning—as in poor Browder's case—and then ring the welkins, on one side, with the most intemperate denunciations and, on the other side—especially in Russia—with the most abject breast-beatings of confessed guilt. We do not berate them for their noise; noise must be. We bemoan the fruitlessness of their ragings. Our noise works the peaceable fruits of discipline, it begets closer inspection of performance and the more circumspect perpetration of policies. Prideful power, as on their side, becomes presumptuous in its pretense and brutal in its practice. In democratic America we support an opposition for the taming of power, and we profit in our two-party system from continuous criticism, of both men and measures. No other way is known of getting much light without the toleration of a certain amount of heat.

Moreover, our phenomenon of national elections, where and when our noise grows differentially uncircumspect, serves fruitfully in another category. Government must depend upon *miranda* not less than upon *credenda*, even granting escape from *horrenda*. The aesthetic element is not to be dispensed with, and so not to be despised, in the governance of men. There is a catharsis operative in political campaigning, however small may

seem the earned increment from such collective parturition. Name-calling substitutes for neck-breaking, and a sense of shame humbles both parties alike when the election is over and the responsible work of Congress sets in. Nobody gets killed in our stridency, and everybody remains to join in the sportsmanship of bipartisan legislation and in the nonpartisan administration of justice.

Political apologetics passes thus legitimately into a paean of praise for democratic procedures as history discloses what it is that democracy saves men from. We know little in America of arbitrary power, less of tyrranical suppression; we know nothing of brazen sadism, nothing of logical presumption, nothing of the falsification of history and the outrage upon individual truth-seekers. And the paean of praise sings itself into a symphony as it takes the high constructive notes. We rid ourselves through national political campaigns and otherwise of many aggressions; we purge ourselves of much extravagance of hope; we achieve party purification through partisan investigations; and we possess ourselves subsequently of correction of policy through the steady criticism of an opposition operating within the framework of *noblesse oblige*. In short, we achieve recreation through continuous self-criticism. We admit the facts of politics as charged, but we claim from the practice of partisan politics not only a product infinitely superior to any alternative but also a resultant of positive spiritual significance.

4. *It is rumored at home, and echoed abroad, that the foundations of our society have grown too secular to replenish the historic springs of our spiritual vitality.*—This seems to me the most groundless, and yet the most insidious, of all the charges hurled today against our democracy. It has deep residence here at home, as it is echoed abroad from religious sources and in other forms already indicated (that we are "materialistic," etc.). So long as such rumors spring from merely sectarian sources, jealous of their own sacerdotal power and ambitious for their own priestly prowess, so long could they be sus-

tained with some degree of complacency. But when such charges spread into all religious denominations at home and then creep as fears into minds independent of organized sectarianism, it is time to meet them head-on.

When something denominated "spiritual" is set over against what is then called "secular," it is almost certain that the two categories overlap too much to be of logical use. When the "secular," for instance, is allowed to cover artistic, scientific, and political impulses, it is clear that if spirituality has anything to do with the human spirit, save to castigate it, then the baby is being risked with the dumping of the bath. If spirituality, on the other side, be confined to something theologically esoteric, then it covers what is not as indispensable to human society as its partisans think.

Theology is something over which the widest differences prevail; in any given form it is deeply divisive; for there is always an opposing form. There is no way, for instance, to prove trinitarianism or to disprove unitarianism. Such "proofs" hold only for those already convinced, and hold equally for them, which leave us where we were. I do not belittle the importance of such issues, and I certainly admit the excitement attending arguments thereon; but I can see that such issues become important for democracy only when they are surrounded by beliefs more amenable than they and, even thus oriented, only when they are pursued with some tolerance and positive *noblesse oblige*. Men have meat to eat that logicians know not of; but meat requires more peace for the eating than arises naturally in a theological climate.

The "spiritual," esoterically conceived, requires, that is, the "secular," as defined, to make "spirituality" safe for democracy. Even religion, as conducive to democracy, has nothing to fear from secularism. It is sectarianism, not secularism, that constitutes the greatest danger to democracy, and to religion as well. If the spiritual does not include the scrupulosity of science, the sensitivity of art, and the sportsmanship of politics, then the spiritual is desiccated out of all relevance to

the democratic way of life. If it includes all these authentic values, then the secular becomes itself a high form of spirituality.

All this was ABC's to our Founding Fathers. Few of the leading ones were satisfactorily "religious" to the religious of their age. And some of the more articulate ones, like Jefferson, were fearfully "irreligious." He advised a young nephew, his ward, boldly to question the very existence of God, on the theory that a deity worthy of a free man's worship would prefer such independence to human servility. As for himself, Jefferson declared that whether a man believed in one God or twenty gods or no god never "picked my pocket nor broke my leg" and therefore was a matter irrelevant to citizenship. He carried it further. "History, I believe," said he, "furnishes no example of a priest-ridden people maintaining a free civil government." He carried the matter much further still. These were his personal opinions; but—and mark this well—he got the fruitage of these personal opinions written not only into the law of Virginia but incorporated in the Constitution of the United States—in as complete a separation of church and state as he was able to devise.

"Congress shall make no law as touching the establishment of religion or prohibiting the free exercise thereof." It is this ringing phrase of our Bill of Rights which still piques and plagues sectarians of every church and creed—to everyone who suspects, if he does not any longer believe, that the salvation of our citizenship depends, not upon religion, but upon his sectarian version thereof. Such fanatics are indeed adequately described, though far from disposed of, by the wisecrack: "Only men who do what God would do if God had all the facts."

Yet it is this darkened spirit which lies back of the campaign today against what is described as the dread secularism of American life. It is this spirit which inspires sectaries to deprecate the public schools and, if they cannot divert part of the tax support, then to foist upon this free system the shadow of their own beclouded vision. Such sectarians actually think that spirituality is a thing so cheap that it can be furthered by some formal reading of scripture in schools or by public prayers desiccated with neutralism, if they cannot be poisoned with partisanship. Little do such provincials remember, as already quoted from Justice Holmes, that "certitude is never the test of certainty." Little do they understand, with that wise man, that "to think great thoughts you must be heroes as well as idealists." Quite beyond them is the truth that it takes more heroism to contain than to perpetrate personal convictions as public policy. Little, in short, do they fathom, with Holmes, the depth of the spiritual life. "Only when you have worked alone," says he with secular saintliness, "when you have felt around you a black gulf of solitude more isolating than that which surrounds the dying man, and in hope and in despair have trusted to your own unshaken will—then only will you have achieved."

It is those who suppose that spirituality can be confined to religion, and that religion can be narrowed to a sect, who stand fearful before the great ocean of truth that stretches from the sensitive soul to the periphery covered by art and science and politics—and then on beyond even these to an immensity not yet discernible to honest eyes.

Despite all such narrowness and fearfulness, this republic, both in its public schools and in the majestic adult tutelage of its politics, is a spiritual enterprise of such magnitude that whoever is caught up in its processes experiences a sense of magnificence never vouchsafed to those who live on the dogmatic droppings of tired spirits. Spirituality is not something to be superadded to function. Spirituality is the spirit functioning in magnanimity through all the specialized reaches of democratic endeavor.

Broadening the purview, let me whisper this parting thought, then, to those who would save us from dogmatic communism by imposing their own dogma in its stead: Communism is not a secularism; it is a new sacerdotalism making irreligion as dogmatic, and as deadly to spirit, as the old sacerdotalism made, and would yet make, its own brand of orthodoxy. I do not thus confide some private intuition, but what can be boldly proclaimed as the official philosophy of America. "If there is any fixed star in our constitutional constellation," says Mr. Justice Jackson in an opinion which now prevails as the judgment of the Supreme Court, "it is that no official, high or petty, can prescribe what shall be orthodox in politics, nationalism, religion, or other matters of opinion, or force citizens to confess by word, or act their faith therein."

America as is, is replete with spirituality; and it has religion enough for its exigencies, if only religious partisans can be got to continue operation under the common canopy of democratic *noblesse oblige*. The secular state has been put over the churches not to interfere with religion but to prevent religions from doing spirituality to death. This "wall of separation" is the symbol of our spiritual strength; it is the parapet from which gleams the searchlight of our national glory. "We are a Christian people," declared Chief Justice Hughes with finality, "but we are also a nation with the duty to survive."

John Stuart Mill gives a classic exposition of two kinds of governmental intervention—the authoritative and the nonauthoritative. It would be authoritative intervention for the government to control the free agency of individuals; it would be nonauthoritative if the government gives advice and promulgates information instead of issuing commands and enforcing them by penalties. The authoritative form has a much more limited sphere of legitimate action. Whatever form is adopted, Mill insists that there must be some area of every individual's life with which no government ought to be permitted to interfere.

The principle of *laissez faire* or noninterference is explored by Mill with reference to political, economic, educational, and other relationships between individuals and their government. It is equally natural for mankind to develop in either direction—toward freedom or toward subordination to tyranny. However, when accustomed to self-reliance and initiative in their common life, people tend to repel tyranny. On the other hand, in proportion as all real initiative and direction resides in the government, and the people are trained to live a role of dependency, there would be, instead of a desire for freedom, an unmeasured appetite for place and power—a chance of tyrannizing.

Thus Mill presents what may be called "the anatomy of state interference," and it will be interesting to apply his principles of analysis to contemporary trends in governmental dominance.

26

OF THE GROUNDS AND LIMITS OF THE LAISSER-FAIRE OR NON-INTERFERENCE PRINCIPLE *

John Stuart Mill

1. We have now reached the last part of our undertaking; the discussion, so far as suited to this treatise (that is, so far as it is a question of principle, not detail), of the limits of the province of government: the question, to what objects governmental intervention in the affairs of society may or should extend, over and above those which necessarily appertain to it. No subject has been more keenly contested in the present age: the contest, however, has chiefly taken place round certain select points, with only flying excursions into the rest of the field. Those indeed who have discussed any particular question of government interference, such as state education (spiritual or secular), regula-tion of hours of labour, a public provision for the poor, &c., have often dealt largely in general arguments, far outstretching the special application made of them, and have shown a sufficiently strong bias either in favour of letting things alone, or in favour of meddling; but have seldom declared, or apparently decided in their own minds, how far they would carry either principle. The supporters of interference have been content with asserting a general right and duty on the part of government to intervene, where-ever its intervention would be useful: and when those who have been called the *laisser-faire* school have attempted any definite limi-tation of the province of government, they

* From *Principles of Political Economy*, Longmans, Green & Co., Ltd., London, various editions 1865, 1909, 1926, 1936. Selection is from Book V, chap. XI, secs. 1–7. (Other editions and pub-lishers from 1848 onward.)

have usually restricted it to the protection of person and property against force and fraud; a definition to which neither they nor anyone else can deliberately adhere, since it excludes, as has been shown in a preceding chapter, some of the most indispensable and unanimously recognized of the duties of government.

Without professing entirely to supply this deficiency of a general theory, on a question which does not, as I conceive, admit of any universal solution, I shall attempt to afford some little aid towards the resolution of this class of questions as they arise, by examining, in the most general point of view in which the subject can be considered, what are the advantages, and what the evils or inconveniences, of government interference.

We must set out by distinguishing two kinds of intervention by the government, which, though they may relate to the same subject, differ widely in their nature and effects, and require, for their justification, motives of a very different degree of urgency. The intervention may extend to controlling the free agency of individuals. Government may interdict all persons from doing certain things; or from doing them without its authorization; or may prescribe to them certain things to be done, or a certain manner of doing things which it is left optional with them to do or to abstain from. This is the *authoritative* interference of government. There is another kind of intervention which is not authoritative: when a government, instead of issuing a command and enforcing it by penalties, adopts the course so seldom resorted to by governments, and of which such important use might be made, that of giving advice, and promulgating information; or when, leaving individuals free to use their own means of pursuing any object of general interest, the government, not meddling with them, but not trusting the object solely to their care, establishes, side by side with their arrangements, an agency of its own for a like purpose. Thus, it is one thing to maintain a Church Establishment, and another to refuse toleration to other religions, or to persons professing no religion. It is one thing to provide schools or colleges, and another to require that no person shall act as an instructor of youth without a government license. There might be a national bank, or a government manufactory, without any monopoly against private banks and manufactories. There might be a post-office, without penalties against the conveyance of letters by other means. There might be a corps of government engineers for civil purposes, while the profession of a civil engineer is free to be adopted by every one. There may be public hospitals, without any restriction upon private medical or surgical practice.

2. It is evident, even at first sight, that the authoritative form of government intervention has a much more limited sphere of legitimate action than the other. It requires a much stronger necessity to justify it in any case; while there are large departments of human life from which it must be unreservedly and imperiously excluded. Whatever theory we adopt respecting the foundation of the social union, and under whatever political institutions we live, there is a circle around every individual human being which no government, be it that of one, of a few, or of the many, ought to be permitted to overstep: there is a part of the life of every person who has come to years of discretion, within which the individuality of that person ought to reign uncontrolled either by any other individual or by the public collectively. That there is, or ought to be, some space in human existence thus entrenched around, and sacred from authoritative intrusion, no one who professes the smallest regard to human freedom or dignity will call in question: the point to be determined is, where the limit should be placed; how large a province of human life this reserved territory should include. I apprehend that it ought to include all that part which concerns only the life, whether inward or outward, of the individual, and does not affect the interests of others, or affects them only through the moral influence of example. With respect to the domain of the inward consciousness, the

thoughts and feelings, and as much of external conduct as is personal only, involving no consequences, none at least of a painful or injurious kind, to other people; I hold that it is allowable in all, and in the more thoughtful and cultivated often a duty, to assert and promulgate, with all the force they are capable of, their opinion of what is good or bad, admirable or contemptible, but not to compel others to conform to that opinion; whether the force used is that of extra-legal coercion, or exerts itself by means of the law.

Even in those portions of conduct which do affect the interest of others, the onus of making out a case always lies on the defenders of legal prohibitions. It is not a merely constructive or presumptive injury to others which will justify the interference of law with individual freedom. To be prevented from doing what one is inclined to, or from acting according to one's own judgment of what is desirable, is not only always irksome, but always tends, *pro tanto*, to starve the development of some portion of the bodily or mental faculties, either sensitive or active; and unless the conscience of the individual goes freely with the legal restraint, it partakes, either in a great or in a small degree, of the degradation of slavery. Scarcely any degree of utility, short of absolute necessity, will justify a prohibitory regulation, unless it can also be made to recommend itself to the general conscience; unless persons of ordinary good intentions either believe already, or can be induced to believe, that the thing prohibited is a thing which they ought not to wish to do.

It is otherwise with governmental interferences which do not restrain individual free agency. When a government provides means for fulfilling a certain end, leaving individuals free to avail themselves of different means if in their opinion preferable, there is no infringement of liberty, no irksome or degrading restraint. One of the principal objections to government interference is then absent. There is, however, in almost all forms of government agency, one thing which is compulsory; the provision of the pecuniary means. These are derived from taxation; or, if existing in the form of an endowment derived from public property, they are still the cause of as much compulsory taxation as the sale or the annual proceeds of the property would enable to be dispensed with. And the objection necessarily attaching to compulsory contributions, is almost always greatly aggravated by the expensive precautions and onerous restrictions which are indispensable to prevent evasion of a compulsory tax.

3. A second general objection to government agency is that every increase of the functions devolving on the government is an increase of its power, both in the form of authority, and still more, in the indirect form of influence. The importance of this consideration, in respect to political freedom, has in general been quite sufficiently recognized, at least in England; but many, in latter times, have been prone to think that limitation of the powers of the government is only essential when the government itself is badly constituted; when it does not represent the people, but is the organ of a class, or coalition of classes: and that a government of sufficiently popular constitution might be trusted with any amount of power over the nation, since its power would be only that of the nation over itself. This might be true, if the nation, in such cases, did not practically mean a mere majority of the nation, and if minorities were only capable of oppressing, but not of being oppressed. Experience, however, proves that the depositaries of power who are mere delegates of the people, that is of a majority, are quite as ready (when they think they can count on popular support) as any organs of oligarchy to assume arbitrary power, and encroach unduly on the liberty of private life. The public collectively is abundantly ready to impose, not only its generally narrow view of its interests, but its abstract opinions, and even its tastes, as laws binding upon individuals. And the present civilization tends so strongly to make the power of persons acting in masses the only

substantial power in society, that there never was more necessity for surrounding individual independence of thought, speech, and conduct, with the most powerful defences, in order to maintain that originality of mind and individuality of character, which are the only source of any real progress, and of most of the qualities which make the human race much superior to any herd of animals. Hence it is no less important in a democratic than in any other government, that all tendency on the part of public authorities to stretch their interference, and assume a power of any sort which can easily be dispensed with, should be regarded with unremitting jealousy. Perhaps this is even more important in a democracy than in any other form of political society; because, where public opinion is sovereign, an individual who is oppressed by the sovereign does not, as in most other states of things, find a rival power to which he can appeal for relief, or, at all events, for sympathy.

4. A third general objection to government agency rests on the principle of division of labour. Every additional function undertaken by the government is a fresh occupation imposed upon a body already overcharged with duties. A natural consequence is that most things are ill done; much not done at all, because the government is not able to do it without delays which are fatal to its purpose; that the more troublesome, and less showy, of the functions undertaken, are postponed or neglected, and an excuse is always ready for the neglect; while the heads of the administration have their minds so fully taken up with official details, in however perfunctory a manner superintended, that they have no time or thought to spare for the great interests of the state, and the preparation of enlarged measures of social improvement.

But these inconveniences, though real and serious, result much more from the bad organization of governments, than from the extent and variety of the duties undertaken by them. Government is not a name for some one functionary, or definite number of functionaries; there may be almost any amount of division of labour within the administrative body itself. The evil in question is felt in great magnitude under some of the governments of the Continent, where six or eight men, living at the capital and known by the name of ministers, demand that the whole public business of the country shall pass, or be supposed to pass, under their individual eye. But the inconvenience would be reduced to a very manageable compass, in a country in which there was a proper division of functions between the central and local officers of government, and in which the central body was divided into a sufficient number of departments. When Parliament thought it expedient to confer on the government an inspecting and partially controlling authority over railways, it did not add railways to the department of the Home Minister, but created a Railway Board. When it determined to have a central superintending authority for pauper administration, it established the Poor Law Commission. There are few countries in which a greater number of functions are discharged by public officers, than in some states of the American Union, particularly the New England States: but the division of labour in public business is extreme; most of these officers being not even amenable to any common superior, but performing their duties freely, under the double check of election by their townsmen, and civil as well as criminal responsibility to the tribunals.

It is, no doubt, indispensable to good government that the chiefs of the administration, whether permanent or temporary, should extend a commanding, though general, view over the *ensemble* of all the interests confided, in any degree, to the responsibility of the central power. But with a skilful internal organization of the administrative machine, leaving to subordinates, and as far as possible, to local subordinates, not only the execution, but to a great degree the control, of details; holding them accountable for the results of their acts rather than for the acts themselves, except where these come within the cognizance of the tribunals; taking the most effective securities for honest and capable appointments; opening a broad path to promotion from the inferior degrees of the administrative scale to the superior; leaving, at each step, to the functionary, a wider range in the origination of measures, so that, in the highest grade of all, deliberation might be concentrated on the great collective interests of the country in each department; if all this were done, the government would not probably be overburdened by any business, in other respects fit to be undertaken by it; though the overburdening would remain as a serious addition to the inconveniences incurred by its undertaking any which was unfit.

5. But though a better organization of governments would greatly diminish the force of the objection to the mere multiplication of their duties, it would still remain true that in all the more advanced communities the great majority of things are worse done by the intervention of government, than the individuals most interested in the matter would do them, or cause them to be done, if left to themselves. The grounds of this truth are expressed with tolerable exactness in the popular dictum, that people understand their own business and their own interests better, and care for them more, than the government does, or can be expected to do. This maxim holds true throughout the greatest part of the business of life, and wherever it is true we ought to condemn every kind of government intervention that conflicts with it. The inferiority of government agency, for example, in any of the common operations of industry or commerce, is proved by the fact, that it is hardly ever to maintain itself in equal competition with individual agency, where the individuals possess the requisite degree of industrial enterprise, and can command the necessary assemblage of means. All the facilities which a government enjoys of access to information; all the means which it possesses of remunerating, and therefore, of commanding, the best available talent in the market—are not an equivalent for the one great disadvantage of an inferior interest in the result.

It must be remembered, besides, that even if a government were superior in intelligence and knowledge to any single individual in the nation, it must be inferior to all the individuals in the nation taken together. It can neither possess in itself, nor enlist in its service, more than a portion of the acquirements and capacities which the country contains, applicable to any given purpose. There must be many persons equally qualified for the work with those whom the government employs, even if it selects its instruments with no reference to any consideration but their fitness. Now these are the very persons into whose hands, in the cases of most common occurrence, a system of individual agency naturally tends to throw the work, because they are capable of doing it better or on cheaper terms than any other persons. So far as this is the case, it is evident that government, by excluding or even by superseding individual agency, either substitutes a less qualified agency for one better qualified, or at any rate substitutes its own mode of accomplishing the work, for all the variety of modes which would be tried by a number of equally qualified persons aiming at the same end; a competition by many degress more propitious to the progress of improvement than any uniformity of system.

6. I have reserved for the last place one of the strongest of the reasons against the extension of government agency. Even if the government could comprehend within itself, in each department, all the most eminent intellectual capacity and active talent of the nation, it would not be the less desirable that the conduct of a large portion of the affairs of the society should be left in the hands of the persons immediately interested in them. The business of life is an essential part of the practical education of a people; without which, book and school instruction, though most necessary and salutary, does not suffice to qualify them for conduct, and for the adaptation of means to ends. Instruction is only one of the desiderata of mental improvement; another, almost as indispensable, is a vigorous exercise of the active energies;

labour, contrivance, judgment, self-control: and the natural stimulus to these is the difficulties of life. This doctrine is not to be confounded with the complacent optimism, which represents the evils of life as desirable things, because they call forth qualities adapted to combat with evils. It is only because the difficulties exist, that the qualities which combat them are of any value. As practical beings it is our business to free human life from as many as possible of its difficulties, and not to keep up a stock of them as hunters preserve game for the exercise of pursuing it. But since the need of active talent and practical judgment in the affairs of life can only be diminished, and not, even on the most favourable supposition, done away with, it is important that those endowments should be cultivated not merely in a few, but in all, and that the cultivation should be more varied and complete than most persons are able to find in the narrow sphere of their merely individual interests. A people among whom there is no habit of spontaneous action for a collective interest—who look habitually to their government to command or prompt them in all matters of joint concern—who expect to have everything done for them, except what can be made an affair of mere habit and routine—have their faculties only half developed; their education is defective in one of its most important branches.

Not only is the cultivation of the active faculties by exercise, diffused through the whole community, in itself one of the most valuable of national possessions: it is rendered not less, but more necessary, when a high degree of that indispensable culture is systematically kept up in the chiefs and functionaries of the state. There cannot be a combination of circumstances more dangerous to human welfare, than that in which intelligence and talent are maintained at a high standard within a governing corporation, but starved and discouraged outside the pale. Such a system, more completely than any other, embodies the idea of despotism, by arming with intellectual superiority as an additional weapon those who have already the legal power. It approaches as nearly as the organic difference between human beings and other animals admits, to the government of sheep by their shepherd without anything like so strong an interest as the shepherd in the thriving condition of the flock. The only security against political slavery is the check maintained over governors by the diffusion of intelligence, activity, and public spirit among the governed. Experience proves the extreme difficulty of permanently keeping up a sufficiently high standard of those qualities; a difficulty which increases, as the advance of civilization and security removes one after another of the hardships, embarrassments, and dangers against which individuals had formerly no resource but in their own strength, skill, and courage. It is therefore of supreme importance that all classes of the community, down to the lowest, should have much to do for themselves; that as great a demand should be made upon their intelligence and virtue as it is in any respect equal to; that the government should not only leave as far as possible to their own faculties the conduct of whatever concerns them alone, but should suffer them, or rather encourage them, to manage as many as possible of their joint concerns by voluntary co-operation; since this discussion and management of collective interests is the great school of that public spirit, and the great source of that intelligence of public affairs, which are always regarded as the distinctive character of the public of free countries.

A democratic constitution, not supported by democratic institutions in detail, but confined to the central government, not only is not political freedom, but often creates a spirit precisely the reverse, carrying down to the lowest grade in society the desire and ambition of political domination. In some countries the desire of the people is for not being tyrannized over, but in others it is merely for an equal chance to everybody of tyrannizing. Unhappily this last state of the desires is fully as natural to mankind as the former, and in many of the conditions even of civilized humanity is far more largely ex-emplified. In proportion as the people are accustomed to manage their affairs by their own active intervention, instead of leaving them to the government, their desires will turn to repelling tyranny, rather than to tyrannizing: while in proportion as all real initiative and direction resides in the govern-ment, and individuals habitually feel and act as under its perpetual tutelage, popular in-stitutions develop in them not the desire for freedom, but an unmeasured appetite for place and power; diverting the intelligence and activity of the country from its principal business to a wretched competition for the selfish prizes and the petty vanities of of-fice.

7. The preceding are the principal reasons, of a general character, in favour of restricting to the narrowest compass the intervention of a public authority in the business of the community: and few will dispute the more than sufficiency of these reasons, to throw, in every instance, the burden of making out a strong case, not on those who resist, but on those who recommend, government interfer-ence. *Laisser-faire,* in short, should be the general practice: every departure from it, unless required by some great good, is a cer-tain evil.

The degree in which the maxim, even in the cases to which it is most manifestly ap-plicable, has heretofore been infringed by governments, future ages will probably have difficulty in crediting. Some ideas may be formed of it from the description of M. Dunoyer * of the restraints imposed on the operations of manufacture under the old government of France, by the meddling and regulative spirit of legislation.

"The State exercised over manufac-turing industry the most unlimited and arbitrary jurisdiction. It disposed with-out scruple of the resources of manu-facturers: it decided who should be allowed to work, what things it should

be permitted to make, what materials should be employed, what processes followed, what forms should be given to productions. It was not enough to do well, to do better; it was necessary to do according to the rules. Everybody knows the regulation of 1670 which prescribed to seize and nail to the pil-lory, with the names of the makers, goods not conformable to the rules, and which, on a second repetition of the offence, directed that the manufac-turers themselves should be attached also. Not the taste of the consumers, but the commands of the law must be attended to. Legions of inspectors, com-missioners, controllers, jurymen, guardi-ans, were charged with its execution. Machines were broken, products were burned when not conformable to the rules: improvements were punished; inventors were fined. There were dif-ferent sets of rules for goods destined for home consumption and for those intended for exportation. An artisan could neither choose the place in which to establish himself, nor work at all seasons, nor work for all customers. There exists a decree of March 30, 1700, which limits to eighteen towns the number of places where stockings might be woven. A decree of June 18, 1723, enjoins the manufacturers of Rouen to suspend their works from the 1st of July to the 15th of September, in order to facilitate the harvest. Louis XIV., when he intended to construct the colonnade of the Louvre, forbade all private persons to employ workmen without his permission, under a penalty of 10,000 livres, and forbade workmen to work for private persons, on pain for the first offence, of imprisonment, and for the second, of the galleys."

That these and similar regulations were not a dead letter, and that the officious and

* *On the Freedom of Work,* vol. ii, pp. 353–354.

vexatious meddling was prolonged down to the French Revolution, we have the testimony of Roland, the Girondist minister.*

"I have seen," says he, "eighty, ninety, a hundred pieces of cotton or woollen stuff cut up, and completely destroyed. I have witnessed similar scenes every week for a number of years. I have seen manufactured goods confiscated; heavy fines laid on the manufacturers; some pieces of fabric were burnt in public places, and at the hours of market: others were fixed to the pillory, with the name of the manufacturer inscribed upon them, and he himself was threatened with the pillory, in case of a second offence. All this was done under my eyes, at Rouen, in conformity with existing regulations, or ministerial orders. What crime deserved so cruel a punishment? Some defects in the materials employed, or in the texture of the fabric, or even in some of the threads of the warp.

"I have frequently seen manufacturers visited by a band of satellites who put all in confusion in their establishments, spread terror in their families, cut the stuffs from the frames, tore off the warp from the looms, and carried them away as proofs of infringement; the manufacturers were summoned, tried, and condemned: their goods confiscated; copies of their judgment of confiscation posted up in every public place; fortune, reputation, credit, all was lost and destroyed. And for what offence? Because they had made of worsted a kind of cloth called shag, such as the English used to manufacture, and even sell in France, while the French regulations stated that that kind of cloth should be made with mohair. I have seen other manufacturers treated in the same way, because they had made camlets of a particular width, used in England and Germany, for which there was a great demand from Spain, Portugal, and other countries, and from several parts of France, while the French regulations prescribed other widths for camlets."

The time is gone by, when such applications as these of the principle of "paternal government" would be attempted in even the least enlightened country of the European commonwealth of nations. In such cases as those cited, all the general objections to government interference are valid, and several of them in nearly their highest degree. But we must now turn to the second part of our task, and direct our attention to cases, in which some of those general objections are altogether absent, while those which can never be got rid of entirely are overruled by counter-considerations of still greater importance.

We have observed that, as a general rule, the business of life is better performed when those who have an immediate interest in it are left to take their own course, uncontrolled either by the mandate of the law or by the meddling of any public functionary. The persons, or some of the persons, who do the work, are likely to be better judges than the government, of the means of attaining the particular end at which they aim. Were we to suppose, what is not very probable, that the government has possessed itself of the best knowledge which has been acquired up to a given time by the persons most skilled in the occupation; even then the individual agents have so much stronger and more direct an interest in the result, that the means are far more likely to be improved and perfected if left to their uncontrolled choice. But if the workman is generally the best selector of means, can it be affirmed with the same universality, that the consumer, or person served, is the most competent judge of the end? Is the buyer always qualified to judge

* I quote, at second hand, from Mr. Cary's Essay on the *Rate of Wages*, pp. 195–196.

of the commodity? If not, the presumption in favour of the competition of the market does not apply to the case; and if the commodity be one in the quality of which society has much at stake, the balance of advantages may be in favour of some mode and degree of intervention by the authorized representatives of the collective interest of the state. . . .

David Lawrence shows that it has become difficult to define the difference between a Republican and a Democrat because the real division of opinion in America today is between conservative liberalism and radical liberalism. This distinction cuts into both parties and is at the heart of many of our present-day problems, both domestic and foreign. This issue goes to the heart of our controversies over the rights of labor and of management, the distribution of income and wealth, and free enterprise, and appears strongly in the trends toward regimentation and regulation of human behavior in the factory, in the counting room, in the school, or on the farm. Fundamentally it is the age-old issue of the proper sphere of a government of a free people in contrast to a government *ruling* a people.

The traditional meaning of liberalism, as it developed in Great Britain after 1776 and functioned until about 1870, was to protect the individual from excessive government; and the functions of liberalism in the United States were similarly directed until the aftermath of the Great Depression. Lawrence's definition of conservative liberalism is a contemporary version of protecting the people from excessive governmental interference, excessive taxation, state paternalism, and the enhancement of governmental powers as a policy. In some respects, the government-action question becomes one of degree, rather than of kind. But radical liberalism clearly emphasizes social values and trends so strongly in the opposite direction that they reveal the influence of socialism, though radical liberals would not like to be called socialists. Lawrence interprets and illustrates the conservative and radical versions of liberalism by listing as objectively as possible the legislative principles and policies which have been sponsored and objected to quite consistently by both groups. It should be understood that there are conservative and radical liberals in both of the major parties—Republican and Democrat. Would it be more realistic then to say that we have in actual practice political parties which should be known as "conservative liberal" and "radical liberal"? Probably not, as in the United States the names "Republican" and "Democrat" still remain more politically powerful terms.

27

CONSERVATIVE LIBERALISM

VS.

RADICAL LIBERALISM*

David Lawrence

We often hear it said that party labels are meaningless.

The reason for this lack of distinctiveness is the fact that another set of political alignments has come into being in recent years.

To define the difference between a Republican and a Democrat is baffling, because the real division of opinion in America today is between conservative liberalism and radical liberalism. It cuts into both parties.

This cleavage not only has split the Republican Party but has kept the Democratic Party from exercising control over Congress in the present session, even though the majority in both houses call themselves Democrats.

For many years it has been assumed that sooner or later a new political party would be created out of comparable groups of Republicans and Democrats. But this now seems unlikely. Third parties have failed.

Rather we shall see the conservative liberals or the radical liberals gradually gaining ascendancy inside one or the other of the two major political parties. As the struggle for control proceeds in each party, the two main labels will remain because they are too closely identified with state and local political systems to undergo any change.

Defining Liberals. How, then, may these growing forces in American politics be defined? What is conservative liberalism? What is radical liberalism?

The true meaning of these terms goes to the heart of our present-day problems, both domestic and foreign. It goes to the heart of our controversies over the rights of labor and of management. It raises the question of a proper distribution of income and wealth. It is related directly to whether there shall be a free enterprise system in America in which the word "free" means license to exploit others, or a system in which the word "free" means freedom of opportunity and initiative and the preservation of the fruits of thrift and labor.

For to be "free" in the operation of one's own enterprise means emancipation from the totalitarian mind which seeks to regiment and regulate human behavior in the factory, in the counting room, in the school or on the farm.

From time immemorial the instinct toward totalitarianism has emerged among good as well as bad peoples. The theory that government is effective only when it regulates the most minute operations of human life begets a desire to pass laws and promulgate regulations for the conduct of nearly everything

* Reprinted from *U. S. News & World Report,* an independent weekly news magazine published at Washington. Copyright 1949, United States News Publishing Corporation. (This editorial is from the August 12, 1949 issue.)

and everybody. This is the genesis of radical liberalism.

Opposed to this theory is the doctrine of conservative liberalism that human beings must be given a maximum of opportunity to develop self-reliance and that they must be permitted incentives which will bring out their best talents and energies.

I—CONSERVATIVE LIBERALISM

The conservative liberal believes in individual responsibility—he condemns irresponsible individualism.

The conservative liberal believes in social responsibility, not only for himself but for the State acting for all individuals in those matters wherein collective action is alone effective as well as desirable.

The conservative liberal believes that the State is the servant and not the master of the people—that government exists for the benefit of the people and not for the benefit of those individuals who happen to hold governmental power.

The conservative liberal believes that he is really his brother's keeper. He is not indifferent to another man's poverty or the plight of his neighbor—whether that neighbor is in the next cottage or in some far-off land gnawed by the pangs of hunger.

The conservative liberal believes in high wages, in good working conditions, and in the right of labor to organize and to bargain for good wages and good working conditions. The conservative liberal believes in these rights of the workers but believes in trade unionism as the servant of the worker and not his master.

The conservative liberal believes not only in improving the standard of living by increasing the wages of labor but also in the preservation of the fruits of labor—the savings of labor—the sole means of sustenance for the widows or the orphans or the disabled.

The conservative liberal does not believe in the confiscation of somebody else's property on the false premise that it is "for the public good."

The conservative liberal attributes to the State—as our forefathers wrote it in the Constitution—all the necessary powers to carry on government. But he does not agree that government possesses all powers inherently and may exercise them at any time it decides to create an artificial or political emergency.

The conservative liberal believes in upholding the Tenth Amendment of the Constitution which states specifically that all rights and powers which were not delegated to the Federal Government are reserved "to the States respectively, or to the people."

The conservative liberal does not believe in usurpation of power by the Federal Government. He believes in allowing the people to limit their own rights only through the proper constitutional processes.

Civil Rights For All. The conservative liberal believes in the Bill of Rights. He believes that civil rights shall be equally applied, irrespective of race, religion or color. For this reason, he opposes legislation which seeks to punish local police officers who are indifferent to mob rule when the victims happen to be of one color and where the disturbances are singled out and put into one class as a matter for federal jurisdiction.

The conservative liberal sees no distinction between lynchings in the South and lynchings outside the factory gates in the North when those engaged in mass picketing overturn cars, intimidate workers and commit other misdemeanors to which local police are indifferent.

The conservative liberal believes in the power of public opinion to stimulate state and local governments to maintain law and order.

The conservative liberal does not, however, hesitate to advocate the use of the power of the Federal Government to maintain law and order when the states show themselves incapable of fulfilling their proper missions under the Constitution.

The conservative liberal believes in freedom of economic opportunity. He believes in equal pay for equal work, irrespective of color, race or creed.

The conservative liberal would seek to

attain these objectives through the process of education and the aggressive power of an informed public opinion.

The conservative liberal does not believe that morals can be legislated, but he does believe that morals can be agitated and that the exposure of wrong-doing at the federal, state or city level is a paramount duty inside and outside of public office.

Freedom of Speech and the Press. The conservative liberal believes in representative government and its principal safeguard—freedom of speech and of the press. To this end, he believes that the press cannot be free if the Federal Government, by invoking the licensing power over newspapers or radio or television, usurps the right to say what shall be transmitted through these media of public expression.

The conservative liberal believes in international cooperation. For this purpose he is willing to vote for large appropriations so as to help the unfortunate people of other countries who have lost their properties and their homes in war and who, in seeking economic opportunities and survival, are dependent upon a helping hand from the United States.

The conservative liberal believes that governmental aid should not be a crutch for permanent support but a temporary help, and that ultimately nations, like individuals, must learn how to support themselves.

The conservative liberal believes in the conservation and development of our natural resources. He recognizes that the sources of electric power in our river areas are the property of the nation as a whole. He believes that these resources must be developed for the benefit of all the people, but he contends that these resources shall be used by government as the servant and not the master of the people.

The conservative liberal holds that, when public resources are developed, the American system calls primarily for leasing of such resources to the highest bidders in private business—leases that are revocable and amendable as the public interest may require from time to time and subject to proper government regulation.

The conservative liberal believes in assistance to individual enterprises in agriculture and industry. This means assistance in the orderly marketing of products of the farm. It means price supports by governmental agencies in order that speculative markets shall not deprive the farmer of the rewards of his labor. It does not mean handouts to one group at the expense of other groups in the community or subsidy for subsidy's sake. It means that government lending should be provided for business when the faucets of private lending are dried up or clogged by fear and panic.

The conservative liberal believes in fair competition. He condemns exploitation either by large or by small business. He believes that the anti-trust laws should be clarified so that no group of people, whether in labor unions or in business, shall exploit their fellow citizens by imposing a monopoly or a restraint of trade.

The conservative liberal does not believe the government should fix any ceiling on profits or wages. He does believe in a minimum wage adjusted periodically to meet living costs.

Fair Use of the Taxing Power. The conservative liberal believes in the collaboration of federal, state and city governments so that their taxing powers shall be utilized harmoniously and without the disruptive effects of over-duplication of taxing devices.

The conservative liberal believes in tax rates that are productive of adequate revenues not only to balance the budget but to obtain a surplus for debt retirement.

The conservative liberal opposes the use of the taxing power to enforce punitive doctrines conceived by radical liberalism.

What, then, in contrast, is the basic philosophy of radical liberalism?

II—RADICAL LIBERALISM

The radical liberal professes to be interested in human rights rather than property rights. This is but another way of saying that he often favors confiscation of property rights as an end in itself.

The radical liberal does not hold that the savings of labor are as important as the wages of labor. He tends to lose interest in the worker at the factory gate.

The radical liberal professes to be interested in the prices that consumers shall pay, which is laudable, but he also insists that private enterprise survive with a minimum of profits.

The radical liberal believes that, when profits happen to be high, they shall be devoted primarily to increases in wages, irrespective of whether these profits are temporary or permanent and irrespective of a fair return to the owners of invested savings.

The radical liberal is opposed to the laying aside of profits to buy tools and equipment or to replace wornout equipment and to expand facilities.

The radical liberal has no interest in seeing investor confidence developed—the only way by which equity capital can be made available to expand American enterprise and industry and provide increasing employment.

The radical liberal is opposed to technological advances that conserve manpower. He regards them all as enemies of labor, when in truth they are the greatest friends of labor.

The radical liberal would keep us in a horse-and-buggy age and would impose royalties upon labor-saving machinery. Many a city ordinance and many a building regulation today prevents the introduction of fabricated housing, for instance, because labor-union monopolies are sufficiently strong to keep intact those regulations.

The radical liberal often dominates the labor union as a dictator dominates a government. This means that freedom of speech inside unions is impaired and that individuals who dare to go counter to an administration can be and often are expelled "for the good of the union." Radical liberals are few in number in unions but they exercise an enormous political and economic power.

The radical liberal believes that picketing is an inherent right, protected by the free speech clause of the Constitution, but that the right of the employer to address his employees, either during working hours or outside of working hours, is a limited right or should be yielded altogether.

The radical liberal believes in the "closed shop" and in compulsory unionization, for he does not really have faith in the efficacy of the trade union to win and hold members through the power of its own ideas.

The radical liberal believes that anything which is big in business is necessarily criminal. He does not draw a distinction between large businesses that serve the public interest with low prices and with necessary goods developed out of years of research and marketing, and those businesses which exploit the people, fix prices and, by collusion with other large businesses, stifle competition.

The radical liberal believes that when businesses become efficient and develop a large sales volume and really benefit the public, they have become eligible for government nationalization.

The radical liberal would put the government in control of the large insurance companies and thus obtain power over their huge deposits of private funds—the savings of labor.

The radical liberal believes in governmental ownership of all systems of communication and transportation.

The radical liberal believes in public ownership and nationalization of major industries.

The radical liberal would use public funds to propagandize and thereby bribe the electorate.

The radical liberal would hand out large sums to farmers, labor unions and business groups—so long as political support is forthcoming.

The radical liberal in public office dispenses favors to lobbyists who are in a position to corral campaign contributions at the proper time.

The radical liberal wants corporations barred from contributing to political campaigns but sees nothing wrong in slush funds obtained by duress from labor-union members.

The radical liberal believes in the one-political-party idea and would discipline labor-union members who refuse to allow their dues to be used to support a political party with which they are not affiliated or in which they do not believe.

The radical liberal would interfere with the freedom of the press by regulating it so as to compel support for the party in power.

The radical liberal believes in maintaining governmental commissions which issue or revoke licenses to radio stations on the basis of political favor and special privilege.

The Way to State Socialism. The radical liberal believes in deficit financing and unbalanced budgets.

The radical liberal really believes in repudiation of the public debt. He is indifferent to the building up of revenues sufficient to balance the budget because he believes in unlimited spending and opposes at every turn any economy in public spending.

The radical liberal seeks to use the power of taxation to reduce individual incentives and pave the way for state socialism.

The radical liberal in politics is to be found in both the Republican and Democratic parties. He would increase the power of government over the individual on the pretext that this is "for the public good."

The radical liberal believes in a "welfare state"—a system in which the government hands out money and favors to the maximum number of voters, irrespective of whether production and the main sinews of our economic system are thereby weakened.

The radical liberal believes in the setting up of a government board or commission to regulate the economy of the nation by fiat.

The radical liberal favors "economic planning" by "master minds" in government bureaus who are to manage and operate our economic system.

The radical liberal professes to be against totalitarianism but he applies the doctrines of totalitarianism in seeking to win his ends.

The radical liberal looks at socialism as an innocuous philosophy which he calls "liberalism." But he forgets that only through the tyranny of suppression and restriction and only through the destruction of private rights and liberties can such objectives of "liberalism" be attained.

To sum up—the radical liberal in his way is as obstructive of progress as the "reactionary conservative" who believes in jungle law and the survival of the fittest.

The Liberalism of Jefferson and Lincoln. The conservative liberal, therefore, is the true liberal. For he is the true defender of private rights as well as public rights—property rights as well as human rights.

The approach of the conservative liberal to the art of government is characterized by a spirit of adjustment as between minority and majority points of view.

For the conservative liberal recognizes that the basic good in representative government is not measured by the number of stalemates provoked or reform proposals adopted. It is measured by the actual progress made year by year toward a better and better society wherein all men are free to acquire wealth and yet are encouraged to regard private ownership of property as a trusteeship in whose custody has been placed the common good of all.

This is the liberalism born in the Democratic Party of Thomas Jefferson, given rebirth in the Republican Party of Abraham Lincoln and modernized by Woodrow Wilson and Theodore Roosevelt. It has been bequeathed to the two major parties of today as an enduring charter of America's political faith.

VI

Changes in Economic
and Political Values

Economic and political changes are to a considerable extent interrelated, though it is possible to emphasize either area of change from the institutional standpoint. Some of the basic ideas and ideologies which have a bearing on economic and political institutions have already been indicated. It would not be amiss, however, to point out other particulars before turning to the readings selected for this chapter.

The root meaning of economic is "orderly" or "methodical." Hence the term is pertinent to the management of the affairs of a government or community with reference to its source of income, its expenditures, the development of its natural resources, etc. It is significant that early treatises in the field used the term "political economy." Economics is a social science which investigates the conditions and laws affecting the production, distribution, and consumption of wealth, or the material means of satisfying human desires. Briefly, economics is concerned with all the institutionalized behavior patterns of man in making or earning a living. Anything which man finds free in nature, equally free to all, would not be included in the concept of economics given above.

The word "political" stems from the Greek word *politikos*, "pertaining to the citizens," thus pertaining to civil government. The word "political" may pertain to the form or constitution of the government of a state, or of any institution or organization similarly administered; it may refer to politics or the conduct of government. With a somewhat different implication, "political" may pertain to the organization or action of individuals, parties, or interests seeking to control the appointment or action of those who manage the affairs of a state. It may also have reference to politicians in their partisan activities. In the political realm, then, we are concerned with institutionalized behavior patterns connected with government.

All institutionalized economic and political behavior or organization is a part of the culture of the society concerned, and social change will necessarily affect some aspects of these institutions. That is, the changes will concern folkways, customs, mores, traditions, laws, forms of organization, etc. But, since social institutions are reciprocally interrelated, changes are likely to involve a plurality of institutional areas. For the present, it is essential to realize that economic changes are not likely to occur completely independent of other institutions, and the same is true of political changes. By their very nature, economic and political changes tend to influence one another directly or indirectly.

Both economic and political institutions are vitally concerned with *property*, which also has been institutionalized. Ordinarily, persons think of property as a "thing." But, for our purpose, property would be defined as an institution, as the exclusive right to possess, enjoy, and dispose of, a thing. Then property applies to any valuable right or interest considered primarily as a source of wealth. Changes may occur with reference to conceptions of property rights, some of which would be defined in legal terms and thus be political.

Property may be owned individually or by a group of persons, or communally, or by a state. Regulations exist concerning such ownership and the methods of inheritance. Property functions change with economic organization, as reflected in the development from a phase of hunting and fishing to pastoral and agricultural pursuits, to the rise of industry and commerce, manufacture and exchange; and more recently the property institution has been affected by the ascendancy of capital, labor, and contract in economic relations. All these economic phases have affected the ownership, possession, and disposition of wealth (property).

Property changes were also indicated by historical systems of production, usually designated as (1) the family or household system, (2) the guild or handicraft system, (3) the domestic or house industry, and (4) the factory system.

Institutional developments during medieval times included the manorial economy, town economy, trade and commerce, and certain formal controls of industrial activity. The manorial economy was headed by the manor lord, and subordinate to him were the villeins, cotters, or serfs. The town economy gave rise to the guild merchant and the craft guilds. The development of trade and commerce was marked by fairs and markets, shops, peddlers, merchants, staplers, merchant adventurers, medieval business associations, medieval currency, and the law merchant. Social control of industrial activity was exercised by the church and by public authorities, as well as by the guilds. The items just mentioned came into being as factors in social change, and served their purpose in the cultural heritage handed down from generation to generation. In all these examples, the interrelations between economic, property and political institutions are apparent. Property is related all the way in economic production, distribution, and consumption of goods and services.

Political aspects of property are evident in that the state owns property in its own right, and even more broadly underlying is the principle of eminent domain which shows clearly how secondary the private ownership of property is to the will of the state. The state may act, through the government, to redistribute property by means of the inheritance tax, the income tax, or through taxes incident to social security programs. The state, acting through its government, may make contracts with business firms or individuals and stipulate conditions for fulfilling the contract. Changes from free enterprise to totalitarianism would inevitably affect the interrelations between property and the economic and political institutions, particularly because of the despotic nature of the power of the state.

Economic Organization. Several forms of business organization have become established institutional patterns in modern economy. These include forms of ownership and control in production and distribution, the market, money, the conception of the business cycle, production factors, occupational grouping, the labor force, unemployment, economic associations, and many other aspects of economic relationships.

Forms of ownership and control of business enterprise have changed from individual proprietorship to partnership, then to the rise of the corporation, the trust, the holding company, etc. Efforts to control business produced the corner, the pool, and the cartel. Abuses of power in industry and in marketing led to legislation on both federal and state levels. Issues in conflict include unfair restraint of trade, price fixing, boycotting, intimidation, collusive bidding, blacklisting, interference, combination, monopoly, or other unfair practices. On the whole, however, giant corporations have become essential in the American economy, although it is important that their operations be kept within the law. Such corporations dominate at least five areas in the economy—manufacturing, mining, transportation, public utilities, and finance. Mere size of a corporation does not constitute a crime or a violation of antitrust laws, though size alone has at times been made a political issue. But Americans are used to bigness in industry. Bigness, inventiveness, and efficiency in industry account for mass production of goods in the United States on a scale surpassing that of all other nations.

Among other economic institutions to consider is the "market," in which money and the banking system are essential. The fluctuations of the business cycle, forming a wavelike pattern of revival, expansion, recession, and contraction, recur at intervals varying from about three to about six or seven years. The factors in production—land, labor, capital, and the entrepreneur (enterpriser)—are to be matched with their specific rewards—rent, wages, interest, and profit, respectively—as the traditional pattern of analysis of free enterprise systems of production and distribution. Within recent decades, however, the state—especially the Federal government in the United States—has become an increasingly important factor in production because of its policies of taxation and control. Occupational grouping and the labor force have increasingly been formalized and institutionalized, as manifested in the U.S. Bureau of Census reports and in the specialized labor unions. Changes in labor organization and functions of unions are reflected in the history of the American Federation of Labor and the Congress of Industrial Organization (AFL and CIO) which merged to form one body in December, 1955. The combined memberships at that time have been estimated at from 16.5 million upward, but the actual number of members in good standing has been subject to considerable variation because of punitive suspension or expulsion of certain unions. Several large unions have remained independent of the AFL, the CIO, and the merger.

The fact that labor unionism is an aspect of the free enterprise system of production is shown by the functions of collective bargaining, and the utilization of mediation, conciliation, and arbitration, all products of social change. If these peaceful means of adjustment fail, unions may legally resort to the "strike," that is, the act of quitting work as a means of enforcing compliance with demands made on the employer. In contrast to this, employers may utilize the "lockout" against their workers. "Blacklisting" has at times been used by employers or by unions; that is, individuals may be listed as deserving of suspicion, censure, or adverse discrimination.

Several elements in conflicts between organized labor and management have become institutionalized concepts of behavior patterns. The closed shop, for instance, is one in which union membership is a requisite for permanent employment, whereas such membership would be optional in an open shop. Company unions of workers are limited to membership within the establishment directly concerned. "Featherbedding" denotes questionable make-work policies on the part of employees. "Sabotage" is malicious waste or destruction of an employer's property by workmen, as may occur during labor troubles. Another bone of contention is the "injunction," which is a writ or process, granted by a court of equity, requiring a party to do or to forbear certain acts. The objective of collective bargaining is the labor contract establishing relations between the employer and the unionized workers, specifying points of agreement, and usually providing for periodical revision in terms of economic trends, or for essential negotiation in the future. All these features of the American economy have been established in response to reforms concerning relations between labor and management mostly between 1890 and the present.

Of special significance among the acts of Congress bearing on labor relations was the Wagner-Connery Act of 1935, usually regarded as one of the signal achievements of the New Deal. But this act favored labor too much, and the Taft-Hartley Act, passed in 1947, was intended to ameliorate the situation. This Bill prohibits closed shops, but allows union shops by secret vote of the majority of employees concerned; it makes unions subject to damage suits for unfair labor practices, such as boycotts or jurisdictional strikes; it requires unions to file financial reports; it also requires union leaders to file statements that they are not Communists. More recently there has been a wave of agitation about "right to work" laws, which have been enacted by a number of states, and possibly other states may follow suit.

Political Institutions. Political institutions are, of course, rooted in law. The state is a political body, a form of social organization; law, as the counterpart of the state, is a social institution. Law, like other institutions, has developed out of the mores, but it would be incorrect to say that all laws have derived directly from the mores. The connection is fundamental, however, inasmuch as laws that are incompatible with the prevailing folkways, customs, and mores are virtually unenforceable. And a law is not a law unless it is enforceable, that is, subject to sanctions. Laws can be classified in various ways according to their subject matter, or more broadly, as criminal law, civil law, canon law, etc.

"Folkways" and "stateways" are in some respects distinctive. A folkway is a localized form of behavior, and may be described as a spontaneous or uncontrived product of the adaptations and adjustments of men to environment and circumstance. A folkway is adaptive, i.e., it can be extended widely by imitation, or it may so uniquely identify itself with the region where it arose or where it was transplanted that it remains unknown elsewhere. Stateways, on the other hand, extend themselves aggressively. The state, as an inclusive social organization, proclaims authority over all individuals residing within defined geographical boundaries and determines what the way of the state is to be, other than the way of the folk. Theoretically, a sovereign state has the power to compel obedience, but this is never quite true. If it were true, there would be no lawbreakers. It is probable that no law ever enacted has been obeyed by all individuals in any group or class of citizens, however respectable. Laws forbidding discrimination on account of color, laws regulating the manufacture and sale of alcoholic drinks, or laws concerning labor-management relations and ideological issues, like those concerning communism, involve public opinion and the mores in emotional ways which make them difficult to enforce. Folkways and stateways thus come into conflict. Folkways of disobedience may nullify laws, and occasionally they defy the stateways. Normally, however, the folkways and stateways tend to arrive at an equilibrium, and then society, through its channels of adjustment, attains a compromise of liberty and security.

The juristic theory of the state conceives government as performing legislative, executive, and judicial functions. But such a conception appears limited in the face of the expanding areas of governmental action. More and more, government is being looked upon as a collection of public services; it has become one of the important instruments through which the common interests of the members of the community are to be furthered. The state renders to its members a large number of services, such as education, scientific research, public utilities, recreation, social insurance, and relief, which cannot properly be described as legislative, executive, or judicial. The functions of government, thus considered, are social control and public service, and the legislative, executive, and judicial provinces of government have become means to those ends, with an emphasis on public services.

All systems of government rest upon a constitution, written or unwritten, by which is meant a system of legal principles designating the highest governmental authorities, the method of their choice or creation, their mutual relations, the sphere of activity of each, and the position of the individual with reference to them. Constitutions may be surrounded by special sanctions. Constitutions may provide for monarchy (one-man rule), for aristocracy (rule by a selected group), for democracy (rule of, by, and for the people), or for other forms. Democracy can be "pure," in which the people have direct participation in lawmaking and government; or it can be conducted through a representative system, commonly known as a republic. But the terms "democracy" and "republic" are not truly synonymous because there are constitutional monarchies which qualify as democracies, and there are authoritarian nations, such as the U.S.S.R. and its satellites, which claim to be republics.

The principal feature of constitutions which concerns us is whether the power to govern is centralized at the top, or is based on popular sovereignty so that power moves from the people upward; these two aspects—a hierarchy of power versus popular sovereignty—are incompatible. In the latter system, safeguards exist against abuse of governing power on the part of either branch of government—the legislative, executive, or judicial; but such safeguards are nonexistent in an autocratic hierarchy. Further safeguards of the liberties and freedoms of the people may be provided in a bill of rights, which in a democratic constitution is meant to be real, and subject to enforcement in the same manner as the rest of the constitution. The bill of rights is particularly important in that it provides areas within which social change can be effected peacefully and legally. In the final analysis, one of the basic functions of law is to provide for peaceful change.

Ideologies emphasize governmental control in different ways. Democracy and totalitarianism are at opposite ends of the pole. Western conceptions of democracy are completely antithetical to those of states or nations motivated by socialist or communist doctrines, as was also the case with Italian Fascism and German Nazism. In states which claim to be democratic in the Western sense, the more they turn toward nationalization of industries and to governmental paternalism—which moves increasingly in the direction of a state-planned economy—the more will democratic principles stand in jeopardy. Political systems, like economic systems, are constantly on trial; the ultimate test is not what politicians and philosophers say about them *but how they work.*

Some of the readings which follow may appear more economic, others more political in emphasis; yet the economic and political factors tend to be interwoven in them and this quality has influenced the sequence in which they are given: "Capitalism and Social Change" by Frank T. Carlton, "The Property Revolution" by Max Lerner, "Automation: a New Dimension to Old Problems" by George B. Baldwin and George P. Schultz, "Toward a Responsible Bureaucracy" by Peter H. Odegard, "Political and Economic Consequences of Totalitarian Dictatorship" by Alfred Cobban, "A Planned Economy: Good or Bad?" by Ruth Shallcross, "Nationalization in Britain: A Sobering Decade" by George B. Baldwin, "The Passing of Keynesian Economics" by Sumner H. Slichter, and "Labor Trends in the United States" by Melvin J. Vincent.

Frank T. Carlton remarks that in capitalism the owners of wealth are free, within changing limitations, to organize and direct business enterprise for the sake of making profits. Capitalism is not static; it has undergone important changes during the last several decades, although people use the term "capitalism" without noticing its transitional phases. Moreover, capitalism in the United States differs from that of England, France, Germany, and other Western countries.

Capitalism in the United States has altered in meaning and function with the expansion in population, market areas, productivity, and changes in the standards of living. It has changed with the methods of cost accounting, scientific management, the nature of industrial agreements, economic planning, the increase in government purchasing, and the growth of standardization because factors of this kind have a bearing on risks in industry. Taxation has become an extraordinarily important factor. Carlton dwells on these and other aspects of corporate organization and function in his interpretation of the reciprocal relationships between capitalism and social change.

28

CAPITALISM AND SOCIAL CHANGE*
Frank T. Carlton

Capitalism may be defined as an economic order in which the owners of wealth are free within changing limitations to organize and direct business enterprise for the sake of making profits. The three basic principles on which the capitalistic system rests are the right of private property, the right of free enterprise, and the right of liberty of contract. All three of these pillars of capitalism have undergone marked changes as the nation moved into the power age. The bundle of rights known as private property rights has lost many of its component sticks. Free enterprise has been restricted because of the growth of large-scale corporate business and the consequent development of semimonopolistic power in the place of the competition of pioneer days. Finally, liberty of contract has been modified by expanding the concept of public welfare or of the police power of the state. However, capitalism has never existed in an atmosphere in which there was no restraint on the part of government.

Capitalism has not been a static institution; it has greatly changed its form within a generation. Many writers and speakers appear to believe that the capitalistic system, as it now exists, is old and inelastic. To believe in perpetualism is a common fault of the individuals of yesterday and today who lack historical perspective. However, a brief study of economic history clearly indicates that capitalism has been subjected to rapid changes in structure. As an inevitable con-

sequence the system is suffering from an extraordinary number of stresses and strains. The capitalism of the period of Franklin D. Roosevelt is quite different from that of the McKinley era, and the latter in turn does not greatly resemble the frontier capitalism which flourished in the Jacksonian epoch. The American capitalism of large-scale corporate industry is far different from the capitalism of the frontier. Furthermore, capitalism in the United States is by no means the same institution as contemporary English capitalism. It also differs from the French or German variety. American capitalism may not be dying, as many of its opponents fondly hope, but it may be undergoing reorganization. New boundaries and limits are perhaps being surveyed.

The capitalism of the machine age is a program or institution adapted to a period of expansion in population, market areas, productivity, and the demand for material goods which make up standards of living. May capitalism be adjusted to carry on in a world in which there are few frontier communities, slow population growth, and markets which must be cultivated intensively rather than extensively? Or is capitalism an institution fitted only for life in the interesting epoch which extends roughly from the discovery of this continent to the end of the first third of the present century? Must capitalism be scrapped as outmoded because the velocity of change in the physical world is slowing

* Reprinted, by permission of the editor, from *Sociology and Social Research*, vol. 28, no. 6, pp. 440–451, July-August, 1944.

down? It may be true that capitalism "cannot live without ever expanding"; but that expansion may not always take the form of widening markets and growing populations. It may take the form of expanding to meet vertically developing markets and rising standards of living for a stationary or nearly stationary population. It may reasonably be suggested that science, the great disturber, may be directed to find new channels for experimentation and new outlets for the restless energy of the scientist. If the end of progress in certain directions has practically been reached, the eager scientist and the engineer will turn to other fields of endeavor. Indeed, the end of the great dynamic epoch in human history may not as yet have been reached. The engineer and the scientist may be laying the foundation for a new and modified capitalism instead of destroying the institution. Capitalism in the power age may be expected to remain dynamic. Inventions, new processes, and new methods of management will continue to appear. The World War may hasten and accentuate changes which have been taking place; but, if the Allied nations win, the suggestion is ventured that the trend of events will not be fundamentally modified.

Capitalism has emphasized the importance of the profit-making motive. The profit-making urge is an integral portion of a wider impulse—the desire for power and prestige, the "wish for worth," or the fondness for significance. The desire for business profits may be fundamentally due to the necessity of obtaining a sufficiency to maintain self and family; but in the case of the great majority of Americans who participate in profits, the desire for power, influence, prestige, or significance has been the potent force which leads to active endeavor. The "customs and habitual assumptions" of the group to which one belongs are also important factors in the determination of the direction of human activity. In the past our American capitalistic system has been one "which flourishes only when business men are disposed to take chances" with a view to money-making.

Today, however, cost accounting, scientific management, formal and informal agreements between business units, the development of large-scale economic planning, the increasing purchasing on the part of governmental units, and the growth of standardization are tending to reduce risks and also the chances to make a killing. On the other hand, taxation is being utilized to take away extraordinary gains or profits which may spring into being in spite of these obstacles.

At the present time a large percentage of the gainful workers are no longer directly affected by the profit-making motive. The relative number of owner-enterprisers has been reduced. Management in large corporations has been quite generally divorced from ownership and is not directly affected by the profit motive. The great mass of workers in manufacturing, mining, transportation, and trade are employees, not owners or even part owners. Many farmers who are owners of the farms they operate are in that occupation primarily for other reasons than profit-making. If capitalism is to continue, either nonfinancial motives must assume prominence or some way must be found to bring a share of the profits to management and workers through a profit-sharing plan. Increasing the stability of the job and giving a guaranteed annual wage supplemented by some bonus because of greater efficiency and better teamwork will tend to reduce the hostility of workers toward capitalism. Such plans would increase the number of active workers interested in the profit motive.

Capitalism rests on a theory of individual responsibility and individual initiative. Private property rights are essential to the existence of capitalism, but the concept of private property rights has undergone many changes in recent generations. Labor and security legislation, building restrictions, zoning regulations, the expansion of the police power of the state, and many other legal restrictions have changed the power of the owner over his property. The right to own property is in reality a miscellaneous collection of rights which may be augmented, changed, or reduced by governmental authority or by custom. Ultimately the definition of property and property rights rests in the United States with the Federal Supreme Court. The earlier idea of property was concerned only with the tangible or corporeal property which could be touched or handled. Later came the idea of intangible value belonging to certain concerns. In 1890 the United States Supreme Court recognized that the reduction of railway rates by a railway commission might constitute the taking of "property," intangible property of the railroad as a going concern. The tangible or corporeal property of the railroad would, of course, be unchanged.

Certain types of private property may be transformed into public property and no longer allowed to exist under private ownership, as recently happened in regard to gold coin and gold bullion. In a similar manner, the scope and extent of capitalism may be and are being modified. The minting of money, the operation of the postal system, and the control of roads have been taken out of the hands of private business. In many countries the railways are governmentally operated. Other projects, like the building of the Panama Canal or the Tennessee Valley development, may be public enterprises. Enlargements in the scope of public enterprise, the limitation of the power of private enterprise to carry on its functions through labor legislation or through legislation such as the N.L.R. Act, or the narrowing of private property rights changes the form of capitalism but does not necessarily indicate that the nation has passed out of capitalism into socialism or into some other form of industrial or economic control.

The pioneer form of capitalism was characterized by small units of property privately owned. The owner was also the manager and director of the property or business. Property in those days signified tangible property which, as someone has suggested, could be hit with a hammer. It consisted of land, buildings, tools, livestock, and the like; it did not consist of notes, bonds, stock certificates, and other paper claims. Soon after the middle of the nineteenth century the modern corporation began to play an important role in the business world. The corporation was granted certain privileges by the state which authorized its existence. It was an artificial or legal person replacing the individual owner and manager; it could sue and be sued; it could make and enforce contracts. The corporation represents a group of owners, many or all of whom may have no active connection with the management of the business. Soon after the turn of the century corporate management took on new aspects. The holding corporation appeared; and the pyramiding of paper certificates became a favorite financial pastime. Then came the investment banker, the investment trust, and combinations horizontal, vertical, and circular. The investor and the owner were bewildered by the maze of intangibles resting on more intangibles. The stockholder or the bondholder has a claim upon tangible operated property, but if the property were split up it would have very little value. Its value depends upon having the property consolidated, unified, and coordinated. For a stockholder to claim and take posession of one machine or one corner of some floor of a factory building or of his share of the total assets of a corporation would lead to confusion and ineffectiveness. The actual managers and the engineers who direct the tangible property which is hidden under the smokescreen of paper securities and values are under orders given by financiers. Pecuniary aims rather than engineering programs were definitely placed in the foreground in the business world. But the breakdown of 1929 cast a dark shadow of doubt upon the wisdom of banker control—unless definitely guided and restricted by governmental authority in the interests of other groups in the community.

The pioneer farmer and the small businessman of over a generation ago did not expect to turn their business property into cash. They possessed little liquid capital. Today, on the contrary, much emphasis is being placed on liquidity, that is, the ability to convert paper claims quickly into cash. Of course, in an emergency this cannot be done readily. If nearly all tried to sell, there would be inevitably few or none to buy. The business world would experience a financial panic.

Almost all our large corporations combine centralized control with diffused ownership among a large number of the middle class. There are about five million separate stockholders. Indirectly, millions of depositors in savings banks and more millions who hold life insurance policies are owners of corporate stocks and bonds. Also, millions of Americans now own United States bonds. Capitalism, with its growing interest in corporate property, is quite dependent upon legislative enactments. The corporation is not a rugged individual; it is brought into being as a result of legislation. Without the law-given privilege of limited liability its life and size would be limited. A return to *laissez faire* or to the free enterprise system of the pioneer would result in a marked change in capitalism—or in its breakdown.

Traditionally, the function of the enterpriser has been to assume risks, to develop new products and processes. Progress has been made by those who are alert, competent, and daring. The development of large corporations with huge overhead expenses and accurate cost accounting systems tends to curb the venturesome leaders possessing initiative and the desire to do things in new ways. In businesses with high fixed expenses, innovations make for financial insecurity. Security becomes preferable to economic adventure, but too great emphasis upon security puts the brake upon the car of progress. Big corporations, confronted only with imperfect or little competition, can afford to pay high wages and cater to organized labor. They can pass the costs on in higher prices. A small business, which is highly competitive, cannot do so without agreements which may easily run counter to antitrust legislation.

Again, the problem of providing commodities for the people of the United States changes greatly as we approach a condition in which we have the requisites in plant and equipment to produce a sufficiency for all of food, shelter, and clothing. Since profit-making business flourishes only under scarcity, as an approach is made toward the sufficient production of a necessity, the price of the commodity drops and profits tend to vanish; the commodity is, therefore, no longer suitable for business activities. Certain necessities which may be produced in sufficient quantities for all families may be expected to pass out of the realm of private into that of public production or distribution; the water supply in many cities and public education are now supplied in this fashion. The sphere of private operation will probably be narrowed and that of public operation broadened, but both public and private business may persist side by side. The engineer and the scientist by increasing national potential productivity are changing and enlarging the field of public service. Unless controlled and directed by business interests, the engineer and the scientist are not hampered by the profit-making motive or by the pecuniary desirability of scarcity. The businessman is. The chief obstacles to greatly increased national productivity in this country are institutional or man-made, not engineering or physical. If not understood before the war began, it is now crystal clear.

A war economy calls for production and more production. When fighting a total war, price is no longer the determining factor in stimulating production. If a war economy sets up any guidepost for peacetime, it is this: if capitalism continues to live, industry must emphasize production rather than the restriction of output. The rewards, pecuniary or otherwise, must go to the management and the men who produce goods and services, not to those who persist in restricting output. Henry Ford, Henry Kaiser, and mass production represent the new points of view.

Certainly the chastening experience of the depression years indicated clearly that new rules and an umpire are needed in the business game. In changing and disillusioned

America the people may be induced to adopt a program located in the broad zone between extreme individualism and collectivism. Indeed, in a complex economic order the preservation of a considerable degree of individual initiative may depend upon governmental control and umpiring in the field of business endeavor, or upon the presence of governmental regulation within the system called capitalism. In 1938 a conservative magazine indicated that every businessman "who is not kidding himself" knows that, if the government took its hands off business and left the enterprise and the enterpriser entirely to their own devices, business in the United States would again be heading for disaster. Whatever may have been the consequences of the AAA, it proved that it is feasible to get a group of individualistic and competing farmers to work along the lines of a program laid down by a central government. It may be reasonably assumed that a similar program applied to other groups in the community could be made to work toward the expansion as well as toward the reduction of output. Many of the ills of the dismal thirties, such as technological unemployment or poverty in the midst of plenty, were the growing pains of a new and rapidly evolving economic and social world. These ills are not the rheumatic pains and stiffnesses of old age in the social and economic order. To "work with change" instead of futilely opposing it is a program which science approves.

In the decade preceding Pearl Harbor the American people possessed the greatest productive mechanism the world has ever known, but it was operated very irregularly and, considered as a unit, very inefficiently. The United States produced during the years of depression only a fraction of what it was capable of producing. Idle men, idle machines, idle buildings, and idle equipment were paralleled by hungry, poorly clad, and badly housed men, women, and children. In the recent depression we were poor financially but not physically. The kind of capital and resources with which the pioneer was familiar persisted. The United States still possessed the machines, materials, men, management, and money or credit necessary to produce a vast flow of needed commodities, services, and capital goods. But markets were neglected, the great business machine stalled because of financial, not engineering, problems. Without going to war, how can the great business and production machine be thrown into high gear and kept in high gear? As population and industrial units become larger, flexibility is reduced and the rigidity of structure increased. Fundamental inventions are not eagerly sought, as considerable change in the technological setup may mean heavier losses in overhead through obsolescence.

Finally, it may be pointed out that under our present system, which we call profit-making, what is particularly desirable for one individual or one corporation may be undesirable for all or for the community. One organization may make large profits if it controls the output of a necessity and restricts its production of that article; but, if every individual and every corporation does likewise with all sorts of produce, obviously production is reduced, standards of living will fall, and a serious situation will be confronted by that society. Universal slackerism is a menace. For one of many competitors to expand his plant and increase the output of his organization might be highly desirable, but if all competitors do likewise it may result in overexpansion or overdevelopment in that industry. It may lead to maladjustment, to idleness of plants and of workers, and to economic waste. Immediate personal expediency may run counter to the best interests of the group.

As long as expansion continued, capitalism and democracy seemed to be harmonious and related institutions. From the geographical point of view there are at the present time no more new lands and continents to conquer, subdue, and exploit. As the period of expansion ended, as the geographical frontier vanished, nationalism with its parochial point of view, with its tariff walls and quotas, and with its particularistic prejudices became a generally accepted doctrine. Better transportation and communication had been mooring the continents in the same harbor; but in this age of insecurity national, political, and economic antagonisms, resting upon a foundation of impulses growing out of the early struggles and the dangerous life of humankind, have been tending at the same time to separate the peoples of the world and to lead the nations back toward the localism of the Middle Ages or beyond. While the technical facilities for international trading have been improving, international trade is declining and markets must be found at home. Capitalism in the power age, in the epoch of nationalism in which tolerance and good will are at a low ebb, and in the period following the long march of expansion across the continents faces new and peculiar problems. Men and women are asking: Can democracy be squared with the new capitalism of today? Or can capitalism be maintained only as a special privilege for minority groups? Certainly it is not easy for men today to discuss calmly the issues involved. Insecurity, which is characteristic of these times, does not make for tolerance; and freedom is a twin of tolerance.

The nineteenth century, with its long list of achievements in science, industry, and technology, has set an intricate stage upon which to enact the drama of today and tomorrow. We now need organized genius and initiative in the economic and political fields. We now need men who are able calmly to take a fresh survey of the intricate cooperative world in which we are living. We now need individuals who can look beyond the immediate and personal to a longer-run social point of view. However, the order in which men and women of today live has tended to emphasize personal and immediate affairs rather than social or long-run matters. The new fields to conquer are found in the balancing of consumption and production on a high level, in the elimination of unemployment, and in the spread of well-being. America has the capital, the power, the natural resources, the labor power, the skill, and the managerial ability to reach these attractive goals. Shall we be able to coordinate and direct effectively the forces now going to waste because of business anarchy? If so, it may be reasonably anticipated that capitalism and democracy may persist side by side as these new economic frontiers are being surveyed and cultivated in the postwar world. War has clearly indicated that a global economy and a world outlook are essential to the welfare, prosperity, and improvement of any one nation or group of peoples.

Property is a fundamental institution in culture, and even among primitive societies it is not as simple as one might think because it is reciprocally related to kinship, marriage, economic, religious, and political institutions. Nevertheless, American conceptions of property were comparatively simple compared with what the concept implies today. Property has become a property complex.

Max Lerner, in the next selection, shows that property has become drastically transformed in the era of "big technology" and the corporate empires. Property of the old sort—family-owned and owner-managed—has become a kind of residual legend. Small property still exists in the form of small farms (though the average farm size is getting larger), small businesses, and tiny shops, but America has become a society not only of "big technology" and the "big corporation" but of "big property." Lerner discusses the factors that have been changing property and the consequences of the new property idea, with particular reference to the United States.

29

THE PROPERTY REVOLUTION*
Max Lerner

In spite of America's role as the chief residual defender of the system of private property in its pristine purity, the position of property in America is neither private nor pure. In a dynamic economy like the American the bundle of legal claims called "property" never remains stable: a change in technical processes, a shift in consumption habits, a new invention in technology or managerial practice, a depression or a war, may give new value to claims hitherto ignored or diminish others hitherto cherished.

Property is not a simple or single right. It has become a property-complex—a tangle of ideas, emotions, and attitudes, as well as of legal and economic practices. As such it has been drastically transformed in the era of Big Technology and the corporate empires. According to the more naïve version of the business legend, private property has always been the American "way of life" and always will be. This has lost much of its meaning. For those who possess property, in the sense of substantial stockholdings and investments, it is mainly a symbol of status for the present and security for the future. For the rest, who may have homes and automobiles but are propertyless in the sense of industrial holdings, it is something they hope to acquire for themselves or their children: this hope, along with the things in their own life that they value and enjoy, serves to link them with the holders of property and power. The forms of property have changed, but the emotions and loyalties it evokes go back deep into the American past.

The American ideas about property were deeply influenced by a trio of English thinkers—Locke, Blackstone, and Herbert Spencer —but it was the structure of American society up until the end of the nineteenth century that gave substance to their theories. The components of the property idea—that a man had a right to the things with which he had mixed his sweat, that his property was linked with his craft and job and therefore his personality, that you could no more deprive him of his property than of his freedom and individuality, that in fact his individuality was linked with the property which made him self-sufficient and self-reliant, and that he could do what he wished with the property that was his—these elements of the property idea had force in a social setting where almost every man owned a piece of land or hoped to save enough on his job to start a small business. In the America of the farmer and the owner-enterpriser, private property was a way of organizing not only the economy but also the personality.

This was reinforced by the underlying theological premises of the Christian idea. The Christian allegory of death and resurrection—the sacrifice for a principle sacred to the personality—gave a militant edge to the crusade for property, which was so closely tied with the personality. The roots of individualism in the Calvinist idea of calling and election

* From *America as a Civilization*, Simon and Schuster, Inc., New York, pp. 297–304. Copyright 1957, by Max Lerner. Reprinted by permission of Simon and Schuster, Inc., publishers.

gave further strength to the secular insignia of success in vocation. The theological premises of St. Augustine's *City of God* and of Bunyan's *Grace Abounding* combined in America to give property the aura of grace. In the moral and emotional climate of the earlier America, entrance into the Heavenly City required that one be shrived of poverty and invested with property. The clinching element of the property idea was the doctrine of natural rights, by which private property came to be accepted as inalienable from the person, part of "the laws of Nature and of Nature's God" that predated human society and therefore could not be changed by human enactment. This theology of the property idea helped the possessors to hold on to their power and invested their position with the support of popular conviction. In a society that regarded property as grace, business enterprise had strong roots in the general allegiance.

But as the conditions of property changed, with Big Technology and the corporate empires, the gap between the property idea and the social reality widened, until property of the old sort—family-owned and owner-managed—became a kind of residual legend, still clung to even when it was stripped of all but a lingering historical memory. Industrial property became centralized, family ownership waned, the corporate form pushed aside the others, the size of the property unit shifted—and America, which had once been a society mainly of small property owners, became a society not only of the Big Technology and the Big Corporation but also of Big Property.

Small Property still exists in the form of small farms, small businesses, and tiny shops, but the independent farmer is a dwindling fraction of the population, the small manufacturer is being crowded by the great corporations, and the little merchant finds himself precariously caught in an economy of big department stores, chain stores, mail-order firms, and discount houses. In the division of the nation among big property, small property, and the unpropertied, big property is increasing in power, small property is increasing in numbers (there were over five million nonfarm enterprises in the mid-1950s, an increase of over a million in a quarter century) but shrinking in power, while the unpropertied are growing in numbers despite the wider diffusion of stock ownership and are as powerless as the unpropertied have always been everywhere.

Before the world wars there still seemed a chance to have the issue fought out between Big and Small Property, and the great names of the Progressive Era—Wilson and Brandeis, La Follette and Norris, J. Allen Smith and Parrington and Beard—were the men who, even in the face of the challenge from the corporate empires, clung to the Jefferson-Jackson-Lincoln conception of an America of small property. It was this issue which furnished one of the great stakes of the social struggle for several generations. The struggle was lost by Small Property, mainly because it was waged not only against the corporate empires but also against their Big Technology, which was even harder to beat. In this struggle the impersonal Big Corporation had the advantage of putting on its enemy's uniform, garbing itself in the emotion-laden insignia of the idea of individualist property that had been shaped in an era of petty trade, small handicraft, and family ownership and operation, and was being invoked to sanction the triumph of the corporation and its new managerial elite.

I do not write of Big Property here as if it were always evil and monopolist, and of Small Property as if it were always good. Neither is necessarily true. The American worship of magnitudes, even when turned upside down to become a cult of the small, still remains an obsession with numbers. The monopoly power—defined as the power to manipulate price and output by being strategically placed to do so—may apply to both big and small corporations that are thus strategically placed, although it is more likely to apply to the big ones. In the ever-greater market of a high-level, mass-production economy the increase in corporate size is bound to keep pace with the growth in the size of the market. The American economy has shown a striking capacity for maintaining its freedom of energy even while changing and seemingly rigidifying its forms.

Two examples may serve to underscore this. One is in the area of competition: to a striking degree price competition in the mass-production industries has been replaced by brand and product competition; for example, technological innovation has made glass, rubber, steel, aluminum, and plastics compete with one another in many industrial and domestic uses. The second example is in the insurance companies, the investment trusts, and the pension funds. During the 1950s it was estimated that at least 80 per cent of all the new venture capital which was supplied to the organized capital market came through these big institutional investors. In a sense it may be said that they act as trustees for the savings and holdings of the ordinary American—a new kind of trusteeship which differs from the vaunted trusteeship of the Big Corporation itself. To the extent that these institutional investors safeguard the property interests of the small man, Small Property may be said to have re-emerged in the investment market even after it had to give way in production itself.

It would be wrong to say that the corporate empires entrenched private property, but even more wrong to say that they destroyed it. A better way is to say that the modern corporation "smashed the property atom," breaking it into constituent particles and re-assigning them. The bond owner now gets one kind of return; the stockholder gets another; the large-minority-bloc stockholders have a hand in corporate decisions, sharing control with the managers, while the small stockholders who may together represent the majority ownership get their dividends but have little power of control except as their interests in the profits and security of their holdings are the concern of the big institutional investors I have discussed. The worker, who once had the hope of becoming a property owner by starting a business, still makes a stab at it in many cases but with a high rate of business failures. His realistic chance of owning property rests on becoming himself a small stockholder. For a fitful moment, during the "sitdown strikes" of 1936 and 1937, there was talk of the worker's property right in his job, but this did too much violence to the whole property tradition, which was emotionally linked with owners and not workers.

What the corporate revolution did was not to strip the propertied class of its power but to extend the reach of that class and change property relations within it. Where the owner had once controlled his own industrial property and capital and received profit from his own management and risk, he still got the profits in the form of dividends, but the decisions and control on which they were based were now bureaucratized, being shifted to the managerial group.

The processes of corporate investment have also suffered a drastic change. A recent analysis of the formation of capital from 1919 to 1947 shows the following: in that period the American capital accumulation was 770 billion dollars; 34 per cent (262 billion) was undistributed profits of the corporations themselves and was plowed back; 40 per cent (310 billion) was in the form of bank credit, used for capital expansion; 26 per cent (198 billion) was individual savings—that is, the savings of the risk-taker in the classical sense. But when the last figure is broken down, one finds that most of it went into savings banks or life insurance or durable consumers' goods which count as personal capital; some of it went into corporate bonds, paying a set return. Only a little more than 3 per cent of the individual savings went into corporate stocks. In 1948, in a year when the national income was 225 billion, only a billion dollars went into new corporate stock, common and preferred.

This means that the big corporation no longer goes out into the market looking for savings. It plows back its own profits. This was foreshadowed decades ago: Charles M. Schwab, the steel industrialist, when asked in 1923 what the future of American industry would be, answered, "Why won't it be in the future as in the past, all the money you make and more put back into the business?" A few recent figures indicate that business has followed his advice. In 1929 the American corporations reinvested 20 per cent of their profits; in 1950 they reinvested 70 per cent.

There are many reasons for this high rate of corporate self-financing. With huge profits, high government taxes, and the desire of the managers to show corporate growth as an index of their own managerial skill and achievement, the corporation has become almost self-sufficient, even in terms of its capital formation. Its new bond flotations are largely taken up by savings banks and insurance companies. This has led to the suggestion that most of the corporate capital today is in a sense "conscripted capital," either plowed back by corporate administrative decision, or invested for individuals by banks and insurance companies, or taken by the government in taxes and invested in public works programs and armament industries. Even more important is the decline of the investment banker. Compare his role in the merger movement of the 1890s and 1900s with his lesser role today, and the change becomes dramatic. There has long been a conviction that whoever controls the money market controls the corporate empires, and that whoever controls credit possesses the crucial power. This conviction was the basis for the economic thinking of Louis D. Brandeis about "other people's money" and for a whole series of Federal investigations of the "Money Trust." It was also the core idea of the European conceptions of American "finance capitalism" from Lenin through Hilferding to the lesser Marxists of today. This is far less true now, given the new trend of corporate self-financing which keeps the economy moving. The American economy during the past half century or longer has shifted from finance capitalism to corporate capitalism.

The consequences of all this for the property idea are far-reaching. It is hard to use the individualist "natural rights" defense of corporate power and talk of the managerial elite mixing their sweat with the soil or with their tools. As for the question of profits and power as a reward for business skills, what has happened is that the profits in the form of dividends go to the stockholders who have to show few business skills except shrewdness in knowing when to buy or sell stocks, while power without profits has gone to those who show the managerial skills.

As for the idea of risk-taking, one of the stock themes of business-minded editorial writers was that risk capital was the life blood of the economy, and that the welfare state might destroy it. But the reality is that risk capital has changed its form and nature. Like the profit motive in business, it was a carry-over from the era of small business enterprise into the Era of the Sure Thing. There is still risk in corporate enterprise. In their measured and ponderous way, corporations do take risks and often very great ones. But the capital they use is not individual entrepreneur capital, and the managers do not take risks with their own money. Nevertheless they have a sense that the corporate capital that they are risking is theirs, that it might otherwise be used for dividends or for strengthening their working funds, and that their own prestige as managers depends upon risking it wisely. In addition there is the generalized risk of violent fluctuations in the economy as a whole, due to the business cycle: the Great Depression confiscated more business values, running into the tens of billions, than the New Deal could ever have done, and when President Eisenhower suffered a heart attack, the loss in corporate values by stock-market quotations was immense.

With its two main underpinnings removed—the profit incentive and the reward for risk—what remains of the original theory of private property? Not much, it must be admitted: the original theory needs drastic overhauling, yet the social reality of private property is still a force in the American economy. Private property has not been abolished, either by Big Government or the Big Corporation: it has taken new forms. It is still private in the sense that it is not statist, but it has ceased to be individualist and has become corporate, institutional, and managerial. The incentives of the owners of Big Property are no longer profit-from-skill but have become profit-from-dividends, security for life, and if possible a "killing" on the stock market.

As for the incentive of the managers, some of them get options on blocs of stock at a low price as part of their salaries and to that extent are corporate owners also. Their salary range is broad: some may get less than $25,000 a year, others more than a quarter million (the highest salaries are in tobacco, liquor, cosmetics, drugs, movies, and broadcasting), and many of them get extra "bonuses," but only a handful are in the millionaire income class. Nonetheless as a group they belong to the big-income class and consider themselves part of Big Property. They know that each quarter they must show a good profits record, along with a good production and sales-volume record and a good labor-relations record.

They are usually able men, college graduates from the Midwest or the Northeast who "get along with people," wear the right clothes, have the right friends, and possess "agreeable" personalities. They work hard, carrying their work home with them at night, are reluctant to retire, and have great pride in their craft. They may be spurred on by the pace of technical advance behind which they dare not lag, or by shifts in the market situation with which they must keep up; but their important incentives are pride, prestige, and self-expression in their work. While they may have few competitors in their own industry, the corporate rivalry is usually intense. Sometimes it is a gamelike rivalry, as with the General Motors–Ford struggle to show which of them will be Number One in the small-car market. Sometimes, as with the automobile manufacturers in the lesser companies, it is a grimmer question of whether they will be pushed out of the market altogether. The cannibalism among corporations is as great as among the tribes in the Congo jungle, although it operates with the sanction of law as well as corporate tribal practice.

One of the great spurs, for both owners and managers, is the sense of power flowing from the massive capital whose investment they organize. This includes the indirect power over legislators, government administrators, and the communications industries, which the possessors of big investments and the dispensers of big advertising can count on. The managers associate themselves with Big Property and have become its agents. A Regent has become King, but he rules in the old regal fashion, in the interests of the dynasty. The freedom to do what one will with property, which is still claimed by the corporate regents as it was once by the individualist business kings, is still the watchword of the champions of corporate "private property"; and the property fears of the managers express themselves as strongly in opposition to "dangerous" ideas at home and abroad as those of the owners ever did.

One change in attitude has, however, taken place. The managers of the big corporations are likely to have a broader vision of the economy as a whole and its place in the world than the individual small businessmen, who are close to the competitive struggle and feel embittered both by their labor difficulties and by the big chunk of their income which the government takes in taxes. No Poujadist movement has arisen among American shopkeepers and small businessmen, as it did in France in the mid-1950s, yet there is a discernible narrowness of outlook in the small sectors of the American economy as well.

There remains to speak of the property ideas of the propertyless. The path to property in the earlier America was either through small landholding, usually on the advancing frontier, or by starting a small firm and making it larger, finally building it into a great established business and even a family fortune. The path to property now is more likely to be by the carving out of a career in the managerial hierarchy. Those who are not managers may shift from one occupation to another, or from industrial worker to white collar or professional, but they remain unpropertied.

Yet it would be wrong to conclude that the property idea has no hold on them. No dogmatically Socialist appeal has ever had much success with them in America, and they have consistently refused to take on the class-conscious bitterness assigned to them by the Marxist writers. However great the gap between the corporate reality and the theory of private property, the propertyless still assign the production record of America and their own increased living standards to the regime of private property. It may be "folklore," but folklore has a way of retaining its hold on the people. They are willing to consider the masters of corporate property the trustees of the private-property system until such time as they themselves or their children (for hope has never died in their hearts) will break into the charmed circle. They are resigned to Big Property not because they believe in some "harmony of interests," or

think there is no conflict between top dog and bottom dog, but because each in his heart hopes still to be a top dog and therefore tends to identify with him. Even American unionism, as Hoxie long ago pointed out, is a property-minded "business unionism."

But I do not want to emphasize too much the identification with the Big Property group. Most of the propertyless are so only when judged in terms of industrial capital or land. Their real concern is with their personal property: a "home," even if it has a mortgage; a car, even an old one; some savings, even if inflation is depleting them; clothes and fashions; a TV set and kitchen appliances; a job, which to most Americans is *theirs* and therefore has property aspects; perhaps even a few shares of stock; and the hope someday of "taking it easy" and "retiring," on a different scale from the rich corporate owner and manager, but in much the same spirit of being invested with property as grace.

Within the last few years automation has been given special emphasis as an issue in management-labor relations. Automation, as represented in controversial propaganda, threatens the security not only of unions but of every industrial worker. But is automation actually so alarming if it is regarded as an aspect of a long process of mechanization and is therefore not entirely a new phenomenon?

George B. Baldwin and George P. Schultz, as joint authors of the selection which follows, discuss three aspects of automation—integration, feedback technology, and computer technology. From the beginnings of the Industrial Revolution, workers have been wary of mechanical innovations which they feared would replace them. Workers now are concerned about the effects of automation in job classification, wage structure, retraining, and the acquisition of new skills; and to the extent that these effects are real, they also are of direct concern to management.

Generally speaking, it may be said that an immediate effect of every technological innovation has been increased unemployment, though readjustments are readily made owing to the expanding demands of industry. Whatever ways may be devised of cushioning the shock of labor displacement because of present phases of mechanization, they are of great concern to industry, unions, individual workers, and the Federal government, especially the latter because of its social-security system. Baldwin and Schultz discuss some of the ways of adjustment in practice at the present time.

30

AUTOMATION: A NEW DIMENSION TO OLD PROBLEMS*

George B. Baldwin and George P. Schultz

By itself, the word "automation" has more romance than meaning. When we try to go behind the word itself and describe the kind of technological change it represents, we quickly come up against complexity and vagueness. Nonetheless, there seem to be three quite distinct developments which together embrace nearly everything that can be brought under the automation rubric.

1. The linking together of conventionally separate manufacturing operations into lines of continuous production through which the product moves "untouched by human hands." This first development, which depends primarily on mechanical engineering for its adoption, we shall refer to simply as integration, a term already in wide use in the metalworking industries.

2. The use of "feedback" control devices, or servomechanisms, which allow individual operations to be performed without any necessity for human control. With feedback, there is always some built-in automatic device for comparing the way in which work is actually being done with the way in which it is supposed to be done and for making, automatically, any adjustments in the work process that may be necessary. This second development we shall refer to simply as feedback technology; it is dependent primarily not on mechanical but on electrical engineering knowledge and techniques.

3. The development of general- and special-purpose computing machines capable of recording and storing information (usually in the form of numbers), and of performing both simple and complex mathematical operations on such information. We shall refer to this aspect of automation as computer technology; it rests primarily on new developments in electrical engineering.

AREAS OF INDUSTRIAL RELATIONS AFFECTED

Some of the ways in which automation will affect industrial relations will obviously depend on the speed and mass with which it strikes the economy. It is less likely to come as a tidal wave than as a succession of ground swells that will reach different industries at different times and with quite different impacts. Most affected industries will probably have quite a bit of time in which to think through the labor problems automation will create and to plan whatever adjustments may be necessary. It is often possible to do things over a period of time that could not be managed if they had to be done overnight, such as letting attrition work off the surplus labor or retraining key employees.

There are also likely to be some effects on labor relations which are independent of the speed with which automation comes; for example, the upgrading of the level of skills

* From *Monthly Labor Review*, vol. 78, no. 2, pp. 165–169, February, 1955. Reprinted by permission of the authors and *Monthly Labor Review*.

required in the labor force and the reversal of the past trend toward more specialized, more routine, and less interesting jobs. These two examples suggest that automation will not confront us solely with "problems" in the labor field, but will confer some benefits on labor directly, as producers, and indirectly, as consumers.

It is important to state quite explicitly that, at this early date, probably no one can predict with confidence the outcome of specific developments or recommend specific solutions to hypothetical problems. What is needed, and what alone seems possible now, is the development of a general awareness of the kinds of changes and problems automation is likely to bring. Here, then, are some general areas that seem likely to be affected by automation:

1. Automation is likely to permit greatly improved *working conditions*, including greater safety and easier housekeeping.

2. Much thinking about *incentive systems*, particularly individual forms of piecework, will have to be revised or discarded.

3. As some traditional processes and factory layouts are changed, the job of pinpointing *managerial responsibility* for the performance of specific manufacturing operations may become easier; buckpassing among departments may be more difficult to get away with. Foremen are likely to take on increased responsibility. On the other hand, there may well be some forms of automation that will work the other way, that is, they may blur the boundaries of responsibilities that are now clear.

4. *Training* (or perhaps retraining) problems will probably require more attention than they have since World War II. The training problems are likely to center on the development of new and complex skills for new grades of maintenance technicians, with shifts in operators' skills being relatively minor.

5. A marked change in the work-content of jobs resulting from automation may find expression in three familiar forms: (a) *Wage structures* may often require adjustment; (b)

the *traditional jurisdictions* of some unions may be disturbed; for example, by the need to unify mechanical and electrical skills in a new class of maintenance workers; (c) the *internal structure* of some unions is likely to undergo changes; in particular, it may be important for some unions to give special recognition to new, small groups of highly skilled workers.

6. Managements and unions, accustomed to thinking in terms of narrow and rigid *job classifications*, may need to broaden the scope of those classifications somewhat. The same thing applies to thinking about *seniority units*.

7. Finally, there is the *employment* effect. The anxiety and fear which stem from uncertainty concerning how employment will be affected by automation give rise to the most difficult problems of all. It is hardly surprising that union newspapers and current contract demands often reflect these fears, though it is worth noting that most unions seem to be approaching automation without hysteria and with a desire to plan intelligently for what may lie ahead. We cannot shrug off people's fears of being left stranded, of having no alternative job or the time and money to find one in the event of layoff; we cannot down these fears by citing the virtues of technological progress, labor mobility, and individualism. Automation seems sure to bring with it increased emphasis on means of cushioning the shock to the worker who is displaced, and of retraining him to a useful and satisfying role in our society.

Each of the areas noted above deserves careful consideration by managements and unions; and each is worthy of considerably more academic research than has been done up to now. Of course, in many respects the problems are entirely familiar and there is already at hand a large body of research and experience for use as a guide in working them out. As one experienced union leader remarked, "Automation? It may look new to the engineers but, to me, it's an old story. Back in the thirties we called it technological change." But, while broadly familiar, the problems associated with automation do bring some new twists, some new dimensions for consideration. We propose to look briefly at three areas, using as a basis for the discussion what we have gleaned from the limited published information available and our own observations. The areas we have selected are these: (1) the effects on the abilities required of the labor force, (2) the effects on rigidly defined job classifications and seniority units, and (3) the problem of displacement.

ABILITIES REQUIRED OF THE LABOR FORCE

What will be the impact of automation on the abilities required of the labor force? Will it leave us with a predominance of dull, routinized jobs, in which people are forced to conform to the dictates of the machine? Or is it more likely to open up jobs with greater intellectual challenge and to raise the skill composition of the labor force?

Any discussion of job mix is, of course, a discussion of proportions, of the relative weights of managerial, professional, skilled, semiskilled, and laboring jobs. Generally, automation appears to bring about a change in the mix, so that the resulting weights tend to emphasize the former, more highly skilled rather than the latter, less skilled types of occupations. We have observed this upgrading effect in a limited number of cases, but the conclusion must rest more on *a priori* reasoning than on statistical grounds. It seems reasonable to expect that the ratio of managers to employees will increase, in view of the increased value of the equipment for which an individual manager would become responsible, and of the increased proportion of the total work process inevitably brought under the supervision of one man. The value and complexity of the equipment similarly indicate a need for a higher proportion of engineers and, especially in the case of the electronic feedback and computer technologies, give rise to what amounts to a new occupation in most concerns, that of electronic technician.

In the factory, the new technology takes over most readily the materials-handling and completely routinized machine operations and tends to emphasize, as far as the average plant workman is concerned, jobs directed at "keeping the process going because we just can't stand downtime." As one plant manager explained, "You can't afford to chase all over the factory for a maintenance man when something goes wrong. He's got to be right there and he's got to know something about electrical and hydraulic problems, not just mechanical." So the proportion of maintenance people is likely to increase as well as the skill required of them. This is not to say that all routine or heavy jobs will be eliminated or to overlook the fact that many skilled jobs may disappear or become less important quantitatively. But in terms of overall proportions, it seems likely that automation will have an upgrading effect on the job mix in those areas of the economy where it is employed. This conclusion may be further bolstered by reference to the oil and chemical industries, where automation has had a relatively long history already.

The quantitative impact of automation on employment in those areas of our economy where it is used is almost impossible to estimate. Obviously, firms install the new equipment because it helps them reduce costs. While labor costs are not the only area of savings involved, they are typically a major consideration, so, on the face of the question, we would expect a reduction in employment opportunities, given some framework of total effective demand. But it is much easier to identify jobs that are being lost to technological change than those it is creating. Neglecting the possibility that greater demand may result from lower product prices, there is the virtual certainty that new products will be made technically or economically feasible, particularly by the feedback control devices now being developed. The question, then, is at least an open one. Neither optimists nor pessimists can afford to be too dogmatic about the long-run quantitative effects of automation on employment.

But suppose we assume that the industries

where automation is used employ a smaller and smaller proportion of the labor force. Despite a direct effect of upgrading on the job mix, there might be, in the overall picture, a downgrading effect if the adjustments that take place are predominantly in unskilled occupations or in such areas as personal services. That seems to us unlikely, however. It seems as certain as any social trend can be that the demand for professional services, especially medical and educational, will increase rapidly during the next 10 years and beyond. And, with the higher standards of living made possible by technological advance, the adjustment may be made through a continuation of present trends toward longer vacations, more holidays, and a shorter workweek. In that event, we may well see another long-term trend continued: a further reduction in the number of unskilled jobs and an increase in emphasis on the more skilled and professional occupations.

In short, our guess is that both the direct short-run and the indirect longer-run effect of automation on employment will call for more and not less skill on the part of our labor force. We are entitled to a cautious hope that automation may afford a partial answer to those who look at the rising educational levels in the country and ask, "What are people going to do with all that education when they find themselves on the dull and routine jobs of American industry?" *Mechanization* may indeed have created many dull and routine jobs; *automation,* however, is not an extension but a reversal of this trend: it promises to cut out just that kind of job and to create others of higher skill.

The training—or the educational job implied—will obviously become more difficult and more important as the speed of innovation increases. Studies of the skilled labor force and its recruitment, training, and movement, such as that on electronic technicians recently made by the Bureau of Labor Statistics,* are given added significance by the technological developments we are discussing. The same may be said for the work of the Bureau of Apprenticeship, and of the many opportunities for adult education in a wide variety of fields. We can expect many of the more alert engineering colleges and community vocational schools to revise their curriculums to take account of automation. Many company apprenticeship programs may be similarly affected.

JOB CLASSIFICATIONS AND SENIORITY UNITS

A frequently noted characteristic of our economy is the tendency toward greater and greater specialization of knowledge and of tasks. Work has typically been organized into the smallest possible units, each one of which is a repetitive part of a total process and is so small in relation to the whole that a sense of identification with the total process on the part of the person performing the job is almost out of the question. In part, this tendency has been a result of the developing technology. But it is also a result, as we all recognize, of the philosophy which says, (1) break the work process down into the smallest possible components, (2) fit jobs into a rigid structure that emphasizes the duties and the boundaries of the job rather than its part in the process, and (3) put everyone possible on an individual or small-group incentive system which gears pay to output on the particular job. This philosophy inevitably has tended to identify the individual with an ever more narrow task, giving him positive incentives to restrict his interests and no incentive at all to think beyond his immediate work environment or to place his own performance in the context of a total operation. This philosophy also brings with it a tendency to think in terms of seniority units as rigid and narrow as the job classifications in many cases.

Automation is likely to challenge these habits of thought fostered by discontinuous and highly specialized methods of production.

* U. S. Bureau of Labor Statistics, Bull. 1150, *The Mobility of Electronic Technicians, 1940–52,* 1954.

From the technical point of view, automation ties operations together physically; in terms of systems, engineering and economics alike, automation requires a new way of thinking about the flow and control of work—a way of thinking that emphasizes continuous movement of work through a total process rather than the stop-and-go progress which is the sum of independent operations.

Almost as a corollary of the reasoning about the effects on skills of automation, it appears that automation will necessitate broader thinking about job classifications and seniority units. For example, when 3 or 4 different types of grinding operations, each now representing a separate job classification, are tied together by automation, one man will be able to operate the integrated grinding line. This man must have a generalized knowledge of grinding; and his changed, broader job classification is likely to carry more pay than any of the old grinding occupations.

As for seniority, existing contract clauses and plant customs may be found unsatisfactory in the light of new needs presented by automation. Where seniority provisions have arisen from a relatively stable operation with long established and clearly defined occupational groups, we suspect that the parties will want to change the rules to provide for increased job changes and transfers of personnel. For example, seniority rules that work satisfactorily in a plant divided into machining, heat-treating, grinding, and assembly departments may not make sense within a new department that combines all these operations in one integrated line; existing rules may also make it difficult to staff a new integrated department with those individuals both parties agree ought to get the new jobs. One management group even suggested that seniority standards would undergo an evolution stemming directly from the need for a more flexible work force. In this view, the development of a work force willing and able to adapt itself to the changing needs of an evolving work process would mean more than mere application of seniority protections to broader units of work. As a standard for continued employment, "ability to learn" would gradually replace "ability to do" the job.

THE PROBLEM OF DISPLACEMENT

It would be silly to pretend that there will not be many jobs which automation will abolish. Whether or not it creates, directly or indirectly, as many jobs as it wipes out, no one can know. Despite the inevitable uncertainty as to the speed and scope of automation's impact, this much at least seems certain: There is bound to be a new influence at work which will strengthen the arguments of people who feel that wage earners ought not to bear the main brunt of technological change.

Social shock absorbers, such as severance pay, the guaranteed annual wage, unemployment benefits, careful timing of laborsaving innovations to coincide with business upswings, and increased information-sharing between managements and unions, seem likely to receive increased attention, as automation spreads. If some of these mobility benefits add to the employer's cost of technological change, that alone would not disturb us greatly. Indeed, it is important to recognize clearly at least two types of costs incurred by the displaced worker: (1) loss of income while looking for a new job; and (2) loss of equities built up on the old job in the form of seniority, pension rights, vacation rights, and so on. While unemployment benefits of one kind or another are clearly a way of approaching the first type of loss, the more general adoption of the principle of severance pay for people with substantial equities in existing jobs may be one appropriate way to share some of the initial gains involved. In addition, such gain-sharing should strengthen the hands of both management and union officials as they confront the inevitable short-run pressures that develop whenever jobs are eliminated.

In developing policies to cushion the impact of automation, as with any major technological change, the toughest situations are not likely to be those in which some new machines and equipment are installed in a given plant; the toughest situations are likely to arise from competition between new plants designed for automation and older ones that are not. Sometimes the two plants will belong to the same company, sometimes not. In cases where automation expresses itself as competition among two or more firms not under common ownership, the policies appropriate to it seem no different from those we would like to see in any competitive situation.

But when automation takes the form of changes within a particular firm, then managements and unions have much greater control over the effects it will have and the ways in which these will be handled. For one outstanding characteristic of automation is that it takes time to install. Even after an exploratory stage has been completed, equipment must be designed and manufactured, men must be hired or trained for new occupations, physical installation and transition problems must be faced. All this takes time—not days or weeks, but many months or years. And with problems like displacement and personal adjustment, time, of course, presents a major opportunity that alert and socially responsible companies and unions can use to good advantage. Social responsibility would mean telling new employees that their jobs were temporary, retraining old employees who have the

requisite ability, permitting those near retirement to claim pension benefits, and so on.

Automation is likely to have its greatest immediate impact on office occupations. In a sense, that is fortunate, since it will affect a class of workers for whom the blow can be softened most easily, namely female employees working in large offices. Not only is turnover markedly higher among female clerical employees, but the demand for them in recent years has been high in most labor markets.

One further point to be made here is both obvious and obviously too important not to mention. In considering the problem of the displaced and unemployed worker, it is not so important to ask why he lost his old job as how much trouble he has in getting a new one, and what kind of new one he gets. This brings to the fore the educational and retraining problems already mentioned. But even more, it serves to emphasize, for an era of marked if not revolutionary change, the importance of government economic policy directed toward the maintenance of "full employment." Change the level of unemployment by a few percentage points, and the problem of displacement changes from a relatively manageable question of adjustment to a social catastrophe of alarming proportions, in which orderly technological progress becomes impossible.

There is a widely current notion that bureaucracy and democracy are somehow incompatible, and to the extent bureaucracy becomes a "rule by bureaus," which is a literal meaning of the term, the notion may have some justification. Nevertheless, a government must have its bureaucracy in order to function at all. As the functions of the state expand and the size and complexity of the bureaucracy increase, the question of responsibility of bureaucrats becomes more important and more intense.

Peter H. Odegard shows, in the following selection, that responsibility implies more than mere accountability for what is or is not done; it implies also a high level of technical competence for the job one is called upon to do; it involves personal character. A truly responsible bureaucrat owes several kinds of responsibility, viz., political, administrative, legal, professional, and moral, and a final responsibility to maintain his own self-respect. These responsibilities are interwoven with responsibility for subordinates, the constitutional division of powers, the representation of the people through Congress, party responsibility, the general welfare versus special interest, and political responsibility versus partisan loyalty. All these aspects of responsibility are discussed by Odegard.

31

TOWARD A RESPONSIBLE BUREAUCRACY*

Peter H. Odegard

A government without bureaucrats is like a centipede without legs, unable to move—even to save itself—and powerless to accomplish any of the goals for which governments are instituted among men. For it is upon the bureaucrats that we depend to see that these goals—or policies—are realized in practice. Without administrative officers—that is, without a bureaucracy to carry them into effect—the most fine-spun schemes for promoting the common defense, insuring domestic tranquillity, promoting the general welfare, and preserving the blessings of liberty to ourselves and our posterity would be stillborn.

Yet there is a widely current notion that bureaucracy and democracy are somehow incompatible—that the bureaucrat and the democrat must forever be at odds. This popular antithesis between bureaucracy and democracy is, as Professor Friedrich says, "an oratorical slogan which endangers the future of democracy. For a constitutional system which cannot function effectively, which cannot act with dispatch and strength, cannot live."

Nevertheless, the fears expressed by the demagogues pose problems which cannot be denied for those who want government to be both effective and democratic. Not the least of these is the problem of enforcing responsibility upon the bureaucracy. For among the so-called immutable principles of democratic theory is the assumption that power and responsibility must go hand in hand. Power without responsibility is the very definition of tyranny, and the transition from arbitrary to responsible government involves more than popular control of the legislature, the so-called policy-making branch of the government. It involves also popular control of the executive establishment and the bureaucracy through which public policies are translated from law into life.

As the functions of the state expand and the size and complexity of the bureaucracy increase, the search for ways and means to make these minions of Leviathan more responsible becomes both more important and more intense. But if bureaucratic accountability is to be real and equitable, the bureaucrat must know for what and to whom he is responsible. The Hoover Commission says:

The President, and under him his chief lieutenants, the department heads, must be held responsible and account-

* Reprinted by permission of *The Annals of the American Academy of Political and Social Science*, vol. 292, pp. 18-29, March, 1954.

able to the people and the Congress for the conduct of the executive branch. [But] responsibility and accountability are impossible without authority—the power to direct. The exercise of authority is impossible without a clear line of command from the top to the bottom, and a return line of responsibility and accountability from the bottom to the top.

IMPLICATIONS OF RESPONSIBILITY

But "responsibility" implies more than mere accountability for what is or is not done, and more too than a strict adherence to policy mandates as they come from the legislature and/or one's administrative superiors and associates. It implies also a high level of technical competence for the job one is called upon to do, a personal character that is loyal, honest, and reliable, a dedication to duty, and faith in the basic values of the society one serves. These values in turn will in final analysis determine the quality of the public service and the character and conduct of its servants.

A truly responsible bureaucrat is, then, a man of not one but many responsibilities. He owes a *political* responsibility to those who have final say as to policy and ultimately to the people who make and unmake them. He owes both a "political" and an *administrative* responsibility to his superior officers. He owes a *legal* responsibility to the courts (both administrative and judicial), lest he transgress the rights of citizens by abusing or exceeding his powers. He owes a *professional* responsibility to his fellow bureaucrats to maintain high standards of integrity and competence, lest he bring dishonor or disgrace to the "guild" of which all are members. He owes a *moral* responsibility to the highest ethical and moral principles of the state and society in which he lives and to which he professes allegiance. And finally he owes a responsibility to his own soul—to the honor and integrity of his own person—for without self-respect he can scarcely be expected to have respect for others or to deserve their respect in turn.

To explore fully these multiple loyalties and responsibilities is beyond the scope of this brief essay. It may, nevertheless, be useful to suggest some of the problems and perplexities that occur in thinking about a responsible bureaucracy in the modern state.

RESPONSIBILITY FOR SUBORDINATES

As far as the mass of bureaucrats have any *political* responsibility, it must be vicarious and not direct. A President, a Prime Minister, and the chief executive officers appointed to serve with them must, above all things, be politicians (and partisans, at that) and, as such, politically responsible not alone for their own acts but for those of their subordinates, however numerous and widespread.

As the leader of the government, and under the principle of collective responsibility as it operates in Great Britain, the Prime Minister is the center and focus of political responsibility. If the deeds of wayward and incompetent civil servants in the Home Office are attributable to the Home Secretary, so in like succession are they—through the Home Secretary—attributable to Her Majesty's Prime Minister. And all together the ministers of the Crown must assume collective political responsibility not only for major lines of policy but also for administrative acts of thousands of civil servants of whose very existence they may be but dimly aware. It is in this combination of individual and collective responsibility to Parliament that the great strength of British democracy is to be found.

Political responsibility for the mass of bureaucrats in the American government is much less clearly defined. The President, to be sure, in final analysis must "take the rap" for what is or is not done. The heads of the major departments are political officers appointed by and accountable to him; and as they must answer for the acts of their subordinates, so the President in turn must answer for them. But the locus of responsibility is by no means as clear as in Great Britain. James Burns says:

> The Founding Fathers did not clearly distinguish between the President's executive authority and the supervisory powers of Congress over administration. On the contrary, they deliberately divided administrative power between the two branches as part of the system of checks and balances.*

THE ISSUE CONFUSED

The President's power to control the bureaucrats derives mainly from his powers to appoint (and presumably by inference to dismiss) "officers of the United States whose appointments are not otherwise provided for" and to "require the opinion, in writing, of the principal officer in each of the executive departments." But these powers are by no means unlimited or exclusive, and at a hundred points Congress has, from the beginning, pared them down and impaired their effectiveness. The organic act establishing the Treasury Department, to cite one example, requires the Secretary "to make report and give information to either branch of the legislature, in person or in writing, respecting all matters referred to him by the Senate or House of Representatives or which may appertain to his office." And, although the Secretary was described in a subsequent law of September 11, 1789, as an "Executive Officer," he and the Treasurer of the United States were nevertheless required to make annual reports to Congress.

Legislation setting up other major departments or executive agencies has not followed this pattern, but Congress has nevertheless found ways and means for interposing itself between the President and his executive subordinates and thus confusing the clear line of bureaucratic responsibility. The creation within major departments of numerous bureaus over which particular committees of Congress and even particular Congressmen exercise

more control than the department chief is but one of several such devices.

Nor is this confusion confined to the central corps of executive departments and agencies. It has been confounded by the creation of "independent" boards, commissions, corporations, and authorities, responsible (if they may be so described) not to the President, but to Congress. This so-called "headless fourth branch of government" has posed problems of administrative organization, management, and responsibility for which no one seems to have found satisfactory solutions.

The mixture of executive, legislative, and judicial powers in these bodies has caused no end of confusion among experts accustomed to a neat tripartite division of political powers. But the Brownlow and the Hoover-Acheson Commissions struggled vainly with the problem of making these agencies "responsible" without at the same time sacrificing their "independence."

CONSTITUTIONAL DIVISION OF POWERS

The problem of the "independent agency" is obviously too complex and too important to be resolved by mere structural or procedural reform. It involves a restudy of at least one basic principle of American constitutional law—the principle of separation of powers. Although not expressly spelled out in the United States Constitution, the principle has always been implied from the language of Articles I, II, and III, vesting the legislative, executive, and judicial powers in three distinct branches of the government. But there is scarcely an agency or official of the government that does not in one way or another exercise two or more of these "distinct" powers.

Wherever an official has discretion to decide controversies among persons or between private persons and the government, he may be said to exercise judicial power; wherever he has power to issue rules or regulations to which penalties for violation are attached,

* James Burns, *Congress on Trial*, New York, 1949, p. 99.

he exercises legislative power; and wherever he has power to direct, or control, conduct in terms of these decisions or rules, he may be said to have executive power. Mean is the official, and humble indeed is his station, who does not in some measure combine these powers in the performance of his duties. To call them *quasi*-judicial and *quasi*-legislative may help the judicial conscience to rationalize departure from fundamental doctrine, but to justify the "independence" and hence the practical "irresponsibility" of an agency of government because it exercises quasi-judicial or quasi-legislative power may be to establish a principle which, if extended to all officials or agencies whose powers may be similarly described, can undermine the democratic principle that public officials—including bureaucrats called commissioners—must be politically responsible to the people through their elected representatives.

REPRESENTATIVES OF THE PEOPLE

It is too often forgotten that the President —no less than the Congress—represents the people, and that it is through him, perhaps more effectively than through Congress, that bureaucrats can be held responsible. Although the political responsibility of bureaucrats is a vicarious responsibility in either case, in the Presidency it comes to fairly clear focus at one time and in a single office, whereas in Congress it appears in fragments and at uneven intervals. And whereas through Congress the bureaucrat's responsibility to his state or local "clients" is emphasized, it is through the President that the bureaucracy can be most effectively held to account for promoting the "general welfare" of all the people. Fortunately it is not necessary to choose between Congress and the President in our search for a responsible bureaucracy. Both are essential, provided we understand what it is we are striving to accomplish.

Not the least of the heavy burdens the President must bear is political responsibility for the conduct and misconduct of the execu-tive establishment. Insolence, inefficiency, incompetence, and corruption in any executive official or agency are properly chargeable to him. He ought not to escape this responsibility, as Grant and Harding, and others too, have sought to escape, by talk of "betrayal" by "faithless men in high places." These men are his agents and for better or worse their deeds are his.

PARTY RESPONSIBILITY

And the President's responsibility is the responsibility of his party. Yet how often have we seen not only the President, but the party whose leader he is, seek (often successfully) to escape responsibility for the "evil deeds of evil men"—forgetting that these same "evil men" were his agents and those of his party! In final analysis political responsibility in a big democracy can be effectively enforced only through well-organized political parties. Hence it is that the search for a more responsible bureaucracy must be sought not merely in administrative reorganization or the redefinition and reallocation of powers and responsibilities, but also through a more responsible party system.

And if this is true of the President, it is equally true of the Congress. Congressmen no less than the President owe their election to the party in whose principles presumably they believe. Without responsible parties to organize and discipline Congressmen in terms of policies upon which as partisans they agree—the Congress itself becomes an undisciplined, irresponsible body of "freewheelers," each seeking his own exaltation and each owing allegiance to state and local pressure groups upon which—rather than the party— his political future comes to depend.

We need to inquire, then, whether party responsibility is more direct and meaningful when applied to Congress or to the President. There is reason to believe that our major political parties—as far at least as concerns the general welfare of the nation— are less responsible at the congressional than at the Presidential level. Although it is true that our major parties may be described as loose federations of state and local parties, it is also true that they function more effectively in Presidential years than at any other time in presenting to the voter meaningful alternatives as to candidates and policies. The higher ratio of actual to eligible voters at Presidential elections is one evidence of this. Another is the identification of the President by the voters as the responsible leader of his party in the nation. It is also true that—for a variety of reasons—party labels mean less at state and local levels than at the national level; and party organization is less efficient and less disciplined at off-year than at Presidential elections.

The relative weakness of the parties at the state and local levels is reflected, as both cause and effect, in the greater power and influence of special interest groups. Many Congressmen, and some Senators, owe more to powerful pressure groups within their states or districts than they owe to the party under whose label they aspire to office. In any case the issues over which congressional campaigns are fought in off years are more likely to reflect state and local interests than the issues over which Presidential campaigns are fought.

What is said here of the relative effectiveness of political parties in enforcing political responsibility in national affairs as between the President and Congress applies, with even greater force, to state and local governments and as between the governor and the legislature. The situation is of course complicated in the states by hydra-headed elective executives and in local governments by the widespread tradition of nonpartisanship.

GENERAL WELFARE VERSUS SPECIAL INTEREST

If this analysis has any validity, it follows that a bureaucracy responsible to the legislature will be more responsive and more responsible to local and special interests than a bureaucracy responsible to an elective chief executive.

It is to be expected that a Congressman quite properly answerable and responsive to the cattle growers of his district should seek to "liberalize" grazing regulations in federal forest reserves or on other federally owned lands within his state. If the bureaucrats responsible for the making and enforcement of these regulations are answerable to the Congressmen, they will find it difficult to restrict such demands for "liberalization" even though they conflict with general policies of the nation concerning the conservation and use of our natural resources. And what is true of grazing regulations is likewise true of countless other policies.

This is not to argue that Congressmen (taken together) are less concerned about the "general welfare" of the nation than is the President. Nor is it to lose sight of the intense pressures from special interests that are felt in the White House. It is, however, to say that the President, because his constituency is the nation, because he has at his beck and call mass communications facilities beyond the reach of any other person, because he is the dominant figure in his party, because of the power and prestige of his office, is less vulnerable to such special or regional pressures than is the average Congressman. Moreover, it is his responsibility to see that the general welfare is *not* sacrificed to special or parochial interests, and where he finds faithless bureaucrats who betray his trust, he has or should have power to discipline, expose, and if necessary remove them.

THE LEGISLATURE AS A SAFEGUARD

But, as I have said, the choice between a bureaucracy responsible to the executive (President, governor, mayor) and one responsible to the legislature (Congress, state legislature, city council) is not to be made in *either or* terms—nor under our system is such a choice open to us.

For, although the weight of constitutional authority, the dictates of practicality, and considerations of democratic theory point to the elected executive as the channel through which the bureaucracy is made responsible to the people, the legislature will continue to challenge this solution and to claim its share of control. And within proper limits it is a legitimate claim. For surely one of the basic functions of a representative legislative body is to maintain eternal vigilance over the bureaucracy to the end that the spirit as well as the letter of the law be observed in its execution and that the liberty of the citizen and the due process of law be not sacrificed to the insolence of office masquerading under "reasons of state."

Legislative bodies discharge this function through the enactment of laws which define the goals and standards of administrative action and the limits of administrative discretion; through the appropriation or denial of funds to administrative agencies, and the examination and evaluation of administrative policies and procedures when budget requests are under review; through more or less continuous inquiries of appropriate legislative committees, and special investigations launched in response to demands for more searching examination of particular agencies; and through the virtually continuous and informal contacts that individual legislators maintain—usually in response to requests from their constituents—with administrative agencies.

All these are legitimate and, under our system of government, inevitable devices available to legislative bodies for enforcing political responsibility upon bureaucrats.

Nevertheless, under present circumstances, it is not easy for the legislature to maintain effective surveillance and control over the vast and far-flung bureaucracy of the modern state. Even in the determination of the basic structure and powers of administrative agencies, the legislature is severely handicapped. To an ever increasing extent it has lost the initiative in the formulation of policy. Moreover, the scope and complexity of the problems with which legislation must now deal require that legislative standards be more general—not to say vague—leaving to the executive great discretion in the development of supplementary legislation (rules and regulations) to meet particular situations.

Nor can the modern legislative body hope to have access to information necessary to effective control of the bureaucracy, except through the bureaucracy itself. Even the power of special investigation may be limited by considerations of national security. The ever expanding scope of governmental activities shrouded in secrecy—if not mystery—makes effective control by a numerous legislative body difficult if not impossible. Congress, for example, is in these days called upon to authorize expenditures of fantastic dimensions for the development of atomic energy, for national defense, for foreign policy, often without the benefit of more than the most sketchy and elementary information. Such information as there is, is in the hands of the executive and subject to his control.

Under these circumstances, a responsible bureaucracy is possible only through a partnership of the legislature and the executive, based on mutual respect, trust, and confidence.

CONGRESSIONAL-EXECUTIVE RELATIONS

Certainly no one observing the American scene in these latter days would argue that such a partnership has characterized executive-legislative relations at the national level. Hearings before committees of Congress take on the appearance of adversary proceedings, with Congressmen as prosecutors and executive officers as defendants. Loose, exaggerated, and often unsupported charges of corruption, incompetence, moral depravity, and disloyalty have been hurled at administrative officers and at entire agencies by presumably responsible chairmen of committees. Observers watching the cold war between the White House and the Hill, even when both are controlled by the same party, might well conclude that the American government had indeed fallen on evil days. The very term bureaucracy has become a "snarl" word, symbol not of loyal and devoted public servants, but of functionless hangers-on—of doubtful honesty, morality, and loyalty. Obviously this is the way to ensure not a responsible, but a bitterly resentful, bureaucracy, crippled by fear, internal disunity, and dissension. Vigilance is indeed the price of liberty under law, but the line between the vigilant and the lawless *vigilante* must be maintained lest we betray the very freedom we seek to defend.

So much has been written about the dangers of executive usurpation and abuse of power that we have become less alert to threats of legislative usurpation. "The legislature," warned James Madison, "is everywhere extending the sphere of its activity and drawing all power into its impetuous vortex," and ". . . it is against the enterprising ambition of this department that the people ought to indulge all their jealousy and exhaust all their precautions." *

Madison's warning has a peculiar timeliness today, when some congressional committees have presumed to exercise not only powers of investigation and legislation normally associated with the legislative branch, but also executive and even judicial powers. Legislative intervention in the appointing power of the President has recently gone far beyond the so-called custom of senatorial courtesy. Attacks on prospective appointees as "security risks," loudly expressed doubts as to the loyalty of incumbents, and riders on appropriation bills forbidding the payment of public funds to named individuals are among the more recent devices of legislative usurpation, although the Supreme Court has branded this latter maneuver as being in effect a bill of attainder and hence invalid.

Illustrations of legislative intervention in administrative management are numerous and occur in virtually every major department of the government. And Senator McCarthy's "negotiations" with Greek shipowners concerning trade with Communist China mark a new level of legislative impertinence and usurpation. Only the so-called Bricker amendment, which would cripple Presidential control of foreign policy, compares with McCarthy's conduct as an example of congressional arrogance.

No better formula for producing a confused, timid, ineffective, and irresponsible bureaucracy could be imagined than this tug of war between the executive and the legislature for control. James Burns says:

> Responsibility for policy and administration becomes shrouded in a fantastically complicated network of ever shifting relationships among President, administrators, staff agencies, Senate, House of Representatives, committees, sub-committees, chairmen, individual legislators and among infinite combinations and permutations thereof.†

There is no easy escape from this situation. No reforms of structure or procedure, and no admonitions concerning good behavior will suffice without strong leadership on both ends of Pennsylvania Avenue.

If the major burden of enforcing bureaucratic responsibility should fall to the elected executive, it is imperative that the executive establishment be adequate, in terms of both the scope and structure of power, to make its control effective. The diffusion and confusion of power in a plural executive (as in the states), the intervention of the legislature in strictly executive functions, and the denial to the executive of power commensurate with his responsibility, all militate against a responsible bureaucracy.

In the far-flung, complex structure of the modern administrative state it is difficult at best for the executive to see or to know more than a tiny fraction of those for whose acts he is responsible. He becomes a prisoner of his top advisers and administrators. And with the multiplication of agencies and functions it becomes increasingly difficult for him to keep in very close touch with more than a handful of these.

The President is not only harassed by congressional interference and usurpation. He is denied many of the powers essential

---

* *The Federalist, or The New Constitution* (1945 ed.), Heritage Press, New York, no. 48, pp. 331, 332.

† James Burns, *op. cit.*, p. 115.

to effective executive control of the administrative machine. He lacks, for example, real authority to determine the organization and structure of the executive branch, and a large number of important executive functions in the so-called "headless fourth branch of the government"—the "independent" agencies—are outside his control. He lacks effective control over the federal budget, is "handcuffed and hog-tied" with line-by-line appropriations, and is denied the item veto. And he has only a limited control over personnel policy and administration, even within the regular executive departments and agencies.

POLITICAL RESPONSIBILITY VERSUS PARTISAN LOYALTY

How far up or down the hierarchy of administrative authority the principle of political responsibility should extend has been a subject of prolonged and intense debate. The issue has been confused by failure to distinguish between political responsibility and partisan loyalty. The former is a salutary and indispensable characteristic of democratic government and should extend from the outermost reaches of the bureaucracy to the White House. The latter, unless carefully confined to top administrative posts which share with the President in the determination of high policy, can become a mask for the place seeker and the spoilsman.

This is not to imply that administrative policy-making is or can be confined to a narrow circle of partisan officials at the top. Policy and administration are the Siamese twins of politics and are associated at virtually all levels of the administrative structure—indeed wherever discretionary power is found. But this is a far cry from saying that *partisan* responsibility for policy should embrace the entire civil service. For the partisan neutrality of the civil service is a cardinal principle of the merit system upon which any sound personnel policy must rest. The tradition, now embedded in law, which bars civil servants from active participation in party politics is based on this assumption. How far this

denial of an important civil right should extend, it is not easy to say. Certainly it should include professional, scientific, and technical workers upon whom we depend for continuity and competence in the public service. Whether it should also include the lower ranks of laborers and purely manipulative employees is not so clear.

To say that civil servants should not be held to any partisan loyalty or responsibility is not to say that they should also be exempt from political responsibility. Political responsibility in this sense implies that the civil servant carry out faithfully and to the best of his ability the policies of the administration, or government, of whatever party, in which the people have placed their trust. As former Prime Minister Attlee once observed, "We always demand from our civil servants a loyalty to the State, and that they should serve the government of the day, whatever its political colour." Anyone who cannot give this elementary loyalty to the state he serves cannot justly claim the security and immunity from partisan responsibility that characterizes membership in the permanent civil service.

LEGAL RESPONSIBILITY

A responsible bureaucracy implies not only political but legal responsibility as well. The legal definition of bureaucratic powers and responsibilities is the heart of administrative law and an important part of the criminal code. Laws against bribery and corruption, fraud and deceit, misfeasance and malfeasance, are, of course, part of the machinery for enforcing this legal responsibility.

In his classic study of the *Law of the Constitution*, A. V. Dicey argued strongly against the importation or infiltration into English law of the so-called *Droit administratif* of France, which (according to Dicey) was designed to give civil servants a preferred status under the law, or at least a status different from that which ordinary citizens enjoyed. Under the French practice, said Dicey, the ordinary courts are incompetent to pass judgment on administrative or official conduct. Redress for wrongful acts by government officials or civil servants must be sought not in the ordinary civil courts but in special administrative tribunals. Moreover, in France, he said, responsibility for such wrongful acts, once established, was assumed not by the individual but by the state.

All this, argued Dicey, was in derogation of the sound English view that responsibility for wrongful acts rests with the individual, without distinction as to his status, whether as private citizen or as civil servant. In England, he wrote, "every official, from the Prime Minister down to a constable or a collector of taxes, is under the same responsibility for every act done without legal justification, as any other citizen." * The public official can no more escape by casting his liability upon the state than can the private citizen. Indeed, the doctrine of state immunity from liability for the tortious acts of its servants ("The King can do no wrong") was a cardinal principle of English law.

American legal theory and practice have followed the English rather than the French tradition. Legal responsibility of the bureaucracy has been enforced through the ordinary courts, and liability for wrongful acts by civil servants has attached to the individual and not to the state. Responsibility of the government for breaches of contract has long been recognized, but a similar responsibility for the torts of its agents has had but a recent and reluctant recognition. Civil and criminal suits against public officials as individuals, plus resort to the great writs—quo warranto, mandamus, injunction, prohibition, habeas corpus—have been the usual remedies for bureaucratic wrong-doing. Proposals to establish a system of administrative tribunals on the French model have been made, but so far without success.

CHANGING LEGAL PATTERNS

Nevertheless there have been significant changes in traditional Anglo-American practice. The theory that a public officer was individually responsible for damages resulting from his wrongful acts may have helped to inspire caution and respect for the rights of others, but it was cold comfort to those actually damaged to know that their only redress was a damage suit against impecunious bureaucrats. So the fiction of individual responsibility has been maintained as the practice of publicly reimbursing officials in the amount of the judgments against them has grown.

Moreover, a distinction between *governmental* and *proprietary* functions has been made, according to which liability attaches to the government for the wrongful acts of its agents when pursuing the latter but not when engaged in the former. This distinction is grounded on the theory that the state derives no pecuniary benefit from its governmental activities—hence no liability—but does from its proprietary activities. However faulty in logic this theory may be, it has helped to extend the area within which government assumes liability for the wrongful acts of its servants.

Significant of the new trend is the Federal Tort Claims Act of 1946, which radically modifies the rule of immunity formerly applied to the federal government. Under this act the United States is made liable "for injury or loss of property or personal injury or death caused by the negligent or wrongful act or omission of any employee of the government while acting within the scope of his office or employment." † There are exceptions, however, including (1) cases where the employees have exercised due care in the execution of a statute whether valid or invalid, (2) discretionary acts, and (3) intentional torts such as assault, battery, and false imprisonment. Where liability attaches, it is declared to be the same as that imposed on a private individual "in accordance with the law of the place where the act or omission occurred."

Reflecting a similar trend in England was

* A. V. Dicey, *The Law of the Constitution* (4th ed.), London, 1893, p. 183.
† 28 U.S.C.A. § § 1346, 2672, 2674.

the enactment in 1947 of the Crown Proceedings Bill. With minor exceptions this act admits state liability for the wrongful acts of public servants. "A person can enforce any claim as of right regarding contracts and torts. The state will admit liability for the wrongs committed by its servants or agents as any private citizen or public corporation does." *

Although we are a long way from the French system of administrative courts, it is possible to point to examples of some roughly analogous institutions in the United States, such as the Court of Claims, the Tax Court of the United States, and the Court of Customs and Patent Appeals. Moreover, quasi-judicial bodies such as the Interstate Commerce Commission and the Securities and Exchange Commission, together with a considerable number of agencies serving the needs of intradepartmental adjudication, might be transformed into something closely resembling administrative courts. But however logical such a plan might be, we are far from adopting it in this country. Moreover, the arguments for the French system, while impressive, are far from conclusive in a country like the United States with a federal system, a strong tradition of local autonomy, and an equally deep-rooted distrust of government in general. For some time to come we shall continue to rely mainly on the ordinary courts to ensure legal responsibility of the bureaucrats.

MORAL RESPONSIBILITY

But a truly responsible bureaucracy will depend as much—perhaps more—upon its own code of professional and civic ethics as upon external controls. Excessive regulation may hinder rather than help in the development of such a code, by cultivating "timidity" and government by rule book at the sacrifice of imagination and initiative. "Infinitely more important than compelling administrative officials to live up to minutely defined require-

ments of control is their acceptance of an ethical obligation to account to themselves and to the public for the *public* character of their actions." †

The growth of professional pride and *esprit* among civil servants, without which no professional code of ethics can have much meaning or effect, has had to wait upon victory over the spoilsman. Although the final battles in that war have yet to be won, it is not too early to make some conscious and concerted effort to create among public servants a greater sense of professional loyalty, discipline, and responsibility. Indeed, signs are not lacking that, in some sectors at least, this new professional spirit has already begun to emerge. Numerous organizations of public servants already exist through which higher standards of competence, integrity, and responsibility can develop.

The experience of other professions—medicine, law, and teaching, for example—can offer stimulus but also a warning to bureaucrats. For too often such associations become primarily concerned not with their responsibility for higher standards and better public service, but with the promotion of narrower and more selfish ends. Associations of civil servants have a special obligation to avoid these pitfalls and to cultivate at all times an intense and pervasive sense of public service and responsibility.

Loyalty to high standards of honesty, "scientific management," and technical competence are, of course, of transcendent importance. But equally important is the bureaucrat's responsibility to know and respect the wishes, values and goals of the community he serves, not in supine response to the pressures of special interest groups, but through a dogged devotion to the basic policies of the state—even though this means resistance to these same special or parochial groups.

Although we have far to go in this country in achieving a truly responsible bureaucracy,

---

* H. Finer, *Theory and Practice of Modern Government*, New York, 1949, p. 921.
† Fritz Morstein Marx, in *American Political Science Review*, p. 1134, December, 1949.

we can take comfort in the progress that has been made. No longer has the patronage peddler or the spoilsman the hold he once had on the federal service. No longer can it be fairly said that American city government is a failure, conspicuous or otherwise. No longer can it accurately be said, as George S. Taylor once said of Britain in the eighteenth century, that politics is "the trade of managing the state in the interests of the men in possession and their friends." Standards of character and competence, of integrity and industry, in the public service will stand comparison with those in other walks of life. But it is not enough that they be "just as good"—they should be better. Just as government should be a model employer, so the public service and the public servant should be models for the community, as I believe they are even now.

It is fitting and proper for the community to expect higher standards among its public servants than in private life. But in the end administrative morality will reflect the morality of the community it serves. A society in which "caveat emptor" is still a basic principle of business, in which the clever man who can make a "fast buck" is eulogized, and in which private peculation is often concealed in acts of so-called public policy, ought not to be surprised if an occasional bureaucrat strays from the straight and narrow path. The ancient English jingle has relevance even to our own times when it says:

The law locks up both man and woman
Who steals the goose from off the common
But lets the greater felon loose
Who steals the common from the goose.

The old aphorism that "every people gets the kind of government it deserves" is at best a half-truth, for the American people probably gets better government than it deserves. In a country where the "politician" is a symbol of corruption and dishonesty, if not dishonor, where a large majority of parents, as reported by the Gallup poll, prefer *not* to have their children enter the public service, where the bureaucracy is regarded as a legitimate object of ridicule and even revulsion and the term "bureaucrat" is a nasty name, how can one expect high standards of public service and responsibility? The wonder is not that we have *not* achieved a competent, devoted, and responsible bureaucracy, but that we have come so close to doing so.

Irresponsible attacks upon public servants are a luxury we can no longer afford—when our prosperity, our freedom, and even our survival may depend upon them. A responsible bureaucracy requires a responsible democracy—and a responsible citizenry. To create the one we must also create the other. To do so will require the best efforts of all who value our democratic institutions, whether they be in education, business, labor, or the professions.

Assuming that state interference develops to the point of being dictatorial or autocratic, what might the consequences be? Alfred Cobban, in the following selection, discusses the economic and political consequences; elsewhere in his treatise he deals with the international effects and the influences on the intellectual, moral, and spiritual life of society. Cobban shows that many of the characteristics of former dictatorships still apply to present-day dictatorships, but a new element has emerged which vitally affects the latter—the development of the totalitarian state.

Cobban discusses several political traits of totalitarian dictatorship in its extreme form: the great extension it gives to the scope of government, the concentration of all powers in the hands of the executive, and the principle of leadership. The role of the dictator in contemporary totalitarian society made it necessary to create a new conception of the state, so that the dictator would be able to make loyalty to himself as the chosen leader identical with patriotism to the state.

It is characteristic of dictatorship to intensify the activity of the state in the economic field. But totalitarian dictatorship has done more than this: it has completed the destruction of the medieval liberties of the privileged classes, though it is important to note that, instead of substituting the liberty of the people for aristocratic "liberties," it has set up the power of the state. Cobban explains that this has been achieved by combining totalitarianism and dictatorship.

Cobban shows that the problem of liberty is not only political but also economic. This relationship is suggested in the more or less popular hypothesis that nineteenth-century liberalism failed because political liberty did not bring with it the necessary economic advantages. Against this could be made another assumption—that nineteenth-century liberalism had run its course and fulfilled the purposes identified with it as a political movement. It is Cobban's belief that ". . . the dictatorships of today have come into being largely because they have promised, in return for the loss of political liberties, to give the people the economic improvements that earlier regimes failed to bring about."

However ambitious contemporary dictators may be to develop economic unity and national self-sufficiency, or autarky, the final motive of dictatorship remains, as always, political power. If a dictator finds that he cannot command prosperity, he may strive after glory. Thus nationalism and dictatorship have become allies. Nationalism, in its new totalitarian form, now serves as an emotional basis for dictatorship. Thus this selection from Cobban's work integrates not only economic and political but nationalist and totalitarian ideologies.

32

POLITICAL AND ECONOMIC CONSEQUENCES OF TOTALITARIAN DICTATORSHIP*

Alfred Cobban

The conclusions which are derived from a study of dictatorship in the past should apply equally to dictatorship at the present day, but the fact that it operates in the new totalitarian state introduces an element which vitally affects its working. The consequences of totalitarian dictatorship therefore call for special examination. They may be considered

* From Alfred Cobban, *Dictatorship: Its History and Theory*, Charles Scribner's Sons, New York, 1939, pp. 266–283. Reprinted by permission of Jonathan Cape, Ltd., London.

. . . under four heads, namely, political machinery, economic consequences, international consequences, and the influence on the intellectual and moral or spiritual life of society. In the first three at least of these fields, moreover, we can legitimately come to some conclusions, without entering the field of ethical philosophy. Thus, to take the political aspect first, we can ask, without denying the existence of other criteria, whether totalitarian dictatorship produces, or can produce, an efficient and stable government and a politically contented people.

The peculiar characteristics of totalitarian dictatorship as a political form are the great extension it gives to the scope of government, the union of all powers in the hands of the executive, and the principle of leadership. Obviously, these factors in themselves greatly increase the power of the state, and it is necessary to bear in mind in this connection the observation of Treitschke that, 'the existence of a government is the less secure in proportion as its activity is extended more widely.' * The greater the scope and power of government, the greater its responsibility, provided, of course, that it is responsible at all. The despotism of the priest-kings of the ancient world was not endangered by their omnicompetence, because the sanction of religious awe bestowed on them the mantle of irresponsibility. In inheriting and exaggerating the powers claimed on behalf of the community by the extremist democrats and socialists, modern dictatorship has inherited not only their problems but also their responsibility. The penalty of failure is loss of power, and not by the peaceful process of a general election. If every failure opens the door wider to revolution, the mighty power of the dictator is only bought at a very heavy price, and this is the first criticism we must make on political grounds.

Secondly, we must ask whether the great concentration of power in the hands of the dictator necessarily promotes efficiency of government. Undoubtedly it provides the most effective, perhaps the only means of rapidly carrying through extensive changes in the structure of the state, and the importance of this in a crisis, or when society is so rotten that only revolutionary changes can save it from decay or destruction, must not be underestimated. A Napoleon or a Caesar may achieve a work of the greatest importance in surmounting a crisis or reorganizing the state. On the other hand, the inability of parliamentary governments to cope with severe internal crises, and their inaptness for effecting great changes in society, however necessary they may be, are notorious.

When we turn to consider the normal government of a country, however, the conclusion is different. In the long run there seems no reason for supposing that the despotism of the chosen of the People will be any more efficient than that of the chosen of God, or a *Führer* more capable of controlling the affairs of a great state with permanent success than a *Roi soleil*—rather the contrary, since the problems of government have become infinitely more complex and less susceptible of solution by arbitrary decree. The defects of despotic government have not changed, and they are too well known to require description.

The revolutionary regime admittedly gives an impetus to the state in its beginnings, and its mastery of the arts of propaganda, along with the absence of criticism, may maintain appearances for a while. But even a degree of efficiency can only be preserved in any state by the establishment of an administrative system based on sound institutions. This it is difficult, if not impossible, for a dictatorship to provide, since in the first place it implies a degree of political stability that dictatorships rarely achieve, and, secondly, dictatorship cannot escape from the fact that by its essential nature it is a government of one man and not an administrative regime. It will have the advantages and disadvantages that personal government necessarily has. Subsequent regimes may inherit the accomplishments of the dictatorship, as later governments in France inherited the Code

* H. W. C. Davis, *The Political Thought of Treitschke*, p. 91.

Napoleon and the prefectoral system, but the dictatorship itself does not find the real sources of its power in such achievements; to estimate what one might call its survival-value, so far as its political basis goes, we must look not to the merit of its institutions, but to the personal loyalty that the dictator is able to evoke. The key to the political success or failure of dictatorship lies not in its laws or institutions but in the psychology of leadership.

As we have suggested in an earlier chapter, the fundamental condition which the dictator has to fulfil in the modern state is that he shall obtain recognition as the leader not merely of a party or a class, but of the nation. The degree in which the dictator is able to identify loyalty to himself as the chosen leader with patriotism to the state, is the measure of his success. This identification is only possible in the presence of a new conception of the state, for the nineteenth-century liberal view was too closely bound up with utilitarian and individualistic ideas to permit the development of strong nationalist emotion and of that organic conception of the unity of the state, which is necessary if totalitarianism and the Leader-principle are to be possible. The modern dictator must be thought of as an incarnation of the unity of the nation, a reconciler of all conflicts, an inspired leader through whom the power and prestige of the state is placed above all the personal interests of its individual members. The political potentialities and limitations of the dictatorial regime depend primarily upon the possibility of satisfying this condition, and this therefore demands detailed examination.

It must be premised that the dictator cannot at first be a truly national leader, because he has to look for support in the beginning to one or other of the warring classes in society, sometimes to a possessing class and sometimes to a revolutionary one. Successful attempts to establish a dictatorship on the latter basis are, however, rare, since the ideology of left-wing movements in modern times has usually been a barrier to the rule of a single man. They have normally been under the influence of liberal and parliamentary principles. Even communism found it difficult to emancipate itself entirely from these ideas; at least in theory it accepted dictatorship only as a temporary phase and at first attributed arbitrary authority not to an individual but to a party, though the principle of dictatorship proved more difficult to tame than the Marxists had expected, and the evolution of the Soviet government showed—as had the development of the revolutionary government in France a century earlier—that a party dictatorship easily becomes a government of one man.

Whether he comes from right or left, however, there is an inevitable dualism in the position of the successful dictator. He must appeal to those possessing power or wealth, those, that is, with something to lose, and at the same time to those still in revolt and dissatisfied. To the former he is a restorer of law and order and social security; to the latter he offers the fulfilment of at least some of their desires. Revolution and reaction meet in his policy: he is the synthesis to their thesis and antithesis. For the dictator, from whichever side he starts, has to grow from a party into a national leader, if he is to complete his ambition and fulfil his national destiny in society. Although he may have achieved power as the agent of a party or a class, he must emancipate himself from its control as soon as he can. He must appear, like the two Napoleons, as a 'saviour of society', governing in the interests not of a small fanatical clique or of a revolutionary class, but of the nation as a whole, if personal dictatorship is to become possible.

The support which the dictator may in this way obtain from general public opinion is not, by itself, however, an adequate basis for his government. Something more concrete is needed, round which support may crystallize. This indispensable nucleus is provided in the beginning by the party or faction organized in support of the potential dictator. Here, incidentally, is a valid reason why a general whose authority is purely military cannot become a true dictator. Even a Caesar, a Pilsudski or a Kemal Ataturk has to make himself a politician, at least to the extent of building up a political faction, if he wishes to become the ruler of the state.

But this association between dictatorship and the rule of a faction raises a further point. The leader of a faction is bound to that faction; if he wishes to emancipate himself from it, he can only do so at the cost of an internal crisis that will shake the whole state. The 'blood purge' of Hitler and the massacre of the so-called Trotskyites in Russia, illustrate what happens when a dictator finds it necessary to remove the faction, or any part of the faction, that brought him to power. But purges are notably lowering to the system, and even such drastic operations as these can rarely be complete. Moreover, although he may destroy those of his own faction who are obdurate, buy over those who are venal, and present himself to the people as a true national leader, the dictator still needs the support that only an organized party can give. However great a wave of popular enthusiasm may have carried him to power, enthusiasm will not provide a permanent basis for government without organized support.

Again, whereas in the small city state the tyrant could be the effective ruler, in a great nation state, even if he is not a mere figurehead he can only be the chief of a body of personal supporters, who in effect govern the country. The dictatorship, although it may attempt to disguise itself under the appearance of being a genuinely national government, is in fact a hidden oligarchy, which according to Spinoza is the worst of all. Government by party seems inescapable in the modern world; but the party will now be not the enthusiasts, the revolutionaries, but the time-servers, the useful hypocrites, the Vicars of Bray, and their loyalty will be bought and will have to be paid for by material advantages.

Here we approach a contradiction: for this reliance on party, however necessary it may be, prevents the dictator from retaining permanently his position as reconciler, above the strife of factions. His party must have been drawn in the main originally from one of the warring sections of society. Even apart from this, its mere existence is sufficient to create a new cleavage, because it forms a new privileged class in the state; and against it and its leader will be concentrated all the jealousies and hostilities of those who are excluded, or who exclude themselves, from its ranks.

If the dictatorship is not to merge into an ever narrower party tyranny and rapidly collapse, the dictator must be able to keep the loyalty of a sufficiently large section of the population outside the immediate ranks of the party. Useless to talk of identifying the party with the nation, for the peculiar characteristic of the party is the possession of an extraordinary loyalty to the dictator, such as the mass of nonpolitical citizens can only experience sporadically. The party must comprise those whose loyalty is preserved by the ties of self-interest and by the possession of particular privileges, which would become meaningless if extended to the whole nation.

Even in the party itself loyalty will be endangered, as the possibility of distributing rewards becomes limited, after the halcyon days of revocations and dismissals, executions and suicides, and a new generation of youth grows up, as we have already said, to find all the posts of advantage in the state occupied by those who were the young heroes of the revolution, and who will not vacate them in the course of nature for another twenty or thirty or forty years. As the prospects of promotion narrow, the circle of discontent widens.

The nation, however grateful it may have been to the dictator in the beginning for having saved the state from anarchy, will not, if it has known the idea of political liberty, continue to accept his government, without a continuance either of the menace that drove it in the first place into the embrace of dictatorship, or of the benefits which were expected to accrue from it. Modern dictatorship, emerging from democracy, must continue to serve, in one way or another, the people, and public opinion is the most insatiable of masters. The dictator must continually re-create the conditions that called him into existence. In so far as dictatorship is the result of a psychological condition of the people, that condition must be perpetuated. If it arose partly as a reaction against some real or supposed menace, such as Bolshevism, Judaism, Capitalist Imperialism, or Trotskyism, then that enemy has to assume a thousand forms and die a thousand deaths that the dictatorship may live.

The modern dictator is thus essentially in the position analyzed by Aristotle. Politically his government has all the traditional weaknesses, and it is the fate of every dictatorship to find itself isolated with increasingly few genuine supporters in a rising tide of disillusionment and discontent. If these are our conclusions, where, it must be asked, is to be found political stability, or even the assurance of effective government? Certainly it is not to purely political forces that totalitarian dictatorship can look for a permanent basis.

But politics, we are often told, are subordinate to economics. Next, then, we must examine the economic consequences of totalitarian dictatorship. We have already agreed that dictatorship arises out of an internal conflict which is generally economic in its motivation. It would therefore be natural to expect that it should have to take decisive steps in the way of economic reform.

All dictatorships intensify the activity of the state in the economic field, at the present day more than in any previous age, because in all of its various manifestations modern dictatorship represents a reaction against the more liberal and individualistic economy of the nineteenth century. But it also signifies the end, along with divine right of kings, of the claims of the privileged classes, who had survived in the shelter of monarchy, and above all of what used to be called the sacred right of property. In this respect dictatorship might be said to be continuing the work of the French Revolution and of nineteenth-century liberalism. Thus at the same time it

marks the culmination and the contradiction of the European liberal movement of the eighteenth and nineteenth centuries. Against the medieval 'liberties' of the privileged classes, which Burke and Montesquieu had associated with political liberty, democracy and socialism have asserted, also in the name of liberty, the rights of the people. Dictatorship has completed the work of destruction, but instead of substituting for aristocratic 'liberties' the liberty of the people, it has set up the power of the state.

The fundamental difficulty is that the problem of liberty is not only a political, but also an economic one. Nineteenth-century liberalism failed because political liberty did not bring with it the necessary economic advantages. Indeed, coinciding with the great industrial revolution, it was accompanied instead by the growth of a huge industrial population, living under appalling conditions. Hence the various schools of socialism were able to erect a damning indictment of liberalism, the essential point in their criticism being in effect that the cart had been put before the horse. They found themselves forced to the conclusion, which Proudhon had already proclaimed in 1848, that social reform did not in fact result from political reform.

The dictatorships of to-day have come into being largely because they have promised, in return for the loss of political liberties, to give the people the economic improvements that earlier regimes failed to bring about. The principle of social equality, although not strictly speaking an economic good, is the first of these.

Hence the appeal of the dictatorships to the proletarian elements in society. On the other hand, it is one of the ironies of history that the middle classes, from the wealthy rentier to the small shop-keeper or office-worker, who by their panic contributed so greatly to the rise of dictatorship in Italy and Germany, are the classes which have probably suffered most and gained least from its economic policy. The poor have at least gained employment and entertainment of a kind; the big pikes in the capitalist fish-pond can always look after themselves; but the middle classes have been the greatest losers by the revolution they themselves made. It is an interesting speculation whether they will resume in consequence their historic role as the truly revolutionary class in European history, or whether the dictatorships, led by Russia, will succeed in squeezing them out of existence. If they do succeed, when middle-class mentality is no more, when the bourgeois—someone who, in the French definition, has 'reserves,' spiritual and material, and is willing to fight to the end in their defence—has disappeared, certain things that have been reckoned not least among the achievements of Western civilization may be found to have disappeared with him.

The principle of equality has been carried a long way in Russia and Germany, not very far in Italy, and up to the present has hardly appeared at all in the other European dictatorships. It is not to be dismissed for this reason as an exceptional phenomenon. The same tendency, though the degree of levelling aimed at may vary, is to be seen in most dictatorships of the past. The reduction of subjects as far as possible to a single level is a classical feature of the technique of tyranny. We need hardly recall Dionysius and the tall poppies or Signor Mussolini and his ministers. Aristotle's observations on this point, Caesar's treatment of the Senate, the tendency in the medieval Italian cities to esteem personal qualities above inherited rank, la carrière ouverte aux talents of Napoleon, and the action of South American dictators, such as Francia, against caste divisions in the state, provide further illustrations.

It might be asked whether liberalism could not do as much, whether indeed in a country such as the United States of America it has not achieved at least as genuine an abolition of social caste as any dictatorship can show. But even if there is some truth in this, in the older countries of Europe the same progress has not been possible. Further, there are more concrete causes of economic discontent, and therefore of the tendency towards dictatorship, which still remain, in the form of widespread poverty and unemployment. A peasantry, living in a system of self-sufficient agriculture, can suffer only the blows of the climate, and for these the government can not very easily be held responsible. The aberrations of the modern industrial and financial machine, periodically producing violent depressions, are less easy to accept as purely natural phenomena, and for these governments are called to account. But this responsibility is precisely what the liberal state rejected in the past.

Whether the failure of parliamentary liberalism is due to its lack of authority in general, or to its particular inability to control and direct to social ends the activities of the great capitalist and financial interests in the state, we need not inquire. The point in either case is that a drastic increase in these powers is necessary to alter the situation. But in the presence of such an increase the state ceases to be liberal in the accepted sense. The question, to which no answer has yet been provided, is: can the liberal state reform itself economically, can it even defend its economic interests as conditions to-day require, and remain liberal?

The urgency of the economic problem and the need for a remedy must be admitted. It does not follow that totalitarianism provides this, but we should not underestimate its achievements in this field. The early years of a dictatorship are often accompanied by economic improvement, resulting from more energetic government, unity of control, increased national confidence, and the appearance of political stability. At the present day it is the proud boast of Soviet Russia and Nazi Germany, the two countries in which totalitarianism has been pushed to its farthest point, that they have abolished unemployment. The whole man power of these countries has been put into operation and great achievements in industry and transport have resulted. Exchange control has prevented the currency fluctuations that are so menacing to contemporary parliamentary governments. Finally, the great emphasis laid in the dictatorial states on physical culture and the constant endeavour to supplement bread with circuses deserve to be remembered.

It is too early to give any final verdict on the economic advantages of totalitarianism. Moreover, since the relevant statistics are mostly provided by dictatorships themselves it would be dangerous to attempt to draw any very definite conclusions from these. One can venture on a tentative opinion, however, that the tightening of the belt which seems to have become an habitual exercise in some dictatorial states does not suggest that the cup of economic well-being is filled to overflowing. Moreover, experience in the U.S.S.R. suggests that dictatorships are not immune from human fallibility and that when they make an economic blunder they make it on a large scale. Russia, however, with its vast, unexploited resources, and its mainly agricultural population, is in an unusually fortunate position, and one which may allow the dictatorship there a fairly long run; but the modern industrial states farther to the West have already begun to show signs of grave economic difficulties.

It would not be very rash to suggest that even in times of comparative plenty elsewhere the totalitarian states have shown that they have not yet solved the economic problem. Whether they will be able to face a world slump successfully we shall doubtless see in due course. Unless totalitarianism succeeds in breaking the economic cycle, the dictatorship, which may have come in with, or even inaugurated, a boom, will, if economic precedents hold, inevitably have to face what is now euphemistically called a recession: and while a government cannot obtain permanent support because of temporary economic advantages, it may have to face revolution because of its economic sins or misfortunes.

All this is in the realm of speculation. Considerations of a different order can be presented, however, bearing on the fundamental nature of the economic activity of the totalitarian state. Its peculiar feature, in the economic as in the political sphere, is that it is a world to itself. It is envisaged as an economic unit. The principle of economic self-sufficiency or autarky, to adopt the Aristotelian term, which has been particularly emphasized in Germany, is sometimes presented as a conclusion drawn from the experiences of the World War; but though doubtless the blockade, and the part the economic weapon played during the last war, has had its effect in intensifying this tendency, it can be found much earlier in German thought. Fichte, at the beginning of the nineteenth century, had already sketched out a whole plan for a closed economic state, and Lassalle represents the same idea in the latter half of the century.

Practical developments have reinforced these theoretical tendencies. A state such as the Soviet Union, which broke away from the existing economic structure, found autarky thrust upon it by the effort of the capitalist states to isolate and if possible stifle a rival economic system. The vast expenditure which the political aims of the dictatorships in Italy and Germany have demanded would have ruined the currency of these countries if it had not been sterilized against exchange variation; but this was only possible by an increasing limitation, as well as by a rigid state control, of economic conditions with the external world.

Earlier dictatorships, for example that of the first Napoleon, made slight attempts at economic self-sufficiency, the most obvious example being the Continental System, used by Napoleon as a means of striking at England, but they are hardly to be compared with modern essays in autarky. Whereas in former periods the only serious consequence might be the deprivation of certain sea-borne luxuries, to-day the state which tries to isolate itself economically evidently suffers a severe loss of raw materials and of articles manufactured abroad, as well as of markets for its own products; the economic sacrifice is so heavy that it is doubtful if any modern state could be persuaded or forced to carry through the full programme of self-sufficiency to the end, except by the most complete tyranny. The work of European capitalism in the nineteenth century cannot easily be undone. It has been the great internationalizing force of the modern world, and has tied the nations together in a nexus of credit and trade that can only be broken at a price. So far as concerns the advanced industrial countries, it is doubtful whether their existing huge populations can be maintained in the absence of the great international trade in dependence upon which they grew up. Self-sufficiency may be merely another way of spelling mass suicide.

Here again, however, we must refrain from dogmatism. By military pressure a dictatorship such as the German may gain economic control of a wide area with diversified products. Given not merely one state, but a large part of a Continent to exploit, the possibilities of economic totalitarianism become immensely greater; but what the future may hold in store for a new Continental System cannot be said.

Even allowing for this development, it must be admitted that the economic disadvantages of autarky so greatly overbalance the initial economic advantages given by dictatorship, that one had to ask why the sacrifice is demanded. With the answer we come to what is the fundamental drawback of dictatorship in the economic field. Economic distress may be a first cause of the rise of dictatorship, but economic improvement is not and cannot be its essential end. The final motive of dictatorship is always political power. Faced with the choice between this and economic welfare, its own nature compels it to choose the former. If autarky seems necessary to the dictator's political ambitions, however great the economic sacrifices it involves, they will perforce be accepted.

It still remains, however, the *sine qua non* of dictatorship that it must continually produce results to justify its existence and keep the support of a sufficient proportion of its people: if economic facts are stubborn, then other motives must be appealed to. We have therefore to pass back from the economic into the political field, only now it is to foreign and not domestic politics that we must turn. If a dictator cannot command prosperity, he may at least strive after glory. The wars which result from this motive, such as the Mexican expedition of Louis Napoleon or the Abyssinian campaign of Mussolini, are sometimes represented as resulting from the need for economic gains; a mere balance-sheet should be sufficient to expose this as a piece of rationalization: the real aim is glory, prestige, for the sake of the internal strengthening of the regime. The willingness of nations to accept foreign triumphs in place of domestic prosperity, and to sacrifice their interests to their vanity, may surprise us, but cannot be questioned. Thus the force to which we are brought back as the true basis for dictatorship is once again the spirit of aggressive nationalism.

It is increasingly evident that in their latest developments nationalism and dictatorship have become essential allies. This is what Spengler has realized, though in saying that nationalism is only the first step towards Caesarism, he makes the former subsidiary to the latter. The dictator may have obtained power through his capacity to profit by the political and economic difficulties of the country, but the foregoing analysis of the political and economic tendencies of dictatorship suggests that these cannot by themselves maintain the dictator in power for more than a limited period, especially since the more successful he is in his initial tasks, the more unnecessary he renders himself. Moreover, every government requires some emotional basis if it is to last. Nationalism, in its new totalitarian form, provides such a basis for dictatorship: through nationalism the dictator may hope to change what was at first only a temporary expedient into a more lasting form of government. This is a return to government by faith: nationalism is the new religion, and the dictator is Pope and Emperor rolled into one. If we wish to know what force from within will overthrow him, we must ask what force, in the modern world, is stronger than nationalism.

In terms of contrasting values, a nation's economy in the modern world is organized either on the fundamental principle of free enterprise or the principle of state control and planning. The tendency in various Western nations—e.g., Great Britain, the Scandinavian countries, and the United States—has been toward a blending and balancing of state ownership, control, planning, and free enterprise. The search for this delicate balance is not an abstract but an empirical pursuit. Apparently each nation has to work out its own formula for such a balance, and many imponderables enter into the equation. In some respects, therefore, the alternatives between collectivist planning and capitalism are rapidly becoming rhetorical.

Ruth Shallcross maintains that there are vital differences between planning by the state or other organizations and a "planned economy." She observes that advocates of planned economy, or the welfare state, have not even recognized the most serious problems of economic organization. Six salient points are discussed briefly to show some of the drawbacks of a government-controlled system in contrast to the accepted values of a free market economy.

33

A PLANNED ECONOMY: GOOD OR BAD?*
Ruth Shallcross

Barbara Wootton, one of the best-known British economic writers on "planned economy," attributes the original interest in the term to the widespread attention attracted by the Soviet Five-Year Plans. Coming, as they did, before and during the most severe economic depression this country had ever witnessed, these plans seemed logical and made individual economic planning seem particularly chaotic. Moreover, with the growing emphasis on technology and on the scientific method, the very word "planning" carried with it a connotation that precluded opposition (and unfortunately analytical thinking) to what seemed to be a necessary reorganization of society along rational lines.

A nation's economy in the modern world is organized either (1) on the fundamental principle of individual determination of economic values in a free market wherein decisions are freely made by millions of producers and consumers and reflected in the prices resulting therefrom, or (2) on the principle that the government (through administrative agencies, economic planning boards, et al.) should determine values by various types of state controls and plans.

The thirties witnessed a tremendous impetus to the idea of a state-directed economy. Many who accepted the concept under the name of "planned economy" (or "a welfare state") have failed to recognize its inherent

*Reprinted by permission of The Scientific Monthly, vol. 71, no. 5, pp. 333–336, November, 1950.

socialist philosophy. Like socialists before them, those advocating a state-planned economy have attacked profits in the free economy because they seem to epitomize the selfish individual acting independently to further his own good at the expense of the public's welfare. For the most part, the new world planners, also like the socialists before them, have accepted in principle, if not as stated, Marx's dictum,* "From each according to his abilities, to each according to his needs," or, as the American Socialists phrased it, "production for use and not for profit"—both concepts implying a centralized economic authority that would determine "need" or "use"; in essence, a state-planned (or controlled) economy.

Few remembered that for a long period of time—one hundred and fifty years—the American public had in fact fared very well with a free market economy now said to be chaotic, in which individuals were allowed to seek their own profit with a minimum of governmental regulation; and, as Adam Smith predicted, great wealth and prosperity for all the people had in fact resulted. The record of improved welfare is clear for all to see. Except for the 1930s, each decade had witnessed more people producing a greater volume (and better quality) of goods per employee than the previous one. Over the past fifty years, the standard of living for all had improved miraculously with a decline of more than one third in the number of working hours per week, with real purchasing power per hour increasing threefold. Joseph Schumpeter states that "if capitalism repeated its past performance for another half century starting with 1928, this would do away with anything that according to present standards could be called poverty, even in the lowest strata of population, pathological cases alone excepted." †

But the fear of loss of property and income, together with evidence of actual loss for a segment of the population during the thirties, clouded the sights of many to this impressive record and to the fact that, even during that depressed period, per capita production was "high relative to the best years of many other countries and to the best years of our not-too-distant past." Even the "government planning" during that era and since, which has created more problems (especially deficit financing) than it has solved, has not dispelled the strong feeling, born of the depression, that the government should guarantee certain economic rights, even at the expense of transforming the economy and eliminating economic freedom. And, moreover, this attitude seems to prevail despite a new critical attitude toward collectivist economic planning in the Soviet Union brought about by the postwar belligerent and openly imperialistic Soviet policy.

Two reasons may be given for this seeming paradox. One is the insecurity caused by the last war and the fear of another. The second is that many government officials have found it politically expedient to promise all sorts of things that could only be delivered, even in a small degree, by having complete power over the economy. Those who are asking for state power to control the economy (or, as they say, to establish the welfare state) are doing so paradoxically "in the interests of saving free enterprise." But why should the state not have complete control over the economy?

Present-day skeptics of a planned economy, or the welfare state, have realized that the most serious problems of economic organization have not even been recognized by those seeking control over the economy, let alone successfully solved. Chief among these is the seemingly simple task of defining and measuring the economic goal of society—the greatest good for the greatest number—in terms that are universally acceptable.

Unfortunately, economics does not have

* K. Marx, "The Criticism of the Gotha Program (1875)," in M. Eastman (ed.), *Capital and Other Writings*, Modern Library, Inc., New York, 1932, p. 7.
† J. A. Schumpeter, *Capitalism, Socialism and Democracy*, Harper & Brothers, New York, 1947, p. 66.

precise yardsticks by which its goals can be accurately measured. But in a free market economy, individual planners (producers) have a very real (even though not precise in a physicist's concept) measure for determining what individuals believe their welfare to be. The measure is prices, which, when uncontrolled, become the common denominator of conflicting ideas of welfare shown in consumers' choice of purchases— the only universally acceptable measure available. But too few understand the intricate working of the price system sufficiently to realize that it is as important a measure in determining the highest economic goal as instrumentation is in determining scientific goals. If any one of the ten million private planners does not promote consumers' welfare, he will be priced out of business. His efficiency, or lack of it, in serving the public shows up as profit or loss. Thus the incentive to promote the public's interests is high. The growth of marketing research substantiates the growing desire on the part of producers to measure consumers' choice more accurately. Imperfect judgments, of course, are to be found in a free market economy as in a controlled one, but the responsibility for economic decisions in a free economy is spread among many enterprising producers and, hence, is not as great as that of a centralized planning board. Moreover, penalties for errors in judgment are restricted to a few in a free economy but affect the entire economy in a centralized planned system.

State economic planners would throw out all the aids to planning that the market economy gives to private enterprisers. They have no magical power of measuring whether, for example, new machines should go into one company or one industry instead of another, but must fumble, and guess, and arbitrarily and authoritatively make a decision. Prices, like a thermostat, are of no value as a measure of economic activity if they are controlled. Profits, if eliminated, cannot determine effici-

ency of production operations. Would the state planners eliminate losses which in a free market system are as effective a measure of inefficiency of production as profits are for measuring efficiency—both being prices (either positive or negative) paid for enterprising activity in risk-taking? Are there to be tests for the planners' efficiency? Or are the planners assumed to be supermen without error in judgment? These are important questions which those in favor of a state-controlled or "planned economy" dislike to discuss. They usually state that the details will be worked out after power has been achieved or they speak vaguely of helping the needy producers (in practice, the most politically expedient needy); but this usually means giving aid to inefficient producers, who, from the public welfare point of view, ought to fail.

Oskar Lange, a socialist economist formerly at the University of Chicago (now purported to be unhappy in a Polish university), has advocated that the state (in a planned economy) should simulate the free market criterion of economic welfare.* But that would be impossible without actually having a free market—a tacit admission that a free market is preferable to any artificially controlled economy.

Sir Henry Clay, in speaking of the economic controls of the British Labour Government, presents the problem of consumer welfare where state planning is not complete in all branches of the economy: †

> The Ministry pays what price it must to secure supplies; being relieved of the necessity of covering its costs out of its receipts, it sells at prices fixed arbitrarily, often in relation to conditions that no longer obtain. The consumer buys, not what he would choose if he had to pay the true cost, but what he chooses at the price (less than the cost) which the Ministry thinks he ought to pay.

* Oskar Lange, quoted by William Diebold, *Am. Econ. Rev.*, vol. 40, no. 2, p. 22, 1950.
† Henry Clay, *Am. Econ. Rev.*, vol. 40, no. 2, p. 3, 1950.

"Nationalization," he goes on to say, "has deprived the consumer of such protection as competition, actual or potential, offers." Maurice Dobb admits that socialism can be achieved only at the price of abandoning the economic freedom of consumers. But socialists or state economic planners would have few followers if they were as realistic.

Half-way planning schemes usually lead to more and more government plans unless the people are constantly aware of and vigorously oppose them. Therefore, a nation can be led step by step, unwittingly, into a full state-controlled economy. This is the method of bringing about socialism deliberately adopted in the nineteenth century by the British Fabians, now influential in the Labour Government, and it is the method most successful in this country. Many who have accepted the goal of a state-planned economy become very emotional over the means to that end. The Fabians have won a large number of adherents to their mild evolutionary methods as distinct from the crude revolutionary and disruptive methods of the communists. However, it is the goal itself that needs to be questioned.

Because of lack of space to develop the myriad facets of a state-planned economy versus a free market economy, the following six points are discussed briefly to show some of the drawbacks of a government-controlled system.

First, a centralized planned economy cannot evaluate individual welfare in terms that are universally acceptable, as was elaborated earlier.

Second, when a centralized plan has been adopted it becomes important that it be carried out irrespective of the opposition from the public and, thus, is inflexible and insensitive to the public's desires. This psychology is evident in discussions with most advocates of a government-planned economy who believe that the public should be forced into accepting an economy that will be "for

its own good." Public welfare is defined by planners in power as something they think is good for the people. The various groups of "planners" argue heatedly over whose blueprint of a new social order will be accepted and forced onto the people. Thus it is evident that most collectivist economic planning is authoritarian in thinking; it assumes that the public is incapable of determining its own welfare and must have superior planners do it for them. It is totally at variance with the democratic ideal which presupposes that people have the right to direct their own welfare and to be free—even to be foolish if they so choose.

Third, planned economies have not proved that they are even as stable as a free market economy, which has been accused of instability. In this regard John Jewkes, of the University of Manchester, comments on the power crisis in England in 1947:

> No country has ever suffered from a more sudden or catastrophic economic seizure. Unemployment rose temporarily to over 2,000,000. The crisis probably lost Great Britain £200 millions of exports. The overall loss of production cannot be estimated with any precision. It is sufficient to say that Great Britain had suffered a crippling blow, the effects of which were largely instrumental in precipitating the balance of payments crisis suffered later in the year.[*]

Erik Lindahl admits that the Swedish monetary system (which he regards as part of the national planning program) has "an inherent instability which can be regarded as a characteristic feature in comparison with the previously existing more automatic systems." [†] Ralph Holben, in discussing state planning in Norway, shows that a planned economy may "substitute one form of instability (that of the balance of payments) for another form of instability (that of domestic prices)," [‡]

[*] J. Jewkes, *Ordeal by Planning,* Macmillan & Co., Ltd., London, 1948, p. 183.
[†] E. Lindahl, *Am. Econ. Rev.,* vol. 40, no. 2, p. 18, 1950.
[‡] R. E. Holben, *Am. Econ. Rev.,* vol. 39, no. 6, p. 1284, 1949.

with the former being especially serious for a small country. He concludes that "one should not be deceived into thinking that once the magic wand of economic planning is waved, the problem of economic stability somehow disappears."

Fourth, a centralized planned economy leads to international conflicts. In peacetime, there is no economic goal higher than individual welfare as determined by the people themselves; during a state of war, consumers are willing to let their own interests be subordinated to the nation's war efforts and will accept, temporarily, whatever goods are offered, shoddy or otherwise. The public is convinced sacrifices are necessary when a real national emergency exists. Because leaders of a planned economy cannot give the people the welfare that they could obtain for themselves in a free market economy, the planners must continue to foment international emergencies. Thus, imperialism and international unrest are far greater in evidence in a strictly controlled economy than when free trade is allowed between private commercial traders who, with the exception of armament makers, have nothing to gain and much to lose from international conflicts. The type of power that is concentrated in the hands of the few state controllers or planners of the economy leads them to use that power for world conquest and more power, as Russia has so very well demonstrated.

Fifth, those who would substitute a government-controlled economy for a market system indict the latter with monopolistic practices which place controls in the hands of a few business leaders. Yet the state-controlled economy would set up a complete state monopoly over all the economy, with all the evils of private concentration of power compounded. Private monopolies without state sanction have in the past been short-lived and frequently have been broken up by the introduction of a substitute product, but this situation could not exist under a planned economy where all industries are nationalized, and, hence, monopolies.

A state-planned economy has been ad-mitted by socialists to be incompatible with free consumers' choice. Thus the last and *sixth* point is that the economic freedom possible only in a free market economy is basic to all other freedoms we in a democracy hold dear. Much evidence exists to show that state economic planning and individual freedom are completely incompatible, the opposition of some spokesmen of economic planning to the contrary notwithstanding. If the state is to take from each according to his abilities (whether by out-and-out confiscation, devaluation of the purchasing power of the dollar, or by progressively confiscatory taxation) and give away the wealth of that production in accordance with need or use (as the welfare planners advocate), someone must arbitrarily and authoritatively determine who shall produce what and where and how much and who is in need. There is no other alternative. Many a Britisher is finally realizing that the applications of the idealistic Fabian phrases are far different in practice than in theory. To be effective, official planning of the economy cannot tolerate those who differ with their plans; thus, free speech is certain to be jeopardized, as Russian planning has demonstrated. The more effective the economic planner, the more dictatorial he (or the planning board) must be and the more the government takes on the characteristics of a complete police state, allowing little freedom for the people.

History is full of the struggles of people seeking freedom from state power. State tyranny has always masqueraded under the guise of promoting the public welfare. Lord Acton has warned us that "power corrupts and absolute power corrupts absolutely"; yet we blithely give the state more and more power over our lives with the vague hope that the officials having that power will, contrary to all historical evidence, use it wisely and in accordance with their promises of welfare and security.

It may well be that the average man really wants the kind of an economy which is completely and authoritatively planned for him, just as many Southern Negroes preferred the slave system to the freedom offered them after the Civil War, because they preferred not to take the responsibility for their own economic welfare. During any postwar period one is tempted by political promises of security. But it is doubtful indeed that the majority of the people want a completely planned and controlled economy.

New debates need to be held by informed public leaders on the role modern government can play in an economy of a free people which would in truth promote their greatest welfare. From these debates, fundamental principles need to be reformulated, as in the days of the Federalist writings, and then maintained with moral conviction. Unless fundamental economic and political principles are held with moral conviction by the majority of the people, they are apt to be lured by false promises or forced into authoritarian schemes by pressure from those who crave power and who would seize it by pretenses that the public welfare makes it necessary.

As the United States stands on the verge of having an economy that is being more and more controlled by the state, or of retaining a free market economy in which the welfare of the people is determined by them through their influence on prices, one might well ponder the statement made by Professor Jewkes: *

For central planning ultimately turns every individual into a cipher and every economic decision into blind fumbling, destroys the incentives through which economic progress arises, renders the economic system as unstable as the whims of the few who ultimately control it and creates a system of wirepulling and privileges in which economic justice ceases to have any meaning.

Several Western nations have experienced some measure of nationalization of industries, among them Great Britain and the Dominions, the Scandinavian countries, also some countries under dictatorial rule. That the United States has been influenced by the ideology of nationalization is reflected in various New Deal and Fair Deal policies involving nationalization. The idea was basic in the Tennessee Valley Authority which was to spearhead similar authorities in other parts of the country; in forms of governmental control over agricultural interests; in ways by which the government virtually entered the banking business; in the nature of the social security system; in proposed programs for Federal intervention in education, medical service, and other activities. Federal legislation and governmental authority in management-labor relations is another representative trend. It becomes obvious, therefore, why Americans should be concerned with some of the effects of nationalization in Britain, as summarized by George B. Baldwin.

Baldwin attempts to determine in the light of British experience how important a relationship there may be between nationalization and labor relations. His general conclusion is this: so far as labor relations are concerned, nationalization is essentially irrelevant. That is, labor relations in a nationalized industry are no different from labor relations in any other industry. But this general statement is subject to many qualifications, and these are the subject of his discourse.

Baldwin observes that the ideological failure of nationalization is forcing a basic re-examination of two vital questions: (1) What can reasonably be expected of nationalization? (2) What changes in the structure, attitudes, and policies of British

* J. Jewkes, *op. cit.*, p. 9.

unions and managements may be necessary to realize the objectives which many had vaguely assumed nationalization would satisfy automatically? To these questions and their principal implications Baldwin addresses himself.

34

NATIONALIZATION IN BRITAIN: A SOBERING DECADE*

George B. Baldwin

In spite of the gains made by workpeople in their conditions of employment and the increase in the power and influence of the unions, there does not seem to have been a commensurate improvement in the climate of industrial relations. There is in every nationalized industry a feeling among rank and file workers that no fundamental change has occurred. The behaviour pattern of the unions does not appear to be significantly different from what it was under private enterprise, and many observers are disappointed at what seems to them to be the failure of the unions to grasp their opportunity to contribute towards making nationalization a success.†

A review of labor developments in Britain's nationalized industries makes sense only on the assumption that there ought to be something special to say arising out of the fact of nationalization. There would otherwise be no excuse for lumping together postwar developments in the coal mining, electricity, transport (railway and long-distance truck-

ing), and iron and steel industries—let alone the Bank of England. For these are, in order, the industries touched by the wand of nationalization between 1945 when the Labour party came in and 1951 when it went out. Its exit was promptly followed of course by the denationalization of trucking and iron and steel, so that a record of experience really exists for only four industries.

NATIONALIZATION AND LABOR RELATIONS: HOPES AND ACTUALITIES

In 1945 there were two reasons for thinking that there might be an important relationship between nationalization and labor relations. First, there were good grounds for believing that in some industries labor problems were so important to the efficient working of the industry, and were in such a sorry condition, that nationalization was necessary to put things right. Through nationalization the workers were to gain justice, the nation a more efficient industry. This argument was conspicuously true of coal mining and only slightly less so of the railways. The second hope was that even in those industries which were to be nationalized primarily for reasons

* Reprinted by permission of *The Annals of the American Academy of Political and Social Science*, vol. 310, pp. 39–52, March, 1957.
† B. C. Roberts, "Trade Unions and Nationalization," *Progress*, Winter, 1954–55.

having nothing to do with poor labor relations, nationalization might nevertheless bring important benefits to the employees in the course of fulfilling its larger economic purposes. This hope was applicable, for example, to the production and distribution of electricity and gas (nationalized mainly to secure co-ordinated development, along with coal, of the nation's fuel and power industries) and to iron and steel. In iron and steel

and in gas, labor relations were among the best in British industry; when iron and steel was denationalized, there was no protest from the leading unions in the industry.

The nub of nationalization is coal mining and the railways, two declining industries whose efficiency depends on the "human factor" to a degree not true of gas or electricity. As Table 1 shows, these two giant industries employ 1.3 million people, or about

TABLE 1. EMPLOYMENT * IN GREAT BRITAIN IN THE FOUR MAJOR NATIONALIZED INDUSTRIES, AND OTHERS, AT THE END OF MAY 1955 (IN THOUSANDS)

Industries	Workers		
	Male	Female	Total †
Four major nationalized industries:			
Coal mining	771	16	787
Railways (excluding shops & ancillary trades for which British Transport Commission is responsible)	464	37	501
Electricity generating & distributing	177	24	200
Gas manufacturing & distributing	130	14	144
Total	1,542	91	1,632
Other nationalized industries and government services:			
Air transportation	23	7	30
Postal, telephone, and wireless communication	199	103	303
National government services ‡	406	163	570
Local government service	544	186	730
Total	1,172	459	1,633
Industries nationalized by Labour, denationalized by Tories:			
Trucking	163	14	177
Iron & Steel	408	49	457
Total	571	63	634

* Total employment in Great Britain as of the end of May 1955 was 21,460,000.

† In a few cases the figures for male and female workers do not add up to the horizontal totals exactly because of rounding.

‡ Excludes armed services and employees of departmental industrial establishments (e.g., ordnance factories).

SOURCE: *Ministry of Labour Gazette*, February 1956. The above figures differ from those representing the number of employees in the service of each "nationalized industry" as reported in their annual reports. The most significant adjustment would be an inflation of the "railways" figure by about 20 per cent to include shopmen and others classified differently by the Ministry of Labour. Nationalization of trucking and iron and steel did not touch more than about half the total employees in those categories because of the exemption of certain large classes of firms left in private hands.

one out of every fifteen in the British labor force. The coal mines and the railways have always been the principal storm centers of labor relations among the state industries, so that if nationalization has any special relationship to labor relations we ought to be able to find it in these two industries. I shall pay much more attention to these two giants than to electricity and gas, industries in which the "labor problem" plays a *relatively* minor role.

There is one overwhelming conclusion to be drawn from the first decade of nationalization that should be stated at the beginning. It is this: so far as labor relations are concerned, nationalization is essentially irrelevant. This is much too strong a statement to make, but it is worth making none the less. It is only another way of saying what it has become almost fashionable to say, that labor relations in a nationalized industry are no different from labor relations in any other industry. Generally speaking, this is a correct judgment on the past decade. But there are so many qualifications to enter against "general statements" that the matter cannot really be left there. As we shall see, nationalization has indeed affected labor relations at a great many points; but it has done little to affect them at precisely those points where everyone's hopes were highest. It does not help much that many of those hopes were foolish.

To say that nationalization has not been a huge success is not to say that it has been a failure. This would be true only if one's judgment were based wholly on the exaggerated hopes with which Socialist ideology had surrounded nationalization. If we put aside the ideological disappointment, we will find that nationalization has indeed meant progress in many areas involving the "human factor" in industry. But it has also meant some loss of the "personal touch" and an increase in the time it takes to make decisions because of the advent of centralized and sometimes remote control.

In Socialist circles it is fashionable to say that nationalization will justify itself if only it is followed by "socialization"—that is, by a progressive extension of industrial democracy. But "industrial democracy" can mean anything from more union representatives on the national Boards to smoother joint consultation or better supervision or employee voting over the price of tea in railway canteens. "Industrial democracy" really means the same thing as "good labor relations," and if we can spell out the one in specific, practical terms, we will already have hold of the other.

QUESTIONS FOR RE-EXAMINATION

If the ideological failure of nationalization has done nothing else, it is forcing a basic re-examination of two vital questions: (1) What can reasonably be expected of nationalization? and (2) What changes in the structure, attitudes, and policies of British unions and managements may be necessary to realize the objectives which many had vaguely assumed nationalization would satisfy automatically? And today many of the disappointments of nationalization are being put down not to bureaucracy and overcentralization, nor to the harsh facts of Britain's economic situation, but to the lack of adaptability of British unions, to the narrow conception of collective bargaining given by British tradition, and to an outmoded conception of industrial management. Added to these lessons concerning industrial relations is the growing realization that many traditional Socialist objectives long sought in part through nationalization (for example, full employment, greater equality, and increased security) are in fact achieved much more satisfactorily through a new conception of fiscal policy and the welfare state. These are the reasons why the first decade of postwar nationalization has been a sobering one and why responsible leaders of both the Labour party and the trade unions are approaching the subject of further nationalization with more caution and less confidence than they approached it during the heady days following Labour's victory in the 1945 election.

So much for some general preliminaries. I want now to turn to a summary review of some more specific developments that seem

to be characteristic of all four of the nationalized industries under review. Later, I
shall discuss a few of these points more fully.

MAIN DEVELOPMENTS SINCE 1945

Collective bargaining in the nationalized
industries has certainly had to be conducted
within the framework of pressures imposed
by Britain's postwar economic situation—
persistent inflation, a continuing balance of
payments crisis, the ever-present fear of hurt-
ing Britain's ability to compete in world export markets, and the huge need for capital
modernization and expansion in nearly all
industries, not just the nationalized ones.
There has been an almost continuous shortage of labor for more than fifteen years.
Finally, Britain's future position in world
export markets has depended on a structural
reorganization of her economy represented by
the need to expand new export lines (for
example, engineering goods, aircraft, electronic and electrical products, and chemicals)
to compensate for the decline in old export
staples such as coal, textiles, and the "in-
visibles" lost during World War II.

Against this economic background, I have
selected thirteen points that I think illuminate specific relationships between nationalization and industrial relations.

Bargaining Atmosphere. Nationalization
has not provided workers with a horn of
plenty into which they could dip their
hands whenever they felt pressed by the
struggle for life. Collective bargaining has
been remarkably like what it is in any large
centralized industry in the United States.
Management has not been "soft" and the
government has not intervened in wage
negotiations any more than has the American
government over the same period. Generally
speaking, wages in nationalized industries
have not risen faster than the general level
of British wages since 1945. In coal, average
wages have improved more than the national
average (but the more important *entry* wage
has barely kept pace); railwaymen's wages
have lagged distinctly behind the general
level; in electricity and gas wage increases

have just about matched the national average.
Many observers believe that the net effect of
nationalization has been to keep wage levels
from rising as rapidly as they otherwise would
have. In 1956, after a decade of close co-
operation with both Labour and Tory governments to restrain wage increases, the
Trades Union Congress broke with this policy
and accused the Eden government of using
the nationalized industries as a "drag an-
chor" to keep down the British wage level.

Dominant Wage Pressures. Nationalization
has greatly diminished competitive forces in
wage determination. In effect, the nationalized
industries still have to compete with other
industries for labor, but competition for labor
by individual operating units has gone in
favor of uniform national or district rates.
True, industry-wide bargaining has produced
a nominal uniformity in many private British industries; but these rates are minimums,
and individual employers have been free to
pay higher rates if they needed to bid for
labor. Thus the nationalized industries have
wage levels that respond more exclusively to
administrative decisions (centralized bargains)
than most other industries. If competitive
influences have been reduced by nationalization, there has been no reduction in the attention which both management and labor
have had to give to problems of wage *structure.* With respect to both internal and external considerations, the intended or unin-
tended shifting of the relative wage position
of specific groups has produced constant
problems. The attempts to rationalize the
wage structures in both coal and railways
have stumbled over this political and psychological problem, involving as it does personal
and institutional rivalries and sensitive questions of status.

Rise in Attention to Welfare Measures.
Nationalization has meant a substantial increase in attention given to safety and welfare, even though capital expenditures have
been necessitated at a time when government
has been forced to choose carefully among
investment expenditures. Coal has benefited
most, the railways least, in relation to need.

Spread of Interunion Rivalries. Ironically, nationalization introduced a period of insecurity for many unions. There has been an unforeseen intensification and extension of interunion rivalries and tension. These have expressed themselves in disputes over jurisdictions, employer recognition, and compulsory union membership. But these were temporary problems associated with getting nationalization started; now that the situation in each industry has been restructured, considerable stability has been achieved.

Absence of Syndicalism. Experience so far has not resulted in any responsible sentiment for a radical extension of "workers' control" in the old syndicalist sense. There are exceptions among some unions, like the National Union of Railwaymen which has long wanted more direct union representation in the councils of management. But while this has led to some grumbling among railwaymen, the NUR has not tried to force its views on the industry through industrial action. Syndicalist sentiments can still be found in many local and national unions as a minority commotion "in the wings." But the British labor movement was far more militant a generation ago than it has been since 1945. This is hardly surprising in view of the responsibility which the unions have brought on themselves by virtue of their historical rise to power.

Industrial Relationships. The approach to more democratic industrial relationships has been primarily through a vast extension of joint consultation, or advisory labor-management committees. This machinery has been kept separate from the negotiating machinery in coal and electricity and at some levels in gas; but in the railways the same machinery has tried to serve both ends. Everywhere the trade unions have been sensitive to the threat which independent consultative bodies represented to their own authority, and they have pressed for and secured substantial control over the membership on such committees.

The system of consultation—essentially a vast experiment in union-management co-operation—has required a great effort but has so far yielded only small results. There is as yet no movement to abandon this new institution (which is also widely used in private industry). Many advocates put their hope in the passage of time to make the system work better; a few are asking if this is the most hopeful way of securing the kind of workers' control over labor matters that Socialists have always wanted. They wonder if the area of collective bargaining might be widened as to topics covered, and deepened by encouraging more local bargaining, than has been customary in Britain. This would help remove some continuing confusion between matters appropriate for consultation and collective bargaining.

Union Structures and Officers' Workloads. Nationalization has greatly increased the workload on trade union officials, and doubtless on most management officials as well. Unions have been very slow to adapt their structures and organization to help them perform better the many new tasks which nationalization requires of them. At a time when the amount of responsibility exercised by the unions has greatly increased, they have not shown any disposition to increase their staffs, their meager research efforts, or their educational work. This unimaginative conservatism is frequently cited to help explain the widespread apathy about union affairs among large sections of the labor movement.

Changed Position of Union Officials. Trade unions have had to assume considerable moral and political responsibility for the performance of the nationalized industries, mainly by trying to resist the pressures to pursue policies that officials know would not be best for the industry. This fact has altered the way union officials have had to think about their jobs, their attitudes toward management, and their political position vis-à-vis their own memberships. They have necessarily developed more understanding of management problems, more sympathy for managers, and they have had to put away their traditional, instinctive response: "Our members' interests, right or wrong." With the continuing low salaries paid British union officials, nationalization has probably decreased the attractiveness of union careers, except as a bridge to jobs in management. These jobs, heavily concentrated in the labor and welfare fields, have opened an important new set of career opportunities for union officials.

Efficient Use of Labor. With some exceptions, nationalization has not made it easier for management to undertake reorganization schemes that involve changes in long-standing labor practices. Such "rationalization" involves the closing of uneconomic canals and branch lines on the railroads and of uneconomic coal mines, the modification of some featherbedding practices on the railroads (such as the abolition of "knockers-up"—a group of about six hundred who used to wake up train crews before the invention of the alarm clock), and the elimination of redundant labor where jobs are found to be overmanned. The Herbert Committee, for example, criticized the Central Electricity Authority for its "passive attitude" towards redundancy for fear that it would be too difficult to handle:

> [This attitude] has caused management at all levels to be disinclined to seek out redundancy because it is known that it will be difficult to deal with that redundancy when ascertained. In consequence we find that work-study, operational research and investigations into restrictive practices are undertaken without enthusiasm, if they are pursued at all. The effect on management itself is therefore bad because the most effective deployment of manpower is never possible. The effect of hidden underemployment upon the workpeople themselves is equally bad and is likely to undermine . . . morale. . . .*

This is an area where some unions have given contractual pledges of co-operation with management in "efficiency" measures, but where practical results have been few because the unions have understandably shrunk from the practical implications of their pledges.

Modernizing Personnel Practices. Nationalization has unquestionably been a powerful instrument for "modernizing" labor relations in the affected industries. The amount of attention now being paid to the training of new recruits, to providing opportunities for higher education, to systematic promotion policies, to job evaluation and work study, to the improvement of methods of wage payment, to personnel records and to personnel research—the attention that management is giving to these subjects is immeasurably greater than it was before nationalization. True, personnel management has not been carried as far in Britain as in the United States. But the nationalized industries, which once included some of the most backward on this score, must now be counted as among the most advanced. Where labor relations only recently exercised a residual claim on management's attention and energies (chiefly at the periodic crises produced by negotiations), today it constitutes an "overhead" claim that is constant, specialized, and formalized. The rapid improvement in personnel policies and their administration is helping to increase vertical mobility in British society.

Spread of Voluntary Arbitration. Nationalization has greatly extended the use of arbitration. In coal, for example, there is a voluntary agreement between the NUM and the Coal Board to submit *all* unresolved disputes to arbitration, including disputes over new contract terms. This does not mean that unions have given up the right to strike under nationalization (the basic arbitration agreement could be scrapped if the union got sufficiently fed up with arbitrators' awards); it simply reflects their feeling that they can now secure satisfactory settlements by less primitive means. The only union-approved strike in any nationalized industry has been

* Sir Edward Herbert, LL.B. (chairman), *Report of the Committee of Inquiry into the Electricity Supply Industry*, p. 73.

the nineteen-day strike of locomotive personnel called in June 1955 by the Associated
Society of Locomotive Engineers and Firemen. Although this stopped 80 per cent of
Britain's rail traffic for nearly three weeks,
there was no serious government proposal to
introduce any special measures for controlling
strikes in "essential industries." The strike
did lead the Trades Union Congress to one
minor reform: it authorized its General Council to intervene at an earlier stage in disputes of member unions.

Persistence of Unofficial Strikes. Despite
the spread of arbitration, the improvement
of management's personnel effort, and the
responsible attitude of union leaders in most
situations, unofficial strikes have presented
major difficulties in every nationalized industry. Management and union officials have
been firm in refusing to negotiate while such
strikes were in progress. These unofficial
strikes seem to have been similar in cause
and in frequency to unofficial strikes in pre-
nationalization days: they do not seem to
represent a substitution of unofficial for official direct action. Since nationalization,
union officials have been much more co-
operative with management in trying to head
off and end such strikes.

The Two "Sides" of Industry. There has
been an unmistakable improvement in working relations—in understanding and respect—
between union leaders and management in
all the nationalized industries, save possibly
on the railways. This new top-level relationship is not duplicated at the employee level—
there has not been any marked reduction in
the "we-they" psychology that has traditionally separated employees and management.
The real question is how strongly this traditional sentiment persists; this is a matter of
opinion very hard to test (statistical measures
of absenteeism, turnover, unofficial strikes,
and so forth are not very helpful). My own
judgment is that there has been some improvement in morale in coal and electricity,
but some deterioration on the railways. Labor
relations in the gas industry have tradi-

tionally been good; nationalization does not
seem to have changed the situation significantly.

UNION SECURITY

One of the ways in which nationalization
impinged on labor relations most unexpectedly was the unsettling effect it had during the early years on the security enjoyed
by particular unions. Although these problems were partly transitional, in moving from
the old order to the new, they have not sunk
entirely out of view. A discussion of these
problems can illuminate some of the more
pedestrian but still very important aspects
of industrial relations in nationalized industries.

A union's security depends upon many
factors—the sincerity and degree of acceptance of its presence by employers; the
acceptance of its jurisdictional claims by other
unions; the satisfaction of various groups
with the service and status given them within
the union and the extent of nonunionism
within the union's jurisdiction. The handling
of these questions differs greatly in Britain
and the United States.

In America there is a long tradition within
the union movement of granting exclusive
jurisdiction to individual unions; this principle is not recognized in Britain. British
unions do indeed have "demarcation" disputes, but they are softened by the absence
of the American principle of "exclusive jurisdiction" and by a tradition of interunion negotiations. These factors structure jurisdictional battles so that British unions "pull
their punches."

Recognition has depended on the employers' will, sometimes forced by pressure
from the union but never by any government
authority (there is nothing comparable
to the National Labor Relations Board in
Britain). Unions recognized by employers
do not enjoy exclusive bargaining rights for
everyone in a well-defined bargaining unit;
sometimes one finds two unions signatory to
a joint agreement with an employer covering

their respective members in a common bargaining unit.

Finally, British unions have rarely sought any kind of "union security" clauses from employers, mainly because they did not regard employers as bent on destroying them at the first opportunity and because the British respect for voluntarism, even among working-class leaders, is so strong that most of them shrink from compelling nonunionists to join or stay in. However, there is a universal contempt for nonunionists, and union membership is normally very high.

These questions of union jurisdictions, union recognition, and compulsory membership were rarely if ever discussed in terms of nationalization. No one seems to have anticipated that nationalization would greatly disturb these rather routine areas of union life. In practice, however, nationalization produced an atmosphere within the affected industries not unlike that produced in the United States by the passage of the Wagner Act in 1935. For nationalization offered British unions prizes something like those offered American homesteaders when the federal government threw open new territories for "staking" a century ago. It was hardly surprising, therefore, that there ensued a lively scramble to stake out new claims, that there was much jockeying and jostling among the contenders, and that the unions' behavior was affected by the ground rules governing the way the game was to be played.

Determination of Bargaining Rights. The most important fact about these "ground rules" is that nationalization formalized them. Each nationalization act, for example, carries a clause similar to this one from the Coal Act of 1946:

> It shall be the duty of the Board to enter into consultation with organisations appearing to them to represent substantial proportions of the persons in the employment of the Board, or of any class of such persons, as to the Board's concluding with those organisations (collective bargaining) agreements. . . .

The effect of this clause was to make the National Coal Board its own "National Labor Relations Board" for determining representation questions. In private industry, which unions were to represent which employees was traditionally left up to the unions alone. Furthermore, the Board was under a legal compulsion to recognize unions that raised their heads for any class of employees (including clerical, technical, professional, and managerial employees), provided only that the union represented a "substantial proportion" of those employees. Without intending anything so subtle, the unions had transferred the right to determine bargaining rights from an internal concern of the union movement into an exclusive right of the employer. The heart of the matter was how the new giant employers would choose to exercise their new authority.

One can imagine the scramble for bargaining rights that developed when one realizes that by 1951 there were more than fifty unions active in five of the nationalized industries. In coal mining and on the railways, two huge industrial unions—unions which had played leading roles in the historic drives for nationalizing their industries—asserted jurisdictional claims over *all* employees in their industries. These claims embraced not only clerical workers but any others who might show any interest in becoming union members. These moves naturally threatened other unions which had long been active among particular classes of employees, as well as outside unions which moved in to seek a place in the nationalized industries.

The reaction of the new employers was to reject these claims and to avoid any direct exercise of their legal power by throwing recognition questions back into the unions' own laps. That is, both the Coal Board and the Railway Executive, in certain important recognition disputes, said that they would recognize whatever unions the Trades Union

Congress suggested they recognize. Several potentially explosive rivalries in coal yielded to this treatment, but on the railways the TUC's inability to persuade rival unions to adjust their disputes left the Transport Commission with no alternative but to make its own choice. When it chose to recognize only unions which had been active in trucking before nationalization, a union which had moved in rapidly only after nationalization withdrew from the field. There was no serious strike threat by the militant NUR to try to coerce the Commission into granting its claim to represent everyone in railroading.

Organization of Nonmanual Employees. So far it is clear that we have been talking only of horizontal rivalries. One important product of nationalization has been the rapid extension of organization among grades of employees not formerly organized, or only slightly so—clerks, technicians, and both lower and higher managerial grades. For these employees, nationalization meant that their employer had become the only employer in their industry, that it had become a somewhat more impersonal employer, that the terms and conditions of employment became more standardized and less personal, and that decisions affecting these matters were now made at a greater distance and with longer delays. The result was to introduce a new feeling of uncertainty and loss of control over one's situation among these clerical, professional, and managerial employees. These grades accepted organization fairly rapidly, if often somewhat apologetically. But one thing became clear very quickly: these special groups wanted to be represented by their "own" unions and resisted the embrace offered by some of the manual workers' organizations. The general rule in all four industries was to grant white-collar and other nonmanual employees representation by unions limited to their own kind. But a great deal of energy and maneuvering went into decisions concerning which unions many borderline classifications ought to belong to.

Break-away Movements. A somewhat similar representation problem has involved "break-away" movements—usually dissident craft groups which were represented by a larger union at the time of nationalization and which hoped to look out for their own interests by securing independent recognition under the nationalization acts. The most important of these break-away movements has involved the attempt of the colliery winding enginemen, a key craft group, to get out of the National Union of Mineworkers and bargain independently. In this bitter dispute between the winders and the NUM, the Coal Board has been caught in a hopeless middle: the winders have repeatedly engaged in strikes to force recognition by the Board; but the Board could not recognize the winders without facing a counterstrike by the NUM to prevent such recognition. The NUM has supplied "scabs" to keep the pits running when the regular winders struck. In civil aviation, the Amalgamated Engineering Union has similarly prevented the British Overseas Airways Corporation and British European Airways from recognizing the Aeronautical Engineers' Association. On the railways, the National Union of Railwaymen has held a similar club over the Union of Railway Servants, a craft union of signalmen that has grown since nationalization but which did not feel it could use the advent of nationalization to win a recognition long denied it under private ownership.

Membership. In this scramble for position in nationalized industry, compulsory union membership might have taken on a new appeal for two reasons. First, union shop agreements would have been one method by which one union could have prevented any others from securing a foothold in a particular bargaining unit. The NUM did in fact submit a closed shop demand to the Coal Board during the first round of bargaining, but the Board rejected the demand "on principle," though it granted a dues checkoff. Second, it might have been thought that the unions would have used the occasion of nationalization to achieve 100 per cent membership by widespread resort to union shop agreements. But nothing like this occurred; there was only a rather timid flurry of interest in such clauses. The British tradition of voluntarism led the employer to reject such demands and led the unions to accept his decision without a fight.

In Sum. To sum up: nationalization had the effect of greatly stimulating interest in union membership among many groups that had traditionally remained outside trade unions, of stimulating many old unions and several new ones to stake out claims in the new industries, of bringing many unions into conflict with each other both horizontally and vertically, of raising delicate and knotty questions of allocating union representation on joint negotiating and consultative boards, and—as a result of all these developments— of putting to a severe test the ability of rival unions to co-operate with each other by settling their rivalries through compromise rather than by force. Despite a few major eruptions, these rivalries were settled with remarkable success. Another effect of some importance was the ending of all employer resistance to recognition of unions representing groups close to higher management, for example, clerical employees on the railways or technical and managerial employees in all four industries. Historically, these were areas where British employers had not recognized unions without resistance—and in which organization was therefore weak and spotty.

The resultant pattern of union-management relations in the nationalized industries is complex and untidy, and the amount of energy expended on these mundane matters by trade union and management representatives has been huge. Although these problems were not foreseen, it is difficult to see how they could have been avoided.

UNION APPRAISALS OF NATIONALIZATION

It is easy to let the ideological disappointment with nationalization tempt people into calling it a failure. But this would be a shallow and superficial conclusion: if all union members over thirty-five years of age were given an opportunity to vote on whether or not, on balance, they preferred life under nationalization to their previous lot, I am reasonably sure that the coal miners would give nationalization a strong endorsement, electricity and gas employees a rather weak and neutral endorsement, and only the railwaymen would probably feel sufficiently disappointed by nationalization to want to return to a private existence. The vote "for" nationalization would run more favorable among union officials than among their membership.

SOCIALIST IDEOLOGY AND ECONOMIC REALITY

Even though nationalization cannot be called a failure, it should have produced a bigger improvement in labor relations than it has. The most important explanation of this gap between hopes and performance is the unreality of the expectations which socialism had historically generated for nationalization. Socialists had long claimed that they could make a unique contribution to the labor problems of modern industry; a decade's experience has shown this claim to be much less valid than many once believed. The main reason for this disappointment is that the ideological symbols of socialism's political struggle are not closely related to the economic and social motivations that determine morale in the workshop. The body of insights and principles developed over the past twenty years in the fields of industrial relations and personnel administration are more important to industrial morale than whether or not an industry is nationalized. This statement might not be true if conditions deteriorated badly in the product market: a nationalized monopoly industry would probably be able to shelter its employees from such pressures better than private profit-minded employers struggling for existence under competition. But the greater ability of nationalized industries to dampen down shocks in the product market might be at some expense to the structural flexibility of the economy. The past decade has not given us any test of nationalization's behavior under deflationary conditions.

NOT ENOUGH HELP FROM BRITISH UNIONS

There is a second explanation, an ironical one. It is that the organization, attitudes, and policies of the British trade union movement present as many difficulties to "making nationalization work" as does the bureaucratic organization of the huge new state employers. This is not a truth widely acknowledged within the British labor movement. But there are enough respected students of the British scene who have come to this conclusion to put it beyond doubt. Here is how one of the most perceptive of these, Professor John Mack of Glasgow, puts the matter:

> Broadly speaking, the formal relationship between trade unions and the wider society in Britain is much the same as it was in 1913. . . . The only new factor in the situation is that the balance of industrial power has swung decisively in favour of the unions. They have increased in weight and influence, but they have retained their former attitudes. They are unwilling to exercise the responsibilities which . . . are a condition of the proper exercise of their growing power.*

He goes on to say that while many leaders wish to exercise the new responsibilities they feel, they are frustrated by a reluctant rank and file. The fundamental shift in the role which nationalization requires of a trade union is that it stop pursuing purely sectional interests and invariably protecting the interests of its members whenever the latter feel injured, rightly or wrongly. No longer can unions afford the luxury of simply standing in protest against society and against employers; under nationalization and the welfare state unions must take some responsibility for seeing that what has to be done is not made impossible. This is an extremely difficult and delicate adjustment to carry through within a framework of freedom, especially for an institution with the deep and democratic traditions of the British unions. For individual British unions are not disciplined by anything like the degree of structural centralization that characterizes the Swedish or German unions, to take two examples from Continental countries whose national economic problems are not unlike Britain's. Without such centralization, it is much easier for irresponsible leadership to throw its weight around at the expense of the general interest. The only restraint on such conduct becomes self-restraint induced by an understanding of the problems of the country and of particular industries. The extent of self-restraint and understanding has not been negligible among union leaders in postwar Britain; but it has served negative rather than positive ends: the unions have seen to it that nationalization did not fail but they have not done much to help it succeed. To do the latter may require far-reaching changes within British unions and in some attitudes toward industrial relations traditional in Britain on both sides of the bargaining table.

NEEDED REFORMS

Some progress might be made if British unions were willing to spend more time and money on education and research, of which there is now very little. There are some structural reforms that seem overdue: the addition of specialized staff to deal with the affairs of the nationalized industries, a rethinking of the kind of workshop organization the unions ought to have (it is now weak in many industries, though not in mining); more attractive terms of employment for union officials. But perhaps the most hopeful source of progress lies in a re-evaluation by labor and management alike of the kind of collective bargaining that would best suit their objectives. For example, by encouraging more local bargaining on local topics it should be possible to eliminate some of the confusion surrounding the proper role of joint

* John A. Mack, "Trade Union Leadership," *Political Quart.*, special number on trade union problems, p. 73, January–March, 1956.

consultation—by defining as negotiable many issues now haggled over on a consultative basis and in so doing to set up a clearer grievance procedure wholly separate from consultative meetings. Again, a more widespread use of "horse trading" in bargaining, instead of the characteristic approach of trying to negotiate separate agreements for each subject "on its merits," would contribute to an easier position for union officials when it comes to accepting measures which they know the industry needs but their members will not like. Management can then be made the chief lightning rod for absorbing the emotional aggression generated by rationalization moves. This is, I realize, a characteristically American reading of some of the difficulties in which the British unions find themselves (and not only in nationalized industries—the difficulties only stand out more sharply there). But some British observers, such as B. C. Roberts, are urging this point upon their countrymen.

NATIONALIZATION NO CURE-ALL

We are brought, then, to a very pedestrian conclusion, one that should perhaps have been obvious in advance before history drove it home. It is that the most significant and most interesting aspects of labor relations in Britain's nationalized industries have comparatively little to do with the fact of nationalization. They have to do either with attitudes and practices that are characteristically *British,* or with the history, technology, and environmental characteristics of a particular *industry.* The form of ownership of an industry is less significant than either of these other two major influences on what labor relations are like within Britain's nationalized industries. This is not to say—as I did say in an unguarded moment at the start of this essay—that nationalization is irrelevant. But its primary relevance is that it provides a more auspiciously structured environment within which the specific labor problems of these industries are being tackled and a more professional and systematic approach to these problems.

If nationalization was to have proved the decisive, almost surgical, solution for an industry's labor problems that many thought it would be, the reality of social relationships would have to be much simpler and human nature much less perverse than history shows them to be.

During the last quarter century, while various countries have been emphasizing government spending as a way of overcoming the effects of the Great Depression, the principal economic theory influencing planners and legislators was that offered by Keynes. Unfortunately, that theory was fundamentally wrong in some very important respects, and Sumner H. Slichter, an American economist, shows why its influence was not an unmixed blessing.

Keynes's theory contributed invaluable tools of analysis to economics, but his theory has turned out to have been wrong in all its essentials because it assumed that advanced economies suffer from a chronic deficiency of demand; instead, they suffer from an *excess* of demand. Keynes erred when he assigned to consumers a relatively passive role in determining the demand for goods; and he overlooked the fact that the development of investment opportunities is itself an expanding industry carried on for profit. Slichter explains these errors and their implications.

Slichter also shows that Keynes's theory failed to comprehend the ethics of borrowing, the demand for capital, and the influence of discovery in industry. The outlook for production, the chronic excess of demand, and rising wages and prices are all inconsistent with the unrealistic Keynesian economics. The new confidence arising in free enterprise is also contrary to Keynes's expectations. Thus Slichter accounts for the passing of the economic theory which so greatly influenced American political policy from the period of the New Deal onward. Not all of its influences could be nullified quickly, but the trend is toward a middle-of-the-road opinion in the United States and in Western Europe.

35

THE PASSING
OF KEYNESIAN ECONOMICS*

Sumner H. Slichter

John Maynard Keynes ranks with Adam Smith and Karl Marx among economists in the influence that his views have exerted on the general public. He had the vision to see that economics lacked a general theory of demand, and he proceeded with boldness and brilliance to construct one.

His theory produced the startling conclusion that highly developed industrial countries suffer from a chronic deficiency of demand, and that this deficiency is bound to grow worse as countries become richer. Hence, Keynes called upon government to assume a new responsibility and a new function—that of closing the growing gap between the power of progressive economies to produce and the size of effective private demand. Keynes suggested two general lines of action—that of controlling the size of the gap through changes in the distribution of income and that of offsetting the gap through greater government spending.

Keynes's theory contributed invaluable tools of analysis to economics and started hundreds of able economists in many lands studying the important problems that the theory opened

up. No one in the history of economics has done as much as Keynes to stimulate good work. But Keynes's theory has turned out to have been wrong in all its essentials. Although intended to be a "general" theory, applicable to all conditions, it was unduly molded by the depressed thirties, the period when Keynes composed it. Advanced economies do not suffer from a chronic deficiency of demand—they suffer from a chronic *excess* of demand. It would be hard today to find an advanced economy that is not struggling to control demand, and most of them are having only partial success.

It is among the undeveloped economies, precisely where Keynes did not expect to find a chronic shortage of demand, that unemployment is endemic and most severe. Keynes's theory that unemployment is caused by an excessive disposition to save obviously does not explain the high unemployment in countries which are too poor to have any savings at all. The high unemployment in undeveloped countries is best explained by Marx's theory of unemployment—that men lack work because savings are insufficient to

* Reprinted by permission of the author and *The Atlantic Monthly*, vol. 200, no. 5, pp. 141–146, November, 1957.

provide the growing labor force with the tools of production.

THE CONSUMER'S ROLE

Why has Keynes turned out to have been so completely wrong? He made two basic mistakes. In the first place, he assigned to consumers a relatively passive role in determining the demand for goods. In the second place, he overlooked the fact that the development of investment opportunities is itself an expanding industry carried on for profit and able to supply the community with a rapidly growing number of investment outlets.

Keynes thought that consumers play a rather passive role in determining the demand for goods because he believed that the amount spent on consumption depends pretty completely upon the size of the national income. Hence, the dynamic influences in the economy, the influences that make the national income and the total demand for goods change, must be found, according to Keynes, outside the spending habits of consumers. Keynes found a single dominant dynamic influence in the rate of investment, which by rising and falling determines whether the economy expands or contracts. As business increases or cuts its buying of investment goods, incomes will rise or fall, and as they rise or fall consumption too will rise or fall.

Had Keynes lived in the United States, he would perhaps have seen that consumers do not let their consumption be determined so completely by the size of their incomes. American consumers, with their strong desire to live better and with their freedom from customs and traditions that decree what ways of living are suitable for people in certain stations, have always been ready to cut their rate of saving, to draw on their capital, or to go into debt in order to buy new things.

Particularly in recent years, consumers have developed a growing willingness to incur short-term debts in order to buy goods. Since the boom year of 1929 there has been an almost sevenfold increase in consumer credit, from a mere $6.4 billion at the end of 1929

to a whopping $41.9 billion at the end of 1956. During this period consumers were obviously not limiting their spending by their incomes. Their spending was being determined, as one would expect it to be, by their total resources, which include their credit, not merely by their incomes. Instead of playing the passive role ascribed to them by Keynes, consumers have been a powerful dynamic influence accelerating the expansion of the economy.

THE ETHICS OF BORROWING

Consumers have been encouraged to play a dynamic role in the economy by the rapidly growing consumer credit industry. This industry is based upon the discovery, only recently made, that consumers are far better credit risks than anyone had dreamed them to be. As a result, there has been a rush by finance companies, banks, mail order houses, automobile dealers, department stores, airplane and steamship lines, and many others to persuade consumers to buy goods on credit. At first consumer credit was limited to tangible goods with a rather definite resale value, such as automobiles or household appliances, but now one may finance trips and vacations on the installment plan. And the proportion of sales made on credit steadily rises. Sears Roebuck reports that in 1954, 39 per cent of its sales were made on credit. Last year the proportion was 44 per cent. With consumers behaving as American consumers are accustomed to behave, Keynes's fear that people will insist on saving too much seems farfetched.

Incidentally, with the discovery that consumers are better risks than had been previously suspected, there has developed a marked change in attitudes toward personal loans—a real change in the ethics of borrowing. Time was when personal indebtedness, except for a few emergencies and to provide the necessary furnishings for a home, was regarded as imprudent or reckless. Today it is seen that debt is a stabilizing and stimulating influence, and that it is a good thing for most young men, particularly married men, to have at least a moderate volume of debts that they are paying off.

THE DEMAND FOR CAPITAL

Although Keynes thought that the dominant dynamic influence in the economy is investment, he conceived of businessmen as a surprisingly unenterprising and helpless lot—unable to do much about the scale of investment. Keynes was obsessed with the fear that, as the country's stock of capital became larger and larger, outlets for savings would be harder to find, and he expressed his fears quite eloquently. He said that he felt sure that the demand for capital is strictly limited in the sense that it would not be difficult to increase the stock of capital to the point where its ability to produce a return would fall to a very low figure.

Keynes's belief that the return on capital would drop very drastically as the stock of capital increased must be ascribed to his failure to appreciate the significance of modern technology. Though a man of affairs, and a highly successful one at that, he failed to see what others saw, the large and growing capacity of industry to discover investment opportunities—a capacity that is far greater in highly developed countries than in undeveloped ones and that grows as the economy becomes richer and more industrial. Technological discoveries are the most important single influence on investment in advanced industrial economies, and yet Keynes's brilliant work contains no discussion of technological research.

THE INDUSTRY OF DISCOVERY

It is ironic that at the very time that Keynes was proclaiming his pessimistic views on the shortage of investment opportunities, the rise of technological research was producing a revolutionary change in the economy. Technological research was becoming an industry. It is convenient to call it the industry of discovery. It consists of many captive laboratories which work only for the company which owns them and a rapidly growing number of firms which do research

under contract. The industry of discovery is one of the most rapidly growing industries in the country. Industry spent $116 million of its own money on research and development in 1930, $234 million in 1940, and about $1.5 billion in 1953, and it has been making even larger outlays under government research contracts. Outlays on research and development would grow even faster were they not limited by the shortage of engineers and scientists.

The revolutionary nature of the rise of the industry of discovery is not appreciated even by economists. Until recently, discoveries have been made mainly in two ways: by the efforts of operating men (incidental to their regular work), who have seen opportunities to improve methods of production or products, and by the efforts of "inventors" who, using their own resources and often driven by much stronger motives than hope of gain, have made industrial applications of scientific knowledge. The revolutionary change is that it has become possible to find a large number of problems or areas of investigation on which money may be spent with a reasonable expectation that the outlay will produce enough useful information and understanding to justify the expense. This means that it has become possible to apply the economic calculus—the balancing of expected expenses against expected gains—to an important new area of human activity, and to have the organized pursuit of gain take over a field of activity where formerly there had only been haphazard individual activities.

Of course, there can be no guarantee that a particular inquiry will produce the required knowledge within the estimated time and cost. When economic calculations are applied to research, the application has to be made in a somewhat different way from the application of economic calculations to the use of known and tried methods of production. Economists as yet do not understand the process by which highly uncertain costs are balanced against highly uncertain returns. But the evidence that some sort of calculus is being applied is found in the enormous growth of research budgets. Industry is not throwing its money away; it is spending on research and development because it has good reason to think that the outlays will prove profitable.

One result of the rise of the industry of discovery is the revelation that the economy was devoting far too small a part of its labor and capital to efforts to develop new products and new methods. The large and rapid shift of resources into technological research is enormously increasing our capacity to develop investment opportunities. An even more important result of research becoming an industry is that we have created an enormous vested interest in expanding research.

Many thousands of able men now make their living by disturbing our lives and by forcing us to discard old equipment, old methods, and old ways of doing things. The more they disturb us, the better living they make. And the vested interests of the people who live by making discoveries cause them to strive to improve the methods and instruments of investigation, thus steadily raising the capacity of the economy to develop investment opportunities. The danger that Keynes feared—namely, that we shall run out of investment opportunities—grows more remote every day, and it becomes most remote in the highly developed economies, precisely where Keynes erroneously believed that it would be greatest.

THE OUTLOOK FOR PRODUCTION

How does the world look when Keynes's theory of demand, constructed in the midst of the great depression, is replaced with one based on the developments of the last twenty years? On the whole, it appears to be a far better world than the one described by Keynes's theory—though not a world from which tough economic problems are absent. The specter of chronic unemployment, slowly growing as wealth increases and as the rate of saving rises, has pretty completely disappeared, at least as far as the industrially developed countries are concerned. Only a series of major blunders in policy could produce the chronic unemployment that Keynes

dreaded. Consumers are a far more dynamic influence than Keynes ever suspected, and industry has far greater power to create demand for goods, mainly through technological discoveries, than anyone a generation or so ago dreamed it might have—and this power is growing.

Of great importance is the fact that the real world also has a far greater capacity to increase productivity, and hence consumption standards, than does the world of the Keynesian theory. Keynes does not discuss the prospects of technological progress, but implicit in his view that investment opportunities will be scarce is the view that technological progress will not be very rapid.

A few followers of Keynes have attempted to reconcile Keynes's pessimistic view of the shortage of investment opportunities with optimistic conclusions concerning the rate of technological progress. They argue that rapid technological progress may co-exist with a chronic shortage of investment outlets, provided inventions increasingly take the form of reducing the amount of capital required per worker. As a matter of fact, however, most inventions are of the opposite sort: they increase the amount of equipment that can be effectively controlled and operated by a worker. Keynes himself did not argue that the shortage of investment opportunities would be the result of a preponderance of a particular form of invention—he simply was not aware of our rapidly growing capacity to make discoveries. Hence, the real world of rapid technological change in which we live is one where the outlook for more production and higher standards of consumption is far brighter than in the world of scarce investment opportunities postulated by Keynes.

A CHRONIC EXCESS OF DEMAND

This is not to say that the real world is lacking in perplexing economic problems. In place of the problems of stagnation and chronic unemployment, the real world is confronted with the problem of a chronic excess of demand, the result of the growing capacity of industry to develop new products and processes. But if demand has a strong tendency to outrun productive capacity, the government will need to maintain rather steady control over the creation of bank credit.

The policy of credit restraint, that has received so much discussion this last year, will be in effect not for a few months but for most of the time in the foreseeable future. The policy of credit restraint is unpopular with a substantial number of shortsighted people who do not like to be prevented from spending all the money they could easily spend if credit were easier. Hence, one of the hazards of life in a period of chronic excess of demand is the danger that public opinion will force the government to abandon the policy of credit restraint. Such abandonment would produce a runaway boom that would end in collapse.

RISING WAGES AND RISING PRICES

Even tougher than the problem of curbing the tendency for demand to outrun productive capacity is the problem of the tendency for wages to rise faster than the productivity of labor, causing a slow rise in labor costs and thus a slow rise in prices. This is a problem that is produced by the combination of full employment and strong trade unions. No one as yet knows a satisfactory way of checking the tendency for rising labor costs to force up the level of prices. A policy of credit restraint can prevent prices from rising faster than labor costs. Indeed, a sufficiently drastic credit policy can prevent prices from rising as fast as labor costs, with the result that unemployment is created, the bargaining position of unions is weakened, and the rise in labor costs is eventually halted. A few extremists advocate such a drastic credit policy. It is safe to predict, however, that such a policy would not last long. Protests from the unemployed and their friends would soon force a relaxing of the policy.

Other persons suggest that rising labor costs can be prevented by persuading unions to practice self-restraint and to abstain from exercising all the power that a sellers' market gives them. But unions are competitive and power-seeking organizations, and they live in a community in which the spirit of competition pervades all manner of activities. The rivalry among unions in winning gains for their members is no greater than the struggle for sales and prestige among soap companies, automobile manufacturers, or makers of tires, radios, or cigarettes. In a community where competition is a way of life, unions alone can scarcely be expected to abstain from trying to outdo one another.

Some people suggest that the way to stop wages from outrunning productivity is to spend more money on technological research. This procedure may partly answer the problem, but it cannot be counted on to do so. The difficulty, as experience shows, is that most technological discoveries increase the demand for capital goods by creating new investment opportunities. Thus they tend to make markets even more favorable to sellers.

There are, however, some types of technological changes that increase productivity without requiring the use of more capital. These are capital-saving changes. Examples of such changes are better selection and training of employees, better scheduling of work, better setting of production standards, better control of raw materials, better maintenance of equipment. Greater emphasis upon these capital-saving changes will raise the productivity of labor while not increasing the demand for goods, and thus will help productivity to keep pace with the rise of wages.

Changes in the corporate income tax would stiffen the resistance of employers to the demands of unions and would thus retard somewhat the rise of money wages. One reason why employers do such an indifferent job of bargaining is that under existing corporate income tax laws, the government in effect pays 52 per cent of any wage increase. The backbones of employers might be stiffened by amendments to the corporate income tax law that would require employers to wait for a year or two before counting wage increases as deductible expenses in computing their liability for the corporate income tax.

Only experience will show to what extent industry and the public will support these several ways of checking the tendency for wages to outrun productivity, and only experience will show the effectiveness of these measures. In the meantime, we shall probably have to live with a slowly rising price level, and the rise in prices may continue indefinitely. The upward creep of prices will itself create problems, but they will be far less serious problems than we experienced from the roller-coaster course of prices during the nineteenth century and most of the first half of the twentieth century. And the problems of a slowly rising price level may be regarded as the price we pay for two desirable conditions that are fundamentally responsible for the creeping price rise: full employment and strong trade unions.

All in all, the real world appears to be a much better place than the world of Keynesian theory—at least better for most people. It is true that the Keynesian problem of stagnation is more amenable to treatment by policy than the real world's problems of excessive demand and creeping inflation. But surely it is preferable to be struggling even with incomplete success with the problems of excessive demand and creeping inflation than to be confronted with a chronic shortage of investment opportunities. Fortunately, there is no incompatibility between creeping inflation and the capacity of the economy to raise productivity.

Undoubtedly, the greatest superiority of the real world over the world of Keynesian theory is in the attitude of people toward the basic economic institutions of capitalism and private enterprise. Keynes was not seeking to overthrow capitalism—on the contrary, when he proposed that the government take on new responsibilities and functions, he hoped to save capitalism. Nevertheless, widespread and continued acceptance of Keynes's theory of

demand would have been disastrous for capitalistic institutions. People could not keep up strong faith in institutions that were unable to provide the community with the needed number of jobs, and institutions in which people lacked confidence would be bound to wither and decay and to be replaced by others.

NEW CONFIDENCE IN FREE ENTERPRISE

The discovery that our economy has far greater capacity to increase the demand for goods than Keynes suspected has naturally produced a great resurgence of confidence in capitalism and private enterprise. Rising confidence in the effectiveness of capitalistic institutions has had the interesting result of causing radicals and conservatives alike to abandon extreme positions. As attacks on capitalism have moderated, the defense of capitalism has become less doctrinaire. In the United States there has been a marked growth of "middle-of-the-road" opinion. The same thing has happened in Western Europe where the Labor and Socialist parties have shifted from advocating nationalization of industry to championing the welfare state— the operation of private enterprise within a comprehensive framework of public policies —and where the principal conservative parties have also accepted the welfare state.

We should be grateful that the world is what it is rather than what Keynes pictured it as being. It is a world in which the energies and aspirations of men are stimulated by expanding opportunities rather than depressed by the constant threat of chronic unemployment. Most important of all, it is a world in which the rapidly growing industry of discovery is creating the possibility of a great cultural revolution. For the first time in history, the high productivity of some countries is enabling their people to have sufficient income, sufficient education, and sufficient leisure so that the good life is ceasing to be the privilege of a favored few and is being brought within the reach of all members of the community.

Labor trends in the United States have been influenced by organized movements in European countries and the principal ideologies that have prevailed there, yet the results have been somewhat dissimilar because American and European economies and political institutions are unlike. Melvin J. Vincent points out the salient factors and events in the American labor movement and shows the impact of the steady growth of union power upon the economic, political, and social life of the United States. This chronicle of events begins in 1778 and carries on to 1955. The principal issues in labor's struggle for improved status in the economy are explained as significant phases of the movement. The high points in about fifty years of labor legislation are enumerated (1903–1947), and the important trends of the labor movement during the past three decades, as summarized by Vincent, reveal the contemporary motivation of the movement.

36

LABOR TRENDS IN THE UNITED STATES*
Melvin J. Vincent

Sociologically, the American labor movement may be looked upon as the story of the struggles of American industrial workers to gain for themselves not only an improved material status but also an improved social status. The former refers to such matters as wages and better working conditions; the latter, to the recognition of workers as human beings rather than mere units of labor energy. These struggles have taken place over a long period of time, and the movement in general has passed through distinct stages and tendencies in its evolution to the present period.

EARLY STRUGGLES FOR MATERIAL
STATUS

Toward the close of the eighteenth century, in 1791, carpenters, shoemakers, and printers created their own organizations in Philadelphia, Boston, and New York in an attempt to secure better wages or to prevent reductions in wages. These early craft unions had their genesis in benevolent societies, just as the first British unions had their origins in the Friendly Societies formed during the middle of the eighteenth century. From these societies came lessons in the benefits and strengths to be derived from solidarity and cooperative efforts. Organizing for economic betterment had thus been recognized by workers long before the idea of permanent working organizations had taken root.

In 1778, the journeymen printers of New York met as a group to demand a wage increase, but abandoned their organization

* From *Analyzing Social Problems*, John Eric Nordskog, Edward C. McDonagh, and Melvin J. Vincent (eds.), The Dryden Press, New York, 1956, pp. 254–261. Reprinted by permission of the author and The Dryden Press (now with Henry Holt and Company).

once that objective was attained. In 1786, the Philadelphia printers carried out the first successful strike in the United States, gaining a minimum of six dollars a week. The Philadelphia carpenters struck for a ten-hour day in 1791, but failed. In the next year, Philadelphia shoemakers organized a craft union for the purpose of securing collective bargaining rights. Thus, toward the close of the eighteenth century, foundations were laid in the United States for some fundamental union techniques.

The successes were moderate, yet they encouraged the growth of the union movement and the idea of labor solidarity. Opposition on the part of employers did not lag since they organized among themselves to resist demands. Two tactics utilized early were the hiring of non-unionites to take the place of strikers, and the appeal to the courts to have unions declared as conspiracies in restraint of trade under English common-law doctrine. In Britain, the Combinations Acts, which declared unions to be conspiracies, were in effect from 1799 to 1824.

APPEAL FOR GOVERNMENTAL ASSISTANCE

The attention of the unions in the United States during the period from 1827 to 1832 became fixed upon political activity as a means to gain certain improvements in working conditions, especially a shorter working day. In Philadelphia, for example, some of the more combative craft unions organized the Mechanics Union of Trade Associations in 1827 and attempted to nominate and elect candidates who were favorably inclined toward labor. The success of the Mechanics Union in this endeavor led to the formation of other local labor parties. However, as the major political parties of the times gained in importance, the labor organizations realized that their best chances for economic gains lay in a better and bigger organization of craft and trade unions. Their political activity called attention to the low economic status of the workers, and state legislatures began to enact laws for at least the protection of children and women in industry. Not

too long after, the framework for a free public-school education was established.

This struggle of labor and the workers may be looked upon as, in part, an effort to interfere with a laissez-faire policy of government, for it reflects the evolution of intervention by the state in labor and industrial affairs. In 1813, Connecticut passed a law requiring a minimum amount of education for child workers. In 1842, Massachusetts enacted a ten-hour law for the protection of its child workers.

Hour laws for men came first in 1840, when President Van Buren ordered a ten-hour day for Navy Yard workers. The first federal legislation for railroad workers was not enacted until 1916. Under the Fair Labor Standards Act of 1938, the forty-hour week was put into effect for workers in interstate commercial carriers.

From 1870 to 1880, seven states had passed minimum-wage laws for the protection of child workers. However, it was not until 1916 that the federal government passed its first child-labor law. Declared unconstitutional in 1918, the second federal law was passed in 1919, only to suffer a similar fate in 1922. At present child workers are safeguarded under a provision of the Fair Labor Standards Act.

Following protective legislation for children came similar rulings for women. The first effective law limiting working hours for women was passed in Massachusetts in 1874. The decision of the Supreme Court in 1908 upholding the Oregon statute introduced an era of laws that were more practically enforceable. In 1912, the first minimum-wage law for women was passed in Massachusetts, but this was a non-mandatory one. By 1923, thirteen states and the District of Columbia had passed mandatory minimum-wage laws. In that year, the Supreme Court declared the District of Columbia's law to be unconstitutional, and thereupon most of the minimum-wage laws of other states became ineffective and remained so for the next ten years. In 1933, under New Deal suasion, six states passed such laws, and in 1937 the

Supreme Court reversed its 1923 decision. Twenty-one states responded to this decision by passing minimum-wage laws for women. Five of these states included men under minimum-wage provisions. At present, the Fair Labor Standards Act of 1938 sets a minimum rate per hour for work performed upon articles sent through interstate commerce; effective March 1, 1956, the minimum wage is one dollar per hour.

Other kinds of legislation for the protection of workers include (1) workmen's compensation laws, which in effect hold that the cost of industrial accidents is part of the costs of production; (2) social-security laws, including unemployment compensation, old-age assistance, and old-age benefits; (3) laws protecting the right to bargain collectively; and (4) fair employment practices acts.

COLLECTIVE BARGAINING RIGHTS

During the early struggles for union survival and after the first important legal recognition of the right to organize (by Massachusetts in 1842), legal protection of bargaining rights all over the United States became an important issue for unionism. It may be said that collective-bargaining rights are the very foundations of working unionism. The first blanket endorsement by the federal government of collective bargaining came in 1917–1918, during the period of World War I. The first federal law to recognize the right of labor to organize was the Railway Labor Act of 1926. For other workers, this right was recognized in 1932, with the passage of the Norris-LaGuardia Act, upholding the right to organize and bargain collectively. This Act also outlawed the infamous yellow-dog contracts, by means of which some employers denied employment to those who refused to promise not to join a union or promote union organization. In 1933, the right to organize without employer interference was reaffirmed with the passage of the National Industrial Recovery Act.

When this Act was declared unconstitutional, in 1935, Congress quickly passed the Wagner Labor Relations Act, which again gave labor the right of self-organization and collective bargaining, forbidding employers to interfere with the workers' selection of representatives. Likewise, it forbade employers to attempt to dominate employee organizations or to form company unions, a practice which was prevalent in the 1920's. Three other practices were designated as unfair: (1) refusing to bargain collectively; (2) discriminating against a union member; and (3) discriminating against a union member who had filed charges against an employer under the law. A three-man National Labor Relations Board was set up to hear charges brought for failure to comply with the provisions of the Act. In 1947, the Taft-Hartley Act was passed as an amendment to the Wagner Act, which had been held to be discriminatory against employers. Under this new Act, the old Board was enlarged to five members, and a General Counsel for the Board was named. Unfair labor practices by unions were listed to protect employers from what was described as the growing tyranny of big unionism. Recognizing the potential threat to the nation involved in communist infiltration into American unionism, the Taft-Hartley Act made it mandatory for unions seeking the services of the NLRB to have their officers file non-communist affidavits.

THE INTERNAL CONFLICT

This story of the struggle of labor to secure governmental interference and protection runs parallel to another story—namely, the struggle within the ranks of the organized workers. Several phases of this struggle may be noted. In the early days, the chief problem was organizational: should there be one great union embracing all workers, or should organization follow along the lines of crafts and trades? During the Civil War period, workers in the Northern states organized nearly three hundred local unions to embrace the skilled workers in factories manufacturing war materials. Some of the unions in the larger cities united to form city federations. In the post-Civil War period, fourteen national unions, including the National Labor Union, were formed. Organized in Baltimore in 1866, the NLU was chiefly economic in aim, but one of its leaders attempted to have it enter the field of producers' cooperatives. The Union also sponsored the National Reform and Labor Party, but the defeat of this party in the election of 1872 brought to an end both the cooperative and the political ventures of the NLU.

Still another attempt to organize all workers into a large union body was made by the Noble Order of the Knights of Labor, which was founded in 1869. Growing slowly from its parent union, the garment workers of Philadelphia, it attained a membership estimated at about 10,000 in 1879. By 1886, it had 700,000 members. Its principal objective was the replacement of a competitive society by a cooperative one. The eight-hour day, public ownership of utilities, and the introduction of cooperatives were all on its agenda, to be achieved mainly through educational and political activities. Internal strife between those who wanted to gain their ends through collective-bargaining practices and those who chose political methods gradually assumed disruptive proportions. Moreover, the skilled workers looked with suspicion upon the Knights because of its inclusion of unskilled workers.

In 1881, six important craft unions—the cigar makers, steel workers, molders, glass workers, and carpenters—formed the Federation of Organized Trades and Labor Unions, under the leadership of Samuel Gompers and Adolph Strasser. About 45,000 workers joined. In 1886, several large craft unions, incensed by the refusal of the Knights of Labor to grant them complete jurisdiction over their own craft affairs, founded the American Federation of Labor at Columbus, Ohio, and soon after amalgamated with the Federation of Organized Trades and Craft Unions. The new organization took the name of the American Federation of Labor and elected Samuel Gompers as its first president, a position which he held, save for one year (1894–1895), until his death in 1924. Com-

bined, the new membership was reported as about 138,000. Its growth was slow at first, but by 1914 the AFL had attained a membership of about two million and had begun to make itself felt as a force in the economic life of the country. In 1920, the AFL could boast a membership of about four million, representing perhaps 75 percent of all union workers. In 1950, the membership had soared to over seven million. The four brotherhoods of railways workers continued to maintain their own independent unions while carrying on friendly relationships with the Federation.

OBJECTIVES OF ORGANIZED LABOR

According to the leaders of the AFL, their organization has always been in the vanguard of the successful fight to raise wages, to secure the shorter working day and week, and to improve conditions through collective bargaining. They also claim to have furthered the battle to extend free public-school education and to obtain protective legislation for women and children in industry as well as workmen's compensation for those injured in the line of duty.

The growing strength of labor was recognized by the passage of an Act of Congress in 1913 creating a Department of Labor with cabinet ranking. William B. Wilson, an AFL unionist, was appointed the first Secretary of Labor. The first Bureau of Labor had been established in 1884, but it had no cabinet representation. One of the legacies left to the AFL by its first and long-time president, Samuel Gompers, was an injunction to remain aloof from partisan politics and to further its objectives through economic means.

During the early 1920's, after several large strikes, especially the great steel strike of 1919, had been lost, union membership began to decline. This decade has been called "the open-shop period." It was also the time of what was later designated as "glorified company unionism" by labor leaders. Many employers had sought to combat unionism by installing management-financed company unions. Using the term "industrial democracy," such employers allowed their workers to form legislative bodies for enacting rules affecting workshop conditions. The power of veto, however, always rested in the employer's hands. In 1932, trade-union membership was at low ebb, with not more than 3,666,-000 members on the rolls. After the passage of the National Industrial Recovery Act in 1933, guaranteeing the right of employees to organize or join unions of their own choosing for collective-bargaining purposes, unionism began to flourish anew.

DIVISION WITHIN THE RANKS—THE CIO

As membership increased, a cleavage took place within the ranks of the AFL. Some officers of the union favored a continuation along the old craft lines; others held that thousands of workers would remain unorganized unless industrial unionism came to the fore. At the 1935 Convention of the AFL in Atlantic City, the plea for the acceptance of a minority report favoring industrial unionism was rejected. Shortly thereafter, six union leaders, headed by John L. Lewis, formed the Committee for Industrial Organization. With four additional leaders, these men began to organize the mass-production industries. The AFL ordered them to desist, but the Committee refused and proceeded to form its own organization.

The Committee held its first annual convention in 1938, at which time it adopted the name of the Congress of Industrial Organizations. Meanwhile, it had established itself as a federation of national and international unions. The new organization, with John L. Lewis as its first president, stimulated the growth of the union movement. By 1950, the CIO claimed a membership of nearly six million workers.

LABOR'S GROWTH IN POWER

World War II gave added impetus to the growing power of labor. Representatives of unions were placed in positions of importance to the war economy on several governmental boards, among them the Management-Labor Policy Committee and the Office of Production Management. The late Sidney

Hillman, then President of the Amalgamated Clothing Workers' Union, shared joint responsibility for the latter agency with its director, William S. Knudsen, President of General Motors. Membership increases and power growth seemed to enhance the rivalry between the two federations. Both the National Labor Relations Board and the War Labor Board were often accused of favoring one rival organization over the other in their decisions until at length the feeling was expressed: "A plague on both your houses."

With the end of the war came a host of readjustments, including the wage problem. Despite government controls, prices had risen during the war. A series of strikes took place over the wage issue, but employers felt that they could not grant increases unless price controls were removed. Attempts were made by the government to keep wages in line with what was then called the 18½-cent-an-hour increase. In the hope that free competition would force prices to seek their own level, the Office of Price Administration was abolished on June 30, 1946, but this action did not stop the rise of prices. As the cost of living continued to rise, more strikes occurred. The new power of labor made itself felt in the negotiations at bargaining tables, and some of the big industrial concerns gave concessions to the more powerful unions, such as the United Mine Workers' and Steelworkers' Unions. Many of the new wage-adjustment plans called for automatic increases based upon or reflecting the changes in the Consumers' Price Index of the United States Bureau of Labor Statistics.

The total union membership of the new merger between the AFL and CIO will be about sixteen million. Several unions, such as the AFL Teamsters' and the CIO Steelworkers', have on their rolls a membership of more than a million workers each.

EXTENSION OF COLLECTIVE BARGAINING ISSUES

In 1949, the Supreme Court held in a case between the Inland Steel Corporation and the Steelworkers' Union that pensions and other welfare benefits were proper subjects for negotiation at the collective-bargaining table. Since that time, collective-bargaining contracts, notably among the steelworkers, miners, and automotive workers, have included what are now known as fringe benefits. In 1954, about seven million workers under collective-bargaining contracts were covered by pension plans, and 11.3 million workers were covered by health and insurance plans. The inclusion of this new subject matter for collective bargaining may be a kind of testimonial to the growing strength of unionism in the United States.

FIFTY YEARS OF LABOR LEGISLATION

The most important labor legislation for the past fifty years serves to indicate in a sense some of the trends of the labor movement in the United States. This legislative program may also throw some light upon the socioeconomic changes of the period as well as illustrate certain changes in the relationship among government, management, and labor. The principal legislative acts for the period mentioned are as follows:

1903: Congress created a Department of Commerce and Labor with Cabinet ranking.

1913: The Department of Labor was installed as a separate Department with its own Secretary of Labor.

1914: The Clayton Act was passed by Congress, limiting the use of injunctions in labor disputes and declaring that picketing and other union practices were not unlawful. AFL's Gompers declared it to be a Magna Carta for Labor.

1916: The first federal Child Labor Law was passed.

1918: The Child Labor Law was declared unconstitutional.

1919: The second Child Labor Law was passed.

1921: The Supreme Court held that the Clayton Act did not necessarily protect unions against the use of the secondary boycott or against picketing.

1922: The second Child Labor Law was declared unconstitutional.

1924: The Child Labor Amendment to the Constitution was passed, but only 28 of the 36 necessary states have thus far ratified it.

1926: The Railway Labor Act was passed, requiring employers to bargain collectively with their employees and prohibiting discrimination against employees for joining unions. It provided that labor disputes were to be settled through mediation, arbitration, and fact-finding boards.

1931: The Davis-Bacon Act was passed, giving to workers employed by private contractors on public works prevailing wage rates.

1932: The Norris-LaGuardia, or Anti-Injunction, Act was passed, outlawing yellow-dog contracts and limiting the use of federal injunctions in labor disputes.

1933: The National Industrial Recovery Act was passed. Clause 7-A of this Act gave employees the right to organize and to bargain collectively without employer interference.

1935: The National Industrial Recovery Act was declared unconstitutional.
The National Labor Relations Act (Wagner Act) was passed, thus establishing the first national labor policy that protected all workers' rights to organize and select representatives of their own choosing, and the beginning of governmental upholding of union security. The Act listed five unfair labor practices for employers and set up a National Labor Relations Board of three members to administer the provisions of the law.
The Social Security Act was passed, encouraging the states to enact unemployment compensation laws, and providing for an old-age and survivors' insurance plan for retired workers.

1947: The Labor-Management Relations (Taft-Hartley) Act was passed as an amendment to the Wagner Act. It listed five unfair labor practices for unions, enlarged the NLRB to five members, required non-communist affidavits from union officers seeking the services of NLRB, and provided for a General Counsel to the NLRB to prosecute its cases. The Act also created a Federal Mediation and Conciliation Service, independent of the Department of Labor.

Among the important trends of the labor movement of the United States during the past three decades are the following:

1. The steady growth of unionism was encouraged by governmental recognition of the legality of organization and the right to bargain collectively. Union security is today protected by union shop, maintenance-of-membership shop, sole-bargaining-agency shop, and by check-off systems.

2. Unionism was established as a factor in the industrial worker's way of life and as a force in the socioeconomic life of the nation. Since 1947, union leaders have declared their intention of utilizing political action when necessary to protect the interest and welfare of workers.

3. Unionization occurred in major and basic key industries.

4. Monopolistic practices were characteristic of both big business and big unions, making for strong power contests.

5. There was a gradual intrusion of government as one of the major parties in industrial affairs. There is a tendency for the states to assume some of the federal practices. Eighteen states have now passed "right-to-work" laws, while the NLRB has limited somewhat its field of jurisdiction. Recently, encouragement has been given to "free collective bargaining"—i.e., bargaining without governmental interference.

6. Unions have a tendency to function as groups giving status memberships, furnishing educational facilities, providing for research activities, training for leadership, and providing for welfare and fringe benefits by means of the collective-bargaining contract.

7. Unions have fought to secure, as a matter of principle, the guaranteed annual wage in the great basic industries, a thing bitterly opposed by many employers, who think that such a wage, if adopted, might result in a rigidly planned and controlled economy. The guaranteed annual wage—or as UAW's Reuther prefers to call it, a "guaranteed employment plan"—may be in effect a partial answer to the rapid growth of "automation," or the application of the machine to work processes formerly performed by men. Under the June 1955 contracts with Ford and General Motors, workers have been assured of unemployment benefits for twenty-six weeks; the money will come from reserves set aside for the purpose by the companies and from state unemployment funds.

8. On February 9, 1955, an agreement was reached by the Unity Committee of the AFL and CIO, later adopted and ratified by AFL's Executive Council and CIO's Executive Board, to "create a single trade union center in America, through the process of merger." On July 20, 1955, the AFL-CIO Joint Unity Committee selected and approved "The American Federation of Labor and Congress of Industrial Organizations" as the name for the merger. The first joint convention to formally ratify the merger was held in December 1955.

VII

Changes in
Religion and Law

Religion and law are closely interrelated social institutions. They are deeply rooted in the mores and are particularly conservative in their cultural functions; yet they must gradually change in harmony with the mores and the other social institutions. A perspective will now be given for religion and law as institutionalized areas of behavior to show the traditional and contemporary patterns within which changes occur.

RELIGION

Religion has been an attribute of man at every stage of his cultural growth and in every period of his history. It is evident, therefore, that religion has had many phases of development. Although the actual origins of religion are unknown, it can be said that religion has developed from the crude and humble elements manifested in animism, idolism, demonism, ancestor worship, fetishism, and totemism to the transitional stages between magic and religion. As anthropologists trace these early or primitive aspects of religion, it becomes clear that religion and civilization have developed together.

In all cultural stages the aleatory element (or element of chance) is outstanding in religion—that is, man has sought protection against uncertain events or contingencies. Man has characteristically been in fear of that which is unknown and inexplicable about him, especially a supernatural and irresistible power. Through religion man makes a deliberate attempt to get into helpful social relationships with powers believed to be able to provide the satisfaction for felt needs. To achieve these ends he has devised customs, rites, symbols, scriptures, altars, temples, dogmas, creeds, churches, ceremonies, various organizations and systems, all of which are institutional devices holding together and perpetuating the ideas of a religious group.

In terms of its universal function, religion is the interpretation and control of man's relations to the forces of his physical and social environment. In primitive

287

terms, these are thought to be under the control of some supernatural power, yet in order to interpret man's relations to these forces there must be some intellectual comprehension of their nature. All religions are built upon the knowledge of the forces of the environment extant at the time of the development of the religion and upon whatever else the founders and leaders themselves may contribute to that knowledge. Evidently, then, religion results from the intellectual powers of man. Whatever the nature of the religion which has been developed, it is an expression of man's deliberate attempt to get into helpful social relationships with powers believed to be able to provide satisfaction for felt needs, to establish some measure of control over the unknown, and to get into harmony with the secret of the universe.

Something of the emergent nature of religion is suggested in its functional phases. In its simpler forms, religion is a means to secure physical comforts, gain security, and obtain a reasonable degree of peace of mind. But religion at its best is man's means of adjusting himself to his physical and social environment and to the universe; at its best, it satisfies his need of being linked up with the ultimate, the universal, and the eternal. Man's conception of these values changes with his advances in thought and experience. Religion at its best offers man the possibility of realizing his spiritual self; it is, finally, the way of a "good life." [1] Thus may be idealized a relationship between religion and progress.

This idealization of religion is not meant to imply that religion has a province of its own separate from the rest of life. On the contrary, religion is expressed concretely in the manifestations of socialized life. Religion is a social institution, the product of society, and evidence of the social emphasis in religion is seen in social service, neighborliness, and humanitarian or social ethics. While these social qualities are commendable and indispensable to society, they are not religion, nor a substitute for religion. They are religion's finest fruits in social life, not its roots. The modern emphasis on humanitarianism and social service testifies to an increasing awareness of certain religious values, though unfortunately there are elements of crassness and corruption in society which have not been brought under control.

Methods of control through religion have significance for social change. The control of individual and social behavior through intellectual powers depends upon habits, attitudes, and information, all of which are subject to change. The types of institutions, the religious ones among them, vary from time to time and from culture to culture, and the methods of exerting control differ accordingly.

Among preliterate groups of people and others somewhat more advanced in culture, various forms of control were based on superstition. As civilization evolved, the knowledge of scientists, philosophers, and political leaders supplanted superstition, and religious institutions became organized to control man's relations to social and physical forces on rational grounds.

Among many primitive peoples no sharp distinction is drawn between religious and political institutions. Not infrequently, religious institutions have developed separately from the political. In such instances, if the political and religious groups have attempted to control the same activities, each has used its own method of

---

[1] Based on interpretation by Joyce O. Hertzler, *Social Progress,* Appleton-Century-Crofts, New York, 1928, pp. 533–535.

control. An example is afforded in the religious and political control of divorce in the United States. Control over civil affairs through religious institutions has tended to weaken when other information and authority has developed, as is evident in the political realm.

Ritual and ceremony may continue in orthodox manner through long periods of time so that people may come to believe they possess inherent powers; on the other hand, differences in beliefs in rituals are evident in the numerous sects which have arisen. All religious institutions depend upon beliefs, knowledge, and training to inculcate their influence upon their members; programs of education and propaganda have been used to persuade their members to accept their doctrines and controls. Nevertheless, in some cases religious institutions have been adapted to harmonize with enlightened, rational thinking. For example, missionaries have emphasized medical service while initiating their religious work among backward peoples. No doubt Albert Schweitzer's work in Africa is the outstanding example. But even more extensively, various denominations have established and maintained hospitals and nursing service for more effective medical aid in Western countries.

Among primitive peoples, religious rituals were commonly required before undertaking hunting, fishing, agriculture, and other economic pursuits, and of course before engaging in warfare. Such practices would now be quite exceptional in the more advanced societies. It is common ritual to begin convocations and meetings of legislative assemblies and the like with prayer, and grace may be said at formal public dinners and in many private homes. For many persons, however, the formalities of prayer are associated with church services and functions. Among primitives, ritual practices of this kind were necessary not only for the welfare of the individual but for the group as a whole. Modern individualism has largely minimized feelings of group solidarity, and the importance of certain religious habits has changed. With the separation of church and state the religious institutions no longer have direct control over political and economic activities of the society in general, and the effect is also noticeable in individual behavior.

For several centuries science and religion have been said to be in conflict; instead, it is now known that the contacts between science and religion have actually been mutually advantageous. There can be no contradiction between the two. The God who reveals Himself in religion does not contradict Himself in the findings of science. Science, as a technique of understanding and using cosmic and social forces, supplements religion in a powerful way. As science has advanced it has narrowed the range of religious investigation and has tended to reduce religion to its fundamentals. Anthropology, folklore, biology, geology, and other sciences have freed religious institutions from faulty or fallacious explanations and superstitions.

In response to the controversy regarding religious and secular education, plans of cooperation have been in the making for religious institutions and public schools. In one plan, children may be dismissed from certain hours of school work provided the religious groups arrange for an effective program of religious training under the direction of trained teachers. A second plan provides that the public schools give credit for religious education taken out of school hours, even on Sundays. A third plan would provide religious training in the public schools themselves.

From the quantitative standpoint, 258 religious bodies in the United States reported having 308,647 churches and a total membership of 103,224,954 for the year ending December 31, 1956. This membership was equal to 62 per cent of the population in Continental United States, and there was a 3 per cent gain over that of the previous year. Protestant membership gained 2.9 per cent, and Roman Catholic membership gained 3.5 per cent over the totals reported for 1955.[2] These rates of annual increase exceed that of the population, which was 1.7 per cent, as computed over a fifteen-year period. In the thirty-year period from 1926 to 1956, Protestant bodies increased in membership from 31,511,701 to 60,148,980, these figures being 27.0 and 35.9 per cent of the population, respectively. During the same period, the Roman Catholic Church increased in membership from 18,605,003 to 34,563,851, these figures representing 16.0 and 20.7 per cent of the population, respectively.

A great number of private colleges and universities have been founded in the United States by religious groups representing various denominations. This type of denominational affiliation with colleges has in some instances been maintained vigorously throughout their existence, while in other cases it has gradually weakened to the point of becoming nominal. Colleges vary in their degree of orthodoxy in theology or dogma, and in their trends toward nonsectarianism in student enrollment and in their faculty membership.

Distinctive characteristics of contemporary religious organization in the United States would include the following:

1. Separation of church and state, which virtually excludes formal religious instruction in the public schools
2. Religious freedom and religious toleration
3. Diversity in forms of religious grouping—ecclesia, denominations, sects, and cults
4. Tendency of religious bodies toward local or congregational autonomy
5. Recognition of lay leadership and democratic control
6. Tendency of religious bodies to remain aloof from political struggles not directly affecting their particular interests
7. Absence of any important trend toward militant or anticlerical movements in the United States
8. Tendency of religious leaders to emphasize the perfectability of man and the possibility of human progress
9. Tendency toward secularization of beliefs, especially among the Protestant groups
10. Occurrence of doctrinal cleavages between orthodox (fundamentalist) and "liberal" Christian beliefs, also to some extent in Judaism
11. The continued influence in American life of the Protestant ethic, i.e. the idea that pursuit of individual salvation through hard work, thrift, and competitive struggle is the heart of the American achievement
12. General open approval of worldly success

[2] Latest statistics are available in *Yearbook for American Churches, for 1958,* Benson Y. Landis (ed.), National Council of the Churches of Christ in the U.S.A., New York, 1958, pp. 257–290.

13. Variance of organizational forms and activities among the local congregations within a given denomination

14. Dependence of religious organizations on formally voluntary contributions for financial support

15. Widespread evangelical activity, missionary effort, and revivalism

16. Tendency of organized religion in the United States toward conformity with, and the preservation of, the main features in the social order.[3]

The functions of religion—its special purposes or ways of satisfying man's social needs—differ according to the cultural heritages or societies and the goals of the persons and groups comprising them. Religions have more than one function, though it is possible to emphasize one of them as outstanding while comparing the traits of a religion with those of other religions. For example, a Tibetan Buddhist turns his prayer wheel and performs other religious duties to further his attainment of the bliss of Nirvana; a Christian's goal is salvation from his sins, while a Moslem's goal is a heaven of eternal delights. But the functions of religion differ not only among the many denominations at given times and places; they change with each developmental phase of a denomination or religion. Salvation in the Hindu religion depends upon which stage of its development is emphasized: if it be Brahmanism, salvation may be obtained chiefly through sacrifices performed by the Brahman priests; if it be Upanishad philosophy, the means of salvation would be one's own speculation upon a pantheistic Supreme Being; if Devotional Hinduism, through personal devotion to a personal deity. All religions that have endured through long periods of time have experienced phases of development, each of which marks something significant in cultural adjustment; and religions or denominations which have more recently come into being are likely to experience situations of competition or conflict which call for accommodation or adjustment.

The Buddhism which originated and survives in India differs from that which has developed in Tibet and other Asiatic countries; that is, Buddhism was diffused from India to other lands and also experienced modification in the new cultural context. Judaism has its orthodox and reformed aspects; various Christian denominations have their fundamentalist and liberal aspects, which indicate drifts away from conservatism. Mormonism is comparatively young as a religious sect—some observers would say it is now a denomination—but it has both conservatives and liberals within its membership. Mormonism, incidentally, has an outstanding record for its program in promoting the well-being of its members and the welfare of the community.

Religion has helped to create and integrate systems of social values defining the nature and content of social obligations. Religious values emerge as the finer essence of a culture and become identified with the social norms. Religion is deeply rooted in the mores, and this may be partly the reason why religious sanctions lend their weight to the enforcement of other institutional norms. The mores are affected all

---

[3] This enumeration has been adapted from Robin M. Williams, Jr., *American Society*, Alfred A. Knopf, Inc., New York, 1952, pp. 315–318; Winfred E. Garrison, "Characteristics of American Organized Religion," *The Annals of the American Academy of Political and Social Science*, vol. 256, pp. 14–24, March, 1948. (This issue of *The Annals* contains other articles describing and evaluating representative religious bodies in the United States.)

the time by changes in environmental conditions and societal growth and by changes in the arts; and religion, as a cultural element, has to follow the mores. The rate of change, based on changes within the mores, is characteristically slow; thus the mores and religion become a resisting inertia to change which gradually must be overcome by the force of social interests. William G. Sumner says the mores of a time are the resultant of the force of interests and the inertia of religion.[4]

Religion helps to integrate and conserve social values.[5] Integration is achieved through the power of doctrine, through the recitation of the tribal myths, through worship—which forms, integrates, and develops the religious group—and, in more advanced societies, through the dogma and the creed. Cultic acts tend to bind together and unite those animated by the same central experience; simple ceremonies and rites integrate the group, whether it is a family, clan, tribe, or nation. The cult appears to be the primary integrating factor in primitive society and the chief agent for the expression of its unity, and the same is true at higher levels of cultural development. Private and public cults symbolized the unity in the life of the city-states of the ancient oriental world—in Israel, Greece, Rome, India, China, as well as in Mexico, Peru, and elsewhere. Religious integration may function within the bounds of narrow provincialism, or if societies yield to a broader sympathy and understanding in world affairs, religious influences may work toward more integration and unity of peoples in the world at large; in fact, there is evidence that this process of integration and unification is bringing about results not only within nations but on an international plane.

On the other hand, some factors which integrate group relations in terms of common interests also work in opposite directions as divisive, disruptive, and even destructive forces. The disintegrative effects of religion are apparent in the multiplicity of sects, cults, and denominations which have not only national but international significance. The divisive and destructive effects of religion have been manifested in conflicts causing schisms in established organizations or in historic wars such as the Crusades in the Middle Ages and the Thirty Years War between the Catholics and Protestants in the seventeenth century. Such events might be thought improbable in the present century, yet the contemporary conflict between Pakistan and India is basically a product of religious and nationalistic motivation.

While religion might be thought of as the finer essence of the culture produced by a society, it should not be overlooked that some religions have justified, in connection with ceremonial occasions, prostitution, intoxication, the use of drugs, sex orgies, or other licentiousness; and religious motivation has served as the rationalization for wholesale murder and rapine against peoples conquered in war. Such negative values are gradually being weeded out by missionaries working among the backward peoples, and of course they are no longer characteristic of modern religions worthy of the name.

[4] William G. Sumner, "Religion and the Mores," *The American Journal of Sociology,* first published in 1910, and reprinted in vol. 60, no. 6, pp. 19–33, May, 1955.

[5] For general coverage of this topic, see Joachim Wach, *Sociology of Religion,* University of Chicago Press, Chicago, 1944, chap. 3. Also cf. Allan W. Eister, "Religious Institutions in Complex Societies: Difficulties in the Theoretic Specification of Functions," *American Sociological Review,* vol. 22, no. 4, pp. 387–391, August, 1957.

The closest logical relation subsists between religion and progress because both words express a process of evaluation. Religion denotes the whole-hearted reaction which a human being makes to life and to the universe in its most significant aspects. The services of religion in this evaluative respect have been so great that its decline would be an immeasurable misfortune to humanity.[6]

What is happening to religion today? The chief difference, intellectually, between the civilization of our own day and the civilization of all former times is, without question, the greater part now played by science. Modern science soon found itself in controversy with the ancient theologies. However, our concern is, not with the shopworn issue of science versus religion, but with the fact that the people of the present age are so engrossed with science that their concern with religion has been lessened, and its social functions are being questioned or being seen in a scientific perspective.

Another factor in the decline of dogmatic religion is the acceptance—throughout almost the whole Western world and much of the Eastern—of the principle of toleration or freedom of thought. There is a third dynamic factor: the moral shock of two great wars which has produced some measure of religious skepticism. For example, if a Divine Person is really existent, ever-present, ever-watchful and omnipotent, beneficent and merciful, and if "God is Love," then why are there wars?[7]

Another conception of what is happening to religion is given by Paul Tillich in his interpretation of "the lost dimension in religion."[8] Tillich says the decisive element in the predicament of Western man in our period is his loss of the dimension of depth—a phrase using scientific analogy to denote the religious dimension in man's culture. Religious depth would be indicated by one's desiring answers to such questions as: What is the meaning of life? Where do we come from, where are we going? And from the purposeful or practical standpoint, what shall we do, and what should we become in the time between birth and death? It seems that man has lost the courage to ask such questions with an infinite seriousness, as former generations did, and he has lost the courage to receive answers to these questions. Why has this change occurred?

The cause cannot properly be attributed to a more widespread impiety of man, for modern man is neither more pious nor more impious than man in any other period. Tillich says, "The loss of the dimension of depth is caused by the relation of man to his world and to himself in our period, the period in which nature is being subjected scientifically and technically to the control of man."[9] The measure of the change is seen in the fact that what Tillich calls the "horizontal dimension" is being emphasized both in scientific and in social thought. For example, man's breaking through of space which is controlled by the gravitational power of the earth

[6] Clarence Marsh Case, *Social Process and Human Progress*, Harcourt, Brace and Company, Inc., New York, 1931. See chap. 12 for development of this point of view.

[7] For development of these changing attitudes toward religion, see The Rt. Hon. the Viscount Samuel, "What Is Happening to Religion To-Day?" *The Hibbert Journal*, vol. 49, no. 3, pp. 211–217, 1951, and successive articles.

[8] Paul Tillich, "The Lost Dimension in Religion," *The Saturday Evening Post*, June 14, 1958, pp. 29 ff. These comments are merely intended to state the approach of the author, details of which are elaborated logically. A careful reading of the article is recommended.

[9] *Ibid.*

into the world-space has influenced his thinking in realms other than physics. Man himself tends to become a part of the horizontal plane; he loses his "self" and becomes a thing among things. In the process of production and consumption, he becomes not only an element, but a victim. He is no longer a free, deciding and responsible self.

But there are evidences that man has not given up in this struggle regarding the religious dimension in man's nature. Tillich shows that testimonials to this effect abound in the works of the novelist, the poet, the painter, the architect, and the philosopher. Religious leaders and laymen in various walks of life are of course being challenged by the reactions of these analysts of the dimensions of life and of religion.

Certain broadly significant aspects of social change in, or involving, religion are developed in the three selections which follow: "Religion as a Source of Creative Innovation" by Talcott Parsons, "God and the Churches" by Max Lerner, and "Our Secularist Age" by Matthew Spinka.

Talcott Parsons shows first that a major religion sets the tone of a civilization in important ways. If one looks backward to the periods of great cultural activity in ancient Greece or India or China or Judea, it becomes apparent that their great systems of cultural values were largely guided by their religions—by the state religion in Greek city-states, by Hinduism in India, by Confucianism in China, and by prophetic Judaism in Israel. In these periods religion evidently was not only a conservative force, but a source of creative innovation.

Attention is then given to two fundamental patterns in the history of Christianity —"universalism" and "activism." These qualities have been especially dynamic in shaping the culture of the West. The keynote in Christianity is doing the will of God, in spite of obstacles that may arise, by overcoming the obstacles. The universalism of ideas, morality, and "truths" is another dominant quality. Christianity's favorable attitude toward active investigation of nature has fostered the development of science. The universalism of law and of individualism, as a quality of Christianity, also works for creative innovation. Parsons objectifies these general principles by citing actual instances of cultural change which have their roots in religion.

37

RELIGION AS A SOURCE
OF CREATIVE INNOVATION*
Talcott Parsons

In most "primitive" societies, and in highly stabilized and traditionalized higher cultures, religion tends to be mainly a conservative force; it is as it were the balance wheel of the society which prevents it from departing from the established ways. So much is this the case that it is highly probable, for instance, that as Max Weber put forward cogently, the fact that a traditional priestly class did not have great social power in classical Greece was an essential condition of the great cultural creativity of the Greeks. Conversely the social ascendancy of the Brahman priestly caste in India is inseparable from the fact that Indian caste society is perhaps the most conservative large scale society the world has ever seen.

But this relationship by no means holds without exception. The very fact of the association of religion with the areas of strain and tension in human life on the deepest emotional levels means that it is likely to be one of the main areas in which responses to such situations are creative rather than traditional. But for the same reasons this creativeness is very likely to be inextricably intermingled with turmoil and many of the types of "irrational" reaction of which we have spoken above. Furthermore the most creative periods

of religious development tend also to be times of social turmoil rather than settled peace.

It is a remarkable fact that roughly the same period saw the development of Confucianism in China, of philosophical Brahmanism and the beginnings of Buddhism in India, and the prophetic movement in Judea, to say nothing of the beginnings of the great development of the classical culture in Greece of the seventh and sixth centuries B.C. which certainly had a most important religious component as well as later religious consequences. In each of these countries, furthermore, it was a period of rapid social change and considerable unsettlement. The warring feudal principalities of China were beginning the process by which eventually a great unified empire arose. India likewise was involved in many internal conflicts, in the difficult relations between the Aryans and the indigenous populations, in feudal wars, and in rivalry for social supremacy between the Brahmans and the Kshatriyas. In Judea the Israelitic Kingdom had already seen its heyday and was gravely threatened by the rising power of Mesopotamia while, finally, in Greece the little city states were maintaining a precarious existence in relation both to each

* From Talcott Parsons' essay, *Religious Perspectives of College Teaching in Sociology and Social Psychology,* originally published by the Edward W. Hazen Foundation, New Haven, Conn. (1951), pp. 29–34. Now available in Hoxie N. Fairchild (ed.), *Religious Perspectives in College Teaching,* The Ronald Press Company, New York, 1952, pp. 315–322. Reprinted by permission of The Ronald Press Company.

other and to the terrifying power of Persia to the east. It was an age of turmoil in some respects comparable to our own across the whole civilized world.

It was in this age that, largely from religious sources, the great cultural systems of values which have guided civilization ever since took their shape. Confucianism, Hinduism and Buddhism have provided the main frameworks of the way of life of the great civilizations of the Orient, with the one major exception of Islam, which came later but was in many ways intimately related to Prophetic Judaism. The Hebrew Prophets were the authors of the world's first universalistic ethical monotheism who dared to say contrary to *all* previous religious tradition that all mankind is subject to the will of a single God and that their history has meaning in terms of His great plan for the development of the world He created. Greek society created the analytical and speculative intellect of Western civilization. Christianity came some centuries later, but in many respects may be treated as a great synthesis of the Hebrew and the Greek traditions. Without the background of Prophetic Judaism there would have been no universalistic ethical monotheism. But without Greek philosophy there almost certainly would have been no rational theology in the Christian sense. Indeed some of the most distinctive features of our Western culture undoubtedly stem from these sources.

Christianity itself arose in a similar situation in which society and human values were in flux. The Jewish people were undergoing, after many experiences in foreign rule, the difficult adjustment of absorption in the Roman Empire. That the adjustment was not easy is attested by the outbreak of Jewish wars only a generation after the crucifixion of Jesus. The prevention of the absorption of the Christian movement in the community of the Jewish people, which was only settled by St. Paul, was one of the most decisive events of the history of civilization. But this could hardly have happened without the peculiar character of Roman imperial society with its extraordinary range of individualism and tolerance.

It was thus the great religious movements of the creative age of the seventh to fifth centuries B.C. which laid the foundation for the fundamental differentiations of the great civilizations for the next two thousand years, as Max Weber so clearly demonstrated in his remarkable comparative studies in the sociology of religion. Without taking the space to delineate the features of Confucianism, Hinduism and Buddhism which differentiate them and the civilizations they have influenced from Christianity and the West, perhaps a few of the distinctive features of the latter may be noted.

The pre-eminent place should, in these terms, undoubtedly go to two fundamental patterns which run through the whole history of Christianity, namely what may be called "universalism" and "activism." Both are deeply involved in the special way in which Christianity conceived the transcendental character of its God, as Creator and Ruler of the world, standing outside and above it, not as an immanent principle of order in the universe, a conception which, with variations, underlies all the great oriental religions.

Activism means essentially that man's goals and values are conceived not primarily as concerned with adaptation to or escape from a given set of physical and social conditions, but with mastery over them. The prototype of the first attitude is found in Confucianism, with its orientation of the organization of a stable social order, sanctioned by a completely stable religion; that of the second is the great mystical religious orientation, the mystical absorption in "nature" of the Taoist, the escape from the Wheel of Karma of the Hindu mystic, or the Nirvana of the Buddhist.

In Christianity, on the other hand, the keynote through all its various forms is doing the will of God in spite of the obstacles presented in the situation, by *overcoming* the obstacles. This may mean, as in early Christian asceticism and of course later, mastery over the flesh without further reference to life on this earth. But this drastic individualism soon gave way to the conception of a more extensive Christian ideal. The mediaeval conception still retained the view that the Christian society existed to prepare souls for the after life; but with what Weber called the "ascetic" branches of Protestantism, notably Calvinism and its derivatives, there emerged the direct conception of the Kingdom of God on Earth, which it was the duty of man to create by Divine ordinance. This whole idea of mastery, then, has oriented man to the control of the world in which he lives as distinct from a fatalistic "acceptance" of things as they are. Such acceptance has of course appeared from time to time in Christian societies and groups, but has never been the dominant keynote to anything like the extent it has been in the Orient. Furthermore, though we have undergone a high degree of secularization, even our secularism is active rather than passive. It is not "floating along on the stream of life," but is an attempt to make over the world by active intervention, in the service of human goals; it is an attempt to create the "good society."

Universalism, as the second dominant strain, is closely connected with activism. Its roots lie in the conception of the universal and only true God of the Prophets and the intelligible world as conceived by the Greek intellect. Neither ideas nor morality can be relative to the particular time and place and social group. There must be universal truths, which are as true for the "heathen Chinee" as they are for any Christian group. And the moral good cannot be defined in terms only of what is good for others, as distinguished from good for me, but the same principles must apply impartially to all men, with allowance for difference of circumstance of course, but nevertheless in principle to all. The enormous significance of this universalistic strain in Western civilization is one of the principal themes of the modern social sciences. And there can be little doubt that without Christianity it could scarcely have developed.

Three fields of application of these two major strains of the Christian tradition may be mentioned. First is the very notable fact that, in spite of the prominence of the "warfare of science and religion," it is only in the Western world that science itself has developed to a really high degree. Beginnings there are elsewhere, but in no case, except for a few specialties, beyond the level attained by the classical Greeks. Many Christians certainly have grave misgivings about where the development of science is leading us. But science is most assuredly a fully legitimate child of Christianity (which, however, is only *one* of its "parents"). It is the *active* and not merely the receptive search for truth. Nature is not merely observed, it is *investigated,* nature is "forced to give up her secrets," not merely contemplated. Man, precisely because he is conceived to be made "in the image of God" is endowed with reason which he is meant to use actively to understand. In Puritanism this strain reached a high culmination in giving direct religious sanction to the great development of physical science of the 17th century. The keynote was that the scientist could come to know God through His Works. The place of universalism in science is too fundamental and obvious to need special comment.

A second fundamental direction of Christian influence is in the field of the universalism of law. This of course was foreshadowed by the great development of Roman law, in part a child of Greek thought, notably that of the Stoics. But after the decline of Rome law in the Western World had sunk to the level of a completely tribal pluralism, there was one law for Goth and another for Frank and so on. It is no matter of chance that it was in the Canon Law of the Church that Roman Law was preserved, and that the great development of mediaeval civilization as a whole soon came to include the revival of Roman Civil Law and the gradual creation of universalistic systems of law. Had a particularistic rather than a universalistic religion dominated Mediaeval

Europe there is little doubt that Roman Law would never have been revived and English Common Law never created.

Finally, we are all aware that there is a fundamental strain of universalistic individualism in Christianity. Each human being has an immortal soul, all of the same religious worth. Though many branches of Christianity have made drastic concessions to social inequality reaching far beyond the minimum needs of a functioning society, generally on the plea that equality applied only to the spiritual realm, there is little doubt of the fundamental character of the contribution of Christianity to the egalitarian strain of modern Western civilization; the most dramatic contrast of course is the religious sanction of caste in Hinduism, the most radical conception of human inequality to be found anywhere. The relation to the conception of the dignity of the human individual, and his right to a fair chance to make his contribution to the life of society and to live his own life independently, is patent.

It should not be assumed that the above argument about the very great influence of religious traditions constitutes a theory of "religious determinism" set over against some version of "economic determinism." There seems to us to be no justification for any simple "single dominant factor" theory of social change. The religious movements we have spoken of were not "immaculately conceived" without roots in all the complex social and psychological forces which influence human action. *Of course* the emergence of Christianity was *in part* economically de-

termined; for example, it is well known that most of its early adherents were the "little men" of the urban communities. That it appealed neither to the rural populations (the "pagans") nor to the upper classes, is partly a function of the economic interests of those groups. It was also dependent for peace and order, and for its opportunity to spread on the political and legal structure of the Roman Empire which was in no sense predominantly a "religious factor." But demonstration of the importance of these things in no way refutes the claim of the importance of creative innovation in the sphere of religious orientation itself. Economic and other "conditions" limit the incidence of a religious movement, for example, they favor or hinder it, but that is a very different matter from "creating" it. Similarly in the course of its very complex history the various developments within Christianity have been intimately dependent on nonreligious features of the situation of the time. It seems to be well attested that Luther's success could not have occurred without support from the secular interests of the German Princes on whom he relied. And could the branches of Protestantism which have flourished in America have had their enormous influence if the little colonies had not had a continent over which to spread? Suppose the French had wrested the control of the seas from Britain a hundred and fifty years ago? With North America under French control from the Alleghanies west, what would the religious complexion of this continent have been? A glance at the Province of Quebec is of some significance to the answer.

Is America a religious culture, or is it a secular culture? Max Lerner explores the implications of this question and notes that both aspects can be answered affirmatively. The American religious heritage was a mixture of theocracy and secularism, of dogma and indifferentism. Religion has lost a good deal of its former hold on the American character and no longer pervades daily living as it once did; nevertheless, religion plays more than a surface part in the conduct of American government and life in general. Lerner notes, among other characteristics, that Americans have been salvation-minded, each believer being engrossed in his relation, not to the church, but to God, in Whom he was to find salvation; yet they have also formed a secular ᴧather than a sacred or hieratic society. The conflict between secular social goals and the religious conscience definitely has colored both the religious and the democratic experience of America. In this manner Lerner explains the interrelated religious and secular elements in American culture, tracing in broad terms the development from colonial times to the present.

38

GOD AND THE CHURCHES*
Max Lerner

Is America a religious culture, shaped by men who sought freedom of worship, with God constantly present in their minds even when the Church has become formalized? Or is it a secular culture, with a "wall of separation" between Church and State, and with religion playing only a marginal role in men's daily lives? Each of these questions can be answered affirmatively, which indicates how deeply the religious ambiguity cuts into American culture. America is as secular as a culture can be where religion has played an important role in its origins and early growth and has been intertwined with the founding and meaning of the society. It is also as religious as a culture can be whose life goals are worldly and whose daily strivings revolve not around God but around man.

De Tocqueville rightly underscored the strong religious base of American life and thought, both in the older Puritan communities of New England and in the new frontier states. The Calvinist doctrine of predestination, which played a dominant role in the early colonies, was a hard and bleak doctrine fitting the mood of communities founded on the "challenge of hard ground." It called for ascetic living, but its asceticism

became part of the secular world rather than the religious and led to an activism which left its mark on American history. Similarly, the earlier intolerance felt by men who had an inner sense of loneliness as they waited for a sign of God's grace was in time replaced by the doctrine of toleration.

This mixture of theocracy and secularism, of dogma and indifferentism, is one of the striking features of the American religious heritage. One finds a clue to it by noting the difference of religious climate at each important stage of American history. The colonies were settled under the stress of religious revolt, in an age of creative religious feeling; American freedom was won at the end of the eighteenth century in an age of Deism and revolutionary freethinking; the major growth of America took place during the century which followed the Jeffersonian era and which was strongly marked by scientific rationalism; in the contemporary Atomic Age there has been a revival of religious feeling under the stress of social tensions and personal insecurity. This mixture of seventeenth-century Calvinism, eighteenth-century Deism, nineteenth-century rationalism, and mid-twentieth-century anxiety may help ex-

* From *America as a Civilization*, Simon and Schuster, Inc., New York, 1957, pp. 703–717. Copyright 1957, by Max Lerner. Reprinted by permission of Simon and Schuster, Inc., publishers.

plain some of the contradictions in the relations between God and man in America.

Religion has lost a good deal of its former hold on the American character and no longer pervades the daily content of living as it once did. Yet we must not underestimate the hold it still has. While there was an atheist strain in the writings of Tom Paine, and while atheism is still protected by Supreme Court decisions, there is less and less room for the "godless" in America, since godlessness is usually associated with Communism and depravity. America is regarded as a "Christian country," with an emphasis on "Christian" that carries it beyond the tolerant deism of the Founding Fathers who wrote of "Nature's God" with an inclusive anthropological sweep. There is no candidate for even minor political office in America today who would dare to mock religion or alienate any of the denominations. In every major speech a President is likely to include what Franklin Roosevelt used to call the "God stuff."

Yet religion plays more than a surface part in the conduct of American government. Woodrow Wilson was a Presbyterian, Franklin Roosevelt an Episcopalian, Harry Truman a Baptist, and Dwight Eisenhower grew up in Kansas among the mushrooming religious sects of the frontier, although he turned to Presbyterianism on the threshold of the White House. Examine the Presidential tenure of each and you will find features of it illumined by the particular kind of religious training he received. The religious ambiguity of American politics is further shown by the fact that every President (and Vice-President) has belonged to one of the Protestant sects, yet few pay much attention to the particular sect to which he belongs.

As the child of the Reformation, Americans took over not only its dominantly Protestant heritage but also its deep individualistic strain. Every European sect that found itself constricted or in trouble emigrated to the New World, which thus became a repository of all the distillations of Reformation thought and feeling. Since the Reformation had broken with the authority of the Church

and left to the individual the meaning of the Scriptures, America became a congeries of judging individuals, each of them weighing the meaning and application of the Word. A Bible-reading people emerged, drenched in the tradition of the Old and New Testaments. This may help explain the stress on the idea of "convenant" in American thought, which Helmut Richard Niebuhr has noted. It also suggests why a people so concerned with the meaning of the Holy Writ has been the first to give a sacred character to a written Constitution but has at the same time remained a nation of amateur interpreters of the Constitution.

Two basic concepts of the Christian belief —the soul and sin—took on a new emphasis in individualist America. Each man was the judge of his own religious convictions, since his possession of an immortal soul gave each man an inner worth regardless of color, rank or station, political belief, wealth or poverty. Thus the foundation was laid in religious freedom for a political equalitarianism which no later history of privilege has been able wholly to extirpate from the American mind. But if each man had an immortal soul to save, it was because it had been steeped in sin. As a Bible-reading people, the Americans took over many of the preconceptions of the Hebraic society in which Judaism and early Christianity were rooted. Among them was the sense of individual—aside from original, or inevitable—sin, without which there could be no individual salvation.

There is a resulting ambiguity between the sin-and-salvation strain in Christian doctrine and the organic optimism of American economic and social attitudes. The Hebrew prophets, as they lamented the disintegration of Biblical society, called on each Jew to ward off God's wrath from his people by cleansing himself of his own inner guilt; the Christian allegory added to the somberness of this conception. But there have been few occasions on which Americans could believe with any conviction in an impending collapse of their social structure and their world. The sense of sin and the sense of doom were therefore importations from the Old and New Testament that somehow flowered in the American soil in spite of the worship of money and success—or perhaps exactly because of this worship, which required a compensating doctrine to ease the conscience.

The result has been an American religious tradition which is at once deeply individualist, anti-authoritarian, concerned with sin and salvation, yet secular and rationalist in its life goals, Bible-reading in its habits, with its emphasis on man's relation to his own conscience and therefore to his private religious judgment. The Americans have been salvation-minded, each believer being engrossed in his relation not to the church but to God, in Whom he was to find salvation; yet they have also formed a secular rather than a sacred or hieratic society. Since they were believing and judging individuals, they did not lean on a priesthood: even their churches were based less on the authority of a hierarchy than on lay presbyters or the congregation itself.

This conflict between secular social goals and the religious conscience has colored both the religious and the democratic experience of America. It underlay the agonized conscience of early New England, the preoccupation with God's way with man in good and evil which characterized American Fundamentalism, the fear-drenched frontier religion filled with literal-minded terrors, the Social Gospel movement; and it will be found in the latter-day movement of neo-Calvinist religious thought, with its Atomic Age setting of apocalyptic guilt and terror. For all its optimism and its cult of action and success, American culture has been overlaid with a sense of both agony and evil.

America owes much of the effectiveness of its democracy, as well as much of its dynamism, to this strain in its religious experience. I am suggesting that the fiber necessary for democracy is not the product of any particular religious doctrine but of the lonely debate within the free conscience. Democracy is the polity of individual choices and of majority consent; it can be run effectively only where there is a habituation to hard choices. Those who are certain of the simplicity of revealed truth make the initial choice of submission and do not have to make any subsequent choices; they do not furnish a fertile soil for the democratic seed. Those who expect miracles will not take the risk of dissent. Those who are sure of dogma given to them will not make the arduous effort of winning the slow and gradual victories of an always unfinished society. Finally those who suffer no conflict within the arena of their own minds will not generate the needed dynamism to transcend the conflict and resolve their conscience.

American democracy, in the sense that it is linked with private judgment and freedom of dissent, is thus also linked with the stir and turmoil of free religious choice. To be sure, the psychic toll of this conflict and dynamism is a heavy one. But the stakes have been great—nothing less than the creation and sustaining of an open society which is based on the judging and choosing individual caught on the battleground of his own mind.

In an era when the threat to democracy is conformism of mind and stereotyping of character, one of the great counterforces is the traditional American religious nonconformism. This nonconformism had its roots, as Arthur G. Parker has put it, in "a religiously inflexible New England, with its mores forged upon the anvil of Jeremiah by the sledge of Calvin." Something of the dark intensity of this religious commitment has persisted in America until the present day. It gave American history some of its Calvinist dourness from the time of the Mathers and Jonathan Edwards to the current revivalists whose chief stock in trade is still hell-fire and brimstone. For all its optimism and its cult of action and success, American history has been overlaid with a brooding sense of agony and evil. One finds it in Hawthorne, Melville, and Poe, as also in Mark Twain and Henry James, Thomas Wolfe and Faulkner. While this strain persists, there is less danger of the flattening out of personality and of a herd-mindedness in opinion.

It is here that American religious Fundamentalism has its roots. The brand of Christianity that the earlier Americans took to their hearts was not the mildness of Jesus's teachings or the doctrine of brotherly love, but the probing of man's relation to good and evil and of God's ways to men. In the mid-eighteenth century, as Perry Miller pointed out, a deeper shadow came over American Puritanism. It remained during the century and more of frontier expansion, forming a frontier religion of the Right Way, filled with literal-minded terrors, with swift rewards and stern punishments. Its basic image was that of life as a hard pilgrimage pursued by temptations and dangers, an unrelenting quest beset with trials and testing. Much of this view has survived even into the contemporary era of diluted and sophisticated religion. Its continuing strength suggests that it fulfills a function—that of keeping alive a ferment of enthusiasm within individuals surrounded by collapsing moral standards, who face denials and frustrations in their own lives. Sometimes, as in the case of the religion of the American Negroes, there is a quality in their religious expression akin to the simplicity and creativeness of the primitive Christian church in its catacomb days. But in many other instances of enthusiastic religion the fervor lacks creativeness and represents a mechanical reassertion of faith in the face of inner fears and emptiness.

One of the striking facts about American history has been the linkage of the "religion of the fathers" with what Mencken delighted to call the "Bible Belt" mentality—a narrow view of life and morals, a belief in the literal inspiration of the Bible, and a reactionary code of political belief. The passion of the "Hot Gospel" and the archaism of the hellfire-and-damnation religion have been put to work as a counterforce to the inherent humanism of the Christian teachings. It has enabled a number of demagogues, especially in the rural Midwest and South, to clothe their racist and reactionary appeals in Biblical references. In the big cities the tradition of Charles G. Finney and Dwight L. Moody

was continued with modern publicity techniques by Billy Sunday, Aimee MacPherson, and Billy Graham. They were evidences of how broad is the gulf in American religion between the loudly committed and the deeply committed. Unlike Puritanism, which with all its excesses embodied an internalized religious conviction—the product of people who wrestled with God as Jacob did—the current evangelism is a form of religiosity externalized in a public spectacle.

The question here is not one of "liberalism" and "conservativism," whether in religion or politics, but of the inner relations between religious attitudes and democracy. There is a curious example in the Populist political movements in the South and Midwest, in which the stress on saving one's soul and preserving religious orthodoxy was linked with an anticapitalist radicalism. The type-figures were William Jennings Bryan and Tom Watson. In them a crusading Populism was fused with a harsh Catonian moralism. The common element was the need for the salvation of the believer from the wickedness of the Cities of the Plain where both wealth and freethinking accumulate. The anticorporate strand was thus intertwined with the moralistic, and Bryan's famous Cross of Gold speech was in direct line with the crusade for Prohibition and the Scopes anti-Evolution "monkey" trial. In its characteristic latter-day form this amalgam has lost its anticorporate militancy, replaced by an antilabor, anti-Negro, and anti-Jewish emphasis. Thus in these areas religious Fundamentalism has damned minority groups along with the urban liberal intellectuals who are vaguely felt to be undermining the tribal traditions.

I take another example from the relation of Christian ideals to the American business spirit. Modern Protestantism and the modern business spirit were born out of the same historical soil. The real problem for religion came with the harshness of the acquisitive spirit. Confronted with this, the churches too often faltered, and instead of challenging business enterprise they emulated its premises, investing business power with religious sanctions. In the case of figures like Dwight Moody, Sam Jones, and Billy Sunday, Christian exhortation either became an apology for the acquisitive and competitive or gave religious confirmation to the caste system in race relations and to the status quo in industrial relations. This approach came to be vulgarized to the point where one writer depicted Jesus (*The Man Nobody Knows*) as the Great Salesman, and the campaigns for the revival of religious faith were mapped out with salesmanship strategy. In the hands of such men religion became conventionalized, status-fulfilling, and smug.

Yet, having said this, one must add to this phase of American church history the Social Gospel phase, given impetus by Washington Gladden and Walter Rauschenbusch, which dedicated the churches to a militant role in economic and social reform. Some of the best energies of the denominations, including the Methodists, Presbyterians, and Baptists—the three sects which also made the greatest headway on the frontier—were turned toward the new pathways of social action in the spirit of a Jesus who had given himself to the poor and been denounced as agitator and revolutionary. In this spirit some of the pastors of every denomination have fought for racial equality and economic justice and have explored settlement work, adult education, and psychiatric pastoral counseling. Wherever this has happened, whether with Catholics, Protestants, or Jews, it has been attacked as a secularizing of religion. It is true that it has turned the main stress of religious energy away from the supernatural to the social, from transcending the human to the serving of human needs. It is also true that such a humanist emphasis has in many instances become theologically thin. It is easy for sophisticates to deride religious liberalism, to caricature the sermon-turned-book-review, to depict the wrestling of the spirit with God in the form of the muscular Christianity of young men in the YMCA gymnasium or in the sports activities of settlement work. Yet it has served the function of making religion a living part of the needs of the people and keep-ing it militantly alert to the furthermost stretches of social possibility.

A reaction has, however, set in against this humanist emphasis. Increasingly the young American intellectuals have been turning not to a social religion but to a new theological intensity which is at once radically pessimist in its premises about human nature and social possibility, and also a return to some of the old Calvinist themes. Theologians like Paul Tillich and Reinhold Niebuhr, while affirming a deep interest in contemporary social struggles, put their chief stress on the corruption of the human enterprise, the limits of human will and action, the difficulties of spiritual growth as well as of social struggle in the process of history, and the heroism called for in the "courage to be."

But the crucial division in American religion is not between fundamentalists and modernists, or between liberals and neo-Calvinists. It is between active and passive belief, between those for whom religion is commitment and those for whom it is lip service or conformist respectability. The Social Gospel and the new Calvinism have at least one trait in common—that of seeking to bring vitality once again to the religious commitment. Both feel the difficulty of the human situation and the unremitting arduousness of the struggle for belief. The enemies of both are smugness, apathy, an easy optimism, and a short-cut conformism. The introspective religion flourishes best where man feels isolated, struggling against the eidola of secular society. The early America, with its lonely frontier communities torn up from their European roots, furnished such a soil. But when American society came into the full swing of prosperity and became itself a great artifact with numberless institutional relationships, the lonely meeting of man and God became more difficult.

Much the same can be said of prophetic religion. Prophecy is the product and sign of social failure, and in the American myths there is no room for failure. Even the mid-nineteenth-century sects which used to forecast the doom of the world at an appointed time could not survive the ridicule of their contemporaries when the time of doom came and the end was not yet. The voice of ridicule was the voice of a culture built on boundless hope and optimism. Even the Fourierist and other Utopian communities of the nineteenth century were the product of millennialism rather than of social despair. Everything in America has seemed to conspire against pessimistic and other-worldly religions. It is hard to talk of the mysteries of Nature where science exploits it, or of compassion in a culture that flees failure, or of humility in an imperial culture that makes an idol out of wealth and power. It is hard to see how a religion of poverty can strike continuing root in the richest civilization of the world, or a religion of denial in one of the most Byzantine.

How then account for the strong pulsation in America today toward a religion which is imbued with a sense of the corruption and weakness of human institutions, and which is once again ridden with pessimism? I suggest that the revival of this impulse comes in an age of anxiety and alienation, when Americans are disillusioned with the idea of automatic progress, when the world struggle and the menace of atomic doom have become pressing anxieties, and when optimism, liberalism, and modernism have come under suspicion. But while this new mood has led some of the best elements in the churches toward new depths of religious feeling, it is part of the dilemma that history presents to American religion. The religion-creating capacity, as witness the great period in the Middle East at the time of the Roman Empire, depends on social failure and catastrophe, while the open society depends on prosperity and peace. To put it another way, the creative soil for religion is social anxiety, which may be the product or the harbinger of democratic failure.

I do not believe that such a sense of failure is likely to thrive long in the American cultural setting. The cultural strains that have given America its power and greatness are those of dynamism rather than despair. Perhaps a new religion will someday emerge from some impending world catastrophe as the religions of the Orient emerged from the collapse of the Greek and Roman worlds. But short of such an apocalyptic vision the American religious future is likely to grow out of the American past, whose chief features have been social optimism, dynamism, and a continuing equilibrium between the conflicting pulls and tensions of American society.

This may offer a clue to the creativeness of the American religious experience. It differs from the religion-creating genius which showed itself in Asia and the Middle East. Its striking characteristic lies in the luxuriant growth of religious denominations splitting off from each other amoeba-wise. Pluralist in so many other phases, the American culture is supremely pluralist in religion. Staying mainly within the broad frame of historic Christianity, Americans have explored new ways of life in new communities (from the Shakers to Father Divine) or proclaimed new particular insights (as with the Mormons, Christian Scientists, Jehovah's Witnesses) or fragmented a denomination into cults and sects. Nowhere else could William James's *Varieties of Religious Experience* have been so congenial to the cultural temper. Nowhere else did the tradition of religious dissent lead to such a spread of denominational forms—not only the broad religious divisions of Protestants, Catholics, and Jews, but also Episcopalians, Presbyterians, Methodists, Baptists, Congregationalists, Unitarians, Friends, Lutherans, Moravians, Christian Brethren, Christian Scientists, Jehovah's Witnesses, Seventh-Day Adventists, Disciples of Christ, Mormons, and the adherents of The Church of God with Signs Following After.

These sects have been derided because they split what might have been religious unity and cast themselves out of the "Eden of infallibility." Yet to attack them for this is to ask America to be other than it is, not only in religion but in every phase of its life. For the pluralism of the American churches is like the pluralism of America's regions, its diverse economic forms, its political localism, its ethnic and immigrant stocks. It is closely linked with religious freedom which, as Madison put it at the Virginia Convention of 1788, "rises from the multiplicity of sects which pervades America and which is the best and only security for religious liberty in any society." The competition of creeds has prevented Americans from erecting intolerance into a principle of government.

There is perhaps less meaning than meets the eye in the figures on the growth of American church membership. It is estimated that, as of 1954, there were ninety-seven million church members (of whom fifty-seven million were Protestant, thirty-two million Catholic, five million Jewish, the rest scattered) comprising over 60 per cent of the population, a larger percentage of the total population than at any time in the past century. This represents a "return to religion" of some sort, but what sort is far from clear. It could mean a new groping for faith as a compensation for the ugliness and danger of life. Or it might mean that in most American communities church membership is a badge of social status, and that membership in them represents safety in a conformist, churchgoing society. Clearly the traditional social nonconformism has been giving way to a conformism which accepts the power structures either as a positive good or as an evil which it would be futile to resist. It is not that the churches practice a conscious hypocrisy about Christian teachings but rather that religious doctrines have been turned into counters in a game men play to bring their consciences to terms with their universe. It is less a question of what the pastors say than the fact that they are no longer listened to; having lost the capacity for belief, they have lost also the power to instill belief.

On the question of the relation of the churches to the class composition of their membership there have been some recent changes of note. On the whole the Protestants and Jews are more strongly represented in the upper and middle classes, while the Catholics draw more heavily upon the lower-income groups, especially among organized workers. Nevertheless the strength of Protestants in the lower class has been growing, especially since World War II. Of the Protestant sects the Methodists, Baptists, and Lutherans have their heaviest membership in the lower class and are lightly represented in the upper class, while the Presbyterians, Episcopalians, and Congregationalists show a higher proportion in the upper class and a considerably lighter one in the lower class. Yet these figures should not obscure the fact that Protestants and Jews, especially the latter, are largely middle-class groups and most typically come from business and the professions and from the white-collar and service strata of the population. The Protestants and Jews also draw from a higher educational level than the Catholics.

The church affiliations of the American Negro offer a special case. The available figures are at least a decade old (most of them come from the year 1946) and there are considerable differences between the figures given in the studies by Liston Pope and William W. Sweet; yet the main outlines of the profile of membership are fairly clear. Sweet estimates that 70 per cent of the fourteen million Negroes in 1946 belonged to churches—a higher percentage than whites. Of the nine and a half million Negro church members, more than eight million were Baptists or Methodists (Pope's figures are six million out of the almost seven million Negro church members). The studies agree that only a small fraction of the Negroes are Catholic (the number has been growing rapidly in the past decade) and, of the Protestants, only a small fraction belong to the predominantly white denominations. The striking fact about Negro church membership is the heavy emphasis upon the all-Negro denominations. This is partly due to the force of white discrimination and partly to the Negro's own desire to control the organization of his church, in which he has found the freest expression of his leadership and his emotional life. The latter fact does not relieve the white churches of their responsibility for religious jim-crowing. The estimate is that less than 1 per cent of the white congregations have any Negro members —usually only a handful—and less than one half of one per cent of the Negroes who belong to these congregations worship regularly with them.

There remains the question of the non-churchgoer and his religious outlook. If 40 per cent of the American population are not claimed as members by any of the denominations, this comes to some seventy million people: taking into account the exaggerated claims of a number of the churches, the figure is probably considerably higher. It does not follow that they do not have religious beliefs. Abraham Lincoln refused to belong to any particular church, yet he was a deeply religious man. No doubt some of the number are atheists, a good many are agnostics, many are indifferent, many are puzzled, many may feel themselves too poor to afford church membership and its social obligations, and still others prefer to keep their religious beliefs to themselves instead of joining a church and worshiping in common with others. Since Americans are, as I have pointed out, a nation of "joiners," the substantial percentage which has stayed out of the life of the church is all the more striking. There is a current tendency to emphasize church membership, which is bound to put pressure upon the nonmembers and reduce their numbers. But it remains true that one of the articles of the democratic belief in America is the disbelief in any state church or any equation between membership in a church and membership in the American commonwealth. This distinction is crucial to the idea of religious freedom as Americans have practiced it.

The issue of religious freedom in America thus goes beyond discrimination and also beyond the pluralism of the sects, to the core principle of the separation of church and state, as embodied in the constitutional prohibition against any "establishment of religion." Given the experience of Europe as well as that of the early Puritan settlers, the generation of Madison's famous *Remonstrance* saw that an official recognition of a "religious establishment" would hamper religious freedom.

There are some polemicists who ask whether a democracy can remain indifferent to religion when its deepest faith is based on religious premises. One might answer that the official religious neutrality of the government does not imply the personal religious indifference of its members. An American President, Senator, or Supreme Court Justice may have his own explicit religious views, including President Lincoln as Protestant, Senator Lehman as Jew, or Justice Frank Murphy as Catholic. But each knew that unless he refrained from using his official power to propagate the strength of his creed, all the creeds would become entangled in a murderous war.

As Justice Rutledge stated clearly, there is a double price Americans pay for religious liberty: one is the self-restraint of the government in noninterference with a man's creed; the other is the ban on the use of governmental machinery by or for any church. That is why the Supreme Court has tried carefully to draw a line of distinction between valid aid to parochial and public schools and the kind that violates the principle of separation. Another problem that confronted the Court involved the sect of the Jehovah's Witnesses, against which a number of local ordinances were directed on the ground that house-to-house visits for the sale of their religious literature created a nuisance. The Court majority ruled against the ordinances, seeing more in these cases than the importunings of a minor religious sect—nothing less than a central principle of American religious freedom.

No creeds have had better occasion to profit from this principle than the Catholics and the Jews, living among a Protestant majority. Swelled by a great immigration from the 1840s to the 1920s, the Catholic population grew from fewer than two million in

1850 to thirty-two million in 1954. Despite some anti-Catholic movements of bigotry, they have grown in popular acceptance, community importance, and power. Nowhere in a non-Catholic society do they enjoy the freedom and prestige they have in America. The same is true of the roughly five million Jews, who—despite sporadic anti-Semitic outbursts—have flourished in the climate of American religious freedom and economic opportunity. It may be noted that no other Catholic community contributes as much to the Vatican world position as do the American Catholics, and that the American Jews form one of the two polar centers (the other being Israel) of the Jewish world community.

In fact, while America is still dominantly Protestant, it can no longer be described as a primarily Protestant culture with Catholic and Jewish minorities: it is close to becoming (in Will Herberg's phrase) a three-religion culture. One might predict that in the latter half of the twentieth century these three religious groupings will harden rather than dissolve. They are becoming increasingly self-contained. There is, for example, greater mobility within the class system in America than among the three religions; to put it another way, an American (especially if he is a Catholic or a Jew) is less likely to marry outside his religion than outside his class. The Catholics are critical of intermarriage, pointing out that Catholics who marry outside their faith are likely to abandon that faith. The Jews, anxious to maintain their identity in the face of world hostility, have also strengthened their resistance to intermarriage. The Protestants, less unified in organization and in religious consciousness, have been slower to join this trend. It is in American politics that the trend toward a three-religion society is most clearly reflected: in a city like New York, for example, the political slates of candidates are likely to be carefully composed of representatives of the three major faiths, and as much care is given to the ingredients of this political-religious recipe as to any recipe of a gourmet—and deviation from it is as sensitively noted.

In the days of the great migrations from Europe, the immigrants brought with them to America their own religious denominational beliefs, along with their language and customs. It was part of the American creed of freedom that while the immigrant was to assimilate "Americanism" in all other respects, he was expected to keep his religious separateness. The second generation often moved away from this religious heritage, and the third and later generations have returned to it—but in a different form. Again a phrase Herberg uses (taken from a study of intermarriage in New Haven by Ruby Jo Kennedy) is illuminating: that the descendants of the immigrants have fused their religious beliefs in a "triple melting pot." For the new generations it is important to be a Protestant, a Catholic, or a Jew "as the specific way, and increasingly perhaps as the only way, of being an American and locating oneself in American society."

This becomes then a new kind of secularism —not outside the churches, as with the seventy million Americans who are nonmembers of any denomination, but inside the churches. The best illustration of this trend is the recent movement to introduce religious teaching into the schools in the form of a stress on "spiritual values." While some Americans, alert to the danger of the erosion of the "wall of separation," have regarded this as a dangerous offensive by the religious vested interests, it may also be seen as a sign of the flattening out of religious belief. This flattening out takes the form of the conviction that religious faith is somehow "a good thing." Or, as President Eisenhower has put it, "our form of government has no sense unless it is founded in a deeply felt religious faith, and I don't care what it is."

It was part of the disquiet and disorder of the era of anxiety that Americans should be seeking some inner link between religion and democracy. One may cite the characteristic intellectual pilgrimage of Russell Davenport, who first sought the meaning of life in the "permanent revolution" of the American free economy, then tried to link it with a Republican political renaissance under Wendell

Willkie, and finally left as his testament an unfinished manuscript asserting that the future of democracy and of the "dignity of man" lies in charting the still uncharted and non-rational elements of religious faith. It might be truer to say, however, that instead of finding their democratic faith in supernatural religion, Americans have tended to find their religious faith in various forms of belief about their own existence as a people. The deepest element of Lincoln's faith, as Edmund Wilson has pointed out, lay in a religious *mystique* of the national Union. If Americans have been turning toward the vague phrases about "spiritual values," it may be because their existence as a unified people is no longer threatened as it was in Lincoln's day.

There is little doubt that the American religious community is linked with democracy, but the linkage is less through "spiritual values" than in the fact of America as an open religious society. What is most striking about it in this sense is the fact that, with its multiplicity of faiths speaking as with a confusion of tongues, there have been no religious wars or massacres. You will find in American history few of those blood-encrusted crimes which in world history have been committed in the name of the only true God and the only true religious way. No other civilization offers a parallel in this respect. There has been marked bitterness between Catholics and Protestants in the struggle for political power, and between the Jews and both of them in economic rivalries. But the principle of the open society, with its rapid class mobility, its religious intermarriage, its respect for the right of religious dissent, has proved a dissolvent force both for bigotries and hostilities.

By the same token it has been corrosive not only of bigotry but also of religious intensity. An example may be cited in what has happened to the religion of American Negroes, whose church affiliations I have already discussed. It has been said that the real inheritors of the creative Christian tradition were not the Protestant descendants of the Calvinists or the powerful Catholic church but the humble and despised Negroes. To them fell the role of continuing the dynamism of frontier religion. Toynbee has written eloquently of the primitive Christianity of the American Negro as one of the few strong growths of spontaneous Christian faith in a "post-Christian era." But as the social lot of the Negroes has improved, their characteristic religion—with its buoyancy, tragedy, and myth-making imaginativeness—has been diluted. With prosperity and a measure of equality has come respectability. Today the middle-class Negro finds himself increasingly caught in the same churchgoing middle class as the white.

A note may be in order on the relation of religion and the economy. The historians of Protestant societies have stressed the doctrine of vocation and its carry-over from religious to secular uses. Given the history of American democracy, one should add another aspect —the inner relation between religious pluralism and a pluralist economy. What both have in common is the process of decision-making through the exercise of private judgment. The free-market economy, as Karl Polanyi has shown, was alien to the ethos and psychology of medieval Europe. It carried in its wake some devastating social irresponsibilities for the human costs of industrialism. But what we have not seen until recently is that the decentralized decisions involved in capitalism put the burden of decision-making on numberless individuals. True, the growth of monopoly has diminished the scope of this, but in great measure it still applies. I do not say that every small businessman or corporate manager or highly skilled worker carries the moral burden of the decision-making well. In many instances he does not. But I do say that a society in which he ceases even to make the attempt is a society in which the habit of decision-making in moral and political terms becomes also constricted. It is a striking fact that the same societies which have maintained a decentralized choice in religion have tended to maintain it also in the economy and in politics.

To those who believe, finally, that it is the religious metaphysic which alone has made American democracy possible and held it together, I would enter a qualification. It is the dissenting pluralist tradition in religion, rather than the religious orientation as such, which has been most strongly linked with American democracy. Religious dissent has carried along with it the tradition of political dissent. It has fostered the democratic idea mainly through its stress on the right of the individual to face and master his own solitariness, according to his own lights. Thus Americans have managed to remain largely a believing people (far more than has been true of other industrial cultures) without the compulsion of imposing their religious beliefs on others—or of imposing *any* religious beliefs, although they hope plaintively that every American will have a set of "spiritual values."

What is the nature of this age of secularism, as it is generally understood? Matthew Spinka sets out to describe it for us. In its essence this secularism is either religious indifference or practical atheism. Although in some instances it has been manifested in militant attack upon religion in either its theological or its ecclesiastical forms, there is also another important aspect—an almost unconscious exclusion from thought or life of all religious concern. Our modern art, a barometer of culture, includes much that is crass and ugly. Contrary to the former ideals which dominated liberal democracies, all totalitarian political thinking subordinates the individual to the state, which possesses all authority over the souls and bodies of men. The political leviathan recognizes no absolute moral law to which it is willing to subject itself, and the same is true of the economic order. As a timely example of the extreme consequences of secularism, totalitarianism in Soviet Russia and its satellites is described and evaluated. The outcome of secularism, thus conceived, is that politics, economy, science, technics, culture in general, all refuse to acknowledge any moral or spiritual law above them. Modern society does not feel bound by any law above itself. Continued movement in this direction may bring the threat of atomistic disintegration and cultural self-destruction.

39

OUR SECULARIST AGE*
Matthew Spinka

We live in an age of secularism. The popular phrase which a short time ago ran "all this and heaven too" has been revised to read "all this, period." Or to put it another way, the deathbed remark of Henry David Thoreau made to the local minister who

* From *Religion in Life*, vol. 21, no. 3, pp. 380–389, Summer, 1952. Copyright 1952 by Pierce and Smith. Reprinted by permission of *Religion in Life* and the author.

came to comfort him, "One world at a time, brother, one world at a time," has been revised by our pragmatic secularists to the effect that this is all the world we have. There isn't any other; let us make the best of it.

I

This mood denotes the last stages of the era of secularist humanism in which the age has turned upon itself in a violent repudiation of its own historic character. For humanism made man the measure of all things. This humanistic phase of our western civilization is passing, as is evident in the entire culture of our day. Humanistic philosophies have become antihumanistic. The latest and most fashionable of them, the atheistic existentialism of Jean-Paul Sartre, denies any ultimate meaning or significance to the universe or man. In this upsurge of nihilism the best that its prophets can do is to exhort the modern man to create for himself, as best he can, a tolerable existence out of the intolerable conditions.

In its essence this secularism is either religious indifference or practical atheism. In some instances it has reached the stage of a militant attack upon religion in either its theological or its ecclesiastical forms. But in its predominant mood it is not so much a conscious attitude or a formulated philosophy as an almost unconscious exclusion from thought or life of all religious concern. The aim of life is physical well-being or esthetic enjoyment. Along with it go immoral and amoral modes of thought or practice. All absolute standards of right and wrong are denied in favor of ethical relativism. Man is judged from a utilitarian point of view. Only in Communism has this apathetic indifferentism been organized into a code contrasting sharply with the generally recognized Christian moral order.

One may observe this secularist view of life in modern literature, which on the whole denies to men and women all spiritual qualities and treats them as if they were mere biological units. Revolting indecencies are thus regarded as "local color." The overconcern with sex, with material and social conditions, predominates. Spiritual aims are rarely envisaged or are treated with ridiculously or tragically inadequate understanding. In such cases the religious analphabetism of the author is plainly revealed. A recent writer characterizes modern American literature as follows:

> Nearly all the old primary assumptions which men once took for granted —the idea of one god and a very few fixed doctrines suitable for his worship, of a fixed code of sexual and social morality, of a fixed dichotomous universe divided between two irreconcilable forces of Good and Evil—have been slowly but relentlessly eroded away by the advancement of natural science, philosophy, and particularly psychiatry; or, to put it more precisely, they have been dissected and atomized until they have lost the authority of a single, integrated body of belief and been scattered into countless fragments of comfortless superstition, vague longings, and abortive guilt. The change, in short, has been from a stable and secure absolutism, in which what was possible was certain, to an unstable and insecure relativism, in which everything is possible because nothing is certain.*

Certainly our modern art, that barometer of culture, registers this antihumanist tendency with even greater clarity. It reveals, in the first place, practically total repudiation of the art of the Renaissance; and secondly, it clearly reflects the chaos, ugliness, and noise of our own decadent civilization. For, not satisfied with the denial of the spiritual nature of man, modernist art goes even beyond that and distorts in a grotesque and repelling fashion even his human form. In a revulsion against the naturalistic or humanistic forms of expression, the various schools of modernist art have either distorted or rejected natural

* C. Hartley Grattan, "The Trouble with Books Today," *Harper's Magazine*, November, 1951

forms altogether and substituted for them fantastic mechanical figures, such as squares, triangles, and other geometrical designs.

I need not even mention such a popular and therefore extremely influential art as that of the film screen, that chief molder of the "mass mind," and for that reason the principal means of debauching the moral standards of the populace.

This tendency to antihumanism, this denial of the spiritual nature of man, has expressed itself in the political and economic fields with particular force. In the former it has taken the form of totalitarianisms, both fascist and communist, with which we have become acquainted during the past thirty-five years. Contrary to the former emphases which dominated liberal democracies, all totalitarian political thinking subordinates the individual to that modern Leviathan, the state, which possesses all authority over the souls and bodies of men. It recognizes no absolute moral law to which it is willing to subject itself. The same is true of the economic order, although not to the same degree. Economic means have been substituted for human ends. Man exists for the economic order, not the economic order for man.

Totalitarianism has reached its most successful embodiment in Soviet Communism, which in its present phase of economic development is really state capitalism or state socialism. Since, contrary to the basic dogma of classical Marxism, it has everywhere seized political power as an insignificant minority, it has had to retain this power by force. For where spiritual bonds have snapped, society cannot be held together otherwise than by force. The vast mechanism of repression, which the Soviet regime has evolved during its thirty-five years of existence and which has been introduced into every satellite country, has made it a life-and-death arbiter over the destiny of the masses. As long as the state is the sole employer of its people, it can starve them into submission by the simple process of denying them an opportunity to earn a living. Any factual description of conditions in Communist-dominated countries

provides ample, even horrifying, evidence and proof of this assertion. This practically unlimited power extends over the minds and souls of men as well. An utterly unscrupulous, fanatically determined loyalty to the aims of the Communist Party is demanded of all its members. The highest virtue is that of blind and unquestioning obedience. The all-dominant principle of this revolutionary morality is loyalty to the cause of the proletariat which means actually to the current policy of the Russian Politburo. Therefore disloyalty, disobedience, is the greatest sin.

Nothing, absolutely nothing, may be preferred to this supreme loyalty. There is no transcendent standard of right and wrong. That is good which aids the cause of the party; that is bad which harms it. The ultimate aim is the conquest of the world. Hence, Communism cannot tolerate any rival, whether it be God or man. Since it demands supreme loyalty to itself, it blasphemously claims for itself the divine commandment, "Thou shalt have no other gods before me." In this, as in some other aspects, Communism resembles dogmatic, intolerant religion. It is surprising in how many ways a good Communist and a good Jesuit are alike.

It follows, furthermore, that since the task of Communism is to overthrow the old order, the quicker and more effectively that is done the better. The enemies of the new order must not be allowed to defend themselves by being given liberty of speech, press, or of other expression or conduct. "Revolutionary justice" deprives them of all property without compensation, denies them all possibility of earning a living, and thus sentences them to speedy oblivion. At any rate, the bourgeois class must be liquidated, exterminated. For no opposition is tolerated. This program is at present being put into execution in countries like Bulgaria, Rumania, Yugoslavia, Hungary, Czechoslovakia, Poland, and China. It had already been largely completed in the Soviet Union.

Thus force is an integral part of the program of Communism, a primary means of attaining the goal. War is an instrument of policy, not merely a means of defense. This is militant secularism in its atheistic form of a most aggressive and virulent kind.

Accordingly, a conflict with any authentically theistic religious loyalty, particularly Christian, is inevitable. The original aim of the Soviet regime, to destroy the Russian Church, was thus nearer to the real intention of the rulers than is the case at present. But even so, by making the present official Church of the Soviet Union a tool for its political aims and a subservient organ for its propaganda, the government, by granting it greater freedom, has accomplished its goal in a second-best manner. This is true of the Christian churches in the satellite countries as well. In Rumania, for instance, the present patriarch, Justinian, was a member of the Communist Party at the time of his election. Elsewhere, even where there had been an initial stage of opposition, in the end the churches have accepted their role as tools of their Communist government. The best record of opposition belongs to Roman Catholicism, which however has a political record not much better than Communism itself. Although in Bulgaria leaders of the insignificant Protestant minority put up enough opposition to earn for themselves long terms of imprisonment, elsewhere, as in Czechoslovakia, Protestant church leaders have voluntarily accepted conditions of spiritual slavery on behalf of their churches.

But it would be a mistake to restrict, even unconsciously, this reign of secularism to the so-called "Iron Curtain" countries. For it is fast becoming a world-wide phenomenon. Western liberal democracies are likewise built upon secularist presuppositions. The difference between such presuppositions of liberal democracies and of totalitarian states is one of degree, not of kind. It would be a fatal mistake to suppose that we of the West are not infected with the virus of secularism. With us the disease has not broken out in its virulent form, but the germ is in our blood.

How has this tremendous change taken place? To answer this question would be a long story stretching over some six centuries. We would have to begin in the early times of the Renaissance when the spirit of humanism was born, the spirit of self-assertion, of this-worldliness, of scientific study of nature, of the assertion of human autonomy as against the divine Will. Much that is noble, much that is of permanent value, has been produced during those six centuries. Human liberties, rights of men, liberal constitutions guaranteeing inalienable freedoms, have been wrested from tyrannous rulers.

First of all, the new humanism asserted itself in the astonishingly powerful artistic activity such as the Western world had not witnessed since the days of Phidias and Praxiteles. Gothic cathedrals, those poems in stone, soared upward symbolizing the lofty aspirations of the men who built them. Giotto and Fra Angelico stand at the beginning of that superbly distinguished line of painters and artists who are the undying glory of our Western civilization. The same outburst of creative energy was seen in literature: in Dante, Chaucer, Shakespeare, and Cervantes. But the Renaissance had distilled poisons from its own body which in the end resulted in the writhing, agonizing throes which we are witnessing today. At first, man strove to conquer nature. In the end, nature conquered him. This naturalistic process finally threw off all religious pretense and showed itself to be lustily, robustly pagan. But even so it was still humanistic. In contrast, in our own day, this tremendous creativity both in arts and literature with which our age began is all but exhausted. For the last century and a half, creative energies have gone into natural sciences and mechanical inventions. The truly cultural or religious interests have suffered decline. We have ended with mechanistic secularism.

In the second place, the humanistic spirit of the Renaissance has shown itself in the political field, particularly in the American and French Revolutions, which represented the assertion of the autonomous, democratic man, of his right to self-government. They fought for liberty, equality, and fraternity.

They repudiated the whole structure of the past along with its social theory which emanated from medieval Thomism. For the Thomistic doctrine of the relation of church and state acknowledged them as co-ordinate spheres, one having to do with the temporal, the other with the eternal concerns of men. But both were ordained of God. The magistrate, the king, and the priest were equally responsible to God. The Reformers held essentially the same view. Luther was driven by circumstances to grant the state virtual autonomy. The church was not to interfere in matters of state, and *vice versa*. Calvin, however, carefully worked out the co-ordination between the two spheres so that the church had a voice in the concerns of the state while the state owed a duty toward the church.

However, the secularist political philosophies which succeeded the medieval systems eventuated in both the American and the French Revolutions and since then in practically every modern state—which not only separated these two spheres, the church from the state, but freed the state from any responsibility to God, deriving its power from the people and making it responsible only to the people. A modern liberal democracy no longer actually regards itself as "this nation under God." It is freed from any recognizable responsibility to God, although the western European and American democracies recognize natural law as a moral norm. In contrast to this, totalitarianisms deny the liberal democratic concept in favor of an extreme and often militantly atheistic secularization which sees in the state the supreme power over both church and state, over both the bodies and the souls of men. Thus the initial humanistic political philosophies have ended in antihumanism.

Another dismal failure of the humanistic era is met with in modern industry. Man at first sought to conquer nature. With the coming of the machine he has succeeded in subjecting nature to himself to a degree unthinkable in any other age. Even those of us who live in relatively modest comforts afforded us by modern industry exceed in these comforts men of old who had great armies of servants at their beck and call. But man has been conquered by the machine: he has substituted economic means for spiritual ends of life. Thus the machine has done much toward destroying human personality. For modern man has been so conditioned by mass propaganda that he passively reflects the environmental influences, instead of having "a mind of his own." Also, he has so far lost the sense of spiritual values as to be willing to surrender liberty for material security and comfort. Both free enterprise and collectivist economy have speeded up mechanization which has dehumanized life. As Berdyaev once wrote, "We are witnessing the process of dehumanization in all phases of culture and of social life. Man has ceased to be the supreme value." Modern technical science has achieved the crowning success of the ages by unhinging the atom. Now we face the supreme danger of being destroyed by the monster our scientists have fashioned.

This, then, leads us to the consideration of scientific culture as a substitute for both the religious and humanistic world views. Scientism, a view that science does or will provide a complete and final answer to all human problems (a view widely held by positivists, whether logical or illogical), repudiates all moral and religious sovereignty and thus becomes a totalitarianism. But these arrogant claims of positivists are fortunately no longer made by the most outstanding of the genuine scientists. Albert Einstein humbly confesses that science does not know, and never can know, what matter is; science is concerned solely with how matter behaves. Nevertheless, there is always a cultural lag among the lesser luminaries, and especially among the "scientific fellow-travelers," who extol scientism as the sole hope of the world.

To sum up, then, our conception of secularism: its chief characteristic is the claim to autonomy, to totalitarianism; politics, economy, science, technics, culture in general, all refuse to acknowledge any moral or spiritual law above them. Modern society no longer possesses a common spiritual center, does not feel bound by any law above itself. Therefore, we are confronted with the threat of atomistic disintegration and cultural self-destruction.

II

What, then, can we of the Protestant Christian churches do in the face of this debacle of the secularist humanistic era? Let it be stated at the outset that we cannot think in terms of a return to some previous political, economic, or social order. We cannot advocate, as the Roman Catholics do, a retrogression to the imagined unities of the thirteenth century, to the mighty scholastic system of St. Thomas Aquinas. We cannot advocate even a return to our own Reformation. There have been valuable achievements of the modern age. Our task is to cherish and preserve the best which the past—both remote and immediate—has produced, but *to embue it with a new spirit,* and consecrate it to the highest social uses. Nations, societies, cultures, economic systems, political institutions, all must become the Kingdom of our God and of his Christ.

Accordingly, I dare say, and say it deliberately, that the religious transformation of society is the chief, yea, the only hope for the future. Even a thoughtful historian like Arnold Toynbee recognizes this truth. He identifies Christians with the "creative minority" which has ever been the saving remnant of culture, and which may again become the builder of a new culture upon the ruins of the old. Authentic Christianity is already represented by a minority, even in lands traditionally designated as Christian. Therefore, even if a ruinous calamity should overtake our present civilization, it is in the Christian church that the hope of the world lies.

Accordingly, let no one be misled by appearances and conclude that totalitarian Communism represents the creative force of the future which will build a new and better world. Never! Communism represents the destructive force of the old world, the last stage of secularism. It enslaves men to a fanatical faith in an obsolescent world view and in an inefficient economy. Hatred, brutal force, oppression, exploitation of the workers, tyranny over the body and the soul, cannot build a better world. It is an integral part of the Christian faith that evil destroys itself.

It is we of the Christian Church Universal who represent, although at present not sufficiently effectively, the constructive forces capable of building a good world. Our task is twofold: first of all, it is a long-term task of the spiritual transformation of human motivation. This is, in my judgment, the primary duty of the Christian church, particularly of its clerical members. For Christian humanism asserts that man is a microcosm comprising a spiritual as well as a physico-mental nature, and a good society can be built only by good men and women. The transformation of humankind is primarily a spiritual task, not merely an economic or political one. Only a radically transformed human will—will to common good, not will to power—can create a better society. Whatever technological, economic, political, sociological, or cultural improvements mankind may achieve, these are good only potentially; for unless they are ethically directed, they may be (and usually are) employed as improved means to unimproved ends.

Judged by these standards, the worthiness or unworthiness of a given society depends on whether it tends toward the development of human personality, or whether it uses man as a tool, as a commodity, as a thing. Is man the goal, or only a means toward some other goal, such as the building of a communist or capitalistic society? According to this criterion, a society which regards economic well-being as the highest social value—and both capitalist and communist societies do—fails to that extent of being Christian. For economy exists for man, not man for economy. "Man shall not live by bread alone."

This, then, is the long-term task of the Christian church. But if some should judge this interpretation as abstract, theoretical, lacking in practicality, I must insist that nothing but this radical spiritual change can ever accomplish the basic reform. Every social evil—injustice, war, economic exploitation, racial hatred—stems from wrong spiritual motivation. It must be eradicated before its consequences can be cured.

But that is no denial of the equally axiomatic principle that the church has a duty to engage in dealing with the immediate evils in society which call for practical action now. This short-term program, without losing sight of absolute goals, adopts practical, realistic, and effective means to deal with the immediate problems. When a house is on fire, the only responsible action is that of putting it out and saving what can be saved, instead of preaching fire prevention. It is this realistic, short-term program in which responsible Christian laymen should be engaged to an incomparably greater degree than is now the case. For the task to be achieved requires the transformation of the very relations in which lay Christians are engaged in earning their living. Thus the absolute goal of the church does not exclude the use of other means and techniques—those of science, industry, culture, politics, agriculture—in a word, of everything that is necessary for human well-being.

Accordingly, since secularism provides the culture climate of our times, we must change that climate by changing the culture. Our task, among others, is an educational one. Our culture must once again be religion-centered. The most immediate task concerns religious education, since this is the aspect which is directly committed to the church. Our public school education in its present form is admittedly one of the chief means of secularization. The rate at which secularization proceeds is frightening. We are right in not advocating segregation such as is represented by the parochial school. But our church school program of religious education is inadequate and often ineffective. Moreover, at best it reaches only a small number of children. There are two suggestions to be made in this connection: since we believe that under the present circumstances the separation of church and state is the only possible arrangement politically, and therefore religious education cannot be integrated into the public school curriculum, should not a vigorous attempt be pressed to solve the problem on the "released-time" pattern? Or better still, should not factual religious content which naturally forms a part of our cultural heritage and pattern be integrated into the subject matter of school instruction (e.g., history)? Moreover, ought not the school, the church, and the family to be integrated more effectively in a co-operative effort to solve their common problems? And ought not Christian nurture of children to be made once more the principal duty of parents, as it has always been?

Furthermore, very much the same situation exists in our church-related colleges and universities. As President White once expressed it, the purpose of Christian education is "to interpret human life, human history, and human society in terms of their relationship to God and his will and his purposes for man." [*] If that is their purpose, then these institutions, by and large, fulfill it inadequately, if at all.

This then, and many similar problems, comprise the areas of practical activity in which the Christian layman ought to be engaged. But he cannot perform such a function adequately and efficiently unless he is trained for it. We cannot expect appreciable results from inspirational but haphazard endeavors. Laymen in large numbers must be trained in professional or semiprofessional skills if they are to be effective. Roman Catholics provide organized guidance and training for such vocations to a much larger degree than we Protestants do. They have groups of trained leaders within organized labor. They have eight social service schools where men and women receive professional training for their work, while we hitherto have had none. No wonder that social agencies are filled with

[*] G. C. White, "Secularism and Christian Higher Education," in Spann, *The Christian Faith and Secularism,* Abingdon Press, Nashville, Tenn., 1948, p. 45.

Catholic personnel! They provide schools of diplomacy. No wonder that our State Department employs Catholics in numbers very much out of proportion to their relative strength.

In short, our task is to revive and revitalize the Reformation doctrine of the priesthood of all believers, lay and clerical alike. Every vocation must be felt as being of divine calling, and as affording an opportunity, yea a duty, of bringing all things into subjection to God. We must learn anew that business, industry, politics, and every other aspect of life which today is dominated by irreligious, secularist, and even demonic forces, must be embued with the spirit of Christ. Secularism thrives where spiritual dynamic is lacking. Only spiritually transformed men and women can provide the dynamic which will transform the world.

LAW

Law and the state are correlated concepts—two aspects of the same thing. Law is the institution corresponding to the association known as the state. What distinguishes the state from other associations is, not the various tasks it performs, but its monopoly of warranted force. The decisive element of organized force separates legal order from custom and usage, yet it is not easy to determine where mere custom ends and law begins. Perhaps one might take as a criterion the point at which somebody with communal approval or sanction does something about the breach of a social norm.

Law, as a social institution, is a form of social rule emanating from political agencies. All social rules, including law, originated in custom or folkways of long standing and are based upon existing conceptions of justice and right in a given community. In time, custom becomes more specifically formulated as law with stipulated sanctions to enforce the will of the community; and in time, unwritten laws or codes may be written and thus become the common knowledge of all concerned.

As customs yield to the status of laws, they become formal, deliberately enacted or adjudged statements in the form of commands or orders. They are not necessarily the result of voluntary consent of the persons against whom they are directed; and they are ordinarily accompanied by punitive sanctions in case of their violation. The deliberate enactment of legal rules is a comparatively modern development.

Modern legislatures have extended the sphere of their action to an almost unlimited range of human activities, and the importance of their work has increased accordingly. As a generalization, it might be said that the enactment of law depends largely upon the power of the groups which lay their claims before the legislative body. In principle, of course, the laws are meant to satisfy the needs of the general community rather than the needs of selfish interests. However, there is no doubt that most of our legislation is passed to satisfy the demands of specific groups or interests. This does not mean that state legislatures or Congress should not pass bills in behalf of individual persons in cases where other legislation fails to cover the situation; in fact, many such individual bills are passed during each session, and justly so.

It is a function of law to establish social order and security necessary for the fullest individual self-expression consistent with general freedom in the community. It is also a function of law to provide for changes in the social order to maintain cultural harmony, and substantive laws themselves must reflect their reciprocal relationships to other elements in the culture.

The nature of law would necessarily change as culture has developed from that of kin-organized to civil society and, within the latter category, through the phases of ancient, medieval, and modern civilization. Law would also differ according to the prevailing political order, whether monarchical, democratic, or totalitarian. Emergent values in law will now be considered in terms of the criteria indicated.

Law in a kin-organized society differed in scope and sanctions from that which developed in an emergent political society where the main bond of social cohesion was no longer kinship. Although political institutions independent of the bonds of kinship or religion were characteristic of the emergent political society, because they were young, weak, and untried their encroachment upon the old kin-based allegiance was wary and hesitating. Social cohesion still seemed based mainly on nonpolitical elements, which therefore were protected. However, by the time political institutions were replacing those of kin-organized society, other social patterns had doubtless changed in economic institutions and organization, in techniques, in customs and beliefs which formerly had been centered about kinship and religion. The status of individuals and families changed in the transition from kinship to civil controls. Conceptions of property had to change.

The rise of commerce brought pressures upon the legal order. Rome, for example, developed its *ius gentium,* a preliminary form of international law for commercial relations; the Middle Ages developed the guilds and the law merchant; usury and other questionable policies had to be regulated. The relations between reason, conscience, equity, and natural law in the common law were gradually clarified and balanced. Eventually the free transfer of property was legalized. Free trade and freedom from monopoly became critical issues. Personal security, due process of law, habeas corpus, and other rights and liberties of individuals were increasingly recognized and established. The jury system came into usage (Henry II laid the foundations for the jury in England in the twelfth century) and more rational modes of trial were practiced.

Expanding industrialism brought both economic and political changes. Conceptions of Roman and English equity had to be revised to suit the contemporary way of life. Legal codes had to be revised in England, France, Germany, the United States. Questions of *laissez faire* and individual liberty became controversial and influenced restrictive legislation. Laws extended the conception of freedom of contract and regulations of restraint of trade were gradually being formulated. Laws to regulate the incorporation of business came into existence—the first one in the United States was "An Act Relative to Incorporations for Manufacturing Purposes," enacted in New York in 1811. Joint-stock companies had become increasingly subject to regulation. Thus, in broad terms, may be indicated the development of law in modern democratic society.

The rise of totalitarian polities and ideologies has emphasized very different values in the development of legal institutions. The following traits of totalitarianism suggest why the laws of Fascist Italy, Nazi Germany, and Communist Russia would reflect social values contrary to those of democracies: nationalistic emotion is exalted to the point of religious frenzy; a single party takes over the power of the state; dissenting opinion is ruthlessly stamped out; the "leader" forms the focus of devotion and patriotism; dogma replaces debate and the press is controlled by the party and the state; culturally the population is isolated in order to prevent it from knowing the real condition of the outside world; immoralism prevails in all forms of political lying and governmental hypocrisy, as well as in state-planned crimes; industry, commerce, and agriculture are controlled by the party and the leader; the economy is motivated by perpetual preparations for war and complete militarization of the population.

Under Fascist doctrine the integral and totalitarian state, called the "people's state," is held to be the condition precedent of law—a doctrine directly opposed to modern thinking which holds law to be the condition precedent of the state. The crisis of the modern state is both the crisis of legal science as evidenced in legal concepts and the crisis of the legal phenomenon, i.e., the sources of law. The Nazi doctrine was underscored by the premise that the spirit of the state was the spirit of the German people and that the Fuehrer had reawakened the spirit slumbering in the subconscious mind of the people, that he gave voice to this spirit, and thus expressed "what everyone felt." The Fuehrer, it was claimed, incarnated the spirit of the German people, and it was his task to give shape to this German spirit.

In the Soviet Union, influenced in turn by Marxism, Leninism, and Stalinism, criminal law, civil law, family law, labor law, agrarian law, and procedural law were and continue to be thoroughly overhauled. Rule by decree is paramount; the secret-police system with its espionage and terrorism, the "popular" courts, which too often constitute an instrument of oppression, the concentration camps and slave-labor camps, the state-regimented economy, and regimentation in education and in practically every area of life—these characteristics suggest broadly the transition in law which has been wrought by the Soviet system in Russia. And trends within the satellite states have shown similar patterns of transformation.[10] Communist China, in spite of any national variations in culture, has largely been forced into a totalitarian way of life imitating Soviet forms of control.

People living in democracies tend to take their legal and other social institutions too much for granted. They fail to realize that their mode of life did not "just happen," but represents and is the product of a matrix of social values whose essence consists of human liberty, freedom, individualism, and respect for the dignity of man. The American way of life is protected by a bill of rights. The government is to serve the people, not to rule it arbitrarily. Deviation from such traditional values would soon mean that Americans would lose their safeguards against arbitrary and autocratic lawmaking and government.

Law, especially in a democracy, should be a live, changing, and adjustable instrument satisfying the requirements of an ever-changing society. And yet it changes slowly. This is partly because of the conservatism of the legalist who sees the law as a

---

[10] For the entire range of legal development beginning with kin-organized society and traced through modern democratic society and finally as it is evident in totalitarian societies, see Sidney Post Simpson and Julius Stone, *Cases and Readings on Law and Society*, West Publishing Company, St. Paul, Minn., 1949.

practical convenience rather than as the reflection of the whole society's effort to order and unfold its life.

Generally the dependence upon precedent in the determination of decisions is also a factor retarding changes in laws and in legal institutions. Although attorneys and judges alike may tend to resist change, there are many cases on record of decisions having been reversed in later opinions rendered. Both common law and formal opinions are meant to guide, not necessarily to arbitrarily restrict, the decision-making power of the judge in cases where he presides. It is common knowledge, however, that "the law is what the judge says it is"; and how the law will be adjudicated depends upon the attitudes the judges have toward it and the pressure for or against it brought by its sponsors and opponents. How the judges decide a case depends upon their outlook upon life, and judges have personalities depending upon their background and training. Whatever their economic and political and other social views may be, judges are supposed to remain as impartial as possible and to interpret the law justly. The judge, through his function of judicial interpretation, "can so construe the written law and select the principles and cases he will follow, that he can almost build a legal foundation for the decision he deems right in the case at bar." [11] Moreover, the judge may, through his interpretation, virtually become a legislator. Democratic legislatures and courts are sometimes criticized for being made up of more or less untrained men with inadequate political equipment. Consequently, law and its interpretation may fail to be as positive as would be desired to insure justice.

Not infrequently members of the bar are accused of aligning themselves with the commercial interests and throwing their influence to the support of these interests even though they sometimes have been predatory in character and their act a gross violation of public interests. There has long been a commonplace saying among corporate executives to the effect that "I want a lawyer not to tell me what I can't do, but to tell me *how I can do legally* what I want to do." Clearly, there are things one can't do, or should not do, and the businessman should want his attorney not to hesitate to inform him accordingly. But the new field of administrative regulation creates many new areas where the distinction between questions of law and questions of policy becomes very thin. Situations of this kind require that the lawyer be brought more closely into the management's inner circle so that all legal aspects may be clarified from the beginning in developing a project. Aspiring young lawyers will find new opportunities as members of the legal department or "house counsel" of large firms or corporations. The opportunities for specialization in law have been growing rapidly.

The pattern of organization followed consistently in the *Annual Survey of American Law* breaks law down into the following major classifications:

Public law in general includes international law, the United States and the United Nations, conflict of laws, constitutional law and civil rights, administrative law, military law, and criminal law and its enforcement.

Public law concerning government regulation and taxation includes the Internal Revenue Code of the year of enforcement, Federal estate and gift taxation, state and

[11] Cf. Hertzler, *op. cit.,* p. 393.

local taxation, trade regulation, labor-relations law, food, drug and cosmetics law; public housing, planning and conservation; local government; copyright law, and patent law.

Commercial law, torts, and family law, as a separate class, includes contracts, agency and partnership, corporations, bankruptcy, commercial law, insurance, admiralty and shipping, arbitration, torts, and family law.

Property and procedure includes the following: landlord and tenant, vendor and purchaser; water law, oil and gas law, and mineral rights; mortgages, future interest, trusts and administration, succession, equity, federal jurisdiction and practice, criminal procedure, and evidence.

Legal philosophy and reform is another area, including jurisprudence, judicial administration, and legal education.

Law is therefore so broad and complex that it is no wonder jurists are conservative about changes, especially in routine procedure. Nevertheless, every area mentioned is subject to change through legislative procedure and through decisions of judges. In many areas where administrative details cannot be specified in the laws creating government bureaus, the latter are responsible for administrative rules and regulations, which in turn are regularly subject to authorized change. When one realizes the magnitude of the functions of legislation, administration, and adjudication embracing government at the federal, state, and local levels, it becomes clear that the legal institutions and changes in them are more comprehensively interrelated with other cultural elements than is commonly known. Even so, much of our daily life moves along without specific awareness of law. The ordinary folkways, customs, traditions, and mores remain fundamentally important guides for behavior; it is when these norms fail that society may find that legislation is necessary.

Consideration of details concerning changes in criminal or civil law in the processing of court trials and in the revision of governmental structure and administration would carry us far afield. Our purpose has been to indicate what law is as a social institution and what general principles give meaning to social change in law as an institution rather than in its counterpart, the state.

The following selections develop special subjects in which law is a factor fostering social change: "The United States Supreme Court and the Segregation Issue" by Rayford W. Logan, "Teen-Age Criminals" by Judge Elijah Adlow, and "The Law and the Future" by Earl Warren, Chief Justice of the United States Supreme Court.

Changes in the status of the Negro in the United States since the 1870s have been facilitated by the influence of World War I, the Great Depression, the New Deal, World War II, and the cold war. Problems of desegregation and integration are reflected particularly in the decisions of the United States Supreme Court, some of the decisions adverse to the Negro, as between 1873 and 1910, and others favorable, as between 1911 and 1955. Legalistic and social elements in the decisions of note are brought into focus and evaluated by Rayford W. Logan.

The segregation issue is especially significant in that it reveals the possible role of the courts of the land in delaying or facilitating the improvement of the social and cultural status of a minority group. The segregation issue is uniquely interesting because it involves the basic question of whether stateways can change folkways; that is, how successful may decisions of the United States Supreme Court be if they are incompatible with the prevailing folkways? In various cases, however, the Supreme Court has, through its decisions rendered during the last forty-five years, altered the American way of life in important ways.

40

THE UNITED STATES SUPREME COURT AND THE SEGREGATION ISSUE*

Rayford W. Logan

From the 1870's to the beginning of this century the status of the Negro in the United States steadily worsened.[1] Then ensued a decade that has been aptly termed "a low, rugged plateau," [2] during which a few Negro leaders and white supporters began to campaign militantly against what is now called second-class citizenship. World War I, the Great Depression, and the New Deal, World War II and the cold war, have greatly accelerated nationwide changes which facilitated gains for Negroes that few persons at the beginning of the century could have envisioned These gains embraced practically every aspect of Negro life, and they have greatly altered the climate of opinion with respect to the status of the Negro in the American democracy. An increasing number of Negro leaders and their supporters, keeping pace with and sometimes moving ahead of these gains, have recently renounced the goal of equality within a segregated society

and have urgently advocated desegregation and integration.

ERA OF ADVERSE DECISIONS (1873–1910)

The decisions of the Supreme Court have both reflected and helped to determine the changing status and goals. From shortly after the Civil War to the end of the first decade of this century, most decisions furthered the declining status of the Negro. The Court virtually nullified the privileges and immunities clause of the Fourteenth Amendment by declaring that it protected only rights that inhere in United States citizenship and that most rights inhere in state citizenship. It held unconstitutional most of the important provisions of the Civil Rights Act of May 31, 1870, the Ku Klux Klan Act of April 20, 1871, and the Civil Rights Act of March 1, 1875. These decisions declared that the Fourteenth Amendment was prohibitory upon states and not upon individuals and that the

* Reprinted by permission of *The Annals of the American Academy of Political and Social Science*, vol. 304, pp. 10-16, March, 1956.

[1] See Logan, *The Negro in American Life and Thought: The Nadir, 1887–1901* (New York, 1954).

[2] Henry Arthur Callis, M.D., Washington, D. C., a student at Cornell University at the time, suggested this phrase.

Fifteenth Amendment was applicable only when the denial of the right to vote was based upon race, color, or previous condition of servitude.[3]

The Court held unconstitutional a Louisiana law forbidding discrimination in interstate commerce on the ground that it placed an undue burden on interstate commerce.[4] In *Plessy v. Ferguson* [5] the Court for the first time sanctioned a state segregation law on the ground that it was a reasonable use of the police powers of the state provided that the accommodations were "equal." The Court repeatedly declined to intervene in cases of alleged exclusion of Negroes from jury service when counsel for the plaintiffs did not show in the trial court that the exclusion was based on race or color.[6] The constitutionality of the Mississippi disfranchising amendment of 1890, which arose collaterally in a case involving exclusion of Negroes from jury service, was upheld.[7] The Court refused to take jurisdiction over the Alabama disfranchising amendment, partly because the question was a "political" one,[8] and also declined to intervene against a Kentucky statute prohibiting Berea College from continuing to admit Negro students, since the charter of the College reserved to the state the right to alter or repeal its charter.[9]

In 1910 in a case involving interstate commerce the Court held that a railway company had the right to require separate coaches for white and colored passengers, ruling that in the absence of congressional legislation the carrier could make reasonable regulations for the conduct of its business. As to what was "reasonable," it was said that this "cannot depend upon a passenger being state or interstate." [10]

The only type of state action that the Court struck down was that which prevented Negroes from serving on juries on account of their race or color.[11] The Court also held that action by individuals in their capacity of state officials constituted state action under the Fourteenth Amendment.[12]

The Circuit Court of Appeals for the Fourth Circuit refused to grant relief to a plaintiff in a case involving the second section of the Fourteenth Amendment on the grounds that its enforcement was a legislative matter and that Congress had not enacted legislation to enforce it. In denying certiorari, the Supreme Court in 1946 held that the question was a "political" one.[13]

ERA OF FAVORABLE DECISIONS (1911–55)

The reversal of the general trend of the Court's decisions after 1910 is the more noteworthy in view of the general inaction of Congress and the belated action of the executive branch with respect to civil rights. There are, however, significant exceptions to the reversal. The scope of the privileges and immunities clause is still limited to United States citizenship. The civil rights decision of 1883 is still the law of the land,

---

[3] The relevant decisions are Slaughterhouse Cases, 16 Wallace 36 (1873); United States v. Cruikshank, 92 U. S. 542 (1875); United States v. Reese, 92 U. S. 214 (1876); United States v. Harris, 106 U. S. 629 (1883); Civil Rights Cases, 109 U. S. 3 (1883). They may be conveniently consulted in Thomas I. Emerson and David Haber (Eds.), *Political and Civil Rights in the United States: A Collection of Legal and Related Materials* (Buffalo, 1952).

[4] Hall v. De Cuir, 95 U. S. 485 (1878).

[5] 163 U. S. 537 (1896).

[6] See, for example, Charley Smith v. Mississippi, 162 U. S. 592 (1896) and Murray v. Louisiana, 163 U. S. 101 (1896).

[7] Williams v. Mississippi, 170 U. S. 213 (1898).

[8] Giles v. Harris, 189 U. S. 475 (1903); Giles v. Teasley, 193 U. S. 146 (1904).

[9] Berea College v. Kentucky, 211 U. S. 45 (1908).

[10] Chiles v. C. & O. Ry Co., 218 U. S. 71 (1910).

[11] The classic case is Strauder v. West Virginia, 100 U. S. 303 (1880); see also Virginia v. Rives, 100 U. S. 313 (1880).

[12] *Ex parte* Virginia, 100 U. S. 339 (1880).

[13] Saunders v. Wilkins, *cert. denied*, 328 U. S. 870.

and the Court in 1913 held that it applied to marine as well as to land jurisdiction.[14] As late as 1920 the Court upheld a Kentucky law requiring separate cars that involved interstate travel between Ohio and Kentucky on the ground that, since the company was chartered in Kentucky, it was subject to Kentucky laws.[15] Attempts to have state poll tax laws declared unconstitutional have failed.[16]

While some of the most far-reaching decisions have been handed down since the entry of the United States into World War II, a few important ones precede 1941. In fact, two—*Bailey v. Alabama* and *Guinn v. United States*—antedate the entry of the United States into World War I and one—*Buchanan v. Warley*—came shortly thereafter.

Peonage and Involuntary Servitude. In 1911 the Court held that peonage violated the Thirteenth Amendment,[17] and since the establishment of the Civil Rights Section of the Department of Justice in 1939 a widespread decline in peonage and involuntary servitude has occurred. In the face of new devices, the Supreme Court acted; for example, in 1944 it struck down as a violation of the Thirteenth Amendment an Alabama statute which enabled employers to force employees in debt on account of advanced wage payments to continue work for them under threat of criminal punishment.

The Franchise. In 1915 in *Guinn v. United States* [18] the Court for the first time declared that the grandfather clause, one of the devices used to disfranchise Negroes, violated the Fifteenth Amendment. A new Oklahoma registration law that sought to circumvent this decision was held unconstitutional in *Lane v. Wilson*.[19] Meanwhile the Court had twice ruled that action by the state of Texas in providing for a white primary violated the Fourteenth Amendment.[20] But in *Grovey v. Townsend*,[21] the Court held that action by the Democratic state convention barring Negroes from the primary was not state action and, hence, not a violation of the Constitution. The Court, however, reversed itself in *Smith v. Allwright*, declaring that "when, as here that privilege [of membership in a party] is also the essential qualification for voting in a primary to select nominees for a general election, the State makes the action of the party the action of the state." [22]

This decision resulted, on the one hand, in a considerable increase in the number of Negro voters in southern states,[23] and on the other, in attempts by several states to circumvent it. In Alabama the Boswell amendment permitted the registration as electors of only those persons who could "understand and explain" any article of the federal Constitution. The Supreme Court affirmed the decision of a United States district court which had held that the requirement violated the Fifteenth Amendment.[24] South Carolina tried to separate completely the Democratic primary from state action by removing all mention of primaries from the state constitution and statutes. District Judge J. Waties Waring ruled that the Democratic primary remained an integral part of the state election ma-

---

[14] Butts v. Merchants and Miners Transportation Co., 230 U. S. 126 (1913).

[15] South Covington and Cincinnati Street Ry. v. Commonwealth of Kentucky, 252 U. S. 399 (1920).

[16] See especially Butler v. Thompson, 97 F. Supp. 17 (E. D., Va., 1951), aff'd, 341 U. S. 937 (1951).

[17] Bailey v. Alabama, 219 U. S. 219.

[18] 238 U. S. 347.

[19] 307 U. S. 268 (1939).

[20] Nixon v. Herndon, 273 U. S. 536 (1927), and Nixon v. Condon, 286 U. S. 73 (1932).

[21] 295 U. S. 45 (1935).

[22] 321 U. S. 649 (1944).

[23] V. O. Key, Jr., *Southern Politics in State and Nation* (New York, 1949), Chap. XXIX.

[24] Davis v. Schnell, 81 F. Supp. 872, aff'd, 336 U. S. 933 (1949).

chinery, and the Supreme Court upheld the decision by denying certiorari.[25] Georgia amended its constitution in 1945 to make eligibility for voting dependent on ability to "correctly read in the English language any paragraph of the Constitution of the United States or of this State and correctly write the same in the English language when read to them by any one of the registrars." County registrars appointed under the Registration Act of 1949 brought suit against a county official who had refused to pay their salaries. The Supreme Court of Georgia held that the Fourteenth and Fifteenth Amendments had not been violated since the case did not involve the right to register to vote; the United States Supreme Court dismissed the appeal.[26] But the Court declared that, since for more than sixty years the county-wide Jaybird Association's candidates had invariably been nominated in the Texas Democratic primaries and elected to office, the election machinery of the Association and of the Democratic party violated the Fifteenth Amendment.[27]

The Court has also invoked Sections 241 and 242 of Title 18, United States Code (1948), to uphold indictments against election officials who had made a fraudulent count of ballots in a federal primary election and who had stuffed ballot boxes in a federal election.[28]

Housing. Shortly after the United States entered World War I the Supreme Court enunciated the basic principle which has governed subsequent decisions. In *Buchanan v. Warley*[29] a unanimous Court declared unconstitutional the provisions of a Louisville city ordinance which denied to colored persons the right to occupy houses in blocks in which the greater number of houses were occupied by white persons, and vice versa.[30]

Later, the Court was faced with the problem of restrictive covenants by which groups of individuals contracted not to dispose of their property to Negroes, Jews, Armenians, Mexicans, Indians, Orientals, Syrians, and other "undesirables." The Court held in *Corrigan v. Buckley*[31] that a restrictive agreement involving action by private individuals did not present a substantial question.[32] State court action to prevent infringement of such a restrictive covenant, however, was held to violate the equal protection of the laws guaranteed by the Fourteenth Amendment.[33] This decision, like *Smith v. Allwright,* provoked various devices to circumvent the clear mandate of the Court. For example, "gentlemen's agreements" proscribe the selling or renting to Negroes outside existing colored districts.[34]

In regard to public housing the Court followed the strict interpretation of state action. It held that the housing project of the Stuyvesant Town Corporation, built under the New York Redevelopment Companies Law, was not state action within the meaning of the Fourteenth Amendment.[35] But in 1951 the New York City Council passed an ordinance to prohibit discrimination or segregation in all private housing enjoying total or partial exemption from city taxes or receiving direct or indirect aid from the city.[36]

[25] Rice v. Elmore, 165 F.2d 387, *cert. denied,* 333 U. S. 875 (1948).

[26] Franklin v. Harper, 205 Ga. 779, *appeal dismissed,* 339 U. S. 946 (1950).

[27] Terry *et al.* v. Adams *et al.,* 345 U. S. 461 (1953).

[28] United States v. Classic, 313 U. S. 299 (1941); United States v. Saylor, 322 U. S. 385 (1944).

[29] 245 U. S. 60 (1917).

[30] See also Richmond v. Deans, 281 U. S. 704 (1930).

[31] 271 U. S. 323 (1926).

[32] See also Hansberry v. Lee, 311 U. S. 32 (1940).

[33] Shelley v. Kraemer, 334 U. S. 1 (1948); see also Barrows v. Jackson, 346 U. S. 249 (1953).

[34] Emerson and Haber (Eds.), *op. cit.* (note 3 *supra*), pp. 1028–34.

[35] Dorsey v. Stuyvesant Town Corporation, 299 N. Y. 512, *cert. denied,* 339 U. S. 981 (1950).

[36] Emerson and Haber (Eds.), *op. cit.* (note 3 *supra*), p. 1052.

Public Accommodations. Morgan v. Virginia [37] concerned a Negro interstate passenger traveling on a bus from Virginia through the District of Columbia to Baltimore, Maryland, who had refused to obey the request of the driver to move to a back seat partly occupied by colored passengers in order to make room for a white passenger. She had been arrested and convicted of violating a Virginia statute which required that she sit in designated seats. The Supreme Court held that the statute was an unconstitutional burden on interstate commerce, largely because of the inconvenience caused passengers by the frequent necessity of changing seats.

To invalidate the denial to a Negro of an unoccupied Pullman seat and of an unoccupied seat in the dining car,[38] the Court invoked Section 3, paragraph 1, of the Interstate Commerce Act of 1887—the provision which makes it unlawful for a railroad in interstate commerce "to subject any particular person . . . to undue or unreasonable prejudice or disadvantage in any respect whatsoever."

Since the Civil Rights Act of 1875 and the civil rights decision did not apply to the District of Columbia, discrimination in the District of Columbia was not affected by it. Discrimination there was forbidden by measures enacted on June 20, 1872, and June 26, 1873, while the District was under a territorial form of government. The Supreme Court held that these acts, especially that of 1873, were still in effect and that consequently a "respectable well-behaved person" had to be served without regard to race, color, or previous condition of servitude by keepers of hotels and certain other public places.[39] Subsequently, not only hotels and restaurants but also theaters, which were not designated in the acts, have generally opened their doors to Negroes.

Until November 7, 1955, Supreme Court decisions with respect to public golf courses have been inconclusive.[40] On that date the Supreme Court in effect applied to public parks and beaches the principle enunciated on May 17, 1954, in the School Segregation Cases that "separate educational facilities are inherently unequal." [41] The Circuit Court of Appeals of the Fourth Circuit had held in March 1955 that segregation in two public parks in Maryland violated the principle enunciated in the public school cases and added: "It is now obvious that segregation cannot be justified as a means to preserve peace merely because the tangible facilities furnished to one race are equal to those furnished the other." The Supreme Court merely affirmed this decision. A federal district court had ordered equal facilities for Negroes on a public golf course in Atlanta, and the Circuit Court of Appeals of the Fifth Circuit had affirmed the decision. The Supreme Court on November 7, 1955, ordered these judgments vacated and the case remanded to the district court with directions to enter a decree in favor of the plaintiffs that would conform with the ruling in the two Maryland cases.[42]

Trade Unions. The Court has also strengthened the rights of Negroes in trade unions. It has held that a state has the power under the Fourteenth Amendment to prohibit discrimination on account of race, creed, or color by any labor union with respect to membership or union services. The Court has also declared that the union as the bargaining agent of the employees selected in accordance with the National Labor Relations Act of 1935 has the duty to represent all employees

---

[37] 328 U. S. 373 (1946).

[38] Mitchell v. United States, 313 U. S. 80 (1941); Henderson v. United States, 339 U. S. 816 (1950).

[39] District of Columbia v. John R. Thompson Co., 346 U. S. 100 (1953).

[40] See Robert B. McKay, "Segregation and Public Recreation," *Virginia Law Review*, Vol. 40 (October 1954), pp. 713–16.

[41] See below.

[42] Washington *Post and Times Herald*, November 8, 1955, pp. 1, 12, news article.

without discrimination because of race or color, and that it can be compelled so to do by judicial action.[43]

Picketing. In *Hughes v. Superior Court*,[44] the Court upheld a California injunction against picketing by the Progressive Citizens of America to induce a retail chain store to institute hiring practices whereby the proportion of Negro to white employees would approximate the proportion of Negro to white customers. California did not have a fair employment practices statute, and the Court held that the state might constitutionally implement its public policy against selective hiring based on race by prohibiting picketing for such a purpose. But in *New Negro Alliance v. Sanitary Grocery Company*,[45] it ruled that picketing in that instance was a labor dispute within the meaning of the Norris–La Guardia Anti-Injunction Act of 1932.

Due Process. In *Strauder v. West Virginia*,[46] the Court had held that state statutes excluding Negroes from juries violated the due process clause of the Fourteenth Amendment. As Ralph F. Bischoff has observed:

Ever since *Patton v. Mississippi*, 331 U. S. 463 (1947) reaffirmed and lent force to the almost forgotten case of *Strauder v. West Virginia* the constitutional intent that Negroes shall not be discriminated against has been more often complied with. Where the defendant in a criminal case makes out a prima facie case of illegal exclusion, it is the state which must present detailed proof to the contrary. . . . A relatively healthy status . . . is apparent from the lack of cases on the subject in 1954.[47]

What is more important is the fact that the Court has adopted the principle that the exclusion of Negroes and other minorities is prima facie presumptive evidence of discrimination.[48]

Moreover, the due process clause of the Fifth and Fourteenth Amendments guarantees the accused a trial free from mob domination or pressure.[49] The Sixth Amendment to the United States Constitution declares that in all criminal prosecutions the accused shall enjoy the right "to have the Assistance of Counsel for his defence." In the famous Scottsboro case,[50] the Court held that "the necessity of counsel was so vital and imperative that the failure of the trial court to make an effective appointment of counsel was likewise a denial of due process within the meaning of the Fourteenth Amendment."

Education. For fifty-eight years the doctrine of "separate but equal" accommodations, sanctioned in *Plessy v. Ferguson* (1896), was the law of the land. But beginning with 1938 the Court defined equality in such a way as to pave the way for the reversal in 1954 of the principle itself. In *Missouri ex rel. Gaines v. Canada*,[51] the Court held that if a state provided legal education within the state for white students it must provide legal education within the state for Negro students. In 1950 in *Sweatt v. Painter*,[52] the Court held that a Negro student had to be admitted to

---

[43] Railway Mail Ass'n v. Corsi, 326 U. S. 88 (1945); Steele v. Louisville & Nashville R. R., 323 U. S. 192 (1944); and Tunstall v. Brotherhood of Locomotive Firemen and Enginemen, 323 U. S. 210 (1944).

[44] 339 U. S. 460 (1950).

[45] 303 U. S. 552 (1938).

[46] 100 U. S. 303 (1880).

[47] "Constitutional Law and Civil Rights," *New York University Law Review*, Vol. 30 (January 1955), p. 54.

[48] Norris v. Alabama 294 U. S. 587 (1935); Hill v. Texas, 316 U. S. 400 (1942); Avery v. Georgia, 345 U. S. 559 (1953).

[49] Moore v. Dempsey, 261 U. S. 86 (1923).

[50] Powell v. Alabama, 287 U. S. 45 (1932).

[51] 305 U. S. 337 (1938).

[52] 339 U. S. 629.

the University of Texas Law School, since the newly established law school for Negroes could not provide substantial equality in such matters as "reputation of the faculty, experience of the administration, position and influence of the alumni, standing in the community, traditions and prestige." At the same time it held [53] that a state after admitting a Negro to graduate instruction must not afford him different treatment from other students solely because of his race.

Finally, on May 17, 1954, the Court unanimously concluded that "in the field of public education the doctrine of 'separate but equal' has no place. Separate educational facilities are inherently unequal." Four cases were decided under the equal protection clause of the Fourteenth Amendment and one, arising in the District of Columbia, under the due process clause of the Fifth Amendment.[54] On May 31, 1955, the Court ruled that "the courts will require that the defendants make a prompt and reasonable start toward full compliance with our May 17, 1954, ruling." If some additional time was necessary, the burden rested upon the defendants "to establish that such time is necessary in the public interest and is consistent with good faith compliance at the earliest practicable date." [55]

CONCLUSION

The decisions in the public school cases have provoked more threats of evasion and defiance than has any decision in recent years. William Graham Sumner's dictum that "stateways cannot change folkways" is gaining new popularity. Any prediction about the extent to which these threats will be successful would be almost worthless. In the meanwhile, other decisions of the Supreme Court during the past forty-five years have greatly altered the American way of life.

Teen-age criminality has been increasing so rapidly for a number of years that the problem has aroused national concern. The problem is not limited to the United States, but has grown in significance in European countries, Russia, and countries in the Near East. Our present interest, however, lies with conditions in the United States.

The revolt of modern youth is especially serious because it bears little resemblance to what was once viewed as juvenile delinquency. Judge Elijah Adlow says that today the crimes of violence in which the young indulge can never be mistaken for boyish pranks, e.g., malicious destruction of property, assaults with deadly weapons, thefts, and holdups. Why the change?

For one thing, the modern youth reacts to environment as grown-ups do; and Judge Adlow points out, as a factor in that environment, that adult America is indulging in an orgy of lawlessness in which more drinking, more gambling, and more widespread indulgence in luxuries and comforts are cited as elements. Among other factors, the authority of parents has been weakened; parents overindulge their children and permit them to do as they please. Modern youth has a great deal of time on its hands. The somewhat general weakening of the moral viewpoint is held to be devastating to youth. Concepts of decency and honor have changed. Class war and unrest on the labor front leave their mark on the youth. Thus Judge Adlow approaches the problem of juvenile delinquency and crime as a function of changing attitudes toward basic values which influence juvenile behavior.

[53] McLaurin v. Oklahoma State Regents, 339 U. S. 637.
[54] Brown v. Board of Educ., Briggs v. Elliott, Davis v. County School Board, Gebhart v. Belton, Bolling v. Sharpe, 347 U. S. 483 (1954).
[55] 349 U. S. 294 (1955).

41

TEEN-AGE CRIMINALS*
Judge Elijah Adlow

I

An attempt to protect juveniles from the contaminating influences of adolescents and adults has resulted in the establishment in many places of separate and independent courts for juvenile offenders. My court has no jurisdiction over juveniles, which means that all offenders under seventeen years of age are handled by the judges of a specially constituted Juvenile Court. This does not mean that the juvenile is a stranger to my court. In fact, one of the alarming conditions that contribute to the contemporary moral crisis derives from the number of crimes which are committed, in whole or in part, by juveniles. For the purposes of this article I shall not limit my observations to those under seventeen years of age, but shall consider all adolescents.

Not long ago two girls, aged nine and eleven, appeared in my court and by their testimony involved fifteen men in charges of most serious sex offenses. It was evident from the testimony given by these girls that in certain instances the girl solicited the men to commit the acts with which they are now charged. This is not the first time that unusually young girls have become involved with men. Since the beginning of World War II the abandonment of domestic responsibilities by many mothers in exchange for jobs in industry has left countless children in America to rear themselves. It was inevitable that some of these children would speedily

show evidences of neglect. The direct result of this absenteeism from the home was noticeable during the war, when many cases involving indecent assaults on children and similar offenses were brought into the courts. The judges expected that with the return to normalcy, and the return of mothers to their homes, the conditions would abate. Unfortunately, a good many mothers who left home for a job are still working, and their families are expected to bring themselves up the best way they can.

What makes the revolt of modern youth serious is that it bears little resemblance to what was once viewed as juvenile delinquency. There was a time when the difference between a bad boy and a playful boy was merely one of degree. Today the crimes of violence in which the young indulge can never be mistaken for boyish pranks. The many cases of malicious destruction of property that have entailed great loss to the public are not the cumulative consequence of youthful exuberance but the product of calculated and planned mischief. The many assaults with dangerous weapons, some of which have had fatal consequence, are the acts of irresponsible desperadoes which differ little from the planned attacks on society by adult outlaws.

More alarming are the thefts and holdups. The petty pilferings that once represented a boy's transgressions were largely restricted to doormats, ash barrels, and milk bottles. But in the past few years I have had an eighteen-

* Reprinted by permission of the author and *The Atlantic Monthly*, vol. 196, no. 1, pp. 46–50, July, 1955.

year-old boy in my court who, while employed by a wholesale electric supply house, loaded $10,000 worth of electric equipment on a freight elevator, lowered the elevator to the ground floor, and then secured a truckman to cart away the loot. Three boys, all seventeen years of age, were before me charged with breaking and entering and larceny. After getting an automobile, these boys broke into a Surplus War Goods Store and carted away $3500 worth of merchandise. Two others in the same age group looted the warehouse of a jewelry novelty wholesaler and carried away $6000 worth of merchandise. After making their getaway they stored the loot in a safe place and canvassed the community until they found an operator of a jewelry store who would buy the goods from them. There is nothing "juvenile" about this kind of delinquency.

Recently four boys, all under twenty-one, brazenly attempted to secure the release of a sixteen-year-old girl who was in the custody of the Massachusetts Youth Service Board at the Lanchaster School for Girls. This is not the first time that young desperadoes have attempted to force the release of inmates in correctional institutions. The bold daring revealed in these escapades merely reflects the cold-blooded indifference of modern youths to the penal consequences of their acts. Nothing is done halfheartedly. So far as youth is concerned, its war against society is total war.

No juvenile groups have yet duplicated the adventures of Murder, Inc. Yet there is ample evidence of their imitation of the extortion and blackmail gangs that have enjoyed nation-wide notoriety. Several months ago five boys between fifteen and seventeen were tried before a Suffolk County jury for extorting money from young boys by threatening them with bodily harm. Despite the conviction of two of these defendants by the jury, the disposition of the cases by probation of the offenders revealed a reluctance on the part of the court to take the entire matter very seriously. In this the court was displaying an attitude consistent with that of courts the country over, of indulging in wishful thinking wherever juvenile delinquency is concerned. If there is a serious juvenile delinquency condition in America today, the courts must share a part of the responsibility for it, but that share is insignificant when compared with the major factors which underlie the condition.

2

We must remember the setting in which the modern youth plays his role. He reacts to environment as grownups do. It would be absurd to expect that at a time when adult America is indulging in an orgy of lawlessness, youth should reveal moderation and restraint. We cannot deny that the standards of communal morality have been lowered by this generation. An age that has witnessed more drinking, more gambling, and a more widespread indulgence in luxuries and comforts than ever before is bound to witness a gradual disappearance of those primitive virtues which sterner and more sober generations nourished and applauded.

The authority of parents has been weakened. And for the impairment of this most important element in character building the parents themselves are to blame. In many homes parents have viewed their responsibilities in a detached and indifferent manner, and their children could really be said to have been left to bring themselves up. I have had frequent occasion in recent years to interview young people who intended to marry and who applied to me for a waiver of the five-day law. I always inquire of these young people whether they have consulted their parents. I have been particularly careful to bring home to servicemen who are away from their parents the propriety of confiding in them before taking such a serious step as matrimony. While some have assured me that they already had obtained their parents' approval, I have been shocked at the number who reply, "Whatever I do is all right with my folks."

A generous application of liberal principles, so called, has resulted in parents' overindulging children and allowing them to do as they please. That they should gratify every whim, express themselves freely, do just as their "little hearts" desire, and have everything they want has been not only tolerated but encouraged. Instead of inhibiting violent tendencies and molding character by strict supervision and guidance, parents have deliberately refrained from stifling the impulses of youth lest some latent talent be frustrated. As a result, bedlam reigns where once was "Home, Sweet Home."

A generation that has been encouraged to express itself freely will little hesitate to join in those "pranks" which amount to vandalism and the malicious destruction of property. The monuments which have been disfigured, the public buildings that have been damaged, and the streetcars that have been wrecked combine to discredit a theory of child guidance which frowns upon restraint. Children can hardly be expected to respect the property of strangers when their destructive tendencies have known no curb in the home.

Frequently these youngsters come from good homes; their parents are excellent people, and no effort or cost has been spared to fit the children properly for their place in society. Consider the hoodlumism revealed by the raids on girls' dormitories by college boys in recent years, and it will readily appear that delinquency is not merely a problem of the slums. If children from the so-called better homes can share in this epidemic of disorder, what can we expect from those who have been denied the care of good and considerate parents? Children who are brought up in an atmosphere of drunkenness and brawling, who witness parents committing assaults upon each other, and who daily see the laws of God and man violated in their homes would have to be more than human if the atmosphere in which they were brought up did not leave its stamp upon them. Such homes are nothing less than breeding places for crime, and the records of our courts go to prove it.

A substantial portion of the young offend-ers brought into court come either from broken homes where the parents are living apart, from homes rendered destitute by the chronic alcoholism of one or both parents, or from homes presided over by parents with long criminal records. The stories disclosed by the police about conditions in these homes are unfit to print. Some are beyond belief. If the conditions which exist in some were ever brought to light, the public would wonder why the delinquency problem is not worse. It can be said with truth that some of these children never had a chance.

3

Modern youth has a great deal of time on its hands. Actually, a shortsighted legislative policy has forbidden young people to engage in many pursuits which once afforded opportunities for wholesome employment. I have seen prosecutions under the Child Labor Law which did more harm than good. I have in mind particularly the owner of a cleaning and dyeing shop whose fifteen-year-old brother helped him after school and who was brought into my court for violating the Child Labor Law. If a young man is not as anxious to work as he might be, let us remember that laws like that have helped estrange him from habits of industry.

There can be no question that the improvement in the condition of the average man, with its increase in earnings, has contributed radically to the change in attitude of parents. Most of them overlook the part which strict discipline, scanty allowances, and hard work played in their moral and physical upbringing. Instead they are determined to give to their children what was denied to them. They buy them better clothes, provide them with larger allowances, enable them to participate in sports, to attend movies, to enjoy summer vacations, and to do all those things calculated to make life agreeable. They not only relieve them of the little tasks or chores which once were a part of a boy's life, but they even frown on the performance of any manual labor, particularly for hire. The industry that was once encouraged in youth as a virtue is now regarded as an interference with the right to enjoy life.

This generosity on the part of parents has had an evil effect on the generation upon which it has been lavished. The little gifts which once provided the great incentive to youth for obedience and industry are now without effect. What was once awaited as an act of kindness and generosity is now demanded as a right. And the kindness of parents which makes occasional work unnecessary has resulted in building up in Young America a pronounced aversion for manual labor and toil. Fifty years ago the popular hero of fiction for our youth was Horatio Alger; today it is Superman. Instead of having its feet on the ground and being conscious of the stern realities of life, our younger generation has its head in the clouds and looks down on its parents as old-fashioned and out-of-date. The parents wanted a generation of "gentlemen" and they got them. They forget that it is important that they be "men" first. On behalf of our youth, it can be said that the parents wanted it that way.

Equally devastating to youth is the noticeable weakening of the moral viewpoint wherever we turn. The nineteenth century may have been hypocritical in its severity, but it extolled virtue and denounced vice and sin. There are serious differences of opinion as to the long-range implications of nineteenth-century austerity and severity, but for youth it meant a high moral standard which served to inhibit lust, to promote modesty and respect, and to encourage obedience to law.

This moral viewpoint has been weakened today by an amazing combination of social, economic, and political factors. One hundred years ago gambling was considered the pastime of the wicked; today it has the sanction of authority in the form of legalized parimutuel betting. One hundred years ago the moral forces in America waged a relentless war against alcoholism and managed to keep the evil under a fair measure of control; today we are paying an exorbitant price for the experiment of Prohibition in the form

of an unlimited distribution of alcoholic beverages. What is called the licensing system is nothing more than a token regulation. As a consequence teen-age drinking has become a major aspect of the problem of juvenile delinquency.

Equally marked are the changes in concepts of decency and honor. We read in the daily paper that a judge has ruled in the Federal Court that even though a man had been convicted on several occasions of violating liquor and gambling laws, he is still worthy of becoming an American citizen. On another occasion we read of a judge stopping deportation proceedings against a criminal who had twice been convicted of manufacturing slugs which could be used in slot machines. This judge's pronouncement to the effect that such a crime did not involve the element of moral turpitude should suffice to alert us to the depreciated moral viewpoint of today.

Let us examine the headlines a bit further. A judge before whom an embezzler stands, makes the injudicious remark, in condoning the offense, "His pay was too low." What effect has such comment on the moral viewpoint of youth? Or let us consider the extreme in official bungling, when a deputy warden in a state prison publicly applauded the conduct of a group of prisoners who had mutinied against prison discipline. When public officials condone lawlessness, is it any wonder that young people become indifferent to high standards?

How has the class war in America affected youth's moral viewpoint? Whether one believes in labor's right to strike or not, it must be apparent to everyone that the chronic condition of unrest on the labor front, punctuated by occasional outbreaks of violence and lawlessness, has had sinister implications for the cause of law and order. Its impact on young people has been noticeable, as is evident from their readiness to join in any mass demonstration promoting any cause.

Several years ago 3000 New York City high school children picketed the mayor's office for four days shouting, "We want more pay for our teachers." On the fifth day there was no demonstration; it was Saturday and there was no school.

In glancing through the newspapers of the last few years, we can find ample evidence of the activities of boys and girls as agitators. They picket City Hall to protest against closing a fire station or abandoning a school site. They join a strike called in protest against a change in the high school curriculum or the transfer of an athletic coach. Possibly these children have serious notions regarding the objectives which such practices promote; but, at the same time, the whole thing coincides with what their juvenile minds regard as "good fun." That the ultimate consequences of these demonstrations are to exalt insubordination and to weaken the arm of constituted authority hardly occurs to them. They have become pawns in the hands of those who thrive on agitation and unrest.

Not only our youths but our grownups have wilted under the spectacle of a viciously waged class war. In no small measure has the indifference of authority to the violence and lawlessness of the labor struggle resulted in a disrespect for law. On the political front the condition is equally disruptive. In recent years there has been an intensification of the struggle for political power in the United States. And the condition is evident at all levels of the political hierarchy. It derives principally from the fact that party government has been supplanted by gang government, and the officeholder wields power by virtue of his personal ascendancy. As a consequence he is campaigning for office 365 days in the year. Those who seek to replace him are equally active and vigorous. This war is being waged with the weapons of the forum; with crimination and recrimination; with sly innuendo and downright bombast. Young people are spectators in this war, and they gaze at the spectacle somewhat bewildered. They emerge from the experience with a feeling that a great many people are being entrusted with the powers of government without regard to their merit

or personal integrity. If youth is waging a revolt against authority today, it is because conditions on the home front have done much to discredit authority.

Recently in Redwood City, California, a schoolteacher took his pupils to a nearby courthouse in order to show them "how justice works." In court the judge helped the show along by asking to see the teacher's driving license. When the judge discovered that the teacher's license had already expired, he immediately issued a summons to the teacher to appear before him on the charge of driving without a license. Such a judge is a menace. Instead of exalting the teacher in the eyes of his pupils, he discredited him and thereby undermined his authority in the classroom. In every sense he was contributing to the delinquency of a group of minor children. Every day in the year, and all over the United States, people who should know better are doing equally stupid things with no other objective than to appear smart.

4

To what extent has the cultural setting in which modern youth lives been responsible for the moral breakdown? No one can deny that the world of today is a much more interesting place for boys and girls than that of the nineteenth century. They have movies, radio, television, and the modern newspaper. Millions of dollars are being spent each day to provide programs that will arouse their interest and entertain them. Some of these items are educational as well as entertaining. Doubtless many of them serve to improve the moral viewpoint of those reached by them. Others have questionable value as educational items, and there are some which are a distinct menace to the morals of the community.

We must never underestimate the role played by suggestion in influencing the behavior of youth. Thirty years ago, in the city of Boston, a boy who had escaped from a correctional institution sent out word that he intended to steal a car and race it through certain streets of Charlestown which were known as "The Loop." No such insane stunt had ever been attempted before. True to his word he appeared on the designated night and entertained thousands who had gathered to watch him, while the police, racing after him on motorcycles, made desperate but futile attempts to apprehend him. Since that night, over thirty years ago, hundreds of boys have imitated his escapade. They have stolen cars; they have killed and injured many innocent citizens. This one insane venture sufficed to set in motion a crime wave which has made the "loop speeder" a chronic problem to authority in Massachusetts.

Let us analyze a few more items which reveal youth's readiness to imitate. Several years ago a slightly deranged veteran stepped out onto the parapet at the ninth floor level of the Hotel Touraine in Boston. For hours he held a crowd spellbound on the street below while he refused to return to a place of safety. It was unfortunate that the episode was publicized. Within a few days similar exhibitionist stunts were staged in different cities in the United States. Need I remind you that every example of unusual behavior reported in the press or portrayed on television is usually followed by a multitude of similar stunts all over the United States? Consider the outbreaks on college campuses. Not even Harvard, Yale, and Massachusetts Institute of Technology could avoid the epidemic of exhibitionism which transformed sections of their student bodies into rioting mobs.

5

If society is bewildered by this spectacle of youth in revolt, its peace of mind has not been improved by the variety of suggestions which have been advanced to meet the situation. These all savor of the new liberalism. They ignore the part which the weakening of parental control over youth has played in precipitating the present crisis. Expanding the probation system, providing more public playgrounds, and raising the age limit for school attendance are but a few of the palliatives recommended. But no sober analysis of the problem can ignore their futility.

Human behavior is linked with character, and the process of character building commences at infancy and acquires its basic strength and quality in the home. No public agency can supply the training and instruction which a well-managed and properly supervised household affords. No one can replace parents in the training of children, and the sooner the new liberalism discovers this the sooner will it be on the right road to a solution. If society wishes to strike at the root of the evil, it must wage its campaign against those parents who refuse to discharge their responsibilities faithfully. The desire of women to retain their place in industry since the war is not without sinister implication. If the condition becomes fixed, we must expect an aggravated delinquency situation. While woman legally has a right to participate in industry, there is no moral sanction for abandoning a much more sacred responsibility. And the great decision which the modern woman must make is whether she prefers the career of motherhood to that of a worker. She cannot undertake both and succeed.

Few people see the long-range implications of juvenile delinquency. Few people realize that a majority of the men in the prisons in America today commenced their criminal careers between the ages of eight and thirteen. Some of these unfortunates had a predisposition to crime; others became criminal through their associations. As for the congenital delinquent, nothing we could have done would have spared him his fate. But the child who might have grown into an honorable career had it not been for the undesirable associations which brought him to his sad estate has a just grievance against a society that did not insulate him from these vicious influences. Policies which deny this protection to the coming generation are policies which will assure a bumper crop of criminals for the future.

I have already mentioned the calamitous consequences to the entire Boston community of the exhibitionism of the automobile-stealing, loop-speeding Jimmy Sheehan. His little crime wave turned into a major outbreak of juvenile delinquency. And the same imitation that multiplied the Jimmy Sheehans and the parapet jumpers is being discovered in the duplication of the crimes portrayed in the movies, on the radio, and on television. Left to his own resources the modern delinquent would still be indulging in the petty pilfering that once satisfied his criminal urge. In an atmosphere filled with suggestion, his criminal aspirations cease to be juvenile. It is because he is so much more dangerous today that he can no longer be treated as a child.

Within a year a seventeen-year-old boy with a record of previous arrests for larceny was apprehended in the act of stealing in a department store. As the store detective put his hand on him, the boy drew a razor and slashed the detective across the face. In my opinion this boy is a confirmed and dangerous criminal. I sentenced him to the Concord Reformatory. He appealed and I learned later that in the Superior Court his sentence was modified to one year in the House of Correc-

tion. Whether this judge's leniency was justified, only time will tell.

Whether the generation which has disquieted our era can be set right is a great question. Some have faith that various expedients of correction and reform provide a ray of hope. In the opinion of realists, however, who have seen society struggling in vain with the problem of crime, a large portion of the delinquent group must be charged off as lost. They are the casualties of the new liberalism. The only hope for the future lies in the resurgence of the home as the basic institution of the modern world. We must recapture the spirit of the home which our parents and grandparents knew, and young people must be brought up and not left to bring themselves up. The position of the parent must be restored to its former place of authority, and the power to govern the household must be asserted with kindness when possible and severity when necessary. Then, and only then, will character thrive and the foundation be laid for a law-abiding society.

Chief Justice Earl Warren looks ahead twenty-five years and considers how the role of law can be widened and deepened here at home as well as in the world. The accelerating rate of scientific and technological change is bound to require changes in legal institutions, and ideological issues in the world political situation will surely have their effect on the law of the future.

The legal heritage of the American people is recounted so that the present nature and functions of our legal system may be understood. Among its basic principles are these: our legal system has been an organic growth; it is adaptable to changing circumstances; and it serves the cause of human justice.

Underlying the American constitutional system is the great tradition which places the fundamental law above the will of the government. Even so, access to justice is not equal in all parts of our country, and American law is subject to procedural flaws and anachronisms, which call for reforms in our system. Turning to the United Nations, it has been an arena of power politics and ideological struggle, but it remains possible that the United Nations may develop into a focal point of world law.

42

THE LAW AND THE FUTURE*
Earl Warren
Chief Justice of the United States

When a man of law tries to peer through the next twenty-five years, he is struck by the probability that all legal systems, and indeed the very concept of law, will be as severely tested as ever in history. The test comes from two sides.

First, the accelerating rate of scientific and technological change in the world makes the pace of legal change look like a tortoise racing a hare. In this same FORTUNE series for which I am writing, it has been predicted by men of science that worldwide transportation may soon become almost as rapid as communication is now; that nuclear developments can make energy almost as cheap as air; that climate control will enable us to turn the Arctic into a tropical garden or alternatively to bring on another Ice Age, as we please. These and like marvels, if achieved, will obviously revolutionize those relationships between man and man, and between man and government, which are the subject matter of the law.

The other test of law comes from the world political situation. The struggle between Communism and freedom, whether hot, cold, or lukewarm, extends not only along the physical frontiers of our civilization, but into its mind and soul, inevitably straining the fabric of all our institutions, the law included. Our legal system is woven around the freedom and dignity of the individual. A Communist state ignores these values.

Ours is the difficult task of defending and strengthening these values while also pursuing a goal that sometimes appears to be in conflict with them—namely, the physical security of our nation.

Such are two formidable challenges to the law which seem to line the corridor of the next twenty-five years.

WHY THE CHALLENGES MUST BE MET

Yet no man who understands the nature and purpose of law will let these challenges go by default. There are at least three reasons why an American jurist must work, hope, and pray that the observance of law, the prestige of law, and the knowledge of law will be far more widespread a generation hence than they are now. I shall give these reasons and then proceed to suggest, as specifically as possible, how I think that hope can be fulfilled.

First of all, the U.S., as Americans have always known and loved it, cannot subsist without law. Our Constitution was designed chiefly by lawyers; it was given bone and sinew by great jurists like John Marshall; and we owe the continuity of our social existence to the respect for law of which our reverence for the Constitution is the symbol and sign. Cicero defined a commonwealth as "an agreement of law and a community of interest." Without their agreement of law, Americans might still have some community of interest, but it would unquestionably take one of those barbaric forms in which order is kept by force alone, and in which the freedom of the individual and the consent of the governed are ignored.

In the second place, it is not just the U.S. that needs law, it is the entire world. The world's chief need in these next decades will be peace and order; and of all human institutions, law has the best historical claim to satisfy this need. Isaiah said that peace is the work of justice. It was an English axiom, framed by Coke, that certainty is the mother of quiet. Justice and certainty are twin aims of the law. When the U.S. entered the late World War, British soldiers sent the following message to our soldiers: "We welcome you as brothers in the struggle to make sure that the world shall be ruled by the force of law, and not by the law of force." Until the millennium, when all men shall be ruled by Christian love, no other means of social peace but these two—the law of force or the force of law—are likely to be known to man.

The third reason the great mid-century challenges to the law must be met is simply this: the nature of man. In all times and places he has had a sense of justice and a desire for justice. Any child expresses this fact of nature with his first judgment that this or that "isn't fair." A legal system is simply a mature and sophisticated attempt, never perfected but always capable of improvement, to institutionalize this sense of justice and to free men from the terror and unpredictability of arbitrary force. Unfortunately, the same human nature that craves justice and freedom under law is too often willing to deny them to others. Thus the struggle for law is never-ending, and our generation is inevitably engaged in it.

The Supreme Court building in Washington is adorned with many statues and friezes. Among the figures represented are Menes, Hammurabi, Moses, Solomon, Lycurgus, Solon, Draco, Confucius, and Octavian, all lawgivers to people who needed and wanted law before the time of Christ; also Justinian, Mohammed, Charlemagne, King John, St.

Louis, Grotius, Blackstone, Napoleon, and Marshall, lawgivers since the time of Christ. The history of law is as old as human nature. By the same token, its proper scope is the world. In fact there is no tribe on the face of the earth, however primitive, and no nation, however tyrannical, that is without some customary or formal code of crime and punishment. The problem of law in the next twenty-five years, therefore, is not so much to introduce law anywhere as it is to improve, strengthen, and civilize law everywhere. Especially must we broaden the scope of that youngest and most fragile of great legal systems, the law of nations.

What is the American share of this great task? To understand that, we must first understand our own legal system, its strengths and weaknesses.

THE INHERITANCE WE BUILD ON

We Americans are peculiarly fortunate in our legal inheritance. One ancestor of our system is Roman law, of which the legal historian Maine said that it had "the longest known history of any set of human institutions," during which history it was "progressively modified for the better." The nearer ancestor of our system is English law, which has for centuries kept peace throughout an empire and commonwealth wider and more complex than the Roman. Our American modification of these systems has served us equally well. With all its imperfections, it can be called an outstanding success. Of the many characteristics of our legal system that can be given credit for this success, three seem to me especially significant.

First, our legal system has been an organic growth, and not the overnight creation of any individual genius. The Founding Fathers wrote our Constitution in a single summer, but in doing so they borrowed unashamedly from long-dead lawmakers and political philosophers from Moses and Aristotle to Locke and Montesquieu. In fact they created no novel or untested principles, but chose the best of those already known; and that is one reason their work has endured. The idea of due process, for example, they owed to Magna Charta; the idea of habeas corpus came to them from sources lost in the mists of the Middle Ages. The natural rights of man explicitly asserted by our Founding Fathers had long been the common-law rights of Englishmen.

Moreover, having written our Constitution, the Founding Fathers did not use it to abolish and replace the laws to which Americans had been accustomed. The new national system was organically grafted on to the state legal systems, not only those of English, but also those of Latin origin, and has grown along with them to this day. I have already mentioned some of the alien lawgivers whose figures appropriately adorn our Supreme Court building, and others could be mentioned—Capito and Labeo, Sabinus and Proclus, Gaius and Ulpian—whose very names are known only to scholars of the law, but who made their contributions to its coral-like growth. And the gallery of American law is not complete without representatives of our own colonial, frontier, and state legal experience: eloquent lawyers like Andrew Hamilton, who defended John Peter Zenger and the freedom of the press; brave judges like William Cushing, who advanced alone against the bayonets of Shays' Rebellion and opened the Massachusetts Court; clear thinkers like Chancellor Kent, whose opinions were carried by the authority of reason far beyond the borders of New York. An organic system like ours requires the faithful work of many men, both famous and unknown.

A second reason for the success of our legal system is its adaptability to changing circumstance. As Pollock said, all courts have a duty, which ours generally try to perform, "to keep the rules of law in harmony with the enlightened common sense of the nation." Even the bicycle forced new definitions of negligence in civil suits; and the thousands of other changes forced by later technological developments indicate that our law can keep up with the still greater changes ahead—so long as "the common sense of the nation" can be discerned. Our judges are not monks

or scientists, but participants in the living stream of our national life, steering the law between the dangers of rigidity on the one hand and of formlessness on the other. Legal scholars may still debate whether the life of the law is reason, as Coke maintained, or experience, as Holmes claimed. I think it is both. Our system faces no theoretical dilemma but a single continuous problem: how to apply to ever changing conditions the never changing principles of freedom.

So far as the Constitution is concerned, it has demonstrated again and again its capacity for adaptation to the most challenging new conditions. Under John Marshall's leadership, it proved it could mold a strong national government, at a time when such a government was needed to protect American liberties. Later the Constitution had to find a path for those same liberties through the iron mazes of our industrial revolution. And while this quest continues through new electronic mazes, still another challenge confronts the Constitution: must a nation that is now the strongest in the world demand, for its own further strength and security, a sacrifice by its own citizens of their ancient liberties? This problem haunts the work of all our courts these days. But the Constitution exists for the individual as well as for the nation. I believe it will prove itself adaptable to this new challenge.

There is a third reason for the success of our legal system: while adaptable to our changing national needs, it serves a greater and unchanging cause. That cause is human justice. Ever since Hammurabi published his code to "hold back the strong from oppressing the weak," the success of any legal system is measured by its fidelity to the universal ideal of justice. Theorists beset us with other definitions of law: that it is a mask of privilege, or the judge's private prejudice, or the will of the stronger. But the ideal of justice survives all such myopic views, for as Cicero said, "we are born to it."

The American legal system was nurtured in this ideal of justice and could not last without it. We have in fact accepted not only the rule of law but, through our unique practice of judicial review of legislation, the reign of law. We have done so in the full knowledge that judges are fallible, procedures slow, and the Constitution itself a product of compromise; but in the faith that it is better to make our final decisions in the name of an eternal ideal. Our courts have occasionally misused their great power of review, but never to the point of justifying its forfeiture. They are kept in line with the other branches of government not only by the words of the Constitution, but by a tradition of self-restraint and impersonality.

LAW AND THE GREAT TRADITION

The American constitutional system is in the great tradition which places the fundamental law above the will of the government. This tradition began with the dawn of our civilization. The people of Israel governed themselves as a federation of tribes, without any central government, under a Constitution —the Covenant they had made with Jehovah. Even after they chose a king ("that we also may be like all the nations") they kept the tradition because the king, too, lived and ruled under the Covenant. When Rome was young, many a similar commonwealth and republic flourished around the Mediterranean; but Rome survived them all because it employed and extended the rule of law, thus making its greatest contribution to our civilization. When the Renaissance broke the mold of medieval Europe, England was not the only monarchy that gave promise of constitutional development. But England alone avoided a serious relapse into despotism, because England secured its public order and individual freedom under the law.

The sign of this great tradition, the tradition which places the fundamental law above the will of the government, is an independent judiciary. We associate it with our system of separated powers and judicial review; but other nations have maintained the tradition with other forms of government. Britain's system of parliamentary supremacy,

for example, can override but does not overawe British justice.

Why, then, have some nations maintained and strengthened the great tradition and not others? For one reason only, that the people were determined to remain free and to keep the law above the government. When the Hitler occupation tried to bend the Supreme Court of Norway to its will, the entire Court risked death by resigning. This act, I am sure, did as much to preserve independent justice for Norway as did *Marbury* vs. *Madison* for the U.S., or as Coke's defiance of his dictatorial King did for England. No form of government, however nearly perfect, can itself secure justice and freedom under law for any country. The true safeguard is the spirit and devotion of the people, a passion for justice and freedom that is widely shared and deeply felt.

To summarize: Americans have one of the great legal systems, but not a monopoly of the sense of justice, which is universal; nor have we a permanent copyright on the means of securing justice, for it is the spirit and not the form of law that keeps justice alive. But as a nation directly challenged by the march of a revolutionary technology, and also by a reactionary antagonist representing the law of force, we have a vital interest in defending and extending the rule of law throughout the world. How then can we go about it?

NEEDED REFORMS OF OUR SYSTEM

Two generations ago Dean Ames of the Harvard Law School pointed out that "the spirit of reform which during the last six hundred years has been bringing our system of law more and more into harmony with moral principles has not yet achieved its perfect work"; and he urged that past advances should encourage effort for future improvement. This advice still needs to be heeded. The proud inscription on our federal courts—Equal Justice Under Law—remains our goal but is not fully secured to all our citizens. The rights promised them by our Constitution are not yet perfected. Some of the defects in our system are inherited; others keep creeping in. Justice, like freedom, needs constant vigilance.

Justice delayed is often justice denied. This kind of denial is a growing problem in our federal courts. Some calendars are so crowded that litigants cannot be sure of trial within four years or more. To our Judicial Conference (composed of the Chief Justice and the Chief Judges of the circuit courts) this has been a problem of increasing concern. It will require a combined effort by the bench, the bar, and the litigating public, as well as some help from Congress, to clear this growing backlog and keep the channels of justice open.

Unequal justice is a contradiction in terms. Yet access to justice is unequal in parts of our country. Suspects are sometimes arrested, tried, and convicted without being adequately informed of their right to counsel. Even when he knows of this right, many a citizen cannot afford to exercise it. There are barely half enough public defenders, legal-aid societies, or other methods available to perfect this right.

American law is pockmarked with other procedural flaws and anachronisms. We have recently made some progress in simplifying methods of appeal in the federal courts, but much remains to be done. Thanks to outside underwriting, our entire system of administering criminal justice is undergoing a detailed survey by the American Bar foundation. The facts already known warrant a continuing crusade by the legal profession for fairer and speedier procedures.

Lawyers are officers of the court and therefore servants of justice. Now that the more cynical forms of "legal realism" are growing less fashionable, it is to be hoped that fewer lawyers will regard their professional training as a mere means of livelihood. But cynicism and apathy are not confined to our profession. Since the instinct of justice is universal, every citizen, lawyer or not, can serve justice by living more consciously in its spirit, and by keeping his own vigilant watch on the rights he shares with his fellow citizen.

Solon, asked how justice could be secured in Athens, replied, "If those who are not injured feel as indignant as those who are."

WHOSE BILL OF RIGHTS?

This is especially good advice at a time when our Bill of Rights is under subtle and pervasive attack, as at present. The attack comes not only from without, but from our own indifference and failure of imagination. Minorities whose rights are threatened are quicker to band together in their own defense than in the defense of other minorities. The same is true, with less reason, of segments of the majority. Churchmen are quick to defend religious freedom; lawyers were never so universally aroused as by President Roosevelt's Court bill; newspapers are most alert to civil liberties when there is a hint of press censorship in the air. And educators become perturbed at every attempt to curb academic freedom. But too seldom do all of these become militant when ostensibly the rights of only one group are threatened. They do not always react to the truism that when the rights of any individual or group are chipped away, the freedom of all erodes.

The moral is that if each minority, each professional group, and each citizen would imagine himself in the other's shoes, everybody's rights would have firmer support. The beginning of justice is the capacity to generalize and make objective one's private sense of wrong, thus turning it to public account. The pursuit of justice is not the vain pursuit of a remote abstraction; it is a continuing direction for our daily conduct.

Thus it is that when the generation of 1980 receives from us the Bill of Rights, the document will not have exactly the same meaning it had when we received it from our fathers. We will pass on a better Bill of Rights or a worse one, tarnished by neglect or burnished by growing use. If these rights are real, they need constant and imaginative application to new situations. For example: the security procedures set up to protect the federal government have been extended to the point where more than eight million Americans must undergo them. As the system expands, everyone is more closely affected by the balance we strike between security and freedom. Injustices carry a wider import. The Bill of Rights must be measured daily against this new problem.

NO U.S. MONOPOLY

By thus improving the administration of justice and strengthening liberty under law in our own country, we will make our greatest single contribution to the promotion of law elsewhere in the world. For as long as the U.S. leads the forces of freedom in the world's great ideological struggle, our institutions will remain under a global spotlight, and what we do will speak much louder than what we say. If our actions continuously testify to our belief in justice, other free nations will be fortified in their pursuit of the same ideal.

A vital concern for the ideal of justice is what all legal systems most need today. The variety of legal systems need not trouble us; they are like different languages. Some languages are subtler or richer, some more logical or straight-forward than others; but all serve the common purpose of communication. So all good legal systems, with their varying histories and environments, serve justice as their people see it; and the best of them serve the great tradition of government under law. But as languages can enrich and extend communication by translations and borrowings, so too can legal systems. The promotion of law in the world will therefore benefit from a revival of comparative jurisprudence, a revival in which American lawyers are already taking an active part.

Twice in our history, in 1883 and 1915, the Lord Chief Justice of England has sat by invitation as an observer on the bench of the U.S. Supreme Court. I was accorded a similar courtesy last summer in Norway, where I heard proceedings before their Supreme Court; and I also met with the members of Germany's constitutional court in their conference room. At Salzburg, I visited the seminar where American institutions, including American law, are interpreted to deeply interested students from all parts of free Europe; Chief Judge Magruder of our First Circuit Court of Appeals was a lecturer this year. Leading law schools both here and in Europe are giving increased attention to comparative law.

It seems clear that this mutual interest and curiosity can profitably be carried much further. Moslem lands, for example, have old and well-developed legal systems about which American jurists know very little, as do Moslems about ours. An agreement among different cultures to exchange full information on basic points of comparative law—such as why, and under what conditions, a man may be jailed—should lead to considerable self-examination and improvement on all sides. In investigating why a thief may have his hand cut off in Saudi Arabia, or be branded on the forehead in other countries, we might also be led to study some debatable forms of punishment still used in some of our states. Habeas corpus, a right we regard as fundamental to a free society, is not so regarded in some other democracies; why not? Why are British court procedures so much more orderly and rapid than ours? To pursue such inquiries in a spirit of mutual truth-seeking could surely yield good results. All of us have much to teach and much to learn.

WORLD LAW AND THE U.N.

The United Nations exists because civilized nations prefer orderly, rational, and peaceful procedures in the settlement of disputes. This preference is the cradle of law. The U.N. can become the growing point of a true international legal system, but only as it grows around the ideal of justice. The U.N. must therefore bend its efforts to make justice the keystone of its arch.

Three ways to do this suggest themselves. First, as justice is a universal goal, so should the membership of the U.N. transcend its origin as a league of wartime allies, and become as nearly universal as an acceptance of the charter obligations permits. Second, peaceful procedures imply that agreements will be inviolable. There will be great need for the strict honoring of U.N. agreements in the next twenty-five years, and the nations with the best record in this respect will have done the most to advance the cause of justice under law. Third, more and more international questions can become justiciable, giving a steadily wider jurisdiction to the World Court.

The U.N. has inevitably been an arena of power politics and ideological struggle. This need not discourage those who hope to see it develop into a focus of world law. It was during one of history's earlier great struggles, the Thirty Years War, that Hugo Grotius of Holland brought to birth those concepts of international law that were to moderate international behavior for three centuries. The U.N. has not succeeded in writing a generally satisfactory Bill of Human Rights. This does not mean that there is no measure of international agreement on this vital subject. Last June an International Congress of Jurists, composed of lawyers, judges, and teachers from forty-nine nations, showed an astonishing unanimity in their so-called Act of Athens, defining the basic characteristics of a free system. They declared that the state is subject to the law, and owes its citizens the means to enforce their rights; that judges should uphold the rule of law in entire political independence; that lawyers of the world should insist on a fair trial for every accused; and that the rights of the individual, to be protected by the rule of law, include freedom of speech, press, worship, assembly, association, and free elections. If by 1980 this writ should run through all the nations whose lawyers helped frame it, then indeed will the great tradition of government under law be established beyond challenge in our world.

Whether or not law can tame the ideological struggles of this era, there is another broad field of human intercourse which can and should be brought wholly within orderly procedures. This is the economic field, where rivalries have sometimes bred wars in the past but need not again. Governments have spent millions of man-hours, as well as billions of dollars, on world economic problems since World War II. They have not solved these problems, but they are learning to manage them. New types of treaties and commissions have proliferated throughout the field of international trade, investment, and finance. Within the free world, if we have the will, these orderly procedures and expert institutions can be made to temper all economic controversies and prevent them from becoming inflammatory. We can reasonably resolve that this whole field will be subordinated to peaceful procedures during the next twenty-five years. Justice in the economic sphere often consists in finding a genuine mutuality of interest. Among the free nations, that mutuality is already great, and can be made permanent.

THE HERITAGE AND THE STRUGGLE

Such are the chief growing points from which the law may extend its influence over the affairs of men in the next generation. In doing so it faces the challenges (already mentioned) of an accelerating technology and a world political struggle for survival.

The challenge of technology to the law is largely to its rate of change. To meet it, the law need not itself get more technically complex than it is now; rather the opposite may be its best course. For in self-defense against a technology which only a few can hope to master, the average man and the common sense of justice will seek an ally in laws which all can understand. As in Blackstone's time, some knowledge of law may become "an essential part of a liberal education"; and lawyers, reaffirming their purpose in life to serve justice, may come in closer touch with the deepest springs of our democracy.

The world political struggle is more dangerous to the future of law. It is a struggle of greater proportions than Americans have known before. In some of our wars, we have briefly succumbed to the temptation of imitating the vices of our antagonist; but the national sense of justice and respect for law always returned with peace. In the present struggle between our world and Communism, the temptation to imitate totalitarian security methods is a subtle temptation that must be resisted day by day, for it will be with us as long as totalitarianism itself. The whole question of man's relation to his nation, his government, his fellow man is raised in acute and chronic form. Each of the 462 words of our Bill of Rights, the most precious part of our legal heritage, will be tested and retested.

By 1980 that heritage can be stronger and brighter than ever, and the ideal of liberty and justice under law made more real in its various forms throughout the world. But it will require a new dedication and a continuing faith from all who cherish the heritage and the goal.

VIII

War and Peace

War and peace are interrelated yet separate problems. War has been institutionalized and is deeply rooted in our culture, an established mode of behavior with ever-changing traits, while peace remains essentially an idealized hope. The issues of war and peace today are of immediate national concern, but they must be understood in their international context. Especially vital are the national ambitions for economic and political power, and the issues implied in the phrase "war versus peace" could well be translated into "international power versus peace." International law and world public opinion are customarily regarded as checks upon war, but neither is capable of regulating the struggle for power and keeping the peace. The members of the League of Nations and of the United Nations have given what might be called lip service to efforts towards disarmament and the actual implementation of peace in the world.

The term "power," in its political context, signifies control over men's minds and actions. It refers to control relationships not only among those who are in public positions of authority but also between those in authority and the public at large. Political power does not depend upon the actual exercise of physical violence, though the threat of violence is intrinsic to political power. Extreme examples of actual violence are capital punishment and war, and, whether threatened or actually carried out, they are tokens of the zest for political power. On the international scene, the resort to warfare indicates that the aggressor has abdicated political power in favor of military power.

Political power is a psychological relationship between those who exercise it and those over whom it is exercised. Armed strength is undoubtedly the most important material factor contributing to the political power of a nation, and war is sometimes referred to as an instrument of politics. But the political objectives of war are varied: the purpose may or may not be the conquest of territory or the annihilation of enemy armies; the political objective may be to force the enemy to yield to the will of the victor, which would involve a change in the mind of the enemy. Economic, financial, territorial, or military policies may be utilized in international affairs to enhance political power.

Present-day conceptions of national sovereignty have become particularly significant in the problems of war and peace. For many people, erroneous implications or inferences have made the term confusing. Sovereignty is strictly an internal characteristic of nations. It means simply that there is no authority above the nation, no state or group of states to legislate for it or enforce legislation within it. It means that no rules and laws are binding upon a sovereign state except those to which it gives consent. Consequently no sovereign state would, because of its "internal sovereignty," be justified in meddling in the internal affairs of other sovereign states. Sovereignty is important in international relations because it denotes respect as an independent state under international law and as a member in the family of nations.

Ideologies characteristic of specific groups sometimes provide the driving force behind social and political action and motivation in time of war. Ideologies may serve as tools in the achievement of political power and in the fomenting of revolution. They sometimes interfere with the rational solution of political problems, not only because they tend to produce cliché-thinking, but because their biased influence may cause people to overlook or disregard facts which are contrary to the tenets or assumptions of that ideology. This ideological role has become abundantly evident in the Communist Revolution's effort at world conquest, which is being directed by the Soviet regime in Moscow.

Emergence of the Various Aspects of War. Rivalry and struggle, even warfare, might be attributed to the animal world, but our concern is mostly with the phases of primitive, civilized, and modern war. It seems reasonable to believe that since each stage began with the emergence of a new type of dynamic equilibrium and was characterized by a new trend of evolution, each can be studied through a new type of evidence. Each phase was marked by certain fundamental inventions; of these the successively improved means of communication have been even more important than improved means of destruction. This is because speech, writing, and printing initiated the ages of man, of civilization, and of the world community, respectively.

War in the psychological sense began with organic nature; war in the sociological sense could not exist as a distinct phenomenon before the emergence of human societies; war in the sense of a legal situation equally permitting groups to expand wealth and power by violence began with civilization; and war in the modern technical sense began with the period of world-civilization. All these phases of war have been analyzed at length by Quincy Wright. As a general introductory statement concerning these four phases, Wright says: [1]

> . . . Animal war resembled modern war only in the psychological sense. War among primitive people, untouched by civilized neighbors, resembled modern war only in the psychological and sociological senses. War among the historic peoples resembled modern war in the psychological, sociological, and legal senses. Only since the advent of continuous world-cultural contacts in the fifteenth century has war existed in the modern technological sense.

[1] Quincy Wright, *A Study of War*, 2 vols., The University of Chicago Press, Chicago, 1942, vol. 1, pp. 40–41. Copyright 1942 by the University of Chicago. Excerpt reprinted by permission of the publishers.

In all its stages war can, of course, be approached from the sociological, legal, and technical points of view as well as from the psychological. In each of these four stages violent behavior has served superindividual functions, has exhibited formal regularities of recurrence and conduct, and has proceeded by describable techniques as well as from understandable psychological drives. Even animal warfare has functions, a theory, and a technique, but they are not the functions, theory, and technique which characterize modern human warfare. While the history of modern psychological drives goes back to the animals, that of modern sociological institutions goes back only to primitive man, that of modern law only to early civilizations, and that of modern technology only to the inventions of the late Middle Ages. Animal sociology rests on different foundations from human sociology, primitive law rests on different foundations from civilized law, and modern technology rests on distinctive foundations. War has changed its character with each of these great transitions.

The material and technological evolution of warfare may be indicated more concretely. Very few of the technologies have undergone such rapid and momentous changes as the art of collective fighting, and in no respects have there been greater changes between ancient and modern wars than in the equipment used in combat. L. L. Bernard [2] points out that the earliest fighters contended with bare hands, teeth, and skeletal muscles, possibly reinforced by stones, sticks, and dry bones used as crude clubs, spears, and hammers. The earliest man-made weapons were clubs, knives, and daggers made of stone and bone or even wood; sharp or sharpened sticks were used as crude spears. The second great advance came with the development of the projectile, which first took the form of the thrown spear and the hurled club; the introduction of the battering ram also belongs to this period. The invention of gunpowder at a later period made it possible to throw small and large projectiles with greater force and accuracy. The fourth great advance in the use of military equipment came with the employment of moving mechanisms in the attack. The fifth type of advance enumerated by Bernard was the employment of chemical warfare, including the use of explosives.

Other changes to note include the greater destructiveness of property and lives in modern wars as compared with the ancient; the changes from personal to impersonal modes of combat; differences in the emotional accompaniments of ancient and modern wars, contrasting the psychological stresses and strains of personal with impersonal combat. The personal cruelty and vindictiveness characteristic of earlier warfare has supposedly been superseded by more humanitarian attitudes in modern warfare. The objectives of ancient and modern wars also have changed. Primitive wars were fought almost exclusively for immediate and material ends—i.e., for booty which was to be obtained by means of raids and other surprise attacks—or for revenge or in defense of violated territory. Modern wars, on the other hand, frequently aim at political or even ideological results, and, if there are material objectives to be gained, they are likely to have future rather than immediate significance.

[2] Adapted from L. L. Bernard, *War and Its Causes*, Henry Holt and Company, New York, 1944, pp. 61–66.

Primitive wars rarely required ethical or legal sanctions, though they do apply to modern war, as evident in international law or custom and in socialized ethics. Primitive and ancient wars were largely regulated by magical considerations, while modern wars are subject to rational control. The "holy war" is one of the psycho-social phenomena of history, but theological holy wars are now definitely on the decline. Present-day attitudes toward war are more negative than positive, to the extent of regarding warfare as outmoded and irrational, yet mankind has not been able to get rid of it. Warfare in its present form as "cold war" involves too many imponderables for anyone to make dependable predictions.

The Causes of War. There is no one cause for war. Situations leading to war are complex, and any classification of so-called causes is purely arbitrary. Broadly considered, the causes may be grouped into psychological, economic, political, and other social categories—each group subject to subclassification.

Among the psychological factors are fear, suspicion, greed, lust for power, hate, revenge, jealousy, and envy. Fear is regarded as one of the powerful emotional factors driving nations toward war today. Fear may be indicated as a feeling of national insecurity, fear of invasion, fear of loss of property, fear of change; it may be specific, as fear of an ideology, or it may be fear of some nation that threatens aggression.

Economic factors as a class would include aggressive imperialism; economic rivalry for markets, energy resources, and essential raw materials; government protection of private interests abroad without reference to the general welfare; disregard of the rights of backward peoples; population pressure; and profits in war. Economic factors depend upon the influences of industrial and technological development upon general social and political relationships which, in their turn, may have not only national but international significance in producing conflict.

Political factors would include the principle of balance of power, secret treaties, unjust treaties, the violation of treaties, disregard of the rights of minorities, the organization of the state for war, and ineffective or obstructive political machinery. Governments may have ulterior motives for encouraging warlike policies. Such is the case with a dictator who encourages war to make himself appear essential, and causes crises to justify his continuance in office. Governments wanting to increase their power may use military situations or the apparent imminence of war to extend control over men and national resources. Ideologies belong in the political category inasmuch as their national influence may be highly militant; socialism, communism, fascism, and national socialism stand out as examples.

Among specific traits which are especially militant in nature are exaggerated nationalism and statism, competitive armaments, religious and racial antagonism, and a general condition of apathy, indifference, and ignorance. War psychology may be created through the press, motion pictures, radio and television, textbooks, and even influences in the home. Social inequalities may contribute to war. Social sanction and the glorification of war as well as a lack of spiritual ideals are cultural factors favorable to militarism.

From this enumeration of so-called "causes of war," it becomes evident that the cultures of "civilized" peoples are motivated toward war rather than toward peace.

If we are ever to be able to counteract this motivation, every factor must be understood and regarded as a culture trait toward which social change may be directed.

Because the nature of warfare has gradually changed throughout history, it is clear that theories about the causes and functions of war in the past would apply in only a limited sense to war in the present century. Willard Waller examines critically some of the current theories about motivation for war and finds in each of them some truth and some fallacy.

Twentieth-century war can be explained only by taking into account the complexities of contemporary culture. Waller analyzes war in contemporary terms—its roots or causes, its leadership, its techniques, its phases, its effects, and the reactions it brings forth. He analyzes several theories of war—the moralistic, the psychological, the instinctivist, the pressure of population upon the food supply, and the pseudo-Darwinian theory. Economic and ideological interpretations of war are discussed because of their pertinence to the present situation. Each of these theories is in some respects true, in other respects erroneous or too limited. Waller attempts to formulate an inclusive theory of what causes war—a theory which is more realistic in its consideration of the multiple-causation factors in warfare as it exists in our culture.

43

WAR IN THE TWENTIETH CENTURY*
Willard Waller

What most of us would like to know about war is why it happens and whether it can be prevented. This is a simple and very important query, and one to which the social sciences have not sufficiently applied themselves. There are a great many theories about the causes of war, each of which has some merit. Let us examine each of these theories in turn, and see whether we can arrive at an understanding of war.

Perhaps the simplest theory and the one most widely held is what we call the moralistic theory. Wars are made because bad

men make them. When a people goes to war, it commonly believes that it is fighting because the wicked leaders of the other people have precipitated the battle by an attack upon a peaceable folk. When the war is over, it often turns out that the supposedly wicked leader of the enemy was only an intensely patriotic citizen who tried to further what he considered the legitimate interest of his country in the way that seemed to him best. Sometimes, indeed, a wicked leader or an irresponsible fanatic does come to power and does start a war, but there are still many

* From *War in the Twentieth Century*, The Dryden Press, Inc., New York, 1940, pp. 3-34. Reprinted by permission of The Dryden Press, Inc. (now with Henry Holt and Company, Inc., New York).

things that require explanation in such a situation. What peculiar set of political processes, what extraordinary moral or economic factors, brought such a person into power? How was he able to impose his will upon other leaders? Why did the masses follow him into war? What delusions did they harbor and how did they come by them? There are, in fact, enough of these subsidiary questions to invalidate the moralistic theory of war altogether. Such a theory is valid only for purposes of propaganda. To say that wicked men make wars does not help us very much. It is well to remember that we nearly always find out afterwards that such beliefs were false.

Another moralistic view is that wars are made to right wrongs and to remedy evils. Germany precipitated the War of 1939 in order to redress the wrongs perpetrated by the Versailles Treaty. The North fought the South in the United States in order to free the Negro and abolish the institution of slavery. There is some merit in this explanation, at least as regards the participation of the average man. Most men must believe their cause is just if they are to be good soldiers. This moralistic explanation, however, calls for another explanation before it tells us very much: How did men come to have these moral ideas and to consider them worth fighting for? Why did the Northern half of the United States discover that slavery was wrong? The fact is that in most wars both sides passionately believe in the justice of their cause. There are earnest and God-fearing men on both sides; neither side has a monopoly of right. If we are to understand war, we must seek to discover the forces behind morality.

A second theory might be labelled the psychological theory. Men fight, it is said, because they have an instinct for pugnacity. It is born in them: men fight for the same reason that bulls fight, because they are fighting animals. A major weakness of this instinctivist explanation is that it certainly is very doubtful that there are any instincts at all in human beings. Even if we have in-

stinct, there is little evidence of an instinct of pugnacity. Suppose we grant that there is an instinct of pugnacity—a very large concession—it still does not follow that this instinct causes wars. There are many channels by which the instinct of pugnacity might be expressed much better than in war. The pattern of conflict pervades our lives. If we wish to provide an outlet for our alleged instinct of pugnacity we may do so by quarreling with our families, falling out with our colleagues, writing a letter to the newspaper, booing somebody on the screen, bullying a waitress, attending a prize fight, by suing somebody for something, or in countless other ways.

War itself, as anyone knows who has seen military service, is an extremely poor way of fulfilling one's combative instincts. Many soldiers never see the enemy; most of them never come to grips with him in close quarters. When fighting occurs, it is a mass affair, with little individual opportunity for hates or heroics. The soldier usually does not see the man he kills. He fights men he has never seen before, men whose very names he does not know, men for whom he can hardly have an intense personal hatred. The soldier's life is for the most part spent in a rather dull routine of training, physical labor, movement from place to place, and waiting. And it is marked throughout by subjection to discipline. Modern soldiers have little chance to "drink delight of battle with their peers." Indeed, if a soldier has a highly developed instinct of pugnacity, it probably does not make him a better soldier but a worse one. A soldier is always under orders; if he gets angry easily, he becomes a discipline problem to his officers. Nor is his lot a happy one if he cannot stand the rough give-and-take of his fellows. Furthermore, if there is an instinct of pugnacity, we must suppose that it is universal among men—but there are peoples which do not know war. And we must suppose, if wars are caused by the instinct of pugnacity, that a once-war-like people will always be so—and yet we know that this is not true. The Scandinavians, for example, were once the scourge of Europe, but now they have become pacific. What has happened to their instinct of pugnacity? Suppose, however, that we pass over all these objections, it still remains true that the theory of an instinct of pugnacity explains only one small part of war. It does not explain why nations go to war, which is an important part of the problem.

If war is the result of an instinct, then we must always have wars, because it is not feasible to change the instincts of man. If, however, there is no instinct of pugnacity, or that instinct is not indissolubly tied to war, then it may be that in a better organized society there will sometime be no war. Proponents of the instinct theory of war are found in very conservative groups. Such persons are so well satisfied with the world as it is that they dislike to think that it could ever be changed in even the smallest particulars. If it would be possible to have a world without war, then who knows what other innovations might come?

Another theory of war is that it results from the pressure of population upon the food supply. A group of people with an unrestricted birth rate remains for some generations within the same territory, which in time becomes crowded. The population then flows over into surrounding regions under the impulse of hunger. There is a measure of truth in this theory. There have been wars for which the pressure of population furnished a principal cause. The great tribal migrations and far-flung conquests of the dawn of history seem to have been conditioned in large part by population pressure. There have been a great many wars in which the pressure of population was a contributing factor. More often than not the pressure of starvation is the ostensible reason for a war, while other and more decisive reasons lie hidden in the background. We remember the case of the Helvetians in the day of Julius Caesar. Their reason for disturbing the peace was that such a mighty people should not be confined within such narrow boundaries, but behind all this was the scheming

of the crafty Orgetorix and who knows what other practitioners of power politics. This situation, in essence, has been repeated many times in human history.

Before we regard population pressure as a principal factor in war, we must explain a number of facts which seem, to say the least, peculiar. In the first place the nations which have the greatest amount of population pressure are often singularly pacific. China and India are densely populated, and, by common report, overpopulated, but, at least in recent times, they have bred no swashbucklers to demand *Lebensraum* with a rattle of the sword. Again, the nations which give population pressure as a reason for aggression frequently proceed to relieve the pressure by annexing or subjugating some poorer and more populous region. How does this remedy the pressure of population upon food supply? Further, those very nations which profess to need room for their existing population are most anxious to keep up the birth rate. It is also quite possible for such nations to relieve the pressure of population by encouraging permanent emigration to other less populous nations, with, of course, loss of nationality, but in fact every attempt is made to combat permanent settlement of nationals abroad. How does this make sense?

The fact is that population pressure alone does not make a nation warlike. When a nation experiences some pressure of population on the food supply, and also has the peculiar economic and social structure of militarism, imperialism, and nationalism, the pressure of population becomes an important factor in the causation of war.

A pseudo-Darwinian theory of war perhaps deserves passing mention, although it is less an attempt to understand the causation of war than a justification and glorification of it. The essential notion of this theory is that war aids the survival of the fit, and is therefore a eugenic factor of the first importance. This is quite untrue. War kills off the fit, and leaves the lame, the blind, and the halt to reproduce the race. Only the physically fit can get into the armies and run the risks of combat. A long series of wars may, therefore, lower the physical standards of a population considerably. War is not a eugenic factor in human society.

THE ECONOMIC INTERPRETATION OF WAR

The so-called economic interpretation of war is widely accepted, and in fact has considerable merit. It is more nearly able to stand on its own feet than any of the interpretations examined so far. Unfortunately, a great many people believe that the economic interpretation of war is a complete explanation which stands in no need of supplementation from other sources, that it contains all that need be known about the causation of war, that it is, in short, the one and only valid theory of war.

The proponents of the economic theory of war usually begin their argument by demonstrating the necessary connection between capitalism and imperialism. Capitalism, the system of production for private profit, developed in the highly industrialized nations, necessarily leads to the production in every nation of more goods than can be sold there. Under the spur of competition and production for profit, capitalism expands the productive plant almost infinitely, so that it becomes necessary to find foreign markets. This surplus, composed not of more goods than can be used within the nation but of more than can be disposed of on the domestic market, must be sold in some way; it is therefore urgently necessary to find a market abroad. But foreign trade with other highly industrialized nations results in a mere exchange of goods; it does not dispose of the surplus of manufactured goods. The search for markets therefore turns to the less developed regions of the world, to predominantly agricultural countries, to peoples who lack manufacturing and machine guns. Several reasons conspire to cause the capitalists of industrial nations to strive to control the trade of these less developed portions of the earth's surface: the desire to dispose of a surplus of manufactured goods, to secure

raw materials at a low price, to exploit the labor and economic naïvité of less sophisticated races, and to build up highly profitable investments in the virgin natural resources of countries on the edge of civilization. There is thus a powerful drive toward the control of less advanced regions implicit in the structure of modern capitalism. This is the reason for the desire for colonies; this is what is behind the demand for "a place in the sun."

The economic interpretation of war then goes on to show that where business interest leads, the state must follow, for the state is only the "executive organ of the ruling class." And the ruling class, of course, is composed of the nation's leading businessmen. It happens inevitably that the business interests of leading nations must often clash in the attempt to control particular areas. When two imperialistic powers come into serious competition, war frequently results. And when the less developed nations resist the rule of the great powers, war may also result from that.

There is certainly a great deal of truth in this interpretation of war. There have been many imperialistic wars in the past few centuries. A principal cause, certainly, of the World War of 1914 was the clash of British imperialism and German imperial aspirations. The European nations have also fought countless big and little wars in order to reduce other people to colonial status, for the task of ruling all races was thought to be "the white man's burden."

Some wars fit this classic picture of imperialism perfectly; others show fragments of it. In other words, the economic interpretation of war fits many of the facts of some wars, and it fits some of the facts of nearly all wars. The American Revolution was a war by means of which colonies which had developed some economic independence finally put an end to their colonial status. The Civil War involved, among other things, a conflict between rival economic systems; the industrialism of the North, whose leaders wanted a tariff, and the plantation economy of the South, whose leaders demanded free trade. In order to get the Civil War into the picture of imperialistic conflicts we should have to regard it as a clash between the industrialists of the North and those of Great Britain for the control of the South; and this is certainly a bit strained. The War of 1812 and the Mexican War were motivated in part by imperialism, but in each case it was largely an agrarian imperialism; industrial leaders and merchants had little part in either conflict. In yet other wars, we can find only traces of the generally accepted picture of imperialistic war. We may find one class controlling national policy in terms of its own self-interest, either by precipitating or avoiding war. An economic analysis of the political process is often revealing in the extreme, showing as it so often does that men vote as they believe their interest dictates. This is true not only of issues of war and peace but of other issues as well.

In recent years we have heard much of a sort of primitivised economic interpretation of war. Wars, it is said, are promoted by munitions makers in order to create a market for their wares; these merchants of death gladly sell arms to the enemies of their country in order to promote business. For other writers, international bankers play the same Satanic role. Enough unsavory facts are known about members of each group to lend some credibility to this view, but it may be doubted that their influence has ever been sufficient to start a major war. We must remember that both the munitions makers and the international bankers of the United States were recently investigated by the Senate, and that this investigation, in the judgment of most observers, disclosed little evidence that either group had very much to do with involving the United States in the first World War.

We must concede that the clash of rival economic systems frequently initiates the friction between nations which later leads to war and that it also sustains this conflict by affording a fresh supply of incidents. Economic interest also supplies influential groups with a powerful motive to promote war. While admitting all this, we must insist that economic factors are not the only factors involved in war. A multitude of things not covered by this theory must necessarily enter into any war. There are always moral and sentimental elements, for men must love their country before they are willing to die for it; most soldiers are not very brave unless they feel that their cause is just. We shall shortly call attention to a number of these non-economic factors in war.

While admitting the presence of these moral, or "ideological," factors in war, the orthodox economic determinist insists that economic factors are always dominant, and that morals and ideology assume the form which economic interest dictates. Here again we are faced with a proposition which contains some truth, but not the whole truth. Morality is influenced by economics, but it also has an independent existence of its own. Standards of right and wrong are not altogether dependent upon self-interest, and sometimes morality runs counter to economic interest. It seems to the economic determinist that economics is the prime mover in society; it *makes* things happen, and other than economic phenomena merely change to conform to economic interest. This notion is simply an optical illusion. The economic determinist starts with the economic factor, and tries to discover changes in other social phenomena conforming to changes in the economic sphere. The changes actually occur, but it is erroneous to believe that the economic factor *makes* them happen, or that the economic factor itself is not determined. If one started with, say, moral ideas, one could make just as impressive a case for morality as the prime mover of society; one could find a vast array of changes in other social fields conforming to changes in moral ideas. If one starts with scientific knowledge, he may see the entire course of human history as a function of the growth and development of the various branches of science. Such interpretations are all equally valid and all equally false. The truth is that all phases of society are closely interwoven; they hang together in nature and can only be separated in the mind of the scientist, and there imperfectly. It is therefore false to say that one of these aspects of society dominates over all the others. A person who is accustomed to study-ing one factor in social change naturally comes to over-estimate its importance, whether the factor he studies be economics, geography, morality, the family, science, edu-cation, or technology. The economist's one-sided view of society can be matched with unilateralisms from all the fields mentioned and from many others; taken together these views furnish an admirable corrective for one another. If specialists could realize how easily they fall into error merely because they know so much about one of the aspects of society, there would be a great gain in our understanding of society.

There are yet other reasons for believing that the economic interpretation of war does not account for it in its entirety. The ma-jority of the men who fight the battles of any war have little or no economic interest in their outcome; frequently they are fighting against their own best interests, but there is no record that they are any less valiant be-cause of that. The economic interpretation may sometimes explain why great men make wars, but it does not tell us why humble men fight in them. Again, it is probably true that in any war a great number of business-men have little at stake, and in some wars the majority of businessmen stand to lose more than they gain. Why does the economic interest of one group predominate over the interests of other groups? If we explain why one economic interest triumphs over an-other and greater interest, are we not al-ready outside the field of economics? Further, there are many wars for which the clearest economic reasons exist, and yet these wars do not take place. One must explain why certain wars, such as an imperialistic war against Mexico by the United States, never come off. In order to answer these questions, one would be forced to consider so-called "ideological" factors in some detail, and per-haps to grant them equal importance with the economic factor.

It is sometimes argued that the economic interpretation of war is the one correct in-terpretation because some economic interest can always be found in every war. Since the economic factor is always present, therefore it must be the one true cause of war. This is utterly fallacious. The fact that there are al-ways economic elements in any modern war proves nothing at all; certainly it does not prove that the economic elements in the war make it happen. Our economic life is now so complex and ramifying that many citizens are bound to profit by any conceivable rear-rangement of our life and many others to lose by it. When the economic consequences, with profit to some and loss to others, of changing the date of the Thanksgiving holi-day by one week are so considerable as to start a nation-wide controversy, we can see how great the effect of a war may be. When the matter of war with some nation comes up for discussion, those who would profit by it naturally attempt to promote it, and it thus seems that they have brought the war about. But these people did not make the war; at most they merely helped it along.

Although the economic interpretation of war affords some illumination, its popularity is greater than its merits seem to warrant. It is popular, no doubt, partly because of its simplicity and because its proponents are kind enough to advance it in a way which does not invite doubt or inflict upon the listener the pain of a divided mind or the tor-ture of suspended judgment. Again, it is a theory which supplies for some persons the need for a personal devil; the men who make wars, the merchants of death, the grasping traders and the international bankers, are obviously very wicked men, and it is a pleas-ure to hate them. Perhaps the greatest ad-vantage of the economic interpretation is its essentially hopeful character. If wars are the product of capitalistic imperialism, then we may hope to do away with them in a so-ciety in which capitalism has been replaced by another form of economic organization.

The economic interpretation is thus justified in part by its relation to a program of action rather than on purely intellectual grounds.

ELEMENTS OF A THEORY OF WAR

We have now passed in review a number of theories of the causation of war. Each of them contains some truth, but not the whole truth; each of them accounts for the phenomena of war only in part. The interpretations reviewed are particularistic. Each one holds fast to a bit of truth, but denies the truth of other explanations. Obviously, a really valid theory of war must not deny the operation of economic or other factors; it must rather show how these economic factors operate in conjunction with other factors in a larger social setting. Someone has said of the drama that the dramatist must learn not to look at life through the eyes of the drama but at the drama through the eyes of life. So the social scientist must learn to correct the bias of specialism by studying life itself.

As we have seen, one of the most striking things about modern war is its total character. It is total war, total in several senses. It affects the totality of society. Above all, its causes are deeply rooted in the whole of modern society; every institution, every ingrained morality is likely to be in some way a cause of war. As difficult as it would be to tear sin from the heart of man, so difficult may it prove to remove war from modern society. We sometimes strive to characterize the age in a single phrase; we say it is the age of machines, or the age of science, or the era of humanitarianism; we say that our culture is extroverted or that our civilization is always catching its trains. It would be more justifiable to say that it is the age of war. European civilization in the twentieth century has to date always been getting ready for a war, fighting a war, or recovering from a war. And these modern wars are not fought by a few adventurous young men in armor or by a handful of hoodlums in professional armies. Everybody fights nowadays. Everybody makes war. Anybody may become a casualty. Any valid theory of war, there-fore, must consider the fact that it grows out of the totality of our civilization.

As a step toward framing an inclusive theory of the causation of war, let us list the elements which such a theory would need to include. We may list the following:

Indoctrination with Warlike Attitudes. Wars would not be possible if men would not fight, and men would not fight if they had not somehow acquired fighting attitudes. These attitudes are implanted in us by suggestions in the years of our youth; they remain latent for some time, and are later called forth by the appropriate stimuli. Such attitudes are the idea that war is glorious, the creed, *Dulce et decorum pro patria mori,* the identification of one's quite personal self with the prestige of his nation, the idea of self-determination of peoples, the notion of national honor, and so on. These attitudes are inculcated upon the young by all the agencies of the family and the community. In the schools children learn a highly provincial sort of history: our country has always been right; our flag has never been sullied by defeat and it has never been raised in an unjust cause; our heroes were braver than those of other nations; we are a glorious people. Such is the history that the child learns in almost every country. If the history teacher makes any departure from the customary fictions, there are plenty of persons to remind him of his duty. In our family life there is likewise much transmission of military attitudes; he who fights is a hero and he who refuses to fight is a slacker. It is the tradition of our family that the Blanks have always been brave soldiers; your grandfather was a major; your father won the *Croix de guerre;* and your uncle's sword hangs over the mantel. In the United States various veterans' organizations have taken special charge of the task of training children to be patriotic; unfortunately, the leaders of such organizations often promulgate a jingoistic brand of patriotism. The church likewise cooperates in inculcating warlike attitudes, in spite of some tenets of the Christian religion which are opposed to war. The culture complex of war ramifies in such a way throughout the whole of the culture that it would be virtually impossible to rear a child to maturity without inculcating the attitudes of the potential soldier.

The Economic System. The economic system of each leading nation is so constructed as to bring that nation into competition with others for the privilege of trading with and building up investments in the less developed regions of the world. The contacts between nations which result in international incidents and wars are usually in some way related to this process of competition. This is the well-known pattern of capitalistic imperialism.

The Agencies Controlling Public Opinion. The development of a war psychology in a democratic people is made possible in part by the character of the agencies controlling public opinion. The press, radio, church, and school are not merely agencies which perform the functions usually attributed to them; they are also attention-getting agencies, and from this ensue certain consequences with regard to war. These agencies are necessarily conducted by persons striving for the attention and approval of the public. Thus a newspaper, when an international incident has occurred, must play up the conflict element in order to sell its papers. Similarly, the radio commentator must uncover and disseminate interesting information, which must often mean information which inflames public opinion. As a crisis gains momentum, more conservative agencies, such as the school and the church, must fall in line. Since all these agencies strive for social approval the stand taken must be strongly "patriotic." The competitive nature of these agencies of opinion brings it about that if any leader of opinion fails to act in the manner described he will shortly be replaced by someone else. The situation is similar to the economic situation which is said to compel all employers to exploit labor if their competitors do so.

Self-appointed Agitators. Many unattached or only partially attached individuals become self-appointed agitators and lead public opinion towards war by stimulating discussion of war. In striving for attention and approval, such persons take an extreme stand. Many of them are minor politicians and politicians out of office who use this occasion as a means of self-aggrandizement. It hardly seems necessary to add that most of these self-appointed agitators are sincere patriots.

Propaganda. Propaganda from interested parties contributes to the general effect. While its influence should not be underestimated, it seems likely that propaganda alone does not suffice to involve a nation in war. Propaganda must work on pre-existing attitudes, and it is probably powerless to reverse established social trends.

Classes. Growing antagonism between social classes may lead to an attempt, more or less consciously planned, to deflect this hostility within the group to objects outside the group. A social class or a political party which finds itself losing its hold may attempt to create a war psychology in order to stabilize internal conditions and perpetuate itself in power. When anciently the people grumbled, their leaders gave them bread and circuses or they gave them war. We have now improved upon this old custom, for modern war combines elements of both of these ancient remedies.

Frustrations of Individuals. Individuals obtain release from their frustrations and internal tensions by the creation of a war psychology. They react to, say, a Panay incident with a vast wave of emotion not generated by the incident itself but only exploded by it. They find in the idea of war a release from their daily routine and an opportunity to discharge repressed emotions. In venting their wrath upon the enemy they momentarily forget and perhaps partially redress the balance for bullying employers and nagging wives. The spacing of wars in time, the manner in which the war psychosis develops in a people, and the analysis of motivations of leaders all seem to show a relation between the causation of war and the life cycle and inner states of individuals. Social machines such as the R. O. T. C. and plans for industrial mobilization may help to create war because of the expectations which individuals build up and hope to realize in the event of war. The economic situation also produces certain effects by working directly on the psychology of individuals; prolonged hard times certainly predispose a people to the outlet of war. It seems certain that the depression of the 'thirties has had much to do with developing the warlike spirit throughout the world today.

Idealization of Past Wars, Including the Last. Immediately after the conclusion of a war, there are many persons who realize its futility and are conscious of its terrible cost. As time goes on, the memory of its unpleasant phases fades from the picture, and its more glorious aspects, its tales of heroism and sacrifice, remain. Those who died in the war are at length forgotten or remembered only through a euphoric haze; those who were impoverished by the war come in time to the end of their struggles and its cripples pass out of sight. The survivors, moreover, grow old and slowly forget their hardships; they remember only the glorious days of their youth. Rationalizations emerge which overcome the sense of futility. The injustices of war or of a peace settlement may after a time come to seem less cruel, for a new set of folkways and mores arises in adaptation to the changed conditions created by the war. Or exactly the opposite reaction may appear, and the injustices done to a defeated nation may come to seem like something that has no parallel in human history. This is particularly likely to happen in the development of opinion in the nation that loses the war. Here, again, idealization is in play, but it is negative rather than positive. The desire to be avenged for a Versailles Treaty or for the loss of a province may thus be a potent factor in causing another war.

In the field of international relations it should be noted that each nation's acts by way of preparation for war are interpreted by itself as legitimate measures of defense but by its neighbors as a threat against their safety. A circular process is thus released which leads to ever greater expenditures for armament, an armament race, and this produces concomitant changes in public opinion.

To this total picture should be added some conception of the workings of the military machine in each nation. The general staffs of armies have in fact great political influence, and are usually aligned with industrial and political groups which also have both influence and power. In fact, alliance with such groups is often very useful to politicians, even in times of peace and in the most peace-loving nations.

WAR AND SOCIAL INTERACTION

All of the elements which we have mentioned undoubtedly have something to do with the causation of wars. They set off processes of change in society which unite with one another to form the major process of going to war. We may say that in the last analysis wars result from movements of public opinion which the factors mentioned combine to create. We have wars because we develop war fever. The process of going to war may be thought of as a sort of spiral movement of public opinion which is largely beyond control. The war process is like certain phases of the economic system: no one wills it, and yet the totality of the process is the result of the interaction of many wills. No one wills that prices shall go up or down, as a rule, and yet they move in response to certain conditions created by a multitude of individual choices. Nobody effectively wills that we shall go to war, and perhaps nearly everyone ardently desires that we shall not, but everyone does his part in bringing a war about. A newspaper, for example, writes headlines and publishes pictures which inflame the public mind, and at the same time argues strongly for peace on its editorial pages; no doubt the editorial comment represents the editor's sincere belief, but in the end the headlines and the pictures win.

The interpretation of war as produced by the development of war fever in a people is, of course, subject to numerous qualifications. It is most true of democratic nations, for in such countries war occurs only when a majority of the people demand it. But even in a dictatorship, a war must be sold to the populace. A modern dictator is only a kind of demagogue who adds the arts of the propagandist to the ancient weapons of the tyrant. He rules by consent and sufferance under the Damoclean sword. So that he, too, can wage only those wars which his people can be induced to support.

THE MILLING PROCESS

It is obvious, too, that the growth of war fever is subject to law. It is a response to economic, cultural, political, social, psychological, and other factors. We may say that these factors co-operate in producing war in more or less the way which chemicals combine to produce different compounds. We may gain a clearer idea of the process of combination by studying the way in which wars usually start. The typical process of going to war may be described as follows:

Conflict begins (if under the international conditions of the past few years it may be said that it ever has a beginning or an end) with certain crises between nations, "incidents," in which there is a definite clash of the power systems of two or more nations. Such incidents are usually occasioned, directly or indirectly, by economic competition, but other than economic elements rapidly become involved in them.

These incidents set off definite conflict, which, however, remains within bounds, that is, it is not so great that diplomatic machinery is unable to handle it. The power systems of the two nations confront one another for a time, and there is difficulty in preventing conflict without loss of face by one side or the other. Public opinion in each nation comes to regard the other nation as a potential enemy. When the conflict subsides into diplomatic interchange, it leaves the situation substantially changed. Each side has now acquired a heightened sensitivity to affronts or challenges from the other. On each side the public appetite for news of con-

flict has been stimulated. One or both sides may feel that they have lost face. In consequence it is much easier for new incidents to occur.

As a result of such a crisis preparations for war increase on both sides. This helps to build a war machine which in time stimulates the war psychology. In addition, this program is interpreted by other nations as a threat to their security.

There now ensues a series of "Incidents," each of which leaves the nations somewhat closer to war. There is a recognized drift toward war, a process which we may compare to the milling of a herd of cattle about to stampede. In each nation the following changes of public opinion tend to take place:

The agencies which control public opinion fall in line in favor of war. Newspapers print an increasing amount of news in which the conflict is featured; headline writers and make-up men give prominence to news which previously went on the inside pages, and editors blue-pencil domestic news in favor of news of the current crisis. Politicians make issues on the basis of foreign policy; domestic issues are forgotten. Self-appointed agitators keep the populace stirred up; they create what the politicians call a groundswell of opinion. Among the agencies controlling opinion, the church and the school are probably the last to take a stand for war. Sooner or later, however, the ministers and the teachers discover that this war is different; this is a holy war.

There is a gradual growth of myths about the other people, a depersonalization of the people and a personification of their government. A vicious stereotype is substituted for other conceptions of the potential enemy; cartoons portray him as a bestial figure; he often comes to be known by names denoting derision and hatred. The first atrocity stories often appear at this time.

War fever gradually takes possession of the masses. There is an increasing loss of objectivity in discussing the issues of war and peace. Attention is rapidly deflected from internal affairs and directed to foreign affairs. Needed internal reforms go by the board because they come to seem of minor importance. Individuals identify themselves increasingly with the nation, and feel that each new incident is an affront to their quite personal selves.

This process may be hastened by propaganda emanating from interested parties. In any case, war fever affects different classes, regions, interest groups, religious and cultural groups, in different ways and to different degrees. Some groups necessarily take the lead in the agitation for strong measures or for war. A vociferous minority often forces into line a majority which at first regards the war passively.

What apparently happens when a warlike climate of opinion develops is that certain propositions get established as unquestioned truths, and everyone accepts them because everybody else accepts them, and it comes to be regarded as bad form to question them. Biased news reports and propaganda furnish a multitude of suggestions which are hard to resist. In addition, these suggestions are reenforced by the powerful sentiments of loyalty to one's country. It becomes a sort of patriotic duty to believe the current slogans. Gradually people become angry, and as anger mounts, their minds close, and they hear arguments against their wrath most reluctantly: they believe ill of the enemy because they ardently desire to believe it. It is not strange that the average citizen should be helpless in such a situation. It is quite understandable that he should be caught up and swept along. It does seem a little odd that the leaders of the people should apparently offer so little resistance to the winds of opinion. In general, the intellectual leaders of the various peoples do not cover themselves with glory when war is in the offing. The disturbance of reasoning during the milling process is seemingly so subtle and insidious that even those persons who but a few years ago or a few months before were violently opposed to war now come to believe that this particular war is both necessary and desirable. None of their beliefs concerning war in gen-

eral has changed, but this war is an exception to the rules. This war is different. Like the man who has been in love ten times before, they believe that this time it is real.

New methods of communication, particularly the radio, seem to have greatly expedited the milling process. They seem also to have given it certain new dimensions. A fighting speech unifies one's own group, but if it is heard in other countries as well, it may also unify the opposition. When a Hitler speaks, the world is his audience, and the effect of his words on this larger audience is great. It is not, certainly, what the German government ought to desire, for the bellicose expressions of a Hitler may do a great deal to alienate the world from himself and his people. The contrast between the crisis of 1914 and those of 1938 and 1939 is explicable in considerable part as the result of modern methods of communication.

INVOLVEMENT OF NEUTRALS

Once a war has begun between two major powers or groups of major powers, there is a tendency for the conflict to spread, other nations taking sides until every great power in the world is involved. Every country must go through something of a milling process before deciding to join in. The gradual involvement of the United States in the Napoleonic Wars and the World War of 1914 illustrates this process nicely. The forces determining whether neutrals shall become involved, and on which side, are many and varied. Neutrals generally tend to take the side of the nations with whom their economic ties are closest. Both sides interfere with the normal flow of economic processes, and there are sharp struggles over neutral rights. If trade is principally with one belligerent, then the other belligerent is cast by nature for the role of the interfering, meddlesome, and ruthless enemy. Loans and investments play an important part, although their influence has sometimes been exaggerated. Still there can be no doubt that if loans are made to one belligerent, a vested interest in the victory of that belligerent is thus created. Modern warfare is particularly likely to spread because of its economic ramifications; in fact, through blacklists and such devices, it enters neutral countries immediately after war begins.

It is also true that a nation tends to take the side of the belligerent to which it is culturally and morally most akin. The Germans, for example, appear to regard the participation of civilians in the defense of their country as the worst of crimes. They make no secret of their ruthless treatment of such civilians, whom they call *franc-tireurs*. It happens that the American does not regard such actions as crime; he cannot help thinking of the Belgian or Polish *franc-tireurs* as brave men defending their homes against the invader. When he sees a picture of a Polish woman *franc-tireur* before a German court-martial, awaiting almost certain death, his sympathies can hardly be on the side of the Germans. The picture referred to was no doubt intended to prove that the Poles were guilty of "sniping," but that is not what it proves to the average American. It is worthy of remark that such pictures should be released by the exceedingly clever German propagandists. Evidently the art of the propagandist does not enable him to span the gulf created by profound moral differences between nations.

STAGES OF WAR

Once a war has begun, a major war which strains the resources of both contestants, it seems to go through several well-defined stages. This is particularly true of war on its mental and social side. A modern war resembles a siege in many respects. It is a long-drawn-out ordeal which gradually wastes away the combatants. Attrition is not, of course, purely physical; morale may be consumed as well as men and goods. The First World War displayed a clearly marked sequence of stages. These stages are demarcated and analyzed below. Although it is possible to find a somewhat similar pattern in many other wars, perhaps it is best to claim no more for this formulation than that it accurately represents the course of the World War of

1914 and suggests certain phases of other wars. For convenience, the sequence of stages is stated in a general form.

War really begins with the milling process which leads to war. After the milling process, the World War of 1914 developed by the following stages:

The declaration of war terminates the milling process, coming when war fever is at its height. This final step is greeted with a strange medley of emotions from which elements of pleasure are not absent. The war releases in the individual a number of emotions founded on the frustration of his daily life; for any routine of life, however gratifying on the whole, involves a considerable amount of denial of natural desires, and any change, even a disaster, releases the individual from some of these blockings. In addition, there is a release of tribal emotions from massing and exerting the power of the group; people commonly believe that the war will be brief and glorious. People have a sense of participating in events of historic importance. The formal declaration of war is greeted with cheers and apparent rejoicing. (This phase of war is quite rudimentary in the War of 1939, probably because of the recency of the previous war, the wide diffusion of knowledge concerning the nature of modern war, and the fact that the mores have undeniably changed.)

With mobilization of troops comes the first disruption of the normal pattern of family and community life. With this begins also the bifurcation of life into civilian and military channels. While the soldier learns to look at war and the enemy in a professional manner, the civilian reaches and maintains a higher pitch of hatred.

In the War of 1939 these dislocations of life, as described by the current newspapers, prove more far-reaching than any that have occurred before. In the first months of the war hundreds of thousands of schoolchildren are taken out of the big cities and put in boarding homes in the country under the supervision of their teachers, that is to say, they are taken from their families and given to the state. Men are taken out of industry, women substituted; and skilled labor diluted with unskilled labor to the danger point. Industries are redirected into war channels and put on a basis of maximum production. Cities are blackened; amusements greatly restricted; private automobiles confiscated or rigidly controlled; the entire transportation system reconstituted; food is rationed, and hundreds of other changes established overnight by executive fiat. The pattern of international trade is shattered and another set of arrangements is quickly substituted; every nation in the world must readjust its economy or suffer scarcities and stagnation.

THE ORGANIZATION PHASE

Each nation then struggles to organize itself for conflict. There is a period of intense tribal emotionalism, the flag-waving period. During this stage any orator or actor has only to point to the flag in order to insure a successful reception for his performance. The nation passes sedition laws, suspends civil rights, hunts spies, persecutes harmless citizens thought to be in sympathy with the enemy, changes the names of its cities and streets, refuses to teach the language of the enemy or to play Wagnerian opera, and indulges in other fantastic displays of solidarity and hatred. National life regresses below the tribal level. The tribal morality, marked by hatred for the enemy and solidarity within the group, now becomes strongly entrenched and imposes itself upon everybody by means of its insinuating persuasions and Draconian penalties. New techniques of publicity help to make the nation's leaders members of every family, and thus to bind the nation together into a close, cohesive group. One hundred percentism, the desire for unanimity characteristic of the close-knit, face-to-face group, now appears and rapidly pervades all phases of life, even those only remotely connected with the war.

Once started, war tends rapidly to become total in all senses. Restrictions on the conduct of war disappear rapidly; hatreds grow; economic and social involvement becomes complete. "We must win the war"—before this slogan all other objectives fade. Intensive propaganda is now unleashed in order to mobilize the resources of the nation. Business as usual gives way to business organized and directed by the government for the purpose of war. There are numerous economic readjustments. Inflation rapidly takes hold and prices rise. These economic dislocations, of course, transcend national boundaries, and are felt in neutral nations almost as much as in nations at war.

The effect of disruptions of family and community life begins to be felt. There is a shortage of able-bodied men at home. The first casualty lists are published and have a sobering effect. The many frustrations of war routine rapidly become irksome. The gap between the mentality of the soldier and the mind of the civilian becomes accentuated. The soldier idealizes home and civilian life. Institutions such as the school and the church are disorganized.

Changes in the moral equilibrium of the community now begin to become apparent. War produces a real awakening of humanitarianism within the group. Several explanations of this incontestable fact seem plausible. Hatreds and antagonisms are deflected to objects outside the group. The enemy outside the group is so threatening that everyone forgets his enemy within the group. Members of the group are bound together by co-operative endeavor, by struggling against the common foe, and therefore sense their interdependence. War accentuates certain social problems, and it becomes clear to leaders of the community that something must be done for the submerged classes. Perhaps the mere accumulation of pitiable cases leads to the determination of individuals to do something for human welfare. There is also a bargaining aspect; underprivileged groups obtain certain concessions by a sort of unspoken bargain in return for their support of the war.

Wartime humanitarianism and increasing national solidarity sometimes produce strange changes in the status of individuals. Liberals and reformers, for example, are in time of peace unpopular dissenters from most of the established creeds by which the nation lives. When war comes, people suddenly find themselves in agreement with these dissenters on many matters of internal policy and plan to carry out liberal reforms just as soon as the war is out of the way. Liberals, on the other hand, find themselves for once in complete agreement with the national objective, which is to win the war; to this end they gladly surrender those personal rights for which in time of peace they struggle unceasingly. Liberals may become very popular indeed in time of war; war is a great time for liberals, if a poor time for their cause, for the achievements of wartime liberalism are in fact either doubtful or shadowy. All of this contributes to the breakdown of liberalism in the period of post-war reaction. There are always, of course, a few liberals, radicals, and dissenters who decline to declare a truce on matters of reform and oppose the conduct of the war. They suffer intensely during the period of war, and may count themselves fortunate if they do not pay with their lives for their opposition to the national program.

The influence of the soldier and the soldier's morality also begins to be observable. Vices and virtues of the military life are not those of civil life. The soldier's morality is primitivised. Since monogamy is hardly ever the soldier's strong point, many violations of sex morality occur. Consumption habits are also modified; there is an increase in the consumption of satisfactions not related to the ordinary pattern of family living and in other hedonistic gratifications. The adjustment of the civilian to army life is not effected without strain. This adjustment was a fertile source of humor to the American soldier during the first World War. Much of the wit which he displayed was of a sort which expressed hostility toward army officers and military regulations.

When war begins, the common man gains a certain importance which he has not previously had. Ordinarily we keep our lives wrapped up in separate packages, and it is our greatest pleasure so to do. Along comes a war, and we are overwhelmed by it; we lose our privacies and refinements and the values which have seemed important to us. But there is also a gain. The nation now has an objective to which even the humblest and obscurest citizen contributes his proportionate share, and this gives meaning to the routine of his life. Perhaps for other reasons, but also in part for these, crime and suicide rates decline. There is, however, an increase in the civilian death rate.

PERIOD OF HIGH MORALE

Now ensues a more or less protracted period in which the nation struggles on grimly. The emotionalism of the early period fades out; flag-waving disappears; other patriotic songs are often substituted for the national anthem. There is a growing respect for the enemy, and a realization of the seriousness of the conflict. There are long casualty lists. The crippled and wounded come home. The state of mind of civilians is about that portrayed by H. G. Wells in *Mr. Britling Sees it Through*.

Hocking distinguished between the first and second stages of war in a splendid essay written toward the end of the First World War. We quote his discussion briefly:

No one going from America to Europe in the last year could fail to notice the wide difference between the minds of nations long at war and that of a nation just entering. Over there, "crowd psychology" had spent itself. There was little flag-waving; the common purveyors of music were not everywhere playing (or allowed to play) the national airs. If, in some Parisian cinema, the *Marseillaise* was given, nobody stood or sang. The reports of atrocities roused little visible anger or even talk—they were taken for granted. In short, the simpler emotions had been worn out, or rather, had resolved themselves into clear connections between knowledge and action.

The people had found the mental gait that could be held indefinitely. Even a great advance finds them on their guard against too much joy. As the news from the second victory of the Marne begins to come in, we find this dispatch: "Paris refrains from exultation."

And in the trenches the same is true in even greater degree. All the bravado and illusion of war are gone, also all the nervous revulsion; and in their places a grimly reliable resource of energy held in instant, almost mechanical readiness to do what is necessary.*

As war goes on, soldiers settle down to the business of war in their age-old manner. They have no illusions, but are determined to do their duty. *Le Feu*, by Barbusse, describes their state of mind. Soldiers now live by their own characteristic morality, which the populace condones. Even those who have formerly been staid citizens develop military mentality marked by bravery and obedience and irresponsibility, by short-time plans and a hedonistic philosophy of life.

Personal, social, and economic dislocations of war are now painfully apparent. People try to take them in their stride. War refugees appear in large numbers, straining the resources of communities. The morale of the refugees is naturally low. Possibly the fortunes of war confront the nation with the task of large-scale social reconstruction in a devastated area. The strain of the war begins to tell upon the health of the people; death rates go up; birth rates fall to surprisingly low levels. Social institutions are disorganized; the education of the young is carried on with difficulties; higher education is crippled. The value of many of the common goods of life, such as soap and cigarettes, is metamorphosed. Food tastes change under the impact of hunger; grease is no longer something to be avoided, and a bar of chocolate is the price of a woman's virtue. A strain of escapism may appear in literature and the arts.

A new set of folkways and mores, adapted to war conditions, begins to become established and accepted. People never thereafter return to the pre-war moral system.

WAR WEARINESS

At length, this period of high morale gives way to war weariness. In the civilian population, bereavements and deprivations weigh heavily upon some, inflation and economic disturbances upon others. The personal-social dislocations of war increase greatly and become very irksome. There are many changes. There are severe health problems, possibly, even probably, epidemics. The engine of war seems to devour men and materials without ever producing any results. It is difficult to carry on any of the ordinary routines of life, difficult to get food and to keep warm in winter, difficult to clothe a family, difficult or impossible to educate children. For most people, all the little luxuries to which they were once attached have gone long since and life seems cruelly hard. There is a feeling that the country has been "bled white," and the desire for peace without victory begins to be expressed. Mysticism and spiritism now appear as a solution for many, especially for bereaved persons.

The soldiers also begin to give way somewhat under the strain of war. They are still resolved to do their duty, but are painfully tired of war. Their state of mind is that described in *All Quiet on the Western Front, Paths of Glory, The Case of Sergeant Grischa, A Farewell to Arms, Journey's End* and similar bits of post-war literature. St. George myths now begin to be credible, as well as stories of comrades who have risen from their graves to carry on the fight. The morale of the soldiers has begun to crack, but at the same time this may be the period when one final, desperate battle becomes possible. Soldiers begin to develop "the sympathy of percussion," that is, they begin to fraternize

* Ernest William Hocking, "Morale," *The Atlantic Monthly*, vol. 122, pp. 721–728, December, 1918.

with the enemy. Perhaps because they feel that the soldier on the opposite side is also at the mercy of the juggernaut, and that the things which all soldiers have in common are greater than those which divide them. (This tendency toward fraternization may, and in the last war did appear quite early. Nevertheless, it is usually regarded as a dangerous symptom of declining morale.)

Opposition to the war grows and becomes articulate. It is fought by propaganda, which sometimes emanates from interested parties. There may be political changes, reflecting the changed mood of the nation. Morale declines more rapidly on the home front than in the army.

The pre-existing moral consensus has by now been profoundly disturbed. Sex mores have been permanently modified; men and women alike have adjusted to the changed conditions of war, and family ties are less binding than previously. Other mores have also been disturbed. There may be a great wave of idealism and social reform, partly as a reaction to mass suffering. Struggles between the social classes, formerly suspended, are now reactivated; there is distinctly a revolutionary situation. The class structure has also been greatly altered by the rise of war profiteers and the damage done to the middle class by inflation. Standards are confused and agencies of social control disorganized. It should be noted that war weariness is a result of the cumulative frustrations and deprivations of war. The greater the sacrifices demanded of individuals by the war, the sooner may war weariness be expected to set in.

POST-WAR REACTION

Victory or defeat emerges from this situation. Then comes the confused post-war period, marked by the following characteristics:

A peace which contains the seeds of further conflict. Social arrangements are set and attitudes engendered in individuals which make war immediately impossible and ultimately inevitable.

There are widespread economic disturbances and disruptions involved in the process of returning industry to a peacetime basis. There may be further inflation in the post-war period, either of the boom type or of the runaway type. In any case, there must be ultimate deflation. These disturbances are, of course, world-wide; neutral nations as well as belligerents must share in them.

There is a changed morality and a very confused morality. The mores have partially adapted to the changed situation but they remain unclear and confused on many points. Those who grew up in the pre-war period are subject to severe conflicts in matters of morality. A generation of post-war youth grows up which escapes the conflict by flaunting many features of conventional morality. The crime rate is usually high in the post-war period.

The struggle between social classes is bitter and intense. Wartime gains in many fields, such as labor, are often largely lost in post-war reaction. Chaotic social conditions make revolution and reaction possible. Liberals are now thoroughly discredited, and the backbone of liberalism is broken.

The soldier struggles to find his way back to civilian life and does not always succeed. The soldier cannot adjust to the moral autonomy, the routine, and the long-term plans of civilian life. The difficulties of this adjustment have been dramatized by the so-called "lost generation," a group of sensitive youngsters wounded and permanently depressed by the horrors of war but also disorganized and confused by the loss of moral landmarks, cut off from their local communities, their families, the hierarchy of social classes and evermore unable to find their place again. There is a bitter reaction to the idealism of war, a burgeoning of futilitarianism, a growth of ivory-tower estheticism, and even a cult of unintelligibility, all of which may be interpreted as a product of idealism and subsequent disillusionment. The common soldier does not become a member of a voluble and endlessly self-pitying lost generation, but he is nonetheless disorganized. It has been said that every war leaves three armies: an army of heroes, an army of beggars, and an army of thieves. In spite of all this, it is likely that most soldiers adjust to civilian life quite easily. Veterans' organizations, though likely to become politically vicious, probably help the soldier to readjust.

An unfortunate remnant of wartime solidarity is the curtailment of civil liberties. Individuals voluntarily give up many of their rights in time of war; at least they make no objection when the rights of free speech and free assemblage and the freedom of the press are abolished and such safeguards as the writ of *habeas corpus* suspended. In the confused period following a war, it seems impossible to restore these rights at once. They are regained, if at all, only after bitter struggles. It is a matter of years before courts and legislators return to their usual procedures. This is one of the least regarded, and in the long run one of the worst, of the consequences of war.

The chaos of a post-war period is almost indescribable. In 1920 James Westfall Thompson felt that the age might justly be compared with the period following the Black Death. He wrote as follows: "It is surprising to see how similar are the complaints then and now: economic chaos, social unrest, high prices, profiteering, depravation of morals, lack of production, industrial indolence, frenetic gaiety, wild expenditure, luxury, debauchery, social and religious hysteria, greed, avarice, maladministration, decay of manners." It would not be easy to find a better summary of the social and cultural aftermath of war.

WAR SETTLES NOTHING

The most unfortunate thing about war is that it accomplishes nothing. All the effort that goes into it is wasted; all its sacrifices are vain. The issues between nations, over which they go to war, still remain when war is done; war does not settle anything. The diplomats at their conventional green tables come to the end of their arguments and their nations go to war. In the end the diplomats must take up again where they left off before, not exactly at the same place, of course, but with the arguments on both sides not very much changed.

War settles nothing because defeated nations will not accept defeat. War is an arbiter whose decisions the contestants refuse to accept as final, for there is always the chance that another trial will turn out differently. If nations go to war over a matter of territory, one side takes the territory and the other side is dissatisfied with the situation. Twenty years later all is to do again, and the war has settled nothing. If it is a matter of right or morality or justice that sets nations at one another's throats, war cannot settle that because force is utterly irrelevant to any claim of truth or right. Arguments concerning a matter of right can be affected by force; one of the contestants can be compelled to withdraw his claim altogether, but the conquered people remains unconvinced; after a lapse of years the vanquished nation will urge the same old arguments and back them with better guns, and it will be seen that the war did not settle the matter.

If war is waged over the status of a minority, it is almost certain to be bootless, especially in Europe. Europe is populated by a large number of peoples—language groups, culture groups, races, nationalities—scattered discontinuously over wide areas. It is impossible to work out the boundaries of nations in such a way that they will include no minorities. Wherever the frontiers of a nation are located, they are certain to include minorities which may consider themselves oppressed. From this side of the Atlantic, it certainly seems that many of the struggles of Central Europe revolve around the question who shall oppress whom. Any solution effected by force is certain to be unstable. The Czechs have lost their liberty, but they say, "We will live again." Many generations of Babylonian captivity failed to crush the nationalistic spirit of the Poles. The only real solution of the problem of minorities would be for all these peoples to abandon their claims to absolute sovereignty and to work out their common destiny together. Such a solution is the moral opposite of a solution by force.

If war arises over the possession of supplies of raw materials it is worse than useless. German industry requires, let us say, some millions of tons of iron ore which Germans must annually purchase in the open market outside of Germany. If Germany goes to war and obtains control of the iron ore, the situation of the German manufacturers and the German people is not materially changed. German manufacturers must still purchase the ore at the price set by economic processes; costs are little if any less now than before. Or let us suppose that the French seize this ore from Germany. It is likely to come about, as a result of the adjustments of international trade, that German manufacturers purchase the same iron ore as before and with relatively little change in the price. It would be wrong to say that war is completely without effect in such cases, but the effect is less than the uninitiated suppose, and it is produced at an exorbitant cost. The impoverishment of a nation by war far outweighs any possible economic gain. There are always two losers in a war.

War does not even mean the end of the fighting. It does not cause people to expend their hate, so that nothing is left; it breeds hate more rapidly than it exhausts it. The war goes on after the war in other forms. A great war is followed by dozens of little wars. The nations of the world have fought with tariffs and other economic measures ever since the Armistice in 1918. War does not end the fighting; it is not the cure for hate. Only compromise and conciliation and the passage of time can cure hate.

The truth is that nationalism is an anachronism. That sort of nationalism which will not renounce war as an instrument of policy has no place in the modern world. The organization of world trade binds the peoples of the world together, so that each is dependent upon all the others, and no one people can live in its accustomed way without the others. The culture of the peoples binds them together; science is international; art and literature are addressed to all men regardless of nationality or creed. The humanitarian spirit is international. Technology has annihilated distance; it has been said that the airplane has made Europe an absurdity. All these things bring the peoples of the world closer together. Only nationalism keeps them apart. War might settle our problems if we waged wars to the point of extermination, but we cannot and will not do that. Our civilization has progressed so far that it will not permit a really decisive war, but it has not progressed far enough to do away with war altogether.

For centuries Western civilization has been periodically devastated by its wars which recur with seeming fatality. While there has been no slackening to date of wars and rumors of wars, there is some reason to hope that we may sometime come to the end of them. Whatever be the case with their governments, no one can deny that the people of Europe have come to look upon war with inextinguishable horror. Their folkways have grown peaceful; there is no people in Europe that has any appetite for slaughter; in no country does any great proportion of the people really want war. The so-called Munich peace was possible only because the masses of the people in Britain and France recoiled with horror from the thought of war. The change in the folkways is certainly not limited to the democratic nations; it shows itself in the dictatorships as well. The flaming protests against war in the 'twenties, the world-wide popularity of such books as *All Quiet on the Western Front* and *The Case of Sergeant Grischa*, the case of the great clergyman who apologized to the unknown soldier for supporting a war, and the English youths who took the Oxford oath—these things seem to have been forgotten now. Have they really been forgotten? Have they disappeared without a trace? It may be that the world has changed more than it seems. It may be that stubborn, resistless changes in the folkways will shortly outlaw war as an instrument of national policy.

Man's hope for peace has been reflected in the works of social philosophers for a number of centuries. Dante (1265–1321) in his book *De Monarchia* proposed a universal federation of peace and prosperity under a single monarch. Pierre de Bois of France in 1305 proposed a plan for securing a peace among all the Catholic princes of Europe. In 1673 Emeric Cruce published a book with a long and imposing title—*The New Cineas or Discourse of the Occasions and Means to Establish a General Peace, and the Liberty of Commerce Throughout the World*. Cruce advocated a union of the nations and the settlement of their disputes in a general conference of arbitrators with the use of force, if necessary, to secure obedience. Two years later, Grotius proposed, not a union of states, but periodic conferences of independent nations in which their disputes, when not otherwise solved, were to be settled by diplomatic negotiations.

Another famous proposal of the seventeenth century was the "Grand Design," devised by Sully, but attributed to Henry IV. This proposal contemplated the establishment of a Christian republic composed of fifteen states with a general senate of about seventy persons from the various European states. William Penn in 1693 wrote an essay, *Towards the Present and Future Peace of Europe*; and in 1712 the Abbé de St. Pierre published *A Plan for Perpetual Peace*, which contemplated a union of all Christian sovereigns with a standing congress in which the king should be represented by deputies. Other details need not concern us here.

About 1788 Jeremy Bentham wrote his *Plan for an Universal and Perpetual Peace*, suggesting a reduction of armaments and an emancipation of the distant independencies of each state. His plan was one of the earliest to renounce armed authority in enforcing decisions. Immanuel Kant, in his essay *Perpetual Peace* (1795), expressed the belief that a representative government would prevent war because the genuine elected representatives of the people would refuse war and favor peace. He considered the possibility of a league of nations with differences settled by law. Several presidents of the United States have tried earnestly to promote the cause of peace. Hague Conferences, treaties for mediation and arbitration, several formal efforts toward limitation of armaments, and the organization of not a few peace societies have served to keep the peace issue alive.

The most significant organizations to promote peace thus far have been the Covenant of the League of Nations and the United Nations Charter. The League of Nations created by the Covenant has been superseded by the United Nations Organization. The United Nations is supposed to consist of "peace-loving nations," yet there is no peace. Instead there is "cold war," and in some places in the world the conflict is hot rather than cold.

Looking backward through approximately 5,000 years of history, it is evident that the world has experienced war at least as frequently as it has peace. In the history of Western civilization, wars have occurred, on the average, every two years. Wars have increased in their horror and destructiveness, and between periods of overt warfare "peacetime" has been merely an opportunity to prepare for the next war.

Peace is not merely the absence of war, and in the next selection, by John Eric Nordskog, it is interpreted as a revolutionary ideal. It is claimed that the realization of peace would require a new mode of life, a reorientation of social values. The motives of our war-tainted culture would have to be superseded by peace motives. Readjustments in social values would have to be made in many areas of our culture—political, economic, legal, educational, and others. To undertake such revolutionary changes would not be easy. Are we willing to make the sacrifices required?

44

PEACE AS A REVOLUTIONARY IDEAL[*]
John Eric Nordskog

Again there is an opportunity to institute peace on earth. Are we willing, after this second World War, to heed the admonition of the Apostle Paul and "follow after the things that make for Peace"? Or follow the prayerful suggestion of Abraham Lincoln, and "do all which may achieve and cherish a just and lasting peace among ourselves and with all nations?" [1] The chief problem before the world is the issue of Peace versus War, and peace does not come out of war. Peace can be won only through a new outlook on life, a reorientation of our civilization.

War is not inevitable and essential in our culture; it is irrational and definitely is not civilized. Each succeeding generation has fallen victim to the ravages of war because our cultures have been oriented to that end. The processes that lead to war can be checked only through rational revolution in our attitudes and culture patterns. Buried deep in the hearts of men lies the hope for peace, though few persons understand how revolutionary would be a genuine peace. In some

groping manner, in the words of Joseph Conrad,[2] "What all men are really after is some form, or perhaps only some formula, of peace." Thus far it has not been learned that "The price of victory does not cover the price of peace." [3] Peace is incompatible with war; it must be institutionalized and developed separately.

War is, unfortunately, a social institution. Its roots are traceable from early primitive society onward through the history of civilization. Modern organized warfare, however, cannot be explained in terms of primitive warfare. In fairness to the primitive peoples it should be pointed out that their scale of warfare has characteristically been trivial and incidental. Their institutions are balanced in terms of group solidarity and simple economy; their cultures are oriented principally for peaceful living. Conflicts, classed with warfare, do of course occur on primitive levels of living, but not the cyclical, organized wars associated with the "higher" civilizations. While a complete historical perspective is desirable, modern warfare can be understood only in re-

[*] From *Sociology and Social Research*, vol. 30, no. 1, pp. 11–20, September–October, 1945. Reprinted by permission.
[1] Second Inaugural Address, March 4, 1865.
[2] In *Chance*, Part II, Chapter 4.
[3] Cited from R. M. MacIver. *Towards an Abiding Peace*, The Macmillan Company, New York, 1943, p. 15.

lation to current institutions with their complexity and diversity of function.[4]

Technology and the material means for war are not in themselves responsible for war, though the psychological and social derivatives may not thus be discounted. Technology, which could have served man peacefully throughout the ages, has characteristically been exploited for war. The epitome of this development is apparent in the relation of industrial science to the present war. The fact that humanitarian values have lagged behind the technological changes in culture accounts in part for the destructive orientation of the latter. Man has become the victim of the machine to such an extent that, as Lewis Mumford says, "war is the supreme drama of a completely mechanized society." [5] As long as man worships at the altar of the machine, and as long as industry and commerce escape rational social control, wars may be expected to continue in cycles. It is wishful thinking to hope that warfare will end because it has become so disastrous; the minorities who, through their government, resort to war are irrational to begin with and do not consider the costs and suffering entailed by war. It is the privileged minorities, who would play the game of conquest and exploitation, that have turned technological agents to destructive purposes, and this full-range motivation has never been more evident than in modern totalitarian warfare. Not only have the usual agricultural and industrial resources of groups of nations been pooled for the present war, but peacetime barriers to protect patents and monopolies have temporarily been lifted.

The issue of peace versus war, and the degree to which the former would be revolutionary, may be indicated by a consideration of the causes of war. We are familiar with such concepts as nation, sovereignty, statism, militarism, economic imperialism, patriotism, and nationalism. Now, the state is ordinarily regarded as above and beyond all law; it is, in the Hegelian sense, amoral; it is sovereign —it possesses "the right to use power without regard to the rights of other states," which, as MacIver remarks, "is sheer irrationality." [6] Conceived as an entity, the state escapes reward or punishment; it possesses no human characteristics. Such views, though useful to instigate warfare, are fictions created by philosophers. In a reorientation for peace, states would be, as groups of human beings, subject to the law and morality expected of persons.[7] Furthermore, if we are to achieve genuine international law, the unit will be not the nation, but the common man, and his welfare must be its chief concern.[8] Thus the common man would have rights and duties not only within his own state or nation but on an international level.

Without the current fallacies regarding the state, nation, and sovereignty, militarists and economic imperialists would have no little difficulty in their resort to warfare; what, however, would they do without patriotism and nationalism as emotional urges? Patriotism is defined as "love of country; devotion to the welfare of one's country." There is an-

---

[4] Comprehensive discussion is available in Quincy Wright, *A Study of War*, 2 vols., The University of Chicago Press, Chicago, 1942. Also useful is Wright's earlier and briefer survey, *The Causes of War and the Conditions of Peace*, Longmans, Green and Company, New York, 1935. For the perspective of the historian, see *War as a Social Institution*, edited by Jesse D. Clarkson and Thomas C. Cochran, Columbia University Press, New York, 1941. There are innumerable individual studies of primitive societies, and several extensive analytical studies: among the latter, W. I. Thomas, *Primitive Behavior*, McGraw-Hill Book Company, Inc., New York, 1937; William Graham Sumner and Albert G. Keller, in *The Science of Society*, 4 vols., Yale University Press, New Haven, 1927, show the importance of understanding primitive cultures in social analysis.

[5] Lewis Mumford, *Technics and Civilization*, Harcourt, Brace and Company, New York, 1934, p. 309.

[6] MacIver, *op. cit.*, p. 22.

[7] Jackson H. Ralston, *A Quest for International Order*, John Byrne and Co., Washington, D. C., 1941, p. 48.

[8] *Ibid.*, p. 166.

other aspect, however, as has been shown by Thorstein Veblen: "Patriotism is of a contentious complexion, and finds its full expression in no other outlet than warlike enterprise; its highest and final appeal is for the death, damage, discomfort and destruction of the party of the second part." [9] Militarists and imperialists know full well that concerted and sustained movement of the national spirit cannot be had without enlisting the community's moral convictions, and they skillfully persuade the common man that right is on his side. Even so, the higher the pitch of patriotic fervor, the more tenuous and superficial may be the requisite moral sanction.[10] Veblen is surely correct in saying that "Patriotism is useful for breaking the peace, not for keeping it," [11] and much the same may be said regarding the sentiment of nationalism as a war drive. In an orientation for peace, patriotism and nationalism would signify loyalty to one's community without contentious elements. There would be loyalties on a higher plane than state or nation because of broader community of interest.

Although the causes mentioned above are among the important ones that would have to be outmoded in an orientation for peace, the problem of cultural reconstruction would be far more complex. The causes of war may be classified, for example, as biological, psychological, political, social or cultural, religious, moral, and metaphysical, each of these being subject to further division.[12] While an emphasis may be placed on any class of causes, there tend to be not a little overlapping, misrepresentation, and rationalization in attributing the causes of wars. The real cause, as Bernard points out, may be economic, yet concealed under political, moral, or even religious disguises, or under some social ideology.[13] Causes of war may develop out of each other in such complex and illusive manner that the people remain in ignorance of the true causes. As MacIver has well said, "No matter whether the cause be small or great, war forgets the 'cause' and engulfs the whole earth." [14] The presentation of far more complex lists of causes would merely fortify the remark that it would indeed be difficult to diagram any plans to change our cultural orientation from war to peace.[15]

---

[9] Thorstein Veblen, *An Inquiry into the Nature of Peace and the Terms of Its Perpetuation,* The Macmillan Company, New York, 1917, p. 33.

[10] Cf. *ibid.,* pp. 34, 36, 37–38.

[11] *Ibid.,* p. 78.

[12] This classification, widely applicable, is discussed in L. L. Bernard, *War and Its Causes,* Henry Holt and Company, New York, 1944, pp. 228–235. A more extensive evaluation is available in Quincy Wright, *A Study of War.* For general background, consult Herbert Hoover and Hugh Gibson, *The Problems of Lasting Peace,* Doubleday and Company, Inc., Garden City, 1943; R. M. MacIver, *Towards an Abiding Peace,* and Mortimer J. Adler, *How to Think about War and Peace,* Simon and Schuster, New York, 1944.

[13] *Ibid.,* p. 233.

[14] MacIver, *op. cit.,* p. 158.

[15] Bernard (*op. cit.,* pp. 228–235) discusses and illustrates a particularized analytical classification which cuts across the departmentalized classification. Listed by opposites, causes may be incidental and fundamental, superficial and profound or surface and underlying, accidental and purposive, unpremeditated and premeditated, temporary and persistent or transitory and continuous, immediate or proximate and remote, efficient and final, initial and ultimate, original and derivative, concrete and abstract, simple and complex, open and concealed, special and general, specific and circumstantial, explicit, obscure, personal and social, single and multiple, contributing, or exclusive. As to validity, causes may be ostensible and real, reputed and actual, quasi and factual, feigned or implied, obscure. Causes may be human and natural, physical and psychological. There may be rationalization, misrepresentation, and confusion with reference to critical incidents, the "white man's burden," presumptions to restore or preserve order, the liberation of peoples, the religious motive, the salvaging of democracy, the protection of small countries, ideological motives, et cetera.

Whatever the underlying causes, wars are conducted by governments, and it has become practically impossible to allocate the responsibility. In so far as this is true, governments, as agents of privileged classes, may actually be a menace to the common peace. Veblen frankly says that governments—monarchies and democratic republics alike—may be criticized for directing the affairs of state too much in behalf of "the kept classes" instead of governing for the welfare of all who live in the community.[16] When war is imminent, one hears so often that "national" interests and "vital" interests are at stake, though this is misrepresentation, for governments as such are not apt to have vested interests in foreign countries. Virtually, it is the private enterprise of privileged groups that is thus clothed in the garb of national and vital interest.[17] In order to preserve imperialistic control over the resources of nature, governments also align themselves in "balance of power" systems. If such a balance is upset, it must immediately be patched up or war is the usual consequence.

In the cultural orientation now characteristic of the Western world, there are other factors which jeopardize peaceful world organization, as, for instance, high tariffs, immigration laws, and power pyramids in industry and commerce, finance, and labor. The power pyramids are all directed toward the glorification of monopoly control, and governments have become closely identified with these avenues toward control. In order that international cartels, for example, may appear to have legal sanction, the tendency for some years has been to have them arranged through government agencies. They are private organizations but become pseudogovernmental. Dozens of exclusive intergovernmental commodity control agreements have thus been created with almost unlimited power over the production and distribution of the commodities concerned. Such a policy may endanger world organization for peace; it is doubtful that international cartels or control agreements are compatible with the principle of free access to natural resources or commercial goods. It is significant that the traditional "balance of power" in Europe is no longer sufficient, and a new world-wide balance of power is being arranged with the Big Five empires as the nucleus. This situation, too, would have to be faced in a reorientation for peace.

The trend has become too clearly a Darwinist struggle of imperialistic nations to survive, not excepting the possible "elimination of the unfit." Fascist nations, of course, boasted of this view, and the fascist leaders also boasted of not being international in program or sympathy. A peaceful orientation would be antithetical to this program. It is not enough to work out a world organization which would "in principle" maintain the sovereignty of nations. There must be protection for small nations against the larger ones; in the final analysis, the people in the smaller nations must be protected against the powerful groups in the larger nations. No superstate would be required for the purpose, though there must be some way to restrain the different nations from action harmful to their neighbors. It is likely that the powers needed would be negative rather than coercive.

Strictly speaking, there is as yet no international law worthy of the name. Peace treaties do not guarantee peace. Treaties between nations are no better than the recognition they receive from the parties concerned. Treaties that appear innocuous may prove to be obstacles to peace. The only true international law would be legislation by some duly constituted authority higher than any and all nations, applicable to international and world affairs, and to this law people, not states, should be subject. International law should in no manner trespass into the realm of purely national matters where local jurisdiction would remain para-

---

[16] Thorstein Veblen, *op. cit.*, pp. 290–92. Cf. Lester F. Ward, *Dynamic Sociology*, Appleton-Century-Crofts, Inc., New York, 1910, vol. II, pp. 212 ff., 227–231.
[17] Cf. Jackson H. Ralston, *op. cit.*, 128–140.

mount. This, it appears to the writer, would be the ultimate achievement in a reorientation of our culture for peace.

National and international values will be found highly reciprocal in working out peaceful organization. One cannot expect international incorruption to come out of national corruption. In a peaceful reorientation, there must be improvement in living conditions within nations. Countless plans have been offered to this end in terms of national interest,[18] with programs that will require years for their fulfillment. While readjustments within nations may not prove easy, it will no doubt be more difficult to implement the new League of United Nations in order that reasonable coordination may be achieved for all in world commerce. In any case, exploitation of the many by the few must cease within nations before it can be dealt with successfully in world organization. Simply stated, people must learn to live together within the nation and thus be prepared to cooperate in what Graham Wallas calls The Great Society.

The transformation which would be so revolutionary if our civilization were to be motivated for peace could not be undertaken without overhauling the educational program. The concepts or values now associated directly or indirectly with the causes of war should not be glorified, but, if taught at all, should be dealt with in negative fashion, as is done with social disease, vice, delinquency, and crime. From childhood onward, the positive rather than negative values should be taught and emphasized. The feasibility of remolding a generation through education and indoctrination has been thoroughly illustrated by several totalitarian countries; by altering the content in the educational programs of the most influential countries, much could be achieved even in one generation in the revolution toward peace. The younger generation would constitute no problem; it is the older group that would be difficult to convert, or "make over."

The price of peace would therefore require a new education in which the values that lead to war would clearly be incompatible. Economic and political institutions would have to be cleansed of their present motivation for war. Maladjustments and social disorganization, so fertile in the discontents which influence people toward war, would need immediate and sympathetic solution. And governments certainly should not rule, conscript, and regiment, as is essential in war, but should protect and serve all without class distinction. There would then be no need for "wars between governments."

It is not the purpose of this essay to evaluate the Dumbarton Oaks proposals or the progress of the Conference at San Francisco in working out a world organization for peace. Others have pointed out strong and weak points in both of them. It would appear that now, during the crucible of war, should be the most opportune time for international and national reconstruction for peace. The most powerful nations, however, do not seem ready to make the sacrifices essential for a genuine and lasting peace. At most we can expect another organization of nations, patterned largely on the first League, with additional developments in connection with regionalism and armed security. The European balance of power will be superseded by world-wide balance of power, which may succeed in holding off war for an indefinite

---

[18] Consider, for example, Lewis L. Lorwin, *Postwar Plans of the United Nations,* The Twentieth Century Fund, Inc., New York, 1943, and his more recent work, *Time for Planning,* Harper & Brothers, New York, 1945. Lorwin has written other books in this field. Louis H. Pink has emphasized the interrelation of domestic and international programs in *Freedom from Fear,* Harper & Brothers, New York, 1944. A symposium, *Problems of the Postwar World,* edited by Thomas C. T. McCormick, McGraw-Hill Book Company, Inc., New York, 1945, deals with economic, political, and international problems. Herbert Feis, *The Sinews of Peace,* Harper & Brothers, New York, 1944, discusses the principal economic issues. For the anthropological approach, see *The Science of Man in the World Crisis,* Ralph Linton (ed.), Columbia University Press, New York, 1945.

period. No one can predict whether it will be a long or short intermission from war. Peace could be expected only through a revolution in social values and a new motivation in basic organization. Military, economic, and moral disarmament would be necessary. We may be moving slowly in the right direction, with the League of Nations and its successor as symbols in the process. It must be fully realized, however, that peace is not an armistice. Far more than that, it is a revolutionary ideal.

The League of Nations and the United Nations were both organized to promote a genuine peace among the nations of the world. That they have failed in that purpose is no doubt due in large measure to their being leagues of states instead of true federations of peoples. Federation, if feasible, should not be an end in itself, but a means to other social objectives.

The functions of federalism in national organization are set forth in the following selection, by John Eric Nordskog, which is based primarily on the experience of the United States, where colonies developed to statehood and finally to nationhood. The American confederation of states failed, but the federation which superseded it has been outstandingly successful and has in some particulars served as a pattern for political organization in other countries. Federations developed in Switzerland, Brazil, pre-Nazi Germany, and in other countries have proved to be practicable and advantageous.

The primary function of federalism is to provide for lawmaking and law enforcement at different but correlated levels of political action (for example, national, state, and local) and at the same time to protect the people from arbitrary or autocratic government. Federalism is in principle thoroughly incompatible with the idea of a superstate. Most people fear the autocratic potentialities of a world state, and justly so. However, experimentation with federalism in international relations would not necessarily result in the creation of a world state or "superstate."

Federalism is already in effect in certain regions of the world, and it could be tried in other areas of common interest where federal organization would be economically, politically, and culturally advantageous.

45

THE FUNCTIONS OF FEDERALISM IN NATIONAL AND WORLD ORGANIZATION*

John Eric Nordskog

Federalism has acquired considerable variation in its forms and functions in the political structure of contemporary nations. The root concept, federal, is derived from *foedus,* meaning league, treaty, compact. But the term *federal* is defined in several ways. It may be applied to a compact between states which surrender their sovereignty and consolidate into a new state, thus forming a federal union. The word *federal* may pertain to a state consolidated from several states which retain limited powers, the central government being designated as federal. A federal system of government may include both central and local autonomy, with the delegation of powers downward or upward; such division and delegation of powers is meant to be real, but may be nominal and pass for federalism.

The fact that federalism may imply or include a "surrender of sovereignty" accounts for traditional fears and prejudices against establishing a world federation of nations, or even a United States of Europe. Such negative attitudes are clearly countered, however, by true federalism, in which the constituent states retain local sovereignty while the central national government is allowed to exercise sovereign powers only insofar as authority has been delegated to it by constitutional procedure. This is the principle of federalism which is richest in functional values. It serves as the model for the writer's analysis of federalism, though examples of exceptions to the model will be cited for comparison.[1]

Federalism is characterized by the following tendencies: to substitute coordinating for subordinating relationships in government; to replace compulsion from above with rec-

* Reprinted by permission of *World Affairs Interpreter,* vol. 19, no. 2, pp. 194–207, Summer, 1948.
[1] This construction is in harmony with usage in the article "Federation," by Arthur W. Macmahon, in the *Encyclopaedia of the Social Sciences,* The Macmillan Company, New York, 1931, vol. 6, pp. 172–177. Macmahon says: "The term federation is variously employed to indicate a relationship, the process of its establishment or the entirety of a complex organization that embodies it. . . . The essential relationship involves a division of activities between the autonomous parts and the common or central organs of the composite whole."

While on the subject of definitions, federalism in the most general sense refers to the federal principle of national organization or its support; federalization is the process of uniting by compact, as under a federal government. To federate, or to confederate, means to unite in a league. A confederation is also defined as a federation, the terms sometimes being used as synonymous; yet a confederation, or league of states, is traditionally regarded as weak and without power of sanctions, while resort to federation overcomes such political and legal deficiencies.

iprocity, understanding, and adjustment; to replace command with persuasion, and force with law. While the basic aspect of federalism is pluralistic, its fundamental tendency is harmonization, and its regulative principle is solidarity.[2] These tendencies represent some of the general functions of federalism—coordination in government, the development of reciprocity, understanding, and adjustment, an emphasis on persuasion and law, the promotion of harmony and solidarity. It will be shown how these and other ends are achieved by federalism.

The idea of federalism is old, though the use of the concept in theory and practice has drifted widely. To the ancient Greeks we are indebted for the concept of federation for peace. Of several federations, the Delphic Amphictyony, founded in 478 B.C., is the most noted; it furnished the nearest approach in ancient times to a working league of nations.[3] On the other hand, the Achaean League, founded in 368 B.C., developed a form which from 281 to 146 B.C. was probably the first to qualify as federal. The twelve member city-states delegated to the League certain powers such as the right to make war and peace, the right to appoint ambassadors, and the right to arbitrate disputes between members. It attempted to reconcile local independence with strong central organization in a way which was virtually federal in texture. The freedom, unity, and generally good government provided by the Achaean League did not again appear in federal form until modern times.

Plans for leagues or federations to establish peace for European states or for the world have been proposed many times from the early fourteenth century to the present.[4] The outstanding authors of such plans have been Pierre Dubois (1305–1307), Dante Alighieri (1310), Marsiglio of Padua (1324?), Henry IV of France (1603), Emeric Cruce (1623), Hugo Grotius (1625), William Penn (1693), the Abbé de Saint Pierre (1714), Jean Jacques Rousseau (1761), Jeremy Bentham (1786–1789), and Immanuel Kant (1795). Some of these authors suggested no more than treaties to form leagues of states to give some measure of political or military security against an aggressor; others apparently conceived of a genuine federation of states. The influences of nationalism and statism then, as now, prevented acceptance of the plans. Present reference to the early plans is for the purpose of showing that there has been a long educational preparation for forming an actual federation of nations, though the best ideas in our cultural heritage of philosophy and history were ignored in the development of the League of Nations and the United Nations. Furthermore, so many successful national federations were available to prove the functional advantages of federations in comparison with any mere league of states that little credit can be given to leaders who were willing to settle for a league.

The most complete form of federalism is that developed in the United States, where self-government is maintained at local, state, and national levels. The essence of it is a division in political jurisdiction, in the power to govern. It operates, along with several other principles, to protect the people against arbitrary government.

One of the principles associated with federalism is that of popular sovereignty. All political powers, whether local, state, or national, derive from popular sovereignty. Residual powers do not belong to the governments at any level, they belong to the people as the source of sovereignty. Whatever sov-

[2] See Mac Hildebert Boehm's article "Federalism" in the *Encyclopaedia of the Social Sciences,* vol. 6, pp. 169–172, for the historical and philosophical setting for these and other values of federalism.

[3] This is the view of Sylvester John Hemleben in his excellent book, *Plans for World Peace through Six Centuries,* The University of Chicago Press, Chicago, 1943, p. xi. It is also known as the Delian Confederation or League, and most writers recognize its historic position.

[4] Hemleben, *op. cit.,* gives the best concise survey of all important plans, including many authors besides those mentioned below.

ereignty is exercised by the national government and by the constituent states is delegated in the fifty-one constitutions which, in a coordinated system of relationships, constitute the American federal plan of government. Once these constitutions have been ratified and begin to operate, the people exercise their sovereignty again when ratifying amendments to either the national or the state constitutions.

Another principle associated with American federalism is the limitation of government. There are definite bounds and restraints on the actions of public officials, whether local, state, or national, and in the national field this is particularly important.

A vital principle which implements American federalism is the separation of powers of government into legislative, executive, and judicial branches, with precise definition of their respective powers and duties. It is the province of Congress to make laws, of the president to enforce them, and of the courts to interpret them. A separation of functions and powers is characteristic also at the state level and is generally observed in local government.

Closely related to the separation of powers is a system of checks and balances, which prevents any one of the three governmental departments from becoming too independent or powerful. The president, for example, can veto laws passed by Congress; the legislature, if it is determined that the law is desirable, can by a two-thirds vote pass the bill over the president's veto. The Supreme Court has the power to declare a law unconstitutional if it exceeds the bounds set forth in that instrument; thus the Court may invalidate legislative or administrative acts contrary to the spirit of the Constitution. It is a function of the Supreme Court to keep the legislative and executive departments within the law of the land. All departments are to be under the law, and none is to be above it. In making treaties, appointments, etc., interdepartmental cooperation is required.

Not satisfied with all these safeguards, the American people have another one which specifically protects the rights of the individual. This is the Bill of Rights, designed to protect the individual citizen from arbitrary governmental practices or against arbitrary individuals who may or may not be government officials. The amendments comprising the Bill of Rights are a part of the supreme law of the land. The states may, of course, also enact a bill of rights.

It is not assumed that any one or a combination of these principles could not be provided without federalism, because non-federal governments do possess some features that are comparable. Joined with federalism, however, the American ensemble constitutes the most complete defense against arbitrary government that has been devised. It is a function of federalism to maintain equilibrium for the entire system.

It is commonly assumed that the national government must be strong and possess a sovereignty higher than that of the constituent state governments, but in the American system it is not strictly a question of which jurisdiction is higher or lower. The national, or so-called federal, government exercises sovereignty only within a specified realm, and to go beyond that realm would be unconstitutional and arbitrary. The state governments similarly exercise sovereignty within their local province, free from national interference in local matters. The sovereignty of the national government applies to interstate, national, and international matters. All authority of national and state governments in their respective provinces is delegated and rooted in popular sovereignty. Residual powers also rest with the people.

It is a function of federalism to form not only a league but an actual union of peoples, as is so well fulfilled in the United States. Federalism thus provides for peaceful organization and economic freedom for all member states. It also provides a means for peaceful change in the interest of all. Change is possible through interpretation of constitutional or statutory law by the courts, through the doctrine of implied powers, or through amendments. These methods apply at both national and state levels. The power of the national government may be increased or reduced by the exercise of popular sovereignty, and the same is true for state governments. It is a function of federalism to keep such changes within due bounds and to safeguard popular sovereignty, which is basic in the United States. Superordination of the national government and subordination of the state governments would be undesirable; instead, better coordination is the objective. National harmony and solidarity are thus promoted. In true federalism, the governments, whether national or state, are not to rule, but to serve. Popular sovereignty stands *above* the government.

The differences in federalism, as it has evolved in various nations, cannot be examined at length, but some examples will be given. In Canada, for instance, there is a reversal of the arrangement of delegated and residual powers. In the Union of South Africa the elected Councils in each of the four provinces have only such powers as are delegated to them by the central government, and each is headed by an administrator appointed by the central government.

As a general observation, the delegation of power to the central government varies among nations according to the need for common defense against aggression or according to the prevailing attitudes toward national paternalism. The trend may in some federal countries be toward nationalization and concentration of power, in others toward deconcentration. It is true that during the present generation a trend toward nationalization has become quite universal, and in this movement not only the influences of war but those of contemporary world-wide revolution should be taken into account. The trend is evident in federal nations as well as other republics and in constitutional monarchies, but federalism can serve to check it. Under no conditions does the Constitution of the United States grant absolute powers to any department of government. In countries where the central government not only delegates or withdraws powers but possesses residual power, security against excessive concentration of power depends on custom, tradition, and the prevailing temper of the people. This would be true in the British Dominions, in which the Prime Minister and Cabinet are responsible to the people. In the Union of Soviet Socialist Republics, which carries the terminology of a federal republic, both federalism and representation are nominal. The government is totalitarian, ruled from the top, and the dictatorship controls all Russia. The so-called autonomy of the sixteen constituent republics may appear to fulfill a federal division of sovereignty, as provided in the constitution, but this condition is nominal. Russia is ruled from Moscow.

In a true federal organization the allotment of powers should not be altered by ordinary legislation. The amendment procedure in the United States may appear slow and cumbersome, but it also secures necessary stability in government. In the Union of South Africa, doubtless under the influence of British parliamentary traditions, amendments to the constitution are handled like ordinary legislation. Cuba likewise has an easy amending procedure. There are variations in the process of ratification. Amendments may be submitted to the authorities of the member states or to their electorates or to the electorate of the union or to a constituent assembly. The amending power may be vested in the central legislative body, some unusual procedure being required to distinguish an amendment from ordinary legislation. An amendment may require an extraordinary majority vote, or repassage in successive sessions, or both. In Brazil the constitution can be changed by a two-thirds majority in the national legislature, and the situation was comparable in Austria and Germany, with certain other exceptions. In the USSR unrestricted power to amend is given to the Union Congress of Soviets, which acts as a periodical assembly. Under totalitarianism, the amending procedure becomes a formality for approval.

Since a considerable degree of fixity in the division of jurisdiction is essential in federal government, a written constitution is also a prerequisite. There must be provision for peaceful change, however. Too much inflexibility would weaken or discredit the federal idea. The Australian constitution has been criticized especially on this account, and the system of the United States has often been regarded as too rigid. The British constitution, on the other hand, provides the utmost flexibility, but Great Britain is not federal.

Judicial control has become a widely accepted element in federalism. The court of last resort, which is commonly a functional part of the central government, offers the final opportunity for relatively impartial justice. The plan developed in the United States has been followed in Australia and in the federalized states of Latin America. Its influence was also evident in Germany, Austria, and Switzerland. In the Swiss federation, however, judicial review over the acts of the legislature is expressly prohibited in the constitution. In Canada another situation obtains: the right of review is vested in the judicial committee of the Privy Council, while Parliament holds the technical power of amendment.

Federal intervention in local affairs is not a part of true federalism, but countries in which it has occurred are still classed as federal republics. In Brazil and Argentina, for example, a certain amount of intervention in local affairs has been exercised by the central executive. During the Vargas administration in Brazil, intervention developed into dictatorship, the federal division of jurisdiction being ignored. After the overthrow of Vargas in 1945, the federal constitutional safeguards became effective.

The allocation of representation in federal legislatures has long been controversial and practices vary. Bicameralism has been favored in the United States, in the federalized countries of Latin America, in Australia, and in Switzerland. Bicameralism may facilitate the institution of federalism, but unicameral-ism has some advantages to offer for government.

The importance of coordinating the central and constituent governments has been mentioned. For this purpose there is need in all federal systems for consultation between federal and state authorities. Simplicity in legislative and administrative procedure as well as in the mechanism of association and conference would be desirable. Federal-state administrative cooperation is possible in many matters, though the division of responsibility is a basic principle in federalism.

It is not the purpose of federalism to remove disparity in the strength of the component parts of a federal union. There is no need for mathematical equality for the member states. In the United States there is considerable difference in the area, wealth, population, and political influence of states and of cities. It may not be ideal for one member state, or even a city, to dominate a federal union, as Prussia did in the German federation and as Buenos Aires does in Argentina. Great inequality does not prevent states from forming a federal union, however, and all members share in its benefits. That racial differences are not obstacles to federalism is shown in the United States, Brazil, Russia, and other countries. That language differences raise no serious barriers is shown in the United States, in Canada, in Russia, in Switzerland. That religious and other cultural uniformity is not essential for federalism is shown in all countries. In fact, there are many sizeable countries which are republics, but not federal in organization, which have all these problems of difference in race and culture to solve. Federalism should facilitate the solution. Federalism postulates not only that the state should join a more comprehensive federal system but that the parts of the state should also be constituted on a federal plan.

So far, the writer has been concerned with examples of national federalism. With centuries of philosophy and history for guidance and many successful federations available for study, are there any prospects for a world federation of nations? That nations have not been willing to go beyond a League of Nations and a United Nations is in some respects discouraging, but the attainment of a league relationship may prove to be the threshold for a federation, as was the case in the United States. National leadership has been too provincial and selfish in outlook. There has been too much conservatism, too much worship of false values, such as nationalism, statism, militarism, sovereignty, imperialism. These are incompatible with federalism. On the other hand, there are other values definitely associated with federalism— peace, economic freedom, political coordination, reciprocity and understanding, harmony, solidarity, etc. Is the meaning of federalism beyond comprehension for world organization? When fifty American states can make a success of federalism, surely sixty or more nations should be able to form a federal world organization. There would be no giving up of sovereignty. But there would be a creation of law and order above the national level, which involves a gain for all nations and not a loss. In a world federation, the world government would not be a superstate, but it would provide a sphere of jurisdiction where international anarchy now prevails. Safeguards against arbitrary power could be provided comparable to those in practice among the nations. In a world federation, the world organization at the center would have no right to interfere in intranational matters. Republics and federations could continue to function internally as they are, though changes in national policies might follow voluntarily. Any system devised for world federation would be subject to revision, just as any national federation must be flexible.

* * *

What the members of a world federation would gain from federalism would depend upon the features selected from examples available for consideration. The federation of the United States offers more than any other as a pattern; it is possible, however,

that some features in other federal countries may prove acceptable for world organization where the American form may seem unduly strict and comprehensive.

The functions of federalism, associated with other practicable principles, would ensure to world government, as well as to regional national groups, such advantages as the following:

1. Federalism would provide for the recognition of popular sovereignty in world organization and in European or other regional federations of nations.

2. Federalism would divide the exercise of sovereign power in world organization as it does on a national level.

3. If the world organization should become truly federal in form, there would be no superstate with arbitrary power over member nations.

4. The central world organization would not have power to interfere in the internal affairs of member states, the latter remaining fully as sovereign in that respect as they are now.

5. Federalism would provide for the separation of world governing powers into legislative, executive, and judiciary, which may also be subject to checks and balances.

6. Federalism may be associated with a limitation of government, with restrictions on the actions of officials.

7. Federalism would give reality to a world Bill of Rights.

8. Federalism would facilitate adjustment in the exercise of power at world, national, state, and local levels, the people being the ultimate source of power. It would provide means for peaceful change in the location of governing power.

9. Federalism would ensure economic freedom for all member nations, as it does within nations or states.

10. Federalism would substitute coordinating for subordinating relations in government.

11. Federalism would replace the tendency toward compulsion from above with reciprocity, understanding, and adjustment.

12. Federalism would replace command with persuasion, and force with law.

13. Federalism would make possible the development of genuine international or universal law and sanctions.

14. Federalism would promote world harmony and solidarity.

15. Federalism would outlaw war and make possible a reorientation of culture for the values of peace.

The social, economic, and technological changes which have knit the world together may have unforeseen consequences for the future of international organization. Change may be destructive as well as constructive. Consideration must be given to change within the existing state system.

Change, in the context presented by Carl J. Schneider, relates to observable differences in the environment within which the struggle for a world order is carried on and in the pressures calling for adjustment today. Schneider discusses the effects of technological change, the changed concepts and techniques of warfare, population changes, and ideologies, all of which have influenced trends in international organization.

46

CHANGE AND INTERNATIONAL ORGANIZATION*

Carl J. Schneider

All our lives long, every day and every hour, we are engaged in the process of accommodating our changed and unchanged selves to changed and unchanged surroundings: living, in fact, is nothing else than this process of accommodation; when we fail in it a little we are stupid, when we fail flagrantly we are mad, when we suspend it temporarily we sleep, when we give up the attempt altogether we die. . . . A life will be successful or not, according as the power of accommodation is equal to or unequal to the strain of fusing and adjusting internal and external changes.†

We must reexamine the facile assumption that the technological unification of the world has so undermined the traditional bases of international relations that in time an integrated international order will inevitably evolve. Hopeful proponents of world federation, European Union, and similar plans for a new international order insist, and no doubt quite properly, that some form of genuine

* Reprinted by permission of the editor from *World Affairs Interpreter*, vol. 22, no. 3, pp. 252–270, October, 1951.
† Samuel Butler, *The Way of All Flesh*.

international organization is a *sine qua non* for the establishment of world peace and prosperity. The urgency of contemporary world politics has, however, obscured the question as to whether "One World" is in reality being retarded or advanced by the forces producing profound changes in our physical and spiritual environment. To attribute the shattering of our hopes for a unified world solely to the machinations of the men in the Kremlin is an oversimplification. We must remind ourselves that the very changes, social, economic, and technologic, which have knit the world together, may have unforeseen consequences for the future of international organization. Change may be destructive as well as constructive.

It is of course undeniable that modern science, technology, and invention have radically altered the fundamental structure of our world. New sources of power, new methods of distribution, new modes of transportation and communication, new techniques of combatting disease and ignorance, new insights into the nature and motivation of human behavior—these have all altered our physical and spiritual environment. The world of today is a world of cities, factories, industrial workers, machines, science, wars of global dimensions, and individuals subject to countless stresses and strains. "The old order changeth yielding place to new."

Distance has been obliterated and opportunities have increased for intellectual contacts and exchange. The line of distinction between domestic and foreign affairs can no longer be sharply drawn. There are more problems of an international character now than ever before, as well as the technical possibility of developing greater understanding and sympathy for other peoples and creating a transnational world. In short, the effect of technologic change has been twofold: the creation of the physical conditions to make possible the establishment of a genuine world community; and the generation of problems which demand solutions on an international level. Recognition of these facts has led impatient voices to demand an ad-

justment in our state system to create an international organization consistent with the technologic facts of life. The vision of "One World" captured the imagination of many people. The day of the nation state is over, it is contended, and it is time to construct more appropriate organizational bases for international relations. The release of atomic energy has again swelled the demand for international cooperation with machinery to implement it. World federation is advanced by many on the ground that to persist in an artificial compartmentalization of the globe into competing nations is not only suicidal but also a refusal to comprehend the true significance of scientific and technological change as an instrument of international unification.

It is important, however, that we do not misunderstand the significance of such change in the nature of our world. Without denying for a moment the existence of fundamental change, or the imperative necessity for heroic measures to reconcile international politics with the objective environment, we must take care lest we make the error of assuming that changes wrought in our society by the wonders of science point inexorably toward a weakening of the nation state and the development of a true international community. It is by no means foreordained that change is working on the side of the angels. Just as the discoveries and inventions of the physical scientist may be used for peace or for war, so all change in our physical and spiritual environment may be both unifying and disunifying in its effect. The unifying effect of change has received ample consideration. Attention will here be concentrated upon that side of the relationship between change and international organization which is frequently overlooked by those who maintain that the nation state is destined for extinction because our physical environment has in effect created a transnational world.

When we speak of change and its effect upon international organization, we must speak first of change within the existing state system. International organization comprises the institutions through which sovereign states conduct their business with one another, the machinery for their intercourse, and the manner in which they arrange solutions to their mutual problems. Originally international organization was relatively primitive, and was based almost entirely upon diplomatic exchange and negotiation. With the rise of democratic forms and institutions, however, international organization assumed more and more a parliamentary or conference form—the League of Nations and the United Nations. Twice the poet's dream of a parliament of all mankind has seemed about to be realized. In other words, the force of change has affected international organization to the extent that attempts have been made to provide a permanent organizational framework for the political integration of the various nations of the world within which problems of mutual concern could be discussed, debated, studied, and solutions voted upon. Traditional diplomatic methodology gave way to a more highly institutionalized pattern of international organization; the technologic and economic changes in the world, along with the rise in importance of the private citizen in the governing process, gave comfort to the idea that it made sense to speak of world unity rather than national exclusiveness.

Nevertheless, the basic unit in international organization has remained the sovereign nation state, completely independent and autonomous in its international affairs. The question then arises whether the continued existence of the nation state is possible in the highly interdependent world of today. There is no real argument against the answer that historically the modern state system has been an obstacle to the enjoyment of international stability and peace; a plurality of independent political organizations cannot easily be fitted into an effective world organization. Change has rendered this increasingly difficult.

"Change" as the term is here used relates to two different, though interrelated, phenomena: (a) the observable differences in the environment within which the struggle for a world order is carried on—the contrast between today and yesterday; and (b) the pressures calling for adjustment today—the forces at work now which will affect the world order either directly or indirectly. When change is used in this sense, a relationship is obviously involved: the effect of change on international organization, and the capacity of international organization to accommodate change and the forces working for further change. The heart of the matter will be found in ascertaining the answer to the following questions. First, what changes have taken place or may be anticipated? Second, what is the effect of these changes upon the state system—weakening or strengthening? And finally, do these changes point to a strengthened international organization or to one of only nominal significance? Unfortunately, much of the ferment of change at work during the twentieth century is ambiguous in its effect; we must constantly remind ourselves that while there is a pull toward a strengthened international organization, there is also a pull in the opposite direction. Before the future of international organization can adequately be appraised, those aspects of change must be examined which have a tendency to undermine the forces facilitating the evolution of an integrated world order.

TECHNOLOGIC CHANGE

One result of technologic change is to increase the economic interdependence of the world. On this fact alone rests much of the case presented by the proponents of the inevitability of world organization. It is demonstrable that economic relations are now international; that modern industry requires raw materials from faraway places; that urban populations require imported food; that a highly industrialized world is necessarily a highly dependent world. It is equally true that no single state is yet so favorably situated that it can completely isolate itself from world commerce and still meet all of the normal wants of its people. For most nations economic self-sufficiency (autarky) is impossible. The logic of the situation therefore seems to demand international planning, international assistance, international supervision of production, distribution and transportation. Unfortunately, though in a world so interdependent the pull toward international cooperation would seem irresistible as a matter of enlightened self-interest, other forces are at work to mitigate this trend. Actually there has been an intensification of economic nationalism and the factors which underlie this intensification are as much a result of technologic change as is our increased economic interdependence.

A resurgence of cultural and economic nationalism is coupled with the demand for political independence in the young and underdeveloped areas of the world, particularly in Asia. The desire of such nations to maintain (or acquire) their political independence has often expressed itself by a form of neomercantilism: the recasting of the economy on a costly protectionist basis. The principle of self-help, inherent in the concept of sovereignty, still prevails. The failure of technologic change noticeably to undermine national egocentricity cannot be attributed solely to traditional xenophobia, human perversity, or the inertia of society. Something more fundamental is involved. In the first place, security now means more than a standing army: it means control of industrial power. Technologic change has made security more precarious. The increasing insecurity of international relations has emphasized the need for stock-piling, self-sufficiency, and cutting the lines of dependency to other countries. Inefficient as such measures may be, economically, they seem indispensable when the very existence of a nation hangs in the balance. It is, of course, argued that self-maintained national security is a snare and a delusion. To argue thus is to ignore the dynamics of the newly released forces of nationalism in the Far East where freedom from all ties with the West is considered essential to political independence. In the minds of many former colonial peoples, political independence cannot be separated

from economic independence regardless of the cost.

Equally important, though frequently overlooked, is another consequence of technologic change. As society becomes more industrialized, mechanized, urbanized; as it becomes more complicated; as the individual finds himself confronted with an overwhelming number of problems which defy solution on an individual, personal basis—then comes the demand for social and economic security guaranteed by the government. The resultant trend towards the positive (or welfare) state, which originates in a basic change in our economy, has strengthened the national state. The individual becomes more dependent upon the state for the conditions of his life which he can no longer secure by his own efforts. The world over, the state is becoming the principal defender against old age insecurity, unemployment, sickness, crop failures, depressions, and similar catastrophes. The state thus becomes more important in the life of each individual citizen than ever before and the individual has a far greater stake in the continued existence of his state. At the heart and center of the problem of world organization lies the relation of the individual to his state. The impact of science and invention has not necessarily weakened the hold of the state on its people; on the contrary, the effect of these forces may easily be simply to intensify nationalism and to entrench the national state. The reaction against *laissez faire* on the part of increasingly large elements of the world's population as a corrective to the insecurities of individualistic capitalism has buttressed the trend towards national self-sufficiency and economic separatism.

Modern science and invention have not resulted in greater political integration; on the contrary, the cumulative effect of major technologic change has been to widen the disparity between states and to create even greater hurdles to the establishment of an international world order. Thus we see an intensification of economic nationalism despite the fact of economic interdependence; the national state system is thereby strengthened.

An interdependent world is also a more complicated world requiring more of its people in the way of understanding and competence than was required in more primitive pre-industrial eras. In his search for peace of mind and stability, the individual quite naturally is tempted to place his trust and hopes in his own government, which is closer to him and more familiar, than in a projected international organization, infinitely remote and strange.

CHANGED CONCEPTS AND TECHNIQUES OF WARFARE

Another area in which change is manifest relates to the techniques and concepts of warfare. The distinction between war and peace is now virtually obliterated—not in international law, perhaps, but certainly in fact. New and terrifying instruments of mass destruction threaten our civilization. They have made neutrality virtually impossible. War and peace are indivisible and global, and both now involve entire populations. The masses are now directly concerned in questions of war and peace—and the stakes are larger, as is the risk. It is quite true that, in consequence, the need for an effective international organization of peace is more widely and more passionately felt than ever before. For generations, optimists have been predicting that the sheer horror of modern warfare would compel mankind to seek a permanent solution to international conflicts. The release of atomic energy has inspired a new hope that now at last this newest weapon has so changed the nature of warfare that the structure of our international organization must be strengthened.

It should by now be obvious that change in our mode of fighting will not necessarily bring about a change in our international organization. It is utopian to expect otherwise, for the very changes in the techniques of warfare themselves may only strengthen the nation state; at the very least, they make more difficult the creation of a viable international order. The risks involved in disarming are greater than ever before, and the problems of assuring protection against international lawlessness are more complicated. Security concepts have changed and the responsibilities of each government for the safety of its people have become enormously complex. Safeguards must now be erected against propaganda, fifth columns, quislings, saboteurs, long range bombers, and economic warfare, as well as against troop movements. An international organization for peace must today be prepared to prevent not only traditional armed hostilities, but a wide variety of new devices whereby one nation can impose its will upon another. Until it can do so, each nation must rely (albeit desperately) upon its own ability to protect itself. Sophisticated arguments about the need to remove the "basic causes of conflict" which ultimately are found "in the minds of men" do indeed reflect a more penetrating grasp of the problems of international relations. Unfortunately the fears and the problems generated by changes in the techniques of warfare are themselves genuine obstacles to the realization of an effective international organization. The old problem of which comes first, security or disarmament, familiar to anyone conversant with the history of the disarmament conferences of the inter-war years, is still with us. Only now it is aggravated because of the changes in the arts of war. In short, the atmosphere created by change in the concepts and techniques of warfare operates to retard the establishment of an effective international organization.

One other aspect remains to be noted. The changes in the techniques of warfare have been brought about by advances in science and technology. Because military supremacy (upon which national security now ultimately rests) is in large measure directly dependent upon scientific discovery, ever widening spheres of scientific inquiry have been brought under the wings of the state. As national security seems to depend more and more upon scientific knowledge, scientific knowledge becomes of direct governmental concern. The result is a frantic rush to preserve "secrets," to prevent the diffusion of scientific data, and to insist upon the national rather than the international aspects of science. That attempts to create a monopoly of scientific discovery are doomed from the start (witness the atom bomb), does not alter the fact that the international community of science, once so real, is under attack because of the close connection between security and science. Thus, one of the genuine forces for international cooperation—the community of scientists—is being lost to the cause of the preservation of the nation state. Scientific advance, it is obvious, does not inevitably pave the way for effective international organization.

POPULATION CHANGES

When we turn to the effect of population trends on the future of international organization, the problem becomes one of interpreting the wealth of statistics which demographers have accumulated. The general picture is fairly clear. The growth of world population is not yet at its peak. In the countries which comprise what we now call the "West" the rate of population increase is slowly levelling off; the great source of population increase is more and more in the countries of Eastern Europe, Asia, and other so-called backward regions. In other words, the future expansion of population will be chiefly in areas not yet fully industrialized and urbanized, and just beginning to profit by advance in medical science, improved methods of food production and distribution, and public health measures. Mortality rates, historically, drop faster than the birth rates. It has been estimated that if India were to reduce her death rate to that of the United States and retain her present birth rate, her population would within one hundred years fill five earths as full as our own; China could do the same, and it would not take the Soviet Union much longer. Such an eventuality may never be realized, but the speculation suggests some of the international implications of the shift in population from country to country and region to region.

These implications are explosive in the extreme. Any international organization which can effectively cope with the disrupting ramifications of this situation must be equipped with more than an abundance of good will—and that quality is, sadly, all too often conspicuous by its absence. It is impossible to predict the objective consequences of this shift in population; it seems obvious, however, that all the various possibilities will tend to disturb the political integration of the world to a greater or lesser degree.

Three possible consequences should be noted, for they portend the greatest danger to an effective international order. First there will undoubtedly be increased pressure on the means of subsistence in the teeming nations of the Far East. The prospect of an increase in the population of India or China before either of those countries is in a position to feed its people is a frightful one; starvation, frustration, low standards of living are the inevitable consequences, providing fertile soil for adventurers and demagogues to sow the seeds of international conflicts. In a world already divided into antagonistic ideological camps such areas become pawns for the game of power politics rather than objects of help and support. The peoples who are now becoming industrialized and who are learning to reduce their death rates are going to feel the pressures of population on their resources more and more as their needs grow; it is exceedingly doubtful whether they will be content with a minor role in world affairs or satisfied to live under conditions of increasingly *felt* hardship. The rising tide of nationalism in the Far East only aggravates an already serious situation.

A second element in the problem is suggested by our historical experience. Nations with a rising population curve tend to be more aggressive, expansive, and inclined to adventurous foreign policies than nations with a declining population curve. Population (manpower) is a source of power, and powerful nations are less likely to feel the compulsions toward international organization. Population growth does not necessarily lead to militarism and national exclusiveness, but it is generally concomitant with other great changes in the social and economic organization of a nation. A different outlook on world affairs may easily result and an expanding, eager population is strongly tempted to flex its muscles, confident in its own destiny and strength.

Finally, and this is actually the basic contingency, the projection of population trends on a global basis may well portend a shift in political power from the West to the East. Changes in population figures have in the past accompanied a change in power alignment and political equilibrium. Marked increases in population have been not only symptoms of great changes within the society, but have also been factors in stimulating economic advance and political exuberance. Once the growth of population begins, it becomes a dynamic factor in forming the structure and organization of the nation's industry and trade and the world outlook of its people. Other things being equal, the West will soon cease to have sole possession of the economic and political advantages of an efficient machine industry and a rapidly growing population to which it has become accustomed.

Demographic change is releasing new forces and creating new problems which render it difficult to achieve the stabilization and integration of the world without which international organization can hardly survive.

IDEOLOGIC CHANGE

Up to this point we have considered some of the implications for international organization created by the changes in the physical environment within which international affairs are conducted. During the past hundred and fifty years great changes have taken place in our habits and in the conditions of our life. The prospect has been opened up for greater mutual understanding and sympathy among the peoples of different nations. Technological change would seem to provide the physical foundation for a true world community—and the sense of a world community is in the long run prerequisite for any successful international organization. Yet,

as we have seen, there is nothing unmistakable in the relationship between physical change and the future of international organization. "One World" may be physically feasible but it is by no means inevitable. Organizational adjustment to the pressures released by change requires a parallel adjustment in the area of ideology, of values, and of convictions before a new fabric of international organization can successfully be woven. And it does not necessarily follow that the changes in our environment will themselves create those changes in the climate of world opinion which are indispensable for a refurbished and effective international organization.

The spiritual and intellectual foundation for a world community remains to be developed. Change in the realm of the nonmaterial operates just as it does in the realm of the material. Our problem now is to appraise the nature of ideologic change in terms of its implications for the future of international organization. It is now axiomatic that we are living in a world in which there are at least two competing moral and political systems claiming universal validity: democracy in the western tradition, and communism, both of which have become identified with particular ways of life and principles. This ideological dichotomy is in contrast with the consensus which prevailed from about 1648 to the French Revolution and from about 1815 to the First World War. There was then a sense of having inherited a common civilization which provided a stability and predictability in international relations and a basis for mutual understanding among the nations —at least all the major powers spoke the same ideological language. The change here is, in a sense, one of degree rather than one of kind; nevertheless, it is true that the twentieth century reveals a growing divergence in standards of behavior, moral and intellectual climate, interpretations of history, and value judgments. To describe this contrast is not, however, sufficient; for our purpose it is necessary first to examine the changes which have brought about the contrast and then to appraise those changes in terms of the future of international organization.

There are two major elements in this change in ideological atmosphere. One relates to the rise of nationalism in the non-western world. The other is a consequence of the industrial revolution which gave rise to mass political movements and new political and economic schemata. Socialism, communism, and the demand of the less privileged for a greater share in the rewards of life represent profound transformations in the entire social process; they represent acute disturbances in the old social order and challenge capitalism, *laissez faire,* and individualism. There has emerged in communism a new formula for peace and prosperity which is in many respects incompatible with established values; moreover this formula postulates a new internationalism based on the community of interest of the working class (proletariat). This unity cuts across old national boundaries and theoretically at least is the antithesis of nationalism. In the clash between the ideologies of democracy and communism we have the makings of a global civil war. Certainly, the difficulties of international organization are accentuated if there is no common agreement on ends or objectives, no basic attachment to the same values of life, liberty, and property. The issues are more than territorial aggrandizement or dynastic competition. Systems of belief and ethical convictions are now at stake. The problems thus posed to an international organization have become acutely serious because of the dynamic and aggressive quality of the new ideology and because the new ideology is not restricted to a few leaders but has become a mass movement.

With respect to the rise of nationalism among former colonial peoples, especially in the Far East and Asia, the struggle for independence and liberty in these areas is not new. What is new is its success and the fact that in many instances the upsurge of nationalism has been strongly influenced by the Leninist-Stalinist theory of imperialism. The teeming millions in the Far East have thus acquired a new significance in international relations. Not only are they successfully demanding national independence (and a voice in the UN), but they have become important factors in the ideological struggle between Soviet communism and the West. For centuries the world was dominated by European culture and traditions; Western concepts provided a modicum of common understanding. Now the Orient, brought up on Confucius, Buddha, Lao Tze, is coming into its own, internationally speaking. The reaction against Western domination carries with it an insistence on local autonomy, local traditions, and local philosophies. Thus diversity is increased in a world where unity is so important. Much will depend on the tempo with which the East becomes strong and the manner in which it uses its power. Even now there are grave problems and pressures which threaten world stability unless controlled by international collaboration. The ideological bifurcation of the world into warring camps makes these problems of even graver concern.

CONCLUSION

Despite technological unification, economic interdependence, and all the technical factors which point toward the necessity for international cooperation, there has been no proportionate unification in the realm of ideology, values, and ways of life. In fact, many of the same forces which seem to demand international organization also pull in the other direction. And it must never be forgotten that modern science has given governments power over their own peoples unheard of a century ago. It is now technically easier for a government to control communications than it once was; thus international understanding is largely dependent upon the willingness of a government to permit the exchange of ideas. The masses of the people have become vitally important factors in politics—hence nations have embarked upon vast propaganda campaigns to bind the citizen to the state and the way of life it espouses.

Changes in the environment of world politics have created many new tensions and conflicts, and social and economic crises. These phenomena have world wide repercussions to be sure, but in the final analysis they concern individual man—his wants, fears, desires, frustrations, and his sense of justice. For each individual these problems are intensely personal and local. The responsibility for the control or accommodation of the effects of these problems is presently in the hands of national governments. If the nation state is unable to summon sufficient good will and patience to solve its problems, what prospect is there for an international organization which is not only remote from the people but has no great tradition from which to draw strength? Before significant strides can be taken toward an effective international organization, the disunifying effects of change must be fully comprehended.

Is any kind of international organization possible under the conditions of today? What kind of international organization can hope to cope with our changing society and the pressures released by these changes? We must answer the basic question: Is universality necessary? Cultural diversity we have always had. Today it has reached the point where international society is disrupted. Under present conditions what seems to be called for is not an imposed or artificial uniformity; nor can we wait until a common doctrine or ideology can be accepted. The immediate problem lies in devising common political procedures for negotiating the inescapable conflicts that arise from our differences. These procedures encompass what we call political democracy. The challenge confronting those who work for a world organization arises from the need to establish procedures and methods for dealing with diversity. Since universality is impossible, there has been a renewed interest in regional arrangements among nations with similar interests and ideological backgrounds. Whether such regional arrangements are capable of coping with the problems presented by our changing environment is still to be determined. In view of the fact that starvation, oppression, depression, famines, epidemics, ignorance, fear and frustration are today of international significance regardless of where they occur, it would seem that nothing less than world solutions would be of any avail.

It is heartening to note that the UN has recognized the interdependency of the world today. A vast set of institutions has been established to deal with the myriad conditions which affect man's relation to man as well as one state's relation to another state. Procedures are available to discuss these problems on an international level, and permanent, expert staffs have been collected to meet them on a technical level; we have at least an embryonic international civil service. These developments all indicate that "change" as here defined is recognized by many of the governments of the world. But there will be no fundamental change in the organization of the world so long as international relations continue to be based upon the nation state operating under the old concepts of sovereignty and nationalism, and dominated by fear and suspicion. Thus the future of international organization depends on the relative force of the pressures released by changed circumstances—whether the pull toward nationalism is stronger than the pull toward political integration. The argument that contemporary international agencies should confine themselves to such problems as are susceptible of technical, rather than political solutions seems unrealistic, for an outstanding characteristic of contemporary society is the impossibility of distinguishing between the political and the nonpolitical.

The momentum of change during the past century has carried the world to the point where a genuine world organization appears not only technically feasible but indispensable for the future well-being of mankind. It is not difficult to postulate the structure of an international organization more in keeping with the objective environment of the mid-twentieth century than the contemporary state system. The actual realization of such an international organization is, however, blocked by the derivative products of the very changes which have encouraged men to dream of world government. The nation-state has in fact not been seriously undermined; on the contrary it has in many respects been strengthened. Nor have the forces leading toward the development of world community been sufficiently potent to destroy national exclusiveness. Diatribes against state sovereignty as an anachronism only obscure the real nature of the problems which must be squarely met before international relations can be organized on a more rational basis.

IX

Civilization on Trial

Civilization means advancement in social culture or, more precisely, a state of social culture characterized by relative progress in the arts, sciences, and statecraft. It is significant that civilization, culture, and refinement are synonyms. Some contemporary anthropologists use the terms "civilization" and "culture" interchangeably and attribute a civilization to primitives as well as to peoples more advanced culturally. More commonly, however, primitives are not thought of as civilized, though they possess a culture.

The term "civilization" is an indirect derivative from the Latin adjective *civilis* and the substantive *civilitas,* which denote general qualities connected with the citizen (*civis*) and more particularly a certain politeness and amiability, especially as shown by superiors to inferiors. In the Middle Ages the meaning of the term was extended to denote the largest and most comprehensive social entity rising above the individual, the family, the neighborhood, and the nation. In the eighteenth century, according to the usage of Voltaire and Dr. Johnson the lexicographer, the emphasis lay on the antithesis of civilization to feudalism and the Dark Ages. The most persistent and pervasive antithesis to civilization is the cultural attainment of so-called primitive peoples.

Whatever definition of civilization is accepted, it is a cultural phenomenon and, like everything in culture, is subject to change. If it denotes enlightenment, it is subject to further enlightenment. All the social processes that operate in the growth of culture affect civilization. Civilization appears to be more evaluative than culture as a generalized concept, yet the fact that culture and refinement and civilization are synonyms indicates the importance of context in arriving at a satisfactory definition.

Civilizations, like cultures, may be thought of as units; but the term "civilization," like "culture," may be conceived in a more comprehensive sense, as in the expression "the civilized world." The object of World War I was said to be "to make the world safe for democracy," yet the nations having or on the way to having democracy differed in important traits of their civilizations.

The fact that ideas and ideologies, technologies, and all social institutions which are components of culture must change in response to social needs indicates that they are on trial, which is merely another way of saying that civilization is on trial.

The underlying meanings of the phrase "civilization is on trial" are brought forth in the selections which follow: "The Problem of Civilization" by N. P. Jacobson, and "Civilization on Trial" by Arnold J. Toynbee.

Jacobson conceives of civilization as a process, and he discusses seven aspects of this process: (1) a growth in the sensitivities of the individual, (2) exercising and maturing of new capabilities of the individual, (3) increasing self-awareness, (4) growing effectiveness of the individual as a source of social change, (5) broadening diffusion, interweaving, and communication of each individual's sensitivities and responses with the thought and action of others, (6) increasing interdependence between men, and (7) increasing assimilation of nonhuman nature into the expanding manifold relation binding men together. These are said to be the crucial characteristics of the process of civilization.

This entire process is a special way of defining socialization involving the threefold relationship of personality, culture, and society—the complete fruition of the process being civilization.

The generic problem of civilization is to promote the growth of individual human beings in mutually compatible, rather than mutually destructive, directions. And it should be realized that "Man was made for civilization; civilization was made for man. In the process facilitating the maximum growth of both self and civilization, man has won his most revolutionary self-discovery."

47

THE PROBLEM OF CIVILIZATION*

N. P. Jacobson

We shall examine in the following order: (1) the concept of civilization, (2) the generic problem of civilization, (3) a solution which becomes ever more clear and coercive as our knowledge about human societies increases, and (4) two root needs in man which suggest that this solution to the problem of civilization will satisfy man's deepest needs and go far to solve the problem that each individual is to himself.

I

The term "civilization" has been used in a variety of ways, seldom with precision and rarely in ways that meet broad response, ever since it became current in the middle of the eighteenth century. It has been used rather loosely to refer to any social organization or to a growth of arts and sciences, or it has been counterposed to barbarism without fur-

* From *Ethics*, vol. 63, no. 1, pp. 14–32, October, 1952. Reprinted by permission of author, journal, and the University of Chicago Press.

ther definition. It is used by Toynbee as a methodological device, each civilization being "the smallest unit of historical study at which one arrives when one tries to understand the history of one's own country: the United States, say, or the United Kingdom." *

Some definitions consist entirely of metaphor. For Spengler, civilizations are organic unities, not otherwise specified, passing through cycles of growth, maturity, and decay. They manifest, successively, the greening shoots of spring, the vigorous warmth of the creative summer, the maturity of autumnal wisdom, and the cold gloom of a disintegrative winter. Out of other specializations and preoccupations, philosophers have sometimes tried to establish the "essence" of civilization in man's mental life, Hegel going so far in this direction as to equate the unfolding of the Absolute Idea with the process of civilization. Some students, Rostovtzeff, for example, find the locus of civilization in the upper classes, as is clearly implied in the questions with which his study of Rome closes: "Is it possible to extend a higher civilization to the lower classes without debasing its standard and diluting its quality to the vanishing point? Is not every civilization bound to decay as soon as it begins to penetrate the masses?" † Nothing could display more vividly the wide variation of linguistic usage in the field than to compare Rostovtzeff's notion with that of C. E. Ayers, who, with the precision achieved by undue truncation, defines civilization as "the continuity of tools," the technological life-stream of mankind. It is evident from this small sampling that the concept of civilization has still to be favored with those common and distinctive elements that circumscribe an empirical reality with care.

Our attempt here to define the concept will seek to reduce what is most essential in civilization to its clearest and simplest terms. Numerous sciences are presently contributing

new insights and sharpening our understanding to a degree that invites the present effort. The following definition, we suggest, identifies the crucial phenomena involved, defines the concept in ways that clarify rather than ignore current usage, and, consequently, should help to establish the study of civilization on a co-operative and fruitful basis.

We suggest that the concept of "civilization" means the progressive diversification and interweaving of relationships joining individual human beings with one another and with the rest of nature. Civilization is not something that *does* this to men; a series of such transformations *constitutes* the process of civilization. To the extent that these transformations are unobstructed by the conditions under which men live—under whatever sun, constitution, racial inheritance, cultural peculiarities, ethical codes, or class alignments —civilization flourishes. Wherever this process is faltering, there civilization is becoming static and commencing to decline and disintegrate.

The implications of our definition are easily elaborated. Analyzed in greater detail, the concept of civilization refers to the following events: (1) a growth in the sensitivities of the individual person; (2) exercising and maturing of new capabilities of the individual; (3) increasing self-awareness; (4) growing effectiveness of the individual as a source of social change; (5) broadening diffusion, interweaving, and communication of each individual's sensitivities and responses with the thought and action of others; (6) increasing interdependence between men; and (7) increasing assimilation of nonhuman nature into the expanding relation-manifold binding men together. These are the crucial characteristics of the process of civilization. That the seven happenings are not merely formal and arbitrary, but identify concrete events occurring all the time in every civilization, can be demonstrated by

* Arnold J. Toynbee, *Civilization on Trial*, Oxford University Press, New York, 1948, pp. 222–223.

† M. Rostovtzeff, *The Social and Economic History of the Roman Empire*, Oxford University Press, New York, 1926, p. 487.

anyone possessing the requisite detailed information regarding any particular unit of historical study. The events gradually disappearing during a period of decline will be found to be the ones to which our concept refers; and, when civilizations are in a state of vigor, these events are occurring with noticeable frequency. This definition sharpens the distinction between higher and lower civilizations and between civilization and barbarism. As men singly and in social constellations are transformed in these respects, they extend the scope and enrich the content of their literature, their art, their science, ethical ideals, technologies, political techniques, and religion. They transmit to the oncoming generations the qualitative meaning, the power, the loyalties, and the forms that have accumulated, with whatever modification may be required to meet changing conditions.

II

Civilization, from whatever point of view it is approached, presents men with problems for which their biological inheritance finds them unprepared. The definition suggested above, however, gives to the phenomena under discussion a certain structure that helps us to identify the basic problem of civilization and extricate our thought from relatively unimportant considerations. This is the problem of promoting the growth of individual men in mutually compatible rather than divisive and mutually destructive directions, as regards the impulses and attitudes of the individual, the relationships between men, and the relationships between men and the rest of nature. This problem is implicit in the very nature of the process of civilization. As soon as the first simple differentiations appear in neolithic societies, this problem commences to badger men thousands of years before they are prepared to understand their problem. This can be inferred from the forms in which they have sought to encompass their growth.

Through the long centuries separating us from neolithic societies, history presents us with one important attempt after another to promote human growth in mutually compatible directions. All these attempts testify abundantly to the creativity of the human species and to the dispersion of creative responses in the broad masses of human beings. It would burden our analysis intolerably to mention more than a few of these efforts to restore equilibrium. Linguistic communication was in no small degree a response to felt dangers of differentiation and interpersonal conflict. But the ability of language to foster equilibrium and compatibility was hampered as long as people lived in primitive hunting bands which were forced to break up as soon as an increase in numbers threatened the balance between consumption and an available food supply. Under such conditions a common language was impossible, the natural growth of language generating numerous more or less distinct dialects. Several generations in the life of a group isolated by the precarious conditions of a hunting, fishing, or gathering culture were sufficient to place numerous disparate patterns of thought and action before the development of civilization. Each developing in an isolation that might be broken by occasional trade or war, these disparate lines of development help to explain why man lived on earth so many thousands of generations before the process of civilization showed any marked acceleration. The development of a permanent food supply through agriculture was probably even more important than language at this early stage for solving the problem under discussion.

The first instances of imbalance and disparity between various lines of human development were undoubtedly restored by resources ready to hand in the form of physical prowess and sexual potencies. The first institutionalized forms of thought and action, indeed, are unique just because they support very closely the basic biological strivings for food, shelter, and sex. The initial co-ordinating thought systems probably could not have survived if they had sought to discredit and penalize man's animal drives. Life was on a far too precarious level. Thousands of years had to pass before men could meet encroaching incompatibility and felt imbalance by submitting their lines of disparate growth into the keeping of patterns that ran counter to those primeval instinctive drives that nurtured man in the beginning. This fact is reinforced when we remember that none of the great world religions has yet survived as long as did the fertility cult.

The most dramatic later attempts that proved eminently successful in solving temporarily the generic problem of civilization were (1) the rise of great empires claiming governance over the entire known world, (2) the development of monotheism in very many forms (Taoism, Buddhism, Judaism, and Christianity), and (3) universal concepts that sought to bring action under control of thought, and thought under control of some unitary, eternal Truth. The development of modern science and the world-wide response that it enjoys testify to the existence of a deep and pervasive feeling that these three innovations are unable to cope with change in its accelerated modern pace. But all four of these patterns are efforts men have made to solve the problem under discussion here while yet oblivious to its real nature. With respect to the three innovations of ancient civilizations mentioned above, Whyte observes that all three appeared very soon before or after 1000 B.C.

The processes which organized human behavior had, it seems, been ready for a swift reorganization; the human pattern had become unstable and now settled rapidly into a new shape. . . . In the ancient civilizations thought and social organization had attained a degree of differentiation which had not yet been compensated by the development of correspondingly extensive co-ordinating ideas. Thus, wherever the traditions of these civilizations were called in question there arose the opportunity and the need for a co-ordination of the new complexity of life and thought within a single comprehensive system.*

Change is endemic in human living, and by far most of the change stems from man himself. Given a chance, man tends to explore his individuality and to exercise whatever potentialities he finds there. This endless seeking for new increments of value in experience, to use Hadley Cantril's phrase, has always operated to unsettle every equilibrium, rendering obsolete in the end every stabilizing form. This is why the only forms to which men have been able to acquiesce for long, in both their intellectual and social behavior, have been abstract and general forms resting loosely upon individual and group and permitting a large measure of deviation and development. This is also why every form, whether intellectual or social, must perish in the end under the impact of man's own historical change.

The generic problem of civilization may be illustrated in more detail with reference to the disintegration of the Roman Empire. The decline of the empire was brought about by failure to promote the growth of men in mutually compatible directions. Originally a creative effort to amalgamate dozens of aboriginal cultures into a unity facilitating creative interchange between men, the empire advertised its failure as a civilizing agency and reality when, as early as the last part of the first century A.D., different lines of social development manifested their inability to appreciate one another.

The army of the empire, at first an important instrument of intercommunication between various parts of the world, became alienated from the rest of the population. The peasant and small farmer, originally the source of Rome's great armies, disappeared from the land as great latifundia tilled by slaves became the typical form of landownership and control. Proletarians huddled together in cities, forced to depend upon either the charity of the emperor or wages kept at

* L. L. Whyte, *The Next Development in Man*, New American Library of World Literature, Inc., New York, 1948, pp. 61-62.

subsistence level through competition with slave labor, proved of rebellious spirit. As early as the end of the civil war of 69–70, Vespasian ceased recruiting the army from the youth of Italy, fearing this rebellious spirit. Formal rebellions in Sicily and Gaul showed this fear to be well founded. At any rate, by the end of the third century A.D. the army no longer represented the broad population of the empire but was a mercenary army drawn from the least civilized parts of the empire. The army as one line of social development had become increasingly sealed off from mutual interchange with the rest of this civilization.

Racial traditions, at first placed in juxtaposition with considerable success, grew increasingly intolerant of each other. Increasingly the racial stocks of the eastern Mediterranean followed their own line of development until, with the aid of the barbarian attack upon the West, they were able to capture political control of an abbreviated empire and become the heir to the Greco-Roman world. Christianity, a religion that had been given its initial form by Eastern races, was probably the only important social pattern that succeeded in directing growth in mutually compatible lines. But even this success was qualified by Coptic, Nestorian, and other schisms and was damaged much more gravely when, partly because of the very racial hostilities here indicated, the Eastern races came forth with Islam as a final notice of the abiding alienation between the Eastern and the Western lines of biological inheritance. The Greek Orthodox church, as well, was in large degree engendered by a continuing alienation between the races. The empire had failed as an instrument of civilization.

The failure of the Roman Empire in its efforts to solve the problem under discussion is illustrated in the progressive alienation of one social group from another, particularly from the closing years of the first century A.D. The imperial court and bureaucracy, with some exceptions such as in the reign of Marcus Aurelius, gradually adopted a line of development that alienated the government from the people. The political bureaucracy became isolated psychologically, socially, and economically, as well as politically, from the people they sought to govern. The emperor became the largest single landowner. His fear of revolt led him to plunder mercilessly the traditional Roman senatorial families, whose lands he frequently expropriated. His interests became progressively at variance with the interests and needs of the people. In the economic province, too, one social group became increasingly alienated from another, especially after the reign of Augustus. Agricultural and industrial property became rapidly concentrated in the hands of a few city bourgeoisie who used slave labor in both factory and farm. The small farmer, once filling the wide gulf between upper and lower classes, was driven out of a functional role, unless one wishes to call the largely unemployed city proletariat a functioning social group.

It is difficult to arrive at a conclusion more heavily documented in history than this: A breakdown of social interaction and communication between one individual or social group and another, instead of bringing the development of either group to a halt, usually only insures that the lines of growth will diverge progressively from one another to engender misunderstanding, hostility, and conflict. This is certainly evidenced by the class structure of the late empire. After several generations of this disparity in growth, no imperial edict was capable of making the lines converge in the direction of mutual understanding. Lines of development followed by one social group in disregard of others finally robbed the empire of its cohesion.

The barbarian invasion in Rome's days of power might have been met by all the people along one common emotional and ideological front. Rome's failure to meet the problem of barbarians at the border was but one major failure following on the heels of many others. The political problem had not been solved, as witnessed by the alienation between the ruling bureaucracy and the people. The racial problem had not been solved, as witnessed by the progressive hostility between East and West. The military problem had not been solved, as witnessed by the alienation of the army from the people it nominally represented. The economic problem had not been solved, as one can demonstrate by the gradual breakdown of economic unity and, finally, the passage from interdependence into self-sufficiency of relatively small units as the fourth century wore on. The increased production that might have enabled the empire to support its unproductive classes was a problem which, like all the rest, was viewed in different and even conflicting frames of reference. The progressive impoverishment of the soil is in large degree another result of the lack of understanding between social groups immediately connected with the soil. Irrigation, drainage systems, and fertilization were not matters on which expert knowledge was lacking, but action was not forthcoming. The labor-saving machinery which might have given the increased productivity Rome required lacked the stimulus that might have brought it into existence. The great army of unemployed, the slave operators, the bourgeoisie, and the ruling bureaucracy tended to view all these problems in mutually hostile frameworks, and lines of disparate development had matured too far to permit a modification of their contradictions. By the end of the fourth century there was no common ground. In the midst of internal disintegration, which evidenced its failure as a civilizing process, the Empire fell apart.

A detailed analysis of any other civilization will probably show with equal force that the "decline and fall" of a particular unit of civilization is but the saturation point as regards disparate lines of growth. Civilization flourishes only in proportion as individuals and social groups so live that they assimilate the viewpoints of one another and develop an appreciative understanding of each other's needs. Whenever a group separates itself from others and begins to develop a framework of preoccupations peculiar to its own separate way of life, the very foundation of civilization is under threat. Developing the tendencies implicit in its own particular way of life, the group's patterns of thought and action become progressively irrelevant to people engaged in other modes of life-activity. In so far as this group insists upon being effective in the culture as a whole, the need grows ever more coercive to persuade others to accept what presents itself to the latter as an irrelevant system of behavior. The monastic line of development in the Middle Ages illustrates this proposition very clearly. Since people outside the monastic orders display tendencies to reject the accumulating monastic doctrines, materials are sought with which to explain this rejection both to the clerical order and to the secular world as a whole. Rejection of the "revealed doctrine" is explained in terms of man's propensity for evil, of his incompleteness and corruption of thought, of the unsuitability of language to convey the Truth, of the crippled conditions of the human mind with respect to apprehending Truth, and of the propensity of man to rebel against the Truth. When these explanations fail to convince, opposition is taken as the indication that more stringent measures are needed. Theories of divine inspiration are brought into the struggle, and claims for an inerrant and divinely instituted clerical hierarchy bring up the rear guard. Over the whole effort resound the threats of excommunication and eternal damnation. Medieval monasticism, modern economic and political bureaucracies, and proletarians living in a completely tangential manner with reference to the wider scheme of things, all bear the earmarks of those disparate movements that witness a civilization's decline. The Protestant Reformation helped immeasurably to invigorate European civilization when it abolished the monastic order and placed every individual on an equal footing before God. This solved the problem of civilization only temporarily, however, since the disparities implicit in the inherited monastic ideology took root in every individual soul and posed the problem that modern civilization must face—the problem of an integrative organization of life that promotes the progressive release of every individual from his own inner disequilibrium.

The problem we are discussing becomes progressively more serious as civilization develops more complex forms of life. This is true for four very important reasons. In the first place, civilization generates power. In the hands of disparate social groups, this power becomes an ever more ominous issue. Power can be used for evil or for good, that is to say, either to support the specific ways of individual or group at the expense of other people or to promote growth along mutually compatible lines of growth. With the discovery of atomic fission, this power assumes the role of a gigantic neon sign spread across the heavens, warning men that traditional modes of solving civilization's generic problem must be supported by more creative solutions than men have yet discerned if the human experiment is not to prove a failure. Second, the more diversified the lines of interest and need-satisfying behavior, the greater the suffering attending personal and social disintegration. The possibilities for intense suffering, therefore, increase in something like geometric proportions as civilization proceeds. People whose patterned lives have grown accustomed to a many-sided manifold of meaningful activities experience far more personal upheaval during a period of social breakdown than people on less complex levels of life. The possibility for frustration and suffering is proportionate in magnitude to the number of diversified cultural activities in which people are actively engaged. Third, social change accelerates as civilization proceeds, since each individual becomes increasingly an effective source of change. This accelerating change proves to be an intolerable burden upon every instrumentality men have thus far employed in directing their civilization. Finally, the growing interdependence among men provides the context in which every dislocation sends a reverberating shock throughout the entire manifold of relationships. Every single occasion of contradictory modes of life becomes a threat to the equilibrium of the entire functioning system. For these reasons in particular, the problem we have been discussing becomes ever more coercive as a civilization passes successfully through other relatively minor barriers. At some point not yet discernible, every civilization must confront as an utter necessity the problem of directing the growth of individual men in mutually compatible, rather than divisive and mutually destructive, directions, as regards both the impulses and attitudes of the individual and the relationships between men.

It should be observed in this respect that, just as men become increasingly self-conscious with reference to the nature of their own individuality, so they become increasingly self-conscious with reference to the nature of civilization. This kind of self-awareness has increased vastly during the last fifty years. The rate of this increase, moreover, appears to accelerate each year. Like our self-awareness in relation to dread diseases and criminality, this appreciation and self-appraisal as a civilization appears to be growing by leaps and bounds. No earlier civilization ever became alert to the presence of decay so quickly as has our own. Rome slept on for two or three centuries after the initial steps toward her own decline had been taken, and she simply could not see until almost the brink of her demise the oncoming avalanche of defeat. She considered herself eternal. Policies intended to stem the tide of Rome's disintegration present the sympathetic reader with a dramatic spectacle in which the best minds of the day were intensely applying patches in the dark. Our own civilization, on the other hand, despite the faster pace at which events now sweep forward, is all about us becoming alert to the danger in our predicament. This alertness is by no means traceable entirely to the ominous threat of the atom bomb, since studies in economic history or in the incidence of mental ailments trace back at least to the close of World War I the growing sense among a people that its major processes and premises of life were under serious threat. This growing self-awareness has been submerged only briefly and superficially ever since. It is entirely possible that ours may become the first civilization to make the discovery which enables the civilizing process to avoid the precipice that has lain athwart the path of the great civilizations of the world. Ours may fan this self-awareness into a solution that need never become obsolete because it solves civilization's generic problem.

III

No political institution, no constitution or ethical ideal, can cope with the problem described above. The most creative and historically appropriate generalizations of thought fail because concepts are notoriously static, perhaps intrinsically so, and they depend upon a concrete social process for both their interpretation and their concrete application. Social institutions seem likewise incapable of being stripped of their inveterate tendencies to resist the social change that is now accelerating. Both concepts and social institutions, unless they are continually transformed in ways that keep them historically relevant, become dangerously divisive, aggravating the problem that must be solved. Moreover, the question of what change will keep ideas and institutions "historically relevant" and which relevancies will prove mutually destructive are matters left completely unresolved. These are the basic points at issue.

When civilization and its generic problem are analyzed as suggested above, a solution appears to have been emerging ever more fully and convincingly in the human mind. Centuries of developing self-consciousness, in the sense of self-discovery and self-knowledge, have been pushing this solution into clarity. It is the location of a process operative within the very stream of civilization, with reference to which our patterns of thought and our social institutions might be given safe and

* Whyte, *op. cit.*, p. 90.

creative direction. When diseases threaten our physical health, we are driven to learn about the progress of the disease in relation to the processes that maintain vital health. In the process of civilization, too, we must learn to identify, to feel, and to serve a process promoting growth in mutually compatible directions and protecting the civilizing process against its enemies of mutual annihilation and destruction. Obviously, this unitary direction of life must not penalize or attempt to obstruct the diversification of the individual's powers, and it must not attempt to combat either social change or the accumulation of social power, since these factors constitute a large part of the civilizing process itself.

The sort of process that we must learn to discriminate in the events transpiring daily about us is suggested by L. L. Whyte. "The organizing processes of a healthy organism ensure that its behavior is such as to facilitate its own development. The fact that man has been able to civilize himself shows that some such self-regulating development has in the main dominated the history of the species." * This process, however, must be given clearer form and more specific concrete reference than the author of this passage provides. It is not sufficient to point to a universal formative tendency, "the tendency for patterns to extend their form," without specifying the form whose extension might now heal our dislocations. The same lack of specificity is found in Toynbee. The three elements and their characteristic functions in the rise and fall of civilizations, the ruling minority, the internal proletariat, and the barbarian proletariat, testify to the dangerous divisive tendencies of civilization without specifying either why the creative minority loses its potency or what might be done to generate mutuality. At this point Toynbee withdraws into metaphor and myth, sometimes offering an other-worldly religion.

How else can we learn to live in the powerful, volatile stream of civilization except by discovering the process with reference to which it can be given intelligent and creative direction? Shall we concede that this cannot be done and that there is no way for civilized men to avoid the personal disintegrations and social catastrophes that presently encroach upon us? Are we prepared to concede that civilization is this sort of curse to man, that while he cannot avoid it, neither can he endure it? Many people are tempted to resign themselves to this diagnosis in much the same temper that others resigned themselves to dread diseases that are now practically extinct. Shall our century take up again the cause of the noble savage? Will we use our atomic radiation to help the sun show forth a man whom civilization has not corrupted?

Were we able to identify a unitary process operating in the midst of civilization as we have described it, it might be possible to solve civilization's generic problem and keep human growth within wholly creative bounds. This is the task to which the remainder of this essay is devoted. We shall attempt to identify one process amid all others which, to the extent that it becomes a point of reference in our thought and the locus of our dominant loyalties, will enable us to make civilization truly one endless continuity of growth.

As it now presents itself, on the basis of what is known of the conditions controlling human growth, this unitary process is constituted by seven types of occurrences, functioning together to promote man's progressive growth, and therefore deserving to be given unitary structure in our thought. The fact becoming increasingly subject to empirical inquiry is that the first occurrence in any kind of individual growth whatsoever is the opening of the individual to a felt need, a sense of requiredness, a feeling of inadequacy. The individual is unique by reason of both his genetic inheritance and the social configuration in which he responds. But no matter how his sensitivities and responses grow and whatever direction and organization they assume, growth occurs only on the hot spots, only on those facets of felt requiredness to which the individual has been alerted from within. Once the psychosomatic processes within the human organism have

been altered so as to produce what we call a felt requiredness, the individual is prepared for an adventure which, under conditions to be described below, will yield a new line of sensitivity and response. It is only by following such lines that the individual becomes effective in new ways in a world whose significance for him is expanding. Because man grows from the inside out, rather than vice versa, the type of occurrence we identify here as the emergence of new need is an intrinsic part of the process of growth whose character man is powerless to alter but whose effectiveness human recalcitrance and ignorance serve to imperil.

Since we do not presently understand how to direct the process of civilization, very little attention is paid to the emergence of new needs. Heretofore, they have been born in the dark, so to speak, and many of them have been kept in the dark, refused, ignored, and both deliberately and unconsciously suppressed. To deal with the needs of the psychosomatic organism in this way is to guarantee that they will become even more active than before, sometimes conducting the individual into schizoid behavior but always continuing a line of development of which the individual may or may not become aware. If civilization is to be given intelligent and feelingful direction, the needs that emerge must become infused with the self-illumination that results when they are freely introduced into conscious awareness and joined with the conditions described below.

The second type of occurrence in the process whereby the individual expands his powers is the emergence of a new sensitivity within the psychosomatic organism. The individual feels something new. On facets where the world formerly was utterly blank, in places where the individual was unresponsive, feelingful interaction emerges to be taken account of. At this stage, the line of development under way lacks self-consciousness, since consciousness involves the appreciation of meaning, and meaning has not yet emerged. Hence, the individual does not know what he needs and feels, perhaps cannot even surmise. He does not think about the new feeling at all; he is being expanded in what he can appreciate and know by a transformation that captures him, so to speak, from the rear.

The potential talents and powers of man slumber on in a totally undeveloped state except as he is transformed organically in these two ways. He may both think and act, but his actions are those of an automaton carrying out the will of another, as though under some hypnotic spell. Except as his own needs and sensitivities lead him, the individual *as such* does not become involved. When new needs and sensitivities are suppressed and ignored, they become increasingly active, passing beyond control. In this state, they disguise themselves in symbolic form that keeps their true identity undisclosed. In this hyperactive and hidden state, they lead the individual to feel himself under threat, so that he is impelled to compensate by undue rigidity in his patterns of thought and action. He may become a bigot in his thought and recalcitrant in social interchange. He may feel it necessary to strive for "moral perfection" in order to relieve the suspicion within and to exaggerate the eminence of his social group. In any case, he is under compulsion, driven by forces which he cannot understand. Such an individual is a subversive element in any civilization, though he may have accustomed himself to using the slogans everyone admires and he may have attained a position of great influence in the economic, political, or religious life of the community. Civilization individuates. Until civilized men understand the nature of this individuating process and learn to direct its novel lines of growth, destructiveness is as apt to result as creative and socialized behavior, with the possibility ever imminent that the increasing power of an undirected process may, like a proliferating cancerous growth, destroy the entire experiment that nature is making in man.

On the other hand, when new needs and sensitivities are deliberately related in thought and action to the events described below, they become an **opening** door through which both individual and community are introduced to a world of expanding quality, meaning, and mutuality.

The third type of occurrence constituting part of the process of human growth, operating yet beyond our conscious awareness in the process of civilization, is the emergence of some new insight, perspective, or qualitative meaning on the trail of emerging sensitivity and need. The organism has now been transformed with more than a feelingful urge. The sensitivity has been illuminated. It has found a relationship with other events in man's conscious awareness. It assumes significance. As sensitivities cross the threshold into conscious awareness, they are comprehended by the human mind; that is to say, they become part of a vast system of symbolic representation wherein events past, present, and still to come may be related in one simultaneous sensitivity. The qualities of the present event are enhanced by this system of relationships, and the mind is enabled to extend its reach far beyond the present experience. Qualitative meaning enables the mind to hold before us precious events and people that are gone. We can encompass in a fleeting moment qualities whose full sweep would overpower our sanity were they not presented in the form of symbols. In the form of such symbolic representation we can subject ourselves safely to experiences which in their raw qualitative concreteness might be full of evil. We communicate by means of these symbols, and, where evil must be encountered, one may die in order that millions may live. We learn to see what others have seen, and what others have discovered becomes a vast storehouse of meaning to help in the illumination of our own sensitized need.

As these meanings form a network of interconnective events comprehending all that is happening in the world, this universe becomes spiritual. It becomes more deeply and pervasively meaningful. It becomes the house of the human spirit, responsive to human need, expressive throughout of hope and fear, joy and sorrow, triumph and failure, defiance and despair, love and fellowship. Events cease to be material things merely and become a language, a prophecy, and a song.*

When these events are related in such a way that they enable us to predict the consequences that follow certain conditions, knowledge is born, and knowledge confers power.

It is important to emphasize the originality of these greening shoots of new qualitative meaning, since the emphasis may save us from the folly (in which civilizations have thus far sought to surpass one another) of leading the individual in ways thought best that he should go. No one can lead another; he can succeed only in misleading him. And a civilization operating blindly in this respect is apt to become a gigantic concentration camp in which no one may be sent to the ovens of Dachau but everyone suffers silently in the framework of thought and feeling imposed by other people, other social classes, or other generations. Western civilization has sought incessantly to bring concrete, spontaneous growth under the control of theoretical constructions, abstractions, generalizations, logical constructs—possibly because its dynamic and changeful nature made it fearfully aware of the need for order. The civilizations of the Far East, on the other hand, have celebrated the individual's spontaneous strivings, somewhat heedless of the need for theoretical organization—possibly because social change in the East has proceeded at a more leisurely pace, with the need for order less urgent. The problem of civilization, we are suggesting, will be found between these two extremes, through the discovery of a kind of unity, and an intellectual comprehension of that unity, which actually promotes spontaneity and individuality as the latter cannot do by themselves unaided by human thought.

Questioning, searching, reaching out for the implications of new sensitivity and need, leaning forward into his own future, the individual is thrown into a quest which, if given the favoring winds of love and respect, can end only in the growth of some new talent or individual power. An original propulsion, rising in a unique individual, reaps a harvest of meanings, insights, and perspectives to illumine the felt qualities of experience. Only in proportion as such windows broaden and vivify an individual's exposure upon the world does a person ever truly find *himself*. In this way, a growing self-consciousness finds a companion in its own integrity. Civilization destroys people and creates in them a terribly destructive social madness when it increases their self-consciousness without providing the conditions in which the growing self can be joined with others and thereby expanded and strengthened.

The fourth type of occurrence in the process under discussion is the exercise and maturation of a new capacity, talent, or power. All that an individual may potentially become and achieve will die unborn except as the events mentioned above open doors through which new talents may be exercised. Human capabilities are strengthened in essentially the same way that one develops stronger muscles—by exercise. An individual's powers are sometimes matured with little conscious attention, but they can never become all they might become until they are favored with deliberate thought and understood in the concrete context of other affairs amid which both resources and liabilities may lie in wait. Talents sentenced to exist *sub rosa*, because they have never been favored with the events mentioned above, frequently make both organic and social contact with strange companions, so that we are treated to the spectacle of creativity being diverted into criminality and genius into insanity.

None of the events mentioned thus far is able by itself to direct the creativity of the human organism so as to solve civilization's generic problem. They must all be taken to-

* Henry N. Wieman, *The Source of Human Good*, University of Chicago Press, Chicago, 1946, p. 23.

gether, in conjunction with the events mentioned below, as constituting one unitary process of growth, a unity that promotes individuality to an extent the latter cannot do by itself. They need particularly to be conceived and related in deliberate action to the social context in which they are always occurring.

What has been discovered must be shared. The meaning of what is new may be ambiguous; it may be in error; it is necessarily of microscopic proportions as compared to the amplifications made possible through sharing. The talent, moreover, that has come under conscious attention may portend such results in the individual's total experience as he would prefer to avoid. Only by sharing the new in social interchange can ambiguity be removed and meaning become clear. The fifth type of event in the process whereby the individual expands his powers, therefore, is the sharing of each new qualitative meaning, perspective, or power with other people in the social manifold, so that it becomes the avenue of repeated interchange. Infused with felt quality, illumined with meaning, vivified and extended with personal power, a new need becomes an occasion for connective growth between people. Favored with a special kind of sharing, each novelty is forced to give an account of itself. Sharing that is overindulgent delivers an individual over into the control of his own unchecked imagination and into the reign of secondhand perspectives that overlay and stifle original growth. Such indulgence fails to provide the tension that strengthens and chastens an individual's powers. Where individuals display genuine care, respect, and love for one another, they *share* their *individuality* with each other, permissively and resiliently, instead of obliterating it. Such sharing provides the resistance of other attitudes and things wherein each impulse is elaborated and its possibilities revealed either for increasing or destroying the "increments of value" all men seek. It is only when these impulses are driven underground by harsh suppression, or treated with overindulgence,

that they become the dark trails along which men are driven without knowing where they go. Among people whose offerings are never the occasion for penalty of threat, the trails of new growth become progressively transparent. *Among such people, evil and error are progressively retired from human history.* As the power of civilized man increases and social change accelerates, these become the only kind of people that can support a civilization.

The sixth type of occurrence in the process under discussion is the integration of each new meaning-illumined, effective sensitivity and need, when it has survived the test of sharing, with all the rest the individual can see, feel, know, anticipate, and do. Amid both an existing apperceptive mass and a system of effective talents and powers, a new pattern of behavior is structured to transform the total organism. These newly patterned powers, merging deep within our person, render us increasingly articulate as a person feeling, knowing, responding. No one is ever able to predict precisely what elements, out of all the trails in which an individual may seek to involve himself, will ultimately be integrated into the psychosomatic organism.

The seventh type of event in the process we are seeking to identify in the midst of civilization is the integrating of the newly illumined, need-driven power into existing avenues of interchange, man to man and man to the rest of nature. Unless the need of the innovator is shared within a social group, a new, reciprocal, and potentially creative relationship between men and the rest of nature will die stillborn as far as the transmission of a culture is concerned. Without this integration, nothing is rescued from the processes of death and decay that overtake each generation. With this integration, all the difference that an individual has made in his world could conceivably be assimilated into the next generation in microscopic detail to become the seed corn for the more meaningful future. Without this integration, nothing survives the creator. With this integration, all of man's strivings may become resources for tomorrow's living. This social manifold hereby becomes progressively deeper and more vivid with felt qualities, and, as these events transpire, each member of the community comes increasingly to be joined to every other along lines of meaningful sensitivity and response that bring the talents of men into focus in a throbbing simultaneity.

These seven events, or types of occurrences, have nurtured the growth of man and society throughout the ages of evolving man. They have functioned together in the long stretch of human history to insure the emergence of the individual from the social group in which he was at first almost totally immersed. They have made this evolving individual increasingly the reservoir of knowledge and expanding capabilities, the exercise of which upon his environment has given man increasingly the power to vary his responses and appreciate himself as an unique individual capable of being effective in a unique way. Out of relatively unresponsive lower animal forms, they have brought forth a being moved less and less by innate responses and increasingly moved by a delicate system of sensitivities, each of which enriches experience by joining the individual in new ways along relationships wherein everything becomes infused with meaning, vivid aesthetic richness, and mutuality.

The process structured as described has facilitated man's emergence from lower animal forms in much the same way that metabolic processes have operated to maintain physiological equilibrium. If men had been oriented in thought, feeling, and action to the operation of this creative process in the past, no civilization should ever have passed into decline. Nothing should ever have been truly lost, and meaning should have been completely corrective and cumulative. No one can wonder that earlier units in the civilizing process passed into decline, however, since men were working in the dark in relation to the events that were of supreme importance for raising them further out of barbarism. Today, however, our knowledge of this process is growing rapidly, and its fur-

ther elaboration and discovery become both possible and far more important than any of the problems presently commanding our rich resources for research. Civilization will never be freed of its tendencies for self-destruction until it masters this task of self-discovery. It must make this process the point of reference for its standards and scales of value. This process must be built into all our social institutions so that the entire cultural matrix shapes thought, feeling and action in ways compatible with its operation. This is just what earlier civilizations were unable to do; it is this wherein ours must succeed, delicately balanced though it now is between further development and self-annihilation. This process, in other words, is the criterion for the continued development of civilization. According to the nature of this process, our cultural matrix must be deliberately shaped so that "the community tradition," as Whyte remarks, "facilitates the development of the individual."

The process described, it will be noted, promotes simultaneously the growth of both individual *as such* and community. All the power of a biological inheritance may now become unreservedly our ally. Knowledge of this process, therefore, is the highest point that man has reached in the expansion of his own self-discovery, and only his growing propensity to make it the central devotion of his living will denote a still higher stage of self-discovery. Already in the knowledge of this process, however, man finally comprehends in manageable abstract form those events that men heretofore have been unprepared to perceive. These abstractions, therefore, are themselves a creation of the process which it is their task to distinguish in experience. And the test of their capacity to fulfil this task in a world of process must not be viewed as an ability to serve endlessly, unwaveringly, unchangingly. The power and the truth of these abstractions, on the contrary, may be tested by their capacity to link man with the process that has raised him from bestiality into civilization. This means that the power and truth of the rational structure we have elaborated as the solution to the problem of civilization will be displayed by the extent to which this rational structure carries within itself the clues to its own self-correction. Men following the guide of this conception will find themselves in relation to the process controlling their maximum development. Their community with others will be progressively deepened, their felt qualities of experience heightened and vivified, the scope of their knowledge and power of control expanded, and the whole world of past and present brought into sharper and richer focus within each individual. With these transformations, men will respond differently to the stimuli about them; they will organize differently their perceptual field, developing new modes of symbolizing what they feel and discern. New aspects of the process described above, aspects as yet unperceived, will undoubtedly displace some of the facets presently of great vividness and importance. It is the concrete process of growth that is of supreme importance for the continuance and enriching of civilization, not the abstract rational structures in which we strive to comprehend that reality.

IV

The process just described not only solves the generic problem of civilization; it provides for the fullest possible satisfaction of two of man's deepest needs: (1) the need to expand one's own powers, to seek "increments of value in experience," and (2) the need for relations of mutual support with other people. Since it is impossible for man to satisfy the former in utter disregard of the latter, these two needs are implicated together in concrete experience to offer powerful dual support for the solution elaborated above.

Man has a need to grow. He has a need to expand the range of what is felt, known, and controlled. His growth has an inner dynamism of its own. This simple fact is supported today by an avalanche of evidence emerging from the research of competent scholars in relatively isolated fields of inquiry. It would burden our essay intolerably to

mention more than a few of these findings. People need relationships with other people and with the rest of nature that free new lines of meaningful response and stir life into richer forms. Without knowing what it is they need, people require a total cultural matrix which, instead of "leaving them cold" as so much social interchange does today, starts new lines of growth stirring in their souls. Everyone must have such a social manifold in which to live, and people who do not find it are diverted into compensatory, compulsive, and essentially neurotic satisfactions that seal the person over with a protective shell of self-destruction.

People differ greatly in this respect, of course, but every human being tends to move outward against obstacles in search of what Hadley Cantril calls "an increment of value in experience."

The ultimate, the most generalized goal of man is what can be called *the enhancement of the value attributes of experience*. This can be regarded as the top standard of human experience, a standard in its own right. It is the capacity man has to sense added value in his experience that accounts for his ceaseless striving, his search for a direction to his activities, for his characteristic unwillingness to have things remain as they are. . . . What is meant by a desired increment in the value attribute of experience can be seen best by observing one's own life and the life of others. The skilled worker who gets the job he wants will soon become relatively dissatisfied if it offers no "future"—if there is no chance for increased responsibility, for increased creative effort, or for greater usefulness in his social group. A young woman may have her whole heart set on marriage. But after marriage she will use this new situation as the springboard for obtaining new, emergent qualities of experience through her children, her new social intercourse, her new community responsibilities. . . . A young man who has acquired the ambition to go to college will rapidly acquire other ambitions as soon as he enters college. He will want to make a certain team or club, or he may strive for a certain academic record. Once he gets into a club or makes a team, the chances are that he will strive within his social groups to raise his status, to become an important member. And once he makes the grades he desires, he will probably raise his sights.*

Passing from psychology to psychiatry, we find Cantril's point corroborated and heavily documented in clinical studies conducted with people from a variety of social levels. Karen Horney has written her latest book within this framework, giving it the title *Neurosis and Human Growth.*

Through his mental capacities man has the faculty to reach beyond himself. In contrast to other animals, he can imagine and plan. In many ways he can gradually enlarge his faculties and, as history shows, has actually done so. The same is also true for the life of a single individual. There are no rigidly fixed limits to what he can make out of his life, to what qualities or faculties he can develop, to what he can create. . . . The basic difference between healthy strivings and neurotic drives for glory lies in the forces prompting them. Healthy strivings stem from a propensity, inherent in human beings, to develop given potentialities. . . . The live forces of the real self urge one toward self-realization.†

Erich Fromm states explicitly that "life has an inner dynamism of its own; it tends to grow, to be expressed, to be lived," and that, among all the psychological and biophysical drives and tendencies of the human being, "the most important seems to be the tendency to grow, to develop and realize potentialities which man has developed in the course of history—as, for instance, the faculty of creative and critical thinking and of having differentiated emotional and sensuous experience." Harry Stack Sullivan is another noted American psychiatrist who spent a lifetime documenting this inner dynamism of the self and the destructiveness resulting from its frustration. The Chicago clinical psychologist, Carl R. Rogers, finds this need to grow evidenced in discoveries he has made along an independent, nonpsychoanalytic line of attack. "The organism," Rogers declares, "has one basic tendency and striving—to actualize, maintain, and enhance the experiencing organism. Rather than many needs and motives, it seems entirely possible that all organic and psychological needs may be described as partial aspects of this one fundamental need." ‡

The evidence we are submitting here should be viewed against the physiological research of W. R. Cannon, whose book, *The Wisdom of the Body,* is a rich documentation of the delicate self-adjustments and reorganizations of which the human body is capable without any conscious direction whatever. The neurologist, C. Judson Herrick, extends the scope of Cannon's work beyond self-adjustment into self-expansion.

The human capacity for inventing new things and original conceptions is the outgrowth of those creative powers that are inherent in all living substance, and the successive steps in the

* Hadley Cantril, *The "Why" of Man's Experience,* The Macmillan Company, New York, 1950, pp. 29–30.
† Karen Horney, *Neurosis and Human Growth,* W. W. Norton & Company, Inc., New York, 1950, pp. 37–38.
‡ Carl R. Rogers, *Client-centered Therapy,* Houghton Mifflin Company, New York, 1951, pp. 487–488.

acquisition of this capacity are open to inspection. This vital creativity, in its turn, has its roots in that directive quality that is apparent in every causal situation, organic and inorganic. Making novelties seems to be nature's chief industry.*

Here then are psychiatrist, social psychologist, clinical psychologist, physiologist, neurologist, each speaking out of competent careers of high rank, and out of studies conducted in widely different frames of reference, each testifying to the tendency in man for self-fulfilment, for growth, for seeking increments of value in experience. A few brief remarks may suggest the even wider extent of this corroboration. Thurnwald finds the need for growth operative in primitive societies. "Work is never limited to the unavoidable minimum, but exceeds the absolutely necessary amount owing to a natural or acquired functional urge to activity.† A student of the modern labor process concludes that "the most potent reason why we work at physical jobs will be found to . . . be some form of the urge in man to realize and express himself as a person." ‡

The nature of this root need of man can be more clearly specified. Most important, the native need to grow cannot find satisfaction amid frameworks of thought and action that are borrowed from another person, social group, or historical epoch. It must be the result of the individual's own integratings of experience, something emerging along the trail of his own needs, sensitivities, capacities, and qualitative meanings. One reason why the process submitted in the preceding section is urgently needed as a contemporary guide is that people have today lost almost completely the ability to distinguish an act of conformity from an original striving of the self. Pressures toward conformity, supported by the fears that stalk throughout the world, inhibiting freedom of thought, speech, press, and assembly, are such as to slaughter in most of us, while we are yet in our prime, the ability to announce, to recognize, and to pursue what is distinctively our own. Considering the nature of civilization, this condition may well herald at least a temporary relapse into barbarism. It is unlikely that this deadening of the threshold of native strivings can be overcome unless the process promoting creative living delivers men from this conformity.

Another imposing mass of evidence might be assembled to show that every man needs relations of mutual support with other people. Unless we find someone, underneath all individual differences, who feels as we feel, thinks as we think, and values what we value, we are lost in our own solitude. This is the solitude of unshared response, the deep isolation of one person from all the rest. People who lack sympathetic response reveal how largely they are driven by the need for mutuality by grasping at even the most superficial and superimposed types of mutuality rather than endure the hollowness of solitude. They collect agates, match covers, dogs, antiques, and everything else under the sun, not because they are pack rats, but because they need to share their experience with others, even if they must invent the means that bring them together. They read magazines dealing with the article in which they are mutually interested; they belong to clubs that bring them together for conventions; they confer credentials upon outstanding collections. People take up hobbies of various sorts to fill the vacuum left by the circumstances of their lives whenever they lack a basis for internal union with others in the ordinary affairs of the day. All these avocations amplify the revealing statement about an outstanding collector of match covers:

---

* C. Judson Herrick, "Integrative Levels in Biology," in Sellars et al. (ed.), *Philosophy for the Future*, The Macmillan Company, New York, 1949, p. 225.

† Richard Thurnwald, *Economics in Primitive Communities*, Oxford University Press, London, 1932, p. 209.

‡ A. R. Heron, *Why Men Work*, Stanford University Press, Stanford, 1948, p. 155.

"Rosen started collecting match covers because he didn't know anyone in Cincinnati." *

So great is the need for mutual interchange with other people that people who have been prevented from developing deeper levels of mutuality will live in the framework of other people's sensitivities and responses, and they will acquiesce to secondhand perspectives and evaluations, if only a relationship with others can be insured. A mere mechanical conformity may become its own justification when our social existence offers nothing more deeply satisfying. It can be taken as an axiom, indeed, that people will accept any avenue for the mutuality of shared experience, no matter how shallow and secondhand it may be, whenever the circumstances under which they live have severed the more genuine and deeper avenues of organic fellow-feeling. What is involved here is not essentially different from the case of the world traveler who, after experiencing increasingly the loss of mutuality as he passes for months among foreigners, is overjoyed to meet a man in Tokyo who had once driven through the traveler's home town. This small shred offered rich mutuality in contrast to months of solitude.

People who lack sympathetic response cannot satisfy their need to grow, since mutual interchange is presupposed for human growth. We have learned from Karen Horney more forcibly than ever how broadly applicable is the explanation of neuroses as a defensive reaction against frustrated processes of personal becoming. Most, if not all, forms of insanity are the result of psychological isolation. And in the Menninger Clinic in Topeka, Kansas, case histories abound which indicate that a cure for such neuroses requires the re-establishment of mutual lines of shared responses, genuinely unfeigned internal person-to-person connection.

SUMMARY

We have conceived civilization to be the progressive diversification and interweaving of relationships joining individual human beings with one another and with the rest of nature. This conception implies that civilization is any form of social interaction which expands the sensitivities of the individual, exercises his capabilities in new directions, promotes self-awareness, renders him increasingly a source of social change, interweaves his responses and sensitivities with other people, increases interdependence, and progressively assimilates nonhuman nature into the manifold of relationships binding men together. These occurrences are to be found wherever civilization, as the term is commonly but obscurely used, exists. This concept reduces phenomena of great complexity to their simplest essential terms.

The generic problem of civilization, we have stated, is to promote the growth of individual human beings in mutually compatible, rather than mutually destructive, directions, and we have described how Rome passed into decline because of failure to meet this problem. The so-called "decline" of a civilization is always the saturation point with regard to disparate lines of growth. We have argued that this problem becomes progressively more serious and difficult as civilization develops.

Some of the measures have been indicated whereby earlier societies sought to restore the equilibrium brought on by increasing differentiation. None of these attempts can meet the problem at its present level of complexity and amid the greatly accelerated rate of change.

The unitary process described will solve this problem because it promotes man's maximum unfolding and does this in mutually compatible directions, protecting the civilizing process against mutual annihilation and decline. While this process facilitates human growth, it does so without incurring the colossal wreckage that has overtaken flourishing social entities of the past. This process is constituted by seven types of occurrences, emerging need, awakening biophysical sensitivity, emerging qualitative meaning, newly

* "How Grownups Play with Matches," *American Magazine*, August, 1950.

empowered talent, sharing of the new amid respect and mutual responsibility, integration of what survives the test of sharing into the total psychosomatic organism to transform the responses structured there, and, finally, integration of a new meaning-illumined talent into the total social manifold that reproduces itself in the young. This is the process that has facilitated man's emergence from lower animal forms into civilization when it had never been done before. It solves the generic problem of civilization. It is the criterion for the advancement of civilization.

Finally, the solution suggested not only is recommended by the nature of our problem and by the state of our increased knowledge with regard to man and society; the solution is also urged upon us by two of man's deepest needs, the need for the individual to grow along his own trails of sensitivity and meaning and the need for sympathetic understanding and mutual response with other human beings. The process described provides powerfully for the satisfaction of these root needs. Much is revealed by this solution that has until now remained hidden. Man was made for civilization; civilization was made for man. In the process facilitating the maximum growth of both self and civilization, man has won his most revolutionary self-discovery.

Would it be unduly pessimistic to think that cultural lag, if allowed to continue unchecked, might bring about the decline of Western civilization? Harry Elmer Barnes, in his prospectus of the American scene today, deals with some of the implications of this hypothesis in the following excerpt,[1] "Cultural Lag: The Gulf between Machines and Institutions."

The most characteristic aspect of our twentieth-century civilization, that which makes our age inevitably transitional in character, is the amazing contrast between the material and the nonmaterial factors in our culture.

Never before has there been such a gulf between technology and social institutions. We have a thoroughly up-to-date material culture, complete, diverse, and potentially efficient beyond that of any earlier age. On the other hand, our institutions and the social thinking through which we seek to control and exploit this material culture are an antiquated mosaic, compounded of accretions from the stone ages to the close of the eighteenth century, with very little from a more recent period actually guiding our lives.

Not only does this vast gulf exist between material culture, on the one hand, and social thinking and institutions, on the other, but we seemingly do everything possible to widen the abyss. We provide almost every imaginable incentive to extend our already top-heavy material equipment. Scientific prizes, patent royalties, industrial profits, social prestige, and every other conceivable reward, are offered to those who will provide us with better machines and more gadgets.

At the same time we set every possible obstacle in the way of those who seek to improve our antiquated institutional machinery. There are no prizes for the social inventor. Indeed, in most modern countries, an individual who shows any real ingenuity in social planning is threatened with a jail sentence. Instead of showering upon the would-be social inventor all sorts of honors, we make him an outcast or deride him as a crank. In this way, the gulf between our material equipment and our institutional life is still more alarmingly broadened.

.   .   .   .   .   .

What has just been said is no mere idle gossip or amusing reading. It lies at the heart of our social crisis. No matter what aspect of our social problems we consider, it is always a secondary manifestation of the chief defect of our civilization—the gulf between machines and institutions. For example, if our economic thinking and institutions were on the same level of efficiency and modernity as our mechanical equipment, we could be living in a veritable utopia where man would have to exert unbelievably little physical effort. If we could handle the problems involved in the distribution and consumption of goods as well as we do the problems involved in their production there would be no crisis. We produce goods with the very latest machinery, but we utilize them on the basis of ideas and institutions which originated a century or more ago.

However lightheartedly some may view this striking discrepancy between our machines and our institutions, it has already exacted a frightful penalty, and may easily exact the supreme penalty of an extensive decline of civilization.

It has produced severe depressions and other economic disasters. It has almost destroyed democracy. It has made our legal system inadequate and produced widespread contempt for law in general. We have an annual crime bill at times equal to a fourth of our total national income, and crime so well organized and protected that the more serious criminals are never even molested by the public authorities. It has bred religious indifference, moral chaos, and educational futility.

The upshot, if we go on as we have so far in the twentieth century, is the impending collapse of Western civilization from internal weaknesses, with the grave probability that the process will be greatly hastened by a devastating world war. If society awakens in time and closes the gulf by bringing our institutions up to date, we may literally 'inherit the earth.' If we continue as we have so far in the twentieth century there is little likelihood of preserving civilization for more than another generation.

For a final word in this analysis of social change, let us turn to Arnold J. Toynbee, famous author of the voluminous *A Study of History* and other works of note.

Toynbee says there is plenty of evidence that civilization is on trial. For example, there is now a recognition of the human rights of peoples of all classes, nations, and races; at the same time, however, there is class warfare, nationalism, and racialism. We now have unprecedented power of production side by side with unprecedented shortages; we have machines to work for us and periods of unemployment.

Specific examples of this kind help point the way, but the subject of civilization on trial requires a much larger canvas. Even the limits of Western Christendom seem narrow in terms of the space dimension; the history of Western Christendom cannot be understood simply within its own geographical limits. Western Christendom is merely one of five civilizations surviving in the world today, out of about nineteen that have come into existence during about six thousand years. The other four surviving civilizations have a longer history, that is, they have survived longer than Western Christendom. And yet, the whole habitable world has now been unified into a single great society, owing to the modern expansion of Western Christendom.

Is it not time, however, to realize that the present Western ascendancy is certain not to last, and that the other civilizations will assuredly reassert their influence?

48

CIVILIZATION ON TRIAL *
Arnold J. Toynbee

I

Our present Western outlook on history is an extraordinarily contradictory one. While our historical horizon has been expanding vastly in both the space dimension and the time dimension, our historical vision—what we actually do see, in contrast to what we now could see if we chose—has been contracting rapidly to the narrow field of what a horse sees between its blinkers or what a U-boat commander sees through his periscope.

This is certainly extraordinary; yet it is only one of a number of contradictions of this kind that seem to be characteristic of the times in which we are living. There are other examples that probably loom larger in the minds of most of us. For instance, our world has risen to an unprecedented degree of humanitarian feeling. There is now a recognition of the human rights of people of all classes, nations, and races; yet at the same time we have sunk to perhaps unheard-of depths of class warfare, nationalism, and racialism. These bad passions find vent in cold-blooded, scientifically planned cruelties;

and the two incompatible states of mind and standards of conduct are to be seen to-day, side by side, not merely in the same world, but sometimes in the same country and even in the same soul.

Again, we now have an unprecedented power of production side by side with unprecedented shortages. We have invented machines to work for us, but have less spare labour than ever before for human service—even for such an essential and elementary service as helping mothers to look after their babies. We have persistent alternations of widespread unemployment with famines of man-power. Undoubtedly, the contrast between our expanding historical horizon and our contracting historical vision is something characteristic of our age. Yet, looked at in itself, what an astonishing contradiction it is!

Let us remind ourselves first of the recent expansion of our horizon. In space, our Western field of vision has expanded to take in the whole of mankind over all the habitable and traversable surface of this planet, and the whole stellar universe in which this planet is an infinitesimally small speck of

* From *Civilization on Trial*, Oxford University Press, New York, 1948, pp. 150–163. Reprinted by permission of Oxford University Press.

dust. In time, our Western field of vision has expanded to take in all the civilizations that have risen and fallen during these last 6000 years; the previous history of the human race back to its genesis between 600,000 and a million years ago; the history of life on this planet back to perhaps 800 million years ago. What a marvellous widening of our historical horizon! Yet, at the same time, our field of historical vision has been contracting; it has been tending to shrink within the narrow limits in time and space of the particular republic or kingdom of which each of us happens to be a citizen. The oldest surviving Western states—say France or England—have so far had no more than a thousand years of continuous political existence; the largest existing Western state—say Brazil or the United States—embraces only a very small fraction of the total inhabited surface of the Earth.

Before the widening of our horizon began —before our Western seamen circumnavigated the globe, and before our Western cosmogonists and geologists pushed out the bounds of our universe in both time and space—our prenationalist mediaeval ancestors had a broader and juster historical vision than we have to-day. For them, history did not mean the history of one's own parochial community; it meant the history of Israel, Greece, and Rome. And, even if they were mistaken in believing that the world was created in 4004 B.C., it is at any rate better to look as far back as 4004 B.C. than to look back no farther than the Declaration of Independence or the voyages of the *Mayflower* or Columbus or Hengist and Horsa. (As a matter of fact, 4004 B.C. happens, though our ancestors did not know this, to be a quite important date: it approximately marks the first appearance of representatives of the species of human society called civilizations.)

Again, for our ancestors, Rome and Jerusalem meant much more than their own home towns. When our Anglo-Saxon ancestors were converted to Roman Christianity at the end of the sixth century of the Christian era, they learned Latin, studied the treasures of sacred and profane literature to which a knowledge of the Latin language gives access, and went on pilgrimages to Rome and Jerusalem—and this in an age when the difficulties and dangers of travelling were such as to make modern war-time travelling seem child's play. Our ancestors seem to have been big-minded, and this is a great intellectual virtue as well as a great moral one, for national histories are unintelligible within their own time limits and space limits.

II

In the time dimension, you cannot understand the history of England if you begin only at the coming of the English to Britain, any better than you can understand the history of the United States if you begin only at the coming of the English to North America. In the space dimension, likewise, you cannot understand the history of a country if you cut its outlines out of the map of the world and rule out of consideration anything that has originated outside that particular country's frontiers.

What are the epoch-making events in the national histories of the United States and the United Kingdom? Working back from the present towards the past, I should say they were the two world wars, the Industrial Revolution, the Reformation, the Western voyages of discovery, the Renaissance, the conversion to Christianity. Now I defy anyone to tell the history of either the United States or the United Kingdom without making these events the cardinal ones, or to explain these events as local American or local English affairs. To explain these major events in the history of any Western country, the smallest unit that one can take into account is the whole of Western Christendom. By Western Christendom I mean the Roman Catholic and Protestant world—the adherents of the Patriarchate of Rome who have maintained their allegiance to the Papacy, together with the former adherents who have repudiated it.

But the history of Western Christendom, too, is unintelligible within its own time limits and space limits. While Western Christendom is a much better unit than the United States or the United Kingdom or France for a historian to operate with, it too turns out, on inspection, to be inadequate. In the time dimension, it goes back only to the close of the Dark Ages following the collapse of the western part of the Roman Empire; that is, it goes back less than 1300 years, and 1300 years is less than a quarter of the 6000 years during which the species of society represented by Western Christendom has been in existence. Western Christendom is a civilization belonging to the third of the three generations of civilizations that there have been so far.

In the space dimension, the narrowness of the limits of Western Christendom is still more striking. If you look at the physical map of the world as a whole, you will see that the small part of it which is dry land consists of a single continent—Asia—which has a number of peninsulas and off-lying islands. Now, what are the farthest limits to which Western Christendom has managed to expand? You will find them at Alaska and Chile on the west and at Finland and Dalmatia on the east. What lies between those four points is Western Christendom's domain at its widest. And what does that domain amount to? Just the tip of Asia's European peninsula, together with a couple of large islands. (By these two large islands, I mean, of course, North and South America.) Even if you add in the outlying and precarious footholds of the Western world in South Africa, Australia, and New Zealand, its total habitable present area amounts to only a very minor part of the total habitable area of the surface of the planet. And you cannot understand the history of Western Christendom within its own geographical limits.

Western Christendom is a product of Christianity, but Christianity did not arise in the Western world; it arose outside the bounds of Western Christendom, in a district that lies today within the domain of a different civilization: Islam. We Western

Christians did once try to capture from the Muslims the cradle of our religion in Palestine. If the Crusades had succeeded, Western Christendom would have slightly broadened its footing on the all-important Asiatic mainland. But the Crusades ended in failure.

Western Christendom is merely one of five civilizations that survive in the world to-day; and these are merely five out of about nineteen that one can identify as having come into existence since the first appearance of representatives of this species of society about 6000 years ago.

III

To take the four other surviving civilizations first: if the firmness of a civilization's foothold on the continent—by which I mean the solid land-mass of Asia—may be taken as giving a rough indication of that civilization's relative expectation of life, then the other four surviving civilizations are 'better lives'—in the jargon of the life insurance business—than our own Western Christendom.

Our sister civilization, Orthodox Christendom, straddles the continent from the Baltic to the Pacific and from the Mediterranean to the Arctic Ocean: it occupies the northern half of Asia and the eastern half of Asia's European peninsula. Russia overlooks the back doors of all the other civilizations; from White Russia and North-Eastern Siberia she overlooks the Polish and Alaskan back doors of our own Western world; from the Caucasus and Central Asia she overlooks the back doors of the Islamic and Hindu worlds; from Central and Eastern Siberia she overlooks the back door of the Far Eastern world.

Our half-sister civilization, Islam, also has a firm footing on the continent. The domain of Islam stretches from the heart of the Asiatic continent in North-Western China all the way to the west coast of Asia's African peninsula. At Dakar, the Islamic world commands the continental approaches to the straits that divide Asia's African peninsula from the island of South America. Islam also has a firm footing in Asia's Indian peninsula.

As for the Hindu society and the Far Eastern society, it needs no demonstration to show that the 400 million Hindus and the 400 or 500 million Chinese have a firm foothold on the continent.

But we must not exaggerate the importance of any of these surviving civilizations just because, at this moment, they happen to be survivors. If, instead of thinking in terms of 'expectation of life,' we think in terms of achievement, a rough indication of relative achievement may be found in the giving of birth to individual souls that have conferred lasting blessings on the human race.

Now who are the individuals who are the greatest benefactors of the living generation of mankind? I should say: Confucius and Lao-tse; the Buddha; the Prophets of Israel and Judah; Zoroaster, Jesus, and Muhammad; and Socrates. And not one of these lasting benefactors of mankind happens to be a child of any of the five living civilizations. Confucius and Lao-tse were children of a now extinct Far Eastern civilization of an earlier generation; the Buddha was the child of a now extinct Indian civilization of an earlier generation. Hosea, Zoroaster, Jesus, and Muhammad were children of a now extinct Syrian civilization. Socrates was the child of a now extinct Greek civilization.

Within the last 400 years, all the five surviving civilizations have been brought into contact with each other as a result of the enterprise of two of them: the expansion of Western Christendom from the tip of Asia's European peninsula over the ocean, and the expansion of Orthodox Christendom overland across the whole breadth of the Asiatic continent.

The expansion of Western Christendom displays two special features: being oceanic, it is the only expansion of a civilization to date that has been literally world-wide in the sense of extending over the whole habitable portion of the Earth's surface; and, owing to the 'conquest of space and time' by modern mechanical means, the spread of the network of Western material civilization has brought the different parts of the world into far closer physical contact than ever before. But, even in these points, the expansion of the Western civilization differs in degree only, and not in kind, from the contemporary overland expansion of Russian Orthodox Christendom, and from similar expansions of other civilizations at earlier dates.

There are earlier expansions that have made important contributions towards the present unification of mankind—with its corollary, the unification of our vision of human history. The now extinct Syrian civilization was propagated to the Atlantic coasts of Asia's European and African peninsulas westward by the Phoenicians, to the tip of Asia's Indian peninsula south-eastwards by the Himyarites and Nestorians, and to the Pacific north-eastwards by the Manichaeans and Nestorians. It expanded in two directions overseas and in a third direction overland. Any visitor to Peking will have seen a striking monument of the Syrian civilization's overland cultural conquests. In the trilingual inscriptions of the Manchu Dynasty of China at Peking, the Manchu and Mongol texts are inscribed in the Syriac form of our alphabet, not in Chinese characters.

Other examples of the expansion of now extinct civilizations are the propagation of the Greek civilization overseas westwards to Marseilles by the Greeks themselves, overland northwards to the Rhine and Danube by the Romans, and overland eastwards to the interiors of India and China by the Macedonians; and the expansion of the Sumerian civilization in all directions overland from its cradle in 'Iraq.

IV

As a result of these successive expansions of particular civilizations, the whole habitable world has now been unified into a single great society. The movement through which this process has been finally consummated is the modern expansion of Western Christendom. But we have to bear in mind, first, that this expansion of Western Christendom has merely completed the unification of the world and has not been the agency that has produced more than the last stage of the process; and, second, that, though the unification of the world has been finally achieved within a Western framework, the present Western ascendency in the world is certain not to last.

In a unified world, the eighteen non-Western civilizations—four of them living, fourteen of them extinct—will assuredly reassert their influence. And as, in the course of generations and centuries, a unified world gradually works its way toward an equilibrium between its diverse component cultures, the Western component will gradually be relegated to the modest place which is all that it can expect to retain in virtue of its intrinsic worth by comparison with those other cultures—surviving and extinct—which the Western society, through its modern expansion, has brought into association with itself and with one another.

History, seen in this perspective, makes, I feel, the following call upon historians of our generation and of the generations that will come after ours. If we are to perform the full service that we have the power to perform for our fellow human beings—the important service of helping them to find their bearings in a unified world—we must make the necessary effort of imagination and effort of will to break our way out of the prison walls of the local and short-lived histories of our own countries and our own cultures, and we must accustom ourselves to taking a synoptic view of history as a whole.

Our first task is to perceive, and to present to other people, the history of all the known civilizations, surviving and extinct, as a unity. There are, I believe, two ways in which this can be done.

One way is to study the encounters between civilizations, of which I have mentioned four outstanding examples. These encounters between civilizations are historically illuminating, not only because they bring a number of civilizations into a single focus of vision, but also because, out of encounters between civilizations, the higher religions have been born—the worship, perhaps originally Sumerian, of the Great Mother and her Son who suffers and dies and rises again; Judaism and Zoroastrianism, which sprang from an encounter between the Syrian and Babylonian civilizations; Christianity and Islam, which sprang from an encounter between the Syrian and Greek civilizations; the Mahayana form of Buddhism and Hinduism, which sprang from an encounter between the Indian and Greek civilizations. The future of mankind in this world—if mankind is going to have a future in this world—lies, I believe, with these higher religions that have appeared within the last 4000 years (and all but the first within the last 3000 years), and not with the civilizations whose encounters have provided opportunities for the higher religions to come to birth.

A second way of studying the history of all the known civilizations as a unity is to make a comparative study of their individual histories, looking at them as so many representatives of one particular species of the genus Human Society. If we map out the principal phases in the histories of civilizations—their births, growths, breakdowns, and declines—we can compare their experiences phase by phase; and by this method of study we shall perhaps be able to sort out their common experiences, which are specific, from their unique experiences, which are individual. In this way we may be able to work out a morphology of the species of society called civilizations.

If, by the use of these two methods of study, we can arrive at a unified vision of history, we shall probably find that we need to make very far-going adjustments of the perspective in which the histories of divers civilizations and peoples appear when looked at through our peculiar present-day Western spectacles.

In setting out to adjust our perspective, we shall be wise, I suggest, to proceed simultaneously on two alternative assumptions. One of these alternatives is that the future of mankind may not, after all, be going to be catastrophic and that, even if the Second World War prove not to have been the last, we shall survive the rest of this batch of world wars as we survived the first two bouts, and shall eventually win our way out into calmer waters. The other possibility is that these first two world wars may be merely overtures to some supreme catastrophe that we are going to bring on ourselves.

This second, more unpleasant, alternative has been made a very practical possibility by mankind's unfortunately having discovered how to tap atomic energy before we have succeeded in abolishing the institution of war. Those contradictions and paradoxes in the life of the world in our time, which I took as my starting point, also look like symptoms of serious social and spiritual sickness, and their existence—which is one of the portentous features in the landscape of contemporary history—is another indication that we ought to take the more unpleasant of our alternatives as a serious possibility, and not just as a bad joke.

On either alternative, I suggest that we historians ought to concentrate our own attention—and direct the attention of our listeners and readers—upon the histories of those civilizations and peoples which, in the light of their past performances, seem likely, in a unified world, to come to the front in the long run in one or other of the alternative futures that may be lying in wait for mankind.

V

If the future of mankind in a unified world is going to be on the whole a happy one, then I would prophesy that there is a future in the Old World for the Chinese, and in the island of North America for the *Canadiens*. Whatever the future of mankind in North America, I feel pretty confident that these French-speaking Canadians, at any rate, will be there at the end of the story.

On the assumption that the future of mankind is to be very catastrophic, I should have prophesied, even as lately as a few years ago,

that whatever future we might be going to have would lie with the Tibetans and the Eskimos, because each of these peoples occupied, till quite lately, an unusually sheltered position. 'Sheltered' means, of course, sheltered from the dangers arising from human folly and wickedness, not sheltered from the rigors of the physical environment. Mankind has been master of its physical environment, sufficiently for practical purposes, since the middle palaeolithic age; since that time, man's only dangers—but these have been deadly dangers—have come from man himself. But the homes of the Tibetans and the Eskimos are sheltered no longer, because we are on the point of managing to fly over the North Pole and over the Himalayas, and both Northern Canada and Tibet would (I think) be likely to be theatres of a future Russo-American war.

If mankind is going to run amok with atom bombs, I personally should look to the Negrito Pygmies of Central Africa to salvage some fraction of the present heritage of mankind. (Their eastern cousins in the Philippines and in the Malay Peninsula would probably perish with the rest of us, as they both live in what have now come to be dangerously exposed positions.)

The African Negritos are said by our anthropologists to have an unexpectedly pure and lofty conception of the nature of God and of God's relation to man. They might be able to give mankind a fresh start; and, though we should then have lost the achievements of the last 6000 to 10,000 years, what are 10,000 years compared to the 600,000 or a million years for which the human race has already been in existence?

The extreme possibility of catastrophe is that we might succeed in exterminating the whole human race, African Negritos and all.

On the evidence of the past history of life on this planet, even that is not entirely unlikely. After all, the reign of man on the Earth, if we are right in thinking that man established his present ascendency in the middle palaeolithic age, is so far only about

100,000 years old, and what is that compared to the 500 million or 800 million years during which life has been in existence on the surface of this planet? In the past, other forms of life have enjoyed reigns which have lasted for almost inconceivably longer periods—and which yet at last have come to an end. There was a reign of the giant armored reptiles which may have lasted about 80 million years; say from about the year 130 million to the year 50 million before the present day. But the reptiles' reign came to an end. Long before that—perhaps 300 million years ago—there was a reign of giant armoured fishes—creatures that had already accomplished the tremendous achievement of growing a movable lower jaw. But the reign of the fishes came to an end.

The winged insects are believed to have come into existence about 250 million years ago. Perhaps the higher winged insects—the social insects that have anticipated mankind in creating an institutional life—are still waiting for their reign on Earth to come. If the ants and bees were one day to acquire even that glimmer of intellectual understanding that man has possessed in his day, and if they were then to make their own shot at seeing history in perspective, they might see the advent of the mammals, and the brief reign of the human mammal, as almost irrelevant episodes, 'full of sound and fury, signifying nothing.'

The challenge to us, in our generation, is to see to it that this interpretation of history shall not become the true one.

Index